Probation Officer/ Parole Officer
Exam

Probation Officer/ Parole Officer
Exam

LEARNINGEXPRESS®

NEW YORK

Library of Congress Cataloging-in-Publication Data:
Probation officer/parole officer exam / by LearningExpress.
    p. cm.
  ISBN: 978-1-57685-582-9
  1. Parole officers—United States—Examinations, questions, etc. 2. Probation officers—
United States—Examinations, questions, etc. 3. Civil service—United States—Examinations.
I. LearningExpress (Organization)
  HV9304P772 2007
  364.6'2076-dc22

                                                              2006100133

Printed in the United States of America

9 8 7 6 5 4 3

ISBN: 978-1-57685-582-9

For information on LearningExpress, other LearningExpress products,
or bulk sales, please write to us at:
  LearningExpress
  55 Broadway
  8th Floor
  New York, NY 10006

About the Contributor ▶

C. Ted Ward serves as director of Ball State's correctional education program. He received his Master of Science in management from Indiana Wesleyan University in 1998, following the completion of his master's project, *Recruiting, Interviewing, and Hiring Quality Candidates for Positions in Corrections*. Ward has taught courses in criminal justice systems, criminology, corrections, addiction and crime, juvenile justice, crisis intervention, research methods, and data analysis.

Contents ▶

ABOUT THE CONTRIBUTOR		v
HOW TO USE THIS BOOK		ix
CHAPTER 1	What Probation Officers and Parole Officers Do	1
CHAPTER 2	Establishing a Career as a Probation or Parole Officer	7
CHAPTER 3	The Written Exam	15
CHAPTER 4	Practice Test 1	31
CHAPTER 5	The LearningExpress Test Preparation System	87
CHAPTER 6	Job Responsibilities	103
CHAPTER 7	Case Studies	111
CHAPTER 8	Reading and Writing Skills	119
CHAPTER 9	Practice Test 2	127
CHAPTER 10	Practice Test 3	177
CHAPTER 11	Practice Test 4	231
CHAPTER 12	Practice Test 5	281
CHAPTER 13	Practice Test 6	313
CHAPTER 14	Practice Test 7	365
CHAPTER 15	The Interview	417
CHAPTER 16	The Physical, Medical, and Psychological Exams	425

How to Use This Book ▶

Congratulations on your decision to become a probation or parole officer! You will find this career path to be both rewarding and financially beneficial. The work is interesting, sometimes exciting, and of course, extremely important. However, there are some hurdles ahead of you. Indeed, you have to beat out the competition and succeed at each step of an arduous selection process before you can be appointed.

Probation Officer/Parole Officer Exam will guide you through each stage of the selection process and will help you strengthen your test-taking skills to improve your chances of success. The following chapters are filled with useful information, advice, and practice exercises that will help you understand both how the hiring process works and how you can best meet the requirements.

The hiring process for selecting probation and parole officers varies among districts. Getting through each phase of the hiring process will require determination and a commitment to your goal of becoming a probation or parole officer. The selection process can be challenging, especially for those who don't know what to expect. You'll probably have serious competition, but you will have an edge over your competition if you use this book and study it thoroughly. It will provide you with the practice and information you need to succeed.

Although there may be some variation among states, most regions require applicants to complete each of the following steps successfully (although not necessarily in this exact order):

1. Application
2. Written exam
3. Physical fitness test
4. Interview
5. Psychological evaluation
6. Medical evaluation

Prepare yourself by taking the practice tests in this book and reading each chapter, so you can avoid the pitfalls that prevent many probation or parole officer candidates from being hired. *Probation Officer/Parole Officer Exam* will help you find out as much as you can about the hiring process and practice the skills you need to succeed at each stage. This book will give you an inside look at the entire process, so you will be less nervous when facing tests, interviews, and procedures, all of which can sometimes be intimidating. Knowing what to expect will help you make better choices and achieve better results than candidates who are just rushing blindly ahead.

CHAPTER 1 ▶ What Probation Officers and Parole Officers Do

Probation and parole officers are charged with the ever-increasing task of providing an adequate alternative to incarceration for criminal offenders. The difference between probation and parole is a subtle one, but a difference nonetheless. Parole supervision always occurs after some type and length of incarceration. Probation supervision usually involves some portion of incarceration being suspended (or withheld) by the court during sentencing. We can say that parole occurs *after* incarceration and probation occurs *in lieu of* incarceration.

A more modern trend is the use of probation officers to supervise the pretrial release of *alleged* offenders during the criminal case processing. That is, before there is a finding of guilt, a defendant may be ordered to adhere to probation supervision as a condition of bond and/or release.

Probation and parole officers are professionals within the criminal justice system and, as such, have ongoing contact with others from the criminal justice system. They regularly communicate with law enforcement officers, department of corrections officials, attorneys, prosecutors, and judges, just to name a few. In addition to the contact they have with members of the criminal justice system, they are also in contact with other professionals throughout the community. It is likely that, for a probation or parole officer to be effective, he or she must also have contact with other resource persons such as school officials, treatment groups, clinicians, and employment and housing professionals.

Much of what probation and parole officers do can be categorized as either an administrative responsibility or an offender supervision responsibility.

▶ Administrative Responsibilities

For probation officers, much of their administrative responsibilities revolve around serving a criminal court. Parole officers, on the other hand, primarily serve the administrative interests of the Department of Corrections via the Parole Board.

Examples of administrative responsibilities would include:

- **Courtroom or parole hearing attendance**
Typically, a trial court of original jurisdiction (Circuit or Superior Courts) requires regular attendance by a probation officer for a variety of reasons. Often, probation officers are aware of information that can or will influence a pending case, whether it is a new criminal charge or some legal action on a pending case. In the event that a defendant with a new case is currently, or has been previously, supervised through probation, the trial court judge may request additional information be provided so that he or she can determine an appropriate bail amount or other pertinent actions that could have additional outcomes throughout the trial process.

Parole officers serve the paroling authority (i.e., the parole board) in a similar way, by providing relevant information that could influence a decision on parole revocation or, in the event of a new decision, to grant parole. Having prior supervision experience with an individual under consideration can greatly affect whether that individual returns to parole for additional time or remains incarcerated.

- **Preparing information and documents for presentation to the court or parole authority**
Probation and parole officers are regularly asked to submit a variety of reports and documents for purposes of decision making by the court or by the parole board.

- **Courtroom testimony**
Probation and parole officers are called upon during courtroom proceedings to provide verbal testimony relevant to pending court actions. Officers will give the court a verbal summation of supervision activities, including both positive and negative experiences with the defendant involved in the case. Officers can be called upon by a prosecutor to identify formally and connect a defendant to a prior period of supervision in an effort to establish a pattern of criminal behavior, which could possibly lead to a harsher sentence. Officers can occasionally provide verbal testimony that is favorable to the defendant, concerning the modification of a sentence or in an early release from supervision.

- **Contacting the victim regarding rights and responsibilities in case hearings**
As concern for victims' rights in criminal trials has grown, the criminal justice system has changed those practices involving probation and parole agents. Often, probation and parole officers are required to contact the victims in an effort to inform them of case-processing activities such as sentencing hearings, parole hearings, revocation hearings, etc. In addition, probation and parole officers will often gather written documents supplied by victims in an effort to provide the relevant information to the court or to the parole board for decision-making purposes. Probation and parole officers work with victims in an effort to afford the victim an opportunity to make statements regarding sentencing or parole-granting decisions or

to supply documents relevant to the repayment of costs for damages suffered by the victim.

- **Completion of interstate or intrastate compact documents**
  Probationers and parolees will often reside or move to an area or state outside the jurisdiction of the original probation or parole office. Therefore, a transfer of supervision must occur and with it are specific rules and regulations governing the process of transferring supervision. Probation and parole officers must follow the requirements of the established interstate/intrastate compacts that exist throughout the various jurisdictions. Failure to do so accordingly could lead to ineffective supervision or additional difficulty in case processing.

▶ Offender Supervision

Beyond those duties to assist the court or the paroling authority, probation and parole officers are responsible for the vigilant supervision of those persons sentenced to probation or granted parole.

Examples of the responsibilities involved in supervising offenders are:

- **Orientation to probation or parole**
  It is important to the process of supervision that offenders understand completely the rules, regulations, and requirements of probation or parole. Probation and parole officers will conduct, either formally or informally, an orientation to the rules of supervision by explaining thoroughly the expectations to be met during probation or parole.
- **Familiarization with probationer or parolee file**
  In order to provide the best possible offender supervision, the probation or parole officer must become expertly familiar with the background of the offender and his or her conduct. Information about the offender's behavior dur-

ing criminal arrests or periods of incarceration, or about the offender's previous experiences of community supervision, is pertinent to the safety of the officer and the community at large during the period of probation or parole. In familiarizing themselves with the offender's case, probation and parole officers can review arrest records, jail and/or prison records, documents supplied by other community agents, and internal probation and parole files.

- **Risk and needs assessments**
  To determine the level of care that must be taken with the offender during supervision, probation and parole officers determine the likelihood of the offender violating the conditions of his or her supervision or committing a new offense. This determination will establish the level and type of supervision that will be implemented during the period of probation or parole. Typically, probation and parole departments use standardized instruments to assess the offender's risk and determine an appropriate level and strategy for his or her supervision.

  Probation and parole officers may employ these standardized instruments again, or simply utilize their specialized knowledge and experience, during the period of probation or parole supervision to address any further needs the offender may have, such as the need for substance abuse treatment, education or job skill development, sex offender programming, or appropriate housing.
- **Referrals to outside agencies for offender assistance**
  In addition to the direct monitoring of probation and parole officers, offender supervision often requires the support and resources of other experts and agencies within the community. These outside resources help the probation and parole officers implement the supervision plan that was developed during the risk and needs assessment activity.

Formal referral of an offender to an outside resource typically involves supplying the offender with appropriate contact information, setting an initial appointment for the offender, presenting relevant documentation to the outside resource, and immediately following up with the resource agent or agency to ensure that the offender appeared at the initial appointment. The completion of these preliminary tasks could greatly influence later proceedings, should an offender fail to comply with the referral, or should other court or administrative action pertaining to the unsatisfactory compliance with the conditions of probation or parole need be taken.

- **Monitoring compliance with terms and conditions of probation or parole**
  Although all of the aforementioned activities and responsibilities are an integral part of being a probation or parole officer, the main responsibility of this position is to ensure that the offender complies with the conditions that govern their period of community supervision. Probation and parole officers are a vital human resource in monitoring the safety of the community through the supervision and support of the offender. In this regard, the probation or parole officer serves as a central source of information on all of the rules, recommendations, and regulations established for any given offender who is under community supervision instead of being incarcerated.

Probation and parole officers conduct visits with offenders in an office setting. Because of increased caseloads, it is usually more efficient to meet with multiple offenders in a relatively short amount of time in an office setting. These visits are necessary at times when the officer needs case or file information, or additional office equipment, in order to do screening or assessment activities. An office visit may also be required if the officer needs to refer the offender to an outside agency or if a confined office area would make an arrest of the offender safer and more controlled.

Probation and parole officers conduct field visits to meet with offenders in their own environments. The purposes of this type of visit are: to confirm what an offender has reported regarding his or her living arrangements; to conduct a search of the offender's home, vehicle, and other property to find any violations of his or her probation or parole conditions or to determine any additional criminal activity; to identify any additional risk factors that could lead to the unsatisfactory completion of his or her probation or parole; and to gain a better understanding of the offender by witnessing his or her place of residence.

Other ways that probation and parole officers supervise include telephone calls to the offender, as well as the offender's significant other, relatives, neighbors, and employers; and collaboration with the offender's treatment counselors to monitor his or her activities and/or progress under supervision. Probation and parole officers may decide to visit the offender's employer or school when they are concerned about his or her attendance at scheduled appointments with the officer or an outside referral resource. An officer may periodically utilize a worksheet or standard-reply form for offenders to supply relevant information about and documentation of compliance with conditions of their supervision such as restitution or supervision fee payments.

- **Documentation of all case-related activity**
  Because of the legal nature of probation and parole supervision and the potential for additional sanctions to be imposed, it is important for officers to collect, maintain, and/or provide or accurate and detailed information, which is then used by many other criminal justice members to make subsequent decisions about the

offender. Again, based on the legal nature of the field, if probation and parole officers do not provide adequate case information, then subsequent actions can be affected adversely.

► Overall Structure of Responsibilities

Various administrative structures exist throughout the field of probation and parole. In general, most probation and parole officers participate in all of the aforementioned activities to complete their assignments. However, depending upon the size of the organization, probation and parole administrators may choose to organize the duties of their officers to better suit the nature and volume of the overall workload within that organization. It is possible that the duties of probation and parole officers are more compartmentalized within a larger organization, leading to a specialization of activities conducted. For example, it is not unusual to find a large organization divided into subunits that are responsible for specific duties, such as hearing-involved activities, report writing, primary supervision, and field supervision. However, a probation or parole officer requires a broad understanding of the entire scope of responsibilities under supervision.

Sometimes the organization separates the various jurisdictions or types of offenders. For example, it is not unusual for an organization to be subdivided into units that handle adult offenders and juvenile offenders separately. Units may be further divided by the type of offense, such as sex offenses or drug- or alcohol-related offenses. Although the nature of these offenders and offenses may require specialized officers, the overall job responsibilities are similar, if not identical, to those mentioned earlier in the chapter.

2 ▶ Establishing a Career as a Probation or Parole Officer

Probation and parole officers are constantly encountering stressful situations that often can include not only dangerous places but dangerous persons as well. A background of knowledge, skills, and experience assists an officer in being able to cope with such situations. Knowledge of the criminal justice system and an understanding of criminal behavior is only a portion of what an officer needs in order to be effective. Officers who can demonstrate cultural awareness and crisis intervention techniques may be more effective in managing the majority of stressful situations that arise in the performance of duties.

Probation and parole officers are considered to be professionals within the criminal justice system, and as such they need to exhibit professional and personal characteristics that will foster success in the work that they do. Most chief administrators in probation and parole would look for officers who are decisive leaders with good physical and emotional health, along with a variety of other qualifications that lead to good probation and parole practice.

▶ Qualifications

Most probation and parole organizations will have a basic outline of qualifications that applicants must meet in order to be considered for the hiring process. Items considered for qualification to become a probation or parole officer typically include a minimum age of 21 (18 in some jurisdictions), a minimum education level, U.S. citizenship, a clean criminal history, a valid license to drive, and examinations of relevant skill and knowledge, of physical agility, and of mental health. The minimum requirements may differ between probation and parole, even within an individual state, depending upon the organizational structure of probation and parole.

MINIMUM EDUCATION REQUIREMENTS FOR PROBATION AND PAROLE OFFICERS		
STATE	PROBATION OFFICER EDUCATION LEVEL	PAROLE OFFICER EDUCATION LEVEL
Alabama	bachelor's degree	bachelor's degree
Alaska	bachelor's degree	bachelor's degree
Arizona	bachelor's degree	H.S. diploma
Arkansas	bachelor's degree	bachelor's degree
California	H.S. diploma dependent upon jurisdiction	some college
Colorado	bachelor's degree	bachelor's degree
Connecticut	bachelor's degree	bachelor's degree
Florida	bachelor's degree	bachelor's degree
Georgia	bachelor's degree	bachelor's degree
Hawaii	master's degree	bachelor's degree
Idaho	not specified	some college
Illinois	bachelor's degree	bachelor's degree
Indiana	bachelor's degree	some college
Iowa	associate's degree	some college
Kansas	not specified	some college
Kentucky	bachelor's degree	bachelor's degree
Louisiana	bachelor's degree	bachelor's degree
Maine	bachelor's degree	bachelor's degree
Maryland	bachelor's degree or may substitute experience for degree	bachelor's degree

MINIMUM EDUCATION REQUIREMENTS FOR PROBATION AND PAROLE OFFICERS		
STATE	PROBATION OFFICER EDUCATION LEVEL	PAROLE OFFICER EDUCATION LEVEL
Massachusetts	bachelor's degree	bachelor's degree
Michigan	bachelor's degree	bachelor's degree
Mississippi	bachelor's degree or may substitute experience for degree	master's degree
Missouri	bachelor's degree or may substitute experience for degree	bachelor's degree
Montana	bachelor's degree	bachelor's degree
Nebraska	bachelor's degree	not specified
Nevada	bachelor's degree or may substitute experience for degree	bachelor's degree
New Hampshire	bachelor's degree	bachelor's degree
New Jersey	bachelor's degree	not specified
New Mexico	bachelor's degree	bachelor's degree
New York	bachelor's degree	not specified
North Carolina	bachelor's degree	not specified
North Dakota	bachelor's degree	not specified
Ohio	bachelor's degree	bachelor's degree
Oklahoma	bachelor's degree	bachelor's degree
Oregon	bachelor's degree or may substitute experience for degree	bachelor's degree
Pennsylvania	bachelor's degree	not specified
Rhode Island	bachelor's degree	H.S. diploma
South Carolina	bachelor's degree	bachelor's degree
South Dakota	bachelor's degree or combination of experience and education	bachelor's degree
Tennessee	bachelor's degree or may substitute experience for degree	bachelor's degree
Texas	bachelor's degree	not specified

MINIMUM EDUCATION REQUIREMENTS FOR PROBATION AND PAROLE OFFICERS		
STATE	PROBATION OFFICER EDUCATION LEVEL	PAROLE OFFICER EDUCATION LEVEL
Utah	bachelor's degree	not specified
Vermont	bachelor's degree or combination of experience and education	not specified
Virginia	bachelor's degree or may substitute experience for degree	bachelor's degree
Washington	bachelor's degree	bachelor's degree
West Virginia	bachelor's degree	bachelor's degree
Wyoming	bachelor's degree or may substitute experience for degree	bachelor's degree

▶ Preferred Qualifications for Probation and Parole Officers

Specific Educational Backgrounds

Candidates who have educational backgrounds in the behavioral sciences—specifically in criminal justice, social work, sociology, or psychology—are preferred over other degree areas. Candidates who have completed internships with probation or parole departments are preferred. Individuals who have specific training in areas of crisis intervention, firearm use and safety, behavior modification programming, self-defense, and first aid are more desirable candidates.

Prior Employment Experience

Administrators are looking for candidates who present themselves with previous employment service in a comparable field. These positions might include previous criminal justice employment as a police officer, a county jail corrections officer, or a youth center/services employee. Persons previously employed in the various capacities with the Department of Family and Children or social welfare organizations might be considered to have relevant working experience. Case management, addictions or other behavioral counsel-ing, Job Corps staff, or other nonprofit human services work would be looked upon favorably as well.

Volunteer Experience

Most applicants considered for employment as entry-level probation or parole officers make their application directly following the completion of an undergraduate degree. Probation and parole officer positions are highly competitive, and as such, decision makers are looking for characteristics in candidates that help to distinguish them from the high volume of applications received for vacant positions. One way to find those qualities is to evaluate what additional experiences a candidate may have that might serve to simulate the probation or parole work environment. Candidates with volunteer experience distinguish themselves by implying that they are willing to go beyond what is expected and to allocate time toward a worthwhile venture, while not expecting financial compensation for that time and effort.

Communication Skills

Probation and parole work is saturated with interaction with others within and outside of the criminal justice field. Probation and parole officers are continuously required to submit various reports and legal documents along with providing courtroom testimony or other verbal statements that impact the supervision of offenders. It is important to the decision makers that their employees represent the department in the most professional way possible. To do so, candidates must be able to demonstrate that they have the ability to communicate effectively both in writing and verbally. Items such as traditional correspondence with other professionals, case notes, witness statements, and complete investigative reports are vital to the successful supervision of offenders and the satisfaction of the wishes of the court and/or administration. Candidates must be able to demonstrate that they can clearly communicate conditions and requirements of supervision to offenders, offer concise statements in court, and respond to other professionals in an informative and professional manner.

▶ Compensation

Salary

Annual salaries of probation and parole officers are generally established either through statute or through a salary schedule. The salary schedule is typically accompanied by a grading system that considers an officer's position, years of service, education level, and specialized training or certifications. Comparable to private sector employment, salaries in probation and parole can be low when workload, level of responsibility, and stress are considered. Although probation and parole officer salaries can vary greatly, most officers currently earn between $30,000 and $50,000.

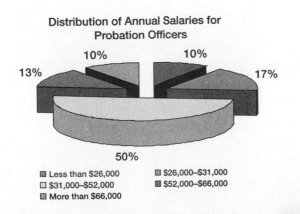

Distribution of Annual Salaries for Probation Officers

10%   10%
13%   17%
50%

■ Less than $26,000   ■ $26,000–$31,000
□ $31,000–$52,000   ■ $52,000–$66,000
■ More than $66,000

Insurance

Probation and parole officers typically enjoy the same life, medical, and dental insurance coverage as other employees within the same government structure. That is, county officers have county benefits, state officers have state benefits, etc. These benefits usually provide for standard group-rate coverage that is contributed by both the employer and the employee. With modern trends in coverage, employees should expect their jurisdiction to subscribe to some form of a managed care provider (for example, an HMO).

Retirement

Consistent with insurance coverage, employees in the field of probation and parole can expect the same form of retirement plan associated with their jurisdiction. However, in some locations, officers have peace officer benefits that are either different from or supplemental to the standard public retirement plan.

▶ Job Searching

Finding Vacant Positions

Positions within the field of probation and parole are expected to continue to grow consistently with other similar occupations in the criminal justice field. In addition to newly created openings, agencies will continue to experience vacancies created because of the replacement of previous employees who have either been promoted, retired, or have otherwise left the organization. It is not uncommon for career-minded people to use these positions to gain experience before applying for other positions in the field. This is especially true of people who underestimate the burdensome workload and high levels of stress associated with probation and parole work.

The creation and retention of positions in the fields of probation and parole are directly connected to the budget constraints of the state and or local jurisdictions that provide oversight of the agency. With recent sentencing guidelines calling for longer sentences of incarceration, the increase in the prison population has placed extreme constraints on the respective budgets. Finding new alternatives to incarceration has become a higher priority as a means to reduce these constraints and to satisfy the goals of corrections. Community corrections, including probation and parole, is far less expensive than keeping offenders imprisoned for lengthy periods.

Positions in probation and parole can be located through advertisements with state employment agencies as well as through local print media. An additional strategy for locating positions is to visit the website of any organization through which a candidate may be interested in pursuing employment. College educators are often resourceful in the location of vacant positions, as they are typically connected to professionals and administrators in those fields.

The Process of Applying

Most positions in probation and parole will require an applicant to submit a resume along with a formal application. A resume is an opportunity for an applicant to outline his or her education, experiences, skills, and abilities to a prospective employer. Agency admin-istrators, or human resource professionals, will expect an applicant's resume to appear organized and contain background information used to screen that applicant for a potential interview.

Steps in the Hiring Process

The actual process of hiring will likely vary from state to state and from jurisdiction to jurisdiction. However, the following should give an applicant an idea of what general procedures will occur:

1. Advertisement of vacant position
2. Review of applicant materials to select for interview
3. Invitation to interview
4. Interview (initial and second, if required)
5. Conditional offer for employment
6. Required testing (physical, medical, psychological, etc.)
7. Preemployment training or academy (not always included)
8. Employment (usually with a review or training period)

Donna K. Horn   1951 Motherly Drive, Muncie, IN 00000
765-555-1951
dkh1951@email.com

OBJECTIVE: To secure a professional position in the field of probation and parole that will utilize the knowledge and skills obtained through previous experience and education

EDUCATION: **Ball State University**   Muncie, IN
                   Bachelor of Science   12/05
                   - *Major area of study: Criminal Justice and Criminology*
                   - *Minor area of study: Counseling Psychology*

Specifically relevant coursework included Community Corrections, Crisis Intervention, Race and Gender, Addiction and Crime, Interpersonal Relationship Skills, and Mediation Techniques

PROFESSIONAL   **Youth Opportunity Center**   Muncie, IN
EXPERIENCE: *Caseworker I*   12/05 to Present
                   - In facility supervision of 30 juveniles adjudicated as delinquent
                   - Risk and needs assessment and reassessment
                   - Treatment planning
                   - Weekly review and case reporting
                   - Courtroom attendance and testimony
                   - Transportation of juvenile offenders to appointments and hearings away from facility

VOLUNTEER   **Juvenile Services of Delaware County**   Muncie, IN
EXPERIENCE: *Casework Intern*   8/05 to 12/05
                   - Assisted casework staff members in the delivery of service to juvenile clientele
                   - Assisted program director in weekly review of case notations
                   - Designed and implemented a change in treatment program created to serve the specific population of substance abusers
                   - Participated as cochair of internal committee created to improve relations with other criminal justice agencies

ADDITIONAL   **Girl Scouts of Wapehani Council, Inc.**   Daleville, IN
EXPERIENCE: *Clerical Staff*   1/05 to 12/05
                   - Assisted with general clerical duties
                   - Provided customer service
                   - Assisted with inventory control and data entry

REFERENCES: Available upon request

The Written Exam

Written examinations will undoubtedly differ from jurisdiction to jurisdiction, but the goal of every examination is to provide as objective an evaluation as possible. These written examinations are designed to identify candidates' strengths and weaknesses, while making determinations as to how well a candidate would perform in certain areas crucial to the field of probation or parole.

▶ Describing the Exam

The examination will use a variety of methods to determine a candidate's previous knowledge, immediacy of response, depth of understanding, applicability, and overall decision making. The following should assist a candidate in understanding the format of the written examination:

Historical Foundations of Probation and Parole

As strong contributors to the criminal justice process, probation and parole can each point to a rich history reaching back more than 150 years. As such, a candidate could be expected to have some basic knowledge regarding the early establishment of probation and parole systems. Additionally, knowledge of primary historical figures in probation and parole would be beneficial to the candidate.

Examinations are likely to cover this area through the use of multiple-choice or true/false questions. It is important for a candidate to be able to distinguish between the major figures in the field of probation and parole. It is also important for candidates to be able to identify major contributions that each of these figures has made to the areas of probation and parole.

Legal Aspects of Probation and Parole

Probation and parole supervision and the respective agencies are established through federal and state legislation, including provisions for when and how probation and parole occurs and for who has authority over its administration. Furthermore, legislative statutes may include specific requirements for agencies and/or agents employed in that capacity.

A candidate should anticipate that basic knowledge, and possibly advanced knowledge, of the legislative statutes and laws governing the practices of probation and parole will be evaluated in the examination. Examinations typically cover this information in a variety of ways, including true/false, multiple-choice, and fill-in-the-blank questions. Candidates should focus on specific statutes granting authority as well as the regulations that exist for agencies and their personnel. Furthermore, with some basic legal knowledge of the overall criminal justice system, a candidate can further understand how probation and parole functions within the legal process.

Confidentiality

Much of the information gathered by probation and parole officers is typically held in confidence. These officers may find themselves dealing with a multitude of information on the offender, his or her family, friends, and associates, as well as on victims involved

in the present case or victims from previous cases. Candidates for employment are expected to understand the protocol for protecting information that could be damaging to a person and to know the circumstances in which that information should be divulged.

The most common method for evaluating a candidate's knowledge on confidentiality is the use of case example questions. Candidates should anticipate a case scenario accompanied by a series of questions that might include true/false, multiple choice, as well as short answer. Examiners are looking for the candidate's ability to make an appropriate decision under common circumstances.

Predicting Offender Compliance

Key to effective supervision is deciding upon the appropriate strategy to address an offender's specific traits and characteristics associated with potential success or failure. There are certain well-known and established variables to be considered when determining the likelihood of an offender complying with the conditions established for his or her supervision in the community. In addition to those constant or static factors would be significant facts concerning the nature of the offender and/or the offense.

Candidates should expect this area to be covered on the examination in a variety of ways. Their basic knowledge of risk factors is likely to be evaluated through multiple-choice questions. However, application of the various risk factors associated with success or failure are typically tested through the use of case example questions or possibly by being asked to provide a written case plan. In these forms of questioning, the candidate should be prepared to be thorough in his or her application of the various risk variables. It is possible that in the written case planning, a candidate's response will be graded according to how thorough each risk factor was addressed.

Determining Offender Needs for Supervision and Programming

Planning for the needs of an offender under supervision is based upon the rehabilitation model of corrections. Recognizing deficiencies and problems in the areas of education, physical health, mental health, substance abuse, housing, employment, and offense-specific programming is the key to reducing the likelihood of recidivism. Often, this function is performed at the point of a presentence investigation or during parole planning, but it is typically an ongoing process with supplemental review stages throughout supervision.

Candidates are most likely to be evaluated on their ability to address an offender's needs through the use of a case example and subsequent case plan or even a mock presentence investigation. Candidates will be expected to have some working knowledge of how these primary areas of needs are associated with the overall success of the community supervision. In addition, it is not uncommon for candidates to be tested on their knowledge and understanding of the current trends in rehabilitation services. This is more likely to be tested through the use of short answer or definition testing.

Evaluating Documents

Probation and parole officers can spend more than half of their time in the processing and intake of external information from various stakeholders involved in the community supervision process. The ability to prioritize the various documents allows officers to be efficient and effective in their assigned duties. In the presentence process, a probation officer often reviews dozens of documents related to the risk and needs of the offender for sentencing purposes. Being able to reference the contents of these documents appropriately during the sentencing process assists the court in providing an appropriate sentence for the offender.

Candidates should expect to be evaluated on their ability in this area through the use of reading comprehension exercises and questions. In addition, a case example question can measure a candidate's ability to recognize documents necessary to complete the case planning.

Documentation

Because of the legal nature of probation and parole supervision, it is vitally importance for these officers to create and maintain as detailed an account of the activities involved in supervision as possible. This documentation occurs in the form of case/supervision notes, periodic reports, and ongoing communication with the offender and/or other stakeholders involved in the supervision. Nearly every document maintained by probation and parole officers is considered to be discoverable. That is, they can be subpoenaed into a court of law. This adds to the necessity that these records be clear, concise, complete, and accurate.

Candidates are likely to be evaluated on their ability in this area through the use of writing examples. These writing examples can be as simple as reviewing a case plan, but more likely they will be in the form of written response to a prompt or upon review of a document. The goal in evaluating this area is to determine a candidate's thoroughness and understanding of the scope of recording information and of what is involved and affected within the process.

Evaluating Offender Compliance

Crucial to the task of community supervision is the accurate determination of an offender's behavior on probation or parole. This determination is often thought of as either complete or incomplete. However, a more effective view of compliance considers the offender's length of consistent compliance, the reasons and explanations for an incomplete requirement, or any violations of a particular condition. Evaluating compliance can be a subjective task, requiring probation and parole officers to interpret the various rules and requirements of community supervision.

Candidates are evaluated in this area through the use of value statements, which require a candidate to respond to statements related to the values they believe are most closely associated with how they think. Additionally, the candidates may be required to prioritize these statements. This can be evaluated through the use of reading comprehension questions, case-planning exercises, and multiple-choice questions. The evaluation of this area can be subjective as well, and, therefore, the candidate may be required to justify his or her responses through the use of logic and through the application of supervision principles.

Responses to Violations of Supervision Conditions

Probation and parole officers are called upon to enforce the conditions of community supervision placed upon the offender. If an offender fails to satisfy a condition or defies a restriction, an officer must respond to that occurrence in an effective way. Officers find success in this area by providing a clear, quick, and, most important, consistent response to a perceived violation. Some violations require court or parole board action, while others can be addressed by making informal changes in the rules or additional changes in the supervision strategy.

Case examples are used to measure a candidate's ability to perceive a violation and to provide an adequate response to that violation. Additionally, a candidate will see the use of multiple-choice or true/false questions related to specific instances of violations.

Ethics

As agents of the criminal justice system, probation and parole officers have a large amount of discretion in the ways in which they handle the supervision of offenders. These officers have an incredible amount of authority over the lives of the offenders they supervise and about whom they provide sentencing information. As such, probation and parole administrators are cognizant of the potential for abuse of that authority and the problems that can occur for the organization as a result.

Candidates are evaluated on their ethics through the use of multiple-choice, true/false, and value statement questions. In a modern trend, the criminal justice industry has followed the lead of the retail industry by administering personality tests and/or situational response tests.

▶ Exam Schedule

When Are Exams Offered?

Schedules for exams differ from state to state and from jurisdiction to jurisdiction, and are most often dictated by the administration an agency falls under. Generally, exams are offered at regular intervals under a preset schedule each month. Typically, candidates could expect to find the exam offered at least monthly; however, it is not uncommon to find exams offered more frequently in states with larger populations. Exams are usually comprehensive, and all portions of the examination are offered within the same setting. However, the exception to this rule could be any form of physical agility testing or personality or psychological testing required in a particular jurisdiction. These are typically administered at the local level, or they are administered during a follow-up examination as a second stage to the examination process.

Where Are Exams Offered?

Exams are offered in a standard location, typically a governmental testing area or within a department of correction or state court administration facility. Typically, there is one testing location for all exams offered within a state. However, exams are also administered regionally in areas with larger organizations and/or larger populations.

These testing locations are generally free from outside noise as well as disruption, and they also provide adequate spacing so that candidates can be an appropriate distance apart for proper testing procedures.

► Implementation of Exam

Materials
Candidates should arrive on-site for the examination prepared with writing instruments such as pens and pencils with erasers. The examiners will provide the exam booklet(s). A candidate might also have access to state statutes or other supplemental materials appropriate to the jurisdiction.

Time Limits
Candidates should anticipate the entire written examination to take four hours or less. Some jurisdictions allow for candidates to begin and end the entire exam at their own pace, while others provide individual time limits for each section of the examination. These time limits are typically adequate for everyone to complete the exam or section of the exam. However, the limits are in place to provide structure and to ensure that a candidate has the desirable knowledge in the area being tested.

Addressing Questions about the Exam
Examiners typically outline the procedures for candidates should a question regarding the exam itself arise. Generally, these procedures call for a candidate to obtain the attention of the examiner who will respond by approaching the candidate at his or her location within the testing area. Examiners are generally responsive to questions regarding testing procedure only and not the content of the examination itself. Therefore, questions regarding the terminology used within the exam are typically outside of the examiners' response ability.

Leaving the Examination Area during the Exam
The procedures for the containment of examinees are typically described at the testing location, just prior to the beginning of the examination. Generally, candi-dates are not allowed to leave the examination for any reason without the permission of the examiner, and it is not unusual for the rules to include forfeiture of the exam attempt should a candidate need to leave the area. The purpose is to ensure that candidates are not seeking outside help in completing the examination.

► Scoring the Exam

Generally, the results of the examination are available to a candidate within a week or two of the examination date. Of course, objective portions of the examination such as multiple-choice or true/false questions are easier to score. However, subjective portions of the examination including short answers and case planning tend to take longer to score.

The scoring format varies from jurisdiction to jurisdiction but generally includes some basic requirement of achievement. These examinations are typically scored on a pass/fail basis and may include a minimum score requirement in each testing category, in addition to the overall score.

► Resource Information

For further information regarding examinations in a particular location, please consult the table of information on page 20.

PROBATION	PAROLE
ALABAMA	**ALABAMA**
Alabama Board of Pardons and Paroles P.O. Box 302405 Montgomery, AL 36130-2405 Phone: 334-242-1695 www.pardons.state.al.us	Alabama Board of Pardons and Paroles P.O. Box 302405 Montgomery, AL 36130-2405 Phone: 334-242-1695 www.pardons.state.al.us
ALASKA	**ALASKA**
Alaska Department of Corrections 310 K Street, Suite 508 Anchorage, AK 99501 Phone: 907-269-7370 www.correct.state.ak.us	Alaska Department of Corrections 310 K Street, Suite 508 Anchorage, AK 99501 Phone: 907-269-7370 www.correct.state.ak.us
ARIZONA	**ARIZONA**
Administrative Office of the Courts 1501 West Washington, Suite 344 Phoenix, AZ 85007 Phone: 602-542-9460 www.supreme.state.az.us	Department of Corrections 801 South 16th Street, Suite 1 Phoenix, AZ 85034 Phone: 602-771-5770 www.supreme.state.az.us
ARKANSAS	**ARKANSAS**
Department of Community Correction Two Union National Plaza, 2nd Floor 105 West Capitol Little Rock, AR 72201 Phone: 501-682-9584 or 501-682-9587 www.state.ar.us/directory/detail2.cgi?ID=1063	Department of Community Correction Two Union National Plaza, 2nd Floor 105 West Capitol Little Rock, AR 72201 Phone: 501-682-9584 or 501-682-9587 www.state.ar.us/directory/detail2.cgi?ID=20
CALIFORNIA	**CALIFORNIA**
Department of Corrections 9825 Goethe Rd., Suite 200 Sacramento, CA 95827 Phone: 916-255-2781 www.corr.ca.gov/DivisionsBoards/BOPH	Department of Corrections 9825 Goethe Rd., Suite 200 Sacramento, CA 95827 Phone: 916-255-2781 www.corr.ca.gov/DivisionsBoards/BOPH

PROBATION	PAROLE
COLORADO	**COLORADO**
Office of the State Court Administrator 1301 Pennsylvania St., Suite 300 Denver, CO 80203 Phone: 303-861-1111 www.courts.state.co.us/dps/dpsindex.htm	Department of Corrections 12157 West Cedar Drive Lakewood, CO 80228 Phone: 303-763-2420 www.doc.state.co.us/index.html
CONNECTICUT	**CONNECTICUT**
Adult Probation CSSD 936 Silas Deane Highway Wethersfield, CT 06109 Phone: 860-721-2167	Board of Pardons and Paroles 55 West Main Street, Suite 520 Waterbury, CT 06702 Phone: 203-805-6683 or 203-805-6685 www.ct.gov/doc/site
DELAWARE	**DELAWARE**
Department of Correction 1601 North Pine Street Wilmington, DE 19802-5007 Phone: 302-577-3443 www.state.de.us/correct	Department of Correction 1601 North Pine Street Wilmington, DE 19802-5007 Phone: 302-577-3443 www.state.de.us/correct
DISTRICT OF COLUMBIA	**DISTRICT OF COLUMBIA**
Court Services and Offender Supervision Agency for the District of Columbia (CSOSA) 25 K Street NE, Room 304 Washington, DC 20002 Phone: 202-442-1275 www.csosa.gov	Court Services and Offender Supervision Agency for the District of Columbia (CSOSA) 25 K Street NE, Room 304 Washington, DC 20002 Phone: 202-442-1275 www.csosa.gov
FLORIDA	**FLORIDA**
Department of Corrections 2601 Blair Stone Road Tallahassee, FL 32399-2500 Phone: 850-487-0558 or 850-488-4839 www.dc.state.fl.us	Department of Corrections 2601 Blair Stone Road Tallahassee, FL 32399-2500 Phone: 850-487-0558 or 850-488-4839 www.dc.state.fl.us

PROBATION	PAROLE
GEORGIA	**GEORGIA**
Department of Corrections #2 Martin Luther King, Jr. Drive SE East Tower, Suite 958 Atlanta, GA 30334 Phone: 404-656-5305 www.dcor.state.ga.us/default.html	State Board of Pardons and Paroles #2 Martin Luther King, Jr. Drive SE East Tower, Suite 1470 Atlanta, GA 30334 Phone: 404-656-5747
HAWAII	**HAWAII**
First Judicial Circuit Judiciary, State of Hawaii 777 Punchbowl Street Honolulu, HI 96813 Phone: 808-539-4585 www.hawaii.gov/psd/hpa.php	Hawaii Paroling Authority 1177 Alakea Street, Ground Floor Honolulu, HI 96813 Phone: 808-587-1295
IDAHO	**IDAHO**
Idaho Dept. of Correction 1299 North Orchard, Suite 110 Boise, ID 83706 Phone: 208-658-2122 www.corr.state.id.us/index.htm	Idaho Dept. of Correction 1299 North Orchard, Suite 110 Boise, ID 83706 Phone: 208-658-2122 www.corr.state.id.us/index.htm
ILLINOIS	**ILLINOIS**
Administrative Office of Illinois Courts 3101 Old Jacksonville Road Springfield, Illinois 62704-6488 Phone: 217-785-7589 www.idoc.state.il.us	Department of Corrections P.O. Box 19277 1301 Concordia Court Springfield, IL 62794-9277 Phone: 217-522-4461 www.idoc.state.il.us
INDIANA	**INDIANA**
Indiana Judicial Center 115 West Washington St., Suite 1075 Indianapolis, IN 46204-3417 Phone: 317-232-1313 www.in.gov/judiciary/probation	Department of Correction Division of Community Corrections 302 West Washington St., Room E-334 Indianapolis, IN 46204-2278 Phone: 317-232-5722 www.state.in.us/indcorrection

PROBATION	PAROLE
IOWA	**IOWA**
Department of Corrections 510 East 12th Street, Suite 4 Des Moines, IA 50319 Phone: 515-725-5732 or 515-725-5725 www.state.ia.us/government/doc/index.html	Department of Corrections 510 East 12th Street, Suite 4 Des Moines, IA 50319 Phone: 515-725-5732 or 515-725-5725 www.state.ia.us/government/doc/index.html
KANSAS	**KANSAS**
Kansas Department of Corrections Landon State Office Building 900 SW Jackson, 4th Floor Topeka, KS 66612-1284 Phone: 785-368-6330 www.ink.org/public/kdoc	Kansas Department of Corrections Landon State Office Building 900 SW Jackson, 4th Floor Topeka, KS 66612-1284 Phone: 785-368-6330 www.ink.org/public/kdoc
KENTUCKY	**KENTUCKY**
Department of Corrections P.O. Box 2400 Frankfort, KY 40602-2400 Phone: 502-564-4221 http://justice.ky.gov	Department of Corrections P.O. Box 2400 Frankfort, KY 40602-2400 Phone: 502-564-4221 http://justice.ky.gov
LOUISIANA	**LOUISIANA**
Department of Corrections P.O. Box 94304, Capitol Station Baton Rouge, LA 70804-9304 Phone: 225-342-6609 www.corrections.state.la.us	Department of Corrections P.O. Box 94304, Capitol Station Baton Rouge, LA 70804-9304 Phone: 225-342-6609 www.corrections.state.la.us
MAINE	**MAINE**
Division of Probation & Parole AMHI Complex, State House Station #111 Augusta, ME 04333 Phone: 207-287-4381 www.maine.gov/corrections	Division of Probation & Parole AMHI Complex, State House Station #111 Augusta, ME 04333 Phone: 207-287-4381 www.maine.gov/corrections

PROBATION	PAROLE
MARYLAND	**MARYLAND**
Department of Public Safety & Correctional Services Division of Parole and Probation 300 East Joppa Road, Suite 1000 Towson, MD 21286-3020 Phone: 410-339-5000 www.dpscs.state.md.us	Department of Public Safety & Correctional Services Division of Parole and Probation 300 East Joppa Road, Suite 1000 Towson, MD 21286-3020 Phone: 410-339-5000 www.dpscs.state.md.us
MASSACHUSETTS	**MASSACHUSETTS**
Office of the Commissioner of Probation One Ashburton Place, Room 405 McCormack State Office Building Boston, MA 02108 Phone: 617-727-7196 www.state.ma.us/doc	Massachusetts Parole Board 45 Hospital Road, Building B3 Medfield, MA 02052 Phone: 508-242-8001 www.state.ma.us/doc
MICHIGAN	**MICHIGAN**
www.michigan.gov/corrections	Parole Board Department of Corrections Field Operations Administration P.O. Box 30003 Lansing, MI 48909 Phone: 517-335-6903 www.michigan.gov/corrections
MINNESOTA	**MINNESOTA**
Department of Corrections 1450 Energy Park Dr., Suite 200 St. Paul, MN 55108-5219 Phone: 651-642-0311 www.corr.state.mn.us	Department of Corrections 1450 Energy Park Dr., Suite 200 St. Paul, MN 55108-5219 Phone: 651-642-0311 www.corr.state.mn.us
MISSISSIPPI	**MISSISSIPPI**
Department of Corrections Community Services Division 723 North President St. Jackson, MS 39202 Phone: 601-359-5600 www.mdoc.state.ms.us	Department of Corrections Community Services Division 723 North President St. Jackson, MS 39202 Phone: 601-359-5600 www.mdoc.state.ms.us

PROBATION	PAROLE
MISSOURI	**MISSOURI**
Board of Probation & Parole	Board of Probation & Parole
1511 Christy Drive	1511 Christy Drive
Jefferson City, MO 65101	Jefferson City, MO 65101
Phone: 573-751-8488	Phone: 573-751-8488
www.doc.missouri.gov/division/prob/prob.htm	www.doc.missouri.gov/division/prob/prob.htm
MONTANA	**MONTANA**
Division of Corrections	Division of Corrections
P.O. Box 201301, 1539 11th Avenue	P.O. Box 201301, 1539 11th Avenue
Helena, MT 59620	Helena, MT 59620
Phone: 406-444-9522	Phone: 406-444-9522
www.state.mt.us/cor/index.htm	www.state.mt.us/cor/index.htm
NEBRASKA	**NEBRASKA**
www.corrections.state.ne.us	Department of Correctional Services
	P.O. Box 94661, Statehouse Station
	Lincoln, NE 68509-4661
	Phone: 402-479-5768
	www.corrections.state.ne.us
NEVADA	**NEVADA**
Nevada Department of Public Safety	Nevada Department of Public Safety
Division of Parole and Probation	Division of Parole and Probation
1445 Old Hot Springs Road, Suite 104	1445 Old Hot Springs Road, Suite 104
Carson City, Nevada 89701	Carson City, Nevada 89701
Phone: 775-684-2600	Phone: 775-684-2600
http://ps.state.nv.us/pphome.html	http://ps.state.nv.us/pphome.html
NEW HAMPSHIRE	**NEW HAMPSHIRE**
Department of Corrections	Department of Corrections
P.O. Box 1806	P.O. Box 1806
Concord, NH 03302-1806	Concord, NH 03302-1806
Phone: 603-271-5646	Phone: 603-271-5646
www.state.nh.us/nhdoc/pandp.html	www.state.nh.us/nhdoc/pandp.html

PROBATION	PAROLE
NEW JERSEY	**NEW JERSEY**
Administrative Office of the Courts P.O. Box 987, Justice Complex Trenton, NJ 08625 Phone: 609-292-1589 www.judiciary.state.nj.us/admin.htm	New Jersey State Parole Board P.O. 862 Trenton, NJ 08625-0862 Phone: 609-943-4671 www.state.nj.us/corrections www.state.nj.us/parole/index.html
NEW MEXICO	**NEW MEXICO**
Corrections Department Probation & Parole Division P.O. Box 27116 Santa Fe, NM 87502-0116 Phone: 505-827-8693 www.corrections.state.nm.us	Corrections Department Probation & Parole Division P.O. Box 27116 Santa Fe, NM 87502-0116 Phone: 505-827-8693 www.corrections.state.nm.us
NEW YORK	**NEW YORK**
NYS Div. of Probation and Correctional Alternatives 80 Wolf Road, Suite 501 Albany, NY 12205 Phone: 518-485-2399 http://dpca.state.ny.us	NYS Division of Parole 845 Central Avenue, East 2 Albany, NY 12206 Phone: 518-457-7566 http://dpca.state.ny.us
NORTH CAROLINA	**NORTH CAROLINA**
Department of Correction Division of Community Corrections 2020 Yonkers Road Mail Service Center 4250 Raleigh, NC 27699-4250 Phone: 919-716-3160 www.doc.state.nc.us	Department of Correction Division of Community Corrections 2020 Yonkers Road Mail Service Center 4250 Raleigh, NC 27699-4250 Phone: 919-716-3160 www.doc.state.nc.us
NORTH DAKOTA	**NORTH DAKOTA**
Department of Corrections P.O. Box 5521 Bismarck, ND 58506-5521 Phone: 701-328-6198 www.state.nd.us/docr	Department of Corrections P.O. Box 5521 Bismarck, ND 58506-5521 Phone: 701-328-6198 www.state.nd.us/docr

PROBATION	PAROLE
OHIO	**OHIO**
Department of Corrections 1030 Alum Creek Dr. Columbus, OH 43209 Phone: 614-387-0809 www.drc.state.oh.us	Ohio Adult Parole Authority 1050 Freeway Dr. North Columbus, OH 43229 Phone: 614-752-1254 www.drc.state.oh.us
OKLAHOMA	**OKLAHOMA**
Department of Corrections 3700 North Classen Blvd., Suite 110 Oklahoma City, OK 73118 Phone: 405-525-4510 www.doc.state.ok.us	Department of Corrections 3700 North Classen Blvd., Suite 110 Oklahoma City, OK 73118 Phone: 405-525-4510 www.doc.state.ok.us
OREGON	**OREGON**
Department of Corrections 2575 Center Street NE Salem, OR 97301 Phone: 503-947-1036 www.oregon.gov/DOC	Department of Corrections 2575 Center Street NE Salem, OR 97301 Phone: 503-947-1036 www.oregon.gov/DOC
PENNSYLVANIA	**PENNSYLVANIA**
Board of Probation & Parole 1101 S. Front Street, Suite 5800 Harrisburg, PA 17104-2538 Phone: 717-787-6134 www.pbpp.state.pa.us/pbpp/site/default.asp	Board of Probation & Parole 1101 S. Front Street, Suite 5800 Harrisburg, PA 17104-2538 Phone: 717-787-6134 www.pbpp.state.pa.us/pbpp/site/default.asp
RHODE ISLAND	**RHODE ISLAND**
Rhode Island Department of Corrections Division of Rehabilitative Services Community Corrections 40 Howard Avenue Cranston, RI 02920 Phone: 401-462-1000 www.doc.state.ri.us	Rhode Island Department of Corrections Division of Rehabilitative Services Community Corrections 40 Howard Avenue Cranston, RI 02920 Phone: 401-462-1000 www.doc.state.ri.us

PROBATION	PAROLE
SOUTH CAROLINA	**SOUTH CAROLINA**
Probation, Parole, & Pardon Services P.O. Box 50666 2221 Devine Street Columbia, SC 29250 Phone: 803-734-9325 www.dppps.sc.gov	Probation, Parole, & Pardon Services P.O. Box 50666 2221 Devine Street Columbia, SC 29250 Phone: 803-734-9325 www.dppps.sc.gov
SOUTH DAKOTA	**SOUTH DAKOTA**
Court Services Department 500 East Capitol Pierre, SD 57501 Phone: 605-773-4873 www.state.sd.us/state/judicial	Board of Pardons and Paroles P.O. Box 5911 Sioux Falls, SD 57117-5911 Phone: 605-367-5040 or 605-782-3153 www.state.sd.us/CORRECTIONS/parole.htm
TENNESSEE	**TENNESSEE**
Board of Probation and Parole Parkway Towers, Suite 1410 404 James Robertson Pkwy Nashville, TN 37243-0850 Phone: 615-532-8129 www2.state.tn.us/bopp/home.htm	Board of Probation and Parole Parkway Towers, Suite 1410 404 James Robertson Pkwy Nashville, TN 37243-0850 Phone: 615-532-8129 www2.state.tn.us/bopp/home.htm
TEXAS	**TEXAS**
Texas Department of Criminal Justice 8712 Shoals Creek Blvd., Suite 290 Austin, TX 78757 Phone: 512-406-5990 www.tdcj.state.tx.us/bpp/index.htm	Texas Department of Criminal Justice 8712 Shoals Creek Blvd., Suite 290 Austin, TX 78757 Phone: 512-406-5990 www.tdcj.state.tx.us/bpp/index.htm
UTAH	**UTAH**
Department of Corrections 14717 South Minuteman Dr. Draper, UT 84020 Phone: 801-495-7702 www.udc.state.ut.us	Department of Corrections 14717 South Minuteman Dr. Draper, UT 84020 Phone: 801-495-7702 www.udc.state.ut.us

PROBATION	PAROLE
VERMONT	**VERMONT**
Department of Corrections 103 South Main Street Waterbury, VT 05671-1001 Phone: 802-241-2270 www.doc.state.vt.us	Department of Corrections 103 South Main Street Waterbury, VT 05671-1001 Phone: 802-241-2270 www.doc.state.vt.us
VIRGINIA	**VIRGINIA**
Department of Corrections P.O. Box 26963 Richmond, VA 23261-6963 Phone: 804-674-3065 www.vadoc.state.va.us	Department of Corrections P.O. Box 26963 Richmond, VA 23261-6963 Phone: 804-674-3065 www.vadoc.state.va.us
WASHINGTON	**WASHINGTON**
Department of Corrections P.O. Box 41126 Olympia, WA 98504-1126 Phone: 360-725-8735 www.doc.wa.gov	Department of Corrections P.O. Box 41126 Olympia, WA 98504-1126 Phone: 360-725-8735 www.doc.wa.gov
WEST VIRGINIA	**WEST VIRGINIA**
West Virginia Supreme Court of Appeals Administrative Office of the Courts Office of Probation Services Building 1, Room E-100 1900 Kanawha Blvd. East Charleston, WV 25305 Phone: 304-558-1045 www.wvf.state.wv.us/wvdoc	Department of Corrections 112 California Ave. Building 4, Room 300 Charleston, WV 25305-0280 Phone: 304-558-2036 www.wvf.state.wv.us/wvdoc

PROBATION	PAROLE
WISCONSIN	**WISCONSIN**
Department of Corrections	Department of Corrections
3099 East Washington Avenue	3099 East Washington Avenue
P.O. Box 7925	P.O. Box 7925
Madison, WI 53707-7925	Madison, WI 53707-7925
Phone: 608-240-5308 or 608-240-5311	Phone: 608-240-5308 or 608-240-5311
www.wi-doc.com/community.htm	www.wi-doc.com/community.htm
WYOMING	**WYOMING**
Department of Corrections	Department of Corrections
700 West 21st Street	700 West 21st Street
Cheyenne, WY 82002	Cheyenne, WY 82002
Phone: 307-777-7208	Phone: 307-777-7208
http://doc.state.wy.us/corrections.asp	http://doc.state.wy.us/corrections.asp

4 ▶ Practice Test 1

This is the first practice test in the book based on the most commonly tested areas on probation officer and parole officer exams. By taking Practice Test 1 before you begin studying for your exam, you
will get an idea of how much you already know and how much you need to learn in order to become
a probation or parole officer.

The skills tested on this exam are the ones that have been previously tested on probation officer and parole
officer exams that focus on job-related skills. The exam you take may look somewhat different from this exam,
but you'll find that this exam provides vital practice in the skills you need to pass your exam.

The practice test consists of 100 multiple-choice questions in the following areas: job responsibilities, case
studies, writing skills, and reading comprehension. You should give yourself three hours to take this practice test.
The number of questions and the time limit of the actual probation officer or parole officer exam can vary from
region to region.

Practice Test 1

1.	ⓐ ⓑ ⓒ ⓓ	36.	ⓐ ⓑ ⓒ ⓓ	71.	ⓐ ⓑ ⓒ ⓓ
2.	ⓐ ⓑ ⓒ ⓓ	37.	ⓐ ⓑ ⓒ ⓓ	72.	ⓐ ⓑ ⓒ ⓓ
3.	ⓐ ⓑ ⓒ ⓓ	38.	ⓐ ⓑ ⓒ ⓓ	73.	ⓐ ⓑ ⓒ ⓓ
4.	ⓐ ⓑ ⓒ ⓓ	39.	ⓐ ⓑ ⓒ ⓓ	74.	ⓐ ⓑ ⓒ ⓓ
5.	ⓐ ⓑ ⓒ ⓓ	40.	ⓐ ⓑ ⓒ ⓓ	75.	ⓐ ⓑ ⓒ ⓓ
6.	ⓐ ⓑ ⓒ ⓓ	41.	ⓐ ⓑ ⓒ ⓓ	76.	ⓐ ⓑ ⓒ ⓓ
7.	ⓐ ⓑ ⓒ ⓓ	42.	ⓐ ⓑ ⓒ ⓓ	77.	ⓐ ⓑ ⓒ ⓓ
8.	ⓐ ⓑ ⓒ ⓓ	43.	ⓐ ⓑ ⓒ ⓓ	78.	ⓐ ⓑ ⓒ ⓓ
9.	ⓐ ⓑ ⓒ ⓓ	44.	ⓐ ⓑ ⓒ ⓓ	79.	ⓐ ⓑ ⓒ ⓓ
10.	ⓐ ⓑ ⓒ ⓓ	45.	ⓐ ⓑ ⓒ ⓓ	80.	ⓐ ⓑ ⓒ ⓓ
11.	ⓐ ⓑ ⓒ ⓓ	46.	ⓐ ⓑ ⓒ ⓓ	81.	ⓐ ⓑ ⓒ ⓓ
12.	ⓐ ⓑ ⓒ ⓓ	47.	ⓐ ⓑ ⓒ ⓓ	82.	ⓐ ⓑ ⓒ ⓓ
13.	ⓐ ⓑ ⓒ ⓓ	48.	ⓐ ⓑ ⓒ ⓓ	83.	ⓐ ⓑ ⓒ ⓓ
14.	ⓐ ⓑ ⓒ ⓓ	49.	ⓐ ⓑ ⓒ ⓓ	84.	ⓐ ⓑ ⓒ ⓓ
15.	ⓐ ⓑ ⓒ ⓓ	50.	ⓐ ⓑ ⓒ ⓓ	85.	ⓐ ⓑ ⓒ ⓓ
16.	ⓐ ⓑ ⓒ ⓓ	51.	ⓐ ⓑ ⓒ ⓓ	86.	ⓐ ⓑ ⓒ ⓓ
17.	ⓐ ⓑ ⓒ ⓓ	52.	ⓐ ⓑ ⓒ ⓓ	87.	ⓐ ⓑ ⓒ ⓓ
18.	ⓐ ⓑ ⓒ ⓓ	53.	ⓐ ⓑ ⓒ ⓓ	88.	ⓐ ⓑ ⓒ ⓓ
19.	ⓐ ⓑ ⓒ ⓓ	54.	ⓐ ⓑ ⓒ ⓓ	89.	ⓐ ⓑ ⓒ ⓓ
20.	ⓐ ⓑ ⓒ ⓓ	55.	ⓐ ⓑ ⓒ ⓓ	90.	ⓐ ⓑ ⓒ ⓓ
21.	ⓐ ⓑ ⓒ ⓓ	56.	ⓐ ⓑ ⓒ ⓓ	91.	ⓐ ⓑ ⓒ ⓓ
22.	ⓐ ⓑ ⓒ ⓓ	57.	ⓐ ⓑ ⓒ ⓓ	92.	ⓐ ⓑ ⓒ ⓓ
23.	ⓐ ⓑ ⓒ ⓓ	58.	ⓐ ⓑ ⓒ ⓓ	93.	ⓐ ⓑ ⓒ ⓓ
24.	ⓐ ⓑ ⓒ ⓓ	59.	ⓐ ⓑ ⓒ ⓓ	94.	ⓐ ⓑ ⓒ ⓓ
25.	ⓐ ⓑ ⓒ ⓓ	60.	ⓐ ⓑ ⓒ ⓓ	95.	ⓐ ⓑ ⓒ ⓓ
26.	ⓐ ⓑ ⓒ ⓓ	61.	ⓐ ⓑ ⓒ ⓓ	96.	ⓐ ⓑ ⓒ ⓓ
27.	ⓐ ⓑ ⓒ ⓓ	62.	ⓐ ⓑ ⓒ ⓓ	97.	ⓐ ⓑ ⓒ ⓓ
28.	ⓐ ⓑ ⓒ ⓓ	63.	ⓐ ⓑ ⓒ ⓓ	98.	ⓐ ⓑ ⓒ ⓓ
29.	ⓐ ⓑ ⓒ ⓓ	64.	ⓐ ⓑ ⓒ ⓓ	99.	ⓐ ⓑ ⓒ ⓓ
30.	ⓐ ⓑ ⓒ ⓓ	65.	ⓐ ⓑ ⓒ ⓓ	100.	ⓐ ⓑ ⓒ ⓓ
31.	ⓐ ⓑ ⓒ ⓓ	66.	ⓐ ⓑ ⓒ ⓓ		
32.	ⓐ ⓑ ⓒ ⓓ	67.	ⓐ ⓑ ⓒ ⓓ		
33.	ⓐ ⓑ ⓒ ⓓ	68.	ⓐ ⓑ ⓒ ⓓ		
34.	ⓐ ⓑ ⓒ ⓓ	69.	ⓐ ⓑ ⓒ ⓓ		
35.	ⓐ ⓑ ⓒ ⓓ	70.	ⓐ ⓑ ⓒ ⓓ		

▶ Practice Test 1

1. The primary function of parole is
   a. to ensure the safety and security of the community.
   b. to provide community resources and services to the offender.
   c. to provide basic supervision of offenders once they are released from prison.
   d. to assist in locating employment.

2. A parolee comes to see you, angry that a potential employer refused to hire him because he is on parole. He wants you to do something about it. How should you respond?
   a. You should tell the offender it isn't your fault; he is the one with a felony conviction.
   b. You should express empathy for the offender and point him to another job lead.
   c. You should sympathize with the offender, pick up the phone, and call the business owner who denied employment, telling him that he discriminated.
   d. You should tell the offender that there are all kinds of people who discriminate and that he has a right to be angry.

3. You have decided to impose the special condition, "You will not have any contact with small children in your home, at work, or any other location in which you frequent," upon a particular sex offender on your caseload. He argues it is unconstitutional and tells you he is going to sue. What grounds do you have to impose this condition?
   a. Simply by being the parole officer, you can impose whatever special condition you want for whatever reason.
   b. The Fourth Amendment provides you with this authority, which has been upheld by the U.S. Supreme Court.
   c. Parole is discretionary, and conditions may be imposed or modified as long as they are reasonable and related to circumstances of the offense and criminal history of the parolee.
   d. You cannot impose this condition.

4. You decide to start revocation proceedings on a parolee on your caseload. The due process rights afforded to the parolee at this time do NOT include
   a. a notice of the violations and time of hearing.
   b. the opportunity to be heard at a hearing and a chance to cross-examine witnesses.
   c. the right to counsel.
   d. a written statement by the fact finders of the final decision.

5. A parolee, who is in jail waiting to be transported back to prison, tells you his Eighth Amendment rights are being violated. What allegation would he be making?
   a. The jail is overcrowded.
   b. There is a lack of adequate medical care and treatment.
   c. The jail is overcrowded, and there is a lack of adequate medical care and treatment.
   d. none of the above

6. You have been told one of your parolees has a gun hidden in her car. Can you search her car, and what provides you justification to do so?

   a. As the parole officer, you can do whatever is necessary to protect society.

   b A parolee must allow his or her car and home to be searched by the parole officer as described in the parole conditions.

   c. No, a search cannot be accomplished without a search warrant.

   d. No, law enforcement officers from the police department are the only ones who can do a search.

7. You are conducting a home visit of one of your parolees. This parolee has been released from jail for only two months and is currently living with his mother. You walk into the home through the front door and hear a disturbance in the kitchen. The parolee immediately apologizes for the "noise" that his mom and her current boyfriend are making. You start conducting your conversation with the parolee when you hear a slap, and then the male voice loudly says, "I'm going to kill you for that." Your parolee is very upset and starts to go toward the kitchen. You should

   a. ignore what is happening in the kitchen and continue talking with the parolee.

   b. follow the parolee into the kitchen and demand to know what is going on.

   c. take your parolee out to the front porch to continue the conversation and explore what options the parolee has of moving out of this type of situation.

   d. put your hands on the parolee to stop him from entering the kitchen.

8. Parole officers perform administrative and discretionary duties. While they are performing those duties without maliciousness, parole officers are given what type of immunity?

   a. quasi-judicial

   b. qualified

   c. absolute

   d. conditional

9. In most states, an adult who is released from prison to supervision is placed on parole. What is this practice called in the juvenile system in most states?

   a. detention

   b. parole

   c. mandatory release

   d. aftercare

10. One of your juvenile probationers who is in detention on a new charge confesses to you and gives you specific details about the crime. You ask him why he is confessing, and he responds, "You are just like my lawyer, and all this is privileged information." What should your next step be?

   a. Figuring that he is in jail and won't get out any time soon, you should falsely agree that his confession is privileged information.

   b. You should agree that his confession is privileged and encourage him to repeat his confession to the detectives.

   c. You should tell him that the confession isn't privileged information because you are not covered under the attorney-client privilege, and that you must tell the prosecutor.

   d. You should tell him that the confession isn't privileged and that you will give him 48 hours to tell the detectives or you will.

11. Probation revocation can be decided only by
   a. the probation officer.
   b. the court.
   c. the probation supervisor.
   d. the county commission.

12. In the matter of a probation revocation, the judge has the option to
   a. continue probation with or without extending the probation term.
   b. modify the conditions of probation.
   c. revoke the sentence of probation and resentence the defendant.
   d. all of the above

13. You have a 17-year-old probationer who has refused to pay her mandatory court costs (fines) and restitution. She claims she will be released from the financial obligation when she turns 18 and is released from her probation. She will turn 18 in three months. Which is NOT an option for your consideration?
   a. to start revocation proceedings because she has the means to pay the fines and restitution but has repeatedly refused
   b. to try talking to her again about the importance of paying off debts, etc.
   c. to avoid making this an issue because you know you can keep her on probation after her 18th birthday
   d. to let the probationer know her facts may not be accurate and that you have asked your supervisor to sit with you while you explain again the importance of paying debts and making amends for the crime, and then, if she continues to refuse to pay, start revocation proceedings

14. _____ is defined as the release of a convicted offender under conditions imposed by the court for a specific time frame during which the court maintains the authority to modify the conditions or resentence the offender as needed.
   a. Prerelease planning
   b. Probation
   c. Community corrections
   d. Parole

15. The man who has been recognized as "the Father of Probation" is
   a. John Augustus.
   b. Alexander Machonochie.
   c. Peter Oxenbridge Thacher.
   d. King Henry VII.

16. You have to go to the facility where your probationer being held while awaiting sentencing. You go to the nearest
   a. prison.
   b. halfway house.
   c. jail.
   d. reentry program.

17. The presentence investigation report is used
   a. by the courts to determine an appropriate sentence for the offender.
   b. by the victim to determine how much restitution is owed to him or her.
   c. by the correctional institutions for purposes of classification and treatment.
   d. choices **a** and **c**

18. You have been asked to complete a presentence investigation report on an offender. When you go to the jail to start this process, the offender tells you that on the advice of his attorney, he is not going to participate actively in this process and you are going to have to find out information on your own. Your next step is to

a. tell the offender that you will see him sit in jail for taking that approach with you.

b. try to convince the offender that it is in his best interest to talk with you, even asking if the offender would like to call his attorney again.

c. leave the jail and go to the judge's chambers to ask him or her to insist that the offender cooperate.

d. leave the jail and go to the records division of the courthouse to start collecting the offender's criminal history and collateral information.

19. You have been asked to prepare a presentence investigation report on a high profile case. You work for hours on this case, only to have the completed report "trashed" by the judge in the open courtroom. You should

a. demand a meeting with the judge to find out what his problem with the report is.

b. ask to meet with your supervisor to go over the report to see how you could improve.

c. ask to receive additional training or attend writing classes, specifically investigation report writing classes.

d. quit because you obviously can't do the job.

20. A juvenile commits an act that is punishable by law. This is called

a. a delinquent act.

b. an act indicating a child in need of supervision.

c. an act indicating a person in need of supervision.

d. an act that should be handled by the adult system.

21. An offender is more likely to abscond if which of the following is true?

a. The offender is frequently unemployed.

b. The offender lives in unstable conditions.

c. The offender is male.

d. choices **a** and **b**

22. Which example is NOT a technical violation?

a. failing to report

b. moving without telling the probation or parole officer

c. associating with people who have committed offenses

d. being arrested for driving under the influence

23. When violations of supervision conditions are committed in a state that is not the state in which the offender committed the original offense, who has the authority to revoke or modify the conditions?

a. the federal courts

b. the state in which the violations occurred

c. the Interstate Compact consortium

d. the state in which the offender was originally placed on probation

24. According to the American Probation and Parole Association, all probation and parole officers must complete which of the following levels of qualifications at the time they are hired?

a. high school plus five years of experience working with offenders

b. a bachelor's degree plus one year of experience or graduate study

c. a master's degree and three months of experience working with offenders

d. both bachelor's and master's degrees

25. Which of the following lists civil rights that have been given to offenders by the courts, unless a compelling state interest can be shown as to why they should not be given?
  a. freedom of religion, freedom from wrongful search and seizure, and the right to bear arms
  b. freedom of religion, freedom of speech, freedom of the press, and the right to assembly
  c. freedom from cruel and unusual punishment, freedom from wrongful search and seizure, the right to vote
  d. freedom of religion, the right to bear arms, and the right to vote

26. A reasonable condition of probation and parole is
  a. directly related to the offense.
  b. a clear punishment.
  c. one that the offender can follow, with a possibility of completing.
  d. explicit, precise, clear, and easily understood.

27. A probation or parole officer who considers his or her role as a "service broker" is
  a. providing counseling to the offenders.
  b. referring offenders to different programs according to their needs.
  c. providing structure regarding the rules and procedures of supervision.
  d. holding offenders accountable, but providing services when requested by the offender.

28. Which of the following is essential as soon as supervision starts?
  a. The offender must submit regular monthly reports to the officer.
  b. The offender must find employment.
  c. The offender must maintain family support.
  d. The offender must schedule meetings for the necessary resources (i.e., drug counseling, Alcoholics Anonymous, sex offender counseling, etc.).

29. An offender wishes to transfer his supervision to another state. In the process of completing the paperwork, you advise him this transfer means he waives the right to
  a. return to the state.
  b. bail.
  c. extradition.
  d. vote in the next election.

30. It is the middle of the month, and you are behind in your paperwork for your caseload. You have accomplished all of the field visits that are required for the month, but you have yet to update the case files on your computer, nor have you completed the mandatory classification tool that is required of all new supervisees. You have received six new offenders on your caseload so far this month. Which of the following should you do?
  a. You should not worry because you have a few working days left in the month to catch up and hopefully you won't have to deal with any offender who has violated his or her conditions.
  b. You should not worry because you know another officer who is three months behind on her casework and nobody has said anything to her yet.
  c. You should plan to work quickly over the next few days to catch up, accepting that you will have to provide only minimal documentation of your field visits and collateral contacts.
  d. You should explain to your supervisor that you are behind in completing your paperwork, and indicate that you plan to do your classification tool first and then will start your documentation with the most severe offenders.

Directions: Read the following case study and then answer questions 31 through 36.

Gerald is serving a ten-year sentence for the sexual assault of a minor. He has served six years and two months of his sentence. He will be released in three months as part of a plan to reduce overcrowding that the department of corrections has developed. Gerald will serve the remainder of his ten-year sentence under community supervision, on parole. Gerald's previous criminal history includes one other sex offense, after which he completed a sex treatment program and was placed on probation, which was revoked because of the current sexual assault charge. All of his victims have been children of family members, who are strongly opposed to his being released. Gerald participated in the sexual offender treatment program while in prison, and the treatment counselor indicated that Gerald has worked hard to learn the triggers he needs to avoid. However, the counselor indicated that Gerald's prognosis is guarded. Gerald has been a model prisoner, earned minimum custody status, and worked in the prison industries. He has indicated that he wishes to be paroled to a halfway house 20 minutes from his family, in a small community where he doesn't know anyone. Family members wish to have a special condition placed upon Gerald to make sure he doesn't have contact with them. For parole planning purposes, Gerald has been accepted into a halfway house program that will provide his only support system. He does not have any job prospects and doesn't have many marketable skills. He plans to attend the aftercare program for sexual offenders.

31. Prior to Gerald being released from prison, you receive several phone calls from the family and friends of the victims indicating that Gerald should not be released into the community. You gently remind them that he is not planning to live in their community and they should not be too concerned about Gerald coming back to their community. They have indicated they will try to block Gerald's release through protests and media blitzes. You should

a. remain professional with the family and friends, listen to their concerns, and offer suggestions on where they can protest.

b. remain professional with family and friends and offer to place a special condition on Gerald that he cannot travel outside the community to which he wishes to be paroled.

c. call the prison where Gerald is being held alerting them to the latest threat of protest.

d. do nothing; because Gerald is still incarcerated, this is still a facility and paroling authority issue.

32. Gerald has arrived at the halfway house safely and has been working within the orientation process for the last two weeks. In your first meeting with Gerald, he indicates he is pleased with being at the halfway house and is comfortable with the other residents. As you are talking, you notice Gerald is unable to maintain eye contact with you, shifts in his chair, and talks quieter when other residents come around. You should

a. do nothing, because this a normal reaction for someone who has just been released from prison, especially considering the amount of time he has spent inside.

b. point out his behavior and demand Gerald tell you why he is so nervous.

c. ask the halfway house staff if they have observed the same behavior you saw during your conversation with Gerald, or if they have knowledge of any problems between Gerald and other residents.

d. point out his behavior, and tell him you think he might have re-offended based on his nervousness.

33. The parole supervisor notifies you that the local newspaper has called to indicate they received a notice of a rally protesting sex offenders. The newspaper's reporter indicates they have heard a rumor that protestors will be marching in front of the halfway house where Gerald is staying. You are told the protestor signs would identify Gerald and another sex offender by name and demand that they be castrated, among other derogatory statements. The parole supervisor asked you to take care of this. You should

a. contact the halfway house manager, alert him or her to the protest plans, and ask him or her to call if you need to do something for Gerald.

b. contact the halfway house manager, alert him or her to the protest plans, and ask for Gerald's itinerary for the following day. If nothing is planned, you should make arrangements for Gerald to spend the day elsewhere.

c. do nothing, as it is not your responsibility to manage the halfway house.

d. contact the police department and ask for additional coverage at the halfway house.

34. The halfway house manager calls to inform you he has been concerned about Gerald's behavior and he thinks Gerald has re-offended. You learn from the manager that Gerald has been caught viewing children's videos on the house television and has visited inappropriate websites on the house computer. Gerald also "disappeared" for several hours yesterday, and the halfway house staff cannot find out from Gerald or the other residents where he was. You aren't scheduled to see Gerald for another two weeks. The first step you should take is

a. to pay Gerald a surprise visit and ask him for an explanation of the manager's concerns.

b. to bring Gerald to the parole office and administer a polygraph test.

c. to have Gerald taken into detention immediately, because waiting for a sex offender to re-offend is political suicide.

d. to tell the manager you just visited with Gerald and ask if Gerald is still participating in his sex offender treatment program.

35. Gerald calls you in your office and asks if you could stop by to see him this week. When you get to the halfway house, Gerald tells you that being out of prison is just too hard and he wants to be returned to custody today. He adds that he likes his prison sex offender counselor better than his halfway house counselor and that he feels more connected to the prison treatment program than his current program. Gerald tells you he is having difficulty staying away from his triggers and is afraid he will re-offend. He also informs you that he has identified the location of a nearby school and what times children walk to and from the school. Under these circumstances, you should

a. tell Gerald to get strong and deal with life as it comes.

b. suggest to Gerald that he start exploring other options for his counseling needs.

c. end the conversation with Gerald, and on your way out tell the halfway house staff of your conversation. You ask the staff to watch Gerald closer.

d. tell Gerald that you are going to put him in jail for a period of time until you both can figure out a way to deal with his relapse. His admission to finding a nearby school and identifying ways to spend time or possibly re-offend with children necessitates this action.

36. The halfway house calls you to inform you that Gerald is missing. Gerald had left for a job interview that morning, to be followed by his sex offender treatment session at 1:00 P.M. The counselor had called the halfway house at 2:30 P.M. to ask where Gerald was. When he realized that Gerald's whereabouts were unknown, the halfway house manager called the police to report him missing. What should you do in this situation?

a. You should issue a parole violation warrant immediately, so that if the police department finds Gerald, there is reason to hold him in jail.

b. You should drive the path you think Gerald might have taken, paying special attention to the schools in and around the treatment program and the halfway house.

c. You should do nothing as the halfway house had already contacted the police department.

d. You should call the victims and let them know that Gerald's whereabouts are unknown.

Directions: Read the following case study and then answer questions 37 through 41.

Jane is a 32-year-old single mother of two boys, ages five and three. She is currently without family support, holds a minimum-wage job, has some college credits, and has indicated to you she is barely making her bills. Jane has been under supervision for one year for a three-year probation sentence for trafficking drugs. Her sentence is a fairly light because the judge considered the circumstances surrounding her arrest: Her then-boyfriend had been being picked up by the local drug detectives who found him "clean"; however, Jane was carrying a small amount of cocaine in her clothing. Still, Jane is considered a mule for one of the local gangs, and is seen with different male gang members at different times throughout the week.

Last week, Jane was arrested at the local airport during a sting operation by the local police depart-ment. The police were looking for a drug lord who was rumored to be using the local airport to get in and out of the nearby large metropolitan area. Local detectives, as well as DEA agents, had staked out the airport waiting for their suspect, and Jane happened to be identified by one of the detectives as a local drug mule. Jane was detained to see if she knew anything of the drug lord and to see just what she was doing at the airport. Jane had been carrying a suitcase. Once she gave permission to open the suitcase, the detectives found it loaded with cocaine with an estimated street value of $50,000. Jane was arrested and booked at the local jail. One of the local drug detectives remembers your connection with Jane and calls you to give you the details of Jane's arrest and her current location. You go to the local jail where Jane tells you she didn't know what was in the suitcase she was picking up. She begs you not to recommend revocation to the judge. She also indicates her children are with her neighbor.

37. Jane's neighbor calls and leaves a message for you at your office about Jane's two children. The message says, "These kids aren't mine, and if you don't come get them, I'm going to set them outside and leave them there all night." How should you handle this situation?

a. You should call the state child welfare office and report the neighbor for potential neglect.

b. You should check the case file to see if Jane listed a close relative who might take the children. If not, then the child welfare agency should be called, and after explaining the situation regarding Jane, ask the child welfare agents to go to the neighbor's house to get the children.

c. You should ignore the message, as taking care of offender's children is not your concern.

d. You should notify the jail that Jane needs to make arrangements for her children.

38. Jane has now spent two full days in jail. From the police report and through conversations with the detectives, you have learned that Jane continues to deny any knowledge that she knew the contents of the suitcase, nor does she know who asked her to pick up the suitcase. You will need to make a decision regarding Jane's probation status by tomorrow. What should you consider when making your decision?
   a. Jane's ability to follow the conditions established by the court
   b. Jane's children
   c. any other violations that have occurred during this year
   d. Jane's current employment

39. The judge has indicated that he is willing to make an exception to the sentencing guidelines and keep Jane on probation for the additional crime. However, he wishes to learn from you what type of expectations you would want Jane to fulfill in this new probation term, if granted. What type of programs would you recommend?
   a. dependency counseling, employment education/counseling, college classes
   b. parenting classes, college classes, employment education/counseling
   c. substance abuse counseling, employment education/counseling, parenting classes
   d. You wouldn't recommend any programs, but would strongly suggest that she move closer to her family.

40. Jane comes to your office and indicates that she knows who the drug lord is and where he is staying. She states she wants to make a deal with the DEA agents, but only if it will help her with her probation. Jane says that she wants to be able to leave with her children and move to her mother's home in another state. After you ask a few questions to ensure she does indeed know the drug lord's name, you
   a. contact the DEA office and tell them about Jane's offer and her conditions.
   b. contact the local drug detectives as you work closer with them.
   c. tell Jane that you don't negotiate probation conditions and no deals will be made. However, now that she has told you she knows the name of the drug lord, she is bound by law to tell you.
   d. tell Jane that she must tell you the name and that you will contact the DEA on her behalf. You will ensure that they will give her the conditions she has asked for.

41. Jane testifies in the drug lord's trial. During the trial, there are hints of retaliation against Jane by several of the gang members who are convicted of other charges. You take the hints and rumors seriously; however, Jane indicates she is not afraid. A detective with the local police department has just called to tell you he has intercepted a message calling for Jane's death. How should you handle this situation?
   a. You should ask the detective to have Jane placed in protective custody and to see if they will move her to a safe location.
   b. You should ask your supervisor if there is any need to be concerned and if the probation department has funds to help Jane out.
   c. You should go to Jane's house, collect her and her children, and take them to a local hotel.
   d. You should call Jane and tell her on the phone what the detectives have learned, and ask her to call the detectives to find out what she needs to do.

Directions: Read the following case study and then answer questions 42 through 46.

An intern, Jonathan, has been assigned to your parole office. The parole supervisor has asked that Jonathan spend the day with you as you have a high-risk offender caseload. Your plan is to spend the morning making collateral visits and then making home visits to three offenders. You ask Jonathan to report to your office at 8:00 A.M. so you can describe the day's activities and answer any questions he may have. Jonathan asks a few questions, and after what seems to be forever, he indicates he doesn't have any more questions. You tell him that, because your caseload is made up of high-risk offenders, you will be going into the homes of offenders who have been convicted of multiple charges, including murder. You intimate that he will need to be on guard to remain safe during these visits, and you ask Jonathan if he has any concerns about this. He asked if you will be carrying weapons, to which you reply no. You indicate that he can watch you do a collateral visit or two, and then he can spend some time interviewing folks in additional contacts if he wants. He seems excited by this prospect.

You were not excited when your supervisor asked for Jonathan to spend the day with you. Your coworkers have not been pleased with Jonathan's attitude when he sits with them during office visits, feeling that he is cocky and rude. Prior to leaving for the day with Jonathan, you again explain that the caseload is full of high-risk offenders and that good communication is essential to your job. You feel that Jonathan understands the activities of the day and that it is essential you both work hard to be safe. Jonathan gives you a sigh and says, "I got it. It's dangerous. Let's go." You anticipate a full day.

42. During your first collateral visit, you ask one of your offender's employers if there are any problems you should know about. You learn the offender has had attendance problems this week, and the employer thinks the offender came into work drunk one morning. You ask what the employer found to make him think that, and you are told that the employee smelled of alcohol and had bloodshot eyes. However, the offender wasn't slurring his words, weaving when he was walking, nor falling asleep at work. The employer indicated, "I'd hate to lose him because when he is here, he works hard." During the interview, you happen to notice Jonathan roaming around the warehouse talking with the workers. On more than one occasion, you notice the workers walk away from Jonathan shaking their heads in a "no" fashion. After you finish you conversation with the employer, you call to Jonathan to meet you in the car. How should you handle Jonathan?

a. You should not say anything to Jonathan as he probably was just asking questions about the offender, which is part of the job.

b. You should indicate to Jonathan what you observed and ask him what he was talking about with the employees. You should them provide appropriate feedback to Jonathan, depending upon what his answer to your question is.

c. You should indicate to Jonathan that this is a learning process and he should stay with you during the first several contacts to learn what type of questions to ask and what type of discussions are appropriate.

d. You should high-five him and applaud his innovation and initiative.

43. Jonathan does a great job in staying with you during the remainder of the collateral visits, and over lunch you thank him for following your instructions. He indicates he has learned quite a bit about how to approach people. He requests that you do a surprise collateral visit and allow him to do the interview. You choose to stop at an offender's mother's home. This particular offender has caused you extreme difficulties in months past, but you feel you have made a breakthrough with this offender, and recently he has been talking freely with you. At the door, you introduce the mother to Jonathan and ask her if she has a few minutes to talk with you both. She agrees and allows you to enter in her home. Shortly after beginning the interview, Jonathan becomes rude in his statements, curses in front of the mother, and generally becomes out of control with his language and accusations. After you interrupt Jonathan and to tell him to stop, you should

  a. ask for a few minutes, step outside to the front porch, and quickly tell him that his attitude and language are unacceptable and that that behavior will stop immediately. Then you should make him go back into the mother's home and apologize to her.

  b. send him to the car so that you can spend time repairing the damage Jonathan has done with the mother.

  c. tell him, in front of the mother, that his attitude and language are unacceptable and that that behavior will stop. Then you should tell him to apologize to the mother.

  d. leave the home, hoping the mother will realize that Jonathan is just learning and didn't mean to be rude.

44. At the second home visit of your afternoon, you inform Jonathan that the offender who lives in this home is a convicted murderer. As you pull up to the front of the house, you notice several cars parked in the driveway that you haven't seen before. You ask Jonathan to write down the license plate numbers of the cars while you review your notes from previous visits. You again remind Jonathan of staying with you so that both of you can remain safe and observant. As you are walking up to the front steps, the door opens and your offender comes out. He is obviously angry as his fists are clenched, his jaw is set, and his eyes are squinted. Jonathan takes one look at the offender, turns about face, and runs to the car. You hear the car doors lock. You ask the offender what is wrong. After calming down, he tells you that he has just had an argument with his girlfriend in their kitchen, and he just happened to come out to the front porch to get away from her and get some air as you were walking up the steps. What should you do?

  a. You should make sure the offender is okay, and then leave as you have had your visit.

  b. You should make sure the offender is okay, and then tell him you think he made the right choice to come to the front porch for air. You should tell him when he is ready you would like to go back into the house as you still need to conduct your home visit. You should ask him if there is anything you can do to help resolve the issues with the girlfriend or if he needs other resources.

  c. You should suggest to your offender that he should stand up to his girlfriend during arguments instead of running away to the front porch for air.

  d. You should explore with the offender the possibility of spending the night away from the girlfriend to avoid an escalated domestic situation.

45. Once you take care of the home visit, you return to the car where Jonathan is still sitting. You ask him to unlock the doors, and when you get in the car, he starts making excuses for not staying with you on the front porch. How should you handle Jonathan's actions?

a. You should make sure that Jonathan is okay and that he understands the situation was scary. You should continue to talk through the events so Jonathan can learn from the situation.

b. You should laugh at his excuses and then continue to make fun of his reaction for the rest of the day.

c. You should remind Jonathan that being scared is not an option and that his behavior embarrassed you. You should admonish him from doing this again.

d. You should end your day, letting Jonathan know that similar situations have happened to you and that you "just get used" to offenders and their behavior.

46. After you return to the office at the end of the day, Jonathan thanks you for the time you spent with him and leaves the parole office. The next day, you are called into your supervisor's office and told that Jonathan has filed a report that you were rude to an offender's mother, you stated inappropriate things to an offender on the front porch of the offender's home, and you spent the whole day speaking to Jonathan in a demeaning tone. He has asked that he never be sent with you again. How do you handle this situation?

a. You laugh the whole thing off, telling your supervisor that the kid is immature and doesn't know what he is saying.

b. You provide your supervisor with explicit details about the whole day and indicate that your documentation will prove who is telling the truth.

c. You tell your supervisor what happened during the day with Jonathan, leave the office, and call Jonathan's college adviser to advise him or her what Jonathan reported, and demand a meeting with Jonathan.

d. You get angry with the supervisor for believing a student's word over yours and storm out of the office after you tell the supervisor, "I don't have to put up with this."

Directions: Read the following case study and then answer questions 47 through 52.

Jordan is a 16-year-old who has been adjudicated a delinquent and given three years probation on drug charges. You have been her probation officer for six months. Jordan has had a comfortable life, as she lives with her father and stepmother, both of whom work in professional jobs. They regularly give her gifts (car, clothes, etc.) when she makes good grades; they feel this is a safe way to reward her. Jordan is popular at school, but has gotten involved with a group of older boys who are actively involved in alcohol and drugs. Her parents can't understand why Jordan can't separate from the boys and try to discipline her, which only makes things worse at home.

In the courtroom, the parents strongly supported Jordan, even defending her choices of friends and activities. The judge, at one point, asked Jordan's parents if they felt Jordan was at fault. They both denied that she actively sought out the drugs; rather they felt she was simply following the boys' lead. As part of the disposition orders, the judge directed the parents to participate in substance abuse counseling with Jordan. The judge explained that the counseling would provide education about the addiction, and may provide insight to the parents as to Jordan's triggers. The parents were furious and said they would not participate.

Since the finding of delinquency, Jordan has withdrawn from all of her friends, except one particular boy. She has stopped talking to her parents, her grades have started to fall, and her parents' denial that Jordan has a problem has gotten more vehement. Jordan has completed her probationary requirements so far, with the exception of substance abuse counseling because her parents refuse to meet with the counselor.

47. During your meeting with Jordan, you finally get her to talk about her home life. She indicates that everything at home is fine, although it is tense because of the judge's condition that her parents participate in counseling with her. Jordan feels that counseling would probably do her some good, but is depressed because she doesn't think she can get her parents to go. She asks you if there is something you can do to help. In this situation, you can

a. talk to the parents to try to convince them that they need to participate with Jordan and to remind them of the benefits that Jordan will experience from the joint counseling.

b. approach the judge to get the condition modified so the parents don't have to go to counseling so Jordan can start going herself immediately.

c. schedule Jordan to meet with the substance abuse counselor as soon as possible. When setting up this meeting, you inform the counselor of the judge's directive and the expectation that, at some point, the parents will join her. You also inform the parents of the upcoming counseling for Jordan and again stress the importance of joining her when the counselor asks them to.

d. tell Jordan that you understand she wants to start counseling and that she has to convince her parents to join her before you will schedule a meeting for her.

48. Jordan has started wearing black clothes and pale makeup that represent the Goth look. She has dyed her hair black, is wearing black nail polish and lipstick, and now has several new piercings in her eyebrows, ears, and tongue. However, she seems happier, easier to talk with, and states she feels good about her life. When asked about the change in her clothing and style, Jordan indicates she is doing this because it makes her parents mad. You talk about her possibly needing a hobby or pastime in life, and she agrees to try to find one. She has not missed school, and her grades seem to be improving. Her substance abuse counselor has indicated that Jordan has made good progress and seems to have a handle on the triggers she needs to avoid. Urine Analysis Tests (UAs) have been pulled on Jordan and indicate that she has been clean from drugs for five months. However, you receive a call from Jordan's father after Jordan's last visit, telling you that he is not pleased with how Jordan has changed since being on your caseload. He is unhappy with the "blackness" she has started to wear and demands that you tell Jordan it is not acceptable. When asked if he feels Jordan is doing better despite her new apparel, Jordan's father stated, "Yes, but not because of your supervision." He ends the call by saying, "I'm going to get her removed from your caseload." You do not have an opportunity to comment on your visit with Jordan before he hangs up. What should you do in this situation?

a. You should do nothing. You deal with parents and their emotions all of the time, and just figure Jordan's father is upset at something else and taking it out on you.

b. You should document the phone call, as well as ensure that you have current documentation on Jordan's progress and her visits. Then you should wait to see if the father makes good on his word.

c. You should document the phone call, as well as ensure that you have current documentation on Jordan's progress and her visits. Then you should take the case file to your supervisor and convince her to keep Jordan assigned to you, as good progress is being made with Jordan and a change in supervision may set her back.

d. You should tell the judge the parents are interfering with your probationer and her supervision, and recommend a meeting with the judge and the parents.

49. During a recent office visit, you tell Jordan she needs to provide a urinalysis test. She hesitates and then indicates she has abused her prescription drugs. When you press for more details, Jordan tells you she is concerned about school, what college she will go to, and her father's temper, and she's worried that she may be pregnant. Jordan indicates that all the pressure got her depressed, and so she took more of her prescription than she should have during the last couple of weeks. This is the first violation Jordan has presented to you. You should

a. tell Jordan you are going to recommend revocation to the judge, and send her on her way.

b. tell Jordan you are concerned that she may have tried to harm herself, and you want her to get a psych evaluation at the local hospital.

c. tell Jordan you are going to call her parents and tell them they have to go to substance abuse counseling with her this week, or you are going to recommend revocation to the judge.

d. tell Jordan you understand life has pressures; however, she is not able to escape by abusing her prescription drugs. You should indicate that she would benefit from counseling, and let her know she needs to call her substance abuse counselor from your office to schedule an appointment for today or tomorrow. You should also let her know it is not acceptable to abuse drugs, and make her aware of the consequences you will impose.

50. One night at about 11:00 P.M., Jordan calls you on your cell phone, saying that she is scared and asks you to come get her. She explains that she is at a party, and there are several teenage boys there who are really drunk and doing stupid things. She doesn't wish to get into trouble and doesn't wish to be revoked. When you ask where the party is, Jordan tells you it is at her house, and her parents are gone for the weekend. You should

a. go to Jordan's house, tell everyone to leave, and then take Jordan to a youth shelter for the weekend.

b. tell Jordan to ask everyone to leave. Then you should advise her to call the police department to tell them the party has gotten out of control, she has asked people to leave, and they have refused.

c. tell Jordan she is on her own, that she thought she could get away with having a party at the house while her parents were gone, and now her probation is in jeopardy.

d. tell Jordan to call her parents, who must insist the teenagers leave the home.

51. Jordan has dated one particular young man most of the time she has been on probation. This young man, Chase, was involved in the initial situation in which Jordan was detained and then adjudicated on the drug charges. Chase was also placed on probation, and in talking with his probation officer, who is also your coworker, you have learned that Chase has had several positive urinalysis tests, and his probation officer is recommending next week that his probation be revoked. Furthermore, the recommendation by your coworker is that Chase spends the next year and a half (when he reaches 18) in a juvenile facility. You know from your conversations with Jordan that this will cause her a lot of anxiety and worry. You are concerned for her health. What should you do in this situation?

a. You should tell Jordan what is going to happen with Chase and tell her she cannot tell him. You should let her know that you are there for her and want her to be okay with the course of action that will be taking place.

b. You should call Jordan's parents and tell them what is going on, as they will need to be prepared to watch Jordan's behavior at home closely.

c. You should do nothing. This is not something upon which you must act. You received this information as a professional courtesy from your coworker.

d. You should go back to the coworker to see if there is a possibility of keeping Chase in the community. You should tell your coworker that you recognize that it is frustrating when an offender refuses to change his behavior. You should even offer to assume supervision of Chase, thinking that a new officer may help.

52. Jordan's father has called you and requested you meet with the family. When you ask why this meeting is important, you learn Jordan has been skipping school. You agree to come to the family home, and when you get there, you find Jordan with a fresh handprint on her cheek. She is crying uncontrollably and cowers when you attempt to talk with her. How do you handle this situation?

a. You proceed to talk with the parents about Jordan skipping school and agree that Jordan needs to face consequences for that behavior.

b. You ask for a few minutes to retrieve something from your car, and once outside the house, you contact your supervisor to ask for advice and guidance.

c. You contact the police department and ask them to make a visit to the home.

d. You ask the father how the handprint got on Jordan's face, and then inform the parents that you are obligated to report the abuse to the child welfare office.

Directions: Read the following case study and then answer questions 53 through 60.

In your parole office, 20 parole officers are supervised by two parole supervisors. There is an additional manager, the parole director, who supervises the parole supervisors. One supervisor is new, well liked, and respected by staff. The other supervisor, Ben, has been in his position for 12 years. It is well known Ben is a timeserver, doing the minimum amount of work with the minimum amount of effort, waiting to retire. Ben has tried and failed to get promoted several times. His failure to get promoted enables his current attitude to continue. Most staff members are eager for the new parole director to start making changes as they hope something will be done about Ben.

The parole director met with all of the staff by the end of her first week. The director then met with the parole supervisors to provide them feedback as to the issues they faced, along with the positives the staff mentioned about the office. The director indicated that the staff was happy about the flexibility on hours, the lack of micromanagement, the welcome use of open forums to discuss difficult cases with peers and supervisors, and the ability to be creative in their supervision with offenders. The challenges of the office included lack of direction from the supervisors, supervisors' inability to make their own decisions, inconsistency in working with officers and their cases, and apparent favoritism. The director asked for comments or questions from the two supervisors. The newer supervisor had several comments regarding the officers' feelings regarding lack of support and inability to make decisions. The newer supervisor and the director began a lengthy discussion regarding how the officers, on the one hand, liked the ability to be creative but, on the other hand, expressed frustration that the supervisors were inconsistent with officers and their cases. Ben did not ask any questions or make any comments.

The parole director stated clearly that the supervisors were to tighten the reigns on their officers and to make sure that cases would be updated with documentation and case reports, that warrants would be issued for the third violation without exception, and that the two supervisors would communicate with each other more to ensure consistency among the officers. The supervisors were also told to ensure that there wasn't a perception of favoritism and to make it clear that all officers would be treated fairly. The director asked if these instructions were clear and understood. The newer supervisor acknowledged the directions. Ben did not verbally acknowledging his understanding and left the office.

53. Rumor has it Ben is upset that his officers had spoken badly of him in their meeting with the new director, and he is going to find out who said what. Two days after the "big meeting," you are in the break room with other officers who are talking about their meetings with the new director. You ask them to stop talking about their meeting because you are supervised by Ben and don't want to be blamed for what they said. All the officers know Ben plays favorites and he will retaliate if he doesn't like you. Ben steps into the break room, and everyone gets quiet. Ben looks directly at you and says, "Oh, talking about me again?" You say no, but Ben tells you that you need to watch your step. He then leaves the break room. How should you handle this situation?

a. You should go directly to the new parole director and inform her of the implied threat that Ben made to you. You should demand that something be done about him.

b. You should go to Ben and convince him that you were stopping others from talking about their meetings. You should go further to convince him you weren't saying anything about him.

c. You shouldn't do anything. You didn't do anything wrong and have nothing to apologize for or explain.

d. You should document what transpired in the break room, including who was there, who said what, and who heard the implied threat. You should file this information in case you need it in the near future.

54. Staff who are supervised by the newer parole supervisor have started complaining that they have to defend and justify all of their actions now that the new parole director has issued some of her new expectations. The staff isn't actually complaining about the extra work they have to do, but rather the lack of extra work being done by Ben's staff. Several of the staff have come to you, as you are viewed as the peacekeeper, and have asked your opinion on how to handle this situation. What suggestion would you give them?

a. The staff members talking with you should go to their supervisor and ask her to talk to Ben about consistency between the units.

b. The staff members talking with you should go to their supervisor and ask her to talk with the parole director.

c. The staff members should just handle their responsibilities according to their supervisor's instructions and not worry about other staff members. You tell them to have faith that the parole director will notice the inconsistencies.

d. The staff members should mind their own business as you are currently supervised by Ben, and you don't want to have to do extra work.

55. You must discuss a case with your supervisor, Ben. At 10:30 A.M., you knock on his closed door and then knock again hearing someone inside the office. You think you heard someone say, "Come in," so you open the door to find Ben sleeping at his desk. What should you do?

a. You should go over to Ben and wake him up. Then you should discuss the details of the case that is concerning you.

b. You should silently close the door and not bother him. Also, you should place a "do not disturb" sign on his door so others won't see him.

c. You should go to the parole director and inform her that, although it is not your intention to get anyone in trouble, you have found Ben sleeping in his office and are concerned for him because this is not his usual behavior. You ask her if there is anything she wishes for you to do.

d. You should close the door and wait an hour or so. Then you should return to Ben's office and see if he is awake. You should let him know that you saw him sleeping earlier, and ask if he is all right. You should then discuss the details of the case.

56. Another parole officer who is supervised by Ben complains to you he and Ben have a philosophical difference regarding community service. Ben has waived the community service hours of several offenders, which is in direct violation of a recent department policy. However, the officer indicated Ben had appropriate justification to do so. The officer asks you what he should do. What do you tell him?

a. You indicate to the officer that nothing should be done because the supervisor has the right to waive compliance of conditions if he has proper justifications.

b. You suggest to the officer that the parole director made aware of this situation as the supervisor has violated policy and should face the consequences.

c. You suggest to the officer that he bring this subject up at the next office meeting, so everyone would have the same understanding of the policy.

d. You suggest the officer go back to the supervisor and complain that he is treating offenders differently.

57. Ben approaches your desk and tells you that an offender, Janie, will not be expected to participate in the job/employment search group that is being held later this week. Ben indicates that tomorrow he will be helping Janie look for employment while you are out on field visits. You ask why Ben is taking a personal interest in this offender, and he tells you that he was asked by the paroling authority to monitor this case closely. You suspect his reasons and think something else is going on between Ben and the offender. What should you do in this situation?

a. You should do nothing. Ben is not doing anything that is not within the scope of his authority.

b. You should monitor the situation closely, changing your field visits schedule so that you have to return to the office during the time Ben is allegedly with the offender. Then you can see if Ben is doing really helping Janie look for employment or if there is something else going on.

c. You should try to convince Ben that he is putting himself in a bad situation and tell him it seems like he is playing favorites with this offender. You should strongly suggest that he remove himself from this offender.

d. You should ask a parole officer whom you trust to monitor the situation between Ben and the offender when she is in the office the next day. Once you learn what actually is going on, then you will decide how to handle this.

58. Ben supervises ten parole officers, including Clare, who is just out of college working her first full-time job. Clare had interned with the parole office during her last semester of college and, according to the interview team, was the best candidate during the interviewing process. The previous parole director had hired her based upon that recommendation. However, several months after Clare's hire, one of the other parole officers who had been part of the interview team makes it known that Clare was, in fact, not the number one candidate. This officer indicates that Clare's responses to the interview questions were incomplete and lacked detail and originality. However, the officer indicates that Ben had pressured the other two officers on the interview team to recommend Clare, and they felt compelled to do so as Ben was their supervisor. The officer asks you for your opinion on this news. In this situation, you should

a. tell the officer not to talk about this with any other probation officer, but rather go to the director to voice his concerns.

b. tell the officer not to talk about interviewing processes after the fact because it would only cause hurt feelings, office stress, and tension and may be cause for legal action.

c. tell the officer to confront Ben about the situation and ask for an explanation.

d. tell the officer to refuse to sit on any future interviewing boards that Ben chairs.

59. You walk into Ben's office and find Ben and Clare kissing. The department has a policy against supervisors being involved with subordinates, and Ben has certainly crossed the line. Ben tells you to forget what you see and get out of his office. How do you handle this situation?

a. You leave and tell the first coworker you see what you saw in Ben's office.

b. You leave Ben's office, knowing you will be called into account by Ben later that afternoon.

c. You go to your office and call human resources to report what you saw, indicating you wish to file a hostile workplace report.

d. You go to your parole director to report what you observed and demand something be done about Ben.

60. The parole director comes to your office and indicates that she is aware you have a documentation file on Ben. She requests you provide that file to her as she has started personnel action against Ben. She informs you that she is aware of the situation she is placing you in, but that she is in need of documentation, as the previous director did not document a thing. You believe your documentation is enough to cause severe action to be taken against Ben. What should you do?

   a. You should provide the documentation as requested. You should then request that once an initial review is completed, you are allowed to copy what documentation she feels she needs to keep in order to maintain your file.

   b. You should tell the director that you will be willing to provide it once you make a copy. Once you are alone, you remove all of the documentation that you feel is not pertinent to Ben.

   c. You should tell the director that if she wants your file, then she will have to get the legal division to get a warrant.

   d. You should tell the director that you need to contact your attorney to ensure that you are protected if Ben finds out you provided the documentation.

61. Which of the following sentences is punctuated correctly?

   a. The juveniles, who said it didn't belong to them, attempted to convince the officer.

   b. The juveniles attempted to convince the officers that the liquor didn't belong to them.

   c. The officer listened to the story. As the juveniles attempted to convince the officer they were not responsible for the possession of the liquor.

   d. The juveniles; who said the liquor didn't belong to them, attempted to convince the officer.

62. Which of the following sentences is punctuated correctly?

   a. According to the driver, he couldn't give a very good description of the suspect.

   b. The driver was unable to give an accurate description of the suspect.

   c. In regards to the description of the suspect; the driver couldn't give a good one.

   d. The driver was unclear about the description, of what the suspect looked like.

63. Which of the following sentences is punctuated correctly?

   a. Tire tracks were visible, with large-sized footprints, leading to them from the broken window.

   b. Footprints and tire tracks. Both were seen from the broken window.

   c. From the broken window, were footprints leading to where tire tracks were also visible in the area.

   d. The large-sized footprints led from the broken window to an area where tire tracks were also visible.

64. Which sentence do you feel is the most clearly written?

    a. The suspect hit several parked cars in the parking lot as he drove away.

    b. The suspect was observed, as he drove away, to hit several parked cars in the parking lot.

    c. The suspect left and several parked cars were hit in the lot it was observed.

    d. It was reported from the parking lot that several parked cars were hit as the suspect drove away.

65. Which sentence do you feel is the most clearly written?

    a. The officer wrote the violation report and then asked the supervisor to read it for clarity and grammar.

    b. For clarity and grammar, the supervisor was asked to read the violation report by the officer.

    c. The supervisor, by the officer who wrote the violation report, was asked to read it for clarity and grammar.

    d. The violation report, written by the officer, was given for clarity and grammar to the supervisor to read.

66. Which sentence do you feel is the most clearly written?

    a. If justification can be given, the compliance of conditions can be waived by the supervisor as you indicate to the coworker.

    b. You indicate to the coworker that nothing can be done, as it is the supervisor's right, with proper justification, to waive compliance of conditions.

    c. The supervisor can, with proper justification, waive the compliance rights, you indicate to the coworker and nothing can be done about it.

    d. The coworker cannot do anything and the supervisor can waive compliance of conditions with proper justifications.

67. Which of the following sentences is grammatically correct?

    a. The facts about the stolen property was given by an informant who was reliable and gives the essential facts.

    b. The informent gave us the essential information on the stolen property, he was known too reliable.

    c. A reliable informent on the stolen property provides the essential facts.

    d. A reliable informant provided the essential facts about the stolen property.

68. Which of the following sentences is grammatically correct?

    a. The officere gave the offender several conditions to follow well sitting in jail.

    b. While sitting in jail, several conditions were gaven to the offender by the officer.

    c. The oficer gave several conditions too the offender while sitting in jail.

    d. The officer gave the offender several conditions to follow while sitting in jail.

69. Which of the following sentences is NOT grammatically correct?

    a. The officer couldn't hear the offender because of the noise level.

    b. The offender could not wheel and deal because the officer was close by.

    c. The offenders did not here the officers message to report too the office.

    d. The officer stayed close to the offender to make sure the offender did not wheel and deal.

Directions: Read the following passage and then answer questions 70 through 74.

School-based probation is a newly developed program that partners juvenile probation departments with local schools. In this program, the probation officers are placed directly into the schools. They report for duty at the school and supervise their caseload daily while their students/offenders attend classes and meetings, before, during, and after school. The students who are targeted for this program have been charged with delinquent offenses and/or are under the supervision of the court. The benefits of school-based probation include: 1) the contact between the officers and the juveniles are increased, 2) the officers are able to check attendance, discipline records, and other information about probationers on a daily basis, 3) the officers are able to communicate with teachers about academic progress, and 4) the officers develop personal relationships with juveniles, which allow the officers opportunities to have better communication with their offenders. Additionally, the presence of a probation officer and the additional supervision offered has led to decreased crime in the schools.

The biggest disadvantage of this program is that the officers are sometimes asked to help settle disputes between students who are not part of this program, as well as to help school administrators with general, school-related issues. Other concerns involve the confidentiality of school records, which the officers may come in contact with, and office space for the officers to conduct their supervision visits, maintain files for the courts, etc.

This is a fairly new concept, so there hasn't been a great deal of research or study completed. However, it is universally accepted that this program has had a positive impact on those juveniles who are involved in the program. There is proof that school-based probation has improved academic performance and is cost-effective. Several other important and proven benefits include closer supervision, better school attendance, fewer instances of recidivism, fewer residential placements, and far fewer placement days, which has resulted in an estimated cost savings of millions of dollars.

Despite the initial evidence that this program is successful, it has not been widely accepted across the nation. Several states have implemented the program throughout their school districts, whereas other states have not started the program because of politics and lack of funding or because they find their current programs are already working well with the juvenile populations. Many critics have said that this type of program crosses the boundaries by allowing probation officers to become involved in the lives of children who are not within the court's jurisdiction. Others say that this is just another program the school administrators are using to avoid facing the violence that has been allowed to manifest in the schools.

70. Which of the following best expresses the main idea of the passage?
   a. States are slow to develop school-based programs, as administrators are afraid of courts taking over their classrooms.
   b. School-based programs were created to make office space available for those who supervise juveniles.
   c. There has been a positive impact on juveniles who are involved in school-based programs because of closer supervision, closer contact, and better communication with their probation officer.
   d. School administrators want this program, as they will gain additional staff to help with the violence that erupts in their schools.

71. The benefits to this kind of school-based program do NOT include which of the following?
   a. better school attendance
   b. better academic performance
   c. better funding for the school
   d. fewer instances of placement for the juvenile

72. The biggest disadvantage for the officer in this type of program is
  a. being pulled into disputes and situations that do not involve juveniles on the officer's caseload.
  b. being in a school that does not offer a lot of space for supervision of the caseload.
  c. being placed directly in the school and not being able to get away from the caseload.
  d. being expected to help decrease the crime in the schools.

73. Students who can participate in this program belong to which of the following groups?
  a. students who attend the school where this program has been implemented
  b. students who have been charged with delinquent offenses and/or are under the supervision of the court
  c. students who have been targeted by school administrators
  d. students who have been caught by school personnel committing a crime at the school

74. This program has not been implemented across the nation because of which of the following?
  a. lack of insight from the school administrators and local judges
  b. local or state politics, lack of funding, or the belief that current programs are already working well with the juvenile populations
  c. insufficient space or personnel in the school to implement this program
  d. insufficient number of juvenile offenders in the school to implement this program

Directions: Read the following passage and then answer questions 75 through 79.

Civil Liability of Probation and Parole Officers

The world has become an endless paper trail of lawsuits. The decisions made by the various courts continue to cast a wider net over who is ultimately held responsible for acts performed by probation and parole officers as ordered by the court or by a paroling authority. The practice of questioning actions through the courts began in the early 1960s and primarily affected prison personnel. Now there is a nationwide pattern of greater liability for all public officials, particularly police, probation, and parole officers. However, state legislatures and Congress appear to be trying to reverse this trend by capping damage awards ordered in state tort cases.

In this age of lawsuits, it is vital that probation and parole officers are properly informed about legal liabilities. Any action, whether intentional or unintentional, within the law or outside the law, can be questioned by anyone an officer comes in contact with (i.e., an offender, victim, or citizen). Civil and criminal liabilities exist at both the state and federal level. In fact, an officer may find him- or herself in a position in which the liabilities are not mutually exclusive; a single serious act may expose an officer to several civil and criminal liabilities under federal and state law. In addition, the officer may be subject to internal disciplinary proceedings that can result in transfer, suspension, demotion, dismissal, or other forms of personnel action.

Officers must understand their inappropriate actions can be classified as negligence and filed under the state or federal tort claims act. Negligence is judged on three levels of severity: slight, gross, or willful. Slight negligence is defined as a failure to exercise great care. Gross negligence is described as a failure to exercise even that care which a careless person would use. Willful negligence is defined as an act of intentional disregard of a known risk or a risk so great that harm is very likely to follow. An example of willful negligence is a citizen being injured by a probationer/parolee and feeling the injury could have been prevented had the offender been appropriately supervised.

There are two types of immunity offered for probation and parole officers: absolute and qualified. Absolute immunity is offered generally to officers who are within the judicial and legislative branches of government. Under this judicial umbrella, officers who perform judicial-type functions that involve discretionary decision making or court functions (i.e., initiating revocation proceedings or presenting a case during parole revocation hearings) are covered under absolute immunity. Qualified immunity is offered to those who serve in the executive branch of government. Courts have found officers are not held liable when their actions are found to be objectively reasonable. Probation and parole officers generally have qualified immunity when performing the administrative or other discretionary functions of their position.

If sued, a probation or parole officer will be offered free legal services from either the department's legal counsel and/or the state attorney general's office. If the free legal counsel believes the officer is guilty of committing a criminal offense, services will not be offered and instead must be found and paid for by the officer. Each agency determines the type of legal representation based upon the situation and case. If found liable, employees of most agencies can expect the state to help pay the costs or fines named in the judgment, but only if the act upon which the finding of liability is based was within the scope of employment and done in good faith.

75. Which of the following best expresses the main idea of the passage?
a. Officers can be sued only if their actions are criminal in nature.
b. Officers must understand the civil liabilities that are involved in their position, along with the types of actions that could be negligent in nature.
c. Officers must conduct their business knowing they are always covered under two types of immunity.
d. If an offender gets upset at an officer, he or she can sue that officer, who must pay for his or her own attorney.

76. Which of the following correctly lists the three different levels on which inappropriate actions conducted by officers can be labeled neglect?
a. small, absolute, and deliberate
b. slight, gross, and willful
c. slight, absolute, and deliberate
d. intentional, unintentional, and injured

77. Which of the following situations would allow an officer to be covered under absolute immunity?
a. discharging a firearm during the fulfillment of the officer's responsibilities
b. testifying in front of the paroling authority during the parole revocation hearing
c. placing the offender in maximum custody supervision, making his supervision more intense
d. an assigned offender injuring a citizen

78. An example from the passage of how an officer can be sued for willful negligence is

  a. a citizen questions whether an officer has the right to start revocation proceedings against his relative, who is the offender.

  b. an offender feels the testimony of the parole officer at the revocation hearing is false and full of hearsay evidence.

  c. a citizen questions whether an offender is supervised when the offender hasn't had to provide a urinalysis test during the month.

  d. a citizen is injured by a probationer/parolee and feels the injury could have been prevented had the offender been appropriately supervised.

79. Officers who find themselves involved in a lawsuit can be implicated in which of the following actions?

  a. lawsuits filed in either state or federal courts with internal department sanctions as a possibility

  b. lawsuits filed in both state and federal courts with internal department sanctions as a possibility

  c. lawsuits filed in both state and federal courts with no other sanctions possible

  d. lawsuits filed in either state or federal courts with no other sanctions possible

Directions: Read the following passage and then answer questions 80 through 84.

Due Process Rights Offered to Offenders in Parole Hearings

Several noteworthy cases have tested the boundaries of which due process rights need to be offered to offenders during the various stages of parole revocations. One of the notable was *Greenholtz v. Inmates of the Nebraska Penal and Correctional Complex* (1979). In this case, the inmates within the Nebraska prison system filed a lawsuit against the paroling authority, indicating that their constitutional rights had been violated when they were denied parole by the Nebraska Board of Parole. The inmates listed three areas of contention: 1) the state's process for hearings, 2) the board's practice of informing inmates of decisions, and 3) the procedure of providing inmates advance notice of their parole hearing.

The U.S. Supreme Court has acknowledged that the parole boards have the extreme discretionary powers necessary for dealing with the various steps of the process afforded under the constitution. The court indicated that the Nebraska procedure afforded opportunities for inmates to be heard, but did not provide the relief sought by inmates. However, the U.S. Supreme Court did establish in this case that inmates require: reasonable notice of a parole hearing date (usually one month's notice); an initial hearing during the revocation process in which the inmate is afforded the chance to present his or her case; and if parole is revoked, written reasons provided to the inmate.

This case also clarified the distinction between parole release and parole revocation as the difference between losing what one has and not getting what one wants. Offenders keep testing the limits of parole being a privilege and revocation being a "slap on the wrist." Paroling authorities are pressured on many sides to keep offenders who revoke their parole within the system, but not for too long.

Society needs to have the feeling that offenders are facing the consequences of violating their paroles; however, funds for additional prisons to house offenders who have had their parole revoked are not easily found within the state budgets. More education is needed for citizens to understand the recidivism rate as well as the pressures placed upon people who work in the system to manage and supervise the offender population (i.e., the paroling authority, prison officials, and community supervision officers).

Additionally, some citizens feel offenders have been given too many rights and take advantage of the due process procedures in order to avoid spending too much time in prison for their revocation. However, cases such as *Greenholtz* and *Morrissey* assure all citizens, offenders included, that officers will treat each offender consistently in providing notification of the parole process and written notification regarding the revocation process.

80. The case of *Greenholtz v. Inmates of the Nebraska Penal and Correctional Complex* brought to light which of the following?

   a. Offenders did not have to have two revocation hearings, because the Nebraska Board of Parole afforded appropriate opportunities for inmates to be heard.

   b. Offenders received appropriate notice of the hearings and results, and no action was needed.

   c. Offenders were to receive advance notice of their revocation hearing, usually one month before.

   d. Offenders didn't have a case as the U.S. Supreme Court found that Nebraska was appropriately following in the process of revocations.

81. Which of the following best expresses the main idea of this passage?

   a. The cases of *Greenholtz* and *Morrissey* give offenders many due process rights.

   b. Society won't pay for prisons that are filled with parole violators.

   c. Officers need to carry out their job responsibilities appropriately so that offenders cannot argue that their due process rights weren't given to them.

   d. Citizens need to understand that cases such as *Greenholtz* help offenders receive consistent treatment throughout the revocation process.

82. The inmates who filed the lawsuit indicated there were three areas of contention. Which of the following was NOT one of the areas listed?

   a. the board's practice of announcing where hearings would take place

   b. the state's process for hearings

   c. the board's practice of informing inmates of its decisions

   d. the procedure of providing inmates advance notice of their parole hearing

83. With its decision in the *Greenholtz* case, the U.S. Supreme Court solidified which of the following ideas?

   a. the difference between losing what one has and not getting what one wants

   b. the difference between never having an opportunity and not getting what one wants

   c. the difference in losing a privilege and not getting an opportunity

   d. the difference in having something taken away and never being given a chance

84. In this case, inmates within the Nebraska penal system indicated that they were not given proper due process in three areas. Which of the following closely resembles the effect of the U.S. Supreme Court's decision on the parole board in Nebraska?

   a. Procedures were correctly done in Nebraska, although various hearings needed to take place.

   b. Nebraskan inmates were given opportunities to be heard in appropriate fashion, and they were given changes to notification and written reasons for denial of parole.

   c. Inmates were given opportunities to be heard, written notice of the charges, and hearings.

   d. The parole board was required to provide inmates with the procedures regarding the intent of the revocation hearing. Otherwise, the U.S. Supreme Court found Nebraska was not at fault.

Directions: Read the following passage and then answer questions 85 through 89.

Female Offenders in the Criminal Justice System

Historically, the female offender population within the criminal justice system has been small, although there has been a rise in the number of female offenders, especially in their participation in violent crimes. The state and federal systems have struggled to determine how best to handle this population and are now being forced to address quickly the issue of gender-specific programs and housing facilities.

According to the statistics, the female offender population in 2004 increased 2.9% from the previous year. Overall, about 8.6% of all persons incarcerated in prison and jails were women. In 2004, 12% of the parolee population and 23% of probation offenders were women.

Women become involved in crime for a variety of reasons; most have risk factors that contribute to their criminal behavior. Some risk factors (i.e., substance abuse, mental issues) are the same as for men; however, factors such as victimization and spousal abuse are for the most part unique to women. Although men can be victims of spousal abuse, the statistics indicate that women are the primary victims in sexual and spousal abuse.

A continuing and now urgent issue for administrators is what programs to offer this rising population as money for programs within prisons and communities is decreasing. Corrections administrators must be creative in developing and implementing new programs for offenders. Many find development time and money better served when programs can be offered to the larger, male population. With such small budgets, administrators are often forced to use their allotted budgets for necessities such as security and staffing and to cut out most programming for all offenders.

Although gender-specific programs have been developed and implemented, only a small number of these programs are available across the country. Some state corrections administrators have been successful in partnering with community resources to provide gender-specific programs to women both inside prisons and on community supervision. Programs such as gender-specific vocational trainings, education classes, and parenting and life skills classes are now offered in all aspects of the system, and are often free or low-cost. Additionally, counseling services are structured so that female offenders who start working on issues within the prison can continue with that process without starting over when they are released under supervision. Some states offering reentry programs to all offenders are targeting women who, once released, become the primary caregiver to their families.

It is evident through research that the rise in the women's prison and probation population was slow to be noticed. However, as more and more women are being placed within the system, administrators must make difficult choices regarding budget dollars for actual housing units, separate facilities, staffing, and most important, gender-specific programming to help with rehabilitation. It will be most important in the years to come for administrators to develop an understanding of the gender-specific issues and concerns within the female population, as well as an understanding of the allotted budgets available to them to run their prison facilities and community supervision programs.

85. Which of the following best expresses the main idea of this passage?
   a. The number of crimes committed by women is on the rise, and more prisons will have to be built.
   b. Female offenders are being put into prisons even though administrators have yet to figure out what to do with them.
   c. Women are committing more crimes and being put into prisons where administrators are having to make tough choices as to how to fund gender-specific programs for their rehabilitation.
   d. Women are committing more crimes and are being transferred to states where gender-specific programs already exist.

86. Has crime committed by women been increasing or decreasing, and for what reasons?
a. decreasing because of many of the same risk factors that contribute to men committing crimes
b. increasing because of many of the same risk factors that contribute to men committing crimes
c. increasing because of similar risk factors that contribute to men committing crimes and a few unique factors specific to women
d. decreasing because of the unique factors specific to women

87. Which of the following best describes what administrators are faced with because of the increase in female offenders?
a. Administrators must be creative in developing gender-specific programs, while spending their department budgets wisely.
b. Administrators must create gender-specific programs for fear they will be sued.
c. Administrators must look for outside dollars to offer gender-specific programs.
d. Administrators must cut all programs for all offenders in order to provide for security and salaries.

88. Which of the following was NOT cited in the passage as having been implemented for female offenders?
a. education and gender-specific training
b. counseling and parenting classes
c. reentry programs
d. community boot camps

89. As cited in the passage, what must corrections administrators do in the future?
a. keep looking for creative gender-specific programs to develop
b. find alternative funding sources for the development and implementation of gender-specific programs
c. keep looking for creative programming for all offenders
d. develop an understanding of how gender-specific issues and concerns are tied to the allotted budgets that are available for prison and community supervision programs

Directions: Read the following passage and then answer questions 90 through 94.

The Questionable Success of Boot Camps
Corrections boot camp programs resemble military basic training in which the staples are physical activity, drill and ceremony, manual labor, and other activities that limit free time. Strict rules govern all aspects of life within the boot camp, especially conduct and appearance. Corrections officers are employed as drill instructors, using verbal tactics intensely at first to break down offenders' resistance and also throughout the program as needed to provide opportunities for constructive changes in their behavior.

Corrections boot camps were started in late 1980s and early 1990s. There has been an ebb and flow of support for the boot camp concept, which has caused changes to the basic program over the years. The first-generation camps stressed military discipline, physical training, and hard work, whereas the second-generation emphasized rehabilitation by adding counseling components and life-skills training. More recently, there has been an emphasis on educational and vocational skills to help provide structure and discipline.

Unfortunately, since 2000, research showing that the recidivism rate of boot camp participants was equal to or higher than those who did not participate in such a highly intense program has led to a decrease in the development and maintenance of boot camp programs. There are several reasons for this decrease: The first is that little or no postrelease programming is available for boot camp graduates as they leave the structured environment. Offenders who had thrived in a disciplined environment find that support suddenly gone and, in turn, easily return to their criminal patterns. The second reason is that the laws and/or goals set by policy makers may not be in line with the objectives of the program. If the goal of the boot camp is to reduce prison population rather than offer an alternative for rehabilitation, then the program is doomed from the beginning. The third reason is that boot camps have drawn so heavily from the military model that they lack a therapeutic component. This lack of treatment allows offenders to fall into the intense structure without examining their criminal behavior and learning how to survive as law-abiding citizens.

If boot camps are to continue, would they reduce recidivism, prison populations, and the cost of housing offenders, and would they offer offenders an opportunity to gain necessary and essential life-changing skills as well? Boot camps have been successful in changing offenders' attitudes and behavior, and they have also provided safer environments for staff and offenders to live and work in. Better attitudes toward incarceration have been noticed in those who have participated. Generally, humans are more likely to succeed when their life is structured. Although the military approach may seem harsh to some, those who have participated in the program have reported higher self-esteem, better problem-solving and coping skills, and an increased likelihood of looking for alternatives to criminal behavior once released. So, the question remains, do we discontinue this type of program for offenders who could benefit from its structure because of those who might not have been placed correctly in the program or who will chose criminal behavior no matter what program they are in?

90. The main idea of this passage is
   a. boot camp programs have offered some improvement in offenders' thought processes, although they may return to prison because of other factors.
   b. boot camp programs have not offered offenders enough incentive to stay out of criminal behavior.
   c. boot camp programs were funded as legislators viewed the program as a way to show their constituency they were trying to make a difference.
   d. boot camp programs have not been successful and should be done away with.

91. Which of the following was NOT listed as a reason that the recidivism rate of boot camps is high?
   a. Little or no postrelease programming is offered to offenders upon leaving the boot camp.
   b. There is no funding for community supervision once the offender leaves the boot camp.
   c. The laws and goals established by legislators may not match the goals of the program.
   d. There is often an absence of a therapeutic component to the program.

92. Which of the following best describes the author's opinion of boot camps?
   a. Boot camps offer opportunities for offenders to learn life-changing skills and should be utilized more.
   b. Boot camps shouldn't be funded as they do not "fix" offenders and are a waste of important budget dollars.
   c. Society should decide if it wants boot camps to reduce recidivism or to offer opportunities to help offenders learn life skills.
   d. choices a and c

93. As stated in the passage, the recent focus of boot camps is
  a. more of a military approach.
  b. more of a combination approach of military training and counseling components.
  c. more of an emphasis on education and vocational skills.
  d. more of a military approach as more programs are closing, and the thought is that offenders will be structured while they do their prison time.

94. Which of the following describes two reasons the author stated for boot camp recidivism rates being high?
  a. Society continues to redefine the program's objective as well as the criteria that identify successful offenders.
  b. Offenders may return to criminal behavior and to prison because they miss the military structure and failed to learn proper ways to be law-abiding citizens.
  c. Offenders may return to prison because proper treatment was not available to them, and they simply find life easier within the prison walls.
  d. Offenders may have been placed incorrectly in the program, or they chose criminal behavior regardless of the program they are placed into.

Directions: Read the following passage and then answer questions 95 through 100.

Job-Related Stress: Whose Problem Is It?

The nature of being a probation and parole officer creates a considerable amount of job-related stress. According to research, the three most frequent sources of stress for officers are high caseloads, excessive paperwork, and meeting deadlines established by risk management tools. These working conditions make it difficult for many to find the time to supervise their caseloads properly, which becomes an additional cause of stress.

Of course, there are other sources of stress worth mentioning, such as low salaries, inadequate supervision, threats of physical harm by offenders, being held accountable for an offender's behavior, family members' stress, and the ever-changing goals of supervision.

Officers often blame the organization for their stress. When blaming the organization, officers will sometimes use the excuse that there is bad office morale or that too much is expected to be done in the workday. It is much easier to blame the organization than to look at one's own contributions to stress levels.

Officers have taken it upon themselves to reduce their stress levels, often to the detriment of the organization and to themselves. One tactic is to abuse their sick leave. When officers use sick leave to alleviate stress, other officers wind up increasing their stress level because they have to assume some additional work from the "sick" officer's caseload. This abuse of sick leave can also lead to disciplinary action against the offending officer, as well as financial concerns for the agency and a decline in the office morale.

Yet officers are not willing to look at their own behavior as being responsible for their stress. They could reduce their stress by giving up some of their break time, not being tardy to work, and avoiding other ways of wasting work time.

To manage the stress successfully, officers must consider the bigger picture. The organization cannot run without rules and procedures, which can actually help officers accomplish their work. It is unfortunate that officers' attitudes and work ethics can, at times, get in the way of keeping stress at a manageable level. Good time management and good problem-solving and communication skills are all necessary for officers to manage the organizational stress.

There are several simple ways to reduce stress. Physical exercise has been known to help because it not only helps the body work off the physical reactions to the stress, but also provides mental stimulus to resolve the stress or conflict. A simple walk is an effective way of taking a break and reducing stress. Communication with a supervisor or counselor is also effective because an officer can "release" the stress by considering the cause of the stress from another viewpoint. Finally, but most important, an officer needs to remember his or her job responsibilities; a full-time officer should work 40 hours and avoid any time-wasting behavior.

It is true that being a probation or parole officer is stressful. Human behavior can provide many unknowns and unpredictable situations, which can be difficult to deal with, especially on a long-term basis. However, officers are trained for that type of stress.

95. Which of the following best expresses the author's viewpoint in this passage?
   a. The organization is the only entity that can fix the stress level of the officers by lowering expectations and caseloads.
   b. Officers must continue to utilize stress reducers such as sick leave in order to deal with the high stress of the job.
   c. Stress comes with any job, and administrators expect the officers to simply work through stress while doing the job.
   d. Stress is inherent in this type of job, and officers must work at controlling their own contributions to the stress level.

96. Which of the following acceptable ways to reduce stress was NOT mentioned in the passage?
   a. exercising
   b. going to counseling
   c. taking vacations
   d. doing the work as required

97. Why do officers blame the organization for stress?
   a. It is more difficult to look at how an officer's own behavior and attitude contributes to his or her stress level.
   b. It is the fault of the organization alone.
   c. The organization continues to add more responsibility and pressure, and it should be responsible to reduce the workload.
   d. The organization doesn't train employees and supervisors to manage stress well, and therefore, the organization is responsible.

98. The author is implying which of the following in this passage?
   a. Organizations simply ask too much of the officers.
   b. Supervisors do not adequately supervise officers, so stress levels climb.
   c. Stress is a integral part of this type of work, and nothing will change as long as humans are involved.
   d. Officers add to their stress level by not managing their daily activities well.

99. Officers who choose to abuse their sick leave cause which of the following for the organization?
- **a.** stress for other officers when they have to assume additional caseload work
- **b.** higher costs that occur when officers have to do overtime because another officer is disciplined for abusing sick leave
- **c.** discontent in the office, which is detrimental to team building
- **d.** all of the above

100. Which of the following causes of stress is NOT created by the organization?
- **a.** low salaries
- **b.** officers being held accountable for an offender's behavior
- **c.** ever-changing goals of supervision
- **d.** inability to get documentation completed on time

► Answers

1. a. Maintaining the safety and security of the community is the main function of community supervision. Choices **b**, **c**, and **d** are all important tasks of a parole officer and are byproducts of choice **a**. If a parole officer accomplishes these tasks well, then the safety and security of the community is likely.

2. b. Choice **a** may be correct, but it is not an appropriate way to handle this type of situation. Choice **c** is incorrect because being on parole is not a legal discrimination category. Choice **d** is also not an appropriate statement for a parole officer to make.

3. c. Parole is a discretionary action and not a right of parolees. Conditions can be modified or added at any time by a parole officer, as long as the condition is reasonable and fits the offender, his or her history, etc. Choice **b** is incorrect because the Fourth Amendment deals with search and seizure and does not apply in this case. Choice **a** is incorrect because there must be a rational reason to add to a parolee's supervision conditions. Choice **d** is simply not true.

4. c. Under *Morrissey v. Brewer*, several due process rights are afforded to parolees who are facing revocation. In addition to at least one revocation hearing, choices **a**, **b**, and **d** must also be afforded to the parolee. *Morrissey* did not provide the right to have legal counsel at any of the revocation proceedings, although it is left to the state's discretion to determine the need for counsel.

5. c. The Eighth Amendment deals with issues of cruel and unusual punishment that have been addressed in the various courts through cases dealing with conditions of confinement.

6. b. As described in standard parole conditions, a parolee must allow a parole officer with reasonable suspicion to search his or her home and car. A parole officer does not have the right to "dig" through dresser drawers or boxes that might be in the truck of a car; however, a parole officer acting on reasonable and reliable information may do more than a plain view search. Choice **a** is legally irresponsible because a parole officer can take only actions that are reasonable. Choices **c** and **d** are simply not true for parole officers. In many states, parole officers are designated as law enforcement by state statute and, therefore, have the same powers as police officers. However, state policy or regulation may restrict parole officers from completing some law enforcement actions.

7. d. Although it is imperative that you not to permit such abusive activity, your first concern is the parolee. It is important to help the parolee focus on moving forward with his supervision, and although this situation is not a positive one for the parolee, he is not able to control how the mother and friends interact. It would be vital to continue to support the parolee so that efforts could be made to remove his from this situation. Choice **a** may be what you wish to do, but it would be impossible if the parolee is not focused on you and your discussion. Choices **b** and **d** could make the situation worse and put more lives in jeopardy.

8. a. In *King v. Simpson* (1999), the court ruled that the parole officer has absolute immunity when acting in a quasi-judicial or prosecutorial function, such as when he or she is initiating parole revocation proceedings. However, choice **b** is incorrect because the parole officer does more discretionary and administrative functions. The courts have given absolute immunity (choice **c**) primarily to parole board members in all decisions to grant, deny, or revoke parole. Absolute immunity protects workers unless they act in ways that are intentional and malicious. Qualified immunity is when actions are found to be objectively reasonable. Choice **d** is not an option because conditions are not based on whether actions are with or without malice.

9. d. Aftercare is a function of the juvenile correctional system whereby the officer provides surveillance and reintegration activities to help the offender get back into family and community. Although the functions are similar to adult supervision, the terms are different for the juvenile system. Choice **b** is terminology for those adult offenders released under supervision into the community. Choice **a** is a term used for the juvenile equivalent to the adult jail system. Choice **c** is incorrect because it is only a type of release from a facility.

10. c. A probation officer does not have the same coverage and responsibilities to maintain confidentiality as an attorney does, and therefore, the officer must provide appropriate personnel with any information that will help solve crimes. Additionally, in some states' statutes, probation and parole officers are considered law enforcement officers and, therefore, have an obligation to provide information received from offenders. Choices **a** and **b** would be irresponsible of a law enforcement officer because they call for deceiving the probationer. Choice **d** does not relieve a probation officer of his or her responsibility.

11. b. The court is the only entity that has jurisdiction over a probationer and his or her sentence. Choices **a** and **c** are incorrect, because those people make recommendations to the court but do not decide on the actual sentence. Choice **d** is incorrect because the county commission is not a lawful judicial entity.

12. d. All of the choices are options afforded to judges regarding the revocation of a sentence of probation.

13. d. Not taking action is not a possibility for a probation officer. Ignoring a condition of probation, even with a short time frame left on probation, is not an appropriate action to take. Although it may be a difficult decision to start revocation proceedings for failure to pay restitution, it is an important and standard condition of probation. It is extremely important for offenders to make amends for their crimes and pay restitution to "make the victim whole." The action an officer should take is choice **d**; however, once you have taken this step, or the step described in choice **b**, then revocation proceedings, choice **a**, would be the necessary action.

14. b. During probation, the judge maintains control over the offender and the offender's sentence. Only the judge has the authority to modify the conditions or revoke the sentence. Prerelease planning, choice **a**, in which the officer and offender determine where the offender will live and work and in which programs he or she will participate, is completed when offenders are working toward their release from detention or prison. Choice **c** is a non-incarcerative option in which offenders serve all or a portion of their sentences in the community-based programs. These programs usually occur at the beginning of the sentence or as a back-end program that assists prisoners in community reentry. Choice **d** is the conditional release of an offender from a correctional institution under the continued custody of the state, to serve the remainder of his or her sentence in the community under supervision.

15. a. In 1841, Boston citizen John Augustus bailed out a "common drunk," took him to his home, helped him with his drinking problem, and taught him a trade (boot making). John then took the rehabilitated man back to the Boston court three weeks later where the reformed man was released after paying a small fine. Choice **b** is incorrect; Alexander Machonochie established an earlier system of parole. Choice **c** is incorrect; Peter Oxenbridge Thacher was a judge who introduced a system of release on recognizance. King Henry VII, choice **d**, provided early sentences to wrongdoers.

16. c. Jail is locally operated detention facility that confines people who are detained (for arrests or transports), awaiting sentencing, or serving a sentence for up to one year. A prison (choice **a**) is a state-run, long-term facility that confines offenders who have been convicted of a felony for a period of one year or more. Choices **b** and **d** are programs into which offenders may be released when they are under community supervision. These programs allow offenders to reenter the community with available resources and support.

17. d. Presentence investigation reports are a major source of information used by the courts to determine what type of sentence is appropriate for the offender. If the sentence includes prison time, then the presentence investigation report is used by the correctional staff to help determine what type of treatment and classification is needed for the offender. Choice **b** is incorrect because, although the victim is able to provide information that may be included in the report, the victim is not provided a copy of the report, which includes the offender's historical information.

18. d. A presentence investigation report does not have to be completed with the offender. An offense-based report is strictly informing the court about the current offense and past crimes. A presentence investigation officer may also be able to collect information regarding the victim, and possibly the offender's family, friends, codefendants, etc. If this information is available, the officer may interview these individuals for possible information to pass along to the court. Choice **b** may be a strategy an officer wishes to attempt before leaving the offender and starting his or her own search, but again the offender's input is not needed to complete the report. Choices **a** and **c** will only cause stress to the offender and to the judge, and are not considered professional conduct.

19. b. You first will need to gain your supervisor's support and confidence in your work. Therefore, asking your supervisor to meet with you to advise on and assist you with the quality of your investigation reports is a good idea. Choice **c** is a nice, second option for additional training after you gain insight from your supervisor. Choice **a** is not really wise, especially if you wish to retain your employment. Judges have the ability to indicate the report was not useful wherever they see fit. It is your responsibility to provide a report that the judge will find useful; it is not the judge's responsibility to tell you what he wants. Choice **d** is would be overreacting to this situation. Everyone has his or her own idea of what specific items should be included in reports. The officer should not take criticism as a personal attack, even if it feels that way.

20. a. There are two types of cases that go to juvenile court: status offenses and delinquent acts. Each is based on the type of act committed. Acts that would not be punishable if committed by an adult are called status offenses, choices **b** and **c**. These acts are also commonly referred to as CINS or PINS. These types of offenders are referred to as status offenders. An act punishable by law, when committed by a juvenile, is known as a delinquent act, or choice **a**, which is the correct answer. These acts have punishments offered under the state's penal code. The age of the juvenile and the type of act committed would determine whether the juvenile is remanded to the adult system (choice **d**).

21. d. Frequent unemployment and unstable living conditions are two factors that can cause an offender to leave supervision. It is important for a parole officer to understand the factors or situations that lead to a return to criminal behavior. Choice **c** indicates that gender has something to do with absconding. Although there are more men within the criminal justice system, research has not shown a connection between being male and absconding.

22. d. Choices **a**, **b**, and **c** are, in fact, three of the standard conditions of any offender's probation or parole.

23. d. The state from which the offender was transferred is responsible for thoroughly and correctly carrying out all of the probation revocation processes. The probationer would be returned from the state in which he or she violated probation conditions (choice **b**) to the state in which the original crime was committed. The only obligation of the state in which the violations occurred would be the necessary documentation of the violations and later testimony, either in person or by phone, if necessary. The federal courts (choice **a**) do not have jurisdiction in these situations unless a federal crime has been committed. The Interstate Compact is an agreement between U.S. states and U.S. territories that allows for the supervision of probationers and parolees across state lines. This is more of an administrative function than a jurisdiction agency.

24. b. Most states require a bachelor's degree for the positions of probation and parole officers. At least 86% of states require a bachelor's degree for juvenile probation officers. Many states allow a combination of education and experi-

ence as a substitute for the bachelor's degree, while others require higher education studies. Choice **a** is the qualification standard (at least the high school portion) for most jobs in the corrections field, but states also like to see a combination of education and experience. Choices **c** and **d** are incorrect because only one state is known to require a master's degree for an entry-level probation or parole job (Hawaii).

25. b. The freedom of religion, freedom of speech, freedom of the press, and the right to assembly are all provided by the First Amendment. Choice **a** includes the right to bear arms, which is a collateral consequence of committing a crime. In other words, when convicted of a crime, citizens lose certain civil rights such as the right to vote, the right to serve on a jury, and the right to own a firearm. Federal law also restricts convicted felons from possessing, shipping, transporting, or receiving any firearms or ammunition. In choice **c**, losing the right to vote is a collateral consequence of the conviction; however, the freedom from cruel and unusual punishment, protected by the Eighth Amendment, and the freedom wrongful search and seizure, protected by the Fourth Amendment, are both rights that offenders do retain after conviction. Choice **d** is also incorrect because only losing the rights to vote and bear arms are collateral consequences of conviction.

26. b. Although choice **d** is important, the correct answer is choice **b**. It is vital that offenders be given supervision conditions that can be accomplished. Choice **a** may be true for special conditions (that is, sex offenders, or substance abusers, etc.). Choice **b** is not a responsibility of your job; the act of providing appropriate punishment is up to the sentencing court.

27. b. Referring offenders to different programs appropriate for their needs is the service brokerage style of supervision. As a service broker, the officer offers resources to the offender based upon his or her needs and upon the reasons that the offender is within the system. This style of supervision also provides the offender with the rules and expectations of the supervision conditions, as well as of the referred programs. In choice **a**, the officer interacts with offenders in a counselor/counselee dynamic; this method does not provide much structure but includes a lot of discussion. The style of supervision in choice **c** is more concerned with providing structure to ensure that the offender adheres to the rules and conditions successfully; however, there is always the risk that the offender may not be able to stay out from trouble once the structure is not provided. Choice **d** allows the officer to hold the offender accountable through rules and conditions, but when asked, the officer will volunteer resources to provide assistance.

28. b. Obtaining employment provides offenders with a sense of freedom to accomplish other goals under supervision. Also, according to a RAND study that measured practitioner recidivism rates in the United States, employed offenders tend to have a better chance of maintaining a successful supervision period and avoiding recidivism. Although choices **a**, **c**, and **d** are important, those accomplishments are not as vital as employment to the self-esteem, self-respect, and livelihood of the offender.

29. c. Transferring supervision to another state means the offender waives his or her possibility of extradition if there is ever a reason the offender needs to appear before a judge or paroling authority in the state in which the original crime was committed. This procedure is outlined in the Interstate Compact, which the offender is required to read and sign. Choice **a** is not an option that the officer can

enforce. Offenders may need to return to their original state for various reasons, and as long as those reasons are legitimate, offenders may request to have supervision returned at any time. Choice **b** is incorrect because bail is available on all charges except probation and parole violations. Choice **d** is incorrect because this is a collateral consequence: Half of the states enforce the loss of this right, whereas the other states do, in fact, allow offenders to vote.

30. d. It is imperative your supervisor know that you are behind and, more important, that you have a plan of action to get caught up. An officer must be current on all classification tools, and to know and be able to explain to others what types of risks the offender might cause the community. Documentation of the most severe cases would be the next priority, then the less severe cases, and finally the least severe cases. An officer's job is to supervise offenders; however, documentation of that supervision is equally important. Choice **c** is incorrect because this action only hides the problem. If you provide substandard documentation, your supervisor will have a more difficult time supporting you if one of your offenders commits extreme violations of his supervision. Choices **a** and **b** are also incorrect because procrastinating or being unconscientious is not a professional or healthy attitude to have when you are charged with protection of the community.

31. b. Parole officers should always remain professional and courteous to citizens and offer to provide assistance in a reasonable fashion. Placing a special condition on travel is certainly within the parole officer's responsibility and scope of authority. Choice **c** is an action the parole officer should consider after dealing with the family, but it should not be the first step. This action would also depend upon what was said by the family and friends and upon the seriousness of the offender's charges. Choice **a** is not a responsible action for an officer of a state agency. Although choice **d** may be factually correct, not taking any action is unacceptable.

32. c. After arriving at a halfway house, all offenders should be allowed a short adjustment period. Choices **b** and **d** do not allow this adjustment period at all. In fact, either of these could damage any comfort level you may have achieved with the offender. Although choice **a** allows for this adjustment period, a parole officer should not forget this is an offender, and the officer should take additional steps to ascertain how worrisome Gerald's behavior is. The correct and responsible response to this situation is choice **c**. It is imperative for a parole officer to obtain and utilize information and insight from the halfway house staff before deciding upon his or her next course of action with the offender. Likewise, relaying your observations of Gerald's behavior may help the halfway house staff better understand Gerald and his interactions with other residents.

33. b. It is important for a parole officer to be a referral and resource agent and to ensure the safety of the offender as much as possible. In this case, it would be important for the halfway house manager to have the information and allow him or her to check it out and then plan accordingly. It is also important to remove the offender, if possible, from such stress. Choice **a** is not a responsible choice because it eliminates action on your part. Choice **d** is not within your authority as you are not the manager of the halfway house, nor do you control staffing at the police department. Choice **c** would be an irresponsible action for a parole officer.

34. a. It is essential that you show support of the halfway house staff and recognize their obser-

vations of behavior as valid and worth pursuing. If you handle the situation correctly, Gerald will respond to your questioning and tell you about his concerns or provide some explanation. You will be able to take action based upon this discussion. Choice **b** would be an option if you had received multiple, successive calls within a specific time frame (i.e., a week or a month). A parole officer would need to take more decisive action after the initial conversations with the offender about his behavior and the need to make immediate changes. Choices **c** and **d** are actions that may not need to be taken upon the first expression of concerns by the halfway house staff. Taking an offender to detention in the early stages may cause conflict in the officer/offender relationship. Telling the manager of a halfway house that you aren't concerned would certainly call for your supervisor's involvement in the situation.

35. d. Although jail is not a place for "shock incarceration," under these circumstances, it is best to place Gerald in detention in order to provide protection to the community. This option certainly provides you opportunities to gain additional resources for Gerald should you chose to let him remain in the community. Choices **a, b,** and **c** would be irresponsible. Not considering Gerald's words, choice **a**, would be inconsiderate and rude. Choices **b** and **c** do not provide safety to the community, nor does choice **c** provide suitable action on your part.

36. a. Even though there may not be an issue, the police department will need to have something from you to hold him in jail until Gerald's whereabouts can be ascertained. For these types of offenses, it is better to be safe. Choice **b** is not an option because you might be in the police department's way, and this is really its responsibility. Choice **d** is legally unsound; at this point, the victims do not need to know that the offender is missing. Choice **c** is also legally unsound because you are the party responsible for supervision, according to the state.

37. b. There are times when a parole officer's responsibility encompasses those people around the offender. In this case, that responsibility involves two minor children. It will help Jane to know her children are at least safe in foster care or wherever the welfare agency can place them. Choice **a** will not really help the children; eventually, the police department would take custody of the children and turn them over to the child welfare agency. Choice **d** is not a viable option because it would be difficult for Jane to make the necessary contacts and arrangements for her children from a locked facility that allows her limited phone privileges. Choice **c** is incorrect and not the action of a responsible and professional parole officer.

38. a. Although it is important to keep in mind that Jane is the mother of two small children (choice **b**), this should not be your first and primary concern. Jane's progress and willingness to follow the rules and conditions established by the court should be the major focus of your decision. Because Jane may be charged with another felony charge (because of the amount of drugs in the suitcase), choice **a** is correct. Jane obviously has not followed the condition of probation that she avoid association with others who may be involved with illegal activities. Whether she knew or did not know what was in the suitcase is not relevant. Jane's association with known gang members is enough to put her in front of the judge for violating her probation. Choice **c** is important only when creating your recommendations for the judge. Choice **d** is not really relevant to

keeping Jane on probation, unless you are not recommending revocation.

39. a. Jane is obviously struggling with several issues, but generally speaking, she has the basic components to be successful. A better job may offer her more opportunities, as well as allow her to make a living rather than just get by, giving her a chance to boost her feelings of self-worth and self-esteem. College would give Jane the opportunity to meet different people and a means to lose contact with the gangs. The dependency counseling would provide her the support and courage to break away from the gangs and would help her understand why she gravitates toward gangs in the first place. Choice **b** is incorrect because the case study did not allude to Jane having poor parenting skills. One cannot assume she is a bad mother because of her associations or actions outside the home. Choice **c** also assumes that Jane has a substance abuse problem, when the case study doesn't confirm that. An offender can be involved with substance abusers, as in this case, without actively abusing the substance. Choice **d** may not be possible for Jane for many reasons; this suggestion may be part of a conversation an officer would have with Jane, but should not be a formal recommendation.

40. b. The correct answer is determined by the working relationship you have with your local police department. Choice **b**, in which the local detectives will work with you and the judge so that all parties have what is needed, is the best answer. However, if your working relationship with the police is not a good one, then choice **a** would be your second choice. Contacting a federal agency may not work in most situations; however, because the DEA was named in the case study as active members of the operation, they would likely be supportive of a call from a local probation officer. Choice **c** is incorrect because negotiations with offenders on compliance with the conditions happen all of the time. It is important to note she is not bound by any laws to provide the name. You are, however, required to report whatever information you may have received to the appropriate authorities. Choice **d** is incorrect because it puts you in the middle of a situation that is not yours to facilitate. Your role is to contact people to have them talk with Jane, not be her mouthpiece.

41. a. It is unfortunate that most probation departments are not equipped for situations like this; however, this situation calls strictly for the police department's involvement. It is important to remember who has law enforcement capabilities and whose responsibility it is to protect citizens. Choice **c** is not a responsible action for a parole officer. Choice **d** would be legally irresponsible and may cause Jane to flee, causing greater issues for her.

42. c. You might need to remind Jonathan that he is to observe and learn, not walk off on his own. You again need to remind him of the dangers of this type of work and solicit a promise that he will stay with you in future collateral visits. Choice **c** is the best response to this situation, although choice **b** would be an acceptable alternative. It is imperative that interns, volunteers, etc., understand that they must learn how to communicate when working with and around offenders. Additionally, it is important for you to convey what you observed to help Jonathan learn what type of behavior you need to watch for and how you should react. Above all, it is important to remind Jonathan about safety issues and concerns and the need to watch out for each other.

43. a. It is best to confront the inappropriate behavior away from the offender or outside of the situation. Taking Jonathan outside on

the front porch and away from the mother saves the mother from witnessing a dressing-down and allows Jonathan to maintain some dignity in the situation. It is important to explain to interns and volunteers why their behavior or action was wrong and how it can be corrected. It is also important in this situation to model appropriate behavior, which is why you should apologize to the mother for allowing this situation to get out of hand. Choice **b** does not provide Jonathan with a learning experience; rather, this action may cause additional anger for all parties involved. Choice **c** does not model appropriate methods of resolving difficult situations. Also, dressing down Jonathan in front of the mother will only embarrass him. Choice **d** is simply not an option, considering the hard work you have accomplished with the offender, who will probably get a call from his mother the minute you leave. Additionally, this choice is not appropriate action by a professional.

44. b. Your first responsibility is to ensure the offender's well-being. Once it is determined that the offender wasn't angry with you or your presence at his home, an officer must not dismiss the expressed concerns, but should spend appropriate time discussing them with the offender. However, it is important to remember the reason for the visit, thus getting into the home to ensure everything is appropriate and legal. Choice **d** is really the offender's decision and may cause conflict between you and the offender. Choice **a** is not appropriate action until you ensure the offender is safe and your responsibility has been completed. Choice **c** is unsound advice from an officer.

45. a. One of the goals of the parole officer is to be a positive role model for offenders, volunteers, and interns. Therefore, it is important to address Jonathan's concerns and issues (choice **a**) and not make him feel as if you are dismissing them (choice **c**). Making fun of Jonathan is also not a good tactic (choice **b**) because it does not teach Jonathan how to work with others in a compassionate way, a skill he will need if he becomes a staff member of the correctional system. Choice **c** would only add to Jonathan's embarrassment and would not reflect positively on you as a teacher or role model. Choice **d** could be an option, depending on how Jonathan upset is. It is wise to make alterations in your schedule so that the day can end successfully. This may mean that you end the day and return to the office or that you attempt to conduct one more home visit, whichever will help the experience be positive.

46. b. It is best to provide explicit details about your day and provide your initial notes to your supervisor when you are questioned regarding any actions you may have done. Documentation is extremely important in a probation or parole officer's job, and sometimes it is your only protection against accusations. Also, conversations in a professional manner will take you farther in the end. Choice **a** may be the natural reaction, but you should always take complaints seriously because your supervisor always will. Choice **c** is again a natural reaction; however, calling the college adviser is your supervisor's responsibility, and it is more than likely he or she has already done this. Your contact with the adviser may only cause more conflict. Choice **d** is not a rational choice and will only make you look unprofessional.

47. c. When a probationer asks for counseling because she says she feels it will help her, counseling should start as soon as possible. The probationer is reaching out, and to ignore this opportunity to help her would be unwise. The officer should also contact the parents to inform them of this action and to reaffirm the judge's expectation that they participate. Choice **a** is not a viable choice because the parents understand they need to participate and probably understand the benefits that their daughter will receive, yet they continue to refuse. Choice **b** isn't an option until all other possibilities have been explored. Choice **d** is incorrect because this is a 16-year-old girl who is already having concerns and issues with her parents; placing this responsibility on her would be counterproductive to her willingness to start counseling.

48. c. Again, documentation is the mainstay of any officer's work. Ensuring your documentation of your offender's progress is current and complete will help solidify any argument you may need to make. Talking with your supervisor to gain his or her understanding and support, as well as forewarning him or her of potential calls from the parents, will also help strengthen your case. However, removing Jordan from your caseload is up to your supervisor and the judge. Choice **b** indicates you are willing to wait to see if the father will call; although this tactic may have to be an option if your supervisor is out of the office, it is always good to prepare your supervisor for citizen calls, especially if they are expected to be negative. Choice **a** is incorrect because not reacting could put you and your offender both in a difficult situation later. Choice **d** is not an option until all other opportunities have been exhausted. The judge does not wish to be bothered with administrative issues unless it is the last resort.

49. d. It is important that an officer not dismiss the probationer's struggles; however, setting limits and clear expectations are also part of the responsibility of a probation officer. Allowing Jordan to establish assistance for her struggles will build rapport between you, which will prove beneficial in the future. Choice **c** will do the exact opposite for Jordan. You may need to involve her parents, but forcing the joint counseling issue in addition to telling them that Jordan relapsed will only cause more conflict. Choice **b** may be a concern of yours, but you should remember that you are not an expert in psychiatry and, therefore, cannot diagnose this. You may need to watch Jordan's behavior and pass on these observations to the substance abuse counselor, so others can be contacted through appropriate channels. Choice **a** is usually not the best reaction on a first violation. Probation officers would fill the jails if they recommended revocation for every violation. It is an expected that offenders will be guided through relapses to learn how to be successful in the end.

50. b. Jordan allowed the party to start in her home, so she must be the one to ask everyone to leave. Giving Jordan a second part to the plan will allow her to feel like she can maintain control, because those who don't leave will have to answer to the police department. Other than the parents, the police department is really the only authority to remove unwanted people from this home. Choice **a** does not allow Jordan to stay in control, and your presence could only cause more issues for Jordan. Taking Jordan to a youth shelter would indicate that Jordan has been abused, neglected, or left without care, none of which seems to be the case. Choice **c** is not a wise choice and would certainly result in the loss of whatever rapport you have established with Jordan and her family. Choice **d** would truly cause more conflict with and problems for Jordan.

51. c. This is not your case or your legal concern. It is important to be trustworthy in this position, particularly with your coworkers. Giving this information to people who do not need to know (choices **a** and **b**) could hurt your credibility and possibly cause the other officer's offender, and your own, to act irresponsibly. Choice **d** is not an option because this is not a decision you are allowed to make. The officer assigned this case has the ability and right to decide how many times an offender is worked with. Likewise, it is the supervisor's job to make case assignments. Negotiating cases is a sure way to cause a supervision issue.

52. b. Contacting your supervisor to discuss situations in which there may be several options is always a good idea. If the situation were more volatile and the abuse more visible, leaving Jordan alone with her parents would not be an appropriate choice. If the situation had been more volatile, then choice **c** would be the correct answer. You must always remember, however, to ensure your safety during the situation or while waiting for the police to arrive. Choice **d** may be an option after the police arrive and inform the father of the potential report. Choice **a** is not an appropriate action because an officer must react to the most pressing situation, which in this case is the volatile situation in the house. Comparatively, Jordan's skipping school seems minor and should be addressed after the more severe situation is resolved.

53. d. Although it seems a threat was implied, being told to watch your step could be interpreted in many ways. Rather than create a larger issue, you should simply document what was said, along with the date, time, and witnesses. It is important to have documentation, regardless of whom the documentation includes. Choice **a** might be an option if the veiled statements continue after the break room situation. Choice **b** could possibly escalate the situation and elicit more harsh statements from Ben. At this point, emotions are high, and you should wait until everyone has calmed down before considering this option. Choice **c** may be true, but documentation is still a necessity.

54. c. If you are viewed as a peacekeeper, then you should advise your coworkers to do as they were instructed by their own supervisor and wait for the changes under the other supervisor to take their natural course. If the parole director is observant, he or she will notice the inconsistencies without you needing to get involved or point them out. Choices **a** and **b** are reasonable, but the staff needs to remain calm and patient. Tensions do not need to escalate, and staff does not need to be separated. Therefore, encouraging the newer supervisor to put themselves in the position of criticizing someone who has seniority is a smart idea. Nor will it do any good, because it is likely that this action could cause further conflict. Choice **d** would only alienate those who feel comfortable with you. You are viewed as a leader, and this is not action a leader would take.

55. c. However, this choice is not an easy one. Ethically, each staff member is obligated to ensure safety in the office. Sleeping in the office is not only a violation of policy, but also a safety concern for the staff. The parole director should know this is happening, and you have an obligation to provide this information. Not doing so would be irresponsible. Choice **d** is an option; however, your priority is to the office and your coworkers' safety, not to Ben and his inappropriate behavior. Choice **b** would certainly be an easier choice, but it is not an ethical one. Choice **a** would also be an easier choice; however, your priority must be ethical behavior and the safety of others in the office.

56. a. It is the responsibility of the supervisor to ensure compliance with policy. If there is appropriate justification to make exceptions to policy, then it is his or her responsibility to determine that as well. Therefore, no action needs to be taken in this situation. Choice **b** would make office conflicts only greater. It is not your responsibility to decide if a superior should receive consequences. Additionally, as long as nothing illegal or unethical is occurring, then there isn't a complaint to be made. Choice **c** might be an option, but raising this issue in an open forum must be done delicately and tactfully. Choice **d** would only cause conflict between Ben and the officer who is questioning his authority.

57. b. It is important for a parole officer to be trustworthy and not to be too hasty in making decisions. In this situation, gathering information would be vital before accusing someone, especially a superior, of wrongdoing. Monitoring the situation and altering your scheduled visits to return to the office would allow you to gain information without bringing anyone else into the situation unnecessarily. Although the second part of choice **a** is true, the first part is not an option. If this is unusual for a supervisor to do, then it is worthy of monitoring and fact-finding. Choice **c** may cause conflict between you and your supervisor, especially if your perception is wrong. If Ben is legitimate in his concern for the offender, then you will be able to see that during the offender's visit the next day. Choice **d** would cause only more conflict in the office and with Ben. Getting someone else in the situation will only cause rumors and will allow a possibly untrue accusation to circulate.

58. b. A personnel matter, which in this case is the interview process, is confidential and should not be discussed in open arenas. Interviews should not be discussed outside of the interview process, even months after the fact. Doing so would only cause more office tension, hurt feelings for the officer being discussed, and that officer, or the rejected candidates, to file legal action. The right time to discuss interview concerns is at the time of the interview and finalization of hiring recommendations. Choice **a** is not a good option because this parole director wasn't involved in making the hiring decision and, therefore, could not reverse it or cause action against the parole supervisor. Choice **c** would also simply cause more office tension. Choice **d** might be a personal choice an officer makes, but it isn't an action for you to insist upon.

59. c. According to federal law, all employees have the right to work in an environment free of harassment. The supervisor made a choice to participate in a display of intimacy that should not be conducted at work. Thus, this situation can be categorized as a type of sexual harassment known as creating a hostile workplace. It is within your right to report it to whomever you feel is appropriate, and this behavior does not have to be reported within the chain of command. Choice **d**, reporting the incident to your director, is an appropriate decision if you feel confident that there will not be any retaliation for reporting this harassment. However, demanding someone face consequences is not within a subordinate's, or the victim's, authority. Choice **a** is not a wise action because it is vindictive and would cause only more office tension. Choice **b** is not an option because most states have a policy that employees must report sexual harassment when they become aware of it.

60. a. If you are given a lawful directive or order, then you are bound to follow that order or directive. It is up to the director to justify how the documentation you provided is used, especially in any type of termination action. Providing documentation may mean you must testify in civil hearings, but doing so is your responsibility under a code of ethics.

Choice **b** might be an appropriate answer if your documentation file holds information on other parole officers or supervisors. Copying information is always a good idea, but it could be done after the director's initial review. Choice **c** is not appropriate, because documents created and maintained during the course of an officer's duties are the property of the department. Choice **d** is also not appropriate because the department's attorneys are also your attorneys and will provide legal representation for you, unless you have been charged with misconduct or have conducted illegal activities.

61. b. This sentence is clear when it is read and punctuated correctly. In choice **a**, the punctuation puts a hesitation in the reading, which is not natural for the sentence. The punctuation in choice **c** creates a sentence fragment. Choice **d** has an inappropriate use of a semicolon. A semicolon would allow two complete sentences to be combined into one thought or sentence. This sentence is not written in that fashion.

62. b. The sentence is complete and punctuated appropriately at the end. Choice **a** and **d** contain sentence fragments. Choice **c** starts with a dependent clause and could not stand by itself.

63. d. The sentence is complete, clear, and punctuated correctly. Choice **b** has a fragment, and as punctuated, this choice does not make sense. The punctuation in choice **a** makes the sentence incomplete. Choice **c** is also a fragment.

64. a. This sentence clearly states the suspect hit several parked cars that were located in the parking lot as he drove away. Choice **b** leaves the reader to question whether the suspect hit the cars or the observer hit the cars. Choice **c** leaves the reader unclear as to who actually hit the cars. Choice **d**, as written, indicates that the parking lot reported that several parked cars were hit.

65. a. This sentence is complete, easy to read, and clear. Choice **b** starts with a phrase, which generally makes a sentence less clear. Choice **c** is neither easy to read nor clear as to what the supervisor was to read for clarity and grammar. Choice **d** indicates what was written by the officer, but the phrase "given for clarity and grammar" implies that the report was written for those reasons rather than for the violations.

66. b. This sentence is complete, with correct punctuation and clarity. Choice **a** could be technically correct, but the sentence structure is awkward and difficult to read. Choice **c** is a series of phrases that do not make sense in this order and create a run-on sentence. Choice **d** indicates a different meaning than intended.

67. d. This sentence is grammatically correct as well as clearly written. Choice **a** has several verb tense issues. In choice **b**, the word *informant* is misspelled, and the sentence is a run-on. Choice **c** also misspells *informant*.

68. d. This sentence is complete, and the reader understands who and what was involved. Choice **a** has several words misspelled and used incorrectly. Choice **b** has a misspelled word and a misplaced modifier. Choice **c** is unclear as to who was sitting in jail and has misspelled words.

69. c. This is the only sentence that is not grammatically correct. Choices **a**, **b**, and **d** are all grammatically correct and have correct punctuation and spelling.

70. c. The author listed the three advantages of the school-based programs. Choice **a** is not an accurate statement; the fact that school-based programs are not being implemented across the nation explains many factors stated in the last paragraph. Choice **b** is not an accurate statement and is not implied anywhere in this passage. Choice **d** is not correct: Although probation officers may help curb violence at schools, it is not the only reason administrators wish for programs to be located in their schools.

71. c. This type of program usually is funded through a federal grant, but funding is only an indirect benefit to the juveniles in this program. Choices **a**, **b**, and **d** are listed in paragraphs 1 and 3 as direct benefits to the juveniles.

72. a. The author cited this as the biggest disadvantage to the school-based program. Additionally, the author indicated that maintaining the confidentiality of school records and the lack of office space are secondary disadvantages. Choice **b** overstates a comment made in paragraph 2. Choice **c** is an advantage of the program, and not being able to get away from the caseload is not mentioned at all in the passage. Choice **d** was mentioned in paragraph 1 and does not capture the full message of the passage.

73. b. This is found in the first paragraph, and court intervention is the only way a juvenile could be under supervision. Choice **a** is incorrect, because the probation officer cannot supervise any student unless he or she has been assigned by the judge to the officer's caseload. Choices **c** and **d** overstate the main idea of paragraph 2.

74. b. The author stated in paragraph 4 the reasons that communities have not implemented this type of program. Many states struggle with the concept of the program, but those aren't cited as the main reasons that the program hasn't been widely accepted. Choice **a** is inaccurate and not cited in the passage. Judges and administrators work hard throughout the country to ensure the best services are offered to the community served. Choices **c** and **d** are not correct; although they may be secondary reasons for not implementing this type of program, this is not a main idea of paragraph 4.

75. b. To ensure actions are legal and within the scope of their duties, officers must be knowledgeable of state and federal laws, as well as of actions that could be deemed negligent. Choice **a** is incorrect, because any action can be questioned in civil and criminal court. Choice **c** is incorrect, because officers are given immunity in every situation or case. Officers must conduct their duties with accuracy or in an objectively reasonable nature. Choice **d** is overstating some of the details of the passage; an offender may sue if an officer upsets him or her, but there must be a cause or reason for the lawsuit. Additionally, if the action were within the scope of the officer's authority, then the agency would provide legal representation.

76. b. Only choice **b** has all the correct terms as defined by federal law. Slight negligence is defined as a failure to exercise great care. Gross negligence is described as a failure to exercise even that care which a careless person would use. Willful negligence is defined as an act of intentional disregard of a known risk or a risk so great that harm is very likely to follow.

77. b. Quasi-judicial functions involving discretionary decision making or court functions are covered under the umbrella of absolute immunity granted to those within the judicial or legislative branches of government. Choices **a** and **c** may be specific discretionary functions of an officer's position and are thus covered under qualified immunity. Choice **d** may be a situation after which a negligence complaint might be filed. If the officer were found to be negligent, but acting within the scope of his or her duties, then he or she would be granted qualified immunity.

78. d. This is the primary basis of a willful negligence lawsuit. Choices **a** and **b** are examples covered under the absolute immunity clause. Choice **c** is an example of an administrative act by the parole officer, and if sued for not properly supervising, the officer could be granted qualified immunity.

79. b. An officer may find him- or herself dealing with both court systems, as one incident could involve civil and criminal liabilities for federal and state courts. Additionally, the department may enforce internal consequences as listed in paragraph 2. Choices **a**, **c**, and **d** are incorrect. It should be noted that, in most circumstances, departments will strongly consider internal corrective action for all situations in which civil or criminal liabilities have been questioned.

80. c. The U.S. Supreme Court found for the inmates in two areas, one of which is choice **c**. Offenders shall receive appropriate advance notice of any hearing regarding their parole or revocation of parole. The other was that, if parole was denied, the inmates should receive written notice of the reasons. Choices **a**, **b**, and **c** are not accurate.

81. d. The author clearly thinks the citizens want offenders locked up, but to be treated fairly in the process. Choice **a** is an expansion on a statement in the last paragraph, but is clearly not the main idea. Choice **b** is partly correct; however, as stated in paragraph 4, this is part of the larger picture presented in the passage. Choice **c** was not stated in this passage but is implied in paragraph 3. Nonetheless, this is certainly not the main idea of the passage.

82. a. This was not in contention in *Greenholtz*; however, this has been part of other lawsuits filed by offenders. Choices **b**, **c**, and **d** were, in fact, the three areas cited by the inmates and are listed in the first paragraph of the passage.

83. a. This was the statement cited by the U.S. Supreme Court in the *Greenholtz* decision. The other choices, **b**, **c**, and **d**, are incorrect; they are simply variations of what was stated in paragraph 3 of the passage.

84. b. As stated in the passage, the U.S. Supreme Court found that the Nebraska Board of Parole offered inmates ample opportunity to be heard throughout the paroling process. However, the court indicated that advance written notice of the parole hearing should be given to the inmate, and if parole is revoked, the inmate should receive written reasons for that revocation. As stated in paragraph 2 of the passage, the U.S. Supreme Court acknowledged that parole boards have a great deal of discretionary powers, which are necessary in dealing with the various hearings. Choice **a** is a combination of sentences in paragraph 2. Choice **c** also combined concepts stated in the passage. In addition, the opportunities to be heard and to be made aware of charges were not the issue in this case. Choice **d** is incorrect because the Supreme Court found for the inmates in two of their stated areas of concern.

85. c. The number of women in prison is increasing across the nation, making administrators work harder to provide programs that will assist in women's rehabilitation, as explained in paragraph 5. Choice **a** is incorrect because the passage says that administrators are not building prisons but rather choosing to put their budgets toward other buildings and programs. Choice **b** is not accurate as explained in paragraph 5. There has been a movement toward development of gender-specific programs in a few but not all states. Choice **d** is incorrect and was not stated in the passage. Actually, in paragraph 5, the author indicates that some states have been successful in implementing gender-specific programs that follow a continuum of services. There is little room in the program and funding for interstate parolees.

86. c. The crime rate among women has increased 2.9% between 2003 and 2004 as stated in paragraph 2. The author offered some explanation for this increase in paragraph 3: In addition to facing similar risk factors as men, women have at least two unique risk factors that may contribute to their criminal behavior. Choices **a**, **b**, and **d** are simply inaccurate. Each population has some unique risk factors, while others may cross the gender lines in a small population. However, research shows that women remain the primary victims in sexual and physical abuse crimes, a statistic that holds true as more crimes are committed.

87. a. Administrators must be creative in the development of programs for all offenders. The author points out in paragraph 5 that some states are partnering with community resources to provide programs that are either free or of cost little to the department. Choice **b** was not mentioned in the passage. Choice **c** may be an option, but it was not an idea expressed in this passage. Choice **d** is an expansion of a statement made in paragraph 4 and is not a main idea of the passage.

88. d. Although developing boot camps for women is a possibility, most states do not feel it is feasible. Also, most states struggle with creating and maintaining coed facilities. Choices **a**, **b**, and **c** were mentioned in paragraph 5 as programs that have been implemented and been successful in a few states.

89. d. The author clearly feels administrators need to understand the connection between programming and budgets. Choices **a** and **b** may be good actions to pursue, but must be considered in relation to the budget. Choice **c** is not a main idea of this passage and is not the correct answer.

90. a. Although according to statistics the recidivism rate is high, the author clearly thinks achieving success with an offender is more than keeping him or her out of prison. An offender who has developed self-esteem, problem-solving skills, and coping skills qualifies as a success, but it is a success that is hard to measure. Choice **b** might be the view of some politicians, as many programs are not easily measured for successes or failures. Choice **c** may be an accurate statement; however, it is not the primary message of the passage. Likewise, choice **d** is also not the message the author is trying to convey.

91. b. This reason was not listed in the passage, and it is an inaccurate statement. All states have funded a community supervision program for offenders. Choices **a**, **c** and **d** are the three listed reasons in the passage.

92. d. The author clearly feels boot camps should be more widely available so that offenders can learn life skills. The author also stated that society should decide if it wants to pay to keep offenders off the streets for extensive periods of time, or if it wants to fund programs such as boot camps to try to rehabilitate offenders. Choice **b** may be a reality when society chooses to lock up offenders rather than rehabilitate them, but this is not the author's point.

93. c. As stated in paragraph 2, the recent emphasis is to provide educational and vocational opportunities to assist in offering structure and discipline to the participants. The first-generation camps stressed more of a military approach, choice **a**. Choice **b** describes the second-generation camps. Choice **d** does not describe any of the generation camps listed in paragraph 2.

94. d. The author states in the last paragraph of the passage that offenders may return to criminal ways because they were incorrectly assigned to a program that did not benefit them; these poor assignments happen when there is a conflict of program goals. Choice **a** was

implied throughout the passage, but not directly stated by the author. Choice **c** is a possibility, but neither reason is stated in the passage. Choice **b** has the two actual reasons cited for high recidivism in paragraph 3.

95. d. There will always be stress caused by the nature of this type of work. It is imperative that officers not add to their own stress level, as stated in paragraphs 6 and 7. Choice **a** is incorrect; the organization cannot relieve the stress of its workers without their cooperation. Choice **b** is incorrect because sick leave abuse only adds to the stress levels of others, and is controlled by the officer who calls in sick, not the organization. Choice **c** is incorrect; administrators must realize that officers cannot "simply work through stress" and will need assistance.

96. c. Taking scheduled vacations is an appropriate way of relieving stress. Choices **a**, **b**, and **d** were all mentioned in the passage as appropriate means for reducing stress.

97. a. The author believes that it is easier to blame something or someone else than look at one's own contribution to stress. The author thinks employees need to assume some responsibility in managing their stress instead of waiting for the organization to address it. Choices **b**, **c**, and **d** point to the organization as being responsible for causing stress as well as for finding a way to alleviate that stress, which is not the main idea of this passage.

98. d. The author believes that officers can control how much they exacerbate the inherent stress of being a probation or parole officer. Managing one's work ethics and responses to conflicts is all within the officer's control and is his or her responsibility. Choice **b** is a brief detail from paragraph 2. Choices **a** and **c** place the responsibility for stress on the organization, which is not the main idea of this passage.

99. d. All of these choices (**a**, **b**, and **c**) are consequences of an officer's choice to abuse his or her sick leave. Each of these consequences can, and should, be avoided.

100. d. Managing time and communicating issues to supervisors appropriately are the responsibilities of the officer, not the organization. Choices **a**, **b**, and **c** are directly linked to the organization's need to operate within a set budget and mission.

5 ▶ The LearningExpress Test Preparation System

CHAPTER SUMMARY

Taking a civil service exam can be tough, and your career depends on your passing the exam. The LearningExpress Test Preparation System, developed exclusively for LearningExpress by leading test experts, gives you the discipline and attitude you need to succeed.

First, the bad news: Taking the probation/parole officer exam is no picnic, and neither is getting ready for it. Your future career in probation or parole depends upon passing the test, but there are all sorts of pitfalls that can keep you from doing your best on this all-important exam. Here are some of the obstacles that can stand in the way of your success:

- Being unfamiliar with the format of the exam
- Being paralyzed by test anxiety
- Leaving your preparation to the last minute
- Not preparing at all
- Not knowing vital test-taking skills: how to pace yourself through the exam, how to use the process of elimination, and when to guess
- Not being in tip-top mental and physical shape
- Arriving late at the test site, having to work on an empty stomach, or being uncomfortable through the exam because the room is too warm or too cold

What's the common denominator in all these test-taking pitfalls? One word: control. Who's in control, you or the exam?

Now the good news: The LearningExpress Test Preparation System puts you in control. In just nine easy-to-follow steps, you will learn everything you need to know to make sure that you are in charge of your preparation and your performance on the exam. Other test takers may let the test get the better of them; other test takers may be unprepared or out of shape—but not you. You will have followed all the steps you need to take to get a high score on the probation/parole officer exam.

Here's how the LearningExpress Test Preparation System works: Nine easy steps lead you through everything you need to know and do to get ready to master your exam. Each of the steps listed below includes both reading about the step and completing one or more activities. It is important that you do the activities along with the reading, or you won't be getting the full benefit of the system.

Step 1: Get Information

Step 2: Conquer Test Anxiety

Step 3: Make a Plan

Step 4: Learn to Manage Your Time

Step 5: Learn to Use the Process of Elimination

Step 6: Know When to Guess

Step 7: Reach Your Peak Performance Zone

Step 8: Get Your Act Together

Step 9: Do It!

If you have several hours, you can work through the whole LearningExpress Test Preparation System in one sitting. Otherwise, you can break it up and do just one or two steps a day for the next several days. It is up to you—remember, you are in control.

▶ Step 1: Get Information

Activities: Read Chapter 3, "The Written Exam," and use the suggestions there to find out about your requirements.

Knowledge is power. Therefore, first, you have to find out everything you can about the probation/parole exam. Once you have your information, the next steps will show you what to do about it.

Part A: Straight Talk about the Probation/Parole Officer Exam

It is important for you to remember that your score on the written exam does not determine how smart you are or even whether you will make a good probation or parole officer. There are all kinds of things a written exam like this can't test: whether you are likely to show up late or call in sick a lot, whether you can be patient when dealing with people, or whether you can be trusted with confidential information. Those kinds of things are hard to evaluate on a written exam. Meanwhile, it is easy to evaluate whether you can correctly answer questions about your job duties.

This is not to say that correctly answering the questions on the written exam is not important! The knowledge tested on the exam is knowledge you will need to do your job, and your ability to enter the profession depends upon your passing this exam. And that's why you are here—to achieve success on the exam.

Part B: What's on the Test

If you haven't already done so, stop here and read Chapter 3 of this book, which gives you an overview of the written exam. Later, you will have the opportunity to take the sample practice exams in Chapters 4, 9, 10, 11, 12, 13, and 14.

▶ Step 2: Conquer Test Anxiety

Activity: Take the Test Anxiety Quiz on page 90.
Having complete information about the exam is the first step in taking control of the exam. Next, you have to overcome one of the biggest obstacles to test success: test anxiety. Test anxiety can not only impair your performance on the exam itself; it can even keep you from preparing! In this step, you will learn stress management techniques that will help you succeed on your exam. Learn these strategies now, and practice them as you complete the exams in this book so that they will be second nature to you by exam day.

Combating Test Anxiety

The first thing you need to know is that a little test anxiety is a good thing. Everyone gets nervous before a big exam—and if that nervousness motivates you to prepare thoroughly, so much the better. Many well-known people throughout history have experienced anxiety or nervousness—from performers such as actor Sir Laurence Olivier and singer Aretha Franklin to writers such as Charlotte Brontë and Alfred, Lord Tennyson. In fact, anxiety probably gave them a little extra edge—just the kind of edge you need to do well, whether on a stage or in an examination room.

Stop here and complete the Test Anxiety Quiz on the next page to find out whether your level of test anxiety is something you should worry about.

Stress Management before the Test

If you feel your level of anxiety getting the best of you in the weeks before the test, here is what you need to do to bring the level down again:

- **Get prepared**. There's nothing like knowing what to expect and being prepared for it to put you in control of test anxiety. That's why you are reading this book. Use it faithfully, and remind yourself that you are better prepared than most of the people taking the test.

- **Practice self-confidence**. A positive attitude is a great way to combat test anxiety. This is no time to be humble or shy. Stand in front of the mirror and say to your reflection, "I'm prepared. I'm full of self-confidence. I'm going to ace this test. I know I can do it." If you hear it often enough, you will come to believe it.

- **Fight negative messages**. Every time someone starts telling you how hard the exam is or how it is almost impossible to get a high score, start telling them your self-confidence messages above. If the someone with the negative messages is you, telling yourself *you don't do well on exams* or *you just can't do this*, don't listen.

- **Visualize**. Imagine yourself reporting for duty on your first day as a probation or parole officer. Think of yourself helping offenders make smooth and successful transitions back into the community. Imagine coming home with your first paycheck. Visualizing success can help make it happen—and it reminds you of why you are working so hard to pass the exam.

- **Exercise**. Physical activity helps calm down your body and focus your mind. Besides, being in good physical shape can actually help you do well on the exam. Go for a run, lift weights, go swimming—and do it regularly.

Stress Management on Test Day

There are several ways you can bring down your level of anxiety on test day. They will be most helpful if you practice them in the weeks before the test, so you know which ones work best for you.

- **Deep breathing**. Take a deep breath while you count to five. Hold it for a count of one, then let it out for a count of five. Repeat several times.

- **Move your body**. Try rolling your head in a circle. Rotate your shoulders. Shake your hands from the wrist. Many people find these movements very relaxing.

Test Anxiety Quiz

You need to worry about test anxiety only if it is extreme enough to impair your performance. The following questionnaire will provide a diagnosis of your level of test anxiety. In the blank before each statement, write the number that most accurately describes your experience.

0 = Never
1 = Once or twice
2 = Sometimes
3 = Often

____ I have gotten so nervous before an exam that I simply put down the books and didn't study for it.

____ I have experienced disabling physical symptoms such as vomiting and severe headaches because I was nervous about an exam.

____ I have simply not showed up for an exam because I was scared to take it.

____ I have experienced dizziness and disorientation while taking an exam.

____ I have had trouble filling in the little circles because my hands were shaking too hard.

____ I have failed an exam because I was too nervous to complete it.

____ **Total:** Add up the numbers in the blanks above.

Your Test Anxiety Score

Here are the steps you should take, depending upon your score. If you scored:

■ **Below 3**, your level of test anxiety is nothing to worry about; it is probably just enough to give you that little extra edge.

■ **Between 3 and 6**, your test anxiety may be enough to impair your performance, and you should practice the stress management techniques listed in this section to try to bring your test anxiety down to manageable levels.

■ **Above 6**, your level of test anxiety is a serious concern. In addition to practicing the stress management techniques listed in this section, you may want to seek additional, personal help. Call your local high school or community college and ask for the academic counselor. Tell the counselor that you have a level of test anxiety that sometimes keeps you from being able to take an exam. The counselor may be willing to help you or may suggest someone else you should talk to.

- **Visualize again**. Think of the place where you are most relaxed: lying on the beach in the sun, walking through the park, or whatever makes you feel good. Now close your eyes and imagine you are actually there. If you practice in advance, you will find that you need only a few seconds of this exercise to experience a significant increase in your sense of well-being.

When anxiety threatens to overwhelm you right there during the exam, there are still things you can do to manage the stress level.

- **Repeat your self-confidence messages**. You should have them memorized by now. Say them quietly to yourself, and believe them!
- **Visualize one more time**. This time, visualize yourself moving smoothly and quickly through the test, answering every question correctly, and finishing just before time is up. Like most visualization techniques, this one works best if you have practiced it ahead of time.
- **Find an easy question**. Skim over the test until you find an easy question, and answer it. Getting even one circle filled in gets you into the test-taking groove.
- **Take a mental break**. Everyone loses concentration once in a while during a long test. It is normal, so you shouldn't worry about it. Instead, accept what has happened. Say to yourself, "Hey, I lost it there for a minute. My brain is taking a break." Put down your pencil, close your eyes, and do some deep breathing for a few seconds. Then you will be ready to go back to work.

Try these techniques ahead of time, and see which ones work best for you.

▶ Step 3: Make a Plan

Activity: Construct a study plan.

Maybe the most important thing you can do to get control of yourself and your exam is to make a study plan. Too many people fail to prepare simply because they fail to plan. Spending hours poring over sample test questions the day before the exam will not only raise your level of test anxiety, but also will not replace careful preparation and practice over time.

Don't fall into the cram trap. Take control of your preparation time by mapping out a study schedule.

Even more important than making a plan is making a commitment. You need to set aside some time every day for study and practice. Try for at least 20 minutes a day. Twenty minutes daily will do you much more good than two hours on Saturday—divide your test preparation into smaller pieces of the larger work. In addition, making study notes, creating visual aids, and memorizing can be quite useful as you prepare. Each time you begin to study, quickly review your last lesson. This routine will help you retain all you have learned and help you assess whether you are studying effectively. You may realize you are not remembering some of the material you studied earlier. Approximately one week before your exam, try to determine the areas that are still most difficult for you.

Don't put off your study until the day before the exam. Start now. A few minutes a day, with half an hour or more on weekends, can make a big difference in your score.

Learning Styles

Each of us absorbs information differently. Whichever way works best for you is called your dominant learning method. If someone asks you for help constructing a new bookcase, which may be in many pieces, how do you begin? Do you need to read the directions and see the diagram? Would you rather hear someone read the directions to you—telling you which part connects to another? Or do you draw your own diagram?

The three main learning methods are visual, auditory, and kinesthetic. Determining which type of learner you are will help you create tools for studying.

1. **Visual learners** need to see the information in the form of maps, pictures, text, words, or math examples. Outlining notes and important points with colorful highlighters and taking note of diagrams and pictures may be key in helping you study.
2. **Auditory learners** retain information when they can hear directions, the spelling of a word, a math theorem, or poem. Repeating information aloud or listening to your notes on a tape recorder may help. Many auditory learners also find working in study groups or having someone quiz them is beneficial.
3. **Kinesthetic learners** must do! They need to draw diagrams, or write directions. Rewriting notes on index cards or making margin notes in your textbooks also helps kinesthetic learners to retain information.

Mnemonics

Mnemonics are memory tricks that help you remember what you need to know. The three basic principles in the use of mnemonics are imagination, association, and location. Acronyms (words created from the first letters in a series of words) are a common mnemonic. One acronym you may already know is **HOMES**, for the names of the Great Lakes (**H**uron, **O**ntario, **M**ichigan, **E**rie, and **S**uperior). **ROY G. BIV** reminds people of the colors in the spectrum (**R**ed, **O**range, **Y**ellow, **G**reen, **B**lue, **I**ndigo, and **V**iolet). Depending upon the type of learner you are, mnemonics can also be colorful or vivid images, stories, word associations, or catchy rhymes such as "Thirty days hath September . . ." created in your mind. Any type of learner, whether visual, auditory, or kinesthetic, can use mnemonics to help the brain store and interpret information.

▶ Step 4: Learn to Manage Your Time

Activities: Practice these strategies as you take the sample tests in this book.

Steps 4, 5, and 6 of the LearningExpress Test Preparation System put you in charge of your exam by showing you test-taking strategies that work. Practice these strategies as you take the sample tests in this book, and then you will be ready to use them on test day.

First, you will take control of your time on the exam. Most exams have a time limit, which may give you more than enough time to complete all the questions—or may not. It is a terrible feeling to hear the examiner say, "Five minutes left," when you are only three-quarters of the way through the test. Here are some tips to keep that from happening to you.

- **Follow directions**. If the directions are given orally, listen to them. If they are written on the exam booklet, read them carefully. Ask questions before the exam begins if there's anything you don't understand. If you are allowed to write in your exam booklet, write down the beginning time and the ending time of the exam.
- **Pace yourself**. Glance at your watch every few minutes, and compare the time to how far you have gotten in the test. When one-quarter of the time has elapsed, you should be one-quarter of the way through the test, and so on. If you are falling behind, pick up the pace a bit.
- **Keep moving**. Don't spend too much time on one question. If you don't know the answer, skip the question and move on. Circle the number of the question in your test booklet in case you have time to come back to it later.
- **Keep track of your place on the answer sheet**. If you skip a question, make sure that you also skip the question on the answer sheet. Check yourself every 5–10 questions to make sure that the num-

ber of the question still corresponds with the number on the answer sheet.

- **Don't rush.** Although you should keep moving, rushing won't help. Try to keep calm and work methodically and quickly.

▶ Step 5: Learn to Use the Process of Elimination

Activity: Complete the worksheet on Using the Process of Elimination (see page 95).

After time management, your next most important tool for taking control of your exam is using the process of elimination wisely. It is standard test-taking wisdom that you should always read all the answer choices before choosing your answer. This helps you find the right answer by eliminating wrong answer choices. And, sure enough, that standard wisdom applies to your probation/parole officer exam, too.

Let's say you are facing a vocabulary question like this one:

"Biology uses a binomial system of classification." In this sentence, the word *binomial* most nearly means
a. understanding the law.
b. having two names.
c. scientifically sound.
d. having a double meaning.

If you happen to know what *binomial* means, of course, you don't need to use the process of elimination, but let's assume you don't. So, you look at the answer choices. "Understanding the law" sure doesn't sound very likely for something having to do with biology. So you eliminate choice **a**—and now you have only three answer choices to deal with. Mark an X next to choice **a**, so you never have to read it again.

Now, move on to the other answer choices. If you know that the prefix *bi-* means *two*, as in *bicycle*, you will flag choice **b** as a possible answer. Mark a check mark beside it, meaning "good answer, I might use this one."

Choice **c**, "scientifically sound," is a possibility. At least it's about science, not law. It could work here, though, when you think about it, having a "scientifically sound" classification system in a scientific field is kind of redundant. You remember the *bi-* in *binomial*, and probably continue to like answer **b** better. But you're not sure, so you put a question mark next to **c**, meaning "well, maybe."

Now, choice **d**, "having a double meaning." You're still keeping in mind that *bi-* means *two*, so this one looks possible at first. But then you look again at the sentence the word belongs in, and you think, "Why would biology want a system of classification that has two meanings? That wouldn't work very well!" If you're really taken with the idea that *bi-* means *two*, you might put a question mark here. But if you're feeling a little more confident, you'll put an X. You have already got a better answer picked out.

Now your question looks like this:

"Biology uses a *binomial* system of classification." In this sentence, the word *binomial* most nearly means
X **a.** understanding the law.
✓ **b.** having two names.
? **c.** scientifically sound.
? **d.** having a double meaning.

You've got just one check mark for a good answer. If you're pressed for time, you should simply mark choice **b** on your answer sheet. If you have the time to be extra careful, you could compare your check-mark answer to your question-mark answers to make sure that it's better. (It is: The *binomial* system in biology is the one that gives a two-part genus and species name like *Homo sapiens*.)

It is good to have a system for marking good, bad, and maybe answers. We recommend this one:

X = bad
✓ = good
? = maybe

If you don't like these marks, devise your own system. Just make sure you do it long before test day—while you are working through the practice exams in this book—so you won't have to worry about it during the test.

Key Words

Often, identifying key words in a question will help you in the process of elimination. Words such as *always, never, all, only, must,* and *will* often make statements incorrect.

Words like *usually, may, sometimes,* and *most* may make a statement correct.

Even when you think you are absolutely clueless about a question, you can often use the process of elimination to get rid of at least one answer choice. If so, you are better prepared to make an educated guess, as you will see in Step 6. More often, you can eliminate answers until you have only two possible answers. Then you are in a strong position to guess.

Try using your powers of elimination on the questions in the worksheet on page 95, Using the Process of Elimination. The questions are not about probation or parole work; they are just designed to show you how the process of elimination works. The answer explanations for this worksheet show one possible way you might use the process to arrive at the right answer.

▶ Step 6: Know When to Guess

Activity: Complete the worksheet on Your Guessing Ability (see page 96).
Armed with the process of elimination, you are ready to take control of one of the big questions in test taking: Should I guess? Some exams have what's called a "guessing penalty," in which a fraction of your wrong answers is subtracted from your right answers. Other exams do not include a guessing penalty. Research your exam before the day of the test to establish if you have anything to lose by guessing.

The more complicated answer to the question "Should I guess?" depends upon you—your personality and your guessing intuition. There are two things you need to know about yourself before you go into the exam:

1. Are you a risk-taker?
2. Are you a good guesser?

You will have to decide about your risk-taking quotient on your own. To find out if you are a good guesser, complete the Your Guessing Ability worksheet, on page 96.

▶ Step 7: Reach Your Peak Performance Zone

Activity: Complete the Physical Preparation Checklist (see page 99).
To get ready for a challenge like a big exam, you have to take control of your physical, as well as your mental, state. Exercise, proper diet, and rest in the weeks prior to the test will ensure that your body works with, rather than against, your mind on test day, as well as during your preparation.

Using the Process of Elimination

Use the process of elimination to answer the following questions.

1. Ilsa is as old as Meghan will be in five years. The difference between Ed's age and Meghan's age is twice the difference between Ilsa's age and Meghan's age. Ed is 29. How old is Ilsa?

- **a.** 4
- **b.** 10
- **c.** 19
- **d.** 24

2. "All drivers of commercial vehicles must carry a valid commercial driver's license whenever operating a commercial vehicle."

According to this sentence, which of the following people need NOT carry a commercial driver's license?

- **a.** a truck driver idling his engine while waiting to be directed to a loading dock
- **b.** a bus operator backing her bus out of the way of another bus in the bus lot
- **c.** a taxi driver driving his personal car to the grocery store
- **d.** a limousine driver taking the limousine to her home after dropping off her last passenger of the evening

3. Smoking tobacco has been linked to
- **a.** increased risk of stroke and heart attack.
- **b.** all forms of respiratory disease.
- **c.** increasing mortality rates over the past ten years.
- **d.** juvenile delinquency.

4. Which of the following words is spelled correctly?
- **a.** incorrigible
- **b.** outragous
- **c.** domestickated
- **d.** understandible

Answers

Here are the answers, as well as some suggestions as to how you might have used the process of elimination to find them.

1. d. You should have eliminated choice **a** off the bat. Ilsa can't be four years old if Meghan is going to be Ilsa's age in five years. The best way to eliminate other answer choices is to try plugging them in to the information given in the problem. For instance, for choice **b**, if Ilsa is 10, then Meghan must be 5. The difference in their ages is 5. The difference between Ed's age, 29, and Meghan's age, 5, is 24. Is 24 two times 5? No. Then choice **b** is wrong. You could eliminate choice **c** in the same way and be left with choice **d**.

2. c. Note the word *not* in the question, and go through the answers one by one. Is the truck driver in choice **a** "operating a commercial vehicle"? Yes, idling counts as "operating," so he needs to have a commercial driver's license. Likewise, the bus operator in choice **b** is operating a commercial vehicle; the question doesn't say the operator has to be on the street. The limo driver in choice **d** is operating a commercial vehicle, even if it doesn't have a passenger in it. However, the cabbie in choice **c** is not operating a commercial vehicle, but his own private car.

3. a. You could eliminate choice **b** simply because of the presence of the word *all*. Such absolutes hardly ever appear in correct answer choices. Choice **c** looks attractive until you think a little about what you know— aren't fewer people smoking these days, rather than more? So how could smoking be responsible for a higher mortality rate? (If you didn't know that *mortality rate* means the rate at which people die, you might keep this choice as a possibility, but you would still be able to eliminate two answers and have only two to choose from.) And choice **d** is unlikely, so you could eliminate that one, too. You are left with the correct choice, **a**.

4. a. How you used the process of elimination here depends on which words you recognized as being spelled incorrectly. If you knew that the correct spellings were *outrageous*, *domesticated*, and *understandable*, then you were home free.

Your Guessing Ability

The following are ten really hard questions. You are not supposed to know the answers. Rather, this is an assessment of your ability to guess when you don't have a clue. Read each question carefully, as if you were expected to answer it. If you have any knowledge of the subject, use that knowledge to help you eliminate wrong answer choices.

1. September 7 is Independence Day in
   a. India.
   b. Costa Rica.
   c. Brazil.
   d. Australia.

2. Which of the following is the formula for determining the momentum of an object?
   a. $p = MV$
   b. $F = ma$
   c. $P = IV$
   d. $E = mc^2$

3. Because of the expansion of the universe, the stars and other celestial bodies are all moving away from each other. This phenomenon is known as
   a. Newton's first law.
   b. the big bang.
   c. gravitational collapse.
   d. Hubble flow.

4. American author Gertrude Stein was born in
   a. 1713.
   b. 1830.
   c. 1874.
   d. 1901.

5. Which of the following is NOT one of the Five Classics attributed to Confucius?
   a. *I Ching*
   b. *Book of Holiness*
   c. *Spring and Autumn Annals*
   d. *Book of History*

6. The religious and philosophical doctrine that holds that the universe is constantly in a struggle between good and evil is known as
   a. Pelagianism.
   b. Manichaeanism.
   c. neo-Hegelianism.
   d. Epicureanism.

7. The third chief justice of the U.S. Supreme Court was
  a. John Blair.
  b. William Cushing.
  c. James Wilson.
  d. John Jay.

8. Which of the following is the poisonous portion of a daffodil?
  a. the bulb
  b. the leaves
  c. the stem
  d. the flowers

9. The winner of the Masters golf tournament in 1953 was
  a. Sam Snead.
  b. Cary Middlecoff.
  c. Arnold Palmer.
  d. Ben Hogan.

10. The state with the highest per capita personal income in 1980 was
  a. Alaska.
  b. Connecticut.
  c. New York.
  d. Texas.

Answers

Check your answers against the correct answers below.

1. c.
2. a.
3. d.
4. c.
5. b.
6. b.
7. b.
8. a.
9. d.
10. a.

How Did You Do?

You may have simply gotten lucky and actually known the answers to one or two questions. In addition, your guessing was probably more successful if you were able to use the process of elimination on any of the questions. Maybe you didn't know who the third chief justice was (question 7), but you knew that John Jay was the first. In that case, you would have eliminated choice **d** and, therefore, improved your odds of guessing right from one in four to one in three.

According to probability, you should get two and a half answers correct, so getting either two or three right would be average. If you got four or more right, you may be a really terrific guesser. If you got one or none right, you may be a really bad guesser.

Keep in mind, though, that this is only a small sample. You should continue to keep track of your guessing ability as you work through the sample questions in this book. Circle the numbers of questions you guess on as you make your guess; or, if you don't have time while you take the practice tests, go back afterward and try to remember which questions you guessed on. Remember, on a test with four answer choices, your chance of guessing correctly is one in four. So keep a separate "guessing" score for each exam. How many questions did you guess on? How many did you get right? If the number you got right is at least one-fourth of the number of questions you guessed on, you are at least an average guesser—maybe better—and you should always go ahead and guess on the real exam. If the number you got right is significantly lower than one-fourth of the number you guessed on, you would be safe in guessing anyway, but maybe you would feel more comfortable if you guessed only selectively, when you can eliminate a wrong answer or at least have a good feeling about one of the answer choices.

Because the probation/parole officer exam has no guessing penalty even if you are a play-it-safe person with lousy intuition, you are still better off guessing every time.

Exercise

If you don't already have a regular exercise program, the time during which you are preparing for an exam is actually an excellent time to start one. And if you are already keeping fit—or trying to get that way—don't let the pressure of preparing for an exam fool you into quitting now. Exercise helps reduce stress by pumping feel-good hormones called endorphins into your system. It also increases the oxygen supply throughout your body, including in your brain, so you will be at peak performance on test day.

A half hour of vigorous activity—enough to raise a sweat—every day should be your aim. If you are really pressed for time, every other day is okay. Choose an activity you like and get out there and do it. Jogging with a friend always makes the time go faster, or take a portable radio or CD player.

But don't overdo it. You don't want to exhaust yourself. Moderation is the key.

Diet

First, cut out the junk. Go easy on caffeine and nicotine, and eliminate alcohol from your system at least two weeks before the exam. What your body needs for peak performance is simply a balanced diet. Eat plenty of fruits and vegetables, along with protein and carbohydrates. Foods that are high in lecithin (an amino acid), such as fish and beans, are especially good "brain foods."

The night before the exam, you might carbo-load the way athletes do before a contest. Eat a big plate of spaghetti, rice and beans, or whatever your favorite carbohydrate is.

Rest

You probably know how much sleep you need every night to be at your best, even if you don't always get it. Make sure you do get that much sleep, though, for at least a week before the exam. Moderation is important here, too. Extra sleep will just make you groggy.

If you are not a morning person and your exam will be given in the morning, you should reset your internal clock so that your body doesn't think you are taking an exam at 3 A.M. You have to start this process well before the exam. The way it works is to get up half an hour earlier each morning, and then go to bed half an hour earlier that night. Don't try it the other way around; you will just toss and turn if you go to bed early without having gotten up early. The next morning, get up another half an hour earlier, and so on. How long you will have to do this depends upon how late you are used to getting up.

▶ Step 8: Get Your Act Together

Activity: Complete the Final Preparations worksheet. You are in control of your mind and body; you are in charge of test anxiety, your preparation, and your test-taking strategies. Now it is time to take charge of external factors, like the testing site and the materials you need to take the exam.

Find out Where the Test Is and Make a Trial Run

The testing agency will notify you when and where your exam is being held. Do you know how to get to the testing site? Do you know how long it will take to get there? If not, make a trial run, preferably on the same day of the week at the same time of day. Make note, on the worksheet Final Preparations on page 101, of the amount of time it will take you to get to the exam site. Plan on arriving at least 10–15 minutes early so you can get the lay of the land, use the bathroom, and calm down. Then figure out how early you will have to get up that morning, and make sure you get up that early every day for a week before the exam.

Gather Your Materials

The night before the exam, lay out the clothes you will wear and the materials you have to bring with you to the exam. Plan on dressing in layers; you won't have any control over the temperature of the examination room. Have a sweater or jacket you can take off if it is warm. Use the checklist on the Final Preparations

Physical Preparation Checklist

For the week before the test, write down what physical exercise you engaged in and for how long and what you ate for each meal. Remember, you're trying for at least half an hour of exercise every other day (preferably every day) and a balanced diet that's light on junk food.

Exam minus 7 days

Exercise: _____ for _____ minutes

Breakfast: _____

Lunch: _____

Dinner: _____

Snacks: _____

Exam minus 6 days

Exercise: _____ for _____ minutes

Breakfast: _____

Lunch: _____

Dinner: _____

Snacks: _____

Exam minus 5 days

Exercise: _____ for _____ minutes

Breakfast: _____

Lunch: _____

Dinner: _____

Snacks: _____

Exam minus 4 days

Exercise: _____ for _____ minutes

Breakfast: _____

Lunch: _____

Dinner: _____

Snacks: _____

Exam minus 3 days

Exercise: _____ for _____ minutes

Breakfast: _____

Lunch: _____

Dinner: _____

Snacks: _____

Exam minus 2 days

Exercise: _____ for _____ minutes

Breakfast: _____

Lunch: _____

Dinner: _____

Snacks: _____

Exam minus 1 day

Exercise: _____ for _____ minutes

Breakfast: _____

Lunch: _____

Dinner: _____

Snacks: _____

worksheet on the following page to help you pull together what you will need.

Don't Skip Breakfast

Even if you don't usually eat breakfast, do so on exam morning. A cup of coffee doesn't count. Don't eat doughnuts or other sweet foods, either. A sugar high will leave you with a sugar low in the middle of the exam. A mix of protein and carbohydrates is best: Cereal with milk, or eggs with toast, will do your body a world of good.

▶ Step 9: Do It!

Activity: Ace the probation/parole officer exam!
Fast forward to exam day. You are ready. You made a study plan and followed through. You practiced your test-taking strategies while working through this book. You are in control of your physical, mental, and emotional states. You know when and where to show up and what to bring with you. In other words, you are better prepared than most of the other people taking the probation/parole officer exam with you.

Just one more thing: When you are done with the exam, you deserve a reward. Plan a celebration. Call up your friends and plan a party, or have a nice dinner for two—whatever your heart desires. Give yourself something to look forward to.

And then do it. Go into the exam, full of confidence, armed with test-taking strategies you have practiced until they are second nature. You are in control of yourself, your environment, and your performance on the exam. You are ready to succeed. So do it. Go in there and ace the exam. And look forward to your future career as a probation or parole officer!

Final Preparations

Getting to the Exam Site

Location of exam site: _____

Date: _____

Departure time: _____

Do I know how to get to the exam site?   Yes ___   No ___   (If no, make a trial run.)

Time it will take to get to exam site: _____

Things to Lay out the Night Before

Clothes I will wear   ___

Sweater/jacket   ___

Watch   ___

Photo ID   ___

Four #2 pencils   ___

Other Things to Bring/Remember

_____   _____

_____   _____

_____   _____

6 ▶ Job Responsibilities

The largest portion of the probation and parole examination will be devoted to determining whether the candidate has the knowledge and ability to carry out the duties and responsibilities associated with being a probation or parole officer. This area of testing will draw upon general knowledge about probation and parole work as well as specific statutes concerning these positions.

▶ Court Responsibilities

In this area, a candidate will be evaluated on his or her ability to understand the process involved with court proceedings. Probation supervision is clearly dictated and influenced by the sentencing court, regardless of the administrative structure of a particular department. An agency may have the ability to establish supervision strategies independent of a trial court judge. However, these strategies are an effort to support the conditions and requirements set forth in the sentencing order initiating probation supervision for a particular offender.

Presentence Investigation

One of the most vital components to the supervision of an offender is the sentencing portion of the criminal case process. For a court to be able to address sentencing properly, further information is needed to assist with their knowledge of the offender. Typically, a presentence investigation will include a review of an offender's previous criminal history, education, employment, family background, psychological and medical health, as well as information about how the victim and his or her family has been affected by the offender.

Interpreting Sentencing and Supervision Conditions

Probation and parole officers must carry out the practical application of the conditions of supervision established by a sentencing court or through the parole-granting authority. These officers should be able to understand, interpret, and implement the various conditions associated with community supervision. Having these skills will allow the officer to prevent further legal proceedings with the offender and ultimately bolster the possibility of a successful supervision period.

Case Supervision

A function of the probation and parole officer position that tends to be favored by most applicants is case supervision. In case supervision, the probation officer works directly with the offender to provide supervision and assistance with issues that could hinder the successful completion of probation or parole. These responsibilities are usually separate and distinct to the supervision strategy utilized by a particular agency.

Emphasizing the Conditions of Supervision to the Probationer/Parolee

The first introduction an offender has to community supervision is some form of orientation or intake. In this session, a probation or parole officer is responsible for ensuring that the offender is aware and understands the conditions he or she must satisfy while serving the period of supervision. A probation officer must first know what those conditions are and how they will be utilized for supervision.

Visits within the Administrative Offices

An officer's contact with a probationer typically occurs within the confines of a probation or parole office setting. Officers and the offenders they supervise must follow a certain protocol to maintain a reasonable structure in supervision visits that occur in an office setting. Additionally, there are advantages and disadvantages to conducting supervision visits within the administrative offices.

Field Visits

A keystone to the successful supervision of offenders, especially those who present a higher risk of re-offending, is the appropriate monitoring of an offender within the community and at his or her place of residence. A probation or parole officer can learn an incredible amount of information about the offender through contact outside of the office setting. Officers will commonly visit offenders in the offender's home or place of employment.

Probationer/Parolee Home

While conducting a field visit in the offender's place of residence, an officer must follow certain protocol to ensure his or her own safety. The probation and parole examination is going to address a candidate's understanding of safe practices associated with this supervision strategy. This area is likely to be tested by asking the candidate to give his or her assessment of a particular case scenario.

Place of Employment

Visits that occur at the offender's workplace must be handled with care and sensitivity because of the stigma that is often attached to someone who has been convicted of a criminal offense and on probation. An offender's coworkers as well as his or her boss may not be aware of the offender's situation. Or if they are aware, they may become uncomfortable with a probation or parole officer visiting the jobsite regularly. Additionally, these visits can hamper the performance of the offender, thereby jeopardizing his or her employment.

Interstate Compacts

The transfer of an offender for supervision in another state can be particularly complex and difficult for the probation or parole officer. Undoubtedly, offenders will be convicted of an offense within a jurisdiction without having any formal ties (for example, family, residence, job, etc.) there. Typically, officers must then facilitate a transfer to the state and jurisdiction where the offender resides. As a part of this process, state administrations agree to follow the procedures that have been set forth by the Interstate Compact. Candidates taking the examination will be expected to have general and specific knowledge about the compact and the procedure it describes.

Taking Court/Administrative Action

When an offender deviates from the requirements and conditions of probation or parole supervision, an officer should respond to that deviation with one of a myriad of options available to him or her according to practice, policy, and statutory code. Often, probation and parole officers encounter what may be considered mild or minor infractions of the rules (i.e., missing a scheduled appointment, late payment on restitution, etc.). Responses to these infractions will be different from responses to major violations such as committing a new criminal offense while being supervised under probation or parole conditions.

A successful officer will know the statutory code for his or her jurisdiction as well as the practices and policies established by the administration. When taking court/administrative action, a probation and parole officer is venturing into an area of moral and legal obligation, as an offender will undoubtedly be further affected by this type of action. Therefore, a candidate testing in this area will have to answer questions related not only to specific responses appropriate to the behavior or action demonstrated by the offender, but also to the nature and consequence of court/administrative actions.

Probation/Parole Revocation

If the offender commits an infraction or violates the conditions of his or her probation or parole, a judge or other paroling authority may revoke the offender's community supervision and incarcerate him or her.

Modifications of Sentence/Supervision/Rules

Beyond revoking an offender's probation or parole, officers and their respective authorities may choose to avoid any legal/hearing proceedings and respond to an infraction of the rules with another strategy. These alternatives to revocation, as they are known, utilize resources available to the officers and eligible to the offenders according to the specific nature of the infraction or based upon the characteristics of the offender.

▶ Practice

Directions: Answer the following practice questions to test your job responsibility question skills.

1. A sentence of probation is affected by a judge's sentencing philosophy, the available resources, a plea bargain, and the recommendations of victims. This statement is
   a. true.
   b. false.

2. Probation officers are asked to do which of the following as a standard part of their job?
   a. provide testimony on a defendant's behavior while under community supervision
   b. select jurors in a criminal case that will assure a revocation of probation
   c. post bail for defendants so that they can keep their treatment appointments
   d. transcribe courtroom testimony and proceedings for the purposes of appeal

3. A presentence investigation interview conducted at the _____ provides the best opportunity to understand a defendant's situation.
   a. office
   b. home
   c. jail
   d. none of the above

4. In a presentence investigation report, where could information regarding recidivism most likely be found?
   a. victim impact statement
   b. official version of the present offense
   c. criminal history
   d. all of the above

5. Which type of conditions of probation or parole is usually tailored to fit the needs and risks of the offender?
   a. special conditions
   b. standard conditions
   c. punitive conditions
   d. reform conditions

6. Ensuring that probation conditions are sufficiently explicit, precise, and easily understood is an issue of
   a. reasonableness.
   b. standardization.
   c. clarity.
   d. constitutionality.

7. Parole conditions are
   a. set out in an order from the sentencing judge.
   b. rules that govern the supervision of an offender in the community.
   c. established by the administrative staff of the correctional facility.
   d. none of the above

8. When probationers are required to perform unpaid work for civic or nonprofit organizations as a condition of probation, it is called
   a. pro bono work.
   b. reparation.
   c. community service.
   d. banishment.

9. Most states severely limit a parolee's Fourth Amendment rights and allow parole officers, without the use of a warrant, to
   a. violate a parolee.
   b. detain a parolee.
   c. arrest a parolee.
   d. search a parolee.

10. What are five reasons that a parole officer requires an offender to meet with him or her in the office?
   1. _____
   _____
   2. _____
   _____
   3. _____
   _____
   4. _____
   _____
   5. _____
   _____

11. Upon arriving at the home of Lou Zerr, a medium-risk offender, you observe what appears to be approximately 30 to 40 empty beer cans scattered across the front porch. Knowing that the offender has a history of violent behavior while under the influence of alcohol, what should you do?

_____

_____

_____

_____

_____

12. Name three reasons that a visit should be made to the jobsite of a parolee.

1. _____

_____

2. _____

_____

3. _____

_____

13. Under the Interstate Compact for Supervision of Parolees and Probationers, the state doing the actual supervision is called the
  a. receiving state.
  b. sending state.
  c. supervising state.
  d. state of original jurisdiction.

14. According to the basic rights of parolees facing revocation under the *Morrissey* decision, parolees have the right to
  a. appeal.
  b. counsel.
  c. confront witnesses.
  d. all of the above

15. When a probationer is facing probation revocation, the court is looking for what in order to rule against the probationer?
  a. proof beyond a reasonable doubt
  b. a bribe
  c. technicalities
  d. a preponderance of the evidence

16. The person who makes the final decision to file for revocation of probation is the
  a. prosecutor.
  b. chief probation officer.
  c. line probation officer.
  d. judge.

17. Probation conditions and/or length of supervision can be modified under which of the following circumstances?
  a. revocation
  b. agreement
  c. probation recommendation to the court
  d. all of the above

► Answers

1. a. Judges often have great discretion when sentencing a convicted person to probation supervision. Their sentencing philosophy will be affected by their tenure on the bench and their previous or current experiences with a particular type of offender or offense. A case involving a plea agreement reached between a prosecutor and the defendant will also influence the conditions imposed by a judge, as the judge is often required to accept the plea as written, without any additional consequences or sanctions imposed. A judge's objective is to ensure that justice is served, and a reasonable request or statement from an involved victim can greatly influence a judge's sentence and the conditions he or she sets.

2. a. Probation or parole officers can be called to provide testimony on the previous behavior of a defendant for several reasons. A prosecutor may utilize the testimony of a probation officer to establish previous periods of probation, thereby illustrating a pattern of convictions when a habitual offending statute has been violated. An officer can also be called to provide statements regarding the offender's behavior, when prosecutors and defense are arguing for a particular sentence.

3. b. A few moments inside an offender's home can provide immeasurable opportunities for the adept probation or parole officer to understand the nature of the offender's daily way of life. It provides an officer with the insight as to an offender's finances, habits, and potential violations of supervision conditions. Furthermore, it gives the officer an opportunity to meet other persons residing at the location.

4. c. Recidivism can be defined as continued criminal behavior. A proper criminal history will outline and chronicle an offender's past legal charges and convictions.

5. a. Special conditions are imposed by a judge or parole board to specifically address either the nature of the offense or the characteristics demonstrated by the offender. Examples of these special conditions could include the repayment of restitution to a victim (not all offenses have a specified victim) or a drug treatment program (not all offenders use drugs).

6. c. *Clarity* is to make or become clear. For a probation condition to be clear, it needs to be explicitly stated, precise in its requirement or expectation, and not too complex for an offender to understand.

7. b. This question is best answered using the process of elimination. It requires that an examinee understand the subtle differences between the administration of probation and of parole. Conditions of parole are established by the parole board and *not* the sentencing judge or the administrative staff (i.e., warden or superintendent) of the correctional institution.

8. c. Community service differs from reparation (choice **b**) in that community service is a sanction imposed with a goal to "repay" the entire community, whereas reparation (sometimes called restitution) repays a particular victim or victims. Banishment is the requirement that an offender cannot ever physically enter a particular jurisdiction. Pro bono work is typically associated with attorneys who perform legal services free of charge as a gesture of goodwill.

9. d. The Fourth Amendment to the U.S. Constitution protects American citizens against unlawful searches and seizures.

10. Answers may vary. Possible answers include high workload not allowing for fieldwork; administrative paperwork and filing; convenience of drug testing; serving of summons or warrant; safety and security of officer.

11. This question is asking for a narrative on the decisions involved following the observation of potential problems. An officer who is aware that an offender becomes violent with the use of alcoholic beverages would proceed with caution in this situation. A correct answer would involve the specifications of precautions to be taken. Depending upon the authority (and equipment) granted to a probation/parole officer, at the very least, of the officer should communicate and collaborate with another officer and/or law enforcement. Then, with the support of another criminal justice professional in the event that the offender presents him- or herself in a violent manner, the officer could approach and confront the offender about possible violations of his or her conditions. If the offender is indeed under the influence of alcohol and in violation of his or her conditions of supervision, he or she should be taken into custody to begin the revocation process.

12. This question requires a narrative statement, and it is looking for proper reasoning on an aspect and practice of probation. Although there are several possible answers, three reasons to include are: difficulty in locating the offender at their place of residence; reports of unlawful behavior at the jobsite; and verification of an offender's employment when other verification attempts have failed.

13. a. The charges may have occurred in the sending state, but the jurisdiction responsible for providing the actual supervision occurs in the state receiving the offender. Choice **c** is redundant, and choice **d** is the same as the sending state.

14 c. The *Morrissey* decision states that, when faced with the loss of liberty that comes with incarceration, a parolee has the right to confront witnesses to address testimony a parolee considers false. This is an extension of the due process rights associated with parole revocation hearings.

15. d. Although in the original trial process a decision of guilt must be based upon proof beyond a reasonable doubt, probation revocation proceedings have a lesser burden of proof: The evidence need only be a preponderance.

16. a. Under probation proceedings, the revocation enters the court of original jurisdiction, and therefore, the prosecutor represents the state's interests associated with the revocation of the offender's suspended sentence and the imposition of incarceration.

17. d. A probationer's conditions of supervision can be altered as a result of formal proceedings involving revocation, by the specific agreement of the offender and the court, or by a recommendation made by a probation officer to the judge.

CHAPTER

7 ▶ Case Studies

A case study is a form of analysis that probation and parole officers may utilize to better understand an offender. On the probation and parole examination, case studies present theoretical material to assess how the candidate would respond in the "real world" of a particular field or function. These theoretical case studies have the characteristics of situations that are likely to be encountered by a probation or parole officer, and they often involve specific circumstances and situations presented by working with offenders. Less commonly, the case studies will address secondary aspects of the job (that is, responsibilities outside of direct contact with offenders), or they may evaluate the candidate's decision-making and prioritization practices.

A case study usually consists of the following:

- Specific character(s)
- Background information on the characters
- Current dilemma presented in the story's details
- Series of questions posed for response

► How Case Studies Are Used in Examinations

The use of case studies is one of the best ways to match theoretical knowledge with practical application. Examinations that include case studies do so to simulate the decision-making process in situations likely to arise in real practice. This analysis helps examiners determine whether a candidate can apply the knowledge and understanding that he or she has obtained in a particular situation.

Case studies require that a decision be reached and, therefore, can expose candidates' viewpoints, preferences, and ability to analyze a situation correctly. Case studies can further allow an examiner to evaluate how different candidates respond to the same or similar situations and determine the possible impact from those responses. Often, case examples include multiple "right" answers, with one answer being "better" than the others. With this format, examiners are trying to isolate the candidates' decision-making process and determine whether their priorities match the best practices within the field.

Case studies provide background information along with specific question prompts, and candidates should expect to address a variety of specific issues. These issues will include tasks, actions, response prioritization, and knowledge of the system. A single case example may present questions in the following areas: effective probation or parole systems, principles associated with community supervision, and laws associated with criminal offenses.

► Reading and Interpreting Case Example Questions and Answers

Case examples are used in examinations for their ability to measure multiple items within the same case and even within the same associated question. Case examples provide real-world scenarios, giving an examiner the opportunity to see how well a candidate understands a particular applied principle or concept. To improve their chances of success, candidates should approach case example questions in the following ways.

The candidate should begin by determining the context the case presents. By understanding the scope of the case and how the background information factors into the questions and answers, a candidate is better equipped to respond favorably. Realizing the scope of the case begins with reading the case in its entirety, instead of attempting to answer the questions without having first read all of the facts associated with the case.

The case should be analyzed to determine the key issues associated with the case, the key player(s), possible problems to be addressed, and the limitations involved with the information from the case.

The questions and the candidates' answers should be considered from various positions and perspectives. This thoughtfulness allows a candidate to determine the merits and shortcomings of each answer choice and to eliminate insufficient answers immediately, isolating possible solutions. There could be more than one justifiable answer, but the candidate must determine which answer is the most correct. That is, case example questions often present answer choices that could be correct but seem less attractive when juxtaposed with more favorable options, given the scope of the situation.

Assumptions and generalizations should be avoided, as examiners are undoubtedly looking for this type of reaction from a candidate and prepare the questions with this in mind. Furthermore, a candidate should attempt to suspend his or her own judgment and to keep an open mind to all possibilities from a systems perspective.

▶ Practice

Directions: Read the following case study and then answer questions 1 through 3.

Allen, an offender with a long history of sex offenses involving boys under the age of 12, faces the five members of the parole board. Allen, now 45 years old and having served five years of the seven-year maximum sentence on his most recent offense, believes that he is ready to be paroled. Allen respectfully answers the questions presented to him by the board, regarding his eligibility and his postincarceration plans.

Toward the end of the hearing, Morty, a recent appointee to the board, presents the following opinion to Allen: "Your institutional record is spotless, and you seem to have a reasonable parole plan including guaranteed employment and an approved residence. Although all of that is in your favor, I still have difficulty voting for your release because you have failed to participate in the sex offender programming offered within the institution." Allen explains that, because of the waiting list associated with entering that program, he decided to become involved in other rehabilitation programs, including vocational training in electronics, substance abuse treatment, and earned employment while incarcerated.

After Allen leaves the room, the board continues to discuss his case and ultimately decides that he should be released in accordance with his original plan of parole. However, that plan does not include any type of treatment or program for sexual offending. One week later, Allen is released and begins living in the home of his sister and her two children, Kevin, who is 14 years old, and Brianna, who is nine years old. Allen holds a job at the television repair shop that is located approximately five city blocks from his sister's home, and he works nine to five, Mondays through Saturdays.

1. Allen has two years of parole to complete, and his parole plan calls for him to have face-to-face visits with his parole agent weekly for the first six months, a schedule that could later be adjusted according to the review and discretion of the parole officer. How would you propose Allen satisfy this commitment of parole supervision as office visits will likely conflict with his work schedule?
   a. I would require Allen to take time off from work to attend his scheduled appointments.
   b. I would discuss with Allen the attitude of his employer and determine a visitation arrangement in which either Allen leaves work for an office visit or I visit him at his place of employment or his place of residence.
   c. I would require that Allen find a new job with a schedule that doesn't conflict with the standard hours of the parole office.
   d. Because Allen is doing so well and working regularly, I would have Allen call for the visit instead of physically reporting.

2. During a visit to Allen's home, you observe that Allen's sister appears to be heavily under the influence of alcohol and/or other mood-altering chemicals. The sister makes the statement to you that she wants Allen to leave, and she doesn't care if he goes back to prison. You locate Allen in his bedroom, where he states that he has been for the last four hours while his sister has been drinking heavily. You ask Allen why his sister would want him to leave, and he tells you because he made a harmless comment to Brianna about how pretty she was. Allen says that he thinks his sister is concerned that he is going to sexually assault Brianna.

  a. You should immediately take Allen into custody and return him to prison for the safety of Brianna.

  b. You should suggest that Allen apologize to his sister and promise not to make such comments in the future.

  c. You should explore with Allen other options for living arrangements and suggest that he stay overnight at the local haven for homeless persons in the meantime.

  d. You should approach the sister about her drinking and the assumptions that she has made because of the influence of alcohol. The discussion should include a plan for her to quit drinking so that she can be a better influence on Allen as well as a better role model for her children.

3. During a routine office visit, Allen discusses with you his feeling of being stigmatized because of his convictions as a sex offender. He says that he has been confronted by neighbors and has apparently been the ongoing subject of the neighborhood association meetings. Allen states that he has been threatened by people who said they would report him to the parole board and say that he has been violating his parole. Allen says that he is afraid the board will believe it, especially because of the comment that one board member made during the hearing. Unknown to Allen, yesterday you received a phone call from an anonymous source expressing concern for Allen living in a neighborhood full of children. Although the caller could not provide any specific example of behavior that would be in violation of Allen's conditions, the caller insisted that Allen was someone who couldn't be trusted. Allen states that if people don't start leaving him alone, he is likely to do something they'll regret. From this information, what determination can you make?

  a. Allen has been sexually assaulting the children in his neighborhood.

  b. Allen is the target of unreasonable suspicion and concern from his neighbors.

  c. Allen would assault the anonymous caller if he knew who the person was.

  d. Allen is at risk for violating the conditions of his parole.

Directions: Read the following case study and then answer questions 4 through 6.

Megan's parents are called to a local convenience store where Megan, who is 11 years old, is being held as a result of attempting to leave the store with a candy bar without paying. Megan swears that it was an accident and that she forgot she had put it into her coat pocket while looking for her money and then became distracted when a friend approached. No charges are filed, and Megan is required by her parents to write a letter of apology to the store's manager. Three weeks later, she is caught again at a different store attempting to run out the door with a cigarette lighter. Again, charges are not filed. Megan goes through several months of being "good," completing chores on time without being told to do so. Her parents are convinced that she has learned her lesson and begin once again to provide her with privileges. Prior to spring break, her parents get a call from Megan's teacher who indicates to them that she has not been submitting her homework. Megan denies what the teacher has said, and indicates to her parents that the teacher doesn't like her and that he must have lost it on purpose so that she would get in trouble.

When Megan is 12, the police are called to the family's home in connection with several problems in the neighborhood. The police ask Megan about her knowledge of several broken car windows on the next block. They also ask her about a fire that occurred in the garage just down the alley from her own home. No arrest is made, but the police indicate to the parents that they are pretty certain that Megan is involved with as many as 15 separate property damage incidents, but that they lack the evidence to file charges.

Now, when Megan is 13, Megan's parents have been called to the local detention center where she is being held as an alleged delinquent child for her involvement in a fight with another 13-year-old child. Megan begs and pleads with her parents to "get her out" and promises to be good forever. Megan remains at the center for two days while she awaits an appearance in juvenile court. The juvenile judge accepted a "plea agreement" whereby Megan admits that she was involved in the fight and whereby the sentence will be at the sole discretion of the judge.

4. You have been asked to submit a predispositional hearing report in an effort to provide the juvenile court judge with background information for sentencing. During routine questioning of Megan and her parents, you determine that Megan was adopted at age three when her biological mother, her adoptive mother's sister, was committed to a mental health facility. Megan's biological mother was released from the facility three years ago and has had occasional contact with the family. With this information, you should

a. recommend that Megan undergo a psychiatric evaluation.

b. require that Megan's biological mother participate in the background investigation.

c. recommend that Megan have no contact with her biological mother.

d. omit this information from the report because Megan's behavior has nothing to do with her biological mother.

5. After the judge gives Megan a 12-month probation, she is scheduled to appear for her initial supervision meeting in the juvenile probation department offices. When Megan arrives for her appointment, she is escorted back to your office. Upon entering, Megan walks over to the window and stares outside. You invite Megan to have a seat at one of the chairs in front of your desk. She looks at you, makes no change in facial expression, and then continues to stare out of the window. You invite her a second time to sit down and talk with you, and when you tell her that she must, she shrugs her shoulders and continues to stare out of the window. What action do you take?

a. You put Megan in handcuffs and return her to the detention center for violating probation by not obeying a lawful instruction.

b. You wait 15 minutes to see if she will voluntarily sit, and when she doesn't, physically place her into the seat so that you can continue the meeting as needed.

c. You call in Megan's parents to see if they can get her to sit down.

d. You explain to Megan that her participation is required and that she will need to return for an additional meeting every day until she can follow your requests or until you file for a revocation hearing with the court.

6. During a visit with Megan in her home, she indicates that performing the 50 hours of community service is easy for her because the person assigned to supervise her service at the placement agency doesn't really watch over her. She goes on to say that, although she is assigned certain tasks each day such as washing windows, taking trash out, and sweeping floors, she rarely completes any of the tasks and even takes a nap in one of the empty rooms. Because the community service portion of probation supervision falls under the direction of another community correction agency, what should you do?

a. You should call the supervisor at the placement agency and tell them that this is unacceptable.

b. You should approach the director of community corrections to explore a plan of action.

c. You should visit Megan at the placement agency to verify her story.

d. You should check with other juveniles performing community service at that agency to see if they have experienced the same thing.

▶ Answers

1. b. This question is measuring the candidate's ability to analyze rules and supervision practices critically. Choice **a** places an additional burden upon Allen and is counterproductive to the requirement of employment. Choice **c** also places an unreasonable burden upon Allen, as it would require him to leave a job at which he seems to be successful and which incorporates the rehabilitation programming he experienced while incarcerated. Choice **d** is incorrect because it is in direct conflict with a stated and specified requirement for the offender to be supervised by face-to-face visits. Furthermore, allowing a sex offender to be supervised by phone calls alone would be cause for concern. Choice **c** allows for input from the offender in discovering the available options that are the least likely to create problems with his or her employer. It is also likely that, because this employment began while Allen was incarcerated, the employer has the expectation that Allen will have obligations under parole that he will need to satisfy.

2. c. This question is asking a candidate to determine the real problem and its possible solutions. Choice **a** is incorrect because, from the information provided, it doesn't appear that Allen has violated any of the conditions of his parole, and therefore, returning him to prison would be an undue hardship and possibly violate his rights of due process. Choice **b** is incorrect because it doesn't address the possibility of imminent volatility, and it assumes that a simple apology will alleviate any concern that the sister has. Choice **d** is incorrect because the parole officer is primarily concerned with the behavior of the parolee and does not have any requirements or expectations to address concerns of family members. Although the action to be taken in choice **d**

could assist the situation and is probably a valid step, choice **c** is the best way to respond immediately to the situation. The officer should be concerned with the presence of alcohol around the parolee because he had been through substance abuse treatment, and because of the sex offender's questionable behavior such as making comments about a child's physical appearance.

3. d. This question asks the candidate to analyze the situation and determine possible occurrences and outcomes. It is unclear from the information provided whether Allen has been sexually assaulting anyone; therefore, choice **a** is wrong. With the increased awareness of the issues involving sex offenders and the public's access to offender registries, neighbors would undoubtedly be concerned about anyone residing within close proximity to them and their children. Calling this concern or suspicion unreasonable would be an opinion, making choice **b** incorrect. Choice **c** is incorrect because it assumes that Allen would take specific action. Choice **d** is the correct answer, because from the information provided, it is reasonable to conclude that Allen is not thinking clearly about the requirements and conditions of his parole because of his anger and frustration. He may, therefore, be considering actions—such as physical violence, vandalism, or even running away under the pressure of the perceived stigmatization—that would lead to revocation.

4. a. Choice **b** is incorrect because, although it is often beneficial to have other family members involved in the planning and programming for a juvenile offender, requiring a person to sever "legal" ties to the juvenile would be improper. If this answer choice had used the word *recommend*, it would mean that this action could have been considered, but not until all other issues involving this person were explored. Furthermore, one might conclude that the onset of Megan's behavioral problems coincided with the release of her biological mother from the mental health facility. Therefore, her involvement with Megan could be detrimental to the child. Although this negative influence is possible, choice **c** is incorrect because it calls for a conclusion that is not supported by hard facts and is contradictory to the already established relationships in the family. Choice **d** is incorrect because omitting this information would not give the judge the full picture of Megan's background or the dynamics of her family's relationships to use when making his or her judgment on Megan's case. However, by selecting choice **a**, an officer can suggest that Megan undergo a psychiatric evaluation, during which further information on the impact of the family's relationship with Megan's mother can be gathered. Furthermore, if Megan's behavior is related to a genetically connected psychological disorder, treatment can be recommended and initiated to reduce the effects that the disorder has on her behavior and, therefore, avoid any subsequent consequences.

5. d. Taking Megan into custody for not sitting down or talking is an overreaction, and therefore, choice **a** is incorrect. Choice **b** is incorrect because a probation officer should not physically restrict or otherwise handle a juvenile except in response to an imminent threat of harm to him- or herself or someone else. Choice **c** is unlikely to yield the desired results and may place the probation officer in a "power struggle" situation with the parents. Therefore, choice **d** is correct because it allows the officer to establish rules with the juvenile and to state the inevitable consequences should the juvenile continue the undesired behavior. Although the response to this type of behavior may need to be become more severe if it continues in subsequent visits, responding this way during the first visit allows for the possibility of more restrictive and intrusive measures in future situations with Megan.

6. b. This question requires a candidate to identify the official protocol to follow when there is a question of unprofessional conduct. Choice **a** assumes that Megan is being truthful about the situation, and it calls into question the ethics of the supervisor without any factual information. Choice **c**, although giving an officer an opportunity to investigate the validity of Megan's story personally, still encroaches into an area outside of his or her direct responsibilities. Choice **d** is incorrect because it involves other offenders instead of other professionals, and possibly alerts them to problems associated with that agency by indicating distrust of the staff. Choice **b** allows an officer to promote communication between criminal justice agencies and places the responsibility of program supervision back in the hands of the supervisor of the community service placement agencies. This may be additional information to what that director has already received, therefore giving him or her the ability to take corrective action and meet his or her obligation.

8 ▶ Reading and Writing Skills

Probation and parole officers are constantly reading documents, reports, sentencing orders, and case notes. The ability to make determinations about content in those various formats is crucial to a manageable caseload and an officer's overall success. Additionally, being able to communicate effectively in writing is essential to the various processes of probation or parole supervision. Officers who do not possess excellent writing skills are not likely to be successful. It has been determined that the average probation officer spends more than 65% of his or her time processing documents and information—that is, reading and writing.

▶ Reading Comprehension

One of the most crucial skills an officer needs is reading comprehension. Most probation or parole examinations include passages for a candidate to read and respond to. It's common for candidates to be asked to read a passage and then answer a series of multiple-choice questions.

▶ Active Reading

People often think of reading as a passive activity. After all, you are just sitting there, looking at words on a page. However, reading should actually be an active exercise. When you read, you should *interact* with the text, paying careful attention and being involved as you read. Whenever you read—for a test, for class, for pleasure, use these active reading strategies to improve your comprehension.

Skim Ahead and Jump Back

Skimming ahead helps prepare you for your reading task. Before you begin reading, scan the text to see what's ahead. Is the reading broken into sections? What are the main topics of those sections? In what order are they covered? What key words or ideas are boldfaced, bulleted, boxed, or otherwise highlighted?

When you finish reading, jump back. Review the summaries, headings, and highlighted information. (This includes what you highlighted, too.) Jumping back helps you remember the information you just read. You can see how each idea fits into the whole and how ideas and information are connected.

Look Up Unfamiliar Vocabulary Words

One of the best ways to build your vocabulary is *always* to look up words you don't know. You need to know what all the words in a sentence mean to understand fully what someone is saying. Remember, a key word or phrase can change the meaning of a whole passage.

So, whenever possible, have a dictionary with you when you read. Circle and look up any unfamiliar words right away. (Circling them makes them easier to find if you lose your place.) Write the meaning of the word in the margin. That way, you won't have to look up the meaning again if you forget it; it will always be there for you to refer to. If you don't own the book, write the vocabulary word and its definition in a notebook.

If you don't have a dictionary with you, try to figure out what the word means. What clues does the author provide in the sentence and surrounding sentences? Mark the page or write down the word somewhere so you can look it up later. See how closely you were able to guess its meaning.

Mark Up the Text

As you read, mark up the text (or use notepaper if the text doesn't belong to you) by:

- highlighting or underlining key words and ideas
- taking notes
- making notes

One strategy used by many readers is highlighting and underlining. By highlighting or underlining key words and phrases, you can make important details stand out. This helps you quickly find the information later when you need to answer a question or write a summary. To highlight key words and ideas, you must be able to determine which facts and ideas are most important.

Here are three guidelines for highlighting or underlining your text.

1. **Be selective.** If you highlight four sentences in a five-sentence paragraph, this will not help you. The key is to identify what is most important in the paragraph. Ask yourself two questions:
   - What is the main point the author is trying to make, or what is the main idea of the paragraph?
   - What information is emphasized or seems to stand out as especially important?
2. **Watch for word clues.** Certain words and phrases indicate that key information will follow. Words and phrases such as *most important*, *the key is*, and *significantly* are clues to watch out for.
3. **Watch for visual clues.** Key words and ideas are often boldfaced, underlined, or italicized. They may be boxed or repeated in a sidebar as well.

Careful, active reading will help you improve your overall reading comprehension skills and make reading a more pleasant experience. It will also be your best strategy for tackling the reading questions on the probation or parole officer exam.

▶ Writing Skills

To test a candidate's ability to write effectively, the examination will require several writing samples for review by the examiners. These samples typically include a case-planning exercise, providing definitions to terminology, and providing short narratives in response to various prompts. It is not unusual for these formats to serve multiple purposes simultaneously. A question that requires a candidate to respond to a prompt may be looking for a candidate's opinion on a certain subject *as well as* his or her ability to formulate the response in writing.

Fulfilling the Assignment

As you respond to a writing prompt, remember to stay on topic. You may think that writing about something other than what's assigned portrays you as an independent thinker, someone who can come up with ideas and doesn't need to be told what to do. But that's not the message you'd be sending. If you're doing your own thing and avoiding the topic, you're telling the examiners that you don't care about what they want, you don't understand the topic, or you don't know enough about the assigned material to write about it.

Fulfilling the assignment, on the other hand, sends a positive message to the examiners. It tells them that:

1. you know how to follow directions.
2. you can handle the subject matter.
3. you can meet the challenge presented to you.

Additionally, in timed situations, fulfilling the assignment shows that:

4. you can organize your thoughts about a specific topic while under pressure.

Understanding the Assignment

In order to fulfill the assignment, you must understand exactly what the assignment is asking you to do. Although this sounds simple, consider that many essay assignments aren't obvious. What does it mean, for example, to "discuss" an experience? How are you supposed to "analyze" an issue?

Breaking down the Assignment

To comprehend an assignment, you need to understand the following:

- What you are to respond to (the topic)
- How you are to respond to it

In some cases, there may be more than one topic and more than one way you are supposed to respond. To find out the expectations, break down the assignment. First, underline the words that describe the topic. Then, circle all of the words that tell you how to respond. These "direction words" include *analyze*, *describe*, *discuss*, *explain*, *evaluate*, *identify*, *illustrate*, and *argue*.

Understanding Direction Words

You've broken down the assignment and isolated the direction words. But what do those direction words really mean? In the following table, you'll find the most common essay direction words and their explanations.

TERM	MEANING
Analyze	Divide the issue into its main parts and discuss each part. Consider how the parts interact and how they work together to form the whole.
Argue	Express your opinion about the subject, and support it with evidence, examples, and details.
Assess	See *evaluate*.
Classify	Organize the subject into groups and explain why the groupings make sense.
Compare	Point out similarities.
Contrast	Point out differences.
Define	Give the meaning of the subject.
Describe	Show readers what the subject is like; give an account of the subject.
Discuss	Point out the main issues or characteristics of the subject and elaborate.
Evaluate	Make a judgment about the effectiveness and success of the subject. What is good and bad about it? Why? Describe your criteria for your judgment.
Explain	Make your position, issue, process, etc., clear by analyzing, defining, comparing, contrasting, or illustrating.
Identify	Name and describe.
Illustrate	Provide examples of the subject.
Indicate	Explain what you think the subject means and how you came to that interpretation.
Relate	Point out and discuss any connections.
Summarize	Describe the main ideas or points.

Brainstorming Ideas

How do you generate ideas? Some writers stare at a blank page waiting for inspiration, while others dive right into a draft hoping ideas will come as they write. Both of these techniques take time and often result in disappointment. There are more productive ways to come up with material for your essay—both in terms of time spent and in the quality of that material. Whether you are assigned a topic, must come up with a topic on your own, or are writing under a time constraint, taking the time to focus and shape your thoughts will result in a better final product.

The most effective technique for focusing and shaping your thoughts is *brainstorming*—allowing yourself some time to make connections with your subject, noting everything and anything that comes to mind. Brainstorming may be used both to generate new ideas and to clarify those you already have. Brainstorming can also be used effectively when you are faced with a number of possible essay topics and must determine which is the best vehicle to express your unique thoughts and experiences.

Freewriting

Freewriting is probably the best-known prewriting technique. It works well when you have some thoughts on a topic but can't envision them as an essay. Freewriting also functions as a developmental tool, nurturing isolated ideas into a cohesive, essay-worthy one. People who use this technique often surprise themselves with what comes out on paper. It is common to discover a thought or point you didn't realize you had.

Specifically, *freewriting* means spending a predetermined period of time writing nonstop, focusing on a specific topic. In fact, freewriting should be called "flow writing," because the most important aspect to this prewriting technique is the flow, or momentum, that comes when you stay with it. It works best when you write in full sentences, but phrases are also effective. The key is to keep writing, without regard for grammar, spelling, or worthiness of ideas. Your speed will help keep you editing or discarding any ideas.

Listing

Listing is similar to freewriting in that it is a timed, flowing exercise meant to elicit many thoughts and ideas on a given topic. However, instead of putting whole sentences or phrases on paper, this prewriting technique involves creating a list. It might contain various individual thoughts, ideas that make sense in a particular order, and/or ideas linked together by association with previous ideas.

Listing is a great brainstorming strategy for collaborative writing projects, which work best when they begin with the entire group collecting ideas. In addition, unlike freewriting, listing works well in a timed

writing situation. Regardless of the time allotted for your essay, spend a few minutes first listing your ideas before beginning to write.

Mapping

Mapping is a graphic (visual) organizer that allows you to investigate the relationships between many diverse ideas. It's a simple process best used for exploring simple topics. To make a map, draw a circle and add spokes radiating from it. Put your central idea or subject in the middle, and add subtopics or related ideas around it in any order. Or, draw a box with your subject written in it and continue adding boxes, connected to one another by arrows, showing the development of your idea. As with other brainstorming techniques, don't judge yourself during this process. Write down any and every thought you have on your subject.

The Benefits of an Outline

Generating an outline before you draft an essay will help you in several ways. First, it will give structure to your ideas. By mapping out the order in which those ideas will flow, you create a roadmap for the drafting process. The roadmap assures that you won't veer off topic, helps prevent writer's block, and speeds up drafting.

Second, an outline will help you determine where you need more support for your thesis. When you create an outline, you'll be able to see any gaps in the development of your ideas. Strongly supported assertions stand out in contrast to weaker ones.

Third, an outline will help judge the plausibility of your thesis. If you jump into drafting without organizing first, you may find during the writing

- If you are not already being timed, set a timer for at least 15 minutes (the more time you spend, the more and better ideas you will probably come up with).
- Write every word or phrase that comes to mind about your topic. If you have not selected a topic, write an answer to the question(s), "What do I have to say to my audience?" or "What do I want my audience to know about me?"
- As with freewriting, do not edit or censor any ideas, and ignore the rules of spelling, grammar, and punctuation.
- When you are finished, look over the list carefully. Cross out useless information, and organize what is left. Categorize similar items.

process that your thesis doesn't hold up. A good outline can help you revise, modify, and/or strengthen your thesis before you begin writing. Specifically, a good outline will tell you if your thesis is:

- **too broad.** If you have trouble including everything in your outline, you probably have too much to say. Your thesis needs to be more focused.
- **too narrow.** If you can't seem to find enough to say, your thesis might be too focused. You need to broaden it to create a viable essay.
- **unreasonable.** If there isn't sufficient evidence to support your thesis, you should reconsider its viability. You may need to take a different stance.
- **underdeveloped.** If you have many gaps in our outline, you may need to do more thinking or research to find sufficient support.

▶ Practice

Directions: Read the following passage and then answer questions 1 through 3.

The sentencing of criminal offenders is often considered the most critical point in the criminal justice case process. Sentencing occurs once a determination of guilt has been made through a voluntary plea or through a trial format. Sentencing is pronounced by a judge in the court where the criminal proceedings were held, that is, by the original trial court judge overseeing the case process. Sentencing is designed to establish some form of punishment related to the offense committed by the defendant. The judge typically has numerous options available in sentencing. Probation is one of the most common sanctions a judge imposes with sentencing. For adult offenders, the use of probation is typically accompanied by a suspended period of incarceration. That is, the judge sentences the offender to serve a certain amount of time in prison, and then suspends the actual serving of that time in exchange for the offender to complete a period of probation. Serving a period of probation will include certain rules for the offender to comply with as well as certain conditions they must meet. The majority of persons sentenced through probation are successful at completing the period without having the suspended sentence imposed.

1. The main idea of this passage is
   a. judges have a tough job.
   b. probation is a structured sanction requiring additional considerations.
   c. most offenders complete probation successfully.
   d. sentencing occurs in a voluntary plea or through a trial.

2. _____ is considered the most critical point in the criminal justice process.
   a. Probation
   b. Incarceration
   c. Trial
   d. Sentencing

3. Which of the following words from the passage means *consequences*?
   a. sanctions
   b. options
   c. sentencing
   d. incarceration

Directions: Answer questions 4 through 6 on the following blank lines. If you need additional space, you may use a blank sheet of paper.

4. The majority of persons incarcerated commit new offenses after being released. Provide a one-paragraph statement to explain why this occurs.

_____

_____

_____

_____

_____

_____

_____

_____

_____

_____

5. Provide an outline of the ten most important factors to consider when presenting the court with a recommendation on sentencing an offender.

_____

_____

_____

_____

_____

_____

_____

_____

_____

_____

6. Write a letter to Olivia Massey, a probationer who has reportedly been using marijuana while under parole supervision, asking her to appear for an appointment in your office.

_____

_____

_____

_____

_____

_____

_____

_____

_____

_____

▶ Answers

1. b. This main idea evolves from the specific statement in the passage to the overall discussion of how probation occurs within the sentencing process. The passage begins at the point of general sentences and arrives at the point of what probation entails.

2. d. The answer is derived from the very first sentence of the passage. The other answers may draw upon a reader's opinion or belief rather than from what the passage has stated.

3. a. Sanctions occur because of an infraction of the rules. Because sanctions are imposed this way, they are thought of as consequences. Choices **c** and **d** are types of consequences, but do not share the definition. With choice **b**, the reader is limiting the definition to what options might be available.

4. Answers will vary.

5. Answers will vary.

6. Answers will vary.

9 ▶ Practice Test 2

This is the second practice test in this book and is based on the most commonly tested areas on probation officer and parole officer exams. The skills tested on the exam that follows are the ones that have been tested on previous probation officer and parole officer exams that focus on job-related skills. The exam you take may look somewhat different from this exam, but you'll find that this exam provides vital practice in the skills you need to pass your exam.

The practice test consists of 100 multiple-choice questions in the following areas: job responsibilities, case studies, writing skills, and reading comprehension. You should give yourself three hours to take this practice test. The number of questions and the time limit of the actual probation officer or parole officer exam can vary from region to region.

Practice Test 2

1.	ⓐ	ⓑ	ⓒ	ⓓ
2.	ⓐ	ⓑ	ⓒ	ⓓ
3.	ⓐ	ⓑ	ⓒ	ⓓ
4.	ⓐ	ⓑ	ⓒ	ⓓ
5.	ⓐ	ⓑ	ⓒ	ⓓ
6.	ⓐ	ⓑ	ⓒ	ⓓ
7.	ⓐ	ⓑ	ⓒ	ⓓ
8.	ⓐ	ⓑ	ⓒ	ⓓ
9.	ⓐ	ⓑ	ⓒ	ⓓ
10.	ⓐ	ⓑ	ⓒ	ⓓ
11.	ⓐ	ⓑ	ⓒ	ⓓ
12.	ⓐ	ⓑ	ⓒ	ⓓ
13.	ⓐ	ⓑ	ⓒ	ⓓ
14.	ⓐ	ⓑ	ⓒ	ⓓ
15.	ⓐ	ⓑ	ⓒ	ⓓ
16.	ⓐ	ⓑ	ⓒ	ⓓ
17.	ⓐ	ⓑ	ⓒ	ⓓ
18.	ⓐ	ⓑ	ⓒ	ⓓ
19.	ⓐ	ⓑ	ⓒ	ⓓ
20.	ⓐ	ⓑ	ⓒ	ⓓ
21.	ⓐ	ⓑ	ⓒ	ⓓ
22.	ⓐ	ⓑ	ⓒ	ⓓ
23.	ⓐ	ⓑ	ⓒ	ⓓ
24.	ⓐ	ⓑ	ⓒ	ⓓ
25.	ⓐ	ⓑ	ⓒ	ⓓ
26.	ⓐ	ⓑ	ⓒ	ⓓ
27.	ⓐ	ⓑ	ⓒ	ⓓ
28.	ⓐ	ⓑ	ⓒ	ⓓ
29.	ⓐ	ⓑ	ⓒ	ⓓ
30.	ⓐ	ⓑ	ⓒ	ⓓ
31.	ⓐ	ⓑ	ⓒ	ⓓ
32.	ⓐ	ⓑ	ⓒ	ⓓ
33.	ⓐ	ⓑ	ⓒ	ⓓ
34.	ⓐ	ⓑ	ⓒ	ⓓ
35.	ⓐ	ⓑ	ⓒ	ⓓ

36.	ⓐ	ⓑ	ⓒ	ⓓ
37.	ⓐ	ⓑ	ⓒ	ⓓ
38.	ⓐ	ⓑ	ⓒ	ⓓ
39.	ⓐ	ⓑ	ⓒ	ⓓ
40.	ⓐ	ⓑ	ⓒ	ⓓ
41.	ⓐ	ⓑ	ⓒ	ⓓ
42.	ⓐ	ⓑ	ⓒ	ⓓ
43.	ⓐ	ⓑ	ⓒ	ⓓ
44.	ⓐ	ⓑ	ⓒ	ⓓ
45.	ⓐ	ⓑ	ⓒ	ⓓ
46.	ⓐ	ⓑ	ⓒ	ⓓ
47.	ⓐ	ⓑ	ⓒ	ⓓ
48.	ⓐ	ⓑ	ⓒ	ⓓ
49.	ⓐ	ⓑ	ⓒ	ⓓ
50.	ⓐ	ⓑ	ⓒ	ⓓ
51.	ⓐ	ⓑ	ⓒ	ⓓ
52.	ⓐ	ⓑ	ⓒ	ⓓ
53.	ⓐ	ⓑ	ⓒ	ⓓ
54.	ⓐ	ⓑ	ⓒ	ⓓ
55.	ⓐ	ⓑ	ⓒ	ⓓ
56.	ⓐ	ⓑ	ⓒ	ⓓ
57.	ⓐ	ⓑ	ⓒ	ⓓ
58.	ⓐ	ⓑ	ⓒ	ⓓ
59.	ⓐ	ⓑ	ⓒ	ⓓ
60.	ⓐ	ⓑ	ⓒ	ⓓ
61.	ⓐ	ⓑ	ⓒ	ⓓ
62.	ⓐ	ⓑ	ⓒ	ⓓ
63.	ⓐ	ⓑ	ⓒ	ⓓ
64.	ⓐ	ⓑ	ⓒ	ⓓ
65.	ⓐ	ⓑ	ⓒ	ⓓ
66.	ⓐ	ⓑ	ⓒ	ⓓ
67.	ⓐ	ⓑ	ⓒ	ⓓ
68.	ⓐ	ⓑ	ⓒ	ⓓ
69.	ⓐ	ⓑ	ⓒ	ⓓ
70.	ⓐ	ⓑ	ⓒ	ⓓ

71.	ⓐ	ⓑ	ⓒ	ⓓ
72.	ⓐ	ⓑ	ⓒ	ⓓ
73.	ⓐ	ⓑ	ⓒ	ⓓ
74.	ⓐ	ⓑ	ⓒ	ⓓ
75.	ⓐ	ⓑ	ⓒ	ⓓ
76.	ⓐ	ⓑ	ⓒ	ⓓ
77.	ⓐ	ⓑ	ⓒ	ⓓ
78.	ⓐ	ⓑ	ⓒ	ⓓ
79.	ⓐ	ⓑ	ⓒ	ⓓ
80.	ⓐ	ⓑ	ⓒ	ⓓ
81.	ⓐ	ⓑ	ⓒ	ⓓ
82.	ⓐ	ⓑ	ⓒ	ⓓ
83.	ⓐ	ⓑ	ⓒ	ⓓ
84.	ⓐ	ⓑ	ⓒ	ⓓ
85.	ⓐ	ⓑ	ⓒ	ⓓ
86.	ⓐ	ⓑ	ⓒ	ⓓ
87.	ⓐ	ⓑ	ⓒ	ⓓ
88.	ⓐ	ⓑ	ⓒ	ⓓ
89.	ⓐ	ⓑ	ⓒ	ⓓ
90.	ⓐ	ⓑ	ⓒ	ⓓ
91.	ⓐ	ⓑ	ⓒ	ⓓ
92.	ⓐ	ⓑ	ⓒ	ⓓ
93.	ⓐ	ⓑ	ⓒ	ⓓ
94.	ⓐ	ⓑ	ⓒ	ⓓ
95.	ⓐ	ⓑ	ⓒ	ⓓ
96.	ⓐ	ⓑ	ⓒ	ⓓ
97.	ⓐ	ⓑ	ⓒ	ⓓ
98.	ⓐ	ⓑ	ⓒ	ⓓ
99.	ⓐ	ⓑ	ⓒ	ⓓ
100.	ⓐ	ⓑ	ⓒ	ⓓ

▶ Practice Test 2

1. The case of *Gagnon v. Scarpelli* defines which of the following?
   a. probation revocation processes
   b. parole revocation processes
   c. diversion processes
   d. community corrections revocation processes

2. Fines and restitution can be named as a condition of probation by
   a. the probation officer attaching them as special conditions to someone's supervision.
   b. the court ordering them and setting the amounts to be paid as conditions of someone's supervision.
   c. the victim requesting that the probation officer set an amount be paid to compensate his or her loss.
   d. being added if the probationer does not successfully complete his or her probation supervision.

3. Which is the most common form of punishment in the United States?
   a. parole
   b. incarceration
   c. diversion
   d. probation

4. The majority of adults are on probation for what types of crimes?
   a. property crimes
   b. drug crimes
   c. violent crimes
   d. public order offenses

5. The main difference between regular probation and intensive supervision probation (ISP) is that
   a. in probation, the officer has more flexibility in supervision.
   b. there is more face-to-face contact between the ISP officer and the offender.
   c. ISP offenders have more resources available to them.
   d. the officer can conduct surveillance on the offenders under ISP.

6. Which of the following lists the three main responsibilities of a juvenile probation officer?
   a. act as alternative parent, enforce the rules and laws, maintain public safety
   b. represent the community, conduct presentence investigations, perform supervision
   c. intake the offender, conduct presentence investigations, perform supervision
   d. enforce the rules and laws, act as community resource specialist, serve as crisis manager

7. What U.S. Supreme Court case established guidelines or principles for juvenile probation officers?
   a. *Miranda v. Arizona*
   b. *Kent v. United States*
   c. *Fare v. Michael C.*
   d. *In Re Gault*

8. Among the most critical issues probationers and parolees must resolve to be successful is/are
   a. employment.
   b. drug and alcohol abuse.
   c. financial obligations.
   d. all of the above

9. Caseloads for probation officers have traditionally consisted of how many offenders?
   a. between 0 and 30
   b. between 35 and 50
   c. between 75 and 100
   d. between 100 and 300

10. Once a probation violation report has been filed, the decision to revoke probation is
   a. decided by the supervising officer.
   b. required by policies of the department.
   c. discretionary on the part of the sentencing court.
   d. mandated by state statute.

11. When an offender is released on parole, the primary responsibility for supervision falls to
   a. probation officers.
   b. parole board members.
   c. correctional officers.
   d. parole officers or agents.

12. Conditions of parole and probation that apply case by case are called what?
   a. general conditions
   b. standard conditions
   c. special conditions
   d. situational conditions

13. Which of the following names the situation in which a parolee violates the conditions of his or her parole but does not commit a new offense?
   a. a law violation
   b. a technical violation
   c. a major violation
   d. a small violation

14. Which constitutional amendment provides defendants with equal protection and due process rights?
   a. Eighth Amendment
   b. Fourth Amendment
   c. First Amendment
   d. Fourteenth Amendment

15. Which of the following names the situation in which an offender must do unpaid service to the community to compensate for harm done?
   a. restitution
   b. community service
   c. court costs
   d. cost of supervision fees

16. Who issues the warrant to revoke probation?
   a. the prosecutor
   b. the probation officer
   c. the local police department
   d. the judge

17. How do the due process rights granted to probationers during revocation proceedings compare to those due process rights afforded to parolees?
   a. They are the same.
   b. They are greater.
   c. They are less.
   d. Probationers have no rights at this point in the process.

18. Residential facilities, such as halfway houses, are filled with which types of offenders?
   a. parole violators, offenders convicted of misdemeanors, and offenders awaiting sentencing
   b. ISP probationers, offenders convicted of misdemeanors, and offenders on trial
   c. paroled offenders, probation violators, and prerelease offenders
   d. prerelease offenders, sex offenders, and offenders who have completed supervision but are homeless

19. Federal probation officers now supervise which of the following?
  a. federal probationers only
  b. federal parolees and offenders released from prison who are now under supervision
  c. offenders on mandatory release and military parolees
  d. all of the above

20. "The state acts like a parent" is the definition of which of the following terms?
  a. *mens rea*
  b. *in loco parentis*
  c. *parens patriae*
  d. *mala in se*

21. What is it called when a juvenile is arrested in the adult system?
  a. taken into custody
  b. adjudicated
  c. taken to intake
  d. arrested

22. A juvenile who commits acts that are not punishable by law is categorized as a
  a. child in need of supervision (CNS).
  b. person in need of supervision (PNS).
  c. delinquent juvenile.
  d. status offender.

23. The court has indicated that juveniles do NOT have the right to which of the following?
  a. freedom of speech
  b. due process
  c. freedom from cruel and unusual punishment
  d. a jury trial

24. A parolee comes to you and says that he has been hired for a ticket sales job that requires him to handle money and certain merchandise. He needs to be
  a. without an arrest record.
  b. bonded.
  c. pardoned.
  d. released from supervision.

25. Probation and parole officers need to understand Megan's Law, which deals with which of the following?
  a. registration of offenders convicted of felonies
  b. registration of offenders convicted of firearm violations
  c. registration of parole violators
  d. registration of sex offenders

26. A parolee has told you his brother is being incarcerated in a neighboring state's prison system. He wants to write to his brother, but doesn't know where he is. The offender asks for your help. You should
  a. remind him that any such contact must be approved by you and the warden of the prison holding the brother.
  b. tell the offender "sure" and get on the phone to the Interstate Compact officer to see if they can find the brother.
  c. tell the offender he really doesn't need the additional stresses in his life that contact with his brother surely will cause him and tell him he can't write.
  d. tell the offender that his mother probably has the address and that he can get it from her.

27. A victim of an offender assigned to your caseload calls to inform you she has received an anonymous letter in the mail that apologizes for the harm done to her. She indicates that she knows it is from the offender and wants you to threaten the offender not to contact her again. What should you do?

a. You should agree to threaten the offender and tell her not to worry anymore about the letter.

b. You should tell the victim to throw the letter away and not worry about it because it was unsigned and there isn't any proof it was from the offender.

c. You should tell the victim to contact the police to report the receipt of the letter and that you will receive a copy from the police department after they process the letter as evidence. Once you get the letter, you will compare the writing and then talk with the offender if appropriate. You should also quickly review the file to see if there is a "no contact" condition.

d. You should tell the victim the date and time of the offender's next office visit so she can come to the office to confront him.

28. The parole supervisor has asked you and your field partner to volunteer to accompany police detectives on a stakeout. The supervisor tells you there aren't any parolees involved, but the detectives want someone from the office to be on-site just in case. You should

a. wait to see if your field partner will volunteer first because you really want to go home and watch your favorite TV show.

b. tell your supervisor you have better things to do and you won't go.

c. agree to go only if the supervisor will give you the rest of the week off.

d. agree to go because cooperation is important between law enforcement agencies.

29. You have been asked to sit in on an interview that is being conducted at the local police department because you are the same gender as the defendant, while the detectives are not. You have no other connection to the defendant. You notice as the detectives get started that they have not advised the defendant of his or her Miranda rights. What should you do?

a. You should stop the interview and point out the need for Miranda rights to be issued.

b. You should allow the interview to continue, and once a break occurs, you should ask if Miranda rights were provided to the defendant prior to arriving for the interview.

c. You should step out of the interview and refuse to participate until Miranda rights are read.

d. You should tell the defendant during a break that he or she should contact his attorney because his Miranda rights weren't provided to him, and everything he or she has already said was obtained illegally.

30. It appears you have only few hours left before you complete your 40 hours of annual training. You love to shoot at the firearm range, which counts toward your 40 hours of training, but you are very far behind in your monthly field contacts. Of the 40 field contacts that need to be made, you have done only 15. What action should you take?

  a. You should go to the shooting range because being adept at shooting is more important to your safety, especially when doing field contacts.

  b. You should tell your supervisor that you are going to the range, but you'll get caught up on your field contacts next month.

  c. You should not go to the range, because your 40 training hours are nearly completed, and field contacts are an important part of your job—if not more important than carrying a firearm.

  d. You should go to the range and then work overtime trying to catch up on your field contacts so your supervisor won't give you grief.

Directions: Read the following case study and then answer questions 31 through 37.

Brian is a 35-year-old, diabetic, white male on parole for burglary. He spent seven years in prison and was released two months ago. This was his first conviction and his only time under any supervision. Brian lives by himself and is supporting his meager lifestyle with an inheritance he received when his parents and sister were killed five years ago. Brian does not have any other living relatives, nor does he have any close friends.

When Brian was released, he talked with you in detail about his medical conditions and asked if you could be his contact person in a medical emergency. You agreed to be the contact person only on a temporary basis. Brian brought you all of medical documents he felt you needed, which you promptly sealed in an envelope and placed in Brian's case file.

During the two months since his release, Brian has reported on time and complied with each of his standard and special conditions. He started his counseling and has attended every session. The counselor has reported that many times Brian is early to the sessions and stays late to help clean up the room. During all of the official visits, you have found that Brian was easy to supervise, pleasant to visit with, and is not really a "supervision" problem. Brian has many times introduced you to others as his parole officer and friend.

31. On one of your home visits, you knock on the door several times and Brian doesn't answer. You know Brian is home because you had called him prior to leaving the office, although Brian had sounded confused and disoriented when you talked with him. Knowing Brian's medical history, what should you do?

  a. You should wait a bit because Brian may have stepped out to go to the grocery store.

  b. You should go ahead and kick in the door because Brian may be in medical stress.

  c. You should check all of the doors and windows to see if there is another entry and to see if you can look into the house to check on Brian.

  d. You should call the police to have them come over so they can gain entry into the house for you.

32. Brian is in medical distress and is taken to the hospital. He is coherent within a few minutes of being treated in the emergency room and can converse about his care with the doctors. When you are allowed in the treatment room to see Brian, he becomes emotional and thanks you for saving his life. You:

   a. brush off his emotional outburst and tell him it was nothing.

   b. acknowledge his thanks and ask what is needed to be done so he doesn't have this type of incident again.

   c. tell him that if he had taken better care of himself he wouldn't have needed saving in the first place.

   d. ask him if he is ready to live in a halfway house because you can't be his lifeline anymore.

33. After this first medical incident with Brian, you have found yourself calling him at his home many times throughout the week. In your calls, you visit about the day, his meetings, counseling sessions, sports, and daily events within the community or state. The conversations are always appropriate, but you are concerned about the impression this is making on Brian. You justify the calls as being "a medical check"; however, you think Brian is becoming too dependent upon you. How should you handle the situation that you have created?

   a. You should continue to make the calls because this is also part of your job responsibility.

   b. You should stop making the calls and tell the offender he needs to find another support system.

   c. You should talk with your supervisor, knowing that you will be told you have crossed the professional/personal line with the offender.

   d. You should talk with the offender about your concern and your role, and then suggest that you set up appointments with available resources within the community so he can start establishing other contacts for his medical and emotional needs.

34. Brian is now involved in mental health counseling and is seeing a dietician for his diabetic condition. You are back to making contact with Brian as per the supervision standards for your office. On a scheduled office visit, Brian informs you he doesn't think he needs to attend all of the counseling sessions with his mental health counselor, because he is feeling good, enjoys his job, and is still seeing the dietician. As the person who set the special condition, you could

a. ask the paroling authority to release Brian from the special condition.

b. modify the special condition again to a reduced number of counseling visits required by the offender.

c. contact the counselor to gain his or her input, and if he or she agrees that Brian doesn't need to attend as much as required, modify the special condition to what the counselor and the offender agree upon.

d. tell Brian that you don't want to find him lying on the floor again and insist he continue to attend the sessions.

35. Your supervisor has approached you with a concern that you have conducted yourself inappropriately with this offender. When asked for specifics as to what you have done, you learn that other officers have told the supervisor you are too close and visit the offender's home too much. Your response should be which of the following?

a. You should tell the supervisor you don't deal with gossip and the supervisor should trust you to do your job.

b. You should tell the supervisor the specifics about the case, the lack of family support, the medical conditions, and what resources you have put into place to help the offender. You should also offer the case file for the supervisor's review.

c. You should demand to know which officers are talking about you so you can confront them with their suspicions.

d. You should tell the supervisor to leave you alone until there are specific allegations to discuss.

36. On another scheduled home visit, you find the screen door to the house unlocked and you can see that Brian is lying on the floor. You call out to him, and when you don't get an answer, you enter the home to find Brian unresponsive and with labored breathing. You contact 911 and then realize that Brian has stopped breathing. While you are still on the phone with the emergency operator, you are told to start CPR. What should you do?

a. Being certified in CPR, you should place the phone by Brian's head and start the reviving process.

b. As you hear the ambulance sirens, you should tell the operator you will wait until the medics get to the scene.

c. You should tell the operator this is an offender and you will wait until the medics arrive.

d. You should hang up and call your supervisor for direction.

37. The police department has notified you that Brian has been found dead in his car, which was found along the interstate highway. The reason for death was listed by the coroner's office as insulin shock. Which of the following might be your next action to take in this case?

a. You close up the offender's file and request another case file from your supervisor.

b. You ask the supervisor for a few days off to deal with Brian's personal effects as well as funeral leave for your loss.

c. You ask for counseling through the employee assistance program because you were fond of this offender and you should get help in dealing with his death.

d. You talk with your peers about the burden this offender was on you and how his death has affected you.

Directions: Read the following case study and then answer questions 38 through 42.

Shawna is an Interstate Compact probationer who is living with her friend in your state. This relationship is only one year old, but they seem to get along well. Shawna's conviction was for theft of property. When Shawna was in the sending state, she had an ex-boyfriend, who is also her codefendant. He had indicated in court the property stolen was to support his drug habit and that Shawna did not use drugs, a statement which was confirmed through tests and interviews with Shawna. However, the judge placed a special condition on Shawna's supervision that she have no contact with her codefendant. Unfortunately, she had contact with her ex-boyfriend and was given two options for this violation: be sentenced to prison time or leave the state. The previous supervising officer indicated in the case file report that Shawna was the youngest child in her family and was given material things by her father in order to appease her temper tantrums. Further reports showed that Shawna didn't report regularly, had, in fact, contacted with her codefendant several times, and had been arrested once for failure to pay parking tickets. The previous probation officer shared in the case file report that Shawna's father was overbearing and demanded weekly to know of Shawna's progress; the officer also shared what efforts had to be made to ensure that father didn't know of Shawna's progress or of her violations.

Shawna is 23 years old, has worked part time only, and continues to receive money from her parents. Shawna has never stood up for herself and has allowed her parents to pamper her and control her actions and decisions. One of the conditions of supervision within your state is that probationer either work full time or work part time while going to school part time. After quite a bit of effort, you finally got Shawna to find a full-time job that she has maintained for now six months.

Unfortunately, Shawna has had some minor violations of her probation, including failure to report. You remind Shawna that she does not have to remain in your state and that she could be forced to return to her home state if she doesn't comply with each condition. She states she really wanted to stay in the state and does not wish to be forced to return.

38. Shawna has approached you and asked for a travel permit to fly home for the holidays, which are in three months. You advise Shawna that
   a. she must comply with every condition for the next two months, and if accomplished, you will process the travel permit.
   b. she hasn't had a successful probation so far, and she must show improvements over the next six months before you will consider any travel requests.
   c. she will receive her travel request.
   d. you needed a good laugh, and you appreciated the request so you could get that laugh.

39. Shawna's father has called you many times in the last three months and seems comfortable when you tell him you can simply indicate that Shawna is fine and still under supervision. However, you just ended a call from Shawna's father during which he was irate that you wouldn't tell him of Shawna's progress. He indicated he wanted your supervisor's name and number. You should
   a. continue to talk with the father with the hope that he calms down so you can reason with him.
   b. provide him with your supervisor's name and number.
   c. tell him that you will have your supervisor call him.
   d. refuse to give him your supervisor's information because you are the supervising officer and he can talk to you.

40. The supervisor has asked you to calm the father down, and you realize that Shawna can help you. Which is the best option that might be suggested to Shawna in order to get this accomplished?
   a. Shawna should talk with her father and, through their conversation, resolve any issues he might have.
   b. Shawna should provide written permission that the supervisor or officer can talk with Shawna's father and answer completely any and all questions he may have.
   c. Shawna should ignore her father's attempt to control the situation because she is an adult and shouldn't be treated this way.
   d. Shawna should move back to live with her father because it is obvious her father doesn't like how she is supervised.

41. Shawna has talked to you often about her fear that her ex-boyfriend will show up at her door and cause problems for her and her friend. She tells you she is anxious all of the time and is having difficulty in coping with these fears. Which of the following steps do you take to assist her?
   a. You tell Shawna she doesn't have anything to fear, that the ex-boyfriend won't be able to get a travel permit from his probation officer.
   b. You ask Shawna if she has heard from the ex-boyfriend and ask why she believes he will travel to see her. You should then contact the sending state (either Interstate Compact or the sending officer) and communicate this information about Shawna's fear.
   c. You contact your Interstate Compact office and ask that they not approve any travel permits for Shawna's ex-boyfriend.
   d. You help Shawna gain control of her feelings by asking what she can do to control the situation if the ex-boyfriend shows up at her door. You remind her of resources, such as 911 and neighbors, and offer to arrange for a counselor, if she would like help with her anxieties.

42. Shawna's friend has contacted you with suspicions that Shawna is doing drugs. The friend insists on confidentiality with this phone call and tells you he is only calling because he cares so much for Shawna. After several questions, you learn that Shawna is behaving strangely toward her friend, is very tired and moody, and thinks she is being followed. Shawna does not have a special condition for drug counseling. How should you handle this situation?

a. You should thank the friend for calling and tell him you will have Shawna submit to a urinalysis on her next office visit.

b. After thanking the friend for calling, you should tell him that Shawna is probably upset because of her concerns about her ex-boyfriend, and that the behavior he describes are because of her concern and fear.

c. You should thank the friend for calling and encourage him to communicate his concerns with Shawna because it will be difficult for you to deal with his concerns, since you haven't seen any of this behavior. You offer to sit with him as he is talking with Shawna or in any other way you might assist.

d. After thanking him for calling, you should tell him that you can't talk to him about his concerns because Shawna is an adult and not under his legal care. You should advise him that if he is concerned enough, he has options that include ending the relationship or kicking her out.

Directions: Read the following case study and then answer questions 43 through 48.

Jesse is a former police officer who was caught stealing drugs and evidence from the evidence room at the police station. Jesse was charged with multiple offenses only after another officer confessed and reported all of the officers and their level of involvement. Jesse contended throughout the trial that she was innocent; however, in the trial it became known that Jesse was taking the drugs for personal use and had developed a severe addiction to a variety of illegal pills. Jesse's attorney convinced her to plead guilty to a reduced charge of possession of narcotics in exchange for her testimony against several of the officers. She agreed, and is now on your probation caseload.

Jesse reports to your office for her first meeting with quite an attitude. She reminds you throughout the meeting that she is a cop, she is pretty important in putting others away, and she needs some leniency because of her relationship with the district attorney's office. You proceed to advise her of the probation conditions and supervision standards the judge has directed, and tell her she will be expected to follow each condition as stated. You also advise her that any leniency given will be within the confines of the law, and she should understand no extra will be given to her for being a former police officer.

43. Jesse leaves your office after the first visit upset and shouting about being a victim of the system and about how she won't stand to be treated this way. You should

a. let Jesse go and then try to contact her tomorrow to see how you can help her process all of her life-changing events.

b. let Jesse go, thinking that she will have to get used to frustration now that she is a criminal.

c. call her back into your office and remind her she is now an offender and will be treated like one.

d. call her back into your office and let her know you don't appreciate her attitude and shouting in the office, which will cease.

44. Jesse had to surrender all of her duty weapons when she was arrested. During a home visit, however, you see a bullet under the coffee table. When you ask about the bullet, Jesse indicates she hasn't cleaned her apartment since her trial, and it is left over from when she was a police officer. How should you handle this situation?

a. You should remind Jesse of her probation condition regarding weapons and ask again if she has any guns, ammo, or other dangerous weapons in her possession or in her apartment.

b. You should demand to conduct a search of her apartment to ensure she does not have any weapons.

c. You should call in the police to do a visual search of the apartment.

d. You should ask Jesse to take a lie detector test to make sure she is being truthful about not having any more weapons.

45. Jesse has complied, reluctantly and with an attitude, with the conditions of her probation, with the exception of her substance abuse counseling. She still maintains she does not have a drug abuse problem and was not taking any of the illegal pills that were taken from the evidence room. Which of the following should you do?

a. You should demand that Jesse attend the next substance abuse class and tell her that, if she doesn't, you will have to talk with the judge.

b. You should ask Jesse if she would be willing to talk with a counselor first because this might help her understand addiction and realize her need to attend the substance abuse program.

c. You should tell Jesse that her unwillingness to attend substance abuse counseling will be reported to the judge, and then dismiss her from the conversation.

d. You should do nothing because Jesse can't be released from probation without your input, and she'll eventually have to attend substance abuse counseling if she wants to complete her probation.

46. Your community is large, with ample resources available to help the citizens in all areas, including but not limited to welfare, employment, and mental and substance abuse counseling. At Jesse's office visit, she is depressed that she can't find a job because of her lack of skills. Jesse is depressed and cynical about her situation. How do you handle this situation?

a. You hand Jesse the want ads, telling her to keep looking for work and assuring her that everything will be all right.

b. You get Jesse connected with the job resource center and with temporary agencies so she can start working, which will make her feel better.

c. You get Jesse involved in a halfway house program, so she can figure out all of her issues without having to worry about working.

d. You tell Jesse she has one month to find employment or you will contact the judge about her violating her probation conditions.

47. Jesse has told you she has been receiving harassing phone calls, knocks on her apartment door in the middle of the night, and hate mail left in her mailbox. She tells you she thinks the officers she testified against, or their families, are harassing her. Some of those officers are on probation, and Jesse wants you to talk with their probation officers to get them to stop. What would you do in this situation?

a. You talk with the other probation officers to ask them to tell their offenders to stop the harassing behavior.

b. You have Jesse consider changing her phone number on a temporary basis and reporting the harassing mail to the post office. You acknowledge her reluctance to report the behavior to the local law enforcement agency, but ensure that she remembers she has a right to do this.

c. You tell Jesse to put a tap on her phone, which will record the phone calls as well as determine where the calls came from. You advise her to get her landlord to put up a camera in the hallway to show who came and went from her apartment, and finally you tell her to get a key for her mailbox, which should be locked.

d. You tell Jesse there isn't anything she can do at this point, because no actual crime has been committed. You remind her that this type of behavior will go away if ignored.

48. During your home visit, you notice that Jesse is listening to a police band radio. What action should you take?

a. There isn't anything illegal about having a police band radio in your home, so you shouldn't take any action.

b. It is unnecessary to have a police band radio in the apartment, and is unhealthy for Jesse. You tell her to remove the radio from the apartment.

c. You place several special conditions on Jesse so she will be so busy that she doesn't have time to listen to the radio.

d. You suggest that Jesse get counseling to help her with her loss.

Directions: Read the following case study and then answer questions 49 through 54.

James is 27 years old and has already been in and out of prison three times. James's original charge was possession of drugs, and when he violated the conditions of his probation, he was placed in prison for three years. James was released early because of good behavior; however, he violated his parole conditions by not reporting and by using drugs. He was released after serving a few months for the parole violations, only to be arrested for drug use within one month of his release. Prior to this last violation for drug use, he lived with a young woman who had a small daughter. James had become very attached to the daughter and had become the primary caregiver while living in the home. James was charged, within a year of his release, of spousal abuse, but he was never convicted because the young woman refused to press charges. He was returned to prison a second time as a parole violator for minor violations of his conditions, and the supervising officer felt James needed to have some "shock parole" time. This is James's third attempt at parole.

Because of his previous criminal history, James is a high-risk offender who has several special supervision conditions, including substance abuse treatment, anger management counseling, a prohibition to contact his former girlfriend, and a halfway house treatment program. Unfortunately, the halfway house in your community is full and has a lengthy waiting list, so James is released to live within the community until he can be moved into the program. James's 62-year-old mother is still living in her home and is James's only living relative in the area. James's mother has been supporting James and has offered to help him. James is upset that he cannot have contact with his former girlfriend, not because he misses her but because he misses being involved with her daughter.

49. James has expressed his concern for his ex-girlfriend's daughter to you. James is now indicating his ex-girlfriend has contacted him and asked him to take the little girl for a week or so. James has checked with his boss who has allowed him to take three vacation days, after which James's mother will watch the little girl while James is at work. James wants to have the little girl with him but is concerned about the special "no contact" condition he has regarding the ex-girlfriend. He asks you if you can help with this situation. Which of the following should you do?

a. You should tell James that the exchange of the little girl should be conducted in the parole office.

b. You should suggest to James that his mother be the primary caregiver of the little girl and that James visit her at the mother's house.

c. You should ask James if there is a relative of the little girl who would be able to watch her, because he isn't supposed to have contact with the ex-girlfriend.

d. You should suggest to James that he simply stay away from this situation all together and that any dealings with the little girl will put him in contact with the ex-girlfriend.

50. James has worked at his current job as a dockworker off and on for the past two years. His employer likes James and held the job for James when James returned to prison for a parole violation. James is said to be a good worker when he is able to stay out on parole. James rides the bus to and from work, his counseling sessions, and the parole office. James has complained that he is spending a lot of money on bus fare and doesn't have enough to pay his bills. How should you best help James with this situation?

a. You should look at James's other expenses to see which can be reduced or eliminated.

b. You should tell James that this is a consequence of not staying out of prison and that he needs to live with the problem or find a better paying job.

c. You should accompany James to a social service agency to see if he could obtain a month's worth of free bus passes.

d. You should have James contact a local church or two to see if they can offer assistance to him.

51. James's ex-girlfriend calls you to report that James has been bringing drugs to her to sell. She wants him to stop coming to her home. You know from past conversations with her and with James that he has shunned her in the past, which made her angry. You should
  a. thank her for the information and, once you hang up with her, call the detectives in narcotics and let them know she is someone they should be watching.
  b. thank her for the call and assure her that you will take care of the problem.
  c. thank her for the call and assure her that you will talk with James to get his side of the story and that if she feels she is being harassed by James or anyone, she should call the police.
  d. thank her for the information and tell her that you feel she is just trying to cause trouble for James and that you aren't going to do anything about this situation.

52. Although it appears that James does not use drugs, you have noticed that James's skin is clammy, he seems to be losing a lot of weight, he is not able to focus when you talk to him, and he seems withdrawn and depressed. He doesn't answer you directly when you ask him if he has been using drugs. You should
  a. conduct an urinalysis.
  b. insist that James go to the hospital to find out what is wrong with him.
  c. call the drug hotline to find out what types of drugs produce these types of symptoms.
  d. call the halfway house to see if you could bring James over to get screened regarding his immediate conditions and to see when James might be able to get into treatment.

53. On a recent home visit, you notice there is a huge hole in the roof of James's house. When asked what happened, James tells you the latest storm made the roof cave in under the weight of the water. He informs you he plans to put a tarp over the hole but doesn't have any plans to get the roof fixed any time soon. What should your response to this be?
  a. You should tell James that you hope it doesn't rain much between now and the time he gets his roof fixed, and you continue with your home visit.
  b. You should insist he get the roof fixed as it is a hazard to his health, and tell him you are placing a special condition on him to ensure that he gets this done.
  c. You should tell him that it isn't safe to live like that and that he must get this fixed soon.
  d. You should strongly suggest he move out of his house until he can get the money together to have the roof fixed.

54. You have been notified there is a bed available in the treatment halfway house for James. When you contact him, James asks to stay out of the treatment program for another two months to work and save money, so he doesn't have to work when he is in the treatment program. Which of the following would be closest to your response?
a. You tell James you understand and you will arrange to hold the bed for months.
b. You tell James that, although you understand his desire not to work while in the program he must go into the program now. Because this is a special condition, he must attend treatment when it is available.
c. You tell James that, although you understand his desire not to work while in the program, you do not believe his attempt to delay entering the program is sincere, and if he doesn't go as scheduled, you will issue a warrant for his arrest.
d. You tell James that he needs to go to the treatment facility and talk to the staff about his request to wait two months, and that you will agree with whatever the halfway house staff decides.

Directions: Read the following case study and then answer questions 55 through 60.

You work in an office that has a parole director, three parole supervisors, and 25 parole officers. For the most part, there is a good balance of teamwork and camaraderie between the officers and supervisors. Everyone understands the office is located in a part of town that has had its share of murders, rapes, and robberies, so security is high at the entrances to the office. There is an official rule that two officers always go together to conduct field visits and an unwritten rule that two officers leave the building together. Although it isn't unsafe to work in this area, everyone in the parole office is comfortable with the rules because it is better to be safe than sorry.

Out of the 25 parole officers, ten have been parole officers for more than seven years. Many of these officers had started in other offices and moved to this office at some point in their careers. Another seven officers have worked at that particular office for five years or so. The remaining eight officers are fairly new within the last two years. There is a lot of joking around between the newer officers and the more experienced officers about being dinosaurs, being just a kid, trying to grow up, or getting too old. You feel this is in bad taste, but others, especially those involved, don't seem to mind.

The supervisors of the office feel they have asked a great deal of the officers and are willing to provide some stress relief" in various ways. One way occurs on the last Friday of each month. The supervisors ask the officers not to schedule any appointments and then allow the officers to stay in the office to catch up on their paperwork. The supervisors bring in pizza or arrange a potluck lunch, and then everyone sits down to eat together.

55. You are aware that some of more experienced officers are not working on case files on the last Friday of each month. You know that, instead, they are reading novels, balancing their personal checkbooks, and in general being unproductive. How should you handle this situation?
a. You should simply do your own work and not worry about what others are doing.
b. You should confront these lazy officers. Why should you be the only one working hard?
c. You should handle personal affairs on this day instead of working on your case files, just like them.
d. You should tell your supervisor about the lazy officers and then go into your office and shut the door.

56. There is growing tension in the office because the less experienced officers feel the more experienced officers are lax about security around the office. Several of the less experienced officers were talking in the break room about the latest example, when an offender was allowed to roam the halls without being escorted. When the offender was stopped and asked where he was going, he simply replied, "Oh, I don't know, I'm just looking around." You are asked for your opinion. Which of the following might be the closest to what advice you would provide?

a. You tell the officers not to worry about it because the offender was probably just looking for the bathroom and didn't want to admit it.

b. You let the officers know that, if they are concerned about this, they should approach the supervisors so that they can reinforce the safety and security rules of the office.

c. You tell the officers to confront the more experienced officers and ask them to remember the safety rules.

d. You tell the officers that they are nitpicking and they need to lighten up like some of the other officers.

57. You have heard that two parole officers, Mike and Jon, have been feuding with each other. The office gossip told you that Mike is telling coworkers that Jon isn't a good officer and that he has had an affair with one of his offenders. You have heard Jon is telling other coworkers that Mike is lazy and has been driving the state car while under the influence. You happen to walk into the break room where three officers are talking about Mike and Jon. What should you do?

a. You should walk right back out; this isn't any of your business.

b. You should sit down and join in, telling them what you have heard; after all, this is your break time.

c. You should tell the officers that gossip isn't good for the office, and they might consider not talking about it, at least in the break room.

d. You should go to the supervisor's office and tell them what you have heard and what is going on in the break room.

58. As you are talking with an offender in your office, you hear Mike and Jon yelling at each other in the hallway outside of your office. After telling the offender that you will be right back, you step outside of your doorway just in time to see Mike grab Jon by the shirt and push him into the wall. Both men are throwing punches at each other. You should

a. step back into your office to prevent your offender from coming out of the office and seeing your peers acting unprofessional.

b. step between the two parole officers and get them to stop fighting.

c. yell at the officers to stop fighting while you wait for other officers to show up; then, when you have help, step between the two officers to stop the fighting.

d. watch the officers to make sure they don't hurt each other, and hope that other parole officers will get them to stop.

59. A less experienced officer tells you that you are one of the dinosaurs in the office and that you are too old for the job. You should
  a. hit the officer in the nose and tell him you aren't too old to do that.
  b. tell the officer you don't appreciate his discriminatory comments and he needs to stop making them to you and to others.
  c. just ignore him; he's just a kid who doesn't know any better.
  d. make a snide comment back to him.

60. Tension in the office is high as two officers have decided to poke fun at other officers by calling them names, kidding them about their age and gender, even telling coworkers things that involve the officers' sexual activities. You have directly heard these two officers joke about their sexual activities and those of others. The human resources manager calls you and asks if you have heard of any discriminating or harassing comments being made by other officers in the parole office. What should your response be?
  a. You should tell the human resources manager that you don't want to get involved and would rather not say anything.
  b. You should tell the human resources manager that you don't appreciate the witch hunt and refuse to respond to any of the questions.
  c. You should tell the human resources manager that you don't know anything, even though you do.
  d. You should tell the human resources manager that you have, in fact, heard comments. You should inform her of the content, date, and time of the incidents, trying to remember as close to the exact wording of the comments as possible.

61. Which of the following sentences is punctuated correctly?
  a. Corrections professionals shall not knowingly exceed their authority in the enforcement of the law or in applying department rules and regulations to the offenders they supervise.
  b. Corrections professionals shall not knowingly exceed their authority. In the enforcement of the law or in applying department rules and regulations to the offenders they supervise.
  c. Corrections professionals, shall not knowingly exceed their authority, in the enforcement of the law or in applying department rules and regulations; to the offenders they supervise.
  d. Corrections; professionals shall not knowingly exceed their authority in the enforcement of the law or in applying: department rules and regulations to the offenders they supervise.

62. Which of the following sentences is NOT punctuated correctly?
  a. Probation officers shall refrain from any conduct in an official capacity that compromises the public's faith and the integrity of the criminal justice system.
  b. Effective and responsive community cooperation, with the criminal justice system, is produced when officers act, with honesty; trustworthiness; and impartiality.
  c. The officer must act in a manner that instills trust and respect from all with whom contact is made.
  d. Probation officers must carry out their duties with integrity, fairness, and impartiality.

63. Which of the following sentences is punctuated correctly?

a. Probation officers must learn appropriate conduct, that is in violation of any law or policy, of this department and shall take necessary action and report the incident to the immediate supervisor.

b. Probation officers must: learn appropriate conduct that is in violation of any law or policy of this department. And shall take necessary action, and report the incident to the immediate supervisor.

c. Probation officers must learn appropriate conduct that is in violation of any law or policy of this department, and shall take necessary action and report the incident to the immediate supervisor.

d. Probation officers must learn appropriate conduct that is in violation of any law or policy of this department and shall take necessary action and report the incident to the immediate supervisor.

64. Which sentence do you feel is the most clearly written?

a. Probation and parole officers shall provide every person in our society, including offenders under their supervision, with professional, courteous, effective, and efficient service.

b. Probation and parole officers shall act in a manner that does not compromise their ability to perform assigned work or duties in an efficient, unbiased, and professional manner, or that of other officers.

c. With professional, courteous, effective, and efficient service, probation and parole officers shall provide every person in our society, including offenders under their supervision.

d. Probation and parole officers, or that of other officers, shall act in a manner that does not compromise their ability to perform assigned work or duties in an efficient, unbiased, and professional manner.

65. Which sentence do you feel is NOT clearly written?

a. A probation and parole officer shall not consume alcoholic beverages or use illegal chemical substances while on duty.

b. A probation and parole officer shall not consume alcoholic beverages to the extent that he or she is rendered unfit for duty.

c. A probation and parole officer shall not report for work with the odor of alcohol on his or her breath or person.

d. Medicine taken which will impair performance, a report to the supervisor the probation and parole officer shall make.

66. Which sentence do you feel is the most clearly written?

a. Sexual harassment offenses, parole officers shall not commit any acts under state law.

b. Domestic battery and/or stalking are two acts as defined by state law that shall not be tolerated by probation and parole officers committing.

c. Probation and parole officers shall avoid ongoing personal and/or off-duty associations with persons who are known to engage in criminal activity.

d. Probation and parole officers intoxicants hallucinogens or controlled substances shall not use.

67. Which of the following sentences is grammatically correct?

    a. Whether by act, omission, or statement, officers shall not espress prejuduce concerning race, color, cred, religious, national origin, sex, marital status, status with regard to public assistance, disability, sexual orientation, or age.

    b. Officers will no if others isn't courteous in there dealings with offenders and the public.

    c. Officers shall advice any peoples of the complaint procedure and how to process complaints.

    d. Officers shall not compromise their integrity by accepting, giving, or soliciting gratuity or gifts.

68. Which of the following sentences is grammatically correct?

    a. Everyone accept the probation officer knew it was true.

    b. Can we talk to the offender about this condition?

    c. The officer done what he was supposed to do.

    d. The officer indicated he did not feel very well.

69. Which of the following sentences is grammatically correct?

    a. The officer made a point with her moralle and ethical actions.

    b. The district attorney's office decided to persecute the offender for the crime.

    c. The officer did especially well with his case file reviews.

    d. The offender has to rise enough money for bail.

Directions: Read the following passage and then answer questions 70 through 76.

Global Positioning Systems (GPS) technology has been used to monitor and pinpoint the locations of offenders. Satellite Monitoring and Remote Tracking, or SMART, is used to locate offenders through a permanent ankle or wrist transmitter device and a microprocessor and antenna, also carried by the offender. The transmitter and receiver the offender carries serves as the connector between the satellite and the central control unit that monitors the various offenders assigned to this program. The receiver records data and transmits it via a cell phone or landline phone. A phone line continuously calls a reporting station to update the offender's location, which is tracked by a computer.

The parole officer can also set "zones" that the offender can or cannot enter without the device sounding an alarm. This is especially useful in making sure that the offender is not traveling to unauthorized areas, because the parole officer can better enforce "no contact" conditions. This system is extremely helpful in keeping sex offenders away from schools or day care facilities, or preventing a compulsive gambler from entering a casino or other gambling establishment. Probation and parole officers now have the opportunity and ability to focus their attention on high-risk offenders, while protecting the community from lower-risk offenders monitored through the GPS.

There are some disadvantages to this system. One disadvantage is the loss of the GPS signal. In some locations, the receiver has trouble picking up the signal from the satellite, or there may be "dead spots," in which cell phones cannot find a signal to use to call in or out. Another second disadvantage is the cost of the system. Ways to reduce costs would include recording data only on high-risk offenders, or collecting data on all offenders every 30 minutes rather than constantly. However, it begs the question: How many crimes could be committed within a 30-minute time frame?

Legal concerns regarding GPS programs have been raised. The issues of equal protection, due process arguments, illegal search and seizure, and violation of privacy have all been presented, and the U.S. Supreme Court has consistently rejected the claims. Electronic monitoring has overcome its constitutional issues and has become an often-used alternative to imprisonment.

70. Which of the following describes the main idea of this passage?
   a. Probation and parole officers now have the opportunity and ability to focus their attention on those high-risk offenders, while protecting the community from lower-risk offenders monitored through GPS.
   b. The legal concerns raised by the use of GPS as a monitoring system are senseless arguments and haven't been accepted by the Supreme Court.
   c. There are more disadvantages to using the GPS monitoring system than there are advantages.
   d. Parole officers can use this system so they don't have to work as hard.

71. Zones can be established in the SMART system for which purpose?
   a. to allow the offender to move freely only in the areas designated by the officer
   b. to notify the offender and the officer when the offender is moving into an unauthorized area
   c. to set off a small electric charge when the offender gets too close to schools or other unauthorized areas
   d. to give the offender a printed map of the authorized neighborhoods in the city

72. Which of the following issues has NOT been addressed by the U.S. Supreme Court regarding the electronic systems?
   a. equal protection
   b. due process arguments
   c. illegal search and seizure
   d. self-incrimination

73. The equipment the offender must carry with the SMART system include
   a. a transmitter, a satellite, and a phone line.
   b. a microprocessor, an antenna, and a landline phone.
   c. a transmitter, a receiver, and an antenna.
   d. a receiver, a control unit, and a cell phone.

74. The two disadvantages of GPS listed in this passage are
   a. the loss of signal and the cost of the system.
   b. having to use a cell phone and the loss of signal.
   c. the cost of the system and the lack of offenders to use the system.
   d. the inability of the system to track offenders for fewer than 30 minutes and the cost of the system.

75. Why would officers prefer this system over traditional face-to-face supervision?
   a. They wouldn't want to use the system because it seems impersonal and is not foolproof.
   b. Officers could track low-risk offenders on this system, while spending their traditional supervision time on high-risk offenders.
   c. This system would be good for only property offenders because it would track the offenders' locations and help solve crimes.
   d. It wouldn't be good for sex offenders, gamblers, and drug users because these offenders commit their crimes in areas that already utilize a lot of technology and satellites.

76. As indicated in the passage, electronic monitoring should be
   a. an alternative to prison.
   b. used with all offenders who are on community corrections supervision.
   c. the only supervision technique used with low-risk offenders.
   d. used only with probationers.

Directions: Read the passage below and then answer questions 77 through 83.

Gagnon v. Scarpelli (1973) is the case that defined constitutional due process rights, including a probationer's right to a lawyer during a hearing. In this case, Gerald Scarpelli was on probation for a felony charge when he was re-arrested for burglary. Scarpelli admitted his guilt to the burglary but later retracted that admission of guilt, claiming that he had been coerced. His probation was revoked without a hearing and without a lawyer present. After serving three years of his original sentence, Scarpelli sought release through a writ of *habeas corpus*, claiming violations of his rights.

In this case, the Supreme Court said the rights provided to parolees in parole revocation hearings are the same due process rights that should be afforded to probationers. The five rights that must be afforded include: 1) written notice of the claimed violations, 2) disclosure of evidence against the parolee, and the opportunity to be heard and present witnesses or evidence on his or her own behalf, 3) the opportunity to confront and cross-examine adverse witnesses (unless there is a good cause for not doing so), 4) a neutral and objective hearing body to review and hear the case, and 5) a written statement as to the evidence relied upon and the reasons for revoking parole. The court indicated that there was no difference between probation and parole revocation because both processes result in a loss of liberty.

Probationers are guaranteed a two-hearing revocation process, as parolees are. In this process of preliminary and revocation hearings, the probationer has the right to waive the preliminary hearing and appear before the judge to present evidence regarding the alleged violations.

The second issue that *Gagnon* questioned was lack of representation. Before *Gagnon*, the courts heard *Mempa v. Rhay* (1967). In this case, the courts held that a defendant has a constitutional right to a lawyer during a probation revocation process that is followed by sentencing. The court held that sentencing is an important phase that requires the presence of a lawyer for the defendant.

The court indicated in *Gagnon*, however, that the right to have a lawyer present at the revocation hearing should be determined on a case-by-case basis—for example, if the probationer is indigent or if a defendant has difficulty presenting his or her case, an attorney would likely be called.

Cases such as *Gagnon* assure citizens that all offenders will be afforded the constitutional due process rights. This case also assures that probationers will receive the same rights as parolees when a revocation process is started. It is clear, however, most probationers do not worry about this process, as the majority of offenders are able to complete probation successfully. Those who do not complete probation successfully, usually by committing new offenses, are returned to court or to the prison system.

77. The case of *Gagnon* decided which of the following?
- **a.** Offenders do not need two hearings if the state feels there is sufficient evidence to prove probable cause.
- **b.** Offenders are to receive documentation and written statements of the process at the final hearing.
- **c.** A judge must hear an offender's case shortly after arrest.
- **d.** Offenders must be afforded the disclosure of evidence held by the officer, and in certain cases, an attorney may be present.

78. Which of the following describes the main idea of the passage?
- **a.** The courts can't decide what rights to give offenders, and they constantly change their minds.
- **b.** Offenders need lawyers to be present at all times prior to and during the revocation process.
- **c.** Offenders are provided due process rights when arrested and during the revocation process.
- **d.** Probation violators usually return to court and then to prison on new charges.

79. Gagnon was arrested for which charge when he was already on probation for another felony?
   a. burglary
   b. theft
   c. murder
   d. auto theft

80. The U.S. Supreme Court ruled in *Gagnon v. Scarpelli* that probationers are afforded certain due process rights. Which of the following closely resembles the rights afforded to probationers by this case?
   a. disclosure of evidence against the probationer, opportunity to confront adverse witnesses, opportunity to be heard and present evidence, an attorney, and written notification of final revocation
   b. opportunity to confront adverse witnesses, opportunity to be heard, opportunity to have the hearing within travel distance of family and witnesses, an attorney at the final hearing, and written notice of reasons for final revocation
   c. written notice of the charges, evidence given in advance so an attorney can build a defense for the probationer, opportunity of cross-examination by the attorney, ability to present a case in defense of the charges, and written notice of every decision made within the revocation process
   d. written notice of the charges, disclosure of evidence against the probationer, opportunity to cross-examine adverse witnesses, an objective hearing body to hear the case, and written notice of reasons for final revocation

81. Which of the following is correct regarding *Gagnon v. Scarpelli*?
   a. This case made probation officers' work more difficult because they must now assure that all offender rights are afforded within a reasonable time frame.
   b. When Gerald Scarpelli was released from prison, he should have been treated as a parolee, not a probationer.
   c. Only the offender has the opportunity to waive any of the due process rights afforded under *Gagnon*.
   d. A probationer can have an attorney present as an adviser throughout all of the revocation proceedings.

82. *Gagnon v. Scarpelli* is closely tied to which of the following cases?
   a. *Mempa v. Rhay* (1967)
   b. *Morrissey v. Brewer* (1973)
   c. *Miranda v. Arizona* (1966)
   d. *People v. Price* (1960)

83. In the author's opinion, why is this case NOT important to probationers?
   a. Most probation officers don't feel the need to inform offenders of these rights because they are covered in the revocation packet that must be presented to the offender.
   b. Most probationers don't realize their rights established by this case.
   c. Most probationers are successful in completing their probation; offenders who violate their probation conditions do so by committing a new offense.
   d. Most probationers are first-time offenders who are given a second chance when they violate their probation conditions.

Directions: Read the passage below and then answer questions 84 through 88.

After several situations and events over the last several years, DNA collection has raised many questions and concerns. Offenders have been released from prison, while others have been convicted and imprisoned, because of DNA results.

Some experts in the field believe that DNA samples should be taken from *all* offenders, from low-level criminals to rapists and murderers. As of now, no state mandates this practice; however, legislatures across the nation are looking into expanding the DNA collection process, arguing that a larger database would help solve both future crimes as well as "cold cases." Currently, 28 states collect samples for some misdemeanor crimes. Five states collect DNA samples from people who have been arrested, but not necessarily charged with a crime (for instance, violent felony and burglary suspects).

This movement toward more DNA collection is coming at a time when complaints about DNA work in criminal investigations are high. These complaints are about mistakes in testing and analysis, which will, some say, only increase in frequency as labs get overwhelmed if states pass legislation that would expand the current collection practices. This expansion must be funded, and many states are indicating that the cost would be burdensome on their already tight budgets. Another major complaint is the backlog of court cases that are on hold until DNA test results are available. The labs are already overworked, some experts say, and this expansion would just exacerbate the current problem tenfold. Finally, the last complaint is a question: At what stage of the criminal justice process should DNA be collected? Some defendants are never formally charged after arrest or are found not guilty in trial; with an expansion of DNA collection, these people, even though they have not been convicted of a crime, would have their DNA collected, stored, and ultimately recorded in the database without their knowledge or approval.

It is clear that, as technology becomes more advanced, our means of solving cases should follow suit. Although we shouldn't take the human component out of the investigation process all together, we must learn how to utilize the advancements of technology to gain justice for those victims affected by criminals.

84. What is the main idea expressed in this passage?
   a. DNA testing will continue to violate citizens' right to privacy.
   b. More DNA testing would allow cold cases to be solved.
   c. Expansion of DNA testing is being considered in many states.
   d. As states consider expanding DNA testing, there are more negative opinions about DNA testing than there are positive ones.

85. The disadvantages to expanding DNA testing listed in the passage did NOT include which of the following?
   a. Mistakes will get only worse as the labs get overwhelmed.
   b. The backlog of court cases will get larger as everyone waits for DNA evidence to be processed.
   c. The cost of the expansion will be more than state budgets will allow.
   d. More staff will have to be hired from an already depleted employment pool.

86. How many states are currently taking DNA samples from offenders who commit misdemeanors?

a. 14
b. 28
c. 5
d. 25

87. As cited in the passage, what is the goal of expanding DNA collection?

a. to help end states' crime waves
b. to make sure that all offenders who are convicted have provided their DNA
c. to create a larger database, which would help to solve both future crimes and cold cases
d. to affect the unemployment pool by offering more available jobs

88. Which of the following opinions did the author give in the passage?

a. We must learn how to utilize the advancements of technology to enhance our investigation skills.
b. Technology is becoming too complicated, and we aren't able to keep up with the funding.
c. We have convicted innocent people, and DNA is a way to free them, as long as we have an expansion of DNA collection.
d. Budgets and labs are already overworked, and the expansion of the collection pool will make the situation only worse, not better.

Directions: Read the following passage and then answer questions 89 through 94.

Officer education versus experience is an ongoing debate when administrators are looking to hire new probation and parole officers. The employment pool has a large number of corrections personnel looking to move out of the prison system and into the community supervision positions. Probation and parole officer jobs are looked at by many as *the* positions to have.

It is interesting that most adult probation and parole officers have a bachelor's degree, at a minimum, and at least 86% of states hiring juvenile probation officers prefer a degree. However, many of these agencies list their minimum requirements as a high school degree. There has been a move within human resources departments to make requirements and qualifications more "diversity friendly," which has for some agencies meant lowered their hiring standards. This move is seen as widening the application pool, not lowering the skill level of the officers hired.

As the emphasis of these community supervision programs has shifted from treatment to public safety and control, a preference qualification has been determined as essential when recruiting for these positions. People who have degrees from criminal justice, criminology, and sociology programs are sought after and enticed to apply for the vacant positions.

However, some in the field believe education doesn't provide all that is necessary for someone to become a quality probation or parole officer. These people insist that experience must be the preferred qualification, because some of the skills needed can't be learned in a classroom or through a book. Quick problem-solving skills, good interpersonal skills, intuition, and leadership skills are honed through experience within the criminal justice system. Some people say probation and parole officers should spend mandatory time working within the prisons prior to becoming an officer. This experience would help develop some of these "soft" skills and help officers learn how to utilize them when supervising offenders, ultimately making the public safer.

Others say that officers who have degrees from criminal justice programs have also had opportunities in which they have honed these skills. Internships, mentoring programs, and ride-along opportunities are available and have been successful in preparing students to become effective employees. Additionally, pre-service and annual trainings allow employees to fine-tune the skills necessary to be a successful officer. It is essential that human resource personnel be open-minded when looking at a candidate's past experiences, to see if they have developed the necessary skills that are required for these positions.

Although this debate will continue, it is certain that the probation and parole officer position is one of the best to have. There aren't too many other positions within the criminal justice field through which employees can make such a positive impact on another human being.

89. The main theme to this passage is
   a. all probation and parole officers should have college degrees at the time of hire.
   b. all probation and parole officers should have a mixture of college and experience at the time of hire.
   c. being a probation and parole officer allows you the opportunity to make an impact on another human being.
   d. being a successful probation and parole officer requires many skills that need to be developed thorough college education or employment opportunities.

90. Which of the following was NOT named in the passage as a way criminal justice students can obtain experience through their college experience?
   a. internships
   b. study- or work-abroad experiences
   c. mentoring programs
   d. ride-along opportunities

91. Which of the following was named in the passage as one of the skills essential to being a probation or parole officer?
   a. coping skills
   b. organizational skills
   c. problem-solving skills
   d. good writing skills

92. Critics of the college degree requirement for probation and parole officers feel which of the following should happen?
   a. Probation and parole officers should be hired based on field experience only.
   b. Probation and parole officers should spend time working within a prison prior to becoming an officer.
   c. Probation and parole officers shouldn't have a college degree, because the required skills can't be learned in a book.
   d. Probation and parole officers should rely more on preservice and annual trainings to gain the necessary skills, rather than on experience or education.

93. Which is the percentage of states who prefer to hire juvenile probation officers with a college degree?
   a. 86%
   b. 50%
   c. 78%
   d. 11%

94. According to the author, what is the purpose of lowering the hiring standards for probation and parole officer candidates?
   a. to help agencies meet their affirmative action quotas
   b. to bring in "trainable" applicants who have the right skills for the job
   c. to widen the application pool from which agencies can select qualified candidates
   d. to bring in people who have military and law enforcement backgrounds and who may have joined the armed forces or police force immediately out of high school.

Directions: Read the passage below and then answer questions 95 through 100.

Fare v. Michael C. (1985) is the case that helped define the relationship between a probation officer and a probationer. In this case, a juvenile named Michael C. was taken into custody as a suspect in a murder case. He was advised of his Miranda rights, and when asked if he wished to have an attorney present during questioning, he asked for his probation officer instead. He was informed by police that his probation officer would be contacted at a later time and that, if he wanted to talk, he could talk to the police. Michael agreed to talk to the police and, during questioning, made statements and drew sketches that incriminated him. When charged with murder in juvenile court, Michael and his attorney moved to suppress the incriminating evidence, alleging it was obtained in violation of his Miranda rights. The judge didn't agree with that argument, and Michael was convicted.

On appeal, the U.S. Supreme Court affirmed the conviction, holding that the request to see a probation officer is not the equivalent to asking for an attorney. Additionally, the court indicated that any evidence voluntarily given is admissible in court.

This case is significant because the Supreme Court helped define the supervisory role of a juvenile probation officer. The first item of clarification is that the communications between the accused and the probation officer are not shielded by attorney privilege. The second item of clarification is that the loyalty of a probation officer is to the state, despite any obligation or relationship with the probationer.

Although this decision makes sense, many probation and parole officers find themselves in difficult situations with juvenile and adult offenders. Offenders often use the officer as a confidante, a hand-holder, a parent, and a friend. Some officers cross the line when they allow their personal opinions and feelings about the offender to get in the way of maintaining a professional demeanor. It is easy to forget that offenders usually have a history of making bad decisions and aren't afraid to manipulate officers to get what is needed. It is then that the officer has put his or her job, credibility, and integrity on the line.

The solution may not be easy for some officers; it may mean that officers have to find a balance between their desire to help and an unshakeable professionalism. Although the officer in *Fare v. Michael C.* did not cross the line, other officers have without hesitation, because of the offender's age, the offender's mental capacity, or the relationship the officer had with the offender. Officers must ask themselves if their conduct with an offender would be viewed as professional by a judge, a supervisor, or higher authority. An officer's commitment to practice professionalism must be reaffirmed each day.

95. Which of the following best expresses the author's viewpoint in this passage?
   a. The case *Fare v. Michael C.* established parameters for juvenile probation officers.
   b. Officers must recognize their relationship with their offenders is a professional one, and not allow themselves to act unbecoming or in an unprofessional fashion.
   c. It is always better to be a hard and direct probation/parole officer, because offenders will always manipulate situations and get officers into trouble.
   d. Probation and parole officers do not have to be notified in a timely fashion when an offender is in custody.

96. The U.S. Supreme Court affirmed the conviction in the *Fare v. Michael C.* case and established which of the following principles?
   a. Juveniles must be provided reasonable notice of charges and counsel appointed by the state.
   b. Juveniles must be read their rights once placed into custody.
   c. Probationer and probation officer communications are not privileged, and the officer's loyalty is to the state.
   d. Juveniles must be given due process rights when transferred from juvenile to adult court.

97. Which of the following is NOT correct regarding *Fare v. Michael C.*?
  a. This case made the probation officer's communications covered under the privileged information.
  b. An offender must ask for an attorney to be present, if that is his or her desire, when he or she is questioned by police.
  c. A probation officer's loyalty must be with the state, not the offender, no matter what the circumstances.
  d. This case made the probation officer's job more difficult, because now they must be careful to watch what is said in conversation with offenders.

98. What did Michael C. do while being questioned by police?
  a. He made statements and drew sketches that incriminated him.
  b. He confessed to the murder.
  c. He refused to answer any questions until his probation officer was present.
  d. He refused to answer any questions until his attorney was present.

99. In the author's opinion, which of the following is the reason that there is misconduct among some probation and parole officers with regard to offenders?
  a. There isn't misconduct with officers with regard to offenders because officers know the line of professionalism.
  b. Officers allow their personal opinions and feelings about the offender to get in the way of maintaining a professional demeanor.
  c. Usually, the officers who cross the line of professionalism have a social work background.
  d. Offenders are really good at manipulation, and all officers will get manipulated by an offender before the end of their career.

100. When a probationer is advised of his Miranda rights, he has the ability to
  a. waive his right to have an attorney present during questioning.
  b. ask for his probation officer to be notified of his arrest.
  c. remain silent until his attorney is present for questioning.
  d. choices **a** and **c**

► Answers

1. a. The *Gagnon v. Scarpelli* case provides constitutional due process rights to probationers prior to and during the probation revocation process. Choice **b** involves processes available for parolees that were established under *Morrissey v. Brewer*. Choices **c** and **d** are not significant cases because diversion is a criminal justice process available prior to probation, and if violations occur, a defendant would revert to a hearing on the original charge and may face probation if convicted. Community corrections revocation processes (choice **d**) would fall under either the probation revocation process or parole, if the offender is a parolee.

2. b. The court must order any fines and/or restitution to be paid. Restitution requires the offender to pay money or provide a service to the victim or to the community. A fine is a cash payment, such as court costs, fees for treatment, or victim compensation, that is determined by the court. Choice **a** is incorrect because the probation officer cannot add or modify probation conditions without a judge's approval. The victim can, in fact, request compensation, but this is usually done through the PSI, and the request is provided to the court, which means choice **c** is incorrect. Choice **d** is incorrect because fines are part of the original sentence, not added as a later punishment.

3. d. As of January 1, 2005, more than four million adults were on probation supervision on a federal, state, or local level. One out of every 53 persons who are 18 years of age or older is on probation. As of January 1, 2005, nearly 1.5 million adults were under the jurisdiction of state and federal prison authorities (choice **b**). Choice **a** is incorrect because more than 700,000 people were on parole as of January 1, 2005. State parolees make up 88% of the adults on parole; the rest are on federal parole. Choice **c** is incorrect; because of the number of court programs used, it is difficult to obtain an exact number of people who have been through a diversion program.

4. a. There are 36.6% of offenders on probation for property crimes (choice **a**). Drug crimes come in second, with 30.7% of the offenders (choice **b**). Choice **c**, violent crimes, make up 19.5%, and public order offenses, choice **d**, account for 12.1% of all probation offenders.

5. b. Because the purpose of Intensive Supervision Probation is to provide more structure to the offender, the ISP officer has more face-to-face contact with the offenders. Choice **a** is incorrect because both programs offer a great deal of flexibility depending on the offender and his or her particular supervision needs. Choice **c** is incorrect because the resources available to probationers should be consistent no matter what level of supervision they have. Choice **d** is incorrect because both programs can conduct surveillance on offenders, although ISP surveillance is more intensive.

6. c. The primary functions of a juvenile probation officer are to do an intake screening, conduct presentence investigations, and provide supervision to the juvenile. Choice **a** lists only two roles a juvenile probation officer must fulfill in the commission of his or her duties. Choice **b** incorrectly lists the function of being a community representative. Choice **d** lists functions that are not part of a juvenile probation officer's responsibilities.

7. c. *Fare v. Michael C.* was the case in which the Supreme Court stated that communication between a juvenile probation officer and an offender is not protected by the same privilege that attorneys share with their clients.

Also, the Supreme Court indicated that the officer's loyalties are to the state, not the offender, regardless of any specific circumstances. Choice **a** concerns the need to read defendants/offenders their rights when they are taken into custody. *Kent v. United States* (choice **b**) concerns juveniles obtaining due process rights when transferred from a juvenile court into an adult court. Choice **d** concerns the leading case for juveniles where they must be given four due process rights in adjudication proceedings.

8. d. All of the issues listed (choices **a**, **b**, and **c**) are vital to the successful completion of any community supervision. Employment will obviously help with financial obligations, but it will also enable an offender to feel self-worth, which may help avoid drug and alcohol abuse. Drug and alcohol abuse (choice **b**) is another critical issue that must be overcome, and an offender must be diligent in obtaining and continuing his or her counseling if they are to be successful on supervision.

9. d. On a national scale, the average caseload for a probation officer is around 127. If a probation officer is assigned offenders who require highly intensive supervision, he or she will have a number of caseloads in the range of choice **a**. Choice **c** is the range of cases (average of 63) that *parole* officers would handle on their individual caseloads. Choice **b** represents the national average for caseloads of special needs offenders (substance abuse, sex offenders, etc.).

10. c. The sentencing court is the only body with the authority to revoke probation. Choice **a** is incorrect because the supervising officer's responsibility is to create the report informing the court of the violations. Choice **b** would eliminate the flexibility officers need while supervising offenders. Some agencies have violation grids that provide sanctions

according to the violation; however, they still allow flexibility in supervision and do not require mandates. Choice **d** is incorrect; this action would fill the jails and prisons quickly and overwhelm the state budgets.

11. d. Parole officers or agents are responsible for the supervision of those offenders who are released from prison so that they may complete their sentence as members of the community. Offenders supervised within the community instead of entering prison would be supervised by probation officers (choice **a**). Parole board members (choice **b**) decide which offender on an indeterminate sentence should be released from prison to be supervised within the community. They establish the supervision guidelines but do not provide supervision to the offenders or to the parole officers. Choice **c** is incorrect; correctional officers supervise incarcerated offenders only.

12. c. Choice **b** names conditions that are offered to everyone under supervision. These conditions are usually established by the judge (for probation) and by the parole authority (for parole). Choices **a** and **d** are not legal terms for conditions.

13. b. In a technical violation, a new criminal offense has not been committed, yet violations of parole conditions have occurred. Choice **a** is, in fact, when a new criminal offense has occurred. Choices **c** and **d** are not technical or legal terms used for violations of conditions.

14. d. The Fourteenth Amendment indicates that no state shall make or enforce any law that shall abridge the privileges or immunities of citizens of the United States; nor shall any state deprive any person of life, liberty, or property, without due process of law; nor deny to any person within its jurisdiction the equal protection of the laws. Choice **a** is a protection against cruel and unusual punishment. Choice **b** deals with the rights of Americans to be safe and secure in their persons, houses, papers, and effects, against unreasonable searches and seizures. Choice **c** deals with the freedoms of speech, expression, and religion.

15. b. Community service, often referred to as a "fine of time," requires the offender to work a specified number of hours in unpaid positions within nonprofit or tax-supported agencies. Choice **c** is a financial penalty that offender must pay for the time the court spent in processing and working with the offender's case. Choice **d** is the established amount of money the offender must pay to be supervised by the agency. Choice **a** is the payment of money made by the offender to the victim as compensation for the harm caused (restitution may be paid to the court who in turn pays the victim).

16. d. Only the judge has the authority to issue probation violation warrants. The probation officer (choice **b**) will write the report requesting the warrant but does not have the authority to issue the warrant. The prosecutor (choice **a**) is not involved in the revocation process. The local police department, choice **c**, will receive the warrant after the judge has issued it.

17. a. Due process rights afforded to probationers are the same as those afforded to parolees in revocation proceedings. Choice **d** would be unconstitutional because the Fourteenth Amendment affords equal protection of the law, including due process. Choices **b** and **c** are simply incorrect answers because they rank one stage of the criminal justice process higher than the other.

18. c. Parole offenders, probation violators, and prerelease offenders are the only clientele who live in residential facilities run or funded by the state department of correc-

tions. Choice **d** is incorrect because an offender who has completed supervision may be in a halfway house, but would not be in a residential center funded by state or federal departments of corrections. Choice **a** is incorrect because offenders awaiting sentencing are usually held in a detention facility. Choice **b** is incorrect because offenders awaiting trial are either out on bond or held in a detention facility because of their risk to the community.

19. d. Federal probation officers are now responsible for supervising people placed under supervision for a federal crime (choice **a**), those who have been released to supervision from a federal prison (choice **b**), and military parolees (choice **c**).

20. c. *Parens patria* is a Latin term that refers to the state acting as a guardian of minors and incompetent people. Choice **a** is the Latin term for "a guilty mind." Choice **b** is the Latin term for "in the place of a parent," referring to the legal responsibility of a person or organization to take on some of the functions and responsibilities of a parent. In *loco parentis* is used mostly to educational institutions. Choice **d** is the Latin term for "wrong in itself," meaning an act that is illegal or inherently evil (i.e., murder or rape).

21. a. A juvenile who is to be charged with a crime in the adult system is arrested as an adult. Choice **d** describes when a juvenile is kept in the juvenile system to answer for the charge. Choice **b** describes the adult trial phase. Choice **c** is usually completed after the juvenile is taken into custody. The intake phase is the most critical processing stage in the juvenile justice system; the juvenile is screened to determine if the case should go further in the juvenile justice system or whether the case can be resolved by utilizing other resources or alternatives.

22. d. A status offender is a juvenile who has committed an act that applies only to juveniles (truancy, for example); if an adult committed the same act, it would not warrant law enforcement action. A delinquent juvenile, choice **c**, has committed an act that is punishable by law and can be adjudicated. Choices **a** and **b** name specific status offenders who are involved in actions such as truancy or incorrigibility and simply need supervision.

23. d. Juveniles do not have the same rights as adults with regard to jury trials, although a state can provide a jury trial if wished. Choice **a** is afforded by the First Amendment. Choice **b** is protected by the Fourteenth Amendment. Choice **c** is afforded by the Eighth Amendment.

24. b. Many agencies will require an offender to become bonded if the position requires the employee to handle money transactions or certain types of merchandise. Choice **a** is a requirement for many employers and many types of positions. Choice **c** is an action that only the governor or the president can take; usually employment does not demand a pardon. Choice **d** is also not a requirement of many jobs; however, if the job required nationwide travel, it might become an issue.

25. d. Probation and parole officers must be diligent in learning about the new laws that are passed nationally to ensure that the offenders are following those laws. In Megan's Law, all sex offenders must register with the designated law enforcement agency, but also the state must make private and personal information on registered sex offenders available to the public. Choices **a** and **b** are incorrect because registration of convicted felons of most other crimes is not a requirement in any state. Specific criminal categories (sex offenders) must register, but, to date, registration is not required for all felons or those convicted

of firearm violations. Choice **c** is incorrect because states do not require parole violators to register with them, but states do have various databases that collect information on parole violators and convicted felons.

26. a. A parole officer must always remember the parole conditions. If the offender requests an action that may be in violation of those conditions, then the officer is bound to remind the offender of that condition. However, the officer should also describe an appropriate alternative process, if one exists—in this case, reminding the offender that he must receive permission from the warden. Choice **b** is not appropriate, because this action circumvents the offender's responsibilities and possibly parole conditions. Choice **c** could potentially cause conflict between the offender and officer. Telling someone he or she cannot contact a family member without giving alternative options and opportunities will only cause hurt feelings. Choice **d** is certainly an option, but it may leave an impression with the offender that the officer isn't willing to help and assist with legitimate requests when needed, and may make the offender stop asking for help all together.

27. c. If the victim has received an anonymous letter that has made her feel threatened, then she should follow the normal course of action, which is to involve the police. If the officer knows of a particular unit or person who might handle this type of situation, then the officer should provide that specific information. The officer should then work closely with the police department to aid in its investigation by checking the files to compare handwriting. A special "no contact" condition might need to be put in place, if it hasn't already been. Telling the victim to throw the letter away could be impeding an investigation and is not wise advice. Also, telling the victim not to worry about the letter (choice **b**) is inappropriate. Choice **a** is the wrong action to take without further investigation into the matter (by the police department). Choice **d** is inappropriate and unwise advice; if your agency has a program in which victims are encouraged to discuss the crime with the offender(s), doing that outside of the program could lead to a potential violation or another crime.

28. d. Joint activities such as stakeouts require and can nurture interagency cooperation and good public relations. Although such activities can interrupt life outside the office, there are usually benefits for the agency and the participating officer. Choice **a** might be an option if your field officer is new or better equipped to handle such an activity (i.e., you have a medical condition that would interfere). Choice **b** is never an option: If you receive a request from your supervisor, you must comply, unless the request is illegal. Choice **c** is also not appropriate, because you cannot demand what is outside of the Federal Labor Standards Act.

29. b. You should wait until an appropriate break in the interview, when you and one or both of the detectives step outside of the defendant's hearing, and tell them about your concern. When you are asked to assist in such activities, you are there only as an observer, not as a primary participant (choices **a** and **c**). Doing either of these actions would damage your relationship with the detectives and/or the relationship between the two agencies. Choice **d** is definitely not an action you should take in this situation. You are there only to ensure the defendant's safety, not to act as his or her advocate.

30. c. Officers must make decisions about priorities on a daily basis, and unfortunately some of the more enjoyable activities must take sec-

ond place when performance standards need to be met (choice **a**). In this case, a certain number of field contacts must be made each month in order for officers to satisfy the agency's requirements. Choice **b** is not appropriate because you are placing your supervisor in a position in which he or she must give you a direct order to complete your job as required. Choice **d** is not appropriate, because generally agencies will not pay overtime unless approved beforehand. Working unapproved overtime puts you at risk to have employment action taken against you.

31. c. There may be another way into the house, but more important, you can check through the windows to see if you can find Brian. If there is another entrance, you need to make sure you announce yourself clearly and loudly. Choice **a** might be an option if the offender doesn't sound disoriented and confused, as is the case in this question. Choice **b** is only an option when parole officers are considered actual law enforcement and when agency policy allows such action; however, most states do not allow this, and doing so could possibly put the officer and the agency at risk for liable court action. Choice **d** is an option if, in your initial check (choice **c**) of the house, through the windows you see something illegal or you see the offender doing something illegal. If the offender is motionless and clearly medically distressed, then an ambulance should be called, to which the police will respond as well.

32. b. Even though some officers have a difficult time accepting praise, it is important to the offender that the officer accept his emotional thank-you. It is also appropriate to tell the offender what steps are necessary to ensure this situation doesn't happen again. Setting up a calling system with a hospice, having a nurse or caseworker come visit, or adopting a proper diet are three examples of steps an officer should suggest to the offender. Choice **a** is incorrect because saving someone's life is important and should be recognized, no matter how uncomfortable. Officers save lives many times and should be proud of their actions and clear thinking. Not acknowledging his thank-you could also give the wrong message to the offender. Choice **c** is not something that should be discussed while the offender is still so emotional; the parole officer may also not be the appropriate person to tell the offender this. However, the parole officer may wish to connect the offender to resources within the hospital or community diabetic organization. Choice **d** is incorrect because it might lead the offender to believe he is more trouble and could cause conflict between the officer and offender.

33. d. Talking to the offender and telling him why you must stop yourself from being overly involved is being honest and clear with the offender. An officer must be able to extract him- or herself so the offender doesn't feel he or she has done anything wrong, a feeling which might lead the offender to take drastic or illegal measures. The officer should also try to replace what is being taken away, which in this situation is the offender's support system. Finding resources or volunteers within the community is also an officer's responsibility.

34. c. Gaining the input from the counselor would be vital in this situation because the counselor should have a good handle on the offender's mental capacity. If he or she agrees that services could be reduced, then the counselor should provide the officer with a new, agreed-upon counseling schedule. This action will validate the partnership you have with the offender as well as the reward system based on appropriate and good behavior.

Choice **a** is incorrect because the parole officer does not need permission to add and modify special conditions, unless specified by state policies and procedures; however, only the paroling authority can remove a special condition. Choice **b** cannot be done without gaining input from the counselor. Choice **d** does not acknowledge the offender's progress nor give credibility to the offender's concerns; however, this may be appropriate action if the request comes shortly after counseling starts or if the offender has not reported for the counseling.

35. b. Telling a supervisor to leave you alone until there are specific allegations to discuss, or demanding the names of other officers who might be spreading gossip (choices **c** and **d**), is not the appropriate or professional way to resolve this situation. Also, choice **a** is not the best response when a supervisor questions your actions because it may cause the supervisor's suspicions to grow or cause the supervisor to look into your actions with more scrutiny. Choice **b** is the correct response to this situation; letting the supervisor know the specifics of your supervision of this offender is the only way to alleviate his or her concerns regarding your conduct. Providing honest and direct information is always the best way to address concerns regarding your work and conduct.

36. a. Not taking appropriate action (choices **c** and **d**) could bring about legal actions and would raise concerns at your agency regarding your unwillingness to offer assistance when needed. Choice **b** is incorrect because officers trained and certified in life-saving procedures must render aid immediately. Failure to act could put you, your certification, and your job in jeopardy.

37. c. The death of a family member, a friend, or an offender always has some effect on the officer.

The supervisor should suggest that the officer attend one or more counseling sessions, but if he or she doesn't, the officer should take it upon him- or herself to seek out this help. Not dealing with death appropriately may result in inappropriate behavior that may be harmful to the officer as well as to others. Choice **a** is not a healthy way to deal with this type of situation, although this may be what most officers do because of peer pressure. Choice **b** is taking the situation to the extreme because funeral leave is offered by agencies only for the death of immediate families. If an officer must deal with personal effects of an offender, it is considered agency business and should be conducted during business hours. Choice **d** may be appropriate to some degree, but peers are usually not equipped to help an officer deal with his or her grief in an appropriate fashion.

38. a. Insisting that offenders follow the rules and procedures of supervision is one tool officers use when offenders request permission to do something. An officer must learn behavior management techniques to assist offenders in earning positive rewards for doing as expected under supervision. The earned reward system also teaches offenders that if they do not behave as required, they will not be granted their requests, for reasons other than "the officer doesn't like me." Choice **b** may be true; however, this tactic is harsh and more of a punishment. It is important to give offenders a achievable goal to work toward. Choice **c** is incorrect because there have been some violations, especially the failure to report, which cannot be forgotten or excused without any consequence. Choice **d** is not an appropriate or professional response.

39. b. Providing the father with your supervisor's name and number is the correct response. This is a reasonable request on his part, how-

ever irate he may be at the time. Your supervisor should talk with you prior to speaking with the father to hear your side of the story. Choice **a** may be an option; however, if someone has asked for your supervisor's name and number, they do not wish to discuss the issue any further with you. Trying to continue the conversation may cause your already difficult relationship with the father to become more problematic. Choice **c** is incorrect because you would be speaking for your supervisor without their knowledge or permission. Choice **d** is never an option. Rather, providing contact information to your supervisor would allow you to give your side of the story, and often the supervisor will support your decision in a calmer tone, so that the other party may be more receptive and accepting to the message.

40. b. It is apparent that the father feels he is not being treated fairly and needs to hear from the supervisor or officer how Shawna is doing. It may also be true that Shawna is not telling her father the whole truth. In order to accomplish your supervisor's request, you must receive Shawna's written permission so that all information (including positive news about her progress and/or what violations there may be) can be discussed. Choice **a** is incorrect because the father is apparently not satisfied with his past discussions with Shawna. It also says in the passage that Shawna is not comfortable with standing up to her father, thus placing the burden on Shawna to diffuse her father's anger is only setting her up for failure. Choice **c** is inappropriate. Ignoring calls or telling offenders to ignore their families will only cause further conflict for the offender. Choice **d** is probably not an appropriate decision to suggest at this point in the supervision period.

41. d. Helping the offender feel in control of this situation will help her feel in control in later situations as well. Choice **b** would be good actions to take *after* you help Shawna learn to control to her fears, and contacting the Interstate Compact office and/or the sending officer would help them enhance their supervision or take precautions regarding that offender. Choice **a** is a response an officer should avoid because it tells the offender her fears are not valid and can be dismissed as unimportant. Also, offenders can find their way onto an airplane without a travel permit: If the ex-boyfriend's intent is to see Shawna, he is unlikely to follow through the proper procedure. Choice **c** is incorrect because the Interstate Compact office is overwhelmed with paperwork and would not be able to provide assistance as immediate as necessary.

42. c. Communicating his concerns to the offender may be difficult, but the friend should understand that the action is essential for all parties. The probation officer has been asked to address the concerns of someone who is not the offender, but the officer should not try to help fix their relationship. An officer must not allow him- or herself to get caught in this web. Simply providing assistance to the offender and the friend in how to communicate about their concerns will be helpful in the long run; any further assistance should come from a counselor referred by the probation officer. Choice **a** is incorrect because officers cannot discuss what supervision needs are necessary for offenders; this may be an option after you meet with the offender to see if she has discussed these concerns with her friend. Or, if you observe the offender's strange behavior, then a urinalysis can be requested; however, the friend should not be informed of this action. Choice **b** is incorrect because again the officer is not permitted to communicate any information learned from the offender, unless danger is foreseen. Choice **d** is not appropriate because the friend made the effort to call, and this type of response implies the officer is cold and uncaring and could have a negative impact.

43. a. Allowing someone to vent their frustrations is important, as long as they are not hurting themselves or others. In this question, Jesse isn't hurting anyone with her comments or by shouting. An empathic officer would contact her either in person or by phone the next day to ensure she is safe and hopefully starting to deal with the frustrations of how her life has changed. Choice **b** is incorrect because a probation officer should not think or feel less of offenders or believe that they have wasted their lives. Choices **c** and **d** are incorrect because these actions would only cause Jesse to become angrier and possibly aggressive.

44. a. It is important to remind the offender of the conditions and ask again if there are any weapons, affording the offender one more opportunity to speak truthfully regarding any other weapons. Choices **b** and **c** will depend on the agency's policy on searches, but usually the police are not called to search an offender's home. A probation and parole officer has the ability to do a visual search of open areas, and upon suspicion, a probation officer would have to return to court. Police must have a warrant to enter a house to do a search. Choice **d** is incorrect because this action could possibly instigate more animosity from the offender toward you and her situation.

45. b. Some offenders often have difficult accepting their loss of authority or the officer's position of power over them. These feelings may manifest in a power struggle between the offender and officer. Choices **a** and **c** would only play into this power struggle and would more than likely allow the offender's hostility to continue. Good communication is often a successful tool to get offenders to comply with conditions they don't understand or like. Choice **b** is the correct action to take, because the offender may have other situations that need attention before she can accept the possibility of a drug problem. Having the offender talk with a counselor may also help get over her fear of being unemployed, her lack of alternative skills, her grief over the loss of her job, and other pertinent issues. Choice **d** would not help anyone move beyond the hostility and denial, nor is it a professional action to take.

46. b. Referring the offender to employment resources should be your first priority. Finding work adds to an offender's feeling of self-worth and eases depression, anxiety, and other feelings that accompany low self-esteem. Choice **a** is not a response that an empathic officer would give. Rather, this action might give the offender the impression that you are not going to help them. This action may cause the offender to give up, leading to even more adverse effects on the offender. Choice **c** would be an option only if the offender's depression or drug use became more of a primary concern. Choice **d** is a law enforcement approach and could have an adverse effect on the offender.

47. b. In this situation, getting the offender to feel like she is in control rather than a victim is important. Even though some of the action that must be taken will be inconvenient, usually taking steps like these suggestions will slow down the behavior. Choice **a** is not an option at this point because there is suspicion of the other offenders' involvement. Convincing the other probation officers to talk with their offenders might only heighten the harassing behavior, especially if the offenders are being unfairly accused of it. Choice **c** is incorrect advice for a probation officer to give. Suggesting a phone tap and a surveillance camera is a bit extreme, although talking with the landlord about the offender's issues is a realistic step. Also, having a locked mailbox is also important, as long as the mail can continue to be delivered. Choice **d** might give the offender the perception that you don't care or that you think her concerns are frivolous.

48. a. It is not illegal to have a police band radio in one's home, so there isn't a violation of probation or an illegal act being committed here. One would question whether it is healthy to do this, but no action needs be taken in this situation. Choice **b** may be true, but telling an offender to remove something from his or her home simply because you don't approve is not a valid action. Choice **c** is inappropriate; an officer should not place special conditions on probationers simply to keep them busy. All conditions must be clear, reasonable, and justified. Choice **d** might be something worth suggesting, although continuously pointing out what the offender has lost will likely have a detrimental effect.

49. b. The offender is intent on having the little girl. The case study indicates that James is very attached to this little girl, which could mean that presenting him with an alternative option could seen as you not trusting him to avoid criminal activities. If his mother is the primary caregiver, he could still visit the child, while the ex-girlfriend contacted the little girl's mother instead of the offender. Choice **a** would not be a viable option because you would be condoning contact between the offender and the ex-girlfriend, leading the offender to believe that further contact would be appropriate. Choice **c** could cause conflict between you and the offender by again suggesting that you do not trust him. Choice **d** is not a helpful resolution because it would certainly cause conflict between you and the offender, and may cause the offender to do it anyway.

50. c. Often, social service agencies will be able to provide free passes to offenders in need of extra services. The agency may ask for community service in their neighborhood to help compensate for the passes. In other states, parole offices obtain extra transportation passes to provide to offenders who are in need. Choice **d** is a good secondary option; many religious groups and clubs are willing to sponsor people with such needs; however, this is not the best answer choice. Choice **a** would only make the offender feel as if he is not trusted, which could have an adverse effect on him. Choice **b** would definitely cause conflict between you and the offender.

51. c. It is the responsibility of the officer to check out information and stories he or she receives. Although it is possible that the offender is not involved, an officer cannot trust that to always be the case. Not checking out information received (choice **d**) would be irresponsible. Choice **b** would leave the impression you are brushing aside her concerns and information, which could lead to future problems for you, especially if her report was correct and violence ensued. Choice **a** would not be a wise choice until you verified the information you received. Calling the detectives could also lead to problems for your offender.

52. d. The case study mentions that James is on the waiting list for a treatment halfway house. Taking James there would allow the staff to screen him to see what the immediate problem is or what drug would produce these symptoms. Although conducting a urinalysis

(choice **a**) would provide results in a day or two, the officer needs to have an immediate explanation for James's symptoms. The halfway house staff is equipped, more so than most officers, to obtain information from offenders regarding their drug use and problems. Choice **b** will not ensure that the officer can obtain the information needed to assist the offender, nor does it ensure the offender will actually go to the hospital unless the officer drives him there. Choice **c** again may tell the officer what drug is causing the offender's symptoms, but this action does not get the offender immediate help and assistance.

53. a. Although this situation is not ideal, nor up to your own standards of living, the offender has the right to choose his living conditions. An officer's questions, requests, and demands must fall within the boundaries of the position, not be based on the officer's own morals or values. Choice **b** is incorrect; special conditions are to be used to protect the community or to help with the rehabilitation of the offender, not impose the officer's personal standards on the offender. Choice **c** may be true, but telling an offender how to maintain his home is not within the officer's realm of authority. Choice **d** is also incorrect. Instead of demanding the offender leave his home, an officer concerned about the safety could only suggest that the offender contact the insurance company or a building inspector to ensure the house is livable.

54. b. Because he was released into the community only because of the waiting list at the treatment halfway house, James has known the time would come when he would need to attend the treatment program. Also, the case study indicates that this is a special condition that must be adhered to. Special conditions can be modified because of circumstances, but in this case, based upon this offender's history and observed behavior, passing up this opportunity would not be in the best interest of the offender. Therefore, choice **a** is incorrect. Choice **c** could cause conflict between you and the offender, when your working relationship seems to be pleasant and productive. Choice **d** is an attempt to pass the decision off to the halfway house staff members, making them act as the "bad guy" in this situation. Officers need to be direct and honest with offenders, while being tactful and professional when providing assistance and guidance.

55. a. As difficult as it is sometimes, doing your own work and not worrying about others will result in longer-lasting, more positive benefits for you than if you tried to even the score in this situation. A supervisor reviewing case files can easily see which officers are caught up on their case files, and thus managing their time well, and which aren't. Choice **b** will only create conflict between you and your coworkers and give others a bad impression of you, especially if you are their peer or lower in seniority. Choice **c** will only make you look unprofessional and will bring consequences when you are not caught up with your files. Choice **d** would certainly create conflict in the office and for you directly; it is important to pick your battles wisely.

56. b. To maintain the relationships within the office and not to add to the growing tension already felt, you should ask the supervisors to get involved, without pointing fingers at the offender or the accuser. Hopefully, the supervisors address this issue without pointing fingers, and everyone would be safe. Choices **a** and **d** would only imply that the less experienced officers' concern, and implied safety, is meaningless, and would serve only to put you in the middle of the conflict. Choice **c** would add to the growing tension and would not

serve any purpose other than to create more controversy in the office.

57. c. Although this action might be difficult for you, it is best to let your peers know the break room isn't the place to be talking about other peers and that they should stop. You can't stop them from talking about it at all, but at least you can request or suggest they gossip about others outside of the office. Choice **a** might be more comfortable for you, but it isn't the responsible action to take. Choice **b** also isn't responsible, and in doing this, you would only be contributing to the unprofessional conduct within the office. Choice **d** would only add to the tension in the office and should not be considered an appropriate first step. As an adult and a professional employee, you should take steps to resolve issues yourself before involving others.

58. c. Yelling at the officers to stop will hopefully provide a diversion for them, and they will stop fighting each other. If they don't respond to the yelling, continue to tell them to stop fighting but wait for help to arrive before doing anything else. Then, once more parole officers arrive to help you, pull the fighting officers apart or step in between them to get them to stop. Stepping in between the fighting officers (choice **b**) may cause you to get injured, but it may be necessary. Do not take this action if you are the only officer available. Choice **a** is not acceptable behavior. The offender in your office has already heard the scuffle and yelling between the officers. Using the offender as an excuse to go back into your office does not diffuse the situation between the fighting officers and allows them time to continue to harm each other. Choice **d** would lead to questions about your actions once the episode is over. Not taking action in this situation would certainly make others question your abilities to protect yourself and others.

59. b. Although it is not necessary that you tell the officer making offensive comments that you are offended, an experienced officer should take the opportunity to educate the less experienced. The less experienced officer may not realize he is making a discriminatory comment about your age, and your guidance may help him to understand why he should stop making such comments. Choice **a** would be unprofessional and possibly cause you to be charged with a crime. Choice **c** might be the easiest thing to do, but it would not stop the behavior. Choice **d** would make you as guilty as the offending officer and is not a correct response in this situation.

60. d. In this situation, an investigation is being conducted after a complaint was made regarding these officers' comments and conduct within the office. Although you were not told of any complaints, you have a responsibility to provide truthful and factual information when asked by an official of the agency. Not providing information (choice **c**) is irresponsible and could lead to employment action being taken against you. Choice **b** is also an inappropriate response. Even if you do not know why the questions are being asked, most agencies have a policy that mandates officers cooperate in an investigation. Choice **a** is also not an option because you are already involved in this situation.

61. a. This sentence is correctly punctuated. This statement is clear and easy to read, with the reader understanding the what, who and where of the sentence. In choice **b**, the fragment needs to be added to the sentence. Choice **c** is incorrect because there are unnecessary and incorrectly used commas and semicolons. Choice **d** is incorrect because of the unnecessary and misused semicolon and colon.

62. b. Choice **b** has several unnecessary commas that inhibit the reader's ability to understand the sentence. Also, the use of semicolons toward the end of the sentence is incorrect. The other sentences (choices **a**, **c**, and **d**) are all correctly punctuated.

63. c. This sentence has two parts or actions that are easily separated with the comma. The sentence remains clear to understand and easy to read. Choice **a** has misplaced commas, which disrupt the flow of the sentence. Choice **b** incorrectly places a colon at the beginning of the first sentence and unnecessarily breaks the sentence into two with a misplaced period. Choice **d** doesn't have any punctuation at all, which makes the sentence hard to digest. Without a comma, there isn't a pause, or breath, to signify the two actions that should take place. The lack of punctuation could lead to confusion on the reader's part.

64. a. Choice **c** indicates officers shall provide every person something, but it is not clear that it is *professional, courteous, effective, and efficient service*. Choices **b** and **d** are incorrect because the reader has to figure out how the phrase *or that of other officers* fits in both sentences.

65. d. Although the reader may be able to figure out the meaning of the sentence, it is not presented in a clear and appropriate fashion. Choices **a**, **b**, and **c** are written clearly so the reader understands what is expected or what action should not be taken.

66. c. This sentence is clear and easy to understand. Choice **a** has a misplaced phrase at the beginning of the sentence; the sentence would be clearer if the phrase *sexual harassment offenses* replaced the word *acts* in this sentence. In choice **b**, it is not clear exactly who is tolerating the acts and who is committing them. Choice **d** is incorrect because the awkward order of the phrases does not allow an easy read and ultimately leaves the reader confused.

67. d. Choice **a** has several misspelled words. In choice **b**, the word *no* should be *know*, the word *there* should be *their*, and the verb *isn't* is in the wrong tense. Choice **c** is incorrect because the word *advice* is spelled incorrectly, and the phrase *any peoples* should be *any person*.

68. d. The words *well* and *good* are often misused. The adjective *good* is used to describe nouns and pronouns; the adverb *well* is used to modify verbs—in this case, it modifies the verb *feel*. In choice **a**, the word *accept* should be *except*. The verb *accept* means "to receive or to approve of," whereas *except* means "to exclude." Choice **b** is technically incorrect because the verb *can* asks if you have the ability to do something, while the verb *may* asks for permission to do something. Choice **c** is incorrect because the verb *done* is not used properly; the sentence should read either "The officer did" or "The officer had done."

69. c. The adverbs *especially* and *specially* are often confused. *Especially* implies that an action is exceptional or noteworthy, and *specially* describes an action that is done for a particular purpose or in a particular way. Choice **a** is incorrect because the word *moralle* should be *moral*. The noun *morale* refers to a person's or group's emotional well-being, while the adjective *moral* is a synonym for *ethical* or *virtuous*. Choice **b** is incorrect because the verb *persecute* means "to harass or afflict," which is probably not what the prosecutor was intending to do. He was probably trying to *prosecute* the offender, because that word means "to bring legal action against." Choice **d** is incorrect because the word *rise* should be *raise*, which means "to increase or generate."

70. a. Parole and probation officers who use this system are able to focus their attention more on high-risk offenders who require intensive supervision. Choice **b** is partially true because the complaints taken to the Supreme Court have been dismissed. Choice **c** expands on a point in paragraph 3; however, there are only two disadvantages listed in this passage. Choice **d** is incorrect because it is never a valid reason for an agency to invest time and money in programs.

71. b. The SMART system establishes zones so officers can determine in which areas the offender should and, more important, should not be. This tool is especially useful in keeping sex offenders away from schools, day care centers, and other trigger spots. Choice **a** is true; however, as cited in paragraph 2, the more important goal of the system is to designate areas that the offender should not be traveling into. Choice **c** is simply not true; the electronic monitoring systems discussed in this passage are for tracking, not punishment, and are unable to transmit electric charges. Choice **d** is also incorrect because as an electronic system, SMART eliminates the need for a paper map.

72. d. Choices **a**, **b**, and **c** have all been argued before the Supreme Court, and as indicated in paragraph 4, the court has consistently rejected the claims.

73. c. An offender must wear a permanent ankle or wrist transmitter device, a microprocessor, and an antenna. The transmitter and receiver that the offender carries connect the satellite to the central control unit that monitors the various offenders assigned to this program. Choices **a** and **d** include items that offenders cannot carry nor have in their possession. Choice **b** includes a landline phone, which is not portable. Also, the offender does not need to carry a phone system to be monitored.

74. a. The loss of the GPS signal is one of the major disadvantages to this system. There are areas in which the signal cannot reach the satellite or the cell phone as necessary. Likewise, the cost of the system does make it impossible for some agencies. Choice **b** is incorrect because a cell phone does not have to be used with this system. There is not a lack of offenders to use this system (choice **c**). Choice **d** is incorrect and an exaggeration of an idea presented in paragraph 3.

75. b. Officers are able to focus more of their traditional supervision techniques on those offenders who need more monitoring, while their low-risk offenders are monitored through GPS. This system is an alternative to imprisonment and should have a huge effect on the supervision of those officers who have low-risk offenders. Choice **a** is incorrect, because although the system may seem impersonal and is not foolproof, it has more benefits to supervision. Choice **c** is incorrect because the GPS system is used for supervision, not crime solving. The system may help provide evidence if an offender commits another crime, but its purpose is to monitor offenders' whereabouts. Choice **d** is incorrect because GPS would allow an officer to set zones for offenders who have established patterns of addiction. If an offender entered one of the zones that the officer has established as off-limits, then alarms would sound for both the offender and the monitoring computer.

76. a. As indicated in the last paragraph of the passage, the author indicated that electronic monitoring should become an alternative to prison for low-risk offenders, but he does not say that it should be the only form of supervision (choice **c**) or that it should take the place of supervision by probation and parole officers. Choices **b** and **d** are incorrect because all agencies should take advantage of this system, not just select ones.

77. d. Probationers are given the opportunity to receive the written statements of the officer and any other evidence that is to be used to ask for a probation revocation. Additionally, the probationer must be given the opportunity to be heard at the hearing and/or to present his or her case, if desired. Choice **a** is incorrect because it is the probationer's decision whether one or two hearings are held, not the state's. Choice **b** is incorrect because the probationer must receive written information of the allegation of violations shortly after his or her arrest. Choice **c** is incorrect because probation hearings are held before a judge; however, Gagnon wasn't contesting who presided over his hearing, rather the fact that he didn't have a hearing at all. It is important to know the distinction between a parolee's hearing officer, who is not an officer of the court, and the judge who hears probation violation cases.

78. c. Choices **a** and **d** are incorrect and exaggerate statements made in the last paragraph of the passage. Choice **b** extends the facts of this particular case to include all offenders and all cases, which is simply not true.

79. a. Gagnon was arrested for burglary one month after being placed on probation for robbery. Gagnon was sentenced to 15 years in prison and paroled after serving three years. Choices **b**, **c**, and **d** are incorrect. Gagnon did not have a violent criminal history, but he was more than a thief.

80. d. These five constitutional due process rights are afforded to probationers and parolees by the *Morrissey v. Brewer* decision and must be adhered to. These rights are in addition to the opportunity to have two hearings regarding the violations and revocation proceedings. Choice **a** is incorrect because having an attorney present is allowed, but it is not a right. Additionally, the disclosure of evidence and the opportunity to be heard are some, but not all, of the conditions established by the court. Choice **b** is incorrect because there wasn't a determination as to where the final hearing should take place in relation to the family or witnesses. Again, having an attorney present is not a right. Choice **c** is incorrect because an attorney is not allowed to cross-examine. An attorney *may* be present if the judge agrees; however, the attorney is only an adviser, not an active participant in the hearing. The attorney does not have the opportunity to cross-examine or to present a case. Remember, an offender does not have the right to have an attorney present at any of the revocation proceedings, but he or she may have an attorney present if the judge feels it is in the offender's best interest.

81. c. Only the judge can determine if the defendant fits the criteria to have an attorney present at the revocation hearing. An attorney could be called to appear in a case that involved a probationer being indigent or a defendant having difficulty presenting his or her case. Choice **a** is incorrect because officers should be ensuring offenders' rights are protected and afforded every day. Choice **b** is incorrect because his claims of a wrong imprisonment were based on his actions while he was on probation. Choice **d** is incorrect because attorneys are present only if and when the judge deems it in the best interest of the offender. This is decided on a case-by-case basis and only if the defendant is not able to represent him- or herself or is indigent.

82. b. *Morrissey v. Brewer* is the case that defined the constitutional rights afforded to parolees prior to and during the parole revocation process. Although closely related in subject matter, *Mempa v. Rhay* (choice **a**) occurred prior to *Gagnon v. Scarpelli* and is related

only by the question of representation, which is a small component of *Gagnon.* Choice **c** was not discussed in the passage, but *Miranda v. Arizona* decided that defendants should be afforded procedural due process rights when placed into custody. Their rights must be read to them, and they should acknowledge their understanding. Choice **d** was not discussed in the passage; *People v. Price* established that a defendant is not constitutionally entitled to a jury in a revocation process.

83. c. As stated in the last paragraph of the passage, most probationers do not worry about this process, because the majority of offenders are able to successfully complete their probations. Those who do not successfully complete their probations are returned to court or to the prison system because of new offenses (choice **c**). Choices **a** and **b** are incorrect because all offenders must be told their rights, usually on the first day of supervision but definitely when there are alleged violations to contend with. Choice **d** is incorrect, although there may be truth to this in some areas. However, this was not in the passage and is merely an implied thought from the last paragraph.

84. c. Many states are looking at expanding their current DNA collection pool to all offenders, but there are some questions and complaints about this movement. Choice **a** is implied in paragraph 3 regarding DNA being collected from people who are innocent or never charged. Choice **b** indicates that more DNA collection will solve cold cases, but as stated in paragraph 2, the hope is that future cases will also be solved using this method. Choice **d** is incorrect. Although there are many negative opinions, proponents of this expansion are working to resolve the complaints in order to expand their testing process.

85. d. More staff will need to be hired as states pass this expansion legislation; this will affect states and agencies budgets, which will need to fund the salaries, equipment, and offices for the new staff who process the DNA samples. However, this disadvantage was not mentioned in the passage. Choices **a**, **b**, and **c** are three of the complaints and concerns listed in the passage.

86. b. As cited in paragraph 2, there are 28 states currently collecting samples from misdemeanors. Five states (choice **c**) are taking DNA samples from people arrested but not necessarily charged with a crime (i.e., violent felony and burglary suspects). Choices **a** and **d** are incorrect and were not listed in the passage.

87. c. As cited in paragraph 2, most state legislatures considering this expansion cite as a benefit a larger database that samples can be run through in hopes of resolving cases, both new and old, more quickly. Choice **a** may be a result of the expanded collection, but it is not the ultimate goal. Choice **b** was not mentioned in the passage. Choice **d** is an expansion of the thought in paragraph 3, regarding one of the complaints about this movement.

88. a. The author states that we must learn to utilize technological advancements to enhance our investigation techniques, and that priorities must be shifted to fund such programs. Choice **b** is incorrect because technology is complicated for some; however, this idea is not presented in this passage. Choice **c** is also partially true because some innocent people have been convicted in the past based on DNA results. However, this is not the author's main idea in this passage. Choice **d** is also partially true; however, the widening of the collection pool may allow systems to run easier in the end.

89. d. College is important, and so is experience. Candidates should be able to obtain the necessary skills and dimensions through a variety of ways, either in the classroom or through real-world opportunities. Choice **a** is not the main theme of this passage, although a great number of administrators feel this way. Choice **b** is not the correct answer, although a candidate with a variety of experiences certainly makes a good candidate for hire. Choice **c** is an end result of this position, but it is not the main theme of the passage.

90. b. However, many colleges are starting transitional components to many degrees, which include studying or working abroad as part of the experience. In this situation, going overseas and conducting a comparative criminal justice study might provide some of the interpersonal skills necessary for an officer. However, this is where human resource professionals must be flexible in how they look at college experiences and education. Choices **a**, **c**, and **d** are all listed in the passage.

91. c. Good problem-solving skills are essential for an officer. Many officers have the ability to identify a problem, but there are many steps in the problem-solving process that officers tend to ignore or not complete (e.g., considering more than alternative for solving the problem). Choices **a**, **b**, and **d** are essential, but are not listed in the passage.

92. b. Critics believe that working inside a prison enhances the "soft" skills and ultimately makes the public safer by having officers who understand how to utilize these skills when supervising a hardened offender. Choices **a** and **c** do represent the critics' position as stated in the passage. The critics believe that education doesn't provide all of the necessary skills for a qualified probation and parole officer. They insist experience must be included as a preferred requirement, without eliminating the need for a college degree. Choice **d** is an exaggeration of a thought from paragraph 5.

93. a. As indicated in paragraph 2, 86% of states recruiting juvenile probation officers prefer a college degree. Choices **b**, **c**, and **d** are not listed in the passage.

94. c. The decision to lower hiring standards, made by the states' centralized human resource agencies, aimed to widen the application pool so agencies could have a large selection from which choose qualified applicants. As the author indicates, this change was not intended to lower the skill level of the officers being hired. Agencies are required by federal law to collect information on the demographics of their applicants and employees, but there isn't an affirmative action quota that agencies must reach. Therefore, choice **a** is incorrect. Choice **b** would be the same as lowering the skill level of the officers being hired, which is not the intent of revising the job requirement. Choice **d** is not the reason that the job requirements were revised. Although the corrections system does attract former military and law enforcement staff, those applicants come into their positions with a great deal of training and skills.

95. b. The main theme of this passage is that officers must be quick to recognize where the line is for professional and unprofessional behavior. It is essential to find a balance between the law enforcer and social worker roles and not allow the offender to prey on emotions and feelings. Choice **a** is not the author's viewpoint, although it is, in fact, true. The Supreme Court helped to clarify responsibilities of the probation officer and established that communications between an officer and an offender are not afforded the same privilege as attorney-client privilege.

Choice **c** is incorrect because being a hard and direct officer is not always the appropriate stance to take with offenders. Also, this is not the author's viewpoint in the passage. Choice **d** is also not the author's viewpoint in the passage, although it is true.

96. c. Communication between a juvenile offender and a probation officer is not considered confidential and must be reported in court. Also, the probation officer's loyalty is to the state, not to the offender, no matter how sympathetic the officer might be to the juvenile. Juveniles are provided reasonable notice of charges and counsel through the case *In re Gault* (choice **a**). Choice **b** concerns the case of *Miranda v. Arizona,* although there are some stipulations to this statement. Choice **d** refers to the case *Kent v. United States.*

97. d. This case did not make the probation officer's job or duties more difficult. An officer should not attempt to control what is or isn't said in conversations regarding a probationer's progress while under supervision. Choices **a**, **b**, and **c** are all parts of the decision made by the U.S. Supreme Court in this case.

98. a. Michael C., in fact, agreed to talk with police and, while being questioned, made statements about as well as drew sketches of the incident that admitted his involvement in the murder. Choice **b** did not happen. Choices **c** and **d** did not happen; although Michael C. did ask for his probation officer, he did not refuse to cooperate at any point in the process. The court indicated in their ruling that the probation officer is not a substitute for an attorney, and a defendant must ask for an attorney if he would like one present.

99. b. Although some offenders are good at manipulation, not all officers will fall for that manipulation (choice **d**). Also, there isn't a particular line of study that prepares officers for this manipulation (choice **c**). Thinking that there isn't misconduct would misguided because officer misconduct is the primary reason for employment actions (choice **a**). Choice **b** is correct because the author indicates that officers cross the line when they are not able to keep their personal and professional feelings separate.

100.d. A probationer can, in fact, waive his or her right to have an attorney present during questioning (choice **a**), or request an attorney and then wait until the attorney is present before being questioned (choice **c**). A probationer can also request that his or her probation officer be notified of his arrest; however, this is not part of the Miranda rights (choice **b**). This request may be done at some point after questioning and when the investigation is under way.

10 ▶ Practice Test 3

This is the third practice test in this book and is based on the most commonly tested areas on probation officer and parole officer exams. Remember, the exam you take may *look* somewhat different from this exam, but you'll find that this exam provides vital practice in the skills you need to pass your exam.

The practice test consists of 100 multiple-choice questions in the following areas: job responsibilities, case studies, writing skills, and reading comprehension. You should allow yourself three hours to take this practice test. The number of questions and the time limit of the actual probation officer or parole officer exam can vary from region to region.

Practice Test 3

1.	ⓐ	ⓑ	ⓒ	ⓓ
2.	ⓐ	ⓑ	ⓒ	ⓓ
3.	ⓐ	ⓑ	ⓒ	ⓓ
4.	ⓐ	ⓑ	ⓒ	ⓓ
5.	ⓐ	ⓑ	ⓒ	ⓓ
6.	ⓐ	ⓑ	ⓒ	ⓓ
7.	ⓐ	ⓑ	ⓒ	ⓓ
8.	ⓐ	ⓑ	ⓒ	ⓓ
9.	ⓐ	ⓑ	ⓒ	ⓓ
10.	ⓐ	ⓑ	ⓒ	ⓓ
11.	ⓐ	ⓑ	ⓒ	ⓓ
12.	ⓐ	ⓑ	ⓒ	ⓓ
13.	ⓐ	ⓑ	ⓒ	ⓓ
14.	ⓐ	ⓑ	ⓒ	ⓓ
15.	ⓐ	ⓑ	ⓒ	ⓓ
16.	ⓐ	ⓑ	ⓒ	ⓓ
17.	ⓐ	ⓑ	ⓒ	ⓓ
18.	ⓐ	ⓑ	ⓒ	ⓓ
19.	ⓐ	ⓑ	ⓒ	ⓓ
20.	ⓐ	ⓑ	ⓒ	ⓓ
21.	ⓐ	ⓑ	ⓒ	ⓓ
22.	ⓐ	ⓑ	ⓒ	ⓓ
23.	ⓐ	ⓑ	ⓒ	ⓓ
24.	ⓐ	ⓑ	ⓒ	ⓓ
25.	ⓐ	ⓑ	ⓒ	ⓓ
26.	ⓐ	ⓑ	ⓒ	ⓓ
27.	ⓐ	ⓑ	ⓒ	ⓓ
28.	ⓐ	ⓑ	ⓒ	ⓓ
29.	ⓐ	ⓑ	ⓒ	ⓓ
30.	ⓐ	ⓑ	ⓒ	ⓓ
31.	ⓐ	ⓑ	ⓒ	ⓓ
32.	ⓐ	ⓑ	ⓒ	ⓓ
33.	ⓐ	ⓑ	ⓒ	ⓓ
34.	ⓐ	ⓑ	ⓒ	ⓓ
35.	ⓐ	ⓑ	ⓒ	ⓓ

36.	ⓐ	ⓑ	ⓒ	ⓓ
37.	ⓐ	ⓑ	ⓒ	ⓓ
38.	ⓐ	ⓑ	ⓒ	ⓓ
39.	ⓐ	ⓑ	ⓒ	ⓓ
40.	ⓐ	ⓑ	ⓒ	ⓓ
41.	ⓐ	ⓑ	ⓒ	ⓓ
42.	ⓐ	ⓑ	ⓒ	ⓓ
43.	ⓐ	ⓑ	ⓒ	ⓓ
44.	ⓐ	ⓑ	ⓒ	ⓓ
45.	ⓐ	ⓑ	ⓒ	ⓓ
46.	ⓐ	ⓑ	ⓒ	ⓓ
47.	ⓐ	ⓑ	ⓒ	ⓓ
48.	ⓐ	ⓑ	ⓒ	ⓓ
49.	ⓐ	ⓑ	ⓒ	ⓓ
50.	ⓐ	ⓑ	ⓒ	ⓓ
51.	ⓐ	ⓑ	ⓒ	ⓓ
52.	ⓐ	ⓑ	ⓒ	ⓓ
53.	ⓐ	ⓑ	ⓒ	ⓓ
54.	ⓐ	ⓑ	ⓒ	ⓓ
55.	ⓐ	ⓑ	ⓒ	ⓓ
56.	ⓐ	ⓑ	ⓒ	ⓓ
57.	ⓐ	ⓑ	ⓒ	ⓓ
58.	ⓐ	ⓑ	ⓒ	ⓓ
59.	ⓐ	ⓑ	ⓒ	ⓓ
60.	ⓐ	ⓑ	ⓒ	ⓓ
61.	ⓐ	ⓑ	ⓒ	ⓓ
62.	ⓐ	ⓑ	ⓒ	ⓓ
63.	ⓐ	ⓑ	ⓒ	ⓓ
64.	ⓐ	ⓑ	ⓒ	ⓓ
65.	ⓐ	ⓑ	ⓒ	ⓓ
66.	ⓐ	ⓑ	ⓒ	ⓓ
67.	ⓐ	ⓑ	ⓒ	ⓓ
68.	ⓐ	ⓑ	ⓒ	ⓓ
69.	ⓐ	ⓑ	ⓒ	ⓓ
70.	ⓐ	ⓑ	ⓒ	ⓓ

71.	ⓐ	ⓑ	ⓒ	ⓓ
72.	ⓐ	ⓑ	ⓒ	ⓓ
73.	ⓐ	ⓑ	ⓒ	ⓓ
74.	ⓐ	ⓑ	ⓒ	ⓓ
75.	ⓐ	ⓑ	ⓒ	ⓓ
76.	ⓐ	ⓑ	ⓒ	ⓓ
77.	ⓐ	ⓑ	ⓒ	ⓓ
78.	ⓐ	ⓑ	ⓒ	ⓓ
79.	ⓐ	ⓑ	ⓒ	ⓓ
80.	ⓐ	ⓑ	ⓒ	ⓓ
81.	ⓐ	ⓑ	ⓒ	ⓓ
82.	ⓐ	ⓑ	ⓒ	ⓓ
83.	ⓐ	ⓑ	ⓒ	ⓓ
84.	ⓐ	ⓑ	ⓒ	ⓓ
85.	ⓐ	ⓑ	ⓒ	ⓓ
86.	ⓐ	ⓑ	ⓒ	ⓓ
87.	ⓐ	ⓑ	ⓒ	ⓓ
88.	ⓐ	ⓑ	ⓒ	ⓓ
89.	ⓐ	ⓑ	ⓒ	ⓓ
90.	ⓐ	ⓑ	ⓒ	ⓓ
91.	ⓐ	ⓑ	ⓒ	ⓓ
92.	ⓐ	ⓑ	ⓒ	ⓓ
93.	ⓐ	ⓑ	ⓒ	ⓓ
94.	ⓐ	ⓑ	ⓒ	ⓓ
95.	ⓐ	ⓑ	ⓒ	ⓓ
96.	ⓐ	ⓑ	ⓒ	ⓓ
97.	ⓐ	ⓑ	ⓒ	ⓓ
98.	ⓐ	ⓑ	ⓒ	ⓓ
99.	ⓐ	ⓑ	ⓒ	ⓓ
100.	ⓐ	ⓑ	ⓒ	ⓓ

► Practice Test 3

1. The case of *Morrissey v. Brewer* defines which of the following?
   a. probation revocation processes
   b. parole revocation processes
   c. diversion processes
   d. community corrections revocation processes

2. You have decided to start revocation procedures on a parolee, but failed to provide him with written notice of the charges within the allotted time frame. What should you do with your offender at this point?
   a. You should keep him detained because failure to provide notice is a small component of the process.
   b. You should review the case to see if it is strong enough that the hearing officer won't dismiss it and release the parolee.
   c. You should release him from detention as his due process rights were violated.
   d. You should write an addendum that describes why the violation report was not presented to the parolee in time, and justifies why the parolee should remain detained and the hearing should continue to take place.

3. A parolee provides you the address and phone number of his living arrangements. When you attempt to do an unscheduled home visit, you learn the address number is located on a vacant lot. What do you do?
   a. You call the phone number the offender provided you and demand an explanation of his living arrangements.
   b. You issue a warrant for his arrest and figure out the truth about his living arrangements later.
   c. You go to his employment and ask his supervisor to allow you a few minutes with the offender.
   d. You wait until the offender's next office visit next month to learn the truth about his living arrangements.

4. The case of *Morrissey v. Brewer* (1972) involved a man on parole who admitted to committing several violations. Which of the following was NOT one of those violations?
   a. buying a car under an assumed name and driving it without permission
   b. giving false statements to the insurance and law enforcement after a minor accident
   c. failing to report as directed
   d. writing bad checks

5. Law enforcement officials contact you and indicate that they have one of your parolees in detention because of a domestic violence situation. However, you learn the parolee was acting in self-defense, and his significant other was the aggressor in this situation. When you ask why the parolee is locked up, you learn there was some pushing done by the parolee. The state law indicates that both parties will be detained if law enforcement can see symptoms of abuse in both parties. What do you do with the parolee?
   a. You issue a parole revocation warrant and leave him detained because he was wrong to push his significant other and perform any other physical abuse acts.
   b. After talking with the parolee, you determine he was not the aggressor, and you release him with warnings.
   c. You do not issue a parole violation warrant and allow the offender to bail out of detention with instructions to report to your office when he gets out.
   d. You talk with the prosecutor and advise him or her that the offender is under supervision, was not the aggressor, and, therefore, should not be charged.

6. A parolee has told you he likes his counseling group and wants to start attending sessions more often. He has requested your assistance in making this happen. When you discuss this request with the counselor, you learn that the parolee is infatuated with another group member and that your parolee is making others uncomfortable. The counselor has requested the parolee be removed from the group sessions. What do you do now?

a. You ask the counselor for a referral into another group session and schedule the offender for that group.

b. You ask the counselor for a referral to a one-on-one counselor because the offender may have other issues that need to be addressed.

c. You talk with the offender about the group being uncomfortable with his actions and tell him to change his behavior.

d. You talk with the offender about his infatuation, how his behavior is inappropriate, and how he should stop acting on his feelings during the sessions.

7. The primary function of parole is to protect the public from released offenders, an objective that can be met through three practices. Which of the following is NOT one of these three practices?

a. the enforcement of parolee restrictions and controls within the community

b. services that help parolees assimilate into a noncriminal lifestyle

c. efforts to boost the public's confidence in the effectiveness of parole services

d. transitional supervision to aid in reintegration and reduce recidivism

8. Which of the following may be a special condition of parole?

a. I will obey all local, state, and federal laws and conduct myself in a responsible manner.

b. I will not engage in a pattern of association with persons who are engaged in illegal activities.

c. I will not have any contact with children under the age of 14.

d. I will notify my parole officer in writing within 24 hours of any changes in my employment or residence.

9. You convince one of your parolees that his participation in the day reporting center (DRC) will beneficial to him. What services will he gain from going to the DRC?

a. He will get tested randomly for drugs.

b. He will get help with his education or his job search.

c. choices **a** and **b**

d. none of the above; participants sit or do housekeeping activities around the center.

10. An offender assigned to your caseload is refusing to make any more child support payments because his ex-girlfriend recently married another man. The parolee indicates he feels the child support payments are going toward drugs instead of food and clothing for his children. Which of the following would be your advice?

a. Child support payments must be paid to the ex-girlfriend because failure to pay will require the parolee to go to jail.

b. The parolee should check with his attorney to see if payments can be stopped because of the recent marriage.

c. The parolee should act upon his concerns and not pay the money owed.

d. If the parolee feels that he separated from his ex-girlfriend for valid reasons and that his children are not suffering, he shouldn't worry about what the child support payments are used for.

11. A local newspaper editor has requested an open records act for a probationer's presentence investigation report (PSI). Which of the following is an appropriate response to this request?
- **a.** Yes, the PSI can be released because an open records act was filed and the information is not privileged.
- **b.** Yes, the PSI can be released, but components of the report that are not public information will be censored.
- **c.** No, the PSI will not be released because it is not a public document.
- **d.** No, the PSI will not be released, because it contains information submitted by witnesses and other individuals who would not cooperate again, if asked.

12. While doing a presentence investigation report, you get information not from the defendant, but from a neighbor. Can you use this information in the PSI?
- **a.** Yes; hearsay evidence is admissible in a PSI because it may help the judge determine an appropriate sentence for the defendant.
- **b.** Yes; hearsay evidence is admissible because it is collected by an officer of the court and is, therefore, valid evidence.
- **c.** No; hearsay evidence is inadmissible because it does not allow the defendant an opportunity to cross-examine the witness who reported the information to the probation officer.
- **d.** No; hearsay is inadmissible during court trials and, therefore, is also inadmissible to any court documents.

13. You are starting to interview a defendant for his portion of the presentence investigation report. What should you do?
- **a.** You should remind the defendant of his Miranda rights prior to interviewing him.
- **b.** You should wait until the defendant's attorney arrives to start the interview.
- **c.** You should remind the defendant to be truthful, that you will be talking to various individuals who know him and that you will find out if he is lying to you.
- **d.** You should start the interview and proceed as normal with your opening statements and explanations of the process.

14. A type of corrections program during which offenders live in a facility but are allowed into the community to go to school or work is called
- **a.** boot camp program.
- **b.** work-release program.
- **c.** day reporting center.
- **d.** reentry program.

15. A parole officer is asked to compute the amount of time an offender lost because of a violation as well as the amount the time the offender must serve in order to be released by law. What is the objective of this task?
- **a.** computing the amount of good time the offender has served and has yet to serve
- **b.** computing the offender's parole eligibility date
- **c.** computing the conditional release date.
- **d.** determining the offender's schedule for seeing the parole board and being released

16. Parole is
   a. an administrative act.
   b. remission of punishment.
   c. an act of forgiveness.
   d. an executive act.

17. In most states, appointments of parole board members are made by
   a. the governor.
   b. the director of corrections.
   c. the chief of the state supreme court.
   d. the legislators.

18. Parole conditions should be
   a. full of legalese and complicated.
   b. clear and reasonable.
   c. relevant and short.
   d. complex and obvious.

19. Conditions of parole and probation that apply to everyone under supervision are called
   a. general conditions.
   b. standard conditions.
   c. special conditions.
   d. major conditions.

20. In a traditional sense, the state is acting upon the behalf of _____ when punishing an offender.
   a. the victim
   b. the community
   c. the offender
   d. the court

21. The amount of restitution is determined by
   a. damages resulting from the original crime.
   b. the public defender's costs.
   c. court costs.
   d. all of the above

22. An officer may conduct a search, if allowed by agency procedures, of which of the following places?
   a. the offender's place of employment
   b. the offender's home
   c. the home of the offender's significant other
   d. the treatment facility at which the offender is being treated

23. An intermediate sanction would be which of the following?
   a. house arrest
   b. diversion
   c. restitution centers
   d. work-release centers

24. A tool used by the supervising officer to conduct an objective assessment to compute the risks posed by the offender and identify the offender's needs is called what?
   a. caseload analysis
   b. classification tool
   c. management tool
   d. workload standard tool

25. Who can modify the probation conditions of an offender?
   a. the probation officer, because this is an executive function
   b. the judge, because this is a judicial function
   c. the probation officer's supervisor, because this is an administrative function
   d. none of the above, because once conditions are set, there is no reason to modify them

26. A sex offender refuses to participate in treatment because there is a component of the treatment that requires him to sign an acknowledgement of all prior sex offenses. The offender claims this is a violation of his constitutional rights against self-incrimination. In this situation, what is your next action?
   a. You tell the offender that he is right and does not have to participate.
   b. You tell the offender that he is under supervision and not to participate fully will mean that he is in violation of this condition and that you will start revocation proceedings.
   c. You tell the offender that complying with this component of the treatment is not a violation of his constitutional rights and that he should participate fully.
   d. You have the offender arrested, because saying that this is a constitutional violation is just his way of trying to avoid participating.

27. A probation officer has identified that an offender must participate in drug abuse counseling, parenting classes, anger management, and some sort of vocational training. What has the officer done?
   a. developed a treatment plan for the offender
   b. added special conditions to the offender's supervision
   c. developed a risk plan for the offender
   d. developed a case management plan for the offender

28. An officer has talked with a neighbor about an offender. What type of contact was made?
   a. face-to-face visit
   b. field visit
   c. collateral visit
   d. home visit

29. Which of the following can jeopardize the authority of a probation and parole officer?
   a. high number of offenders on a caseload
   b. having a specialized caseload
   c. lax supervision
   d. poor documentation

30. A probationer has had his probation revoked and is now sentenced to spend time in prison. In a visit, the probationer asks you if the time he spent on probation counts toward the prison time. How would you answer this question?
   a. Yes, the judge provided a sentence that included all options of probation and prison.
   b. No, the probation time is not counted, but the jail time while waiting for sentencing or transportation is.
   c. No, the prison sentence starts when the offender arrives at the prison.
   d. You don't know the answer so you tell the offender to ask that question when he arrives at the prison.

Directions: Read the following case study and then answer questions 31 through 36.

Winslow is an African-American male who has just been released from prison after returning to prison twice for violating his supervision conditions. In the past, Winslow violated his supervision conditions when he was caught stealing several hundred dollars worth of meat from a grocery store, in addition to not reporting and not participating in counseling as directed. Winslow has always told you he can't report or go to counseling because he has to work. This release is his third attempt at community supervision, and he indicated he is ready to stay out of prison and finish out his time on parole.

Winslow is 27 years old, the oldest son in a large family. He is living with his mother while on parole, because he supports his mom and six younger siblings when he is working. Winslow doesn't have many special conditions to his parole, because there haven't been notations in any of his records that indicate substance abuse or a mental problem. Winslow has always exercised, and is a very large and muscle bound man. He looks intimidating and tends to scare people who are seeing him for the first time. Winslow is well known within the police department because he was pretty aggressive when they first arrested him. Officers still talk about that fight and how massive Winslow still is. Because you have worked with Winslow in the past, you have a good relationship with him and find him pleasant to supervise, even when he is violating his conditions.

Other than the original charge of attempted murder, Winslow has not shown any tendencies of aggression within the community. The victim of the original charge was the ex-boyfriend of Winslow's mother who still shows up from time to time at the mother's house. Winslow is not comfortable with this man being around the house, but Winslow doesn't have anywhere else to go when he is released.

31. Winslow comes in to report and tells you that he has been approached by some guy who is looking for a hit man. Winslow indicates the hit is being requested by his mother's ex-boyfriend's son, and the son's wife is to be killed. Winslow doesn't wish to be involved, but he also doesn't want anyone to be killed. What should your course of action be?
   a. You should have Winslow bring the man looking for a hit man into your office so you can hear about the deal.
   b. You should have Winslow go with you to the police department to tell the local detectives what he was told and to help however he can.
   c. You should go to the police department yourself to tell the detectives what you heard so they can follow up with an investigation.
   d. You should tell Winslow not to do anything because his mother's boyfriend and son are just trying to get Winslow in trouble.

32. A police detective approaches you and asks you what type of drugs Winslow takes to get such big muscles. When you tell him there is no record of substance abuse, the detective snickers at you and says that you aren't doing your job and you just haven't caught Winslow doing anything. He walks away mumbling that "steroids can't be found on those stupid tests anyway." How should you respond?
   a. You should continue the conversation with the detective to explain how the drug tests work, what the statistics are on the success rate of the testing, and that Winslow has passed all the tests with nothing detected.
   b. You should find the chief detective and complain about the detective's attitude toward your offender.
   c. You should continue the conversation and debate the facts of the drug testing system, the collection process, and the statistics on the drug vendor or company, and then challenge him to tell you why he thinks the tests do not work.
   d. You shouldn't do anything.

33. During parole planning, Winslow indicates that he wants to move out of his mother's house but feels that he can't find work that will support her household and an apartment of his own. He worries that she will not provide for the siblings if he doesn't live there and makes sure there is food on the table. In this situation, what advice would you give to Winslow?

a. You help Winslow figure out how his mom is supporting his siblings while he is in prison, and then assist him in finding a way to suggest to his mom that she continue doing that while he gets his own apartment.

b. You help Winslow see that he has a responsibility to his mother and that the best thing is for him to return to live with her.

c. You suggest to Winslow that he should not worry about his mom, because she will find a way and means to provide for the siblings.

d. You suggest that he be paroled to another city so he doesn't have this conflict.

34. During one of his weekly visits, Winslow indicates that his mother's boyfriend has moved back into the home. Winslow is uncomfortable with this situation, because he suspects that the boyfriend has sexually abused one of the younger siblings. He tells you that one of the younger girls told him the boyfriend had touched inappropriately on several occasions while Winslow was in prison. Winslow feels it would be best to move back into his mother's home. How should you handle this situation?

a. You tell Winslow that he cannot move back home and that he will simply have to trust his mother to take care of the younger siblings.

b. You present Winslow with the different options that are available to report suspected abuse, and after he has chosen the option he would like to pursue, you offer him assistance. You continue to explore other ways of resolving this situation without having Winslow move back in.

c. You tell Winslow to move back in, confront his mother with his suspicions, and have her kick the boyfriend out.

d. You tell Winslow to confront the boyfriend about his suspicions and then kick him out of the house.

35. Winslow tells you he wants to fight in a tournament held by the local fighting club. The tournament will be at the community center and the grand prize is $2,000, of which he said he would give his mom half. Winslow works hard to convince you that he could win this fight and that his mom could really use the money. Because fighting is obviously in violation of his parole conditions, you tell Winslow no. He asks you to reconsider because this is an organized sport with mandatory practices supervised by trainers, with rules, referees, and other sanctions so fighters won't fight on their own. How would you handle this situation?

a. You tell Winslow, because this is an organized sport, to register for the fight, knowing he has a good chance of winning.

b. You talk with your supervisor, telling her about the situation and about what you told Winslow. You indicate Winslow should not be involved as this is an act of aggression.

c. You talk with your supervisor and attempt to convince her of the need for Winslow to be involved in the fight tournament.

d. You tell Winslow no again, and then document the conversation in your case file. You don't talk to anyone else as it is unnecessary; you told Winslow no and he will follow that directive.

36. Winslow tells you the police stopped him last night while he was driving. Winslow says the police officer told him he was stopped for playing loud music, but Winslow swears he didn't have his music that loud. He states he had to get out of the car, was handcuffed, and then, after his car was searched, Winslow was released and told he could leave. Winslow says he believes that he was a victim of racial profiling and wants to file a complaint. He asks for your opinion as to what to do. You should

a. encourage Winslow to go on with his life and not worry about such things; this type of thing happens to everyone.

b. suggest that he hire an attorney and file a discrimination case against the city.

c. talk to Winslow about what he was doing just before he was stopped, and then comment on the events, pointing out that the police didn't have the right to search his car.

d. tell Winslow his options, which include going to the police department to file a complaint, altering his routes to avoid that area for a while, and making sure his music is low. You should then tell Winslow which action he takes is up to him.

Directions: Read the following case study and then answer questions 37 through 42.

Sam is 34 years old and has been a parole officer and your coworker for several years. Sam is currently divorced and is renting an apartment with a friend. Over the last several months, the parole supervisor has talked with Sam about his inappropriate conversations regarding his female friends and their social activities. Additionally, it has been noticed that Sam has started to show his temper with offenders in the office. Sam's caseload isn't any more stressful than others' caseloads in the office, but he is constantly complaining about the workload, all of the documentation, and the bad office morale.

Sam is scheduled to spend today out in the field conducting field visits, but his female field partner called in sick. Because the office has a "two-out" policy (two officers conducting field visits together), your supervisor asks if you would go out with Sam. You have heard rumors that Sam doesn't actually do his field visits but feel he will conduct himself appropriately because you are with him. After about an hour of doing your field visits, Sam drives to an out-of-the-way park, stops the car, and then turns to you and asks if you want some ecstasy. When you decline, he then asks you if you have wanted to have sex with an offender. You demand that Sam take you back to the office, to which he responds that he was just kidding around with you and he thought you could take it.

37. When you walk into the office, another parole officer, Jordan, approaches you and asks what had happened. You tell him what Sam said and that you are going to file a report. Jordan walks into Sam's office calling Sam several vulgar names. Sam grabs Jordan by the shirt collar and shoves him up against the wall. You manage to break them apart before the supervisor can become aware of the situation. In this situation, your next step is to
    a. tell Sam that you will be filing a report of what he said as well as about the physical altercation with another officer.
    b. walk out of Sam's office and immediately go to the supervisor's office to report what Sam said to you and the physical altercation between Sam and Jordan.
    c. tell Jordan to leave the parole office to calm down, while you proceed to your office to document what happened.
    d. call the police department to report the battery of a law enforcement officer.

38. In this situation, is there sufficient cause to file a sexual harassment charge? Why or why not?
    a. Yes, there is sufficient cause to file a charge, because federal law indicates one incident, if severe enough, is enough to file a charge.
    b. Yes, there is sufficient cause to file a charge, because you were offended by his question and any reasonable person would be offended. If an officer is offended, he or she has the right and responsibility to file a sexual harassment charge.
    c. No, there is not sufficient cause to file a charge, because, although sex was talked about, the implication wasn't for the two officers to be involved.
    d. No, there is not sufficient cause to file a charge, because although the officer's question was inappropriate, it does not fall within the regulations governing sexual harassment. This situation certainly warrants a misconduct action and possibly other illegal actions, but not a sexual harassment charge.

39. You feel the intensity of the investigation is focused on the physical altercation between the two officers rather than the questions of drugs and sex with offenders. You ask your supervisor for information regarding what is being done about your part of this situation, and you are told that the battery charge is the more important charge. Which of the following should you do?

a. Nothing, because you didn't want to be involved in the first place and focusing the issue on you would only cause you to have to be a witness in a court hearing.

b. Nothing, because you know the department lets the local jurisdiction run its investigation prior to conducting any internal investigation regarding violations of policy and procedure.

c. You should talk with your supervisor to ensure that there is an investigation into whether the officer was involved with drugs and/or the solicitation of abuse of offenders. You should ask if further documentation is required and if you can speak to the investigating officer.

d. You should talk with your supervisor and demand the focus of the investigation be shifted from the misconduct toward your accusation. If you don't get an affirmative answer, then loudly tell the supervisor that you are getting an attorney to file charges of your own.

40. The prosecution has gathered enough evidence against Sam and has charged him with possession of narcotics, battery of a law enforcement officer, and sexual exploitation. You have learned that Sam has selected a hotshot attorney who has been known to badger witnesses. As the hearing date grows closer, you decide to prepare yourself, although the district attorney's office has worked with you on your testimony. To prepare yourself, you should

a. stand in front of your mirror at home and recite your testimony just as you have been taught.

b. hire your own attorney to help you with your testimony and to be present in court in case you need one.

c. ask the agency trainer to help you with a mock trial so you can go over your testimony again.

d. contact the assistant district attorney handling the case and ask if there is someone who could work with you to ease your fears.

41. A few weeks after the hearing, Jordan approaches you and asks if the rumors are true. When you ask what the rumors are, you learn that you supposedly have had an affair with Sam and have been visiting him while he is in jail. Jordan says the whole office has heard this rumor. What action should you take?

a. You should ask the supervisor to call an office-wide meeting so you can set the record straight that you are not having an affair.

b. You should go to your office and send out an office-wide e-mail that states you know of the rumor and deny being involved with Sam in any inappropriate fashion.

c. You should do nothing; office rumors happen all the time, and next week someone else will be the subject of the rumor mill.

d. You should talk to your supervisor about the rumor, make assurances you have not been involved with Sam, and then go about your business in a professional fashion.

42. Sam is found guilty of several misdemeanors and placed on probation. He is to be supervised by a probation officer who is a seasoned employee of the probation department. You know you will see Sam at times when he is reporting because the probation department is in half of the building and the parole division is in the other. You were a key witness in Sam's trial, and his attorney really questioned you hard, implying you had asked Sam for sexual favors and had been instrumental in getting Jordan to harm Sam physically. With that in mind, you are uncomfortable with Sam sitting in the lobby or accidentally bumping into him when he is reporting. How should you handle this situation?

a. You should talk with your supervisor to see if Sam could report anywhere else.

b. You should talk with the probation officer to get a schedule of Sam's office visits so you can schedule your field visits at those times.

c. You should talk with your supervisor about transferring to another parole office so you don't have to worry about running into him.

d. You should go about your business as usual because Sam is responsible for his actions and conviction, and you do not have any need to adjust your life. If Sam does something else to you, then you can take the appropriate actions.

Directions: Read the following case study and then answer questions 43 through 48.

Sarah is a 23-year-old first-time offender who has been placed on probation. One of Sarah's probation conditions is that she enters into the local intensive supervision program (ISP) and abides by its guidelines for a one-year period. The judge indicates that Sarah needs intensive supervision because of her lack of good judgment and history with gangs. Sarah's original crime of aggravated battery is reduced to a theft charge because of a plea arrangement. In the plea agreement, Sarah agrees to testify against several of the gang members who are charged with more severe crimes.

Sarah's parents have professional jobs and are in the middle to upper social economic class. They had hired one of the town's better attorneys, which is how the plea agreement was reached. Because of her parents' connections, Sarah has a job as office manager at one of the local banks, drives a fairly new car, and rents an apartment in one of the nicer parts of the town. She graduated from the local high school with a 3.9 GPA, but had always suffered from low self-esteem. The attorney has been seen visiting Sarah at her office, and the two have been seen having lunch many times throughout the week. The attorney has made it well known that Sarah will never see the inside of a prison, no matter how badly she does in the ISP or on probation.

43. During an unannounced employment visit, you notice that Sarah is wearing slinky, revealing clothing and jewelry her salary cannot support. She is vague when you ask her where she obtained the jewelry. What should you do in this situation?

a. You should ask Sarah to provide receipts for the jewelry as well as a list of her recent associates, and then you should place her under surveillance.

b. You should tell Sarah she must return all the jewelry and provide you with receipts of those returns. You should tell her that she should not be associating with the gang members, and place her under surveillance.

c. You should ask Sarah why she is wearing clothes that are so different from those you have seen in the past, and if her style change has anything to do with old associates. You should remind her of her conditions to avoid people who are associated with illegal activities. You should allow Sarah a chance to provide you with information, and you should then place her under surveillance if she does not provide you with a legitimate reason.

d. You should document the style change and the jewelry that Sarah is wearing. You should continue to monitor the situation and do more unannounced visits to see if the pattern continues.

44. Sarah has had one positive urinalysis test, has recently failed to report as directed, and has moved without providing the new address. You have not had any contact with Sarah for one month. In attempts to find her, you contact Sarah's attorney and explain that Sarah has failed to report as directed. You are told that she is just fine and will report when she is ready to. Which of the following should you do next?

a. You should explain to the attorney that you are only following the orders of the judge based on the plea agreement that was accepted by all parties, and it would be in Sarah's best interest to report to your office as soon as possible or you will start action for a hearing before the judge.

b. You should contact the judge and tell him or her that the attorney is prohibiting you from fulfilling your duties as an ISP officer, and request some intervention from the judge's office.

c. You should write Sarah a letter and send it to her last known address, knowing this action is a futile effort but will afford you the evidence you need to initiate proceedings to get a warrant for Sarah's arrest.

d. You should contact Sarah's parents and ask for their help in getting their daughter to report as soon as possible.

45. The manager of the bank where Sarah works calls you and complains that some of Sarah's associates have been hanging around the bank lobby waiting on Sarah to take breaks, go to lunch, or get off work. Based on the description the bank manager gives you, you recognize that it is gang members waiting on Sarah. You ask if Sarah is doing anything wrong, and you are told, "No, she continues to do her job well." The manager says that these people are scaring his older customers and that he wants them out of his lobby. He asks you to tell Sarah to get these people to quit coming to the bank. Your response should be to

a. tell the bank manager you will come to the bank immediately and talk to Sarah.

b. suggest the bank manager either have his security move these people on or call the police if they are unwelcome.

c. suggest the bank manager tell Sarah to have these people leave, because he is responsible for the bank environment.

d. say that this is not your concern because Sarah is not doing anything wrong and that you hope his problems get resolved soon.

46. During a recent office visit, Sarah says that her parents have given her a plane ticket to the Bahamas for her 24th birthday. She wants to obtain approval to travel next month. When you start to ask questions about whom she is going with and where she is staying, all Sarah would say is that a friend is going with her. You ask why the Bahamas, and again Sarah gets quiet and refuses to provide any details of the trip. She asks for the paperwork, saying that she will fill it out and bring it back within the week. What should you do?

a. You should tell Sarah while she is still in the office that there isn't any way you will approve a travel request.

b. You should let Sarah fill out the paperwork to see who is going with her before you make any decisions.

c. You should tell Sarah that you doubt you will agree to this travel plan and you suggest she wait to use the ticket when she completes probation.

d. You should tell Sarah that, until you get details about the trip, you aren't giving her the paperwork to complete.

47. You are called to your supervisor's office and informed that a motion to have Sarah's probation terminated has been placed on the judge's docket. You are directed to put together a report of Sarah's progress while in the ISP and then provide a recommendation for the motion. You argue that Sarah has not been a model offender and should not be released from supervision. Your supervisor tells you to quit talking about it and get the report done. What should you put in the report, and what would the recommendation be?

a. The report should be factual and list all of the violations with a recommendation that Sarah remain on probation, in the ISP, for another six months.

b. The report should be factual and list all of the violations with a recommendation the Sarah's probation be terminated, because it will happen no matter what your recommendation is.

c. The report should not list any of the violations, because the judge will do whatever he wants whether you recommend termination or extension of probation.

d. The report should not list any of the violations but recommend that Sarah remain on probation for the remaining time originally established by the court.

48. In conversations with Sarah, you find she might benefit from participating in a women's counseling group. In this group, the focus is on helping women learn self-esteem, self-worth, and good problem solving. You mention this to Sarah, who leaves your office having signed the special condition paperwork and is ready to participate in the group. However, an hour later she contacts you and says that she would rather not join the group because she doesn't want her concerns and business aired to strangers. How should you handle this?

a. You should tell Sarah that she has already signed the paperwork committing to participate and she is expected to do this.

b. You should ask Sarah what has happened to change her mind, and ask her to reconsider her decision. You should even ask if she will meet with the counselor one-on-one for a while.

c. You should tell Sarah that you will remove the special condition and there won't be an issue.

d. You should call Sarah's father, because you are sure that is where the pressure is coming from for Sarah to not participate in this. You tell him he is not letting his daughter gain all of the resources she needs to be successful and ask him to reconsider his stance.

Directions: Read the following case study and then answer questions 49 through 52.

As a parole officer, you have always taken pride in the fact that you are up to date on your documentation and contacts. You also take pride that your work ethic allows you to keep your desk and office clean, which is not so for the parole officer, Brett, in the next office. Your office does not have piles on the desk, table, or floor, nor is your wastebasket overflowing daily with candy wrappers and soda cans. In general, you would classify Brett as a slob, but he is a nice guy and is quick to help you out whenever you need or ask for it. Brett is a long-term parole officer and is usually given the more difficult offenders to supervise. Brett normally works from 6:00 A.M. to 6:00 P.M., and leaves his desk only to take smoke breaks. The parole director seems to like Brett because they take breaks together and often spend time in Brett's office discussing sports, guns, cigars, and other personal interests.

You notice when you arrive to work in the mornings that your desk and file cabinets have been rummaged through. In fact, you speak to your supervisor about the possibility of the janitorial people taking their breaks in your office because of your feeling that someone has been in there during the evening hours. You report to your supervisor that you have a feeling someone has been going through your desk and file cabinets, but nothing has been taken and your office is just not as neat as you left it the night before.

Your supervisor asks in a unit meeting if anyone else is having concerns about his or her office. Other than the janitorial people not emptying wastebaskets, no other complaints are discussed. The supervisor tells you after the meeting that you are probably being over-sensitive about your office and not to worry about it.

49. You happen to come into the parole office late one evening and find Brett in an office across the hall from both of your offices. He is wearing latex gloves and is going through one of the desk drawers. You ask him what he was doing in that office with gloves on, and he glares at you, demanding to know what you are doing in the office at that time in the evening. You again ask Brett what he was doing, and he goes into his office and shuts the door. You look in the office that Brett came out of, but don't find anything amiss. What should you do?

a. You should get what you came for from your office, go home, and talk with your supervisor in the morning.

b. You should leave the parole office and call your supervisor immediately to report what has transpired with Brett.

c. You should go into your office, turn on your computer, and type an account of what has transpired so all of the details are accurate. When you are finished, you should put the hard copy of your documentation under your supervisor's door.

d. You should knock on Brett's door, go into his office, and confront him again as to what he was doing in someone else's office with latex gloves on.

50. After a thorough investigation into Brett's behavior in the other office, Brett isn't at work for a full week. Speculation among other officers is that Brett was suspended for a full week for his misconduct. Because personnel matters are confidential, no one is told whether he was suspended or is just taking a vacation. When Brett returns to work however, he is very tense around you and takes up activities that cause you grief. He bangs a rubber ball against your wall, acts as if he is going to trip you as you walk by him, and does other things that are annoying. What action, if any, should you take?

a. You should ask Brett if he has an issue with you and if he would like to talk about and resolve it.

b. You should tell your supervisor you would like to move offices and, until you move, spend more time doing field visits and contacts.

c. You should tell your supervisor what Brett is doing and that you want it to stop immediately. You should tell him that, if Brett continues, you will file a complaint against him.

d. You should go to a toy store and buy rubber balls, bubbles, and other toys that you can use to irritate Brett as much as he is irritating you.

51. An offender assigned to your caseload comes in for a scheduled office visit and asks how you are. You find this unusual and ask why he is concerned. He then tells you the word on the street is that Brett is out to get you and is using his offenders to try to set you up. Your offender tells you that he heard it was to happen on your next scheduled field day. You should

a. ask this offender if he will tell your supervisor of this information and then coordinate that meeting.

b. tell the offender that everything is all right, and you will be conducting your field day as you see appropriate. Then, you should reschedule all of your field visits for another day.

c. finish your meeting with the offender and then confront Brett with this information.

d. finish your meeting with the offender and then continue your day, because you don't believe Brett would hurt you or anyone else in the office.

52. You are meeting with a male offender who is new to your caseload. You announce to this offender that you would like to have him participate in a urinalysis test. The offender gives you excuses as to why he can't provide a sample today, and you tell him that he can wait in the lobby for a bit until he can produce a sample. You escort him to the lobby and then proceed through the office to find a male officer to assist you. The only officer available is Brett. You ask him for assistance, and he says that he will meet you and the offender by the sample site. As you and the offender proceed down the hallway toward Brett, the offender slams into you and pushes you against the wall. In the few minutes it takes to get the offender under control, you become aware that Brett is playing a large part in subduing the offender. What should you do in this situation, if anything?

a. You should just tell him thanks, because all of his actions are part of his job responsibilities.

b. You should say nothing to him, because you are still upset about the allegations of setting you up.

c. You should tell him thanks in a sincere manner and make sure the supervisor knows of the situation and of Brett's help.

d. You should send an e-mail reminding other officers of security concerns and telling how Brett really came to your assistance today.

Directions: Read the following case study and then answer questions 53 through 57.

Oscar has been in prison for 22 years on a murder charge. He went to prison when he was 28 years old and is now being released for community supervision for the first time. During parole planning, Oscar met with the prison parole officer and indicated he did not wish to be paroled and he was scared to be out on the streets.

Oscar is 50 years old now and went to prison when the world was very different from the world that exists today. He does not know how to use computers, does not know a DVD is, and does not understand the concept of the high-speed Internet. Oscar's marketable skills include working on cars, woodworking, and cooking. Prior to going to prison, Oscar had become a lucrative businessman, selling cocaine out of his garage.

Oscar is now paroled and living with an old girlfriend because he doesn't have any family left in town. Prior to leaving, Oscar's family sold his home, garage, cars, and other personal belongings, and then used the money to relocate. They did not visit Oscar while he was in prison, nor did they offer to have Oscar live with them when he was released.

The victim's family adamantly opposed Oscar's release to the paroling authority. Oscar has learned of their opposition and has expressed remorse for his crime, and some fear that the family will try to take their revenge.

53. During your first meeting with Oscar, you ask what his priorities are for his parole time. He indicates he would like to find a job and get an apartment or house of his own. However, he complains about how expensive things are and says he would really like to go back to prison. How do you convince him to make the effort to stay within the community?

a. You tell him that going back to prison is the easy way out and that he needs to be strong and work through his fear.

b. You tell him his priorities are good, and he should look to accomplishing those goals in about six months. Until then, you inform him he just needs to stay put with his old girlfriend and learn about the world.

c. You hand him the classified ads and tell him that, if he wants a different place to live, he needs to find a job first. You offer him bus tickets so he can go apply for jobs.

d. You schedule him to see the job coordinator and structure his daily time for the next week. In this schedule, you connect him with job and living resources as well as a counselor. Also, you schedule yourself some time to pick him up or meet him at job centers or employers who you know are hiring.

54. Oscar has been out on parole for a month and doing well. He is still living in his girlfriend's house, but he has a new job making more than minimum wage. The on-duty officer calls you at home at 9:00 P.M. and indicates Oscar is in jail. You are asked if a warrant should be issued to keep him there for a possible parole violation. When you ask what Oscar did, you are told that he threatened a man with a knife. Do you leave him in jail and start revocation proceedings in the morning?

a. Yes, because Oscar's original crime was a violent one and he exhibited more violence with this charge.

b. Yes, because you know Oscar did this just to return to prison where his life would be easier.

c. You leave him in jail until you can all the information about the charge, but you do not start revocation proceedings until you learn what will happen with the new charges.

d. Yes, because you are tired of hearing Oscar whine about how expensive the world is now.

55. Six months into his supervision, Oscar informs that you he now has enough money to rent his own apartment. You know he has been working hard but have some suspicions about how Oscar got the extra cash. However, he provides you with a new address to an apartment complex and indicates he will be moving next week. You congratulate him on getting his new apartment. What might be your next action?

a. You make note of the new address in Oscar's case file and schedule an unscheduled home visit for next week.

b. You make note of the new address and provide it to the surveillance officer, because you know that Oscar is dealing drugs again, which is how he obtained the extra cash.

c. You contact the local drug detectives and ask them if there is any known drug activity around this apartment complex, and then you let them know that Oscar is moving into that complex, so they may want to watch it more.

d. You do nothing and know you will talk more with Oscar next month when he comes in for his scheduled office visit.

56. Oscar tells you that one of his brothers wants to come and live with him in his new apartment. When you start asking questions about the brother, you learn he was one of the family members who sold everything Oscar owned and used the money for his own purposes. You also learn this brother was involved with Oscar in his drug-dealing business. Which of the following would be an appropriate response to Oscar in this situation?

a. You tell Oscar that the brother cannot come to live with him right now, because Oscar has made such good progress and should not be sidetracked. You suggest that the brother can come live in a year.

b. You let Oscar know how proud you are of his progress over the last six months, and ask how you can help him stay crime and problem free while his brother is here. You also ask if there has been any discussion about how long the brother expects to live with Oscar, and then react to that information by offering assistance in getting the brother connected with housing authorities, welfare agencies, and other necessary resources.

c. You remind Oscar of the progress he has made, and ask if there is any way the brother could live somewhere other than with Oscar.

d. You ask Oscar to put a time limit on the brother's visit and insist that the visit not interrupt Oscar's work schedule. You remind Oscar of his good progress and tell him that he should be proud of the steps he has taken. You wish him a good visit.

57. Oscar's employer contacts you and informs you that he put Oscar's name in for a community award without thinking that Oscar may not want citywide recognition. The employer indicates that he was told this morning that Oscar won the award and that there will be a banquet next week to present Oscar with a plaque. The employer says that the press would be there and that the city manager wants to do a full spread in the paper about Oscar and the success he has had. When the employer told Oscar about this award, Oscar told him he would not go, and if forced to go, he would quit his job and return to prison. The employer wants you to help convince Oscar to attend the banquet and accept the award. What should you do?

a. You should agree to help and to encourage Oscar to attend the banquet. You should assure the employer that Oscar will cooperate with any event scheduled for the banquet.

b. You should agree to talk to Oscar to encourage him to attend.

c. You should ask the employer to contact the city manager to determine his flexibility on the publicity of the event, because you know the exposure is what Oscar is avoiding. If the publicity plans are flexible, then you should agree to talk with Oscar about what he is willing to do.

d. You should tell the employer that this is his problem and you want no part of convincing Oscar to attend this banquet. You should also tell him that you wouldn't want public recognition either and that you support Oscar's decision not to go.

Directions: Read the following case study and then answer questions 58 through 61.

Mary was the victim of a heinous crime committed by an offender assigned to your caseload. You worked closely with Mary throughout the trial process, even though your offender was the perpetrator. Mary sent several letters of appreciation to your boss, the agency's chief, and the governor, and because of those letters, you received a letter of commendation along with a nomination to a national criminal justice association.

Mary is now 34 years old and, in group and individual counseling, has worked through many of her issues caused by the crime. She has married and has, it seems, been able to move forward in her life. Mary has stayed in touch with you through the years, even inviting you to her wedding. You both feel comfortable in your relationship and have lunch once a month to catch up with each other. You try to remind her that you are an officer, but you appreciate her friendship.

Mary has told you about her plans to have more kids, get a better job, and maybe start a counseling group for survivors. She has asked for your opinions and has taken your advice well.

58. Mary calls you in tears because she has received notice from the victim notification office that the offender who committed the crimes against her is coming up for parole. Although you haven't been notified of this hearing, you really don't think the parole will be granted. You try to tell this to Mary, but she is beyond consolation. What steps would you take next?

a. You contact the victim notification office and tell a coordinator about the victim's distress. You yell at him or her for not sending notification of the pending parole hearing to the parole office first or for not calling the victim prior to sending a letter.

b. You contact the victim notification office to see if the letter is correct and to ascertain why the victim was not called prior to receiving the notification letter by mail. You describe the victim's distress and ask that someone from that office contact the victim as soon as possible to provide assistance.

c. You notify your supervisor in writing of Mary's phone call and request that something be done to ensure this doesn't happen to another victim, like it happened to your friend.

d. You leave the office and go to Mary's house to console her.

59. The victim notification office contacts you two weeks prior to the offender's public comment hearing and asks if you would consider appearing to offer support for the victim, Mary. What do you do in this situation?

   a. Although you have a personal relationship with Mary, it is not appropriate for a parole officer to appear in support of the victim, and so you decline. However, you indicate that you will appear at the hearing in an official capacity.

   b. Because you have a personal relationship with Mary, you quickly accept the request for your support by appearing at the public comment hearing.

   c. You recognize the possible conflict by appearing at the public comment hearing in support of the victim and tell the notification office coordinator that you do not wish to become any more involved than you already are.

   d. Because you will more than likely be the offender's parole officer again if he is paroled, you decline because appearing at the public comment hearing in support of the victim would create a conflict of interest.

60. Mary's husband calls and tells you this public comment hearing and the possibility of a parole hearing for the offender has taken its toll on Mary. He tells you that Mary is not sleeping, not eating, and is having visions of the crime. He is worried about her. He asks if you would talk to her. In this circumstance, you

   a. agree to come to their home and talk with Mary.

   b. agree to talk with Mary, but ask that Mary be brought to the parole office.

   c. indicate that it would be better for Mary to talk to her counselor instead of you.

   d. suggest that you, Mary, and her counselor meet, and ask her husband if he thinks you or he should make the arrangements.

61. The public comment hearing is held, and Mary does a great job of providing her thoughts about any pending parole possibilities for the offender. Parole is denied for the offender, and another parole hearing date is set for three years. Mary contacts you and asks if you can meet for lunch. During the events leading up to the public comment hearing, you had felt very conflicted about this relationship and the strains it placed on you in your position. Which of the following should you do at this point?

   a. You should tell Mary that your relationship has caused you stress at work and that you are not able to have lunch or meet with her anymore.

   b. You should just not return Mary's phone calls anymore and hope she will get the message.

   c. You should call Mary's counselor and ask him or her to intervene and tell her how unhealthy it is to have a connection with the offender's parole officer.

   d. You should tell Mary how much you have enjoyed her visits in the past and that you would like them to continue; however, there may be times when your position as a parole officer must come first, and you hope she will understand your restraint or reluctance.

62. Which of the following sentences is punctuated correctly?
   a. In this program, the probation officers are placed directly in the schools to supervise their caseload while their students/offenders attend classes and meetings, before and after school.
   b. In this program. The probation officers are placed directly in the schools to supervise their caseload while their students/offenders attend classes and meetings, before and after school.
   c. In this program: the probation officer are placed directly in the schools to supervise their caseload while their students/offenders attend classes; meetings; before and after school.
   d. In this program; the probation officers are placed directly in the schools to supervise their caseload while their students/offenders attend classes: meetings, before and after school.

63. Which of the following sentences is punctuated correctly?
   a. The parole officer showed great restraint with the offender; after the offender threw his cup of soda at the officer.
   b. The parole officer showed great restraint with the offender after the offender threw his cup of soda at the officer.
   c. The parole officer, showed great restraint with the offender, after the offender threw his cup of soda at the officer.
   d. The parole officer; showed great restraint. With the offender after the offender threw his cup of soda at the officer.

64. Which of the following sentences is punctuated correctly?
   a. The victim was upset the offender was paroled without having special conditions attached to his parole.
   b. The victim was upset the offender was paroled without having special conditions attached to his parole?
   c. The victim was upset. The offender was paroled without having special conditions attached to his parole.
   d. The victim, was upset, the offender was paroled without having special conditions attached to his parole.

65. Which sentence do you feel is the most clearly written?
   a. When there are many temptations facing them, offenders have a difficult time staying within the boundaries of the laws.
   b. Offenders have a difficult time staying within the boundaries of the laws when there are many temptations facing them.
   c. Offenders have a difficult time, when there are many temptations facing them, staying within the boundaries of the laws.
   d. Within the boundaries of the laws, offenders have a difficult time staying when there are many temptations facing them.

66. Which sentence do you feel is the most clearly written?

   a. The parole officer found it easiest to update the case file immediately after the parolee left the office.

   b. Immediately after the parolee left the office, the parole officer found it easiest to update the case file.

   c. It was found easiest to update the case file immediately after the parolee left the office, the parole officer found.

   d. The parole officer found, immediately after the parolee left the office, it was easiest to update the case file.

67. Which sentence do you feel is the most clearly written?

   a. Parole officers must be ethical and trustworthy; it is important to understand.

   b. Parole officers, must be ethical and trustworthy, it is important to understand.

   c. Important to understand, parole officers must be ethical and trustworthy, it is.

   d. It is important to understand why parole officers must be ethical and trustworthy.

68. Which of the following sentences is NOT grammatically correct?

   a. It is important to understand the different styles of supervision.

   b. Unimportant rules can be forgotten and disregarded by the officer.

   c. It can't never be disregarded by the officer, because they are not the final authority.

   d. The final authority is usually the paroling authority, and they could disregard some rules.

69. Which of the following sentences is grammatically correct?

   a. The cop stopped the offenders in their car because they were playing their music too loud.

   b. The cop stopped the offenders because they were playing there music to loud in there car.

   c. The cop stopped the offenders because they is playing their music too loud in their car.

   d. The cop stopped the offenders because they was playing their music too loud in their car.

70. Which of the following sentences is grammatically correct?

   a. While sitting in jail, the offender told other offenders that he committed the crime.

   b. The offender told ofer ofenders that he committed the crime while setting in jail.

   c. He commited the crim while setting in jail, the offender told other offenders.

   d. The offender, while setting in jail, committed the crime he tole other offenders.

Directions: Read the following passage and then answer questions 71 through 77.

The case of *Morrissey v. Brewer* defined constitutional rights afforded to parolees prior to and during the parole revocation process. The case started when Morrissey was on parole after serving time for writing bad checks. Seven months later, Morrissey's parole was revoked when he violated several of his parole conditions, involving buying a car under an assumed name and driving it without permission; giving false statements to the police about his address and insurance company after a minor accident; and failing to report as directed to his parole officer. Morrissey admitted to all of the violations, and his parole was revoked without a hearing. Morrissey filed suit believing that his revocation was unconstitutional because he was not provided an opportunity for due process. Ultimately, after the case made its way through the legal system, the courts ruled that parolees do, in fact, have five main constitutional due process rights.

The five rights that must be afforded include: 1) written notice of the claimed violations, 2) disclosure of evidence against the parolee and the opportunity to be heard and present witnesses and/or evidence on his or her own behalf, 3) the opportunity to confront and cross-examine adverse witnesses (unless there is a good cause for not doing so), 4) a neutral and objective hearing body to review and hear the case, and 5) a written statement as to the evidence relied upon and the reasons for revoking parole.

In some states, *Morrissey* is interpreted to mean that parolees are entitled to a two-hearing process—the preliminary and revocation hearing—in addition to the aforementioned five rights. In other states, *Morrissey* is interpreted more loosely, as not mandating two hearings. Parolees do have the right to waive the preliminary hearing and be moved to the location where the final revocation hearing will be held.

If not waived by the parolee, a preliminary hearing must be held shortly after the time of arrest and detention to determine if there is probable cause to believe the offender has violated the conditions and terms of supervision. If the hearing officer determines that the offender has committed any violations, then the offender is returned to prison as a parole violator where he awaits his revocation hearing with the paroling authority. This is the only time that guilt or innocence is determined and parole may be revoked.

Cases such as *Morrissey* assure offenders that they will all be afforded their constitutional due process rights. Some citizens feel offenders should not be given such rights, nor should they be afforded further opportunity to harass people by cross-examining them during the first hearing. Other citizens believe that offenders are not able to offer a significant defense and should be afforded an attorney during all stages of this process. However, all citizens agree that there are too many offenders returning to the system as parole violators.

71. The case of *Morrissey v. Brewer* established which of the following?
- **a.** Offenders do not need to have two hearings if the state feels there is sufficient evidence to prove probable cause.
- **b.** Offenders are to receive documentation and written statements of the process at the final hearing.
- **c.** A judge must hear the case shortly after arrest.
- **d.** The court must disclose the evidence against the parolee and allow him or her the opportunity to be heard and present witnesses and/or evidence on his or her own behalf.

72. Which of the following restates the main idea of the passage?
- **a.** Offenders are given too many rights, and citizens are tired of it.
- **b.** Offenders need to have lawyers present at all times prior to and during the revocation process.
- **c.** Offenders are provided due process rights when arrested and during the revocation process.
- **d.** Society won't continue to pay for prisons that are filled with parole violators.

73. Morrissey felt he needed to file a lawsuit because
- **a.** the parole officer didn't like him and revoked his parole without cause.
- **b.** his parole was revoked without due process.
- **c.** when his parole was revoked, his car wasn't returned, and he'll need it when he is paroled again.
- **d.** he was not afforded an attorney at any stage of the process.

74. Which of the following was NOT a violation Morrissey committed that led to the revocation of this parole?
  a. He gave a false statement to the police and insurance company regarding his name and address.
  b. He stole several checks from his insurance company.
  c. He bought a car using a false name.
  d. He failed to report to his parole officer as directed.

75. The decision of the hearing officer at the preliminary hearing must meet which criteria?
  a. A sufficient amount of probable cause exists to show that the parolee violated the terms and conditions of parole.
  b. The same level of determination of guilt must be found during the revocation hearing process as during a court trial.
  c. An officer of the court must provide a sufficient amount of probable cause that led to the reasonable suspicion that violations occurred.
  d. Guilt or innocence isn't determined at the revocation process, so no set amount of evidence is required at this time.

76. Which of the following lists the rights afforded to parolees in *Morrissey v. Brewer*?
  a. disclosure of evidence against the parolee, opportunity to cross-examine witnesses, opportunity to be heard and present evidence, opportunity to have an attorney present at the hearing, and written notification of final revocation
  b. opportunity to cross-examine witnesses, opportunity to be heard and present evidence, opportunity to have a hearing within travel distance of the parolee's family and witnesses, opportunity to have an attorney present at the hearing, and written notice of reasons for final revocation
  c. written notice of the charges, evidence given in advance so an attorney can build a defense for the parolee, opportunity of attorney to cross-examine witnesses, ability to present a case in defense of the charges, and written notice of every decision made within the revocation process
  d. written notice of the charges, disclosure of evidence against the parolee, opportunity to cross-examine witnesses, an objective hearing body to hear the case, and written notice of reasons for final revocation

77. Which of the following is NOT correct regarding *Morrissey v. Brewer*?
  a. This case ensured offender rights are afforded in a reasonable time frame.
  b. Once the hearing officer finds probable cause, he or she will revoke parole and return the offender to a correctional facility.
  c. Only the offender has the opportunity to waive any of the due process rights afforded under *Morrissey*.
  d. A parolee can have an attorney present as an adviser throughout any of the revocation proceedings, if it is allowed by the hearing officer and/or paroling authorities.

Directions: Read the following passage and then answer questions 78 through 83.

Mandatory reporting of child abuse is a growing issue across the United States. Probation and parole officers, as statutory law enforcement agents, are required to report child abuse and neglect. Statistics have shown a decrease in substantiated child sexual abuse and maltreatment since the 1990s. Some believe this decline can be attributed to the efforts to catch and incarcerate offenders, along with publicizing their crimes and arrests. Others believe this decline is caused by the efforts to educate children, family members, schools, and neighborhoods about this issue.

Despite these efforts, many cases of maltreatment go undocumented, even by mandated reporters. There are five possible reasons reporters do not file a child abuse claim: 1) They may believe reporting the abuse won't make a difference; 2) They may not be open to the possibility that child maltreatment is actually happening and may deny it is occurring; 3) They may find the laws confusing and are not clear on exactly what should be reported; 4) They may not thoroughly understand what authority they have as law enforcement (probation and parole) officers in these situations; and 5) They may be afraid of reporting too many incidents or reporting incidents that do not meet the definition of abuse or neglect.

Many states have laws that indicate that mandatory reporters must report suspected child abuse and maltreatment when they have reasonable cause to believe that a child known to them in their official capacity is being abused or neglected. Communication between an officer and an offender is not considered privileged information and, therefore, not a valid justification for failing to report suspected abuse. Probation and parole officers must report offenders or the offenders' family members if they observe a child they suspect of being abused or neglected, or if the offender tells them about the abuse or neglect of a child who is within the offender's living arrangements.

This mandatory reporting is part of the probation or parole officer's primary goal of protecting the children within the community. However, the officer's commitment to this goal may lead to a poor working relationship with the offender and/or the offender's family. A probation or parole officer needs to be comfortable with his or her choices, even if those choices are difficult to make and/or will have long-term effects on the officer and the offender.

78. The main idea of this passage is best expressed by which of the following?
   a. Probation and parole officers do not fall within the mandatory reporting obligation, as they aren't true law enforcement officers.
   b. Probation and parole officers must follow the laws of their state, which allow them to report any suspected abuse of anyone, anywhere.
   c. If probation and parole officers are classified as law enforcement within the state, they are obligated to report any suspected child abuse and neglect of a child known to them in their official capacity.
   d. Probation and parole officers are not officers of the court and, therefore, do not have to follow the letter of the law. If they see or hear of abuse, they can decide what to do after considering the consequences of their decision.

79. Probation and parole officers should monitor the statistics regarding national trends toward child abuse and neglect to determine which of the following?

a. If the national trend is down, they do not have to be as careful when observing their offenders and the children within proximity of their offenders.

b. Statistics shouldn't influence whether a probation or parole officer reports suspected abuse and neglect; suspected cases must always be reported.

c. If the national trend is up, they need to watch their offenders more closely to observe and report the abuse that is surely happening.

d. Statistics shouldn't influence the probation or parole officer because they reflect national trends, not what is happening in the officer's own community.

80. Which of the following was NOT listed in the passage as one of the five reasons that probation and parole officers do not report suspected cases of abuse or neglect?

a. They believe reporting the abuse won't make a difference.

b. They may find the laws confusing and are not clear on exactly what should be reported.

c. They may not thoroughly understand what authority they have as law enforcement (probation and parole) officers in these situations.

d. They are unable to choose which agency they report the suspected abuse to.

81. There has been a decline in substantiated child sexual abuse and maltreatment cases since the 1990s. Which of the following did the author identify as reasons for this decline?

a. efforts to catch and incarcerate offenders, publicity about offenders' crimes and arrests, and efforts to educate members of the communities

b. efforts to embarrass the offenders by televising their arrests and prosecution of all offenders

c. removal of the abused children from their families and publicity about the offenders as a warning to other families

d. efforts to arrest and incarcerate the offenders so they can be rehabilitated and returned home to take care of their kids

82. Probation and parole officers should report which of the following situations as a suspected case of child abuse or neglect?

a. A child is spanked by the offender because the child was running with a fork in the house.

b. A child has a dazed look and was left in a diaper filled with fecal matter.

c. During a home visit, you hear a child whimpering from the locked closet.

d. When on the phone with the offender, you hear him threaten to kill the child when he gets off the phone.

83. In mandatory reporting, the probation or parole officer's responsibility is to

a. the child.

b. the offender.

c. him- or herself.

d. the officer's employing agency.

Directions: Read the following passage and then answer questions 84 through 90.

Drug courts began as a trend within the criminal justice system in the late 1980s, when a deluge of felony drug convictions strained the courts and crowded the jails and prisons. Drug courts were developed as an alternative to prison and as a way to handle this type of offender outside of traditional courts and correctional systems, which could then focus on other, more severe cases. Drug courts encourage defendants to enter and remain drug treatment programs until they benefit from them.

More than 1,500 drug courts were operating in the United States as of December 2005, and almost 400 more are being planned and developed. As a drug court is planned and implemented, several key components for success are considered: the target population, the judge's role and attitude toward the likelihood of success among drug court participants, treatment resources and issues, and cost-benefit analyses.

One of the advantages of a drug court program is that the members of the drug court team work with each offender to give them a proper assessment, create a treatment plan, review and secure services, and determine what types of performance reporting and results are necessary (including drug test results). Team members are educated in addiction and substance abuse theories, various current treatment approaches, and relapse prevention, all to ensure that offenders' needs are met. Another advantage of the program is the offenders' opportunity to interact with a single drug court judge, who becomes one of the most important influences they have while in the program. The judge's ability to communicate clearly, work through any legal issues quickly, and be available to offenders through an open-door policy is paramount to offenders' success in this type of program. These offenders are more likely to comply with program demands quickly and without further problems than offenders in larger communities and programs.

There are some disadvantages with drug courts, starting with the availability and quality of drug and alcohol treatment programs. A program in one community is simply not enough when you are attempting to make a significant impact on a targeted population. The program must be up to date in the therapeutic tools, to help those who need to have a long-lasting behavior change. Treatment programs that utilize a shotgun approach to the treatment may produce counterproductive results and/or behavior.

Drug courts have, in fact, reduced recidivism in some areas across the country. However, it is difficult to determine exactly what aspect of the program positively affects the offender and what type of offender responds best to this program. Also, the allocation of resources is based on a demonstrated benefit, which can be difficult to determine because data is not readily available on drug court programs.

84. Which of the following might be one of the themes of this passage?
   a. Drug courts work at reducing recidivism, although it is difficult to determine which aspect of the program is positively affecting the participants.
   b. Drug courts have too many disadvantages to make a significant impact on the participants.
   c. The program offers a lot of support both from its staff and through outside resources.
   d. Drug courts were trendy in the 1980s, but are now outdated.

85. The advantages to drug court programs did NOT include which of the following?
  a. Program staff members work together to develop a treatment plan.
  b. An assessment of the offender is completed to secure services and determine what types of performance reporting are necessary.
  c. The offender is able to stay within the community and pay restitution to the victim.
  d. The offender interacts with the same judge throughout the duration of the program.

86. Which of the following key components that must be considered when implementing a new drug court program in any community was NOT mentioned in the passage?
  a. targeted population
  b. available staffing
  c. treatment resources
  d. cost-benefit analyses

87. What was the reason that drug courts were developed in the 1980s?
  a. Drug courts were developed because federal money could be obtained if a program was implemented, and they soon became the latest fad among correctional agencies.
  b. Drug courts were developed so various members of the criminal justice system could start working together as a team to help offenders.
  c. Drug courts were developed to help maintain the community's substance abuse and mental health resources.
  d. Drug courts were developed as an alternative to prison and as a way to handle this type of offender outside of traditional courts and correctional systems, which could then focus on other, more severe cases

88. The treatment staff working with drug court participants conducts which of the following?
  a. assessments so that a proper treatment plan can be developed
  b. supervision of the participant so there isn't a relapse
  c. admission records so that the participant can be admitted for inpatient treatment
  d. a risk assessment to determine the type of risk the participant poses to the community

89. Which of the following was named by offenders in the passage as their most significant influence while in the program?
  a. the treatment team
  b. the probation officer
  c. the judge
  d. the program itself

90. Which of the following is mentioned in the passage as a reason that it is difficult to determine which aspect of the program makes the most positive impact?
  a. There are too many resources involved in this type of program, so it is difficult to pick just one.
  b. Data is not readily available on drug court programs, so it is difficult to prove which method of treatment works best.
  c. The allocation of resources depends upon the success of various treatment methods; and funds are awarded to the program that uses the most successful methods.
  d. There aren't many drug courts available across the United States; therefore, a first-rate program hasn't been developed yet.

Directions: Read the following passage and then answer questions 91 through 95.

The presentence investigation report is a tool that helps the judge decide upon the most appropriate sentence for the defendant. At the state level, this report provides the judge with information about the defendant's life, past criminal history, educational and vocational skills and needs, and substance abuse and mental health issues, as well information regarding the victim. There is usually an informed recommendation from the probation officer regarding the possible sentences and any other needs that should be addressed by the defendant if placed under supervision upon conviction. Generally, evidence shows a high correlation between the report recommendations made by the officer and the sentence imposed by the judge. Based on that information, many defense attorneys feel that due process requires access to the presentence report. Many attorneys believe that there is a distinct interest in liberty at this stage and that they should have access to the report and to its author.

At the federal level, the rules of criminal procedure require that presentence reports include information about the defendant's history and characteristics, including any prior criminal record, financial condition, and any other details that may be helpful in imposing a sentence or correctional treatment.

Most likely, all or part of the presentence report will be disclosed to the defendant and attorney because of state statute, court rule, or the exercise of judicial discretion. Third parties have made requests to have access to presentence reports, but those requests have been denied. However, these decisions are being challenged.

It is important for the probation officer to exercise great care in choosing materials to include in the presentence report, and in ensuring that all information is correct. The officer should also exercise great care in avoiding any situation that would place him or her in contempt of court or in tort and possibly criminal liability action. Probation and parole officers should know that intentionally including information in a report with knowledge of its falsehoods or with reckless disregard for the truth will receive strict consequences.

There have always been questions about the distribution of the presentence report and whether any further action should be taken against its author (i.e., cross-examination). Defense attorneys have long claimed that it is the right of the defendant to know what has been written about him or her as well as to know the recommendations made. It is further argued that the defendant should have the opportunity to have the report's author cross-examined during the hearing or trial. The ability to argue points made in the presentence report have bogged down the court proceedings and has caused the actual crime to get lost amid the fighting over terminology or the process of collecting materials.

The presentence report should be viewed as a court document, not as a document the defense attorneys have the right to tear apart. If probation officers are trained appropriately and officers who have exhibited good judgment, good communication skills, and strong ethics are hired, then the report should be valid, accurate, and appropriate. There shouldn't be any reason for the defense attorney to cross-examine a court official as to the validity of the material.

91. The general message in this passage is best restated as
   a. presentence investigation reports are usually full of falsehoods and misinformation.
   b. presentence investigation reports are important factual documents that help the judge find an appropriate sentence for the defendant, who has the ability to see the report prior to sentencing.
   c. presentence investigation reports are strictly for the defense and are used to bog down the court system by initiating arguments over the information that is presented by the probation officer.
   d. probation officers must create documents that tell of the defendant's life and criminal history so the defense attorneys can plan a strategy.

92. The author implies that the presentence report is used for what purpose?
  a. to help the judge give a harsh sentence
  b. to help the victim ensure that justice will be done
  c. to help the defendant and the defense find a strategy to get a lighter sentence
  d. to help the probation officer win points with the judge

93. The author mentioned several components of the presentence report. Which of the following was NOT listed in the passage?
  a. educational and vocational skills and needs
  b. past criminal history of the defendant
  c. information regarding the victim
  d. physical and medical information

94. It is important the presentence report be which of the following?
  a. accurate, factual, and appropriate
  b. appropriate information that the judge needs to hear, whether or not it is in the best interest of the defendant
  c. accurate to a point, but in the best interest of the defendant
  d. information that the judge wants to hear and is presented professionally

95. In general, what information is different in the federal presentence reports from in the state presentence reports?
  a. past criminal history
  b. financial records
  c. medical and physical information
  d. education and vocational skills and needs

Directions: Read the following passage and then answer questions 96 through 100.

Family support programs are becoming increasingly important for agencies to recognize as a vital part of their employee assistance program. In some cases, job stress affects the family as much as, if not more than, the employee. Stress factors for employees and family members have been identified in various studies and include handling severe conflicts, "use of force" incidents, and quick-decision-making situations, as well as the everyday tasks that take a toll on an employee. Agencies must readily identify the stress factors and quickly develop programs to alleviate the stress that is caused by the job responsibilities. Agencies' adoption of services may be useful, but their true value will be recognized in the officers' knowledge of and willingness to use these programs.

Officers use employee assistance programs (EAPs) when an event happens in their personal life or when an emergency happens at work and then manifests itself at home. Another reason that employees utilize EAPs is that they are sometimes required to participate in a certain program for specific job-related stress. Given the choice to gain assistance through EAPs or to tough it out, officers typically will not utilize the services available to them. Seeking help does not often fit within the tough image that law enforcement and corrections staff must maintain at work, nor does a staff member want to be burdened with the perceived label that will be attached when he or she goes to an EAP service. Officers are extremely sensitive to being labeled because there is a perception that seeking services is a sign of weakness, which could prevent future promotions and/or assignments.

Many agencies do, in fact, have sufficient programs or services that are offered free or of minimal cost to the employees, so that stress of life can be dealt with professionally. Offering services, however, is simply not enough if employees are left to decide if they participate or not in these services. The mere existence of the programs is not enough and cannot help if they are not utilized. Agencies must be more receptive to marketing the benefits of using these programs and the fact that management is supportive of anyone who should need to use the programs, without retribution, real or perceived. The focus should be on developing strategies to raise the credibility and trust of these programs and reduce the stigma that exists in asking for help, rather than on developing more, flashier programs.

96. Which of the following best summarizes the author's viewpoint in this passage?
a. Officers must get over their fears and use the programs that the agency offers.
b. Agencies must find ways to convince officers to trust the EAPs offered, and management must show their support of the utilization of the programs.
c. Stress is inherent in this type of job, and the officer and his or her family must work at resolving their own conflicts and contributions to their stress levels.
d. Agencies should be worried about offering assistance only to their employees; family members are not the agency's concern.

97. Which of the following was NOT included in the list of ways that agencies can encourage employees to utilize the assistance programs more?
a. Agencies must be more proactive in marketing the benefits of the programs.
b. Agencies must make the programs more accessible to family members, offering the programs on evenings and weekends.
c. Management must be supportive of anyone who needs to use these programs and allow them to do so without retribution, real or perceptive.
d. Strategies must be developed to raise the credibility of the programs and reduce the stigma that exists in asking for help.

98. What did the author identify as the one true advantage of employee assistance programs?
a. Agencies offer them free to the employee and his or her family.
b. Agencies have developed strategies to raise the credibility of the programs.
c. The employee has the knowledge and willingness to use the programs.
d. The employee utilizes the programs when his or her family is in crisis.

99. Employees utilize employee assistance programs for themselves or their family members for which of the following reasons?
a. an event happens at their home that causes stress
b. an event happens at work, which manifests itself as more stress at home
c. an event occurs that puts the family in crisis
d. all of the above

100. Which of the following is listed in the passage as a type of stress officers must deal with?
a. domestic violence situations
b. quick-decision-making situations
c. investigations of violations and offenses
d. paperwork that must be done on a daily basis

► Answers

1. b. *Morrissey v. Brewer* is the case that established constitutional due process rights to parolees prior to and during the parole revocation process. Choice **a** involves processes that were established for probationers under *Gagnon v. Scarpelli*. Choices **c** is incorrect because diversion is part of a criminal justice process available prior to probation, and if violations occur, a defendant reverts back to a hearing on the original charge and faces probation if convicted. Community corrections revocation processes (choice **d**) are part of the probation revocation process, or the parole revocation process if the offender is a parolee.

2. c./d. Depending on a particular state's procedure, there may be two appropriate responses to this situation. In most states, the action described in choice **d** would be the correct answer. The parole officer should write an addendum to the violation report explaining why the written charges were not presented to the parolee in time. Usually the delay occurs because the parole officer is still gathering evidence to include in the violation report. If this is an acceptable reason, then the hearing officer will determine whether the justification for late notification was valid. The alternative answer is choice **c**: Many states feel a time frame of 48 hours is sufficient for any parole officer to provide notice. If the parole officer is not able to give written notice of the charges in that amount of time, then the parolee is released from detention. Choice **a** is incorrect because keeping the parolee in detention is a violation of his or her due process rights, without cause or justification. Choice **b** is also incorrect; simply to hope that the hearing officer won't dismiss the case is not an acceptable protection of a parolee's constitutional rights.

3. c. If the strategy was to make an unscheduled home visit, then make an unscheduled employment visit and ask to speak with the offender for a few minutes and promise that your conversation will be brief. When you speak to the offender, you need to remember to keep the conversation focused on finding out his living arrangements, and ask the offender to report to your office either at the end of his shift or the next day to discuss the matter further. It is important to remember the offender may be defensive and may chose to abscond if he or she is conducting other criminal behavior. Choice **a** is an option; however, if the parolee is at work, he is more than likely not able to take phone calls. Choice **b** might be a too hasty and unnecessary step, which may also have a long-term impact on your relationship with the offender, especially if he has a valid reason for the address being wrong. Choice **d** is not an option because the parole officer should require the offender to provide a valid address as soon as possible, not in a month.

4. d. This was Morrissey's original charge, not one of his parole violations. Choices **a**, **b**, and **c** were all violations that Morrissey admitted to, and the parole officer revoked the parole based on those admissions.

5. c. Waiting to issue a probation violation warrant will allow the court system to figure out the specifics of the domestic situation. Because law enforcement at the scene determined that the offender was not the aggressor, he or she is not a risk to the community with this situation. If the offender makes bail, he can then report to your office, where you can advise him of new special conditions or other supervision issues that would be pertinent to discuss. Choice **a** means the state assumes the cost of the offender, and the actual domestic abuse situation becomes a secondary situation. If this situation had happened before, then this might be a correct action. Choice **b** is incorrect; you can't release him, because you aren't the one holding him in custody. Only the prosecutor could release the offender by dismissing the charges. Choice **d** is incorrect. In all reality, a parole officer should not talk with the prosecutor to negotiate for the parolee. Although this action may be taken in extreme circumstances, this situation is not that extreme. A parole officer should allow the prosecutor to do his or her job, and then figure out if the action is severe enough to start revocation proceedings.

6. b. If the group counselor wishes for the offender not to participate in the group setting any longer, then the parolee needs to be moved. However, the offender's issues and inappropriate behavior need to be addressed by a counselor. Once the parolee stops having inappropriate feelings and thoughts, then the counselor can help establish the parolee in another group setting. Choice **a** is incorrect because it would not address and deal with the offender's behavior problems, and because passing the parolee onto another unsuspecting group is a not responsible action. Choice **c** is incorrect and would only make the parolee upset and cause him to become possibly more secretive in his efforts to show his feelings toward the other group member. Choice **d** should be a conversation between the parolee and a counselor, not the parole officer, because the counselor is more equipped to deal with the offender's feelings and other concerns.

7. d. Although these were originally goals of the parole system, the objectives of parole have had to become more realistic. Although a

desired outcome, reduced recidivism is not a practical goal because of the many obstacles that parolees face in today's world. Choices **a**, **b**, and **c** are all ways to protect communities and states from released offenders.

8. c. This is a special condition that might be placed on parolees who are sex offenders. The conditions listed in choices **a**, **b**, and **d** are standard conditions for parolees across the nation.

9. c. Day reporting centers will help offenders stay off drugs, pursue their education, and find employment. Participants also learn life skills, participate in treatment programs, and receive slightly more supervision than they would with a parole officer.

10. d. Because he and his ex-girlfriend are no longer together, the parolee cannot enforce what the child support checks are used for. He can maintain a watchful eye to see if his kids are being mistreated. If he feels that they are, the parole officer can suggest contacting agencies or other means within the legal system to help resolve the issue. Otherwise, he doesn't have a say in how the money is spent and must pay the child support as ordered. Not doing so would be a violation of parole as well as the court order. Choice **a** is good advice in this situation, but being so direct with the offender may cause a negative reaction. Choice **b** is incorrect because the court has ordered the parolee to pay child support, and that order must be followed. A parolee would not have to pay support as directed only when the child(ren) reach legal age or are not in school. Choice **c** is incorrect because the parole officer is advising the parolee to disobey a court order, which will eventually lead the parolee into other legal difficulties.

11. c. The presentence investigation report is not a public document and is not covered under the open records act. Certain components of this report are public information (i.e., the crime and other criminal history), but the witness statements—individuals speaking about the offender's past employment, education, and substance abuse (choice **d**)—are not public information and are privileged to the court. Choices **a** and **b** are incorrect. The open records act does not force agencies to provide documents that are normally not available in routine methods of information collections. The court, however, can provide directives to releasing certain information, but great care is taken to protect those citizens who offered assistance and do not wish for any publicity.

12. a. Hearsay evidence is admissible in a presentence report, because it may be helpful to the judge in determining an appropriate sentence. The judge must be given every opportunity to review current and useful information during the sentencing phase. Choice **b** is incorrect because the officer of the court, the probation officer, does not provide anything above what is offered to and for the lawful purpose of the report. Choices **c** and **d** are incorrect because the hearsay evidence can be admitted, but the officer can be cross-examined about the validity of the information. The report is ordered by and for the court; however, hearsay evidence is included in the PSI and can be placed into a court hearing with cause.

13. d. You should start the interview and explain to the defendant what a presentence investigation is and describe the process you will be working through to complete the investigation. Choice **c** will probably anger the defendant and cause conflict between you, the defendant, and possibly his attorney. Choice **a** does not have to be done; appellate courts have held that Miranda rights do not need to be read to the defendant before interviewing him for the PSI because the investigation does not elicit the defendant's right against self-incrimination. Choice **b** is incorrect because the defendant does not have the right to legal counsel during the PSI interview, although the probation officer may allow an attorney to sit in. This is not an adversarial situation because the probation officer is conducting this interview as an arm of the court, not as an arm of the prosecution.

14. b. A work-release program is a restrictive environment (more restrictive than a halfway house), in which offenders live within a facility, follow program rules, participate in treatment and mental health programs within the community, and work outside the facility. Offenders usually pay a stipend toward rent, must pay their restitution and other financial obligations, and must have a savings account. Choice **a** is a military-style program in which offenders are pushed physically and mentally until they have changed their criminal behavior and thinking. Choice **c** is a center to which offenders report on a daily basis, either in person or by phone, but live in their own living quarters. Choice **d** is a program that brings community resources, law enforcement, courts, and corrections together to offer services to offenders so they may be successful.

15. a. *Good time* is the legal term for the result of computing an offender's time already served (minus any time lost because of violations), to reduce the length of his or her sentence before becoming eligible for parole or before being released from parole supervision. Choices **b** and **d** are incorrect because these decisions have already been made and acted upon if the parolee is on parole. Choice **c** is incorrect because this task is required of parole officers by the states that offer good time to offenders.

16. d. Parole agencies are commonly organized under a state agency within the executive branch of state government. Federal probation and parole offices, however, are currently administered as part of the judicial branch of the federal courts. Choices **a**, **b**, and **c** are all incorrect and are not legal terms or divisions.

17. a. In states that have parole boards, members are usually appointed by the governor. Although there are ideal qualifications for members, there aren't set criteria that parole board members must meet in order to be appointed. Choices **b**, **c**, and **d** are not involved in the appointments of parole board members. However, the director of corrections must be able to work with the board members because their decisions have a direct impact on the prison population. The chief of the state supreme court and legislators do not have much of an interest in the process; however, legislators in some states validate the selection through the legislative processes.

18. b. Parole conditions should be clear and reasonable, not complex (choice **d**) or full of legalese and complicated (choice **a**). The length of the conditions is a concern, as long as the condition is relevant (choice **c**)—but, more important, clear and reasonable.

19. b. Standard conditions is correct. Choice **c** are conditions that are used for individuals who need a specific area of concern to be addressed. Choices **a** and **d** are not legal terms for conditions.

20. a. Because the victim is not able to administer punishment legally, the state takes this action, to make the victim whole. The community (choice **b**) as a whole is not considered the victim of a crime. Choice **d** is not able to be "the victim" in any official capacity; the judge, if the victim of a crime, would proceed through any court proceedings in his citizen capacity rather than his official capacity. Choice **c** does not make sense.

21. d. Choices **a**, **b**, and **c** are all used to determine how much the offender should owe to the victim and to the community.

22. b. The only place an officer may conduct a search is an offender's home. An offender can approve a search conducted by an officer or by law enforcement only of areas that he or she has control over or owns. Choices **a**, **c**, and **d** do not legally belong to the offender, unless his or her name is on the lease (i.e., a significant other's home). In these cases, the only person who can approve a search of the area, is the significant other, the employer, or the treatment facility manager.

23. a. House arrest is one of the intermediate sanctions available when offenders, particularly low-risk offenders, need physical restriction but not incarceration. Intermediate sanctions provide offenders with options that vary in terms of their supervision levels and treatment plans. Choice **b** is a sentencing option that the court may offer prior to the offender entering into the prison system. Choice **d** is an option for incarcerated offenders who have exhibited good behavior, have reached minimum supervision custody, and are within a reasonable time frame of being released. Choice **c** is available for offenders who are incarcerated and have yet to make substantial efforts at paying restitution.

24. b. A classification tool, often called a "risk and needs" assessment, is used to determine what risks the offender poses to the community, what needs the offender has, and how to best supervise the offender. Choice **d** is a tool that calculates the number of hours required to supervise an offender, based upon that offender's level of supervision. Choices **a** and **c** are incorrect.

25. b. The judge is the only one who can set and modify the conditions and length of probation. The probation officer (choice **a**) enforces the conditions and terms, and can develop a plan for how a probationer will abide by those conditions. Choice **c** becomes involved only when approval is needed to take the offender and the modification request before a judge. Choice **d** is incorrect because probation conditions are always in flux and may need modifications frequently.

26. c. In *McKune v. Lile* (2002), the U.S. Supreme Court held that an acknowledgment of all prior sex offenses does not violate the Fifth Amendment's protection against self-incrimination. The court justified its decision by indicating that acknowledgment of past offenses is the beginning of rehabilitation and acceptance of responsibility for his or her actions. Choice **a** is incorrect and would probably create conflict between you and the offender. Choice **b** is incorrect; presenting "win or lose" ultimatums will certainly create conflict for the officer. Choice **d** should not be a first step but may become necessary if the officer feels there are no other alternatives and other programs and counseling have been tried.

27. a. The officer has developed a treatment plan for the offender. A treatment plan is a plan of actions that will bring about a change in the offender's conduct or well being for the purpose of reintegration and rehabilitation. Choice **c** is a measurement of the risk or danger the offender poses to the community because of his past criminal history. Choice **d** is an overall plan to identify specific supervision issues about and strategies for working with the offender, including treatment and risk control. Supervision includes conditions (choice **b**) as well as consequences for not fulfilling those conditions.

28. c. During a collateral visit, the officer attempts to verify the offender's progress with people not directly involved with the offender's employment or living arrangements. A

neighbor, a treatment staff member, or a religious figure are all people you should seek out for a collateral visit. Choice **a** occurs when an officer meets with an offender. Choice **d** takes place when an officer and an offender meet in the offender's home. Choice **b** is a visit that is conducted somewhere other than the offender's home or place of employment (i.e., a local restaurant).

29. c. Lax supervision and failure to deal with offenders who persistently violate the terms of their supervision can and will jeopardize an officer's authority. Choice **d** is incorrect, although poor documentation can prevent officers from supervising their offenders properly and thoroughly. Choices **a** and **b** are inconvenient and stressful but do not jeopardize authority.

30. b. Time served on community supervision does not count and is not credited as prison time (*Bruggeman v. State*, 1996). Essentially, it is wasted time if an offender's probation is revoked because of violations. Jail time accrued while waiting to be sentenced or to be transported does count toward the prison sentence. Choice **d** is incorrect, but it is better than providing false information. Giving the responses in choices **a** and **c** would be providing false information.

31. b. It is extremely important that Winslow provide the police details of the conversation and descriptions of the man who contacted him. Choice **a** is not a good choice for several reasons: The safety of you and Winslow should always come first, and bringing in the individual who was looking for a hit man would likely cause trouble, and not yield any more information. Choice **c** would be an option *only* if Winslow repeatedly refuses to cooperate; the police department could then pick up Winslow and interview him in a more suitable environment. Choice **d** is not a reasonable action for a law enforcement officer.

32. d. Debating an issue regarding your offender will not help your offender; your priority should instead be assisting him or her. Choices **a** and **c** are incorrect because it really doesn't matter whether a police detective agrees with the agency's drug-testing methods. A continued debate would not serve any constructive purpose. Choice **b** is not a reasonable action to take when the detective is merely expressing his opinion, not acting inappropriately or making discriminatory comments. Taking this action would only cause conflict between you and the detective.

33. a. Winslow needs to learn how his mother was supporting his siblings while he was in prison. A parole officer's responsibilities require him or her to assist parolees in a many ways, and in this case, you must encourage Winslow to talk to his mother about how she can financially support her family while he lives separately. Choice **b** is not reasonable, because your responsibility is to the parolee, not his family, and you should help him achieve goals that will lead to his success. Choice **c** is also not a reasonable suggestion to give a parolee who is struggling with issues of family and financial responsibility. His concern is valid, and dismissing his concern will not yield a positive result. Choice **d** may be part of the discussion in which you explore his available options, but this should not be your first suggestion.

34. b. As a parole officer, you are often a broker of services. In this situation, it is your responsibility to make parolees aware of the available services and options for difficult situations. Then it is your responsibility to offer assistance in whatever way possible. Because this is a potentially difficult family situation, you should encourage the parolee to talk with his

mother and express his suspicions, and then work toward a resolution with her through the available resources. Choice **a** has the potential to exacerbate Winslow's issues and concerns. In the scenario, Winslow has a concern for his younger siblings and to tell him to let his mother handle the situation will not alleviate his concern and may cause him to resort to other actions without talking to you first. Choices **c** and **d** are incorrect because Winslow does not have a say in who lives in his mother's home. Also, this action would certainly escalate the situation without resolving the issue.

35. b. Because of Winslow's original charge, the officer should describe the situation and conversation with the offender to a supervisor. It may be decided that surveillance or other actions are needed to ensure Winslow's compliance. Choices **a** and **c** are incorrect and would be irresponsible considering Winslow's original charge. The deliberate participation of an officer in an offender's violation of his supervision could lead to a public relations and political nightmare. Choice **d** is incorrect; the situation should be documented in the offender's file, but the supervisor should also be made aware of the offender's request and your denial of that request.

36. d. The offender is asking for advice, not a decision. The parole officer should simply provide options and then let the offender make his or her own decision. Choices **b** and **c** are incorrect because the parole officer is hearing only Winslow's side of the story, and the police officers' "inappropriate" actions are, at this point, only hearsay. Suggesting that Winslow hire an attorney and sue the city or critiquing another law enforcement agent is only inviting conflict. Dismissing the offender's feelings of being singled out (choice **a**) could alienate the offender from the officer.

37. b. It is best to report any inappropriate and/or illegal actions directly to the supervisor, who should take immediate action to protect the evidence, the officers involved, and the parole office environment. Choice **d** is an action that should be taken by the afflicted parole officer, in conjunction with the parole supervisor. Because you were not involved in the physical altercation, it is not your responsibility to make this call. Choice **a** is incorrect because telling him about your plan of action is unnecessary and could endanger you if Sam continues to be angry. It is important to provide documentation (choice **c**); however, sending the officer out of the office is an action for the supervisor, and doing so could impede an investigation, if the officer is needed by the supervisor.

38. d. Although Sam's questions are very inappropriate, neither rise to the level of sexual harassment as defined by federal regulations. However, these questions should be further investigated by the agency or the local police department. Choice **a** would be correct if Sam had propositioned the officer to have sex, but Sam had only asked if the officer had ever wanted to have sex with an offender. The federal regulation indicates one incident, if severe enough, would be sufficient to file a sexual harassment charge; this situation does not meet that standard. Choice **b** is incorrect because, although an officer can file a sexual harassment charge at any time, he or she should do so only when the federal standards have been met, to avoid filing frivolous cases. Choice **c** is incorrect because the two questions, as asked, are not in violation of state and/or federal laws.

39. c. Your supervisor should be able to provide some information about the focus of the investigation and how far along it is. Although personnel action is confidential, the supervisor should be able to provide some assurances as to what the process might be and what your involvement will be. Choice **d** is not appropriate; there may be bigger issues at stake than the misconduct toward you. Issuing threats is not professional and may hurt your reputation and credibility. Choice **b** may be a good assumption, but doing nothing will certainly not ease your discomfort about the situation. Choice **a** is incorrect because officers should always be willing to ensure that other officers in the field are conducting themselves appropriately and professionally.

40. d. Contacting the assistant district attorney (ADA) who is handling the case will allow you to obtain the correct advice and counsel for this situation; also, you will be letting the ADA know that one of his or her key witnesses is nervous, so he or she will need to work hard to prepare you for being on the stand. Choice **b** is incorrect because hiring your own attorney seems unnecessary, even if you had the extra income to afford it. It may help your nerves to repeat your testimony over and over (choice **a**), but the mirror will not provide you critical feedback. Choice **c** is incorrect because witnesses should not discuss their testimony and the case with anyone, and doing so would place you and the trainer in a difficult situation with the prosecution, the judge, and potentially the agency.

41. d. As difficult as it is to be the subject of a vicious rumor, the best action is to ignore it and continue working in a professional manner. It is important, though, to speak with your supervisor and assure him or her that the rumor is unfounded; losing your supervisor's trust could hurt you in the long run. Choice **c** says that rumor mills change quickly, which is true; however, it is incorrect because it suggests that nothing should be done. Choices **a** and **b** are incorrect because they humor the rumor; not reacting to the pettiness of others is not easy, but it will make you appear more professional.

42. d. After being convicted of misdemeanor charges, the officer will only face more consequences if he acts on his frustration or anger toward you, and his probation officer should convey that point. You should remain professional and go about your business as usual. Choices **a** and **c** may be attractive options, but they are a little extreme and, therefore, unrealistic. Choice **b** is incorrect because altering your schedule and/or lifestyle to avoid the offender would be inappropriate.

43. c. In this situation, the change of clothing is the most important detail. The jewelry may have been a gift from the offender's parents, a friend, or another significant person, or if the offender bought the jewelry for herself, she should not have to produce any receipts. It is important to give the offender an opportunity to tell the truth, but if the offender does not tell the truth, then an officer should employ an investigation/enforcement style of supervision. Choice **d** is incorrect; documenting observations and monitoring the situation with more unannounced visits are good supervision techniques, but an officer should always address any suspicions with the offender. Choices **a** and **b** are incorrect because the officer would be jumping to conclusions by taking these steps. These actions would be part of a direct supervision style and should be used only if the offender has a pattern of lying or withholding all of the facts.

44. a. Sarah's attorney is her representative and can be asked to cooperate. It is hoped that the attorney will contact Sarah and convince her

that it is in her best interest to report to the probation/ISP office. Choice **b** is incorrect; this action would severely damage your working relationship with the judge and the attorney. Additionally, you do not wish to appear incompetent to the judge who may have appointed you. Choice **c** is incorrect because it is not the most productive step in this situation. Choice **d** is incorrect because contacting the parents after the attorney contact may be viewed as manipulative.

45. b. Because Sarah is not violating her conditions while at work, this situation is not your concern. Suggesting to the bank manager that he get extra security or involve the police is the best advice you could provide. Also, it would be wise to talk with Sarah about her associations during her next office visit. Choice **a** is incorrect because you would be assuming responsibility for this situation and dealing with people whom you do not have jurisdiction and authority over. Choice **c** may be a realistic option, but it gives responsibility for the situation to Sarah, who may not be strong enough to handle it, which jeopardizes her employment. Choice **d** is an inappropriate response.

46. c. Usually, an officer's hunch that an offender is hiding something is correct. In this case, the offender did not give details when asked for them, or gave vague information about who was going with her or why. Traveling to another state is a privilege, not a right, which must be approved by the parole officer. In choice **c**, which is correct, the officer denies permission but reminds the offender that she can take the trip when her probation has been completed. Choice **a** might also be an appropriate response, but the tone is a little harsh and may cause the offender to take drastic action (i.e., travel to the Bahamas without your permission). Choice **b** might satisfy the officer's curiosity, but an officer takes a gamble that the information on the forms may force the officer to grant the request. Issuing threats (choice **d**) will not prove productive for the officer in the end and should be avoided.

47. a. Because a motion has been filed, the officer needs to put together a factual record of the offender's progress. Also, an officer should make a fair recommendation that would be consistent with his or her recommendations for other offenders. Putting an offender on supervised probation rather than in ISP may be a nice compromise and would allow the judge to keep the offender under supervision but support the political agenda. Choices **b**, **c**, and **d** are incorrect because the officer is not maintaining his or her consistency and credibility. Having a reputation for playing favorites will not serve the officer well.

48. b. A probation officer should utilize a counseling style of supervision when helping offenders find ways to start something new. Many offenders have negative feelings about counseling, and officers must be patient and willing to compromise to gain the desired outcome (in this case, offender goes to counseling). Being direct, as in choice **a**, will probably get more resistance from Sarah against this program as well as others you may want to have her participate in. Choice **c** is incorrect because, once paperwork has been signed and all special conditions have been agreed to, usually the only way to remove a condition is to complete it. In probation cases, judges have the authority to order special conditions, but in most ISP situations, the condition can be issued and the judge's signature can be obtained later. Choice **d** is incorrect; Sarah is an adult, and calling her father is not an appropriate action. Even if the father is responsible for Sarah not participat-

ing in the program, an officer's obligation is to the offender, not the family members.

49. b. Because misconduct is being done, you are safer outside of the parole office. The parole officer's judgment should be questioned, especially if he is going to the trouble of wearing latex gloves while searching offices. You do not know this officer's breaking point, so it is best to leave the office and immediately call the supervisor to inform him or her of what you saw while the details are fresh in your mind. Choice **a** is incorrect because more immediate action should be taken. Even though the office is empty until morning, the parole officer may take more drastic action now that he has been caught in misconduct. Choice **c** would not be a safe action to take, especially because you do not know how the officer will react now that you have observed him in misconduct. Documentation is necessary, but it does not have to be done at the parole office, and certainly not slid under the supervisor's door while the parole officer is still in the office. Choice **d** would be very unsafe and unwise during the evening after business hours, with just the two of you in the office. Although it is unthinkable that one parole officer may hurt another, it is always better to put safety first when dealing with everyone: offenders *and* coworkers.

50. c. The actions taken against you in this situation might be reason to file a complaint. There are various options for policy violations such as a sexual harassment/hostile workplace policy (based on sexual orientation or gender), a grievance policy, or a workplace violence policy if there is an implication of threat or an actual threat. However, if told about the actions, your supervisor will put a stop to them and put Brett on notice that his misconduct should cease. Choice **a** only gives the officer the attention he wants and may lead to further disagreements between you. Choice **b** might be an alternative option if other actions don't work first. However, supervisors should be able to handle this situation properly, and moving shouldn't be necessary. Choice **d** is certainly not an option in this situation and would escalate the conflict between you.

51. a. Threats, implied or real, should always be investigated in a calm fashion. If the threat is not real, and the situation has been controlled, then no one else should know of the matter. Your supervisor should be the first person you contact in all situations in which a threat has been made (choice **a**). In this case, the offender telling the supervisor allows the supervisor to ask questions and make decisions based upon facts rather than hearsay. Choice **b** may allow you to appear unaffected by the information, but it is not wise to ignore threats, real or otherwise. Choice **c** would not be wise, because a confrontation would only escalate the conflict. Choice **d** would be nice to believe; however, safety should always be on the minds of parole officers.

52. c. You should always recognize assistance from others. In this case, you should also ensure that your supervisor is aware of the need to restrain an offender within the parole office, and once the situation has been brought under control, you should tell your supervisor about the officer's quick action helping to restrain the offender. Choice **a** is appropriate, but the situation probably warrants more than just a quick thank-you. Choice **b** would bring on only more conflict between you and the other officer. Choice **d** is an action that should be taken by a supervisor, not you.

53. d. Parole officers must sometimes use a "parent-style" of supervision, in which an officer must retrain an offender to utilize basic life skills such as interviewing, managing a bank account, and/or handling transportation needs. This type of supervision may take extra time and planning. Choices **a** and **b** are both actions that would cause conflict between you and the offender and, therefore, are not appropriate responses in this situation. Officers must be patient and remember that, for some offenders, living within the community is very challenging. Choice **c** is incorrect because the tone of the response is a little harsh, but it would be an appropriate action in a direct style of supervision.

54. c. It would be best to keep Oscar in jail on a revocation warrant until you learn all of the facts of the situation and the prosecutor has made decisions regarding the new charge. There may be more to the story, including a valid reason for Oscar's actions. If charges are filed, then you can make a decision how to deal with the technical violations. Choices **a** and **b** are incorrect because you would be taking the easy way out of the situation, instead of doing everything in your authority to help the offender. Choice **d** is incorrect because listening to and responding to an offender's complaints are part of your job responsibilities. Also, if you persevere in working through problems and obstacles with offenders, you are providing them a valuable example of an important life skill.

55. a. Conducting an unscheduled home visit is always a good way to verify an offender's address, to check up on the activities of the offender, and to let the offender know he should be prepared for you checking on his progress in this way. Making notes about any changes or other new and pertinent information regarding the offender in the case file is also important. Choices **b** and **c** are incorrect because at this point these actions may be inviting more stress for the offender, but they may be steps an officer would take if the offender has had a positive urinalysis. Choice **d** would not be a prudent response because waiting for any period of time to verify an address may result in the offender changing locations again and/or deciding to abscond.

56. b. Even though Oscar's family are no longer part of his life, you must not assume that other family members are not important to the offender. Denying the visit (choice **a**) or putting stipulations on the visit (choice **d**) may cause conflict with the offender and lead him to resist future requests and directives. Although this action could be seen as helpful, choice **c** could also give the impression that you do not approve of this new situation, which may also cause additional stress for or conflict with the offender. In this case, the correct answer is choice **b**: acknowledging the offender's hard work and good progress and then suggesting several issues to think about and actions to take, in the hope that Oscar will continue to make good choices while the brother moves in. Suggesting means of assistance for the brother would also be seen as helpful, not judgmental.

57. c. Because most offenders do not want attention drawn to them, Oscar may be shying away from the publicity, not the award itself. If the officer can find a compromise to offer to the offender, then he is more likely to participate. Choice **a** would be in the direct style of supervision and, in this situation, would probably cause a great deal of conflict with the offender, to which he may respond by absconding. You can only provide the offender an outlet to discuss his fears or concerns about the situation; you cannot push the offender to do something that makes him uncomfortable (choice **b**). Choice **d** is incorrect because it is not a reasonable response to a citizen's request.

58. b. The first and most important action is to obtain facts, and in this case you should first find out if the offender is, in fact, being granted a parole hearing. Once that information has been confirmed, then you should verify the process of notification (which may be designated by policy). Choice **a** would not resolve the immediate problem that the victim is confused and afraid, and would serve only to upset more people. Choice **c** would be stepping outside the boundaries of your position and authority. Choice **d** is incorrect, because it shows the officer has crossed the personal/professional line and forgotten that his or her first priority is to act as an officer; no matter how close you are to the victim, the victim notification office should be your first point of contact in this situation.

59. a. Although states have different regulations about the relationship between parole officers and victims, officers must always remember their role and responsibility. Most states employ a victim coordinator, whose sole responsibility is to support the victim throughout the criminal justice process. The officer's responsibility is first to the community and then to the parolee, and an officer should always communicate with his or her supervisor if he or she is unclear about these priorities.

60. d. Because in this case, you have established a close relationship with the victim, it would be unwise to turn away from the victim at this point; however, the victim's well-being is officially the counselor's concern. A conversation between you, the victim, and the counselor is the best resolution to this request. Choice **a** shows compassion but may be crossing the personal/professional line. Choice **b** is incorrect because the victim is already distraught and bringing her to the parole office could only aggravate her condition. Choice **c** is incorrect because the officer should not avoid the victim in this way; this response could hurt the victim's feelings and end whatever relationship the victim felt she had with you.

61. d. An officer should always be truthful, but honesty is especially crucial when dealing with victims, who have already suffered. The victim probably doesn't realize the situation you are in, and would probably understand that you need to scale back the relationship. Choices **a**, **b**, and **c** are not acceptable, because victims need closure and none of these options provide that, nor do they leave the officer in good standing with the victim. Not returning calls is never appropriate when you are in an official capacity, and asking for intervention from others is simply not necessary.

62. a. This sentence is punctuated correctly. Choice **b** has a fragment that should be connected to the sentence. Choice **c** is incorrect because it uses a colon when a comma would be more appropriate and because the semicolons after *classes* and *meetings* are incorrect. Choice **d** is incorrect because it uses a semicolon when a comma would be more appropriate and because the colon after *classes* should be replaced with the conjunction *and*.

63. b. This sentence is punctuated correctly. The semicolon in choice **a** indicates two sentences, which are not actually sentences and do not make sense unless they are combined. Choice **c** uses commas when none is needed. Choice **d** uses necessary and confusing punctuation.

64. a. This sentence is punctuated correctly. Choice **b** is incorrect because this sentence is a statement and should not end with a question mark. Choice **c** uses a period to divide this thought into two sentences, which is unnecessary. Choice **d** uses commas where none is needed.

65. b. This sentence is complete, easy to read, and is clear. Choice **a** begins with an introductory

phrase, which is not incorrect, but is not the clearest way to present a thought. Choice **c** moves that phrase to the middle of the sentence, where it sounds awkward and makes the sentence's meaning unclear. In choice **d**, the wrongly ordered phrases confuse the meaning of this sentence.

66. a. The sentence structure and grammar leave little for the reader to question with regard to the sentence content. Choice **b** is awkward but could easily fixed by moving the introductory phrase to the end of the sentence. Choice **c** has a confusing syntax; the subject should be moved from the end of the sentence to the beginning. In choice **d**, the wrongly ordered phrases confuse the meaning of this sentence.

67. d. This sentence is clearly written. Choice **a** reverses the beginning and end of the sentence and divides them with a semicolon Choices **b** and **c** also reorder the phrases in the sentence, which makes them difficult to understand.

68. c. This sentence has double negatives, which should always be avoided in writing because they unnecessarily muddle the meaning of the sentence. Choices **a**, **b**, and **d** are all grammatically correct.

69. a. This sentence is grammatically correct. Choices **b**, **c**, and **d** have grammar and word choice issues.

70. a. This sentence is grammatically correct. Choices **b**, **c**, and **d** have several words that are misspelled and out of order.

71. d. Parolees are given the opportunity to read the written statements of the officer and any other evidence to be used in the parole revocation hearing. Additionally, the parolee must be given the opportunity at the hearing to present his case and speak on his or her own behalf, if he or she chooses to do so. Choice **a** is incorrect because the state does not have a choice in the matter; the parolee decides whether one or two hearings are held. Choice **b** is incorrect because the parolee must receive written information about the alleged violations shortly after his arrest and detainment. Choice **c** is incorrect because none of these hearings are held in front of a judge or in a court of law; rather, a neutral and objective body, usually employed by the state but not an officer of the court, acts as the hearing officer.

72. c. Choices **a**, **b**, and **d** are incorrect and misconstrue statements made in the last paragraph of the passage.

73. b. Morrissey was returned to the Iowa state prison without due process. Choice **a** is incorrect because there is no mention of the parole officer or the officer's feelings toward Morrissey in the passage. Choice **c** is incorrect; although Morrissey's car was taken, this was not mentioned in the passage as a reason for the lawsuit. Choice **d** is incorrect because obtaining or having an attorney provided was not a right afforded to parolees in the final decision by the Supreme Court.

74. b. Morrissey was never charged with theft or stealing. However, choices **a**, **c**, and **d** are all violations that Morrissey admitted to committing while on parole.

75. a. If a hearing officer believes that there is sufficient evidence to support the allegation that an offender has committed parole violations, he must determine that there is *probable cause*. Choice **b** is incorrect because the required level of evidence for a court of law is higher than the required level of evidence for revocation. Choice **c** also refers to a court of law and reasonable suspicion, both of which are not part of parole revocation proceedings. Choice **d** is incorrect because a standard must be met in order for a parolee to be returned to the facility; however, guilt or innocence

isn't determined until the final revocation hearing.

76. d. There are five constitutional rights of due process that are afforded to parolees and must be adhered to. These rights are given in addition to the opportunity to have two hearings regarding the violations and revocation proceedings. Choice **a** is incorrect because having an attorney present is allowed but not a right. Additionally, the disclosure of evidence and the opportunity to be heard constitutes one of the conditions established by the court, not two. Choice **b** is incorrect because there is no stipulation that the final hearing should take place near to the parolee's family or witnesses. Again, having an attorney present is not a right. Choice **c** is incorrect because an attorney is not allowed to cross-examine. An attorney *may* be present if the hearing officer agrees; however, the attorney can only act as an adviser, not be an active participant in the hearing.

77. b. The paroling authority is the only body that has the ability and responsibility to revoke a parolee's parole. The hearing officer can only return the offender to prison once probable cause has been established and the final revocation hearing can be held. Choice **a** is true according to the findings of Morrissey. Choices **c** and **d** are also true statements and, therefore, incorrect answers.

78. c. If probation and parole officers are classified as law enforcement within the state, then they are also considered mandatory reporters of child abuse and neglect. Statutes in some states may classify probation and parole officers as treatment officers, which also makes them mandatory reporters. Choice **a** is incorrect because most probation and parole officers across the nation are either classified as law enforcement or agents of the court, which means that they are an extension of the court of law. Choice **b** is incorrect because officers must act as mandatory reporters only when their state requires them to do so; however, officers should always report abuse they observe while acting in their official capacity. Choice **d** is incorrect because any officer of the court must follow the letter of the law and report any suspected cases.

79. b. Choices **a**, **c**, and **d** are incorrect because nationwide statistics have nothing to do with probation and parole officers' responsibility to act as mandatory reporters. Also, statistics are usually released a few years after the data was collected and, therefore, may not present an accurate picture of the current situation. Also, choice **d** is incorrect because nationwide statistics do not exclude certain parts of the country.

80. d. In all states, agencies will collect reports of suspected child abuse so officers do not need to worry about which one is the "right" agency. Choices **a**, **b**, and **c** were all listed in the passage as reasons officers may not report suspected abuse cases.

81. a. The decline in substantiated abuse and neglect cases can be attributed to the efforts of law enforcement in catching, prosecuting, and incarcerating abusers. Additionally, publicizing the crime, arrest, and consequences causes embarrassment, which can deter offenders from committing further abuses. Last, the efforts to educate the community have been instrumental in getting people, especially children, to either not allow the abuse to happen or report the abuse they witness in their neighborhoods. Choice **b** is incorrect because it only mentions embarrassing the offenders and because it exaggerates a statement made in paragraph 2. Choices **c** and **d** are incorrect because sometimes the abused children are returned to their homes and not all offenders are incarcerated.

82. c. Locking a child in a confined room goes beyond reasonable punishment. You may not agree with spanking (choice **a**), but it is not abuse if the child is not physically harmed by the action. The use of physical punishment may be a cultural or learned behavior and may be appropriate for the situation (running with a sharp object). Choice **b** may seem like neglect, but there may be a medical reason that the child looks dazed, and the offender may not have had a chance to change the child's diaper. In this situation, an officer may have to ask if there is a medical issue before a determination can be made. Choice **d** is incorrect because, although this threat is inappropriate, no physical harm has been done to the child at this time. If you were to do a home visit within a short time of the phone call, and the child appeared to have been physically abused, then you would report the situation and the threat made during the phone call.

83. a. As stated in the last paragraph of the passage, part of the probation or parole officer's primary goal of protecting the children within the community is mandatory reporting. Also, the working relationship between the officer and the offender (choice **b**) may suffer if the office has to report a suspicion of abuse on the part of the offender. Choices **c** and **d** are incorrect because an officer would consider him- or herself or the agency only if he or she was afraid of making a false report about suspected abuse; however, not reporting suspected abuse would result in worse consequences for the officer or the employing agency.

84. a. As stated in the last paragraph of the passage, recidivism is reduced; however, it is difficult to determine exactly what aspect of the program positively affects the offender. Choice **b** is incorrect because, although disadvantages to the program were listed in paragraph 4, the author did not say that those disadvantages outweighed the good of the program. Choice **c** is incorrect because the program staff is always available, but outside resources are not. Choice **d** is incorrect; there were 1,500 drug courts operating in the United States as of December 2005, as stated in paragraph 2.

85. c. Choices **a**, **b**, and **d** were all listed in paragraph 3 as advantages to the drug court participants.

86. b. The author did not mention staffing availabilities in the passage. Although the need for available staff is a valid concern, most communities have available and qualified citizens to fill staff positions, or they have the resources to recruit staff. Choices **a**, **c**, and **d** were all listed in paragraph 2 as key components that must be considered when a community plans to implement a successful program.

87. d. As stated in the first paragraph, drug courts were developed to provide an alternative to prison and to reduce the number of these types of cases going through the courts so that more difficult cases could be handled. Choice **a** is incorrect because, although drug courts proliferated across the country during the 1980s; this is not the reason for their popularity. Choices **b** and **c** are incorrect because these are results of but not reasons for the implementation of drug courts.

88. a. The treatment staff conducts assessments in order to develop a treatment plan that identifies the various services the participant needs as well as the means of measuring his or her success. Choice **b** is incorrect because this is a function specific to the probation officer, who is a part of the treatment team. Choice **c** is incorrect because inpatient treatment may not be the best service for all participants.

Also, any admission records for inpatient treatment would be completed by the inpatient treatment staff. Choice **d** is incorrect because a risk assessment will be conducted by the probation officer, not the treatment team.

89. c. The offenders in the passage felt that working with a judge who communicates clearly, works through legal issues quickly, and has an open-door policy was their most positive experience in the program and had the greatest influence on their likelihood for success. Although important, choices **a** and **b** were not considered as important as the judge. Choice **d** is incorrect; although if the program weren't available, the participants would not have the opportunity to interact with the judge.

90. b. Data on these programs simply hasn't been captured as well as that on other criminal justice programs, so it has been difficult to determine which components of the drug courts have been the most successful and beneficial. Choice **a** is incorrect because there aren't too many resources available; rather, most successful programs are looking for as many resources as they can find to offer to the participants. Choice **c** is incorrect because it exaggerates a sentence in the last paragraph. Choice **d** is incorrect because there are plenty of drug court programs across the nation, but there isn't enough data on them to determine which part of the program has had the most impact.

91. b. Presentence reports are factual documents given to the judge, who uses them to determine an appropriate sentence for the defendant. The defendant may see the report or will be told about it by the defense attorney. Choice **a** is incorrect; the probation officer must take great care to ensure that all information is accurate and factual to avoid unjustified consequences. Choice **c** is incorrect because this is a court-ordered document, not a document of the defense. Also, defense attorneys do not purposefully try to slow down the system, but they do what it takes to give their client the best defense possible. Choice **d** is incorrect because again this documents is a tool for the judge, not the defense attorney.

92. c. The author implies that the defendant, through the defense attorney, can use the presentence report to help obtain a lighter sentence by arguing the points of conflict, cross-examining the probation officer, or building a defense for sentencing options. Choice **a** is incorrect because the judge must use the sentencing guidelines available in the report to determine a reasonable sentence. Choice **b** is incorrect because the victim contributes in small part to the report, but his or her personal wishes for the offender are not included in the report or considered by the judge. Choice **d** is incorrect; the probation officer should only worry about making sure that the information in the report is correct and accurate. Doing one's job thoroughly and appropriately will ensure that the judge remains pleased with the officer.

93. d. Physical and medical information may be important if the defendant has a known condition or disability; however, this information is generally not included in a presentence report. Choices **a**, **b**, and **c** are all included in presentence reports.

94. a. As stated throughout the passage, probation officers must present information that is accurate, factual, and appropriate to the case. Choices **b**, **c**, and **d** are incorrect because this report should not be biased for or against the offender, but rather should be an objective review of the defendant, the particulars about his or her life, the crime, and the victim.

95. b. The federal courts want to see the financial records of the defendants. Choice **a** is included in both state and federal presentence reports, according the first two paragraphs of the passage. Choices **c** and **d** are required by the state courts, but not the federal courts.

96. b. Agencies must find ways to support these programs as well as those employees and families who utilize them. Visible managerial support of the program will help to reduce the fears employees have about the impression that using the services gives. Choice **a** is incorrect because this mindset has led many officers to not deal with stress appropriately, which can have a larger negative impact on the family. Choice **c** is incorrect; it is because stress is inherent in this line of work that agencies must be willing to address these stress factors and not leave family members out of the assistance process. Choice **d** is incorrect; as stated in the first paragraph, stress felt by the employee affects the family as well. Agencies cannot ignore the reality that work stress goes home with the employee each night, and many times has an negative effects on the family.

97. b. This statement was not discussed in the passage. According to the author, agencies must be more receptive to marketing the benefits of the programs (choice **a**), management must be supportive of employees who use the programs and not cause them to fear retribution (choice **c**), and strategies must be developed to raise the programs' credibility and reduce their stigma (choice **d**).

98. c. The true advantage of the program is simply that the employee knows that the program is available at no cost to him and his family whenever they need to utilize it. This usually means that the agency has to promote the positives of the program and support the employee's use of the program and not make him or her feel there will be any retribution. Choice **a** is true, but if the employee does not know about the program or does not feel he can utilize it without retribution, the program goes to waste. Choice **b** is incorrect; strategies to raise the programs credibility are not an advantage to the program, rather actions that agencies must take to ensure that the programs are being used. Choice **d** may be true but is not identified as an advantage of the program.

99. d. Stress affects employees in many ways and has an impact on their work or homelife even if they don't think it does. Unfortunately, officers often do not utilize the programs soon enough because they fear the stigma or retribution, and so they wait until the stress has already affected their work or homelife or until they or their family is in crisis.

100. b. Quick-decision-making situations usually cause officers more stress than situations in which the officer has time to receive guidance from other officers or resources. Choice **a** is incorrect because, although it is a stressful situation, it wasn't listed in the passage. Choice **c** is incorrect because investigations can usually be conducted in a calm and reasonable fashion. Choice **d** is incorrect; paperwork can be stressful, especially if you are not good at time management.

This is the fourth practice test in the book based on the most commonly tested areas on the probation officer and parole officer exams. The practice test consists of 100 multiple-choice questions in the following areas: job responsibilities, case studies, writing skills, and reading comprehension. The number of questions and the time limit of the actual probation officer or parole officer exam can vary from region to region. Set aside three hours to take this practice test.

Practice Test 4

1.	ⓐ	ⓑ	ⓒ	ⓓ
2.	ⓐ	ⓑ	ⓒ	ⓓ
3.	ⓐ	ⓑ	ⓒ	ⓓ
4.	ⓐ	ⓑ	ⓒ	ⓓ
5.	ⓐ	ⓑ	ⓒ	ⓓ
6.	ⓐ	ⓑ	ⓒ	ⓓ
7.	ⓐ	ⓑ	ⓒ	ⓓ
8.	ⓐ	ⓑ	ⓒ	ⓓ
9.	ⓐ	ⓑ	ⓒ	ⓓ
10.	ⓐ	ⓑ	ⓒ	ⓓ
11.	ⓐ	ⓑ	ⓒ	ⓓ
12.	ⓐ	ⓑ	ⓒ	ⓓ
13.	ⓐ	ⓑ	ⓒ	ⓓ
14.	ⓐ	ⓑ	ⓒ	ⓓ
15.	ⓐ	ⓑ	ⓒ	ⓓ
16.	ⓐ	ⓑ	ⓒ	ⓓ
17.	ⓐ	ⓑ	ⓒ	ⓓ
18.	ⓐ	ⓑ	ⓒ	ⓓ
19.	ⓐ	ⓑ	ⓒ	ⓓ
20.	ⓐ	ⓑ	ⓒ	ⓓ
21.	ⓐ	ⓑ	ⓒ	ⓓ
22.	ⓐ	ⓑ	ⓒ	ⓓ
23.	ⓐ	ⓑ	ⓒ	ⓓ
24.	ⓐ	ⓑ	ⓒ	ⓓ
25.	ⓐ	ⓑ	ⓒ	ⓓ
26.	ⓐ	ⓑ	ⓒ	ⓓ
27.	ⓐ	ⓑ	ⓒ	ⓓ
28.	ⓐ	ⓑ	ⓒ	ⓓ
29.	ⓐ	ⓑ	ⓒ	ⓓ
30.	ⓐ	ⓑ	ⓒ	ⓓ
31.	ⓐ	ⓑ	ⓒ	ⓓ
32.	ⓐ	ⓑ	ⓒ	ⓓ
33.	ⓐ	ⓑ	ⓒ	ⓓ
34.	ⓐ	ⓑ	ⓒ	ⓓ
35.	ⓐ	ⓑ	ⓒ	ⓓ

36.	ⓐ	ⓑ	ⓒ	ⓓ
37.	ⓐ	ⓑ	ⓒ	ⓓ
38.	ⓐ	ⓑ	ⓒ	ⓓ
39.	ⓐ	ⓑ	ⓒ	ⓓ
40.	ⓐ	ⓑ	ⓒ	ⓓ
41.	ⓐ	ⓑ	ⓒ	ⓓ
42.	ⓐ	ⓑ	ⓒ	ⓓ
43.	ⓐ	ⓑ	ⓒ	ⓓ
44.	ⓐ	ⓑ	ⓒ	ⓓ
45.	ⓐ	ⓑ	ⓒ	ⓓ
46.	ⓐ	ⓑ	ⓒ	ⓓ
47.	ⓐ	ⓑ	ⓒ	ⓓ
48.	ⓐ	ⓑ	ⓒ	ⓓ
49.	ⓐ	ⓑ	ⓒ	ⓓ
50.	ⓐ	ⓑ	ⓒ	ⓓ
51.	ⓐ	ⓑ	ⓒ	ⓓ
52.	ⓐ	ⓑ	ⓒ	ⓓ
53.	ⓐ	ⓑ	ⓒ	ⓓ
54.	ⓐ	ⓑ	ⓒ	ⓓ
55.	ⓐ	ⓑ	ⓒ	ⓓ
56.	ⓐ	ⓑ	ⓒ	ⓓ
57.	ⓐ	ⓑ	ⓒ	ⓓ
58.	ⓐ	ⓑ	ⓒ	ⓓ
59.	ⓐ	ⓑ	ⓒ	ⓓ
60.	ⓐ	ⓑ	ⓒ	ⓓ
61.	ⓐ	ⓑ	ⓒ	ⓓ
62.	ⓐ	ⓑ	ⓒ	ⓓ
63.	ⓐ	ⓑ	ⓒ	ⓓ
64.	ⓐ	ⓑ	ⓒ	ⓓ
65.	ⓐ	ⓑ	ⓒ	ⓓ
66.	ⓐ	ⓑ	ⓒ	ⓓ
67.	ⓐ	ⓑ	ⓒ	ⓓ
68.	ⓐ	ⓑ	ⓒ	ⓓ
69.	ⓐ	ⓑ	ⓒ	ⓓ
70.	ⓐ	ⓑ	ⓒ	ⓓ

71.	ⓐ	ⓑ	ⓒ	ⓓ
72.	ⓐ	ⓑ	ⓒ	ⓓ
73.	ⓐ	ⓑ	ⓒ	ⓓ
74.	ⓐ	ⓑ	ⓒ	ⓓ
75.	ⓐ	ⓑ	ⓒ	ⓓ
76.	ⓐ	ⓑ	ⓒ	ⓓ
77.	ⓐ	ⓑ	ⓒ	ⓓ
78.	ⓐ	ⓑ	ⓒ	ⓓ
79.	ⓐ	ⓑ	ⓒ	ⓓ
80.	ⓐ	ⓑ	ⓒ	ⓓ
81.	ⓐ	ⓑ	ⓒ	ⓓ
82.	ⓐ	ⓑ	ⓒ	ⓓ
83.	ⓐ	ⓑ	ⓒ	ⓓ
84.	ⓐ	ⓑ	ⓒ	ⓓ
85.	ⓐ	ⓑ	ⓒ	ⓓ
86.	ⓐ	ⓑ	ⓒ	ⓓ
87.	ⓐ	ⓑ	ⓒ	ⓓ
88.	ⓐ	ⓑ	ⓒ	ⓓ
89.	ⓐ	ⓑ	ⓒ	ⓓ
90.	ⓐ	ⓑ	ⓒ	ⓓ
91.	ⓐ	ⓑ	ⓒ	ⓓ
92.	ⓐ	ⓑ	ⓒ	ⓓ
93.	ⓐ	ⓑ	ⓒ	ⓓ
94.	ⓐ	ⓑ	ⓒ	ⓓ
95.	ⓐ	ⓑ	ⓒ	ⓓ
96.	ⓐ	ⓑ	ⓒ	ⓓ
97.	ⓐ	ⓑ	ⓒ	ⓓ
98.	ⓐ	ⓑ	ⓒ	ⓓ
99.	ⓐ	ⓑ	ⓒ	ⓓ
100.	ⓐ	ⓑ	ⓒ	ⓓ

▶ Practice Test 4

1. When can the parole board be sued for making a bad decision regarding an offender's parole?
   a. Never, because the parole board has immunity.
   b. when the parole board releases an offender in error
   c. when the parole officer makes a mistake in its supervision
   d. when the offender is not granted all of the available "good time" credit prior to release

2. Which of the following should be the first steps a parole officer should take when an offender absconds from supervision?
   a. The officer should issue a warrant for the offender's arrest, ensuring this action is reported to local, state, and nation crime information databases.
   b. The officer should wait for the offender to be stopped by the local police department.
   c. The officer should contact the offender's family, friends, and employer to see if they know the offender's whereabouts.
   d. The officer should contact the public utility companies to see if a new account has been created in the offender's name.

3. The safety and security of the community is the primary function of which of the following?
   a. probation services
   b. parole services
   c. prison facilities
   d. jail facilities

4. Which of the following is a type of program that brings community resources, law enforcement, courts, and corrections together to offer services to offenders?
   a. boot camp programs
   b. work-release programs
   c. day reporting centers
   d. reentry programs

5. Conditions of supervision should be which of the following?
   a. full of legal language and complicated
   b. clear and reasonable
   c. relevant and short
   d. complex and obvious

6. The judge determines the amount of restitution the offender owes from which of the following?
   a. the presentence investigation report
   b. the victim
   c. the prosecutor
   d. the probation officer

7. A tool that helps determine the risks that an offender poses to a community is called
   a. a case file.
   b. a treatment worksheet.
   c. a "risks and needs" assessment.
   d. a workload standard tool.

8. Your daughter is sick and has to be hospitalized. Because you are the primary caregiver, you ask your supervisor if your time with your daughter is covered for leave. He tells you that she is covered, but you will need to fill out and submit paperwork. Which of the following legislative acts of leave time is your daughter covered under?
   a. Family and Medical Leave Act
   b. Federal Labor Standards Act
   c. Medical and Insurance Act
   d. Federal Sick Leave for Family Act

9. Which of the following is the main difference between probation and parole?
   a. The supervision conditions and standards of parole are harder than those of probation.
   b. The type of offender on probation is different from the type on parole.
   c. Probation is supervision prior to incarceration, whereas parole is supervision after incarceration.
   d. Parole is supervision prior to incarceration. whereas probation supervision is after incarceration.

10. A parole officer visiting an assigned parolee in the hospital learns that the parolee may be contagious. When the officer calls his supervisor to report that he may now be contagious, what should his supervisor advise him to do?
   a. The officer should report to the hospital that deals with work compensation injuries and be checked out thoroughly by the doctors.
   b. The officer should stay home on sick leave until the incubation period is over.
   c. The officer is probably not contagious because he wasn't with the offender that long, so he should go back to the office and get to work.
   d. The officer should bring a written medical explanation of the situation from the doctors to the supervisor, who will then make a decision as to what to do next.

11. You have to go to a nearby facility where your offender is being detained pending arrest and, ultimately, a trial. You go to the nearest
   a. reentry program.
   b. halfway house.
   c. prison.
   d. jail.

12. A peer complains that he has received a letter of reprimand for abusing his leave balances. Which of the following has he most likely done?
   a. abused his sick leave
   b. worked overtime without taking the necessary compensatory time off
   c. abused his vacation leave
   d. worked overtime without approval

13. You receive a phone call at home in the middle of the night from the local police department, telling you that one of your assigned parolees has been arrested for a gang-related incident. What action should you take?
   a. You should roll over and go back to sleep, because processing the offender at the jail will take several hours to complete.
   b. You should immediately issue a parole violation warrant so the offender cannot make bail.
   c. After a call to your supervisor to inform him of the arrest, you should go to the jail to talk to the offender to determine what happened.
   d. You call the night sergeant at the jail and ask him to keep the offender from bailing out for about five hours, until you can get a chance to get to the jail with a warrant.

14. A probationer has been arrested for driving while intoxicated. When you talk with him about his arrest, the probationer states that he has been taking prescription medication and had three drinks at a friend's home. After driving for a few miles, he realized he couldn't drive home, so he pulled over to the side of the road to sleep off the medication and alcohol in his system. The police say the offender was driving erratically and nearly drove into a ditch before they stopped him. Because you have two conflicting stories, what do you do?

a. You take the side of the police, because they would never make up a story like this.

b. You take the side of the probationer because what he said made sense, and you know that he has been taking the prescription medication, which probably made him drowsy.

c. You allow the courts to decide which side of the story is accurate, and then you make a decision regarding the offender's probation.

d. You ask for the case to be reassigned to another officer because the probationer obviously lies.

15. The judge has ordered Sam to pay restitution of $400 per month. Sam has found a job that gives him $1,650 per month, which pays for rent and half his monthly bills. The $850 left does not give him enough money to pay for food and monthly expenses such as gas, bus tickets, car insurance, etc. Sam has asked for your help—what should you do?

a. You should tell Sam to get either a different job or a second job to help with the costs.

b. You should suggest to Sam that he cannot make it on the streets and that it would be easier to be incarcerated.

c. You should tell Sam that this isn't your problem and that you don't know how he is going to fix this.

d. You should connect Sam to resources in the community that would be able to provide him assistance with utilities, food, and clothing, as well as teach him money management skills.

16. You are preparing to request a probation violation warrant from the judge on an assigned probationer. Which of the following describes the actions you should take?

a. You should talk to the probationer to tell him of your request and then write the report.

b. You should write the request, present it to the judge, and when the warrant is issued, call the offender to ask him to report to the office.

c. You should call the police to give them a forewarning of the warrant, write the request, and present it to the judge.

d. You should write the request, call the probationer and ask him come to your office, and then take the report and the probationer to the judge.

17. Which of the following due process rights are probationers NOT entitled to during the two-stage revocation hearing process?
   a. written notice of the alleged probation violation
   b. the right to confront and cross-examine witnesses
   c. the right to judgment by a neutral hearing body
   d. the right to have an attorney present at all stages in the process

18. A defense attorney has argued that his 16-year-old client (the defendant) should be able to exercise the same rights as adults in the courts. If the juvenile is being tried in an adult court, which of the following is true?
   a. The juvenile was emancipated.
   b. The juvenile's case was kept in the juvenile system but heard by an adult court judge.
   c. A "transfer of jurisdiction" decision was made to move the case to the adult court.
   d. The defense attorney argued his client would have better chances in the adult court, and the juvenile judge agreed and excused himself from the hearing.

19. You are a juvenile probation officer, and a reporter from the local newspaper has asked you how many offenders you have on your caseload, who they are, and what charges they were convicted of. What information are you allowed to give the reporter as a matter of public record?
   a. the juveniles' names only
   b. the juveniles' names and convictions only
   c. the juveniles' names, convictions, and conditions of probation only
   d. the juveniles' names, convictions, conditions of supervision, and the lengths of their probation

20. You have had a juvenile arrested on a probation violation warrant. The parents of your offender want him to remain in their custody while waiting to have the revocation hearing in front of the judge. Which action is best in this case?
   a. to allow the probationer to remain in the parents' custody until the hearing
   b. to hold the juvenile in custody in a juvenile facility until the hearing
   c. to place the juvenile in a foster care home until the hearing
   d. to have the juvenile stay with his best friend's family until the hearing

21. Your agency requires juvenile probationers to submit to fingerprinting as a condition of supervision. One of your probationers has refused to give his fingerprints and claims this is a violation of his privacy rights. What did the courts say about this situation?
   a. If a juvenile does not wish to provide fingerprints, then he or she may be incarcerated, and his or her fingerprints will be taken upon intake into the detention facility.
   b. Fingerprints should not be taken of juveniles for any reason, because it is a violation of their rights.
   c. Providing fingerprints does not violate any basic rights and holds value in providing a rehabilitative purpose of probation.
   d. Providing fingerprints is not a violation of the First Amendment and should be done to protect the juvenile in future circumstances.

22. A female probation officer must conduct a field visit at a home in which a particularly violent juvenile lives, and she asks a local police officer to accompany her on the home visit. During the visit, the police officer sees drugs in the home. Which of the following actions best applies what the court has ruled about the seizure of the drugs to this situation?
   a. The police officer cannot seize the drugs.
   b. The police officer can get a court order to seize the drugs from the home.
   c. Only the probation officer can seize the drugs because she is responsible for the situation and is the authority in charge.
   d. The police officer can legally seize the drugs as long as he is in the home legally and the drugs are immediately recognizable as seizable.

23. Which of the following departments fall under the judicial branch of government?
   a. parole
   b. probation
   c. pardon
   d. clemency

24. One of your juvenile probationers and her mother come in for the scheduled office visit. During the visit, the juvenile's mother starts scolding the juvenile for her late-night activities. Before the juvenile stops her mom, her mother has unknowingly confessed that the juvenile has committed four probation violations. What action should you take?
   a. You should confront the juvenile with this information and determine whether the violations actually happened. You should ask for the mother's help in providing structure and discipline at home. Then, if the violations are not severe or new offenses, you should write appropriate special conditions.
   b. You should ask the mother to step out of the office while you confront the juvenile about the violations. Then you should reprimand the juvenile and send her on her way.
   c. You should take the juvenile to juvenile detention and start the revocation process based on the mother's testimony.
   d. You should begin proceedings to remove the juvenile from the home, because it is obvious the mother cannot control the juvenile.

25. Which of the following is NOT a difference between juvenile and adult courts?
   a. terminology
   b. a jury
   c. an objective hearing body
   d. confidentiality

26. A parolee recently been assigned to your case-load has the word *pitcher* tattooed on his arm. You know from the case file that this offender was heavily involved in prison gangs. Which of the following defines what *pitcher* means in prison gangs?

a. The offender is involved in a baseball gang.

b. The offender likes to drink lots of beer.

c. The offender has killed using his fist.

d. The offender is sexually aggressive.

27. Which of the following civil rights is lost when an offender is convicted of a felony?

a. the right to privacy

b. the right to vote

c. freedom from search and seizure

d. the right to due process

28. At the beginning of the first hearing in an offender's revocation process, you learn that the offender's witnesses haven't arrived. When the hearing officer asks the offender if he was able to contact his witnesses, the offender indicates that he had contacted them and they had refused to come. What should the hearing officer do at this point?

a. He should cancel the hearing and reschedule it when the offender can convince his witnesses to appear.

b. The hearing officer should find that the offender violated his conditions because the offender cannot produce evidence or witnesses to support his claims.

c. The hearing officer should ask the offender if he is willing to proceed with the hearing, even without the witnesses, and let the offender know he can have the witnesses appear before the paroling authority at the last hearing.

d. The hearing officer should ask the parole officer to contact the offender's witnesses to see if they would testify by phone at this hearing.

29. The hearing officer at the offender's first hearing of the revocation process is handed a list of 15 witnesses who wish to testify on behalf of the offender. When the hearing officer asks what they will testify to, the offender says that each of the witnesses will talk about how upstanding of a citizen the offender is. When asked if these witnesses know about his violations, the offender replies no. Which of the following should the hearing officer do?

a. The hearing officer should go ahead and listen to all 15 witnesses.

b. The hearing officer should ask the offender to pick three character witnesses who can represent the 15 witnesses.

c. The hearing officer should tell the offender that character witnesses will not help prove whether or not he committed the alleged violations, and so none of the 15 witnesses will be heard.

d. The hearing officer should tell the offender he doesn't have time to waste, and should find that the violations were committed because the offender could not produce any other witnesses to provide evidence to the contrary.

30. An offender assigned to your caseload has brought you flowers as a thank-you for helping him through a particularly difficult time. How do you respond to this situation?

a. You thank the offender for the lovely flowers and place them on your desk.

b. You tell the offender that you cannot accept the flowers and throw them away.

c. You tell the offender you cannot accept the flowers and suggest he give them to his mother or significant other.

d. You thank the offender for the lovely flowers and place them in a central location so the whole office can enjoy them.

Directions: Read the following case study and then answer questions 31 through 36.

Rita is an attractive, tall, blond woman who was incarcerated on a "conspiracy to commit murder" charge. She had contracted an undercover police officer to have her boyfriend murdered. Rita's boyfriend had been abusing her, and she couldn't figure out any other way of getting away from him other than having him killed. In the jury trial, she was sentenced to 15 years in prison for her role in the conspiracy.

Rita didn't have a drug problem when she arrived at the prison, but she quickly developed one. She also became romantically involved with another female prisoner, who liked being called "Mark." Mark ran the side of the cellblock that her and Rita's cells were on, and. Rita soon found that Mark provided her a lot of protection and became comfortable with the lifestyle that Mark offered.

A public hearing was held prior to Rita's parole hearing, and 15 people spoke against Rita being paroled. Rita's mother and Rita's friend argued for parole. Eventually, Rita is paroled and released to a halfway house. There is some concern among citizens in the community, but the problem quickly resolves itself when Rita seems to make good progress and doesn't cause problems in the community. When Rita was paroled, she had had hopes of having Mark join her in the program, but found out Mark was not approved for parole and would have to stay in prison for another several years.

Rita has now been on parole for four and a half years without issue. She rarely misses an appointment, nor has she had any other violations of her parole. She quit using drugs shortly after being released and has completed all of the mental health and drug counseling programs and halfway house programs she was asked to participate in.

31. The agency's public information officer (PIO) contacts you and indicates that a national television reporter is coming to the state to interview Rita, the halfway house staff, and you regarding Rita's case and progress under supervision. The television show is about murderers and their lives after the murder, and will air in a few months. The PIO indicates that the agency has approved these interviews and wants you to contact Rita to tell her. When you do, she adamantly refuses to participate. How should you handle this?
   a. You should tell Rita that the interview has already been approved, and she really doesn't have a choice in the matter.
   b. You should tell Rita that you had hoped she wouldn't cooperate because you don't want to be interviewed for national television.
   c. You should tell Rita that it is her right not to want to be a part of a national television interview and that you will pass the message along.
   d. You should ask Rita to come to your office to meet with the PIO so she can get a better understanding of the television show. Then she can make her own informed decision.

32. Rita receives a letter from Mark, who wants Rita to sponsor her when she is released. Mark wants to live at Rita's house until she can find her own place. Rita doesn't want to be involved but doesn't want to tell Mark that. She has asked for your opinion. Which of the following do you tell her?

  a. You encourage Rita to tell Mark the truth and to tell Mark the reasons Rita would rather live by herself.

  b. You tell Rita that you will contact the parole officer doing Mark's parole plan investigation and will stop the plan before Rita is talked to.

  c. You tell Rita that having Mark live with her is a violation of Rita's conditions.

  d. You encourage Rita to tell Mark that Rita has found a new boyfriend and that she doesn't have room for Mark in her life anymore.

33. When you tell Rita she needs to provide a urine sample, she hesitates and then tells you that she has been using cocaine. How would you handle this situation?

  a. You take Rita at her word and have her contact the drug treatment counselor she had worked with earlier in her parole.

  b. You let Rita know she has violated her parole, ask why she felt she needed to do drugs, and then have her provide the sample.

  c. You tell Rita you are going to need to take her to jail because she has violated her conditions of parole.

  d. Because she confessed, you tell Rita to stop doing drugs and focus on doing well on her parole.

34. Rita is asking you for a travel permit to go to Texas. When you ask why she's going to Texas, she responds, "Mark." She tells you she is visiting as just a friend. She is close to completing her parole and has done well under supervision. Which of the following should you do?

  a. You should tell Rita that she cannot go, because you don't approve of same-sex relationships and you won't be a party to creating one.

  b. You should tell Rita that she can go after she gets off parole.

  c. You should complete the appropriate paperwork because Rita's relationships are not your concern as long as they do not involve illegal activities.

  d. You should ask Rita to invite Mark to your community, because you would rather Rita stay within your state.

35. Rita calls you early on a Monday morning to inform you she was the victim of a hate crime over the weekend. Someone wrote sexually obscene words on her car and house and then put a burning stake in her yard. Which of the following actions should you take?

  a. You should ensure that Rita is all right and that she contacted the police department to report the crime.

  b. You should tell Rita that you will be right there to investigate.

  c. You should jokingly ask Rita what she did to them mad.

  d. You should issue a warrant for Rita's arrest because she must have done something illegal to warrant this type of neighborhood reaction.

36. You receive notification that Rita's discharge date is in two months. You notice on the paperwork that the victim's family has been notified of this development. You have had to work with the victim's family quite a few times throughout the past several years because they thought Rita was doing something wrong and would call you to complain about her. Which of the following should you do?

a. You should call the victim notification office and angrily ask why the victim's family was notified because your workload will now increase because of all their phone calls.

b. You should call the family to answer their questions and talk them through their grief.

c. You should send the victim's family a letter explaining that Rita's parole will be completed and nothing can be done to stop it.

d. You should do nothing. This is the natural course for offenders within the criminal justice system, and there is nothing you can do to help or to stop it.

Directions: Read the following case study and then answer questions 37 through 42.

Rob is a 17-year-old on probation after his first conviction on possession of drugs charges. Rob was initially charged with two felonies and three misdemeanors, and the possession charge was the result of plea bargaining efforts of his attorney. Rob is a senior at the local high school, is quarterback for the varsity football team, drives a new car provided by his parents, and has a very active social life. Rob actually was caught during a raid on another high school student's house, when Rob had drugs and was high. He was arrested, charged, and convicted despite the outcry from his parents, local politicians, and a state legislator who was a friend of Rob's parents.

The district attorney's office took a lot of political heat by continuing its case against Rob; however, they wanted to make an example out of him. The district attorney charged each of the teenagers caught in the raid, and they all were convicted, either on the charges or through a plea bargain.

Rob has made an effort to comply with all of his probation conditions, but is about to start his senior year and is pushing to gain favors on his supervision. His parents are also putting pressure on you, your supervisor, and the district attorney to get the supervision period reduced or to eliminated.

37. One of Rob's probation conditions is to have a curfew. During the summer months, you established a 10:00 P.M. curfew during the weeknights and a midnight curfew on Fridays and Saturdays. With school starting soon, Rob is complaining that he is missing a lot of parties and get-togethers that are held during the week. He wants a midnight curfew for all nights. What should your response be?

a. You should indicate to Rob that together you should have a conversation with his parents to gain their input on his request.

b. You should remind Rob that partying at a friend's house got him in trouble the first time, and his curfew will stand.

c. You should tell Rob that it is hard for you to say no, but you are good at it, and no change will be made to his curfew.

d. You should tell Rob that his parents should petition the court to have him removed from supervision, and then he can do whatever he wants in the evenings.

38. The whole town has rallied behind the football team and especially your probationer, who is the quarterback of the team. Rob's arrest and conviction was widely publicized, and the town was divided over whether or not he should have been convicted. When you go to games, people always stop and ask how Rob is doing on probation, which of course you don't answer. However, one father stopped you and told you that you were wrong for putting Rob on probation in the first place. He continued by saying that Rob is the star of the football team and shouldn't be penalized for doing one little thing wrong. What should your response be to this father?

a. You should tell this man he needs to get out of your face with his complaints or you'll have him arrested.

b. You should calmly tell this man that you were not the one who convicted Rob, and if he feels that strongly about this, he should make an appointment with the judge to express his feelings.

c. You should turn away from the man and ignore him throughout the rest of the football game.

d. You should let the man know that he is entitled to his opinion and that you will do your job professionally no matter what that entails.

39. Rob calls to tell you that he is being pressured by his girlfriend to drink. He says this usually happens when they are out at night, and she has even brought a six-pack with her on their dates. He indicates to you that he knows if he drinks he will start doing drugs again, and he doesn't want that. He wants to know how to handle this situation with his girlfriend. What response should you give him?

a. You should tell him to dump his girlfriend because she is a bad influence on him, and he doesn't need that kind of pressure.

b. You should encourage Rob to tell his girlfriend's parents that she is drinking and that you would be willing to take her to an Alcoholics Anonymous meeting.

c. You should encourage Rob to connect with his substance abuse counselor and suggest that you would be willing to help him make that connection. You should encourage him to attend Alcoholics Anonymous meetings and make a counseling appointment, so he can learn to manage his triggers.

d. You should suggest to Rob that he is not allowed to go out at night with his friends until he learns to manage his triggers.

40. Rob tests positive for drugs. When you confront him with the results, he begs you not to tell his parents, who have still been pressuring you to have Rob released from supervision. What should you do?

a. You should tell Rob you will not tell his parents if he gets his parents to stop pressuring you.

b. You should ignore the offender's request to withhold this information from his parents, tell them about Rob's drug usage, and ask them to stop bothering you about releasing Rob from supervision.

c. You should tell Rob to continue to attend his Narcotics Anonymous meetings and that the situation will work out in the end.

d. You should continue to ignore the parents' repeated requests and place a special condition on Rob that he reenter and complete substance abuse treatment immediately. You should remind Rob that his drug use is a violation of his probation and you expect him to stop.

41. You had agreed that Rob could travel with the football team to the various "away" games as long as the coach would guarantee that Rob would travel to and from the games on the team bus. Rob's parents and coach agreed, but you find out that Rob has been traveling back from the games with his friends. What should you do?

a. You should tell Rob that, because he violated your agreement, he cannot play at away games anymore.

b. You should ask for a meeting with Rob, his parents, and his coach to discuss what you have learned to find out if it is true, to determine if the parents knew about it, and to agree on a resolution.

c. You should ask for a meeting with the judge to see if the judge could talk to the parents about enforcing the supervision conditions.

d. You should call the coach and demand to know why he is letting Rob violate this condition of his supervision.

42. The judge has requested a report from you on Rob's progress while on supervision. He wants the report by the end of the next workday; however, you had planned to take the rest of this afternoon and tomorrow off. You should

a. tell the judge of your vacation plans and ask if you could submit the report to him the day after your vacation.

b. cancel your vacation day and stay to work on the report.

c. ask your supervisor to do the report for you.

d. ask the supervisor if he or she would ask the judge to give you an extra day to finish the report.

Directions: Read the following case study and then answer questions 43 through 48.

Robin is a 62-year-old white woman who was released on parole last week after serving 24 years for attempted murder. File material indicates that Robin's violent behavior has not changed over the years. In 1959, Robin was sent to a mental hospital for shooting a man she said had raped and assaulted her. In 1969, she was charged in another state for aggravated assault with intent to kill. In 1980, Robin stabbed a boyfriend, but he did not want to press charges. In 1983, Robin was charged with the present offense and convicted after her attorney unsuccessfully presented a defense based on Robin having battered woman's syndrome. The judge indicated during sentencing that Robin posed a serious threat to any man with whom she is in a relationship.

You believe that Robin is a danger to the community and that she will attempt to seriously harm or kill someone again. The parole board indicates that they understand the risk but feel that Robin should have a chance of rehabilitation within the community. The parole board specifically requests that Robin be placed on high supervision and, in an effort to avoid any further violence between Robin and her significant others, that she not be allowed to live with anyone.

Robin has never used illegal drugs but has been known to abuse her prescription drugs. She did not participate in treatment while in the prison, because she spent most of her time in segregation units. In prison, Robin was violent and made many accusations against some of the male corrections officers. She has been assigned a psychiatrist, whom she is supposed to see on a weekly basis.

43. One of the parole board members calls you directly and warns you to be careful with this offender. He tells you that you can place any special condition on her that you would like. You should
   a. ask the board member why the board paroled this offender if they are so concerned about her, and why it didn't establish more special conditions if the members thought they would be necessary.
   b. thank the board member for his call and concern and assure him that you will be placing additional special conditions on this offender.
   c. ask the board member if he wants to place a bet on how long you keep this offender on the streets.
   d. tell the board member that he should really be talking with your parole director, and you would prefer to transfer the call.

44. In some of your conversations with Robin, she has tried to convince you she should have gotten a lighter sentence because she has battered woman's syndrome. She becomes adamant that you agree with her. You should
   a. continue to steer the conversation back to how important it is for her not to hurt anyone else.
   b. remind her that you don't care if she was battered and that she should move on.
   c. remind her that her defense was stupid and ask her, if the jury didn't believe her, why should you.
   d. remind her that she is well past the trial stage and that she should be concerned with her progress on supervision, not what has already happened.

45. Since she has been released, Robin has cooperated with you fully. She reports regularly and complies with all of your requests. She is living in her own apartment, working, and paying her bills on time, and has generally been doing well under supervision. However, other officers keep making comments such as "When is she going to kill her next man?" or "You better make sure she leaves her gun in the car," or the receptionist tells you, "Annie Oakley is here to see you." How do you handle this situation?

a. You advise each of the parole staff when he or she makes these comments that they are inappropriate and that you want them to stop.

b. You tell your supervisor about these comments and ask him or her to get the staff to stop making them.

c. You wait until the next month's unit meeting, which is three weeks away, and then make a general announcement to the whole office.

d. You do nothing, because this is what the office staff does to relieve stress.

46. While you are conducting a home visit, you notice that Robin is becoming more and more agitated. She shouts at you to leave her alone and then she apologizes for being rude. When you ask her if she has been taking her medicine as directed, she quietly says you that you should probably leave now and sits in the chair staring at you. You notice the pupils of her eyes are quite large, and she is sweating profusely. What should you do?

a. You should leave because she probably just has premenstrual syndrome.

b. You should ask her if she is all right and if she wants to go to the hospital.

c. You should tell her you are going to get her some help and leave the apartment. Then you should call the parole office to request a warrant so the transport team can escort her to jail.

d. You should tell her you are going to get her some help and leave the apartment. Then you should call Robin's psychiatrist to report her behavior and together figure out how to help her.

47. After your last visit with Robin in the psychiatric ward at the local mental hospital, you became more concerned about her mental capacity. You should

a. go back to the office and tell your coworkers of your concern.

b. tell Robin she should consent to stay voluntarily in the hospital, because you believe it is too difficult for her to be in the community.

c. tell the psychiatrist your concerns and discuss what options may be available to keep Robin safe.

d. tell the hospital staff members that you are concerned and ask them to pass the message on to Robin's doctors.

48. The victim of Robin's last offense contacts you and tells you that Robin has called him numerous times over the last week. You know that Robin could not be making those calls, because she is in the psychiatric ward at the hospital; however, you are not able to tell him that information. The victim insists that Robin has called him and says that he is fearful that she will come back to kill him. With his fear in mind, how should you handle this situation?

   a. You should tell the victim where Robin is, so he will rest easier.

   b. You should encourage the victim to talk with a counselor about his fears.

   c. You should encourage the victim to talk with the police about the harassing phone calls and to get a temporary phone number until the matter is dealt with.

   d. You should tell him that it isn't possible that Robin has been calling him and that you aren't able to help him.

Directions: Read the following case study and then answer questions 49 through 54.

You are one of nine probation officers under one supervisor, and you all work in an older building located across the street from the county courthouse. Your town has a population of 12,500 people and is a suburb of the larger city that is about 50 miles east. Each probation officer carries a caseload of about 160 offenders. The supervisor carries a smaller caseload of 45 juveniles, in addition to supervising the probation officers.

Each probation officer is responsible for supervising offenders and completing presentence investigation reports (PSIs). Because caseloads are large, your supervisor has requested in next year's budget two additional officers to handle specialized caseloads. One officer would conduct all of the PSIs, and the other would handle substance abuse offenders and all juveniles.

Even though the town is relatively small, the officers do not socialize much outside the office. The officers have a camaraderie, and they ask one another for help when they need it. Everyone seems to get along well despite occasional annoyances or disagreements. No one has ever made an official complaint about another officer.

The judges work hard to maintain good communication with the probation department. Your supervisor knows there have been some complaints from the judges about reports not being submitted in a timely fashion or about officers showing up for court late or looking disheveled; however, your supervisor hasn't addressed those complaints with the offending officers, because she feels these complaints are minor and not really important to the overall mission of the job.

49. Your supervisor comes to your office and asks if you are going to court today. When you respond yes, she informs you that you will have to go home (on unpaid time) to change your clothes. When you ask what is wrong with what you are wearing, the supervisor replies, "The judges won't like your outfit." What should you do?

   a. You should tell the supervisor that you are dressed professionally so you aren't going to change.

   b. You should ask if there has been a complaint about your attire and what would be more appropriate for court appearance.

   c. You should tell your supervisor that you aren't paid enough to buy more clothes and that, until you get a raise, you aren't going to worry about what the judges think.

   d. You should point out one of your coworkers who always wears wrinkled clothes and ask why the supervisor hasn't said anything to him or her.

50. Trent, another probation officer, comes to your office upset because your supervisor made him go into her office and iron his pants. Apparently, while he was in her office, she came in to get some papers off her desk. Trent says he was standing behind the ironing board wearing only his shirt, underwear, and socks. He says the supervisor commented on his legs and the color of his underwear. He tells you he is embarrassed and he thinks he should go home because he just can't concentrate on his work. He asks for your opinion. Which of the following would be your response?

a. You encourage Trent to contact the human resources department to report what the supervisor did and find out if her behavior qualifies as sexual harassment.

b. You inform Trent that the supervisor is just having trouble dealing with the judges and that he should just give her a break. Besides, you think he has nice legs, too.

c. You agree with Trent that the supervisor acted inappropriately, and you encourage him to start a petition to remove her from her position.

d. You tell Trent that you think this situation is entirely his fault because he wears wrinkled clothes.

51. After your supervisor leaves one day around 3:00 P.M., the administrative judge calls and asks you to be the acting supervisor effective immediately and to run the office until further notice. He tells you your supervisor has been suspended for 30 days, but he doesn't want the other probation officers to know that. What should you do?

a. You should tell the judge that you don't believe whatever the supervisor did warrants a 30-day suspension and that you would rather not be the acting supervisor.

b. You should tell him that you are glad the supervisor has been given time off, because she had been acting weird in the office and maybe this break will give her time to get her act together. You should accept the assignment gladly.

c. You should accept the assignment and tell the judge you are happy to help out however you can. You should ask if there are specific meetings or tasks the judge wants you to participate in and assure him you will keep good communication with him.

d. You should let the judge know that you are not the most senior probation officer and ask if he would rather appoint someone with more experience as the acting supervisor. Then you should reluctantly accept the assignment.

52. The other probation officers took the news of your new, temporary position well, and any tension in the office regarding the supervisor's absence seems to have dissipated. In fact, the officers have made a habit of eating lunch together in the break room since the supervisor has been gone. You walk into the break room and hear the officers gossiping about the supervisor. You should

    a. sit down with the officers and fill in the gaps of the story.

    b. walk out of the break room quickly, hoping they didn't see you.

    c. walk out of the break room but stand by the doorway to hear what is said about the supervisor.

    d. tell the officers that it is inappropriate to gossip about a coworker and ask them how they would feel if they were talked about. You should thank them for changing the subject of their conversation and tell them to enjoy their lunch.

53. Since assuming the acting supervisor role, you have learned one of the officers, Jan, has not been keeping accurate documentation in her assigned presentence investigation reports. In fact, you have discovered she made up information in order to get one report finished on time. You don't believe she falsified information in any other reports, and a quick review of Jan's PSIs proves this theory. What should you do?

    a. You should tell the administrative judge about the flawed report and indicate that you would like to provide additional training to the officer who submitted the report.

    b. You should tell the administrative judge that a flawed presentence investigation report was used for sentencing purposes and that the officer who submitted the report needs to be reprimanded.

    c. You should not tell the judge anything and deal with the officer internally and quietly.

    d. You should not tell the judge anything and not let the officer know you found the flawed report. This way, you can monitor her reports and, the next time she does this, recommend that she be fired.

54. During your tenure as acting supervisor, your friend's performance review date comes up. The human resources director calls and asks if you would complete the review so her records will be current. When you tell her that you and this officer are friends, the director says she trust you to be objective. Unfortunately, you know that your friend is not working to her potential and that there are problems with her caseload documentation. What should you do?

a. You should call the human resources director back and tell her that you just cannot be objective in this case and refuse to complete the review.

b. You should ask the administrative judge if he would complete the review if you provided him all of the paperwork.

c. You should call your friend into your office, explain the situation, and ask her to call the human resources director to approve a delay of the review.

d. You should go to your friend's office and ask to speak with her. You should explain the situation of completing the review, tell her you know about her problems with her caseload, and ask for her help in completing the review.

Directions: Read the following case study and then answer questions 55 through 60.

Jeanne is a 32-year-old white woman who has been paroled after serving 12 years of a 20-to-life sentence for murder, sexual abuse of a child, and child endangerment. She was convicted of killing her two children (daughters aged two and four). She was also convicted of sexually abusing the children, locking them in closets, and refusing to feed them. Jeanne's boyfriend was also convicted of sexually abusing the girls but was acquitted of the murder charge.

Jeanne's case file indicates that her defense attorney argued that Jeanne's boyfriend had intimidated her into committing the crimes. Jeanne asserted, in court and while in prison, that her boyfriend had abused the older girl, and when Jeanne found out, he threatened to take the girls away if she didn't participate in "the game." She reported to the prison chaplain that she was physically sick about what the girls had to endure, and according to the chaplain, she has shown great remorse for all of her actions.

Because of her crimes, Jeanne's life in prison was not easy. The other inmates avoided her, refused to room with her, and when they had the opportunity, they abused her. She would often spend her days in administrative segregation, praying.

Jeanne has been "born again" through the ministry of the chaplain, and she has found a Christian family willing to sponsor her on parole. She is hoping to live with this family for a brief time and then move into her own apartment. The church where Jeanne will be working is located down the street from where she will be living. She will walk to work and will ride the bus if she needs to go anywhere else in town.

55. During your parole planning meetings, you met several of the women from the church where Jeanne will be working. In your conversations with them, you realize that the women do not know about the crimes Jeanne was convicted of committing. For their safety, you should

a. tell the women what charges Jeanne was convicted on as well as the details of the crimes.

b. not say anything about the crimes; because this information is public record, you decide that if the women want to know about the crimes, they can go to the courthouse and find out themselves.

c. indicate that Jeanne will have some things to tell the women when she is paroled.

d. encourage the women to ask Jeanne directly about her crimes.

56. Jeanne has been out of prison for one week and has reported to the office. She says that her work is good and that she gets paid each Monday. She asks about the possibility of regularly giving you money to hold for her so that she can eventually buy her daughters a headstone. How should you respond?

a. You should tell her that you would be happy to hold the money for her because it is for a good cause.

b. You should encourage Jeanne to ask the financial administrator of the church to withhold money from her paycheck and save it for her.

c. You should encourage Jeanne to go to a nearby bank and set up a savings account for this purpose.

d. You should suggest that Jeanne ask the family she's living with to buy a small safe that she can put her money in.

57. Jeanne has been on parole for several weeks when she calls you crying. She says a trustee's wife found out that Jeanne killed her daughters, and the woman is now refusing to leave her children in day care at the church and is demanding that Jeanne be fired. Jeanne wants your guidance and advice about what she should do. Which of the following would you tell her?

a. You encourage Jeanne to talk honestly with the trustees and with the minister about her crimes and to tell them how being in the church has affected her life.

b. You encourage Jeanne to talk with the woman to let her know Jeanne has changed and will not harm anyone's children.

c. You suggest that Jeanne quit the job and find something else.

d. You suggest that Jeanne not do or say anything because she hasn't violated her parole conditions, and this is the woman's issue, not Jeanne's.

58. The minister, who is aware of Jeanne's charges, calls and asks if Jeanne has a special condition that she not have contact with her ex-boyfriend. When you reply yes, the minister tells you that the boyfriend has started coming to church on Sunday mornings. The minister says that he didn't believe that Jeanne spoke with her ex-boyfriend, but he can't be sure. What should you do with this information?

a. You should do nothing, because the minister doesn't believe Jeanne has violated her conditions by having contact with her ex-boyfriend.

b. You should find out which officer supervises the ex-boyfriend and talk with him or her about getting the boyfriend to stop going to that particular church.

c. During Jeanne's next office visit, you should tell her that you heard her ex-boyfriend has been worshipping at her church, and that you don't want her to violate her special condition that she not have contact with him. Then you should ask her to find a resolution to this situation, and offer her your assistance in doing so.

d. You should remind Jeanne about the special condition that she not have contact with her ex-boyfriend, and let her know that if he keeps coming to worship at her church, she will have to find another church to attend.

59. The parole board established a special condition that Jeanne get counseling to help her develop self-confidence and leadership skills. The board felt that Jeanne committed her crimes because she couldn't stand up to her ex-boyfriend. Jeanne has been participating in counseling and is doing well—so well, in fact, that Jeanne has been acting somewhat insubordinate to you when you are conducting an office or home visit. Jeanne has been belligerent, even hostile at times, and has sometimes simply refused to comply with your instructions. How should you handle this situation?

a. You should tell Jeanne that it is not appropriate to talk to you that way and that she will go to jail the next time she does it.

b. You should run an urinalysis on Jeanne during the next office visit.

c. You should cancel Jeanne's counseling sessions because they obviously worked, too well.

d. You should talk with Jeanne's counselor and report what is happening. You should ask the counselor if steps can be taken to teach Jeanne not to act this way or if there are other methods, such as drug therapy, that you should be aware of.

60. Jeanne calls you on the phone crying. After she calms down, you learn that the members of the church have collected enough money for Jeanne to put a headstone on each of her daughter's graves. She had just wanted to share that with you. How should you respond?

a. You should tell her that is great news and wish her a good day.

b. You should encourage her to find a way of thanking the congregation publicly this Sunday.

c. You should suggest that she not accept the donations because the church has given her enough already.

d. You should suggest that she take the money she has saved, combine it with the donations, and buy her daughters a monument instead of a headstone.

61. Which of the following sentences is punctuated correctly?

a. The offender asked, "Where is the application that needs filled out?"

b. The offender asked "Where is the application that needs filled out"?

c. The offender asked, Where is the application that needs filled out?

d. The offender asked Where is the application that needs filled out?

62. Which of the following sentences is punctuated correctly?

   a. Although working and maintaining a high level of mental awareness takes a good deal of time; the effort pays off in the long run.

   b. Although working and maintaining a high level of mental awareness takes a good deal of time, the effort pays off in the long run.

   c. Although working and maintaining a high level of mental awareness takes a good deal of time: the effort pays off in the long run.

   d. Although working and maintaining a high level of mental awareness takes a good deal of time. The effort pays off in the long run.

63. Which of the following sentences is NOT punctuated correctly?

   a. Sally came into the office to report about her job, her employment, and her counseling sessions.

   b. Sally came into the office to report, about her job, her employment, and her counseling sessions.

   c. Sally, came into the office to report; about her job, her employment, and her counseling sessions.

   d. Sally came into the office, to report: about her job, her employment, and her counseling sessions.

64. Which sentence do you feel is the most clearly written?

   a. The murder, when it took place, astounded the entire community, which was in the urban area, with its brutality and racial overtones.

   b. When the murder took place, it astounded the entire urban community with its brutality and racial overtones.

   c. When the murder, with its brutality and racial overtones, took place, it astounded the entire urban community.

   d. The murder, with its brutality and racial overtones, astounded the entire urban community.

65. Which sentence do you feel is the most clearly written?

   a. The primary function of parole is to protect the public from released offenders.

   b. This goal is accomplished, in three objectives, that include the enforcement of parolee restrictions and controls in the community.

   c. Providing services that help parolees integrate into a noncriminal lifestyle is also an objective of parole.

   d. Increasing the public's confidence, as an objective of parole, in the effectiveness of parole services.

66. Which sentence do you feel is the most clearly written?

a. Mass media, it was decided that radio, television, movies, and comic books have contributed to juvenile delinquency.

b. It has been decided that radio, television, and movies along with crime and horror comic books contribute to juvenile delinquency, produced by mass media.

c. It was decided that mass media is contributing to the country's alarming rise in juvenile delinquency through radio, television, movies, crime and horror comic books, and other types of printed matter.

d. The radio, television, motion pictures and crime and horror comic books have contributed to juvenile delinquency produced by mass media it was decided.

67. Which of the following sentences is NOT grammatically correct?

a. The officer saw that the judge was coming to the officer's office.

b. There's was a happy working relationship.

c. The officer saw the accident and reported it, too.

d. The officer saw the offender to her office and then pulled the file.

68. Which of the following sentences is NOT grammatically correct?

a. The officer told the offender to set the paper down.

b. The offender brought in the perscription for the officer to copy for his case file.

c. The officer met with the offender and established the parameters of their relationship.

d. The hearing was postponed because of the parole officer's illness.

69. Which of the following sentences is grammatically correct?

a. Comic books, television, and movies have been known to contribute to juvenile delinquency.

b. Movyies commic books and television have ben known to contribute to juvenile delinquency.

c. Comic books, television, and movies has been known to contribute to juvinile delinquency.

d. It has been said that comic boocs, televesion, and movies have bein nown to contribute to juvenile delinquence.

Directions: Read the following passage and then answer questions 70 through 77.

Club Drugs

Probation and parole officers must constantly keep updated on the various illegal drugs and the ways teenagers acquire them. The latest popular drugs for teens and young adults, known as "club drugs," are MDMA (ecstasy), rohypnol, GHB, and ketamine. These three drugs are now part of the lifestyle that also includes going to nightclubs, bars, raves, or trance scenes. These drugs can generally be bought at a low cost and give intoxicating highs that only enhance the rave or trance experience.

What is dangerous about these drugs, besides the drugs themselves, is how raves and other parties manipulate parents and guardians into believing their children will be safe. Many times, the rave is advertised as alcohol-free, which gives parents a sense of false security in allowing their child to attend. However, parents may not be aware that illegal drugs are sold and used at these parties. The number of people at a party could be minimal (30 people in a small bar), or could grow to be as many as a few thousand in an open field.

To some adults, club drugs may seem harmless, but in reality, these drugs can cause physical and psychological problems—even death. MDMA (ecstasy) can cause users to grind their teeth, so the people who go to raves, known as "ravers," often suck on baby pacifiers or lollipops to offset this effect. Ravers also use glow sticks and flashing lights to heighten the effect of the visual distortions brought on by MDMA. Other symptoms include increase of heart rate and blood pressure (often to a dangerous level), a prolonged sense of confusion, depression, and difficult paying attention, and possibly fatal respiratory problems. Low-dose amounts of ketamine can result in an impaired ability to pay attention, learn, or remember. Rohypnol and GHB are odorless and colorless, and can often be ingested without knowledge. These drugs are all central nervous system depressants.

The members of the criminal justice system must become partners with the community in its attempt to curb these raves and parties. There are movements in many communities to ban or curb the ability to host raves. Some communities are passing new ordinances that establish juvenile curfews and licensing requirements for large public gatherings. Other communities are enforcing existing fire codes and health, safety, and liquor laws for establishments at which raves are allowed to be held. Yet, one must ask if criminal justice professionals could be doing more. Do probation and parole officers ask enough questions of their assigned offenders when they talk of going to an alcohol-free event at one of the neighborhood bars, or do the officers ask what else is going on at that free concert besides listening to music? Do the officers interrupt their own family time to show up to one of these events to ensure our offenders are safe and not involved in illicit drug use?

In 2005, a anonymous national survey was sent to teenagers to find out more about their drug use. Approximately 2.8% of eighth graders, 4.0% of tenth graders, and 5.4% of 12th graders reported using MDMA. Also, 3.1% of eighth graders, 4.1% of tenth graders, and 4.5% of twelfth graders reported using methamphetamines. It is time criminal justice professionals step outside of their comfort zones to ask more questions, spend more time in the field after normal

working hours, and visit more with the parents or family members to learn what is really going on with the offender during evening hours. It is time to educate parents on these types of events and parties and encourage them to ask more questions before their child leaves for a party. It is time to make an impact on juvenile delinquency by talking to parents at the back door, rather than by showing up to arrest an offender at the front door.

70. Which of the following restates the main idea of this passage?
   a. Drug use has not increased among teenagers and young adults since the last generation.
   b. Drugs are being sold at events advertised as alcohol-free, and the effects of those drugs are just as dangerous as alcohol, if not more so.
   c. Teenagers are being more manipulative and sly in finding ways to use drugs.
   d. Criminal justice professionals haven't been doing their jobs, and this incompetence has caused an increase in drug use among teenagers.

71. Which of the following was NOT mentioned in the passage as a way that criminal justice professionals could help with this community issue?
   a. Officers should step outside of their comfort zones and ask more questions of the juveniles.
   b. Officers should spend more time in the field after normal working hours visiting offenders and their parents.
   c. Officers should go undercover and act as juveniles to learn what drugs are sold at different events.
   d. Officers should educate parents about raves and other types of drug parties in the community.

72. Which of the following was NOT listed in the passage as a side effect of using MDMA (ecstasy)?

   a. teeth grinding

   b. depression

   c. increased heart rate and blood pressure

   d. the ability to think and talk really fast

73. Which of the drugs discussed in the passage is odorless and colorless?

   a. MDMA (ecstasy)

   b. ketamine

   c. rohypnol

   d. cocaine

74. According to the passage, how are communities attempting to stop or curb the drug use?

   a. by establishing curfews and licensing requirements for large public gatherings

   b. by establishing neighborhood watches comprised of teenagers' parents who are responsible for watching for events such as raves in their areas

   c. by enlisting the cooperation of law enforcement, parents, mental health and corrections staff, to pool their resources to educate teenagers about the problems caused by using drugs

   d. by convincing teenagers and young adults not to participate in these types of illegal activities and to become involved in helping their peers

75. Why does the author think these drugs are attractive to teenagers and young adults?

   a. because teenagers and young adults view experimenting with and using drugs as a rite of passage

   b. because these drugs are low cost and give the user a high that deepens the rave or trance experience

   c. because these drugs are easy to buy and sell

   d. because the supply of these drugs is plentiful and because people can use their established businesses as a front to sell these drugs to teenagers

76. Which of the following does the author imply in the passage?

   a. Teenagers are going to do drugs no matter how much effort is made to try to stop them.

   b. Business owners and landowners must be punished when they allow raves, trances, and other drug parties to occur on their property.

   c. To help curb this problem, criminal justice professionals must do more within their official capacity to be visible, ask more questions, and get more involved in juvenile offenders' lives.

   d. Parents must do more to help stop this problem.

77. According to the passage, what percentage of eighth graders reported using MDMA?

   a. 4.0%

   b. 2.8%

   c. 4.1%

   d. 5.4%

Directions: Read the following passage and then answer questions 78 through 85.

Questions have been raised about the objectivity of the interviewers and the politics of hiring in the traditional interview process. All agencies want to find the right person with the right skills for the job. Competency-based interviewing, which has become more and more popular in corrections agencies, is a style of interviewing that eliminates many of the concerns about traditional interviewing and raises the bar for qualified candidates.

Competency-based interviewing allows a candidate to show how he or she can accomplish a skill or task by identifying past experience in which he or she performed that skill or completed that task. The candidate is asked questions that begin, "Tell about a time when. . ." or "Describe a time when. . ." In this type of interview, there isn't a right or wrong answer, but rather a short, vague answer or an answer that is detailed, specific, and relevant.

Competency-based interviewing allows the candidate to champion his or her skills in communication, problem solving, leadership, and other areas the employer has determined necessary for a successful probation or parole officer. This type of interviewing also allows the employer to see what the candidate's qualities are and whether or not the candidate would be an asset to the agency.

This type of interviewing assures the employer that the interviewers are being objective, not letting their personal impressions cloud their judgment of the candidate's ability, and eliminates misunderstandings or perceptions that occur in traditional interview settings.

Unfortunately, this process is not without shortcomings. Candidates can obtain sample questions and answers from a variety of sources, and then can come to the interview with practiced answers rather than natural responses. Another problem is that competency-based questions take time to develop. The human resources staff is busy enough without having to take additional time to develop quality-based questions for each interview board. Many times, the same questions are used in interviews at different agencies, allowing candidates who interview at more than one agency to memorize the question and provide a stock answer. However, the greatest concern comes from the candidate. Candidates who have years of experience and are comfortable with the traditional style of interviewing are not sure about themselves in this new style of interviewing. Because of this apprehension, highly qualified candidates may withdraw from the application process once they learn they will have to participate in this style of interviewing. Additionally, they may convince themselves to apply, only to do poorly in the interview. These candidates often become bitter or angry, which can lead to other problems for the agency.

Agencies cannot say for sure that competency-based interviewing is the best method of assessing candidates; however, they can say that traditional interviewing doesn't help their employee retention rate. The cost of advertising, interviewing, and training a new employee gets higher and higher every year. Agencies want a foolproof method for finding the right person with the right skills for the job.

78. The main idea of this passage is that
   a. agencies are using competency-based interviewing as a way to learn what skills a candidate has and what training the candidate would require.
   b. candidates are not able to get a fair interview if they are asked traditional questions.
   c. candidates can talk about their skills by telling stories about their experience, and the interviewers don't know if the candidates are telling the truth or putting themselves in a positive light.
   d. agencies don't like this interviewing style, but they think it's better than the traditional style.

79. What was listed in the passage as a shortcoming of the traditional style of interviewing?
   a. The passage doesn't list any shortcomings of the traditional style of interviewing.
   b. Candidates aren't comfortable with the traditional style of interviewing, because they can't figure out what the questions would be.
   c. The objectivity of the interviewers and the politics of hiring caused concern among employers who used the traditional style of interviewing.
   d. The traditional interview was usually short, which didn't give the candidate time to talk about his or her experience.

80. Which of the following are candidates are expected to do in a competency-based interview?
  a. simply talk and talk until the interviewers indicate they have enough information
  b. provide an answer that may be embellished in order to tell the interviewers what they want to hear
  c. answer a question that hypothetically asks what the candidate would do in a future situation
  d. answer in detail a question that asks how the candidate handled a past experience, and show how he or she used his or her skills to succeed

81. Which of the following was NOT listed as one of the problems with competency-based interviewing?
  a. Candidates can sell themselves better using the traditional interviewing style.
  b. Candidates can obtain sample questions and answers ahead of time because of the widespread use of this system.
  c. The questions are recycled often, which can elicit stock answers from candidates.
  d. Candidates who are uncomfortable with this style of interviewing may become bitter and angry if they do not do well in the interview or may not apply for the position at all.

82. This style of interviewing assures employers of which of the following?
  a. Candidates aren't hired based upon their looks.
  b. Candidates have sold themselves enough on their skills that they would be competent if hired.
  c. The interviewers are objective and not using their personal impressions to identify a qualified candidate.
  d. Candidates cannot have stock answers to the questions, because they have to give specific examples from their own lives.

83. According to the author, which of the following should a candidate do to have a successful competency-based interview?
  a. Tell several stories when answering a question.
  b. Give specific details about what he or she did, said, and decided in the story about his or her experience.
  c. Dress for success and be mentally sharp when going to the interview.
  d. End every story with an example of his or her leadership or problem-solving skills.

84. Which of the following is NOT an action taken by candidates who are uncomfortable with the competency-based style of interviewing?
  a. Candidates may not talk others into applying for positions that require a competency-based interview.
  b. Candidates may not apply for a position if they have to participate in a competency-based interview.
  c. Candidates may not research the competency-based process on the Internet.
  d. Candidates may not stay employed with an agency that uses competency-based interviewing.

85. Which of the following was NOT mentioned in the passage as a quality that competency-based interviewing can help an employer identify?
  a. integrity
  b. leadership
  c. problem-solving skills
  d. good communication skills

Directions: Read the following passage and then answer questions 86 through 93.

The Family and Medical Leave Act (FMLA) is a federal law that grants up to 12 weeks of unpaid leave during any 12-month period to eligible employees who work for qualified employers. The purpose of this law is to afford employees time away from work to handle specific personal issues, knowing that their position is being held for them for a specified time frame. Acceptable reasons for taking this time include: the birth and care of a newborn child (after an adoption as well), the care of an immediate family member (spouse, child, or parent) with a serious health condition, and the treatment of an employee's own serious health condition.

Employees may also use the 12 weeks of FMLA leave on an intermittent basis. Intermittent use may be needed if the employee, as a primary caregiver or having a serious medical condition, needs to go to treatments, appointments, the doctor, etc. throughout the duration of the illness. An employee can choose to substitute vacation time and/or sick leave for any of the unpaid leave under FMLA. An agency may insist FMLA leave run concurrently to the use of the employee's sick leave and vacation time taken for medical treatments, appointments, or other business related to the illness.

A problem arises when the sick time or the illness does not qualify under FMLA. Often, employees are not aware of what is covered and what is not. Human resources managers who are knowledgeable about the law, what is covered, and how to count the FMLA time may not know about an employee's leave for an FMLA-approved reason until they receive the employee's time sheet at payroll time. By then, it may be too late to cover the employee, and failure to offer coverage to the employee could potentially place the agency in liability.

Some employees have tried to manipulate the system by claiming FMLA-approved conditions in order to abuse their sick leave. When a supervisor confronts an employee and alleges an abuse of sick leave, some employees will attempt to protect themselves by claiming that the illnesses were all related to an FMLA-covered medical condition. The most common excuses include back pain, migraines, depression, and work-related stress. These conditions are all covered under FLMA and are experienced by many employees legitimately; however, employees who abuse their sick leave have used these conditions as excuses for their absences.

It is difficult to track intermittent time-off completely and accurately. The employee who is chronically late and uses a health condition as the excuse is not only hard to track time-wise, but also hard to supervise. More than 30% of FMLA-covered employers report that intermittent leave has a negative impact on office productivity and morale. Some employers believe the misuse of the law is exaggerated; they indicate that if an employee is chronically late and blaming his or her fictional back pains, the problem is not because of a medical issue, but because the employee isn't happy with his or her job and/or employer.

FMLA is available to help those employees who have a life-changing event such as the birth of a child or who need time to get themselves or their family member treatment. It is a shame that some employees see FMLA as a program they can abuse. What would they do without the law if it was truly needed? Or if they lost their jobs because they abused it?

86. FMLA is a federal protection provided to eligible employees who work for covered employers. What does the acronym FMLA stand for?
   a. Family and Medical Leave Act
   b. Farmers Medical Labor Association
   c. Family and Medicine Labor Association
   d. Family Mitigation Law Act

87. Which of the following was NOT listed as a reason employees may be eligible for FMLA leave?
   a. childbirth or adoptions
   b. hospitalization of a family member
   c. an employee's serious health condition
   d. the care of an immediate family member who has a serious health condition

88. Which of the following restates the author's main point?
   a. Employees who need to use their sick leave should do it anytime, because they are offered 12 weeks of unpaid time through FMLA.
   b. Employees don't know enough about the law to know whether or not their medical condition is covered under FMLA.
   c. Employees who work for covered employers may have their job protected for 12 weeks of unpaid time for certain medical reasons. However, some employees attempt to manipulate the system to abuse their sick leave.
   d. The law that allows employees to take 12 weeks of unpaid leave is being manipulated by employees who abuse their sick leave and create fictional illnesses.

89. The author cited the statistic that _____ of employers feel intermittent leave has a negative impact on office productivity.
   a. 15%
   b. 18%
   c. 30%
   d. 52%

90. According to the passage, which of the following common conditions do employees who abuse sick leave NOT use as an excuse?
   a. migraines
   b. back pains
   c. hysterectomy
   d. depression

91. According to the passage, an agency may insist employees do which of the following when they have an FMLA-approved condition?
   a. Use their sick leave and vacation time concurrently with their FMLA leave.
   b. Use their sick leave and vacation time and then use their FMLA leave.
   c. Use their FMLA leave and then their vacation time only, so employees will still have sick leave available after they recover.
   d. Use their FMLA leave and their sick leave, but employees cannot use their vacation time.

92. Human resources professionals can often aid the supervisor and employee with FMLA processes. However, according to the passage, what is one situation that could cause liability for the agency?
   a. An employee uses all of his or her vacation time and sick leave before the human resources office notices.
   b. The human resources office is not informed of the illness until the end of the payroll period, which may be too late to get the employee covered.
   c. An employee tries to manipulate the system by abusing his or her sick leave and claiming FMLA on his or her time sheets.
   d. The human resources office is notified of an employee's illness but does not provide him or her the necessary paperwork.

93. According to the passage, why do employees try to manipulate FMLA?
   a. Employees know they can get more money if they try to use FMLA.
   b. Employees know they won't get caught when they use FMLA.
   c. Employees know they have used too much vacation time, and their supervisor is angry.
   d. Employees know they have abused their sick leave and are now trying to get their time covered under FMLA.

Directions: Read the following passage and then answer questions 94 through 100.

Reentry Plans

States are trying to deal with the constant increase in the number of offenders who are being released from prison every year. In addition to the number of offenders being released from prison on parole for the first time, states are facing a crisis of recidivism. Fewer than half of all released offenders are able to stay out of trouble for three years after their release.

Administrators from law enforcement, corrections, and community service agencies have collaborated in many communities to monitor offenders while assisting them in the implementation of specific reentry plans. The reentry programs represent a community approach to utilizing all of its available resources, identifying means to gain additional resources, and supporting those offenders who return to their community successfully. Some programs are created through federal and state grants, while others may already exist or have been updated.

A successful reentry program will begin its work while the offender is still incarcerated, to help the offender transition out of prison with the goal of becoming stable within the community. A successful program has three phases. The first phase, to protect and prepare, is designed to prepare the offenders to reenter the community. Services provided in this phase include educational programs, mental health and substance abuse programs, job training, and mentoring. The second phase, to control and restore, works with offenders prior to and immediately after release, to provide a continuation of education, substance abuse and mental health counseling, mentoring, and life and job skills. In the third phase, to sustain and support, community-based support programs work with offenders as they near their date for release from supervision. These programs are long term and will assist the offender in the transition from being controlled by the system to providing one's own structure by providing ongoing support and services.

Underlying the success of such programs is the understanding that corrections is not solely responsible for the offenders who return to the communities. Recognizing that the reentry population is also the responsibility of public health departments, workforce development agencies, housing authorities, counseling services, and welfare agencies is much of the battle. National attention has been brought to this subject as President Bush called for action to expand (in part) job training and placement services to help newly released prisoners. Also, national reports (published by the Council of State Governments) provide an analysis of elements that are essential to increasing the likelihood that adults released from prison will become productive member of communities. Reports such as these represent vision statements for the safe and successful transition of offenders from prison to the community.

So far, these programs have not been in existence long enough to yield good statistical evidence of their success. However, the programs are a good step in maintaining our efforts to keep communities safe. The message that it "takes a village to raise a child" takes on a special meaning when looking at the effectiveness of these types of programs.

94. The main theme of this passage is which of the following?
   a. Offenders are being released from prison in large numbers and are victimizing the communities they are returning to.
   b. Offender recidivism rates are not helping the overcrowding issue, because fewer than half of all released offenders return to prison after their release.
   c. Reentry programs are a right step into assisting offenders' transition from the prison to the community.
   d. Reentry programs are coming to communities only because national attention has been placed on the concern about recidivism rates.

95. Which of the following was NOT listed in the passage as one of the three phases in a successful reentry program?

a. to protect and prepare

b. to identify and provide

c. to control and restore

d. to sustain and support

96. Reentry programs have been developed in various communities because of which of the following?

a. Communities have found ways to keep community agencies funded and growing through the use of federal dollars.

b. Communities are tired of all service programs being implemented inside the prisons only, so they developed these programs to help others within their communities.

c. The reentry concept forces many community agencies to work together, which only helps the community become stronger.

d. Large numbers of offenders are released back into the community without a great deal of support, which allows offenders to victimize the community and results in the offenders being sent back into the prison system.

97. Which has brought more national attention to this community problem?

a. the U.S. Department of Justice, by offering communities grant money

b. President George W. Bush's 2004 State of the Union address, by indicating that action needed to be taken to expand the job training and placement services to help newly released prisoners

c. the reentry report by the Council of State Governments

d. a heinous crime committed by an offender who wasn't properly supervised

98. According to the author, the underlying success of reentry programs is what?

a. the understanding that corrections agencies are not solely responsible for the offenders who return to the communities

b. the understanding that corrections agencies must take the lead and coordinate all of the service agencies before deciding what is needed for the various offenders

c. the understanding that service agencies are beholden to corrections agencies for keeping their doors open to serve offenders in the communities

d. the understanding that, no matter what a community does, offenders will not stay out of prison unless they want to change their behavior, no matter how many programs are available to help them

99. What was the main idea of this passage?

a. Offenders will not stay within the community unless they want to change their behavior, no matter how many programs are available to help them.

b. Community leaders have vision and insight as to how to make communities safer for everyone.

c. It will take a village to help an offender make changes in his or her behavior and to learn to be a productive citizen.

d. Thoroughly funded programs will make a difference in offenders' lives, so they can stay out of prison and be productive.

100. Which of the following have become community partners with corrections programs?

a. schools

b. mental health and substance abuse programs

c. workforce development programs

d. all of the above

► Answers

1. b. If the parole board releases an inmate by mistake, that offender is able to stay under supervision within the community, according to the Supreme Court (*Hawkins v. Freeman,* 1999). Choice **a** is correct because the parole board members have immunity in all decisions to grant, deny, or revoke parole (*King v. Simpson,* 1999); however, when mistakes are made, members must be held accountable. Choice **c** is incorrect because the parole board does not supervise the parole officers. Choice **d** is incorrect because the parole board does not oversee or act upon granting or denying good time, other than when a dealing with a revocation decision.

2. c. An officer should always check with family, friends, and the employer first before doing anything else in regard to where the offender may be. Generally, the offender will tell someone that he or she is going away and when he or she may return. Choice **a** would then be the second action an officer would take to find an absconder. The third action taken to find the offender would be choice **d**. It is generally in this fashion that offenders who truly abscond are located and arrested. Finally, choice **b** would be the last step taken by the officer. Once the warrant is issued, there really isn't anything else to do but wait until the offender is stopped or arrested on a new crime.

3. b. Parole has the primary goal of providing safety and security to the community. The goal of probation services (choice **a**) is to provide safety to the community as well treatment to the offenders. Choice **c** is incorrect because prisons hold incarcerated offenders to keep them out of the communities. Choice **d** is not the correct answer because jails detain people who may be guilty or innocent.

4. d. Reentry programs are fairly new and bring together all types of resources so that offenders can be offered services in order to be successful while under supervision. Choice **b** is incorrect. A work-release program creates a restrictive environment (more restrictive than a halfway house) in which offenders live within a facility, follow program rules, participate in treatment and mental health programs within the community, and work outside of the facility. Offenders usually pay a stipend toward rent, must make payments on their restitution and other financial obligations, and must have a savings account. Choice **a** is a military-style program in which offenders work through a program to change their criminal behavior and thinking. Offenders are not allowed to leave the program until they have completed the requirements. Choice **c** is where offenders report on a daily basis, either in person or by phone, while they live at their arranged living quarters.

5. b. Parole conditions should be clear and reasonable, not complex (choice **d**) or full of legal language and complicated (choice **a**). The length of the conditions is not in question as long as the condition is relevant (choice **c**) but, more important, clear and reasonable.

6. a. The probation officer (choice **d**) compiles all of the relevant information into the presentence investigation report to give to the judge, who will use that information to make an informed decision. The prosecutor (choice **c**) may provide costs, but usually court costs are established through other means. Choice **b** is incorrect; the victim will be able to provide information on damages and any other costs to the probation officer who is completing the presentence investigation report.

7. c. Choice **d** is a calculation of the number of hours required to supervise one offender based on that offender's level of supervision. Choice **a** certainly provides the historical data of the offender's past criminal history, but it may not have captured all of the incidents and crimes and, therefore, may not tell the whole story. Establishing a risk number is important in order to know how to supervise the offenders. A supervision plan cannot be established with inaccurate or incomplete data.

8. a. The Family and Medical Leave Act (FMLA) covers primary caregivers when they are taking care of a family member or themselves, or when they have had or adopted a child. These criteria must be met in order to qualify, which is explained in the paperwork that is sent. Choice **b** deals only with labor situations such as time and hours worked, overtime and compensatory time, etc. Choices **c** and **d** are incorrect and are fabricated terms.

9. c. These two terms are often confused by citizens. Choice **c** is the correct answer because probation supervision occurs prior to incarceration, not the other way around (choice **d**). The supervision conditions of both probation and parole (choice **a**) are very similar and may have standard and special conditions that may be the same in some areas. The type of offender (choice **b**) is the same for both.

10. a. If an officer is hurt or injured while on duty, then the officer must be seen by the work comp contractor to determine a course of action for the officer. The course of action will include what the officer should do as well as who pays for the care given, the company or the employee. Choice **b** is incorrect because the supervisor doesn't have proof of the contagious stage, if there really is one. Additionally, personal sick time is used only for the first seven days of a work comp situation. Choices **c**

and **d** indicate that the supervisor is making medical decisions that could impact the whole office. It is best to make a decision to be safe rather than sorry, and the officer should go to the work comp contractor.

11. d. Jail is a locally operated detention facility that confines offenders who are detained while awaiting processing on charges or trial, awaiting sentencing, or serving a sentence for up to one year. Choice **c** is incorrect because a prison is a long-term facility that is either state or federally run and confines offenders who have been convicted of a felony for a period of one year or longer. Choices **a** and **b** are programs in which offenders may go to live or obtain resources in order to complete their supervision time successfully.

12. a. In general, consequences are brought down on employees who take sick leave in a pattern of days or when employees have a "use it or lose it" attitude of sick leave. Vacation leave (choice **c**) is viewed as the employee's to use as he or she sees fit. However, agencies see sick leave as time that should be available for the employee to use when he or she or his or her family members are actually sick, not when a mental health day is needed. Choices **b** and **d** are generally not punished; however, these issues are federal labor standards issues, and if abused, consequences could result.

13. b. Some agencies do not have the luxury to employ on-call officers who will take care of situations like this. In that case, the officer must get out of bed and take care of the paperwork necessary to hold this offender in jail. Any time the police department has evidence of gang-related activity, that information should be taken seriously and acted upon accordingly. Choice **c** is incorrect; calling a supervisor is a necessary step, but a parole officer should not plan to talk with the offender until decisions regarding his or her parole are made. Choice **d** is never an option. This type of request would certainly place the sergeant and the jail in a potentially liable situation, especially if the offender was capable of making bail. Choice **a** would be irresponsible action on a parole officer's part.

14. c. In this situation, you allow the offender to remain within the community until the courts hear both sides of the story to determine what the truth is. While the offender is in the community, he should attend counseling where alcohol-related consequences are discussed. Choices **a** and **b** are incorrect, because you are not the judge, nor can you determine what was seen by whom because you weren't there. This action may also cause conflict between you and the probationer. Choice **b** is incorrect for the same reasons. Choice **d** would certainly cause conflict with quite a few people, such as the probationer, your supervisor, and the probation officer who would get the case if it was transferred. This action is not relevant to the situation nor helpful to the offender.

15. d. An officer's responsibility is to be a referral agent as well as to ensure the safety and security of the community. To assist this offender and to keep him crime-free, the officer should ensure the offender is connected with the resource agencies that provide help and support to low-income citizens. Choices **a**, **b**, and **c** are not appropriate answers and reactions for an officer when an offender requests assistance.

16. b. To begin this process, the probation officer must write a factual report that describes for the judge why a warrant should be issued. The report should then be given to the judge, or judge's staff, for processing. Once the warrant has been issued, then the office can give the probationer a call and direct him to report to the office so the police can detain him there and not out on the street where

harm is more likely to come to all parties. Choice **a** is incorrect. Talking to the probationer prior to writing the report and obtaining the warrant could make the offender abscond supervision, ensuring a more difficult process for the offender. Choice **c** is incorrect because you cannot be sure the police department will not go find the probationer prior to receiving the warrant. Choice **d** is incorrect because the judge wants to ensure all facts are present, issue the warrant, and then will see the probationer at the revocation hearing.

17. d. This is the one right that is not available to probationers during the two-stage revocation hearing process. Under *Gagnon v. Scarpelli* (1973), attorneys may be present at the hearing stages only on a case-by-case basis as determined by the judge. Choices **a**, **b**, and **c** are all due process rights offered to probationers as well as parolees when revocation has been started.

18. c. A transfer of jurisdiction is the process by which a juvenile's case is sent to be tried in the adult justice system. This transfer can be accomplished in many ways, whether it be through a hearing, a certification by the juvenile court judge, a statutory exclusive, or a direct file by the prosecutor. Choices **b** and **d** are incorrect because this process is not haphazard or without process and procedure. It would be rare for an adult court judge to sit in for a juvenile judge or to handle a juvenile case without the legal process of transferring the case to the adult court. Choice **a** is incorrect because it means the juvenile has been judged to be responsible for him- or herself, and usually there isn't a criminal case or juvenile violation involved.

19. a. A probation officer may disclose the name of a juvenile on probation; however, what the juvenile is on probation for (choice **b**), the conditions of probation (choice **c**), and the length of probation (choice **d**) cannot be revealed, unless directly ordered by the judge to do so. It should be noted some state statutes may prohibit the disclosure that a juvenile is on probation.

20. b. Generally, juveniles who have been arrested on a probation violation warrant are held in custody in a detention facility pending the hearing. Not that having the parents involved (choice **a**) is bad, or that they aren't able to provide the necessary structure, but holding the juvenile in a detention facility will ensure he or she is available for the hearing without delay or issue. Choices **c** and **d** are incorrect. These placements would be for juveniles who have not made bad choices that caused them to be under supervision. Children who are in need of supervision, in need of care, or neglected usually are placed in foster care or another adult's home.

21. c. In a case heard by the Arizona court of appeals in 1998, fingerprinting of juveniles does not cause a violation of due process or constitutional rights and has a bearing in the rehabilitative process of probation. Choices **a**, **b**, and **d** are incorrect because of the details regarding what the court decided about fingerprinting.

22. d. The police officer, if escorting the probation officer, may seize the illegal substances under the plan view doctrine. However, if the police officer suspects drugs are in the home and asks the probation officer to help him enter the home, then a warrant would be needed (choice **b**). Choice **c** is incorrect because the police officer does not lose his authority just because he is providing escort to the probation officer. Choice **a** is incorrect because the drugs can be seized.

23. b. Probation services generally fall under the judicial branch of government, with probation officers often appointed by judges.

Choice **a**, parole, is generally within the executive branch of the government, because parole services is under the direction of a commissioner appointed by the governor. Choices **c** and **d** are actions the governor or president can grant. These actions are usually to "forgive" the criminal punishment, not the act or crime.

24. a. It is important in this situation to acknowledge that the mother may be frustrated with the juvenile and is using this setting to gain some assistance. With that in mind, choice **a** is the best choice for a response. Gaining assistance from the parent in enforcing structure at home may help the mother immediately as well as help the juvenile be more successful under probation. All violations should, however, result in some type of consequence; if the violations aren't severe, then special conditions should be added to the juvenile's supervision. Choice **b** would cause damage to your relationship with the mother and would cause more stress at home for the juvenile. Choice **c** is incorrect, unless the violations are so severe that the juvenile and the community would be at risk if the juvenile returned home with the mother. Again, the judge would issue the warrant to have the juvenile detained, not the probation officer. Choice **d** is not action the probation officer can take and is not within reason for this situation.

25. c. An objective hearing body is the common factor between the two types of court systems. There are attorneys present at all adult hearings and are generally present in all juvenile cases. However, a child advocate, rather than a defense attorney, may be speaking for the child. The other choices **a**, **b**, and **d** are all differences between juvenile and adult courts.

26. d. Gangs use slang and regular words to mean different things while in prison. Choices **a**, **b**, and **c** are incorrect.

27. b. Civil rights are rights that belong to a person by virtue of citizenship. The right to vote is a civil right that is lost upon conviction of a felony, along with the right to own or possess a firearm, the right to hold public office (with some restrictions), and the right to serve on a jury. Choice **a** refers to the rights protected under the First Amendment. Choice **c** refers to the rights protected under the Fourth Amendment. Choice **d** refers to the rights protected under the Fourteenth Amendment.

28. c. The hearing officer should let the offender know that the witnesses can still appear if they wish at the last hearing in front of the paroling authority. Also, the hearing officer should ask to proceed with this hearing. Choice **d** should not be requested of a parole officer; however, the parole officer does have an obligation prior to the hearing to help the offender locate and possibly contact his witnesses. Choice **a** does not allow the offender to have his hearing within the allotted periods. Also, this may be a possible attempt by the offender to manipulate the hearing officer and the legal progress. Choice **b** does not provide the offender with the opportunity for due process.

29. b. The hearing officer should attempt to hear some of the witnesses provide character testimony. Even though that information will not be used in the findings, the witnesses traveled to the hearing and courtesy would dictate this action. Choice **a** would not be a time-worthy decision. Choice **c** would be rude and would cause a negative reaction from the witnesses and the offender. Choice **d** would not allow the offender to have ample due process because he can still provide testimony and evidence to whether the violations did or did not occur.

30. c. This situation is difficult, because you don't wish to appear rude; however, an officer should never accept gifts from an offender. The acceptance of gifts, even flowers, could put you in jeopardy of being accused of becoming too familiar with the offender. Thanking the offender sincerely but telling him that you cannot accept the lovely flowers and then suggesting he take them to his significant other or his mother will ensure the offender hasn't wasted his money. Choice **a** would give the impression to the office and to the offender that you are too familiar with the offender. Choice **b** would be rude and will certainly cause the offender to be hurt or angry. Choice **d** may also give the impression of being too familiar. This is appropriate when vendors send baskets, food, or candy to the office; those gifts should be shared with the office. However, offenders should never be allowed to bring or leave gifts for a particular officer or for the office.

31. d. Asking Rita to gain more information in order to make an informed decision is the best way to assist in this situation. Rather than become the "messenger" with bad news for both parties, arrange for a meeting so the PIO can provide what information he knows and then the offender can inform him of her reluctance to participate. Choice **c** is a quick fix but will place the officer in the middle of a situation that is difficult. Choice **b** is incorrect because it doesn't matter what the offender's decision is in relation to your wishes. If the offender doesn't wish to be interviewed, then he or she has the right to be excluded. Choice **a** is inappropriate and untrue. This action would certainly establish a conflict for the offender.

32. a. Telling the truth may be uncomfortable, but encouraging the offender to act responsibly in this situation is showing the offender how to handle situations in the appropriate way. Choice **b** is assuming this problem as your own, and will certainly cause conflicts for you and the offender in the future. Choice **c** is incorrect. There may be a condition in which offenders cannot associate with other offenders, but this condition is usually tied to offenders being involved in illegal activities. Living together would not be an absolute guarantee that illegal activities would be done. Choice **d** is not appropriate. Encouraging someone to tell a lie is not professional action or good decision.

33. b. Even though Rita understands, it is important to inform her, or any offender, that his or her action is a violation. Doing this will ease any confusion in future meetings. It is important to help the offender figure out what her trigger was, and then get the sample anyway to ensure that cocaine is the only drug she is taking. Choice **a** is never an option. Leaving the offender to do something will not ensure that it is done, especially after he or she confessed to committing a violation of parole. Choice **c** is not an option, especially if this is the first violation the offender has committed. If there are a string of violations, then that is another issue; however, that was not true in this case study. Choice **d** is not an option. A parole officer must react to violations and give some sort of consequence or action to the offender. "Brushing this under the rug" will only cause more harm in the long run.

34. c. If state procedures allow this type of travel and if the offender has progressed well in parole, as in this case study, there shouldn't be any issue in letting an offender go. The officer, in fact, does not have a say in the offender's lifestyle or sexual preference as long as the offender is not doing anything illegal (choice **a**). Choice **b** is not a correct response because the offender is probably

going to go without approval. This response could be viewed as being sarcastic and flippant, and would probably cause conflict with the offender. Choice **d** may be an option if the offender has not progressed well. However, in that case the offender shouldn't be having out-of-state travel.

35. a. A parole officer's first concern in this situation should be the safety and welfare of the offender. Asking if she is all right should be the officer's professional response. Ensuring the offender has reported the crime should be the next order of business. If not, then the officer should help the offender get to the police department to do so. Choice **b** is not the parole officer's duty or responsibility. Choice **c** would be a very inappropriate reaction of a parole officer. This offense is obviously beyond vandalism and has serious implications for the offender and the community. Choice **d** would be highly inappropriate because simply thinking the offender did something illegal is not proof nor a justified reason to take someone's freedom away.

36. d. Nothing can be done at this point in the process other than to help the offender process all of the paperwork involved in being discharged. Choice **a** is not an appropriate action because it is the parole officer's job to answer questions and concerns from the public. The victim coordinator was doing his or her job in providing notification to the victim. Choices **b** and **c** are not the officer's responsibility if the agency has a victim coordinator. The parole officer should always be available, though, to help refer family members to counselors more appropriate to work through their grief.

37. a. The parents must be involved in making decisions such as setting curfew because, for the most part, they are the ones enforcing those boundaries. In this case study, gaining their input is also important to help ease the pressure the parents are placing on you by asking them to be accountable for their son's progress while under supervision. Choice **b** is not an option, although it is true in this case study. Replying in this fashion will make the officer appear insensitive and could cause more conflict. Choice **c** would also make the officer appear insensitive and unprofessional. Choice **d** should not be advice given from a probation officer. It is not a probation officer's responsibility to advise probationers how to get off probation by any means other than fulfilling the conditions.

38. b. You should calmly tell this man whom he should contact to air his complaints. Telling this man to get out of your face or get away from you (choice **a**) could possibly anger him more. When emotions are involved, the possibility of a scene or the use of force is greater. An officer's responsibility is to help ensure the safety of the public, even at football games. Dealing with the public means working with a calm attitude and approach. Choice **c** will only anger the man more and possibly cause future encounters with this man or others in the future. Choice **d** may be true but could appear to be flippant and not professional. This action would not help to calm or resolve the situation.

39. c. When an addict feels out of control, the best advice an officer can give is to get reconnected with his counselor or attend a meeting. In these settings, an offender can refocus on his efforts to stay clean and not allow his triggers to pull them back into the addiction. Choice **a** would only cause the offender to be angry with you because this action is also not the officer's decision to make. Choice **b** would certainly cause conflict between you and the offender, and is not wise advice. Choice **d** is

not advice that a teenager would ever take, and would give the impression that the officer doesn't care and is insensitive.

40. d. The immediate priority is getting the offender back into treatment for the substance abuse. Placing a condition on the offender will ensure that the offender is committed to doing this treatment. Telling the offender that this is a violation of his supervision will also make it clear that he did something wrong and that he will receive consequences. Ignoring this situation (choice **c**) will give the offender the wrong impression. The next action, not mentioned in this answer, would be for the officer to establish a time for the counseling to start. In this situation, the parents' request is really not an issue for the officer to be concerned about. Therefore, choice **a** is not appropriate action. An officer should never "bargain" for compliance or to gain favor. Choice **b** would not be appropriate; however, the offender should be encouraged to tell his parents and face the consequences of his actions.

41. b. Without getting all of the facts from all of the people involved, it is difficult to make informed decisions. This is a good action to take especially if you aren't sure of the credibility of the person who told you about the situation. Choice **a** is not in the best interest of the offender, and would probably bring a lot of conflict to you and your agency. Choice **c** could be one of the options if the parents were blatant about letting the offender violate the conditions of his probation. At this point, that doesn't seem to be the case. Choice **d** is not a professional manner in which to handle this situation. This is especially true if you don't have all of the information gathered.

42. a. You should have a comfortable, professional relationship with the judge. Telling the judge of your vacation plans and asking tactfully if the report could be submitted a day later is a responsible way to handle this time conflict (choice **a**). Choice **b** may be the action to take if the judge indicates he cannot wait; however, this is not the action to take in any other situation. If you have vacation plans or plans for the day, make sure you take that time. Most of the time, supervisors and judges will understand your situation. Choice **c** would not be appropriate action to take. Choice **d** is incorrect; the only time this action should be considered is when you don't have a comfortable relationship with the judge.

43. b. The parole board member is obviously concerned about this offender's time on supervision and has called you directly to talk about the offender. Taking the time to thank him for the call and concern, and then assuring him you have the situation under control is exactly what is needed. Choices **a** and **c** are inappropriate responses to a parole board member, or anyone else for that matter. Betting on someone's freedom is not appropriate, nor is questioning someone's decision-making abilities. It is irrelevant why the decision was made, especially since the offender is already on parole. Choice **d** would not be wise because the board member called you directly. Transferring the call to the parole director would be a brush-off and would be considered rude on the officer's part.

44. d. You should remind the offender that, at this point, it doesn't matter what her defense was or what happened at the trial. It is important to keep the offender focused on the present and future rather on what the jury believed or didn't believe. Choice **a** may be a part of a conversation that is begun by choice **d**, but it shouldn't be the first answer. Keeping offenders focused on the positive should be the officer's goal. Choice **b** would seem insensitive to the offender and would cause hurt feelings or other emotions. Choice **c** would certainly

cause you conflict with the offender and would be insensitive to say.

45. a. Though difficult, this is the best action for a parole officer to take. Telling people tactfully that they are making inappropriate comments will hopefully stop the behavior while maintaining the working relationship. Choice **b** is one way to damage a working relationship. Having the supervisor deal with other officers once you "snitched" on them is not always the best course of action. Choice **c** would not be appropriate because the meeting isn't for three weeks, and there is a chance the offender will overhear the comments. Also, you would have to put up with the comments for a longer period. Choice **d** is not a wise decision. It is never appropriate to be unprofessional, no matter how stressful the job is.

46. d. It would be vital to communicate with the offender's psychiatrist to inform him of what you are seeing with the offender and to find out what to do. Staying by the apartment will ensure that the offender doesn't leave in her current condition. Also, this tells the offender she is not alone, which may be heard through her emotion and cause her relief. Choice **a** would not be appropriate, especially knowing you are dealing with a mentally unstable person. Choice **b** would be good questions if the offender wasn't already exhibiting behavior that she isn't all right. Choice **c** would be a resolution if the offender had caused harm to someone else. In this case study, there wasn't any harm done that you know of and she is in obvious mental distress, and jail would not be the answer for that.

47. c. It would be important for an officer to communicate his or her concerns to the psychiatrist and to work together to plan for the offender either to return to the community with support or to stay institutionalized. The psychiatrist would be the one with priority supervision, and the parole officer should work diligently with the doctor. Choice **a** is inappropriate and unprofessional. It is never appropriate to make fun of someone else's problems or pain. Choice **b** is not appropriate, because the offender may not be in a state to make such decisions rationally, or the conversation may cause the offender to become emotional, which may set back her treatment. Choice **d** is not appropriate because an officer should not assume concerns will be passed along, although most of the time they are. If an officer is concerned enough about the offender and the public, then time should be taken to talk with the appropriate people.

48. c. Even though you know it isn't possible for your offender to be the perpetrator, it is still the responsibility of a parole officer to provide assistance as needed. In this case study, finding a quick resolution to the man's fears would provide some relief. Contacting the police department and obtaining a temporary phone number would allow the victim to gain some control over the situation and over his fears. Also, this would not put you in jeopardy of reporting confidential information. Choice **a** would be a violation of an officer's ethics and may cause employment action or consequences against the officer. Choice **b** would not provide immediate relief or control, which is what the victim wants by calling you. This, however, is a good suggestion to make after you help him work on getting the phone calls stopped. Choice **d** would simply cause more emotion in the victim, and isn't helpful to anyone. This response may also appear flippant and uncaring.

49. b. Though this is difficult, the officer should remain calm and not personalize this complaint. Asking what would be more appropriate would help you understand what the judges may find offensive or more acceptable. It would be best to go home during a lunch hour or ask if you can alter your time so you aren't affecting your pay. Choice **a** is not appropriate because your supervisor is telling you something is wrong with your outfit. This response could be seen as insubordinate. Choice **c** could also be seen as insubordinate. Neither the judges nor your supervisor is typically in charge of your pay range, and using this is simply an excuse to be insubordinate. Choice **d** is not appropriate, because the supervisor didn't come to your office to talk about another probation officer. When you point the finger at someone else's issues, you are trying to deflect the attention rather than accept responsibility for your own actions or issues.

50. a. Asking an employee to iron his clothes in a place of business is not appropriate, but then to walk in while the employee is semidressed and to comment on his body could border sexual harassment. The employee should be encouraged to contact the human resources office for guidance. Choice **b** is incorrect because it places you in the same situation as the supervisor by being borderline harassing. Choice **c** is not a professional response. Talking negatively about your supervisor will not help you to maintain a positive attitude in the office, and petitioning to remove a supervisor will only cause conflict. All employees have some sort of due process protocol afforded to them. Petitions are not a satisfactory way of moving someone out of their position. Choice **d** is not a helpful comment. The employee is obviously distressed about what has happened to him, and blaming him would not be helpful or logical.

51. c. The administrative judge has called to ask you to fill in. The best scenario for you is to accept gracefully and ensure you know his expectations for meetings and tasks that are important to him and to the position. Assuring the judge that the office will be taken care of is all the judge really wants to hear. Choice **a** is not a smart or wise answer to give to the administrative judge. The judge didn't ask for your opinion about a confidential employee matter, rather he is trying to ensure the office will continue to function. Your opinion about this matter is irrelevant. Choice **b** is also irrelevant information. The judge doesn't want to know your opinion of the supervisor's behavior but wants to know if you will assume the position on a temporary basis. Answering in this way will only cause conflict in the long run. Choice **d** makes you appear not to have confidence in your work and may make the judge wonder why he is selecting you to assume the supervisor position.

52. d. Telling the officers to stop gossiping and to focus on their task (lunch) is the appropriate and responsible thing for a supervisor to do. Choice **a** would not be responsible. Because you are the acting supervisor, you cannot afford to lower your professional standards to the level of gossip. Choices **b** and **c** are inappropriate, because nothing is done to stop the gossip, and in choice **c**, your standing by the door listening shows only that you were unwilling to take action or afraid of confronting the officers.

53. b. A supervisor must provide this type of information to the appropriate judge so the defendant can be dealt with fairly. Consequences must be given to the officer because this behavior and action is a violation of the code of ethics and is possibly illegal. This violation cannot be overlooked or handled passively (choice **a**); training may be an option after the consequence is provided. Choice **c** is not acceptable because the defendant has the right to a fair trial and sentencing. The PSI is used to provide the judge with information about the defendant so that he or she can

determine a sentence. If that information is not accurate, then the defendant cannot be dealt with in a fair and reasonable fashion. The failure to notify could be possible liable action. Choice **d** could be possible liable action against you as well as the employee and is generally an unacceptable action for a supervisor to take.

54. d. Explaining the situation to her and asking for help is the best resolution to this situation. Also, keeping her in her comfortable environment when you tell her you know of her performance issues will allow her to feel comfortable and not be defensive about her deficiencies. If she is your friend, then she will work with you to provide a good review. Choice **c** puts her in an uncomfortable position with you and the human resources director. Choice **a** is not an option. As the acting supervisor, you really do not have an opportunity to tell someone at a higher level that you aren't going to do something, unless of course it is an illegal action. Choice **b** would not be in your best interest. The administrative judge placed you in an acting position and trusts you to do the work required, not pass it off, especially to him.

55. b. More than likely, the women have made decisions regarding Jeanne through their conversations with her. The women may know about some of the crimes and are choosing not to care or be concerned. Choice **a** is incorrect because it is not your place to tell all of the details of the crime. If you are asked, it is acceptable to talk of the charges, but you shouldn't relay all of the details. Choice **c** would put Jeanne in an uncomfortable position, and it should be the offender's decision to talk about her criminal history. As long as people are not being harmed or manipulated, the charges are not relevant to Jeanne's current situation. Choice **d** would really serve no purpose other than to create conflict and confusion for the offender.

56. c. Officers should not accept money for any reason (choice **a**), whether or not it is for a good cause. Establishing a savings account would help the offender take care of her money, and a bank is the logical place to hold money. Choice **b** is incorrect because an officer should encourage parolees to learn to depend upon themselves as a resource and not always lean on others. Choice **d** would stretch the limits of being a landlord. Most landlords will not purchase such items for tenants and suggesting that the offender ask for this may put her in a bad position.

57. a. People react in different ways to offenders who have been convicted of heinous crimes. Offenders may receive a lot of opposition to where they work, live, or eat. Choice **d** is incorrect. Certainly, the offender may not wish to say anything because she has had a successful parole so far; however, her success on parole will not make a difference to people who cannot move past the crime. Choice **a** is the correct answer. Encourage the offender to talk honestly to the trustees who hired her, to provide answers to their questions, and to tell them how the church has changed her life. The trustees and minister can either believe the passion or not. Choice **b** is incorrect because the woman is already upset about Jeanne working in the church. The woman probably would not wish to have a conversation with Jeanne, and suggesting Jeanne take this action may be setting the offender up for disappointment or hurt. Choice **c** may be a last resort if the situation gets unbearable for Jeanne.

58. c. Reminding the offender of the special condition that she not have contact with her ex-boyfriend and the consequences of violating that condition is the best step. An officer can simply remind offenders of the conditions and consequences and then help the offender find ways to resolve the issue. Choice **a** may be true; however, offenders have a history of making bad choices, and an officer should offer to assist the offender in ensuring a successful transition or parole. Choice **b** would potentially cause more conflict for you and for your offender if this action were taken. In the case study, you were not aware that any violations had occurred, so this would be a knee-jerk reaction. Choice **d** is incorrect, although it may be a last resort Jeanne may have to consider.

59. d. The conversation will inform the counselor of your concerns about Jeanne's behavior and may help you to make sense of the situation. A plan of action can then be developed as to how to help Jeanne know when it is appropriate to be assertive and when it is not. It is not appropriate for an officer to threaten a "loss of liberty" action for a personality trait that may or may not appear (choice **a**). It is appropriate to indicate how you wish offenders to talk with you, but it is not okay to threaten. Choice **b** is incorrect; if this is the only behavior change you've witnessed, a urinalysis would not be justified. Choice **c** would not be a good action to take; ending the sessions is the counselor's call, not the officer's.

60. b. Although Jeanne probably knows this, reminding her to be gracious and thank people as soon as she can may help the offender stay focused on the good that was done for her. Choice **a** may appear to be insensitive and rude to the offender. Choice **c** would also appear to be insensitive to the congregation. This suggestion would put the offender in a very difficult position and is not good advice. Choice **d** would be senseless and would make the offender seem ungrateful.

61. a. This sentence is punctuated correctly.

62. b. A comma is the correct punctuation for this sentence.

63. a. This sentence is punctuated correctly, with the commas used after *job* and *employment*. Choice **b** is incorrect, with commas after *report* and *employment*. Choice **c** is incorrect, with a comma after *Sally* and a semicolon after *report*. Even though there seem to be multiple items for a list, using a semicolon makes two sentences, which does not make this sentence correct. This makes the sentence very disjointed and difficult to read. Choice **d** is incorrect, with a comma after *office* and a colon after *report*. These punctuation marks are inappropriate and make the sentence difficult to read.

64. d. Choice **a** includes unnecessary or misplaced clauses that cloud the meaning of the sentence. Choice **b** is a little awkward and could be written more directly by avoiding the introductory clause. Choice **c** also has misplaced phrases and clauses and, therefore, is difficult to read and understand.

65. a. Choice **b** is written in the passive voice and misuses commas. Choice **c** is not incorrect, but the syntax is overly complicated and not easy to follow. Choice **d** is missing a verb and is, therefore, not a sentence.

66. c. This sentence is clearly and directly written. Choice **a** is awkward and makes it confusing how exactly mass media fits in with the rest of the sentence. Choice **b** is written in the passive voice, which leaves the reader questioning what is produced by mass media. Choice **d** is worded awkwardly.

67. b. *There's* refers to a place; however, the pronoun *theirs* should have been used here.

68. b. The word *perscription* is spelled incorrectly. Choice **a** shows the correct use of *set* (to put something down) versus *sit* (to be seated). Choice **c** is correct; *parameter* means to establish a variable or boundary, and *perimeter* means the border or line around an object.

Choice **d** is correct because it uses the phrase *because of* instead of *due to*. *Due to* means "owed to" and should not be used to mean "caused by" or "for the reason that."

69. a. This sentence is grammatically correct without misspellings or improperly used words. Choice **b** is incorrect, with several misspelled words and no punctuation. Choice **c** has a misspelled word and uses the wrong verb tense. The subject of the sentence is plural, so the verb tense should be plural as well. Choice **d** is incorrect, with several misspelled words: *books, television, been, known, delinquency*.

70. b. Often, illicit drugs are sold at events advertised as alcohol-free, thus giving parents a false sense of security when they agree to let their child attend the event. These drugs cause problems and produce dangerous side effects for those who use them. Choice **a** is not the main idea of this passage; in fact, this wasn't mentioned in the passage at all. Although choice **c** may have merit, it is not the main idea of the passage. Choice **d** is certainly not the author's main idea in this passage.

71. c. Many times, local law enforcement agencies will have one of their new recruits go undercover in the early stages of that officer's employment. However, it is not suggested that a probation or parole officer do this. Choices **a**, **b**, and **d** were suggested in the passage as ways that criminal justice professionals can help with this community problem.

72. d. This is the only side effect of MDMA (ecstasy) not mentioned in the passage. Choices **a**, **b**, and **c** are all discussed in the passage.

73. c. Rohypnol is the trade name for flunitrazepam, which falls within the drug class known as benzodiazepines. Rohypnol is a central nervous system depressant and can incapacitate victims, making them unable to resist sexual assault. This drug produces "anterograde amnesia," or a temporary amnesia that will make persons not remember events they experienced while under the drug. This odorless and colorless drug can be lethal when mixed with alcohol or other depressants. Choice **a** is incorrect because MDMA, or the "safe" drug, has both stimulant and psychedelic properties. This drug gives the users feelings of well-being and stimulation, and distorts time and sensory perceptions. Choice **b** is an anesthetic that can be injected, snorted, or smoked. It has been approved for both human and animal use in medical settings since 1970. About 90% of the ketamine sold legally today is intended for veterinary use. Choice **d**, cocaine, was not listed in the passage.

74. a. Establishing curfews and licensing requirements for large public gatherings will certainly not stop such activities from happening, but it will make people responsible when they agree to host one of these events. When adults are held accountable for what happens in their establishments, they may make themselves more aware of what is going on at the event. Choices **b** and **c** were not listed in the passage, although they are good suggestions to consider. Choice **d** is always a good idea when addressing community concerns. However, choices **b**, **c**, and **d** were not listed in the passage.

75. b. Choice **a** is incorrect; the author does not say this, nor is it true for every teenager and young adult. Choice **d** is incorrect because it also was not discussed in the passage and is untrue. Choice **c** is incorrect; drugs may be easy to obtain, but that is not the only reason they are attractive to young people.

76. c. It is believed that criminal justice professionals must do more outside of their comfort zones and working hours to help curb illegal activities within their communities. Choice **d** is incorrect; it refers to the idea in paragraph

4 that criminal justice professionals should teach parents how to ask more questions. Choices **a** and **b** were not discussed in the passage.

77. b. In a 2005 anonymous national survey, 2.8% of eighth graders responded that they had used MDMA (paragraph 4). Choice **a** is the percentage of tenth graders who responded to the survey. Choice **c** is the response of tenth graders who indicated in the survey they had used methamphetamines. Choice **d** was the 12th graders' response on MDMA use.

78. a. As mentioned in paragraph 3, agencies use this type of interviewing to see what a candidate's qualities are and whether or not the candidate would be an asset to the agency. Choice **b** is incorrect, although it is mentioned in paragraph 5 as a thought some candidates may have. Choice **c** is incorrect and exaggerates a point made in paragraph 5. Choice **d** is incorrect; this thought in mentioned in the first sentence in paragraph 6, but it is not the main idea of the passage.

79. c. As indicated in the first paragraph, the traditional interview has been conducted for many years, but the results were often clouded by doubts about the interview, the objectivity of the interviewers, and the politics involved in the hiring. Choice **b** is incorrect; it is the opposite of the point made in paragraph 5 regarding the concerns of competency-based interviews. Choice **d** may be true but was not discussed in this passage.

80. d. Candidates should answer in detail how they have handled a task in their past that would show how they have used their skills and experiences in order to be successful. Choice **a** would not be a successful action in any type of interview. Choice **b** is incorrect, because embellishments of any kind are never recommended. Choice **c** is not the purpose of a competency-based interview. The goal is to discuss past experiences, which will show how the candidate has handled those experiences, information that serves as a predictor of future behavior.

81. a. Choices **b**, **c**, and **d** were listed in paragraph 5 as problems associated with competency-based interviewing.

82. c. The only thing employers can be assured of in any interview process is that the interviewers had the opportunity not to be influenced by their first impressions. In this type of interview, answers must be ranked according to a rating system, which helps justify the final score given. If the score is high but evidence isn't substantial, then the score must be questioned. Choice **a** is something employers can be assured of in this process. Looks, hygiene, and other outside factors can be determined in second interviews. However, these factors are not scored or rated during a competency-based interview. Choice **b** is also something that employers cannot be assured of. Some candidates are simply good storytellers, and no interview process can provide a guarantee that whoever is hired is competent. Choice **d** also cannot be guaranteed. As widespread as this process is, questions and answers are available. Candidates can use the experiences of others and sell them as their own.

83. b. The measure of successful interviewing in this type of system is when the interviewers can "see" the story through the details of how the candidate became involved, what the candidate did, said, and decided until the end of the story with the conclusion. Choice **a** is not a wise decision because interviewers will ask questions that will allow the candidate to tell similar stories that involve the same competencies. Telling multiple stories for one answer may cause the candidate to report inappropriate stories or may cause the candi-

date to run out of examples. Choice **c** should always be done, no matter which type of interview is conducted, but this was not mentioned by the author in this passage. Choice **d** is not wise, because each question has a set of competencies to be rated or scored. Not every example, as well, may be a good representation of the candidate's leadership or problem-solving skills, which cause the candidate to appear to be rambling.

84. b. Experienced employees may not wish to adjust to this new style and, therefore, will not apply for positions. Choice **a** may also be an aftershock of an agency going to a new interviewing system, but this wasn't listed in the passage. Choice **c** is probably true for some experienced people because they may not be comfortable with technology, but this wasn't listed in the passage. Choice **d** may also be an aftershock of adopting a new interview system. Employees may be so uncomfortable with the process they may have to go through to be promoted that they simply leave the company to go where they are more comfortable. However, this was not in the passage.

85. a. Although this is a valid competency that can be reviewed through good interview questions, the author mentioned only choices **b**, **c**, and **d** in the passage.

86. a. The Family and Medical Leave Act provides up to 12 weeks of unpaid leave during any 12-month period to eligible employees who work for covered employers. Choices **b**, **c**, and **d** are fabricated answers and do not exist.

87. b. In fact, if a family member is hospitalized and remains under a doctor's care, FMLA time should not be granted to the employee. If the employee is simply visiting the sick family member, he or she is not providing care. However, when the family member is home and the employee stays with him or her to ensure his or her care and safety, then that time is counted as FMLA. Choices **a**, **c**, and **d** are all reasons listed within the law that are covered under the FMLA.

88. c. Employees who are eligible and work for covered employers have the ability to protect their position during 12 weeks of unpaid time off, taken for certain medical reasons. The author does explain that some employees do attempt to manipulate the system in order to abuse their sick leave. Choice **a** is not the author's main point in the passage. Employees are offered 12 weeks of unpaid leave through FMLA, but the author is not indicating those employees who use their sick leave should be able to be covered for every condition. Choice **b** is true, but the author explains that it is the responsibility of the human resources office to provide employees with information regarding this and other employment laws. Choice **d** is mentioned in the passage in paragraphs 4 and 5, but this is not the main point of the passage.

89. c. The passage says that 30% of covered employers feel the use of intermittent leave has had a negative impact on office productivity and morale. Most employers say that employees with verified illnesses who see employees with fictional illnesses get similar time off feel they have a right to ask about the fairness of the system. Additionally, when someone is out of the office for whatever reason, others must assume some of the duties and responsibilities. If someone is abusing his or her leave, then coworkers must pick up those duties, which only increases the loss of productivity. Choices **a**, **b**, and **d** are not listed in the passage.

90. c. Although not mentioned in the passage, having and recovering from a hysterectomy is a verified FMLA condition, and an employee may receive 12 weeks of unpaid leave for this

procedure. Choices **a**, **b**, and **d** were conditions listed in the passage as conditions that are serious and do legitimately exist in employees. However, these conditions are also used as an excuse by some employees who simply want the day off.

91. a. Agencies may require that employees use their sick leave and vacation time at the same time they are covered under FMLA leave. This requirement is acceptable under the FMLA law. Choice **b**, listed in paragraph 2, is another option that agencies can elect to use as their tracking method. Choice **c** is incorrect because sick leave time must be used for sick leave, and FMLA is not used in place of sick leave. Vacation time can be used for sick leave (choice **d**), but sick leave cannot be used for vacation time.

92. b. As noted in paragraph 3, the human resources professionals are knowledgeable about the law and understand the necessity of timeliness of notification. However, the problem often comes when the human resources office is not notified of an employee's illness or consistent use of sick leave until the end of the payroll period. The agency is put in a situation in which the failure to provide notice of the employee's rights may place the agency in a liability situation. Choice **a** would rarely happen because the human resources office must account for an employee's time and leave in each payroll period. Choice **c** is incorrect because again the human resources office monitors each employee's sick leave each pay period. Any mention of FMLA on a time sheet would be questioned. Choice **d** would be highly unlikely, unless the human resources office was extremely busy. Most notifications happen on time and promptly.

93. d. In paragraph 4, the author indicates that many employees who find themselves in trouble over their abuse of sick leave will look to utilize the FMLA system to cover the time they have been gone. If they can find a doctor who will certify that their days off were for FMLA-covered reasons, then they will be protected for at least some of their leave. However, most employees aren't that lucky. Choice **a** is incorrect and not possible. Choice **b** may be the belief of some employees but is not the case. Choice **c** doesn't apply because employees can use all of their vacation hours upon approval of their request.

94. c. Reentry programs aim to assist offenders as they transition out of prison and into the community, with the hope that they will become productive citizens and not return to the prison system. Choice **a** is true but not the main theme of this passage. Choice **b**, stated in the first paragraph, is also true but again not the main theme of this passage. Choice **d** expands on a thought in paragraph 4, but is not the main point of this passage.

95. b. Choices **a**, **c**, and **d** were the identified phases. Choice **a** is the phase in which offenders are prepared to reenter the community. Choice **c** is the phase in which programs work with offenders prior to and immediately after release to provide a continuation of programs and trainings. Choice **d** is the phase in which the offenders receive support from long-term programs and resources after they are released from prison.

96. d. As stated in the first paragraph, communities were being victimized by offenders who were released into communities without a great deal of support. The offender was then sent back into the prison system and, later, released to start the cycle all over again. Communities had to find someway to stop that cycle. Choice **a** may be an exaggeration of information in paragraphs 1 and 2. Some agencies did use federal money to make programs available outside of prisons to offend-

ers and other citizens (choice **b**). Choice **c** is also true but not the reason reentry programs were developed within communities.

97. b. In paragraph 4 of this passage, the author discusses several reasons that attention has turned to this problem. President Bush started this movement in earnest when he mentioned this community concern in his 2004 State of the Union address. Since that time, the U.S. Department of Justice (choice **a**) has offered more than $100 million in grants to states to promote the development or expansion of reentry programs. Choice **c** was released sometime after 2004. In this report, more than 100 leading elected officials, policy makers, and practitioners, along with representatives from ten professional service agencies, developed a report which analyzed the elements essential to increasing the likelihood that adults released from prison would avoid crime and become productive citizens. Choice **d** can be one way a movement begins, but, in this case, national leaders are given the credit.

98. a. The author indicates in paragraph 4 that the underlying success of reentry programs is the understanding that all agencies must work together and be responsible for the offender population. Choice **b** is close, but reentry programs work through partnerships, so no single agency is the coordinating agency. Responsibility lies with all of the programs, not just one. Choice **c** is incorrect and was not the message of the passage. Choice **d** is a pessimistic viewpoint. Offenders do have the ability to make changes in their behavior; the community must provide them with a reason to do so.

99. c. The author implies in the last paragraph that the saying "It takes a village to raise a child" takes on a special meaning with these types of programs. Choice **a** is not true because some offenders do see the benefit of transitional programs. Many offenders wish to change their behavior but do not have the programs to assist them while they make that transition. Choice **b** is not the message of the passage, although it is true. Community leaders must have vision and insight into how to keep their communities safer. Choice **d** is also true, but rare, as budgets continue to shrink. Taxes are used more and more to help salvage service programs, but at some point, community leaders will not be able to raise any more money.

100. d. As discussed in paragraph 3, all of these service providers (choices **a**, **b**, and **c**) are included in the partnership, in addition to other programs such as public health departments, housing authorities, and welfare agencies.

12 ▶ Practice Test 5

This is the fifth practice test in the book based on the most commonly tested areas on the probation officer and parole officer exams. The following 100 multiple-choice questions deal with the following skill areas: job responsibilities, case studies, writing skills, and reading comprehension. Remember, the number of questions and the time limit of the actual probation officer or parole officer exam can vary from region to region. Allow yourself three hours to complete this practice test.

Practice Test 5

1.	ⓐ	ⓑ	ⓒ	ⓓ
2.	ⓐ	ⓑ	ⓒ	ⓓ
3.	ⓐ	ⓑ	ⓒ	ⓓ
4.	ⓐ	ⓑ	ⓒ	ⓓ
5.	ⓐ	ⓑ	ⓒ	ⓓ
6.	ⓐ	ⓑ	ⓒ	ⓓ
7.	ⓐ	ⓑ	ⓒ	ⓓ
8.	ⓐ	ⓑ	ⓒ	ⓓ
9.	ⓐ	ⓑ	ⓒ	ⓓ
10.	ⓐ	ⓑ	ⓒ	ⓓ
11.	ⓐ	ⓑ	ⓒ	ⓓ
12.	ⓐ	ⓑ	ⓒ	ⓓ
13.	ⓐ	ⓑ	ⓒ	ⓓ
14.	ⓐ	ⓑ	ⓒ	ⓓ
15.	ⓐ	ⓑ	ⓒ	ⓓ
16.	ⓐ	ⓑ	ⓒ	ⓓ
17.	ⓐ	ⓑ	ⓒ	ⓓ
18.	ⓐ	ⓑ	ⓒ	ⓓ
19.	ⓐ	ⓑ	ⓒ	ⓓ
20.	ⓐ	ⓑ	ⓒ	ⓓ
21.	ⓐ	ⓑ	ⓒ	ⓓ
22.	ⓐ	ⓑ	ⓒ	ⓓ
23.	ⓐ	ⓑ	ⓒ	ⓓ
24.	ⓐ	ⓑ	ⓒ	ⓓ
25.	ⓐ	ⓑ	ⓒ	ⓓ
26.	ⓐ	ⓑ	ⓒ	ⓓ
27.	ⓐ	ⓑ	ⓒ	ⓓ
28.	ⓐ	ⓑ	ⓒ	ⓓ
29.	ⓐ	ⓑ	ⓒ	ⓓ
30.	ⓐ	ⓑ	ⓒ	ⓓ
31.	ⓐ	ⓑ	ⓒ	ⓓ
32.	ⓐ	ⓑ	ⓒ	ⓓ
33.	ⓐ	ⓑ	ⓒ	ⓓ
34.	ⓐ	ⓑ	ⓒ	ⓓ
35.	ⓐ	ⓑ	ⓒ	ⓓ

36.	ⓐ	ⓑ	ⓒ	ⓓ
37.	ⓐ	ⓑ	ⓒ	ⓓ
38.	ⓐ	ⓑ	ⓒ	ⓓ
39.	ⓐ	ⓑ	ⓒ	ⓓ
40.	ⓐ	ⓑ	ⓒ	ⓓ
41.	ⓐ	ⓑ	ⓒ	ⓓ
42.	ⓐ	ⓑ	ⓒ	ⓓ
43.	ⓐ	ⓑ	ⓒ	ⓓ
44.	ⓐ	ⓑ	ⓒ	ⓓ
45.	ⓐ	ⓑ	ⓒ	ⓓ
46.	ⓐ	ⓑ	ⓒ	ⓓ
47.	ⓐ	ⓑ	ⓒ	ⓓ
48.	ⓐ	ⓑ	ⓒ	ⓓ
49.	ⓐ	ⓑ	ⓒ	ⓓ
50.	ⓐ	ⓑ	ⓒ	ⓓ
51.	ⓐ	ⓑ	ⓒ	ⓓ
52.	ⓐ	ⓑ	ⓒ	ⓓ
53.	ⓐ	ⓑ	ⓒ	ⓓ
54.	ⓐ	ⓑ	ⓒ	ⓓ
55.	ⓐ	ⓑ	ⓒ	ⓓ
56.	ⓐ	ⓑ	ⓒ	ⓓ
57.	ⓐ	ⓑ	ⓒ	ⓓ
58.	ⓐ	ⓑ	ⓒ	ⓓ
59.	ⓐ	ⓑ	ⓒ	ⓓ
60.	ⓐ	ⓑ	ⓒ	ⓓ
61.	ⓐ	ⓑ	ⓒ	ⓓ
62.	ⓐ	ⓑ	ⓒ	ⓓ
63.	ⓐ	ⓑ	ⓒ	ⓓ
64.	ⓐ	ⓑ	ⓒ	ⓓ
65.	ⓐ	ⓑ	ⓒ	ⓓ
66.	ⓐ	ⓑ	ⓒ	ⓓ
67.	ⓐ	ⓑ	ⓒ	ⓓ
68.	ⓐ	ⓑ	ⓒ	ⓓ
69.	ⓐ	ⓑ	ⓒ	ⓓ
70.	ⓐ	ⓑ	ⓒ	ⓓ

71.	ⓐ	ⓑ	ⓒ	ⓓ
72.	ⓐ	ⓑ	ⓒ	ⓓ
73.	ⓐ	ⓑ	ⓒ	ⓓ
74.	ⓐ	ⓑ	ⓒ	ⓓ
75.	ⓐ	ⓑ	ⓒ	ⓓ
76.	ⓐ	ⓑ	ⓒ	ⓓ
77.	ⓐ	ⓑ	ⓒ	ⓓ
78.	ⓐ	ⓑ	ⓒ	ⓓ
79.	ⓐ	ⓑ	ⓒ	ⓓ
80.	ⓐ	ⓑ	ⓒ	ⓓ
81.	ⓐ	ⓑ	ⓒ	ⓓ
82.	ⓐ	ⓑ	ⓒ	ⓓ
83.	ⓐ	ⓑ	ⓒ	ⓓ
84.	ⓐ	ⓑ	ⓒ	ⓓ
85.	ⓐ	ⓑ	ⓒ	ⓓ
86.	ⓐ	ⓑ	ⓒ	ⓓ
87.	ⓐ	ⓑ	ⓒ	ⓓ
88.	ⓐ	ⓑ	ⓒ	ⓓ
89.	ⓐ	ⓑ	ⓒ	ⓓ
90.	ⓐ	ⓑ	ⓒ	ⓓ
91.	ⓐ	ⓑ	ⓒ	ⓓ
92.	ⓐ	ⓑ	ⓒ	ⓓ
93.	ⓐ	ⓑ	ⓒ	ⓓ
94.	ⓐ	ⓑ	ⓒ	ⓓ
95.	ⓐ	ⓑ	ⓒ	ⓓ
96.	ⓐ	ⓑ	ⓒ	ⓓ
97.	ⓐ	ⓑ	ⓒ	ⓓ
98.	ⓐ	ⓑ	ⓒ	ⓓ
99.	ⓐ	ⓑ	ⓒ	ⓓ
100.	ⓐ	ⓑ	ⓒ	ⓓ

▶ Practice Test 5

1. Transferring a juvenile to the criminal court system is known as
   a. incarceration.
   b. emancipation.
   c. waiver.
   d. diversion.

2. The longer the period of intensive probation supervision,
   a. the higher the rate of recidivism.
   b. the lower the rate of recidivism.
   c. the sooner the offender will pay restitution.
   d. the more likely the offender will abscond.

3. The person most closely associated with the establishment of probation is
   a. Alexander Maconochie.
   b. Zebulon Brockway.
   c. Walter Crofton.
   d. John Augustus.

4. Critics of probation claim all EXCEPT which of the following about the use of probation as an alternative to incarceration?
   a. that it does not punish an offender at an appropriate level
   b. that it does not prevent recidivism
   c. that prison sentences are more appropriate for criminal offenses
   d. that it assists the community by alleviating prison overcrowding

5. Conduct that would not be considered a criminal act if it were to be committed by an adult is known as
   a. status offense.
   b. recidivism.
   c. delinquency.
   d. restitution.

6. _____ is an order issued by the court for a probationer to pay for the supervision services provided by the probation department.
   a. Restitution
   b. User fees
   c. Bribery
   d. Diversion

7. Which of the following is NOT considered a responsibility of parole supervision?
   a. assisting the offender with adjusting to life in the community
   b. enforcing the conditions of supervision
   c. revoking a parolee's release so that he or she can be reincarcerated
   d. providing guidance to a parolee to ensure his or her successful completion

8. House arrest should primarily be used for
   a. parole violators.
   b. violent offenders.
   c. female offenders.
   d. nonviolent offenders.

9. Sentencing alternatives to incarceration include all EXCEPT which of the following?
   a. community service
   b. treatment facilities
   c. confidential informing
   d. electronic monitoring

10. Staff qualifications that affect the quality of parole or probation services include all EXCEPT which of the following?
   a. education/degrees
   b. experience
   c. specialized training
   d. political affiliation

11. Statewide probation was enacted first by which state?
a. New York
b. New Hampshire
c. Massachusetts
d. Minnesota

12. Sentencing a person to probation by the court following a conviction is most likely to occur under which circumstance?
a. regular probation
b. deferred prosecution
c. diversion
d. none of the above

13. A sentence that is established in statute and that does not allow for the discretionary release by a parole board is known as
a. determinate.
b. indeterminate.
c. retributionary.
d. indecisive.

14. Which of the following should receive the least consideration by a probation officer when determining the appropriateness of a recommendation for probation supervision at the time of sentencing?
a. needs of the offender
b. costs of incarceration
c. protection of society
d. maintenance of social order

15. _____ is a situation in which a person is incarcerated for a portion of his or her sentence and then released for a probationary period for the remainder of his or her sentence.
a. Work release
b. Split sentence
c. Judicial reprieve
d. Parole

16. The offense-based presentence investigation report (PSI) is likely to focus on which of the following?
a. causes of the behavior
b. a defendant's potential for change
c. loss experienced by the victim
d. all of the above

17. During a presentence investigation, an aggravating factor used by a probation officer in the evaluation and recommendation of a sentence may include which one of the following?
a. a victim younger than 12 years of age
b. imprisonment causing undue hardship
c. the crime resulting from circumstances unlikely to reoccur
d. no previous criminal convictions

18. _____ requires that a probation officer secure a court order or written permission from the defendant in order to obtain certain information regarding the defendant or case.
a. Confidentiality
b. Criminal history
c. Collateral information
d. Privatization

19. The type of probation conditions imposed on all offenders in a jurisdiction is
a. clear conditions.
b. standard conditions.
c. reform conditions.
d. special conditions.

20. Which of the following is NOT a standard condition of probation?
a. You shall commit no new offenses.
b. You shall attend Alcoholics Anonymous meetings.
c. You shall report to the probation officer as directed.
d. You shall maintain employment.

21. All of the following satisfy an important purpose of a victim impact statement in a presentence investigation report EXCEPT
   a. to provide a description of the harm done to the victim in terms of financial, social, psychological, and physical consequences of the crime.
   b. to provide the judge with information about the victim's feelings about the crime.
   c. to provide the judge with the victim's feelings about a proposed sentence.
   d. to provide the judge a chance to confront the victim regarding the validity of his or her testimony.

22. The most important component in conducting a presentence investigation is the
   a. victim impact statement.
   b. defendant interview.
   c. prosecutor's recommendation.
   d. judge's philosophy.

23. A probationer not wishing to "tell the truth" about information that could lead to not only a probation revocation but also new criminal charges is an issue relating to the _____ Amendment.
   a. Fourteenth
   b. First
   c. Fourth
   d. Fifth

24. Which of the following would be considered a standard condition of parole?
   a. You shall perform 100 hours of community service.
   b. You shall attend anger management treatment weekly.
   c. You shall not commit a criminal offense.
   d. You shall have no contact with the victim in this case.

25. The procedure for determining the risk posed by the offender, identifying the supervision issues, and selecting a supervision strategy is called
   a. risk assessment.
   b. ranking.
   c. diagnosis.
   d. classification.

26. Informal juvenile probation differs from formal probation because informal probation is used
   a. in status offenses.
   b. after confinement.
   c. before adjudication.
   d. in misdemeanor cases.

27. Sandy, a parole officer, has discovered through her neighbor that one of her parolees has recently been involved with drug trafficking. Of the following choices, which is the best for Sandy?
   a. to wait for the parolee to report for an appointment and confront him or her with this behavior
   b. to plan a strategic visit to the parolee's home to explore the possibility that a new offense or violation has occurred
   c. to contact local police officers to inform them of the alleged offense
   d. to ask the neighbor to gather evidence of the alleged offense, while continuing to administer drug tests to the parolee during office visits

28. When probationers transfer to another state for supervision under the Interstate Compact, it involves
   a. bail during revocation proceedings.
   b. the right to counsel.
   c. due process rights.
   d. extradition.

29. Generally, probation can be revoked only during the probation term EXCEPT when
   a. the probationer is convicted of another crime.
   b. the court finds the probationer falsified reports.
   c. the warrant was issued prior to probation expiring.
   d. the probationer fails to pay restitution.

30. For Mike the probation officer to have a revocation warrant issued for Tom the probationer, what does he need?
   a. convincing evidence
   b. a reasonable suspicion
   c. probable cause
   d. preponderance of the evidence

Directions: Read the following case study and then answer questions 31 through 36.

Leonard is a 36-year-old man who was recently convicted of "operating a motor vehicle while intoxicated" as a felony offense. According to the information gathered from Leonard during the presentence investigation, he had been at a party with some friends on the night of his arrest for the present offense. Leonard had arrived at the party and started to drink alcohol around 10:00 P.M., and the arrest occurred at approximately 2:00 A.M. the following morning. Leonard estimates that he had consumed approximately 14 beers along with three shots of whiskey prior to being arrested. Leonard states that he did not feel intoxicated at the time he was arrested, which was why he made the decision to drive a vehicle home from his friends' house.

Leonard has been convicted on three other occasions for alcohol-related offenses, including one charge of "illegal possession of alcohol by consumption," public intoxication, and "operating a motor vehicle while intoxicated" as a misdemeanor. He admits that there have been numerous other occasions in which, according to law, he could have been arrested but wasn't because either he did not come into contact with law enforcement or an officer decided not to arrest him. Leonard consumes alcohol about four days each week, having approximately six beers per drinking episode. Additionally, on two of the four days, he consumes enough alcohol to become intoxicated. Leonard has attended an alcohol abuse education class as a condition of a previous period of probation.

Leonard attended public school, where he completed the tenth grade prior to being expelled in connection to his first alcohol-related offense. He is recently divorced from his second wife, and she has custody of their two children. Leonard works for himself, performing tree trimming and other odd job services when he can. Leonard states that his income could be better, but it is usually enough to get by. Leonard currently owns no home or automobile and, at the time of the interview, was complaining of some pain in his side, but has not been seen by a physician in 20 years.

31. Which of the following seems to be the most appropriate special condition of probation?
   a. license suspension
   b. no consumption of alcohol
   c. gainful employment or enrollment in a program of education
   d. drug and alcohol abuse assessment and recommended treatment

32. What is likely the main cause of Leonard's arrests?
   a. alcohol consumption
   b. lack of education
   c. lack of structured employment
   d. being in the wrong place at the wrong time

33. What factor is NOT a concern when measuring Leonard's risk of violating the conditions of his supervision or committing another criminal offense?

a. alcohol consumption

b. lack of education

c. lack of structured employment

d. being in the wrong place at the wrong time

34. You are conducting a home visit with Leonard one evening when you notice an odor of alcohol coming from him. You perform a portable breath test on him, and it registers 0.02 blood alcohol content (BAC). Leonard explains that he had just used mouthwash to freshen his breath. What is the likelihood that Leonard is telling the truth, and should there be cause for concern?

a. It is very likely he is not telling the truth, because if he had drunk alcohol, the BAC would have been higher on a portable breath test; therefore, there is no cause for concern.

b. It is likely he is not telling the truth; therefore, there is cause for concern because of Leonard's past history of consistent alcohol use.

c. It is likely he is telling the truth; therefore, there is no cause for concern because there are no alcoholic beverage containers in the house.

d. It is very unlikely he is telling the truth, because mouthwash does not contain alcohol; dishonesty is cause for concern.

35. Leonard is arrested over the weekend for driving a motorcycle without a license. After receiving a copy of the arrest report, you discover that the officer detected an odor of an alcoholic beverage but did not administer any test of Leonard's blood, breath, or urine to confirm the assumption. How would you respond in this situation?

a. You would visit the jail and get Leonard to confess to his alcohol usage.

b. You would file for a revocation of Leonard's probation, because he violated a condition of his probation, as well as the law.

c. You would file for a revocation of Leonard's probation, because less proof is needed to revoke probation than to convict on a new offense.

d. You would wait to see if Leonard is convicted of driving the motorcycle without a license before taking any action.

36. Based on his background, what is the most likely risk classification for Leonard?

a. high risk for violence

b. moderate risk for violence

c. low risk for violence

d. no risk for violence

Directions: Read the following case study and then answer questions 37 through 42.

After being recently convicted on a "possession of marijuana" charge and for resisting law enforcement charges, Janice was placed on probation for a period of one year. She must also serve an intermittent period of incarceration of 20 days to be served on ten consecutive weekends.

According to the arrest report, Janice was a passenger in a vehicle stopped by police for suspicion of drunk driving. When police officers approached the vehicle, they detected the odor of marijuana smoke. The driver and Janice were asked to exit the vehicle and were subsequently searched. Janice had approximately 22 grams of marijuana on her person, contained in a baggie, along with rolling papers usually associated with marijuana cigarettes.

When informed that she was going to be placed under arrest for possessing the marijuana, she began to argue with the police officers. As the argument increased, Janice pulled away from the officer's grasp and began to run from the scene. She was apprehended approximately 50 yards from the vehicle. Once in custody, she was handcuffed and shackled by the police officers, while she continued to struggle physically with and verbally abuse them until she was incarcerated at the county jail.

37. Which of the following seems to be the least appropriate special condition of probation for Janice?
  a. periodic drug testing
  b. anger management therapy
  c. no contact with the driver involved with her arrest
  d. drug abuse assessment and recommended treatment

38. What is likely the main cause of Janice's arrest?
  a. her negative attitude toward the police
  b. her habitual usage of marijuana
  c. her poor financial situation, causing her to participate in criminal activity
  d. the results of a police sting operation to catch marijuana users in the act

39. What factor is NOT a concern when measuring Janice's risk of violating the conditions of her supervision or committing another criminal offense?
  a. marijuana use
  b. Janice's income level
  c. her intermittent sentence of incarceration
  d. her resistance to the commands and the arrest made by police officers

40. Janice's first drug urine sample tests positive for the presence of cannabinoids (marijuana). When you confront her about this result, she states that she has not smoked marijuana since the night before her sentencing hearing. What should be the next step in this case?
  a. A revocation petition should be filed immediately because she violated a condition of her parole by using drugs.
  b. A second drug urine sample should be taken to check the validity of the first sample.
  c. A reasonable amount of time should be allowed to eliminate the possibility that Janice's admitted marijuana use prior to the hearing is causing the positive result in the current drug testing.
  d. Nothing else should be done; Janice wasn't required to abstain from marijuana use.

41. Janice's employer calls you to expresses his concern for her behavior on the jobsite. He thinks that Janice is coming to work under the influence of some chemical substance. The employer says that her attendance, attitude, and job performance have been worsening over the past few weeks. What would be the appropriate way to respond?
  a. You take no immediate action and wait to bring up the employer's concerns during Janice's next scheduled office visit.
  b. You call police officers to have them take Janice into custody for a violation of her supervision conditions.
  c. You ask the employer to fire Janice.
  d. You make a visit to the jobsite, so that Janice can be confronted about her behavior and tested for drugs as quickly as possible.

42. Janice comes into your office after six months of supervision and requests that you no longer serve as her probation officer. How should you respond to her request?

   a. You should tell her that you will look into the possibility of having one of the other officers take over the supervision and, in the meantime, schedule her next visit.

   b. You should tell her that you have been assigned to be her probation officer and that she cannot pick and choose whom she wants to have as an officer.

   c. You should ask her to elaborate on what her grievances are and pursue a meeting with your supervisor to determine the appropriateness of the request.

   d. You should convince one of the other officers to provide supervision for Janice, by agreeing to take over the supervision of a difficult probationer assigned to that officer.

Directions: Read the following case study and then answer questions 43 through 48.

As a parole officer, Stephan has always been told that he is held to a higher standard of conduct than most citizens. He knows that if an officer behaves in a disruptive manner, make an offensive joke, or is otherwise uncivil, even while not on duty, community members can react with distrust and contempt. Stephan knows that a parole officer is expected to be an idealist, even though he or she consistently confronts human nature at its most disillusioning.

As a parole officer, Stephan is considered to be a keeper of civil order and must exemplify civil behavior. Committed to the ideals of justice and truth, Stephan must practice fairness and accuracy, even when speaking. Although the rights of parolees are diminished, Stephan knows that he must nonetheless treat each of them with respect.

Maintaining this higher standard of civil conduct is not merely a matter of community relations, but it speaks to the essence of Stephan's role as a parole officer. For the same reason, Stephan wants to be treated with respect, just as he is required by his job to adhere to a higher standard of tolerance, understanding, moderation, and civility.

43. Which of the following best expresses Stephan's understanding of his role as a parole officer?

   a. High standards should apply to businesspersons as well as to parole officers.

   b. Parole officers are held to unrealistic standards of behavior.

   c. Parole officers must remain idealistic, despite the disillusioning nature of their work.

   d. A parole officer should uphold common ideals, both as expressed in law and as required to keep order and safety in the community.

44. Stephan should refrain from using racial slurs for all of the following reasons EXCEPT

   a. as generalizations, such slurs are unfair and inaccurate.

   b. such slurs are disrespectful.

   c. such slurs are hurtful to the morale of a multicultural parole department.

   d. such slurs may be used in the context of testimony as direct quotations and used as commentary evidence.

45. Which of the following should be most important to Stephan in his role as a parole officer?

   a. defining civil order

   b. earning respect

   c. his own civil conduct

   d. being tolerant

46. Why does civil conduct speak to the essence of a parole officer's role?
a. because a parole officer is a public servant
b. because a parole officer who behaves in an uncivil manner elicits public distrust
c. because civil conduct is necessary in order to keep order in the community
d. because a parole officer upholds the law and reasonable expectations of the paroling authority

47. According to information from the passage, which of the following is NOT mentioned as a quality Stephan understands to be part of his role as a parole officer?
a. politeness
b. courage
c. justice
d. moderation

48. Stephan witnesses one of his fellow parole officers telling a joke to one of his parolees that is likely to be offensive to women. What should Stephan do?
a. He should have a conversation later with his fellow parole officer to encourage the end of such behavior.
b. He should report the fellow officer's indiscretion to the supervisor.
c. He should immediately apologize to the parolee for the officer's behavior.
d. He should ignore the situation and do nothing.

Directions: Read the following case study and then answer questions 49 through 54.

Tom has been working as a parole officer for nearly two years for a department that actively supervises 1,200 adult parolees with 14 officers. On average, Tom has supervised between 40 and 60 parolees at a time since he became a parole officer. Tom works a standard schedule of 8:00 A.M. to 5:00 P.M., Mondays through Fridays, along with a shift on Saturday evenings for field work once every three weeks.

Prior to becoming a parole officer, Tom worked at a local mental health facility, where he provided case management services to adult and juvenile clientele while completing his degree in criminal justice. Because Tom worked full time at the mental health facility and could attend school only part time, he took nearly six years to complete his degree. Tom admits that, at times, he was not nearly as alert in his courses, and that he did not study as much, as he should have been.

After experiencing his own father going to prison on child molestation charges, Tom became focused on creating a career for himself in criminal justice. Parole seemed to be a good match for Tom; however, Tom has never shared with his coworkers that his father is currently serving a total of 20 years of incarceration for his charges.

49. Tom has become involved as a volunteer with a local youth ministry group, and is having trouble getting to some of the sessions on time because of his work schedule. Tom sees value in his work, but he also sees that he can make a difference in the lives of the youths participating in the ministry group. What should Tom do?
a. Tom should participate with the youth group only outside of his office hours, regardless of how late he has to be.
b. Tom should take vacation hours on the days of the meeting, so that he can leave work early enough to make the meetings on time.
c. Tom should go ahead and leave work early on the meeting days and make up the time in some other way.
d. Tom should discuss a possible schedule change with his supervisor.

50. From the information contained within the passage, what would you expect risk distributions of Tom's caseload to be?
  a. mostly high-risk offenders with a few medium-risk offenders
  b. equal amounts of high-, medium-, and low-risk offenders
  c. all medium- and low-risk offenders
  d. all high-risk offenders

51. While Tom was working as a caseworker at the local mental health facility, he had attended a music concert. At the concert, one of Tom's friends convinced him to use some marijuana. He did not use marijuana before that and has not used it since then. Tom supervises a parolee who has tested positive on a urine drug screen for marijuana use, and the parolee explains that he used the marijuana in a situation almost identical to Tom's. What should Tom do given these circumstances?
  a. He should file for a revocation hearing.
  b. He should discuss with his supervisor his own use, and let the supervisor make the decision about the parolee.
  c. He should utilize the standard practices and policies defined by his department.
  d. He should take no action because he is as guilty as the parolee.

52. You are Tom's supervisor. You notice that Tom's desk is cluttered with supervision case files as well as other unfiled correspondence from treatment agencies. What is the primary concern you should have?
  a. Tom is allowing the possibility of public access to confidential information.
  b. Tom hasn't been properly addressing information from collaborative agencies.
  c. Tom is careless with his supervision methods.
  d. Tom's behavior will influence the behavior of other parole officers.

53. Tom has been asked by a local business group to present information about his job responsibilities and experiences at a lunch gathering, and his supervisor gives him the approval to do so. Which of the following is NOT a reasonable consideration for Tom's participation?
  a. increasing Tom's network of contacts in the community
  b. supplementing Tom's low salary with the fee he will receive for speaking
  c. providing factual knowledge and direct connections about the work of parole officers
  d. responding in a positive way to a group of citizens' request to build public confidence

54. Tom's father was released from prison yesterday under a five-year period of parole, with supervision to be provided through Tom's department. What is Tom's obligation regarding this information?
  a. to let everyone in the office know that his father was convicted and is being paroled and that he will be supervised in the department
  b. to quit his job as a parole agent, because he cannot work in the same department that provides supervision to his father
  c. to let his supervisor know of the situation, because it was not part of the application or interview process
  d. to keep this information to himself, because his dad is likely to receive bad treatment if everyone knew that they were related

Directions: Read the following case study and then answer questions 55 through 60.

Kecia began her unlawful activity at age 11, when she was caught by security at the supermarket for trying to leave the store without paying for a candy bar that she had placed into her coat pocket. She explained desperately to her parents when they came to pick her up that she was trying to help her friend Missy carry some items to the checkout and had forgotten she put the candy bar in her pocket.

About two months later, she was discovered with a necklace from a store in the local mall. Kecia was taken to the juvenile detention center but was released to her parents' custody. No charges were ever filed, and Kecia then went through a period of about six months of good behavior. Her grades began to improve, and the family began to trust her again.

A couple of years later, Kecia was suspected of being involved with some of her peers in the destruction of property in the neighborhood. The police had received numerous reports of damage to vehicles, graffiti, and even two incidents of arson in which garages were set on fire. Although the police lacked evidence necessary to charge her formally, the parents agreed to a voluntary period of house arrest for Kecia while the investigation is being conducted over the next several weeks. Although two of Kecia's closest friends were charged with delinquent offenses, Kecia was never charged for any of her alleged involvement.

Now that she is 15, Kecia's parents have been called to the local detention center, where she is being held as an alleged delinquent child for her involvement in a burglary offense at the residence of her school principal. Kecia promises never to do anything bad again if her parents will just get her out of there so she can go home. Kecia was required to remain at the center for two weeks following her initial appearance in juvenile court. The juvenile judge eventually accepted a "plea agreement," in which Kecia admitted to her involvement in the burglary and the judge established her sentence in according to the results of the predispositional hearing report.

55. As a probation officer, you must submit a predispositional hearing report in an effort to provide the juvenile judge with as much information about Kecia as possible. During routine questioning of Kecia and her parents, you learn that Kecia had been adopted at age 3. Her biological mother, her adoptive father's sister, had been committed to the state department of corrections. Kecia's biological mother was released from the facility about four years ago and has occasional contact with the family. Kecia's adoptive mother indicates that the biological mother has been treated most of her life for schizophrenia. With regard to this information, should you

   a. recommend that Kecia undergo a psychiatric evaluation.
   b. require that Kecia's biological mother participate in the background investigation.
   c. recommend that Kecia have no contact with her biological mother.
   d. omit this information from the report, because Kecia's behavior has nothing to do with her biological mother.

56. After the judge placed Kecia on a 12-month period of probation, she was scheduled to appear for her initial supervision meeting in the juvenile probation department offices. When Kecia arrives for her appointment, she is escorted back to your office. Upon entering your office, Kecia walks over to the window and stares outside. You invite Kecia to have a seat in one of the chairs in front of your desk. She looks at you, makes no change in facial expression, and then continues to stare out of the window. You invite her a second time to sit down and talk with you, and when you tell her that she must, she shrugs her shoulders and continues to stare out of the window. What action do you take?

  a. You place Kecia in handcuffs and return her to the detention center for violating probation by not obeying a lawful instruction.

  b. You wait 15 minutes to see if Kecia will voluntarily take a seat, and when she doesn't, physically place her in the seat so that you can continue the meeting as needed.

  c. You call in Kecia's parents to see if they can get her to sit down.

  d. You explain to Kecia that her participation is required and that she will need to return for an additional meeting every day until she can follow your requests or until you file for a revocation hearing with the court.

57. While you are visiting with Kecia in her home, she indicates that performing the ten hours weekly of community service is easy for her because her supervisor at the placement agency doesn't really watch over her. She goes on to say that although she is assigned certain tasks each day such as folding clothes, painting, and picking up trash, she rarely completes any of the tasks and even sees other juveniles smoking behind the facility. Because the community service portion of probation supervision falls under the direction of another community correction agency, what should you do?

  a. You should call the supervisor at the placement agency and tell them that this is unacceptable.

  b. You should approach the director of community corrections to explore a plan of action.

  c. You should make a visit to Kecia at the placement agency to verify her story.

  d. You should check with other juveniles performing community service at that agency to see if they have experienced the same thing.

58. Kecia's biological mother contacts you, wanting to know if Kecia has been keeping her grades up at school. Which of the following is the best response?

  a. You give her Kecia's telephone number and tell her that she needs to call to find out directly from Kecia or her adoptive mother.

  b. You invite her to the next scheduled supervision appointment with Kecia so that she can be active in the discussions.

  c. You refuse her request, citing that she has no legal right to the information and that you are not permitted to give her the information.

  d. You make a copy of Kecia's latest report card and send it to the biological mother in the mail.

59. Kecia's principal calls you with concern for Kecia's behavior in the cafeteria. Kecia is believed to have stolen lunch money from one of her peers. The principal says that he has also noticed Kecia's attendance, behavior, and performance declining over the past three weeks. What would be the proper way for you to handle this?

a. You make a visit to the school, so that Kecia can be confronted with her behavior as quickly as possible.

b. You ask the principal to expel Kecia from school.

c. You call police officers to have them take Kecia into custody at the juvenile detention center.

d. You take no immediate action and wait to bring it up during Kecia's scheduled visit to your office.

60. Kecia is making good progress and is nearing the end of her probation period. But she has not yet completed her community service hours. Although you have just given permission for Kecia's parents to take her on a family camping trip away from town, you realize that Kecia has about ten days total to complete 15 hours of community service and will be out of town for seven of those days. The community service placement agency can accommodate community service workers only for about three hours each day. Which of the following would be the best option?

a. You waive the remainder of Kecia's community service hours because of her recent positive behavior.

b. You file for revocation, because Kecia has failed to complete the hours as required.

c. Upon their return, you work with Kecia and her family to establish a reasonable time frame for the completion of the hours. Then you complete a formal agreement with them extending her probationary period until the completion of that time.

d. You request that, through her parents, Kecia donate to charity an amount equal to the minimum wage for each hour she has not fulfilled by the day of her release from supervision.

Directions: In questions 61 through 67, choose the answer choice that best rephrases the underlined portion of the given sentence.

61. <u>This was the fifth of five speeches the author gave during this the month of May.</u>
   a. This was the fifth of the five speeches the author gave during this the month of May.
   b. Of the five speeches the author gave during May, this was the fifth one.
   c. Thus far during the month of May, the author gave five speeches and this was the fifth.
   d. This was the fifth speech the author had given during the month of May.

62. The troposphere is the lowest layer of Earth's <u>atmosphere' it extends</u> from ground level to an altitude of seven to ten miles.
   a. atmosphere, it extends
   b. of which it extends
   c. atmosphere. Extending
   d. atmosphere; it extends

63. <u>Along with your membership to our health club or</u> two months of free personal training.
   a. Along with your membership to our health club and
   b. Along with your membership to our health club comes
   c. With your membership to our health club,
   d. In addition to your membership to our health club being

64. The <u>people that are at the back of the line</u> should move to the front.
   a. people, who are at the back of the line
   b. people who are at the back of the line
   c. people, that are at the back of the line,
   d. people who, are at the back of the line,

65. The students asked whether I thought there would be a woman <u>president within the next decade?</u>
   a. president within the next decade!
   b. president, within the next decade.
   c. president within the next decade.
   d. president, within the next decade?

66. This is the first time you have ever been to a probation <u>conference isn't it?</u>
   a. conference, isn't it?
   b. conference, is'nt it?
   c. conference, isn't it.
   d. conference isn't it.

67. Chicken <u>pox a virus</u> is very contagious.
   a. pox, a virus,
   b. pox, a virus
   c. pox, a virus
   d. pox a virus,

Directions: In questions 68 through 74, a portion of the sentence is underlined. The answer choices show four ways of phrasing the underlined word(s). Choice **a** shows the original underlined portion; the other three choices provide alternatives. Select the choice that best expresses the meaning of the original sentence. If the original sentence is better than any of the alternatives, select choice **a**.

68. The tip about the probationer's illegal behavior came from an <u>anynonimous</u> source.
   a. anynonimous
   b. anonimous
   c. anounymous
   d. anonymous

69. The field supervision team made <u>less arrests today than they did</u> last Monday.
   a. less arrests today than they did
   b. lesser arrests today than they did
   c. few arrests today than they did
   d. fewer arrests today than they did

70. Nobody on the unit <u>marches more graceful than me.</u>
  a. marches more graceful than me.
  b. marches more gracefully than I do.
  c. marches gracefuller than I do.
  d. marches more graceful than I do.

71. Many criminologists <u>maintain, that severe</u> sentences do deter crime.
  a. maintain, that severe
  b. maintain that, severe
  c. maintain that severe
  d. maintin—that severe

72. <u>The Mississippi River, it originates in Minnesota,</u> empties into the Gulf of Mexico.
  a. The Mississippi River, it originates in Minnesota,
  b. The Mississippi River, that originates in Minnesota,
  c. The Mississippi River, who originates in Minnesota,
  d. The Mississippi River, which originates in Minnesota,

73. <u>There wasn't never an officer that was busier.</u>
  a. There wasn't never an officer that was busier.
  b. There never was a busier officer.
  c. Never was there an officer more busier.
  d. There was never an officer more busier.

74. The parole officer presented a(n) <u>ultimatum</u> to offender Migel regarding the paraphernalia found in his car—next time, he will be returned to prison.
  a. ultimatum
  b. petition
  c. question
  d. inquiry

75. Three of the sentences below contain one or more grammatical or spelling errors. Select the answer choice that is correct as is.
  a. Ethics and the law having no true relationship.
  b. There is no true relationship between ethics and the law.
  c. Between ethics and the law, no true relationship.
  d. Ethics and the law is no true relationship.

76. Three of the sentences below contain one or more grammatical or spelling errors. Select the answer choice that is correct as is.
  a. Some people say jury duty is a nuisance that just takes up their precious time and that we don't get paid enough.
  b. Some people say jury duty is a nuisance that just takes up your precious time and that one doesn't get paid enough.
  c. Some people say jury duty is a nuisance that just takes up precious time and that doesn't pay enough.
  d. Some people say jury duty is a nuisance that just takes up our precious time and that they don't get paid enough.

77. Three of the sentences below contain one or more grammatical or spelling errors. Select the answer choice that is correct as is.
  a. The criminal justice professor, along with several of her students, is planning to attend the exhibit opening tomorrow evening.
  b. The criminal justice professor, along with several of her students, are planning to attend the exhibit opening tomorrow evening.
  c. The criminal justice professor, along with several of her students, plan to attend the exhibit opening tomorrow evening.
  d. The criminal justice professor, along with several of her students, have planned to attend the exhibit opening tomorrow evening.

78. Three of the sentences below contain one or more grammatical or spelling errors. Select the answer choice that is correct as is.
  a. A longer happier life, caused by one's owning a pet.
  b. Owning a pet, for one to live a longer, happier life.
  c. To live a longer, happier life by one's owning a pet.
  d. Owning a pet can help one live a longer, happier life.

79. Three of the sentences below contain one or more grammatical or spelling errors. Select the answer choice that is correct as is.
  a. One of the first modern detectives in literature were created by Edgar Allen Poe.
  b. One of the first modern detectives in literature was created by Edgar Allen Poe.
  c. Edgar Allen Poe having created one of the first modern detectives in literature.
  d. In literature, one of the first modern detectives, created by Edgar Allen Poe.

80. Three of the sentences below contain one or more grammatical or spelling errors. Select the answer choice that is correct as is.
  a. I don't like fish as well as my sister does.
  b. I don't like fish as well as my sister.
  c. Fish isn't liked by me as well as my sister.
  d. My sister likes it, but I don't like fish as well.

81. Identify the sentence that contains a mistake in capitalization, punctuation, grammar, or spelling. If you find no mistakes, select choice **d**.
  a. Our class took a field trip, going to the art museum.
  b. There are rocky cliffs along the coast.
  c. We saw Dr. Mason because our doctor was on vacation.
  d. no mistakes

82. Identify the sentence that contains a mistake in capitalization, punctuation, grammar, or spelling. If you find no mistakes, select choice **d**.
  a. Make sure your seatbelt is fastened.
  b. I'm afraid of spiders George is too.
  c. Yes, I will bring the dessert.
  d. no mistakes

83. Identify the sentence that contains a mistake in capitalization, punctuation, grammar, or spelling. If you find no mistakes, select choice **d**.
  a. They traveled south and hiked in the desert.
  b. "Don't shout at me," she yelled back.
  c. Joshua enters lots of contests, therefore he knows he can't win.
  d. no mistakes

84. Identify the sentence that contains a mistake in capitalization, punctuation, grammar, or spelling. If you find no mistakes, select choice **d**.
  a. Where's my blue jacket?
  b. The prizes were awarded to Juan and me.
  c. After midnight, you will turn into a pumpkin.
  d. no mistakes

85. Identify the sentence that contains a mistake in capitalization, punctuation, grammar, or spelling. If you find no mistakes, select choice **d**.
  a. When I heard the alarm, I jump out of bed.
  b. Mr. Fox is the president of his own company.
  c. At night, I listened to jazz on the radio.
  d. no mistakes

86. Identify the sentence that contains a mistake in capitalization, punctuation, grammar, or spelling. If you find no mistakes, select choice **d**.
  a. The muffins cost more than the bread does.
  b. Roberta and I were in the same watercolor class.
  c. The temperature was colder today than it was yesterday.
  d. no mistakes

87. Three of the sentences below contain one or more grammatical or spelling errors. Select the answer choice that is correct as is.

  a. After renting him the room, Alvin discovered Mr. Morris owned a cat.

  b. After renting him the room, a cat was discovered to belong to Mr. Morris.

  c. A cat belonging to Mr. Morris was discovered by Alvin after renting him a room.

  d. After renting him a room, Mr. Morris was discovered by Alvin to own a cat.

88. Three of the sentences below contain one or more grammatical or spelling errors. Select the answer choice that is correct as is.

  a. We ate the popcorn and watch the movie.

  b. While watching the movie, the popcorn was eaten.

  c. Popcorn, while watching the movie, was eaten.

  d. We ate the popcorn while we watched the movie.

89. Three of the sentences below contain one or more grammatical or spelling errors. Select the answer choice that is correct as is.

  a. Parole Officer Richardson phoned his supervisor every day when he was in the hospital.

  b. When his supervisor was in the hospital, Parole Officer Richardson phoned him every day.

  c. When in the hospital, a phone call was made every day by Probation Officer Richardson to his supervisor.

  d. His supervisor received a phone call from Probation Officer Richardson every day while he was in the hospital.

90. Three of the sentences below contain one or more grammatical or spelling errors. Select the answer choice that is correct as is.

  a. Some of the case transcripts I have to type are very long, but that doesn't bother one if the cases are interesting.

  b. Some of the case transcripts I have to type are very long, but that doesn't bother you if the cases are interesting.

  c. Some of the case transcripts I have to type are very long, but it doesn't bother a person if the cases are interesting.

  d. Some of the case transcripts I have to type are very long, but that doesn't bother me if the cases are interesting.

91. Three of the sentences below contain one or more grammatical or spelling errors. Select the answer choice that is correct as is.

  a. For three weeks, the chief received taunting calls from an arsonist, who would not say where he intended to set the next fire.

  b. The chief received taunting calls from an arsonist, but he would not say where he intended to set the next fire, for three weeks.

  c. He would not say where he intended to set the next fire, but for three weeks the chief received taunting calls from an arsonist.

  d. The chief received taunting calls from an arsonist for three weeks, not saying where he intended to set the next fire.

92. Identify the sentence that contains a mistake in capitalization, punctuation, grammar, or spelling. If you find no mistakes, select choice **d.**

  a. Science and math are my two best subjects.

  b. We met senator Thompson at a conference last June.

  c. Did you see the movie *Babe*?

  d. no mistakes

93. Identify the sentence that contains a mistake in capitalization, punctuation, grammar, or spelling. If you find no mistakes, select choice **d.**

a. "I'll come and stay with you, grandma," I said.

b. "Don't ever tell a lie," he warned.

c. "Why won't you play with us?" he asked.

d. no mistakes

94. Identify the sentence that contains a mistake in capitalization, punctuation, grammar, or spelling. If you find no mistakes, select choice **d.**

a. He's the best officer in the department.

b. We were planning to go, but the meeting was canceled.

c. "Okay," she said, I'll go with you."

d. no mistakes

95. Look at the four numbered sentences below. Choose the sentence order that would result in the best paragraph.

1) During the parole period, he is supervised by a parole officer.

2) The parole officer must also be concerned, however, about the safety of the community.

3) After a prisoner has served his sentence, he may be paroled to the county where he was tried.

4) A parole officer has a certain amount of latitude in supervising her parolees' transition from prison life.

a. 1, 4, 2, 3

b. 2, 1, 4, 3

c. 4, 1, 3, 2

d. 3, 2, 4, 1

96. Look at the four numbered sentences below. Choose the sentence order that would result in the best paragraph.

1) For example, a man in Texas was convicted of stealing the guns belonging to Clayton Moore, television's Lone Ranger.

2) For example, drivers are ordered to place a bumper sticker on their car that publicizes their crime.

3) In addition to a fine and probation, the gun thief was ordered to complete 600 hours of community service cleaning the Houston police department's horse stables.

4) In recent years, courts have begun handing down criminal sentences that include an element of humiliation.

a. 1, 4, 2, 3

b. 2, 1, 4, 3

c. 4, 1, 3, 2

d. 3, 2, 4, 1

97. Look at the four numbered sentences below. Choose the sentence order that would result in the best paragraph.

1) Visits, especially from family members, can aid in a prisoner's rehabilitation.

2) Usually, this means that a prisoner and his visitors may not have physical contact with each other.

3) Therefore, they are separated by a pane of glass and must talk by phone.

4) However, in order to maintain prison safety, family visits cannot be unrestricted.

a. 2, 4, 1, 3

b. 1, 4, 2, 3

c. 1, 2, 3, 4

d. 3, 1, 2, 4

98. The following question consists of four numbered sentences. Choose the sentence order that would result in the best paragraph.

1) Therefore, persuading another person to commit a crime by discussing a specific crime with the intention that it be carried out is considered solicitation.

2) First, the person must have persuaded another person to commit a crime.

3) Second, the person must have been discussing a specific crime and must have had the intention that the act would be done.

4) Police officers may become aware of a person who did not actually commit a crime, but solicited another person to do so.

  a. 1, 3, 4, 2
  b. 2, 4, 1, 3
  c. 4, 2, 1, 3
  d. 4, 2, 3, 1

99. The following question consists of four numbered sentences. Choose the sentence order that would result in the best paragraph.

1) Murder in the first degree is usually defined as the willful and premeditated killing of another.

2) A third definition of murder in the first degree is the killing of a police officer or community corrections officer.

3) Finally, in some states, killing of a person while attempting to escape from lawful custody may be defined as first-degree murder.

4) It may also apply to situations in which a person is killed during the commission of a felony crime.

  a. 4, 3, 1, 2
  b. 2, 1, 3, 4
  c. 3, 2, 4, 1
  d. 1, 4, 2, 3

100. The following question consists of four numbered sentences. Choose the sentence order that would result in the best paragraph.

1) No search of a person's home or personal effects may be conducted without a written search warrant issued on probable cause.

2) This means that a neutral judge must approve the factual basis justifying a search before it can be conducted.

3) The Fourth Amendment to the Constitution protects citizens against unreasonable searches and seizures.

4) However, there are exceptions to the Fourth Amendment, such as when evidence is in plain view.

  a. 2, 4, 1, 3
  b. 1, 4, 2, 3
  c. 1, 2, 3, 4
  d. 3, 1, 2, 4

► Answers

1. c. Incarceration is the imprisonment of an offender or alleged offender, which may not always occur under a waiver. Emancipation is a process in which a juvenile is legally separated from the care of his parents. Diversion is a preadjudication/conviction program that allows an offender to avoid conviction in exchange for the completion of specified conditions.

2. b. The longer the period of intensive supervision, the longer the period of support and control of the offender, therefore reducing the risk of further criminal law violations while under supervision. Being supervised for a longer period of time does not coincide with reducing the duration it takes for an offender to pay restitution. An offender is less likely to abscond under intensive supervision.

3. d. John Augustus is considered to be the father of probation. Alexander Maconochie and Walter Crofton are figures involved with the early development of parole. Zebulon Brockway is known for his work at the Elmira Reformatory, specifically with his system of release, which was a predecessor to the formation of an indeterminate sentence model.

4. d. Critics would not provide testimony to the positive effects of reducing prison overcrowding, especially in attempting to denounce the practice of probation.

5. a. Status offenses include charges of truancy, curfew, runaway, incorrigibility, and illegal possession of alcohol. Recidivism is often defined as repeat criminal activity. Delinquency is defined as criminal activity committed by a juvenile. Restitution is the process by which an offender repays a victim for his or her losses caused by the crime.

6. b. User fees help the supervising agency recover part of the costs associated with providing supervision of an offender. The theory behind user fees is that, because the offender created the situation, he or she should reimburse the jurisdiction for those costs. Restitution is the process by which an offender repays a victim for his or her losses caused by the crime. Bribery is an unlawful act whereby someone offers something of value to someone else in order to gain favor. Diversion is a preadjudication/conviction program that allows an offender to avoid a conviction in exchange for the completion of specified conditions.

7. c. Revoking a parolee's release would be a negative reaction to the supervision service provided. Although this situation happens, even with some regularity, ultimately the responsibilities of supervision are those named in the other choices.

8. d. House arrest is an intermediate sanction between probation and institutional incarceration. Therefore, parole violators, by the nature of having already been incarcerated and failed, would not typically make good candidates. Violent offenders would pose too much of a risk of committing further violent acts if they were not incapacitated through imprisonment. Assigning a program of supervision that is based solely on an offender's sex or gender would be discriminatory; offenders have the right to fair application of their supervision. Nonviolent offenders pose the least risk of physical harm to the community at large.

9. c. Confidential informing is a process by which an individual agrees to provide information to police officers to help them investigate criminal acts or enterprises. Although offenders sometimes enter presentence plea agreements that require their testimony against other alleged offenders, a judge would not utilize this program as a sentencing alternative.

10. d. Officers increase their education level by earning specified degrees and gain valuable experience through their professional or other collateral work. Specialized training and certification is often sought and achieved in connection with education or work assignments. An officer's political affiliation is not a qualification.

11. c. Probation was formalized in the commonwealth of Massachusetts in 1878. The other states listed followed the practice in the years following.

12. a. Regular probation is a broad term covering the standard use of probation supervision. Deferred prosecution is the process by which the prosecution of an individual in a criminal case is delayed and, ultimately eliminated, if a defendant agrees to complete a set of sanctions and conditions that may include probation supervision. Diversion is a preadjudication/conviction program that allows an offender to avoid a conviction in exchange for the completion of specified conditions.

13. a. Determinate sentences are firm in their requirements of specified amounts of incarceration time connected with a particular classification of offense. An indeterminate sentence is the mechanism that allows for discretionary release through the parole board's authority. Retribution is a sentencing ideology that calls for an offender to pay his or her victim back for his or her actions.

14. b. Probation officers constantly balance their duties with respect to the offender, the safety of the community, and the overall maintenance of social order. Although sometimes important to the general understanding of the system's processes, the costs of incarceration hold the least amount of consideration for a probation officer when deciding what to do with a particular case.

15. b. Don't be fooled by the fact that an offender "splits" his or her time between the community and incarceration under work release. Parole occurs after a period of incarceration, but is considered a continued custody situation and is completely separate from probation. Judicial reprieve occurs when a judge removes a sentence for a particular interval of time, thus providing some liberty while postponing other sanctions in the process.

16. c. The offense-based PSI is typically used in jurisdictions requiring certain sentencing guidelines and, therefore, restricts a judge's ability to consider items specific to the convicted offender. Therefore, the reasons or explanations for an offender's behavior and his or her ability to make changes are not as important to consider as the loss experienced by the victim as a result of the offense.

17. a. Aggravating factors are the details of a case that tend to increase concern regarding the offense, but do not necessarily warrant an increase in the offense classification. A particularly young victim of a criminal offense would tend to cause concern, because he or she may be more vulnerable to criminal actions and, therefore, may play a role in the offender's decision to commit an offense against them.

18. a. Probation and parole officers deal with a multitude of information and documents, and many of these are governed or secured by confidentiality statutes that protect the information of the defendant. Collateral information obtained is sometimes confidential, but it doesn't necessarily have to be. An offender's criminal history is typically public record, and privatization is a practice whereby agencies or tasks are handled by private practitioners.

19. b. The conditions that any offender placed on probation can expect to abide by are known as standard conditions. Special conditions may also be ordered to address the needs or risks of a particular offender or type of offense. Reform conditions are considered special conditions and are typically based in a sentencing ideology.

20. b. The other choices are standard conditions, while a condition that requires attendance at Alcoholic Anonymous meetings addresses specific needs or risks posed by an offender. It is unlikely that all probationers supervised in a jurisdiction would be required to attend this type of meeting.

21. d. The judge has no obligation, purpose, or right to confront victims on their testimony. This is left to the due process of law and the established legal practices. Therefore, a probation officer provides the impact statement to the judge so that the judge can properly consider the impact of the offense on the victim as well as his or her subsequent losses, both real and anticipated.

22. b. Although the other choices are integral parts of the process of investigation, an interview with a defendant often provides insight into multiple factors considered during sentencing. A defendant is likely to disclose previous criminal involvement that may not have been uncovered during other investigative practices, or he may disclose information about family, education, employment, and mental health history.

23. d. The Fifth Amendment deals with an individual's right against self-incrimination.

24. c. It is reasonable to expect that no probationer be allowed to commit a new criminal offense while on parole; otherwise, he or she should not have been released from incarceration. The remaining conditions would be imposed to address the specific nature of the offense or needs or risks of the offender.

25. d. Classification is the result of risk assessment as well as the matching of strategies and

resources available to a supervising officer. Diagnosis determines what problems may exist, and can be either formal or informal and would probably be factored into the risk assessment and, subsequently, the classification.

26. c. Informal sanctions are preferred to a more formal process because they help a juvenile avoid the stigmatization or label often associated with the adjudication process. Informal sanctions are imposed when it is clear that they would yield the same result as a more formal process.

27. b. Choice **c** is worth considering as a possible solution if this parolee starts to be uncooperative. Choice **a** is less likely to yield positive results, because the offender is unlikely to admit to criminal behavior. Choice **d** is unreasonable because a private citizen lacks the skills and abilities to conduct investigative work, and their participation in such activities would not only be unsafe and risky, it would be unethical. Choice **b** gives the best opportunity for a detailed investigation, and the parole officer has the potential to invite police officers into the search. A search may result in additional charges for new criminal offenses in addition to revocation of parole on the original sentence.

28. d. The main issue here is the fact that a probationer is not being supervised in his or her original jurisdiction, and, therefore, the laws that govern the transportation of offenders suspected of criminal activity between states must be considered. The other issues are certainly a part of the overall process, but extradition is directly related to supervision through the Interstate Compact, while the others are not.

29. c. This question addresses the time limits involved in probation revocation practices.

The other answers are specific types of violations.

30. c. Probation officers use reasonable suspicion to initiate a further search of an offender or his or her property. Probable cause is determined once that reasonable suspicion becomes supported through evidentiary procedures. In the revocation hearing, a judge or paroling authority will determine whether to revoke community supervision based on a preponderance of the evidence, whereas original trial processing requires a person to be guilty beyond a reasonable doubt.

31. d. Choices **b** and **c** are usually considered to be standard conditions. Choice **b** could be considered a special condition, but it is applied as standard to a class of offenses involving alcohol or drugs. Choice **a** is an appropriate condition, but choice **d** specifically addresses the underlying cause of Leonard's recent conviction. Without the completion of this condition, it is unlikely that Leonard will successfully complete supervision and is likely to commit further alcohol-related offenses.

32. a. Although a lack of education and formalized employment are risk factors associated with recidivism, they alone do not present a problem for many people. In Leonard's case, he is a chronic user of alcohol, and as such, he participates in risky behavior, such as operating a motor vehicle while intoxicated.

33. d. Choices **a**, **b**, and **c** are all considered valid risk factors when assessing the likelihood that an offender will continue with criminal behavior or technically violate the conditions of supervision. Choice **d** is incorrect because the idea that dumb luck plays a part in assessing the behavioral risks of offenders is ridiculous.

34. b. The 0.02 BAC could be explained by the minimal consumption of an alcoholic beverage, possibly a 12-ounce can of beer or less within the previous hour. Or, larger quantities of alcohol consumed at an earlier time may not yet have metabolized or been expelled from his system. He may not have consumed the alcohol at his own residence, or he could have already removed the containers from his home. Most mouthwash brands contain at least some levels of alcohol.

35. b. Choice **a** raises issues of Fifth Amendment rights and proof of violation. Waiting to see if a conviction in the new offense occurs, as suggested in choice **d**, is problematic, because the length of time that is typically needed for criminal case processing is substantial. Choice **c** is possible given the information provided; however, it is not the best choice. Filing a revocation based on the law violation gives the best, most timely response, because the burden of proof for a revocation is less strict than for a new conviction and doesn't necessarily require a conviction on the new offense.

36. c. Nothing in the narrative indicates any form of violent behavior. Choice **d** may be tempting. However, to say that there is no risk for violence from Leonard is inappropriate, especially when considering that Leonard has a history of using alcohol, which is a mood-altering substance that can lead to unpredictability.

37. c. Choices **a** and **d** seem tailored to the details of Janice's offense of marijuana possession and probable use. Choice **b** could be appropriate to address her attitude and behavior at the time of her arrest. Choice **c** could be imposed but would be considered the least likely to decrease her risk for recidivism while under probation supervision.

38. b. We do not know if choice **a** or **c** is correct based on the information provided in the passage. Choice **d** seems unlikely because the passage indicates what the initial traffic stop was made for. Choice **b** is an assumption; however, it is an assumption that is likely considering the facts provided in the passage.

39. b. Drug use, knowledge of an impending incarceration period, and a history of unlawful behavior are good indicators when predicting violation or new offense risks. Her income level has very little to do with whether or not she will satisfy the conditions of her community supervision, with the exception of covering the costs of supervision and imposed fines and fees.

40. c. With marijuana particularly, a drug urine test can detect the presence of a drug for approximately 30 days following consumption. Although any marijuana use is likely a law violation, drug testing is not usually accepted as proper evidence to prove possession.

41. d. This is a classic example of how proper fieldwork is necessary to address the immediate risks of a particular offender. It is unlikely that an employer would take the time to call a probation officer if he or she was not truly concerned, or even convinced, about what has been happening with the offender.

42. c. A conflict of style or personality between an officer and an offender is not unusual. However, an officer should be mindful of manipulation techniques employed by offenders in order to reduce the amount of structure and restriction experienced by the offender as a result of probation supervision. Ultimately, the supervisor has the responsibility of case assignment and, therefore, reassignment. Utilizing choice **d** would be undermining the supervisor's authority.

43. d. The case deals not only with the sphere of law but also with the sphere of values and civil conduct specifically. Nowhere does the passage say that parole officers should be idealistic, as suggested with choice **c**.

44. d. Fairness and accuracy, respect for individuals, and the importance of maintaining community relations are all reasons racial slurs should be avoided. Maintaining morale on a multicultural force is also important. When quoting the statements of other individuals for the purposes of testimony, the officer must use the *exact* language and statement observed to ensure accuracy of and convey the context of the testimony.

45. c. The importance of a parole officer's conduct is mentioned several times throughout the case study.

46. c. The first sentence of paragraph 2 states that Stephan is committed to civil order.

47. b. Moderation is explicitly referred to in the case study. Justice and politeness are synonymous with fairness and civil conduct. It's true that most parole officers are courageous, but courage is not mentioned in the information provided.

48. a. Stephan should bring the behavior to the attention of his fellow parole officer, who may not be aware of the consequences of his or her behavior. Doing nothing would be an endorsement of the behavior, whereas interrupting the session with the parolee would be disrespectful to the fellow officer. If the fellow officer's behavior continues after the conversation, then Stephan should inform the supervisor.

49. d. Parole officers are human beings with life circumstances, obligations, and interests, and there may be times when an officer has a conflict with his or her personal schedule. Cultivating a personal life outside of work is key to any worker's success, but especially to professionals who work in high-stress positions. In choice **c**, Tom is probably violating departmental policy. However, if he openly discusses his needs with his supervisor, together they may be able to formulate a plan that will work for Tom and still satisfy the needs of the department.

50. a. Because Tom's average number of supervised offenders is markedly fewer than the overall average, it is likely that Tom does not supervise any low-risk offenders. However, his caseload is not small enough to allow the assumption that he has only high-risk offenders. We may expect a caseload of only high-risk offenders to be somewhere near 20 or so cases, considering the total number of parolees supervised by the department.

51. c. Following the standard practices and policies of the agency is always a great way to make decisions regarding the treatment of offenders.

52. a. Although choices **b**, **c**, and **d** are certainly cause for concern, the primary concern is maintaining confidential records. Tom's practice of making supervision case files available to anyone entering or exiting Tom's office to view, observe, or to remove them is unacceptable. Tom should be required immediately to place these papers in a file cabinet or desk drawer that locks or is away from open access.

53. b. Although it is unlikely that Tom would receive financial compensation for this presentation, it would unethical to consider Tom's salary as a justification for him to participate. Doing so would set a precedent whereby Tom and other officers may begin to look for ways to use their position to earn additional compensation. This practice creates, at the very least, the appearance of impropriety and, at worst, illegal or unethical behavior.

54. c. The main issue that Tom should consider when deciding to inform his supervisor about his father is the stigma that is attached to offenders convicted on child molestation charges. The best option for Tom would be to go ahead and discuss the situation with his supervisor. It is not unusual for parole or probation officers to have family members or friends who have been convicted of criminal law violations and who are subsequently supervised in a community setting. Departments typically have practices and procedures to address these situations when they occur.

55. a. Choice **b** is incorrect because, although it is often helpful to have other family members involved in the planning and programming for a juvenile offender, requiring participation from a family member who is no longer "legally" connected to the juvenile would be improper. The officer could *recommend* that the family member become involved, but that should not be an option until other issues involving that family member were explored. Furthermore, it may be concluded that the onset of Kecia's behavioral problems coincided with the release of her biological mother from the correctional facility, and therefore, the biological mother's further involvement with Kecia could be even more detrimental to the child. Although further harm is possible, choice **c** is incorrect because it calls for a conclusion that is not supported by hard facts and is contradictory to the already established relationships of the family. Choice **d** is incorrect because omitting this information would eliminate possible issues to address during the programming portion of the sentence, information that would provide the judge with a better understanding of the family's dynamics. However, in choice **a**, an officer can suggest that Kecia undergo a psychiatric evaluation to gain further information about the impact of the family's relationship with Kecia's mother. Furthermore, if Kecia's behavior is related to a genetic psychological disorder, treatment can be recommended and undertaken to reduce the impact on her behavior and to avoid the subsequent consequences.

56. d. Choice **a** is incorrect because taking Kecia into custody for not sitting down or talking would be inappropriate. Choice **b** is wrong because a probation officer should not physically restrict or otherwise handle a juvenile except in response to an imminent threat of harm to him- or herself or someone else. Choice **c** is unlikely to yield the desired results and may cause conflict with the parents. Choice **d** gives the officer the ability to establish rules with the juvenile and state the consequences should the juvenile continue the undesired behavior. Although the officer's response may need to become harsher if this type of behavior continues in subsequent visits, responding this way during the first visit allows for more restrictive measures to be taken later.

57. a. This question requires a candidate to identify the professional protocol that should be followed when there is a question of inappropriate conduct. Choice **a** would require an officer to assume automatically that what the juvenile has said is correct, and it calls into question the ethics of the placement agency supervisor without any factual information. Choice **c**, despite giving the officer an opportunity to investigate the validity of Kecia's story personally, still encroaches in an area outside of his or her direct responsibilities. Choice **d** is incorrect because it involves other offenders instead of other professionals and possibly alerts them to problems associated with that agency by indicating distrust of the staff. Choice **b** allows an officer to promote communication between criminal justice agencies and places the responsibility of program supervision back in the hands of the person responsible for supervising the community service placement agencies. This information may be in addition to other complaints the director has already received, thereby giving him or her the ability to take corrective action.

58. c. Kecia's biological mother no longer has legal rights as Kecia's parent; those rights have been granted to the adoptive parents. As such, the biological mother is restricted from certain information about Kecia. Providing her the telephone number, as suggested in choice **a**, could be dangerous or otherwise harmful to the family, who may not want to be involved with Kecia's mother.

59. a. Given Kecia's recent history as described by the principal, an immediate visit to the school to confront Kecia is most appropriate. This visit will allow you the opportunity to make an assessment of the causes of the situation and then react accordingly. Without further investigation, having Kecia expelled from school would seriously conflict with her need for an education. With only a suspicion of a theft, taking custody of Kecia may not be necessary. This situation is serious enough that it cannot wait to be discussed at Kecia's next office visit.

60. c. Although the other options are sometimes possible, this choice provides the best opportunity for Kecia to complete what she has started and has committed to finishing, in the least restrictive way possible.

61. d. This is the only choice that does not contain excessive wordiness or redundancy. In choice **a**, the phrase *the fifth of five* is redundant. Choice **b** also repeats by using both *five* and *fifth*. Choices **c** and **d**, although constructed differently, make the same error.

62. d. The correct punctuation between two independent clauses is a semicolon. Choice **a** is wrong because it creates a run-on sentence. Choice **b** creates faulty subordination. Choice **c** creates a sentence fragment.

63. b. This choice is the only complete sentence.

64. b. The sentence does not require any punctuation other than the period at the end. Also, *who*, not *that*, should be used with *people*.

65. c. This is a declarative sentence; it asks an indirect question, so a question mark is not needed. Also, the comma is unnecessary.

66. a. The sentence requires a comma before the phrase *isn't it*.

67. a. The phrase *a virus* is a nonessential element in the sentence and needs to be set off with commas.

68. d. *Anonymous* is the correct spelling.

69. d. When a comparison is made, the word *fewer* is used with nouns that can be counted; the word *less* is used with quantities that cannot be counted.

70. b. This is the only choice that uses the adverb correctly and establishes the appropriate comparison. Choices **a**, **c**, and **d** are incorrect because an adverb (*gracefully*) is required to modify the verb *marches*.

71. c. No punctuation is necessary; in fact, any use of punctuation would unnecessarily separate the verb *maintain* from its object.

72. d. This is the only sentence that uses the correct pronoun, *which*. Use *which* when introducing clauses that are not essential to the information in the sentence—when the clause refers to people, then use *who*. The second clause in choice **c** is referring to a river, not a person, so the use of *who* is incorrect.

73. b. This is the only sentence that does not contain a double negative or a double comparison.

74. a. An ultimatum is a final, nonnegotiable proposition, condition, or demand. This definition best fits the context of the sentence.

75. b. Choices **a** and **c** are sentence fragments. Choice **d** represents confused sentence structure as well as a lack of agreement between subject and verb.

76. c. The other choices contain unnecessary shifts in person, from *people* to *their* and *we* in choice **a**, to *your* and *one* in choice **b**, and to *our* and *they* in choice **d**.

77. a. The subject of the sentence *criminal justice professor* is singular and takes the singular verb *is planning*.

78. d. This is a complete sentence; the other choices are fragments.

79. b. This is a complete sentence. Choices **c** and **d** are fragments. In choice **a**, the verb does not agree in number with its subject, *one*.

80. a. This sentence is clearest. In choice **b**, the speaker likes his or her sister more than fish. Choice **c** is confusing. Choice **d** has an unclear pronoun: The use of *it* makes it unclear whether fish or the sister is being referenced.

81. a. This sentence has faulty subordination; the word *going* should be deleted, and the comma should be eliminated.

82. b. This is a run-on sentence.

83. c. The connecting word between the two clauses creates an illogical statement. The word *therefore* should be changed to the word *but*.

84. d. There are no errors.

85. a. This sentence makes an illogical shift in tense—from the past to the present tense.

86. d. There are no errors.

87. a. In choice **b**, the cat seems to be renting the room. In choice **c**, it's unclear whether *he* refers to the cat or to Mr. Morris. Choice **d** implies that Mr. Morris rented himself a room.

88. d. In choice **a**, the lack of agreement in tense makes the sentence unclear as to time; choice **b** doesn't make it clear who ate the popcorn; choice **c** implies that the popcorn watched the movie.

89. b. In the other choices, the pronoun reference is ambiguous; it is unclear who is in the hospital.

90. d. The other answers contain unnecessary shifts in person from *I* to *one*, *you*, and *a person*.

91. a. The other choices are unclear because they are awkwardly constructed, obscuring who intends to set the fire.

92. b. *Senator* should be capitalized because it refers to a particular senator.

93. a. *Grandma* is used as a proper name and should be capitalized.

94. c. To set off the dialogue, there should be quotation marks before the contraction *I'll*.

95. c. Sentence 4 is the topic sentence. Sentence 1 provides detailed information and sentence 3 provides further detail about the information in sentence 1. Sentence 2, with the word *however*, adds to the information.

96. c. Sentence 4 is the general topic sentence. Sentence 1, with the phrase *for example*, gives a specific case. Sentence 3 gives the details of the example. Sentence 2 provides another more general example.

97. b. Sentence 1 provides a general rule. Sentence 4, with the word *however*, notes an exception to the general rule. Sentence 2, with the word *usually*, gives an example of the exception. Sentence 3 tells how the example is applied in practice.

98. d. Sentence 4 introduces the topic of solicitation and explains how it may come up. Sentence 2 gives the first part of the definition of *solicitation*; sentence 3 gives the second part of the definition. Sentence 1 refers to all the elements mentioned in sentences 2 and 3.

99. d. Sentence 1 introduces the topic, murder in the first degree. The phrase *it may also* in sentence 4 indicates a second definition of the topic; sentence 2 is a third definition; sentence 3, beginning with the word *finally*, gives the last definition.

100. d. Sentence 3 introduces the topic, the Fourth Amendment. Sentence 1 details what the Fourth Amendment protects against; sentence 2 explains what was detailed in sentence 1. Sentence 4, introduced by *However*, tells that there are exceptions to what was stated in the previous three sentences, and gives an example of one of those exceptions.

13 ▶ Practice Test 6

This is the sixth practice test in the book based on the most commonly tested areas on the probation officer and parole officer exams. The practice test consists of 100 multiple-choice questions in the following areas: job responsibilities, case studies, writing skills, and reading comprehension. The number of questions and the time limit of the actual probation officer or parole officer exam can vary from region to region. Set aside three hours to take this practice test.

A version of this practice test is available through the LearningExpress online link, if you prefer to take it on the computer.

Practice Test 6

1.	a	b	c	d		36.	a	b	c	d		71.	a	b	c	d
2.	a	b	c	d		37.	a	b	c	d		72.	a	b	c	d
3.	a	b	c	d		38.	a	b	c	d		73.	a	b	c	d
4.	a	b	c	d		39.	a	b	c	d		74.	a	b	c	d
5.	a	b	c	d		40.	a	b	c	d		75.	a	b	c	d
6.	a	b	c	d		41.	a	b	c	d		76.	a	b	c	d
7.	a	b	c	d		42.	a	b	c	d		77.	a	b	c	d
8.	a	b	c	d		43.	a	b	c	d		78.	a	b	c	d
9.	a	b	c	d		44.	a	b	c	d		79.	a	b	c	d
10.	a	b	c	d		45.	a	b	c	d		80.	a	b	c	d
11.	a	b	c	d		46.	a	b	c	d		81.	a	b	c	d
12.	a	b	c	d		47.	a	b	c	d		82.	a	b	c	d
13.	a	b	c	d		48.	a	b	c	d		83.	a	b	c	d
14.	a	b	c	d		49.	a	b	c	d		84.	a	b	c	d
15.	a	b	c	d		50.	a	b	c	d		85.	a	b	c	d
16.	a	b	c	d		51.	a	b	c	d		86.	a	b	c	d
17.	a	b	c	d		52.	a	b	c	d		87.	a	b	c	d
18.	a	b	c	d		53.	a	b	c	d		88.	a	b	c	d
19.	a	b	c	d		54.	a	b	c	d		89.	a	b	c	d
20.	a	b	c	d		55.	a	b	c	d		90.	a	b	c	d
21.	a	b	c	d		56.	a	b	c	d		91.	a	b	c	d
22.	a	b	c	d		57.	a	b	c	d		92.	a	b	c	d
23.	a	b	c	d		58.	a	b	c	d		93.	a	b	c	d
24.	a	b	c	d		59.	a	b	c	d		94.	a	b	c	d
25.	a	b	c	d		60.	a	b	c	d		95.	a	b	c	d
26.	a	b	c	d		61.	a	b	c	d		96.	a	b	c	d
27.	a	b	c	d		62.	a	b	c	d		97.	a	b	c	d
28.	a	b	c	d		63.	a	b	c	d		98.	a	b	c	d
29.	a	b	c	d		64.	a	b	c	d		99.	a	b	c	d
30.	a	b	c	d		65.	a	b	c	d		100.	a	b	c	d
31.	a	b	c	d		66.	a	b	c	d						
32.	a	b	c	d		67.	a	b	c	d						
33.	a	b	c	d		68.	a	b	c	d						
34.	a	b	c	d		69.	a	b	c	d						
35.	a	b	c	d		70.	a	b	c	d						

▶ Practice Test 6

1. The main goal of a treatment agent working with probationers and parolees is to
   a. understand and change the probationer's or parolee's behavior.
   b. find appropriate community services that can help meet the needs of the probationer or parolee.
   c. campaign for the rights of probationers or parolees who have been unfairly treated by society.
   d. enforce the court-ordered conditions of probation with no concern for changing behavior.

2. Most probation and parole officers feel uncomfortable in their role as a treatment agent largely because
   a. society is opposed to the treatment approach in probation and parole.
   b. they lack the skills and education necessary to "do therapy."
   c. they have problems maintaining the confidentiality of issues discussed in treatment sessions.
   d. the majority of officers prefer a law enforcement approach.

3. A probationer who you have supervised for one year approaches you with a request to have his curfew modified, from 10:00 P.M. to midnight. Records reflect he has paid his court costs and is up to date on his probation supervision fees. He reports consistently and is in compliance with the conditions of his probation. You decide to
   a. inform the probationer that conditions can never be amended for the duration of the sentence.
   b. inform the probationer that conditions can be amended only if there are repeated technical violations or a new arrest.
   c. inform the probationer that, as a result of satisfactory compliance with court orders, you will request that the judge amend the probation order to drop the curfew.
   d. request that the judge amend the probation order to move the curfew from 10:00 P.M. to 8:00 P.M.

4. Which of the following would most likely result in revocation by the court?
   a. failure to pay probation fees for two months
   b. a new arrest for robbery
   c. missing the last curfew check
   d. requesting travel out of the jurisdiction to a concert

5. Without the assistance of the probation officer, a probationer convicted of grand larceny finds employment as a clerk at a local convenience store and does not inform the employer of his criminal record. Shortly after his employment begins, he steals $2,500 from the store. The employer sues the probation department for failure to warn about the offender's criminal record. Can the probation department be held liable for the offender's actions?

a. Yes, because the officer had a duty to inform the employer.

b. No, because probation and parole officers are immune from being sued.

c. Yes, because the officer failed to provide adequate supervision.

d. No, because the probationer secured the job without the assistance or knowledge of the probation department.

6. A payment that probationers are required to pay the victim for the expenses of the crime is called

a. restitution.

b. retribution.

c. probation supervision fees.

d. a fine.

7. "As an offender, you must pay your debt to society and get what you deserve." This statement would be consistent with what purpose of punishment?

a. retribution

b. incapacitation

c. rehabilitation

d. deterrence

8. Which of the following may NOT be considered in the assessment for parole release?

a. length of time served

b. institutional record

c. prior criminal record

d. number of dependents

9. A parolee has been under parole supervision for one year. He commits a new burglary offense and is arrested and detained. Within a week, he is sent back to prison to serve the remainder of the sentence. Six months later, he appeals the revocation on the grounds that he was not given a revocation hearing nor granted an attorney. Does he have a legitimate case?

a. No, parole is a privilege, and the offender was not entitled to a hearing or counsel because he violated the terms of that privilege.

b. Yes; because he was losing conditional freedom, he was entitled to a hearing and representation by counsel.

c. He was entitled to a hearing, but not representation by an attorney because he had no interest in being protected.

d. No; because parole is administrative, due process does not apply.

10. Ten probationers on your caseload have been classified as "absconders." What is the definition of an absconder?

a. An absconder has had his or her probation revoked.

b. An absconder has had no contact with the probation officer.

c. An absconder has been classified for special treatment.

d. An absconder has fulfilled his or her financial obligations and can be terminated early.

11. After a night of drinking, two young men steal a tractor and drive it down the middle of a main street in the city. Later, they attempt to steal a telephone booth but are arrested in the process. The presentence investigation report indicates that both of these young men have had some "alcohol issues" in their past. As part of their probations, which of the following special conditions is the judge likely to impose?
  a. The offenders must attend school or get a GED.
  b. The offenders must not get within 100 feet of any place where there are children.
  c. The offenders must attend Alcoholics Anonymous meetings.
  d. The offenders must do 500 hours of community service.

12. *Street time* is a term used in probation and parole for the
  a. time from the commission of the offense to the arrest of the offender.
  b. time from arrest to conviction.
  c. time that the probationer or parolee spends in the community under supervision.
  d. time that the probationer or parolee spends in prison after being revoked.

13. The Director of Probation and Parole Services has asked you to write a concept paper about the value of volunteers at probation and parole agencies. Which of the following would you use to illustrate the need to initiate a volunteer program for your agency?
  a. Volunteer programs provide a way for well-meaning but bored upper-class housewives to do something with their time.
  b. Volunteer programs give officers the opportunity to train citizen volunteers when they have little or no work to do.
  c. Volunteer programs can train workers to replace ineffective or disgruntled officers.
  d. Volunteer programs can provide unbudgeted staff assistance and ancillary services to assist offenders in community reintegration.

14. A woman comes to your office requesting that you confirm whether or not a neighbor of hers is on probation. You respond by
  a. checking out the probationers supervised by your office and providing her with the information about his case.
  b. informing her that you cannot confirm or deny that kind of information because of confidentiality issues.
  c. having her arrested for invasion of privacy.
  d. having security remove her from the office after lecturing her about prying into others' business.

15. A probationer informs you that her son's fourth grade class will be taking an overnight field trip to the 4-H Camp 200 miles away. His teacher, explaining that they don't have enough parents going on the trip, has asked her to serve as one of the chaperones. The school and her son are not aware that she is on probation with limitations on her travel; she does not know what to do and asks for your advice. How do you respond?
  a. You inform her that she will have to explain to her son and the school that she will have to decline.
  b. You encourage her to make up an excuse to give the teacher.
  c. You request an amended probation order to allow her to travel for the specified period of time.
  d. You call the teacher to explain the mother's legal problems.

16. A standard order relating to parolees arrested for technical violations or a new arrest is to "detain without bail." Why is this important?
  a. The parolee has nothing to lose and may disappear.
  b. The parolee should sit in jail and think about the crime that he or she has committed.
  c. Time in jail will make the parolee plead guilty to avoid the time and expense of court.
  d. The parole board operates with complete autonomy and can do whatever it desires.

17. You learn that an inmate appearing at the upcoming parole board hearing has been making contact with his victim and threatening harm if she appears before the parole board. As the institutional parole officer who has supervised this case for the past five years, what do you do with the information?
  a. You do nothing, because he has been a model prisoner.
  b. You contact the parole board directly so that it may stop the parole process.
  c. You accuse the victim service officer and victim of being vindictive and dismiss the claims made by the victim.
  d. You discuss the matter with the senior officer and the warden to determine how to proceed.

18. An alternative to incarceration that allows an offender to remain under supervision in the community with court-ordered conditions describes
  a. parole.
  b. commutation.
  c. probation.
  d. a pardon.

19. Which of the following defendants is more likely to be granted probation?
  a. a repeat violent offender
  b. a first-time offender convicted of forgery
  c. an offender facing his third incarceration for burglary
  d. a parolee who commits another violent offense

20. As a probation officer, you may be required to collect supervision fees for probation/parole services to clients. If you were opposed to the collection of fees, which of the following arguments would you use?
   a. Offenders are already burdened with court fees, fines, victim restitution, program costs, etc.
   b. It is appropriate to collect fees from correctional clients who are granted the privilege of probation or parole.
   c. The collection of probation and parole fees for supervision allows departments to provide more services to clients.
   d. Fee collection makes correctional clients responsible for some of the costs of supervision.

21. Which of the following characteristics is most desirable for probation and parole officers?
   a. having a judgmental temperament and an eye for details
   b. being intimidating and authoritative
   c. being easily intimidated by opposition
   d. having a knowledge of the social and behavioral sciences

22. You have been appointed as a new probation officer and eventually will have a caseload of 250 probationers, 50% to 60% of whom are required to report weekly, biweekly, or monthly. In addition, you are required to make field visits, write reports for the court, and conduct presentence investigations. Which of the following will be most valuable in surviving in your new job?
   a. the ability to recognize and classify dangerous offenders
   b. successfully convincing your supervisor to reduce your workload
   c. the ability to manage time and organize your work effectively
   d. the ability to represent yourself and the agency well in the community

23. A juvenile whom you supervised in juvenile probation committed a new offense—a robbery. The original crime was processed in juvenile court. But after the case was adjudicated and in the dispositional phase, the judge decided that the juvenile court had exhausted its efforts to rehabilitate this young man. He decided to waive jurisdiction and transfer the case to try him as an adult in criminal court. As you read the comments of the judge, you become alarmed because
   a. you know that this young man will never survive in an adult prison.
   b. you are afraid that he will only become a more dangerous criminal in adult prison.
   c. you know that his family cannot afford to hire a criminal defense lawyer.
   d. you know he can't be tried twice for the same crime.

24. You have just received a new probationer on your caseload. In reading the file, you discover that there are some mental health concerns. The offender had spent six months in jail awaiting trial prior to probation. During that time, he underwent extensive psychiatric evaluations, but none were conclusive. The first three weeks of supervision consisted of him coming to your office and sitting and talking to himself for approximately 15 minutes. He is unable to complete the probation report form or communicate with you. At first, you think that it is just a game, but as you think about his behavior and reread his case file, you recognize that there is a problem. You decide to

   a. request revocation of probation because there is nothing you can do to help him.

   b. refer the case back to the court psychiatrist for further evaluation, reporting his behavior over the past months.

   c. let him continue to do what he was doing; it makes your job easier because you don't have to do much.

   d. file a report with the state's attorney reporting the judge who placed the young man on probation knowing that he was mentally incompetent.

25. The stress and burnout among probation and parole officers is a major concern in the field. Which of the following is NOT likely to be a cause of officers' stress and burnout?

   a. pressures within the organizational bureaucracy

   b. low salaries and few rewards

   c. temptation to engage in criminal behavior

   d. interference with family and social life

26. Annie, a 55-year-old probationer on your caseload, is an alcoholic. In the three years that you have supervised her, she has been in drug rehabilitation four times. She reports that for the past ten years her husband, who is also an alcoholic, has abused her. She also says that he has become more violent and she has become more afraid. You have suspected it, and her presentence investigation report indicated an abusive relationship. You decide to

   a. do nothing because she is used to the abuse.

   b. ignore her because the alcohol is probably making her imagine things.

   c. refer her to the court for provoking the assaults from her husband.

   d. refer her to the domestic violence shelter for battered women.

27. In recent years, there has been an attack on rehabilitation, as the public demands tougher punishment for criminals. Probation has been viewed as too lenient or just a "slap on the wrist." As an advocate for community corrections in general and probation in particular, which of the following statements would you make to convince citizens that probation is really punishment for offenders?

   a. Probationers are subjected to random drug tests, unannounced home and employment visits, and tighter control and stricter enforcement of the conditions of probation.

   b. Many jurisdictions have dropped curfews as unnecessary and unenforceable.

   c. Because of limited resources and larger caseloads, there is less opportunity to adequately supervise probationers.

   d. Because of overworked courts and crowded court dockets, judges are requesting that technical and even some new arrest violations be handled in the probation department.

28. A recent college graduate who has been hired as a probation officer in your office believes that, if he can gain the probationer's trust, he or she will cooperate and obey the rules. He tells you that, at least twice a week, he goes to happy hour with several of his male and female probationers. As an officer for the past 12 years, you respond by

a. telling him to do whatever it takes to get the job done.

b. reporting his behavior to the department supervisor.

c. discussing with him the dangers of developing that kind of unprofessional relationship with probationers.

d. saying nothing. What he does after work is his business.

29. As a field parole officer, you have been asked to verify the employment plan of an inmate who is being considered for parole. He has indicated that he would be working in maintenance at a wellness center. When you arrive, you discover that it is really a hospital that specializes in pain management using narcotics as well as other techniques to manage chronic pain. You look at his file and discover that he has been convicted of possession of controlled substances. Further checking reveals that he has a past conviction for the sale of controlled substances. You decide to

a. say nothing because, as a maintenance person, he will not have access to drugs.

b. provide the information as a part of your report to the institutional services.

c. contact the inmate's family to ask for money to keep quiet about this information.

d. contact the parole board directly to make sure that it gets the information.

30. You have just discovered that one of your probationers, with a history of drug use, is HIV positive. As you discuss this issue, you discover that this information has not been disclosed to anyone but you. You are also aware that he is married and has been involved in at least one extramarital relationship. You feel that you have a duty to warn these additional parties who may be at risk of being infected. Yet there are rules of confidentiality that must be followed. What do you do?

a. You notify the wife and the girlfriend so that they can be tested.

b. You request that probation be revoked so that the probationer can go to prison where he will no longer be a risk.

c. You seek the advice of your supervisor to ascertain the correct procedure and protocol relating to this situation.

d. You do nothing because he has probably already infected these significant others in his life.

Directions: Read the following case study and then answer questions 31 through 33.

Diane is a 21-year-old woman serving a ten-year term for six counts of theft and receiving stolen property. She has two juvenile arrests for possession of marijuana and the burglary of her mother's home. As an adult, she has six arrests and five convictions for retail theft, receiving stolen property, burglary, and possession of drugs. Three of her sentences were concurrent for three years. She was granted parole after six months on the condition that she enters a residential drug treatment program. Her participation was unsuccessful, and she refused to comply with other conditions of her parole. She was sent back to prison to serve the remainder of her sentence.

Diane is the younger of two children. Her parents were divorced when she was one year old. She lived with her mother until her mother remarried. She did not fit into her mother's new lifestyle, so her grandmother and her aunt raised her. When her grandmother and aunt could no longer take care of her, she was turned over to the Department of Child Welfare, who placed her in and out of foster care. She lived on the street for a while, making her living mostly through prostitution. When she was 16, she had a child, whom she gave up for adoption. She has very little contact with any of her family members. She last saw her biological father about five years ago.

Diane got married four years ago because she was pregnant. Her husband was an addict, and subsequently she became addicted. They separated after a year because he was physically abusive and she realized that she could not "kick the habit" as long as he was around. She began keeping company with another man, got pregnant, and had another child. She abandoned the child in a parking lot when she was trying to avoid an arrest. Although her husband is in prison, she is still legally married, and her child is in the care of the Department of Child Welfare.

Diane dropped out of school in the ninth grade. She confessed that she did not really want to go to school anyway. Diane has never held a full-time job or developed any kind of work history. The defendant has been hospitalized for drug overdoses and has had hepatitis four times. She is presently in good health. Her extensive drug history begins at age 12, and by age 16, she was addicted to heroin. She has now been clean of drugs for about 11 months.

31. Diane has informed you that she wants to get a job, find suitable living arrangements, and regain custody of her children. She admits that she does not know how or where to start because she does not have any skills or education that would help her get a job. She admits that her family refuses to help her because they gave up on her a long time ago. As her probation officer, you are the only person she has who can provide some guidance. You should
   a. inform her that providing this kind of advice is not a part of your job but wish her luck with her goals.
   b. encourage and assist Diane in developing realistic goals as well as a plan for reaching those goals.
   c. express your doubts about the seriousness of her desires for a better life.
   d. tell her that she is still too young and that the state would never return her children.

32. Diane confides that she ran into some old friends who convinced her to get "high" with them. She admits that she was feeling a bit "depressed," and she feels guilty and says that she doesn't want the drug life. You respond by
   a. notifying the judge that Diane has violated probation and recommending that her probation be revoked.
   b. demeaning her for her lack of self-control.
   c. being a broker and referring her to a drug treatment program or a counselor who can help her at this time.
   d. suggesting that she try to get arrested and revoked; prison would solve her job and housing problems.

33. Diane calls to tell you that her husband is being released from prison. A family member told her that he plans to "get her" when he gets out. He said it was her fault that he got busted. As her probation officer, you verify that he is going to be released and

    a. inform her that domestic issues are not your responsibility.

    b. inform her that this is only hearsay and she should ignore it.

    c. call his family and threaten to have them arrested for frightening your client.

    d. because there is a history of abuse, refer her to the domestic violence program that can provide safe shelter.

Directions: Read the following case study and then answer questions 34 through 37.

Johnny is a 28-year-old man on probation for burglary, theft, and receiving stolen property. He was sentenced to a ten-year probation term, ordered to pay $5,000 restitution, and has a combined fine and court cost totaling $2,000. He is in his second year of the ten-year term. His criminal record indicates five juvenile arrests and convictions, all for property crimes. He was also on juvenile probation. As an adult, he has three felony arrests and two convictions for burglary, auto theft, and receiving stolen property. He also has two misdemeanor convictions for simple assault and theft. He previously served a five-year probation term after pleading guilty to two charges of burglary. His only incarceration has been one year in the county jail on a burglary charge.

Johnny is the second child of four brothers and two sisters born to his mother and father, who never married but lived together for more than 20 years. He had a close relationship with both parents but was closest to his father. His father was a strong disciplinarian who kept the house in order. After he died, his mother was not the strong disciplinarian and often let the children do what they wanted. Later, his mother remarried a man who left after a year and took the family savings with him. One of Johnny's brothers was killed during a robbery, and his youngest brother is wanted in several states and is characterized as a thief.

Johnny married at 20, and the marriage, which lasted only one year, produced one child. He married again at 23 and has had three more children. The marriage has been shaky because of his drinking and his irresponsible behavior.

Johnny dropped out of high school in the tenth grade. Therefore, he has had only unskilled laboring jobs. In the last two years since being on probation, he has quit three jobs and been fired from two. He receives public assistance to take care of his living expenses. He was in the army and was discharged after going AWOL three times. He is emotionally immature and seems to be in constant distress.

Johnny has no assets or debts, and as noted, public assistance covers most of his living expenses.

34. As you read Johnny's case history, how would you characterize him?

    a. Johnny is a decent guy who has just had a few bad breaks.

    b. Johnny's history shows a pattern of irresponsible behavior and immaturity.

    c. Johnny has been unfairly labeled, which has left him trying to prove himself.

    d. Johnny's dysfunctional relationship with his father has left deep scars.

35. How would you characterize Johnny's criminal history?

    a. There is a strong pattern of aggressive and violent behavior.

    b. There is a pattern of drug distributing.

    c. There is a pattern of petty victimless crimes that should not have been prosecuted.

    d. There is a pattern of property offending as a juvenile and as an adult.

36. How would you characterize Johnny's home and family life when he was growing up?
   a. It was dysfunctional from the day that he was born.
   b. It was a home in which children saw and experienced violence on a regular basis.
   c. It was a home that appeared to be stable but became dysfunctional after his father died and his mother remarried.
   d. It was a home that appeared to tolerate and encourage criminal behavior in order to survive.

37. On his most recent monthly visit to your office, Johnny informs you that he would like to enroll at the local junior college to pursue an associate's degree in a trade. You respond by
   a. laughing in his face at his latest project that he will never finish.
   b. encouraging him but allowing him to take the initiative to explore the programs, start the application process, and talk to advisers at the college.
   c. threatening to request probation revocation if he doesn't get a job.
   d. questioning why he would want to get a trade and a job when he's already receiving financial assistance from the state.

Directions: Read the following case study and then answer questions 38 through 41.

Carolyn is a 34-year-old woman on probation for robbery. She took $50 from a cab driver who picked her up along the interstate. Carolyn turned herself in and repaid the cab driver. She was given probation because the victim didn't think that she should be incarcerated, she never showed a gun, and she returned the $50.

She has one juvenile arrest for shoplifting, for which she served a six-month juvenile probation term. This is her first offense as an adult.

Her childhood was basically uneventful. She came from a stable family in which both parents worked to support the needs of the family. She has an older brother and sister whom she sees frequently. There is no history of criminal activity in the family; they all support her and are willing to help in any way they can.

Carolyn married at age 17 because she was pregnant. She admitted during the presentence investigation that she was mentally, physically, and sexually abused during her two-year marriage. Her son's paternal grandmother has legal custody, and she is allowed to see him once every two months. At age 23, she married her present husband, who is also on probation for possession of a gun without a license. Although the marriage has had its rough spots, it has lasted for more than ten years and appears to be stable.

Carolyn graduated from high school despite her poor grades. Before being placed on probation, she enrolled in a course to become a medical technician but had to drop out because for financial reasons. She says that she would like to be a nurse's aide or a medical assistant. She has had only one job, at a meatpacking plant. She was laid off because of a knee injury.

She has been drinking since she was 16 and has been hospitalized for depression and alcoholism.

38. You receive Carolyn's file prior to her initial visit. What is your overall assessment of this case?
   a. This woman has no business on probation; she should be in prison.
   b. Prison would have been more harmful to her, because it is obvious that she is more in need of treatment than punishment.
   c. She has an extensive criminal history, which the judge didn't consider before sentencing her to probation.
   d. She appears to be a danger to herself and society and should be locked in prison or a mental hospital.

39. Which of the following would be an important advantage in Carolyn's rehabilitation?

  a. having a supportive husband and family who are willing to help in whatever way they can

  b. being 34 years old with only one child and no plans to have any more

  c. being unemployed and having no skills

  d. being a white female

40. Carolyn tells you that she drinks mostly during the day when she is home alone and bored. She would like to go back to her medical technician course and get a job. You respond by

  a. encouraging her to explore the amount of time that she has left to complete the course and then help her to explore ways to pay for her study.

  b. advising her to get any job because she is in violation of probation conditions.

  c. advising her to stay at home and try to be the best wife that she can be.

  d. advising her that, because she started the course before she was placed on probation, your helping her or advising her about it is inappropriate.

41. After supervising Carolyn for a month, you observe that she is depressed. She expresses fear that she will start to drink again. She is unwilling to seek counseling on her own, so you respond by

  a. doing nothing. You hope that the problem will get better on its own.

  b. requesting that the probation order be amended to include counseling as a condition.

  c. attempting to counsel her during her monthly visits.

  d. waiting for her to violate her probation conditions so you can request revocation of probation.

Directions: Read the following case study and then answer questions 42 through 44.

Billy is a 26-year-old man sentenced to 15 years of probation for burglary and retail theft. He was convicted on eight counts of burglary and one count of retail theft. He has five prior arrests as a juvenile but no convictions. His adult record includes seven felony arrests and convictions. Offenses included larceny, receiving stolen property, and failure to stop at the scene of an accident. He was sentenced to ten years for these convictions but was paroled after three years.

Billy grew up in a dysfunctional family. His father has been married and divorced seven times. There was no financial stability because the father had an unstable work history with periods of unemployment. His mother left the family when Billy was four years old and took two of the five children with her. A neighboring family adopted one child, while his paternal grandparents raised Billy and his sister.

He married two years ago, but the marriage is shaky. He has worked only unskilled laboring jobs and has no real employment history. While in prison, he developed a heroin addiction and has used as much as $400 to $500 dollars worth of heroin a day. Much of his criminal behavior is related to his drug addictions. Drug treatment has failed in the past, and he believes that there is little hope of him ever kicking his habit.

42. As you read Billy's case file, you conclude that

  a. Billy's drug addiction is probably a major factor in his criminal behavior.

  b. Billy is violent and should be incarcerated.

  c. Billy is probably better off in prison because of his unemployment and lack of skills.

  d. Billy's wife should get a divorce.

43. After you have read the case file, you conclude that Billy has many problems that need attention. Which of the following would NOT be one of Billy's major problems?
a. lack of job skills and unemployment
b. drug addiction
c. violent or hostile behavior
d. irresponsible behavior and hopeless attitude

44. As you read Billy's case file, how would you characterize his chances for probation success?
a. Excellent; he knows what prison is like and doesn't want to return.
b. Good; the support from his family, especially his father and wife, will help him through.
c. Good; he understands that he will lose his family, job, and conditional freedom by returning to prison.
d. Poor; he's unemployed and has a poor job history, limited skills, little family support, and a drug addiction that he admits he cannot overcome.

Directions: Read the following case study and then answer questions 45 through 47.

Randy, a 15-year-old male, has been referred to juvenile court several times since he was ten years old and has always appeared before the same juvenile court judge. When he was ten, he was referred to the court for habitual truancy from school. He began associating with a bad crowd, which lead to his delinquent behavior. He appeared in juvenile court for shoplifting and was placed on probation for six months. He was eventually charged with one count of burglary and, at age 14, was placed in a juvenile institution. After seven months, he was released conditionally on aftercare. During the next year, he was involved in several law violations, usually involving liquor. He violated his conditions of release and spent another four months in a juvenile institution.

After his release, he stayed out of trouble for about three months before being arrested again for burglary. The loss of property is estimated at $15,000. The district attorney wants the juvenile tried as an adult so that he may receive adult punishment and incarceration in a state facility. The district attorney believes this to be in the best interest of the community, because Randy has not responded to the care, treatment, and supervision of the facilities of juvenile court.

Once the juvenile court waives its jurisdiction, the case will be sent to the grand jury for indictment. Because of Randy's record and the fact that the case is a felony, the sentence will be probation or possibly incarceration in prison.

Two issues of concern to the juvenile court judge are the effects of adult prison on the juvenile and his responsibility as judge to protect the community. Should the severity of the case warrant the child be tried as an adult or should the boy be protected under juvenile court in an effort to rehabilitate him?

As the juvenile probation officer who has done intake on Randy as well as been his probation officer, you are responsible for giving the judge some advice regarding this case.

45. As you read the case information, you conclude that
a. incarceration has had no positive impact on his behavior.
b. his delinquent behavior is caused by the lack of care and concern for him by others.
c. Randy has a pattern of aggressive behavior that should be controlled.
d. incarceration contributed to his behavior; his felonies began after placement in a juvenile institution.

46. Based on Randy's case history, you present reasons to the judge that Randy should be given another chance in juvenile court. Which of the following would be your strongest argument for keeping him under juvenile court jurisdiction?

    a. There is no program or punishment left in juvenile court to deter him.

    b. Statistics indicate that juveniles placed in adult prisons are often beaten, sexually assaulted, or taught to be better criminals.

    c. It costs twice as much to house a juvenile in an adult facility than an adult.

    d. Incarceration will protect society from Randy's uncontrolled criminal behavior.

47. If you believe this case should be transferred to adult court, what would be your argument for more severe punishment?

    a. Randy is only 15 years old and believes that his offenses are only childish pranks.

    b. The offenses are only property offenses and not that serious, so they should receive severe punishment.

    c. Randy has not been deterred by the punishment or rehabilitation efforts of the juvenile court; more severe punishment is needed.

    d. Randy is too young and immature to understand the seriousness of his behavior.

Directions: Read the following case study and then answer questions 48 through 50.

Robert has been sentenced to a five-year probation term for burglary and forgery. His presentence investigation report (PSI) indicates that he is gay man and has made his living by dancing at gay bars. He is 19 years old and dropped out of high school in the tenth grade. When you interviewed him for the PSI, he came dressed in female attire: slacks and blouse and, high heeled shoes. He says that he has never been employed in a "real" job and claims that no one will hire him,
even though he has had interviews. A man in the community takes care of Robert and has made himself responsible for paying any fees that are owed; this man is well respected and wants to remain anonymous. Robert has a tendency for violent behavior and has been arrested several times for assault. There have been rumors that he carries a switchblade and will not hesitate to attack someone who provokes him. There is also indication that he may have a drinking problem.

48. During his initial meeting in your office, Robert indicates that he has been fired from his dancing job and has trouble finding other employment. He further indicates that he really does want a job but has no skills. When he asks you for advice, you

    a. dismiss him because he is not serious about wanting a job.

    b. look at his attire and think that he'll never get a job.

    c. refer him to "Workforce" for career counseling.

    d. start preparing the paperwork to request revocation of his probation.

49. A condition of Robert's probation is that he keep out of bars and taverns, even if that means he must quit his dancing job. One day, you receive a call that he has been dancing frequently at the local bar. You respond by

    a. filing a delinquency report about this technical violation of probation conditions.

    b. warning him about his behavior and reminding him of the conditions and consequences of violating those conditions.

    c. using other probationers to spy on him and report back to you.

    d. requesting that police go into the bar undercover and arrest him.

50. Robert's presentence investigation report indicates previous problems with alcohol and some violent tendencies. How should the probation officer address these issues during the initial visit?

  a. The officer should wait until there is a problem with violence or alcohol before addressing these issues.

  b. The officer should inform Robert that he or she is aware of possible alcohol and violence problems and should suggest counseling.

  c. The officer should refer the case back to the court for further processing.

  d. The officer should completely ignore these issues as possible problems.

Directions: Read the following case study and then answer questions 51 through 56.

Joyce is a 20-year-old woman serving a five-year sentence for forgery. She found some social security checks, which she signed and cashed. The victims were two elderly residents who lived in the same housing project as Joyce.

Joyce has had several arrests and convictions for drugs and property offenses, and she has been on probation twice and has spent time in the county jail. This is her first incarceration in prison. She has served 18 months and is presently being considered for parole. For the first six months of her prison stay, she had some problems adjusting. She has received several disciplinary actions for fighting and has a reputation with the staff and inmates as being "bad." She works in the prison laundry and seems to get along well with her inmate coworkers at the laundry.

As she prepares to go before the parole board, there are a number of concerns regarding her release. She denies having a drug problem. Although Joyce completed high school with above average grades, she has no marketable skills and has been unemployed most of the time since graduating from high school. She has stated that she will be living with friends

because she and her mother do not get along; her mother was always harassing her about going to college. It should be noted that these friends are suspected drug dealers and users; this house is currently under surveillance, even though it has not been raided or entered with a search warrant.

The probation officer conducting the presentence investigation is somewhat concerned that Joyce is always extremely well dressed. Throughout her prison stay, she has been receiving money and supplies from "friends." Although unconfirmed, there is a rumor that Joyce is selling drugs in prison for those "friends."

51. As her institutional parole officer, you assist Joyce in preparing her parole plan. How would you view Joyce's chances of success if released on parole?

  a. Good; she has friends who are supportive and will help her make the adjustment once released.

  b. Excellent; although she had problems initially, she has made satisfactory progress while in prison.

  c. Fair; although she has a drug problem, she has made progress in other areas of her life.

  d. Poor; she has no employment, unknown living arrangements, a possible drug problem, and friends who are suspected drug dealers.

52. How would you characterize her adjustment to prison life?

  a. Overall, her adjustment to prison has been satisfactory, but there are some questions about her continued associations with people on the outside, who may be involved in drugs.

  b. Joyce has learned the "con" game and uses it to her advantage.

  c. Joyce has constantly gotten into fights throughout her 18-month prison stay.

  d. Her overall adjustment to prison has been very poor; she is a bad influence on the other prisoners.

53. Joyce has informed you that she would like to enroll in the prison cosmetology course, because she has realized that she has no job skills for employment when released. You respond by
   a. discouraging her from applying because you don't feel that she is serious.
   b. dismissing this as an attempt to impress the parole board.
   c. encouraging her and then helping her to enroll in the course.
   d. recommending to the parole board that Joyce be denied parole because she has violated prison rules.

54. You hear inmates discussing Joyce's suspected criminal activity and you decide to
   a. report this information to the parole board to support your recommendation for denial of parole.
   b. use snitches to spy and report on her illegal activity.
   c. do nothing; you would not want to jeopardize her chance for parole.
   d. talk to Joyce about her alleged criminal activity and warn her of the consequences.

55. If Joyce were granted parole release, what would be your recommendation for her living arrangements?
   a. You would recommend that Joyce should live with her mother for no less than one year.
   b. You would allow her to live anywhere people are willing to let her move in.
   c. You would recommend that Joyce live with her friends because they stuck by her even when she was in prison.
   d. You would recommend that Joyce secure her own apartment before leaving prison.

56. If Joyce is released, which of the following conditions should the parole board NOT give as a condition of probation?
   a. The offender must enroll in drug treatment.
   b. The offender must work with the police department to catch her friends who are suspected drug dealers and users.
   c. The offender must not associate with criminals or those suspected of criminal activity.
   d. The offender must maintain suitable employment.

Directions: Read the following case study and then answer questions 57 through 60.

John has been placed on probation for aggravated assault with a deadly weapon. You notice in his PSI that this is not the first violent offense on his criminal record. Excluding the present charge, he has committed three previous offenses of simple assault. He was convicted on only one of the assault charges. He was placed on misdemeanor probation and completed the two-year term without incident. He also has one prior conviction for burglary. He has never been sent to prison, although he did spend nine months in jail on the burglary charge. He had been granted probation, but it was revoked after he was arrested for simple assault. He is now on probation for a new assault charge. He shot a "friend" after the friend accused him of cheating in a card game. His criminal history indicates that he was first arrested and taken to juvenile court at the age of 14 for cutting a student with a razor after school. He was given probation and sent to counseling for his behavior.

John's first visit to see you since leaving court and getting his probation conditions was scheduled for 9:00 A.M., but he fails to show up. Then, at about 10:30 A.M., the receptionist announces that John is in the waiting area. When he comes into your office, he slumps into the chair. He hands you the report form, which has been completed incorrectly and in a handwriting that is not legible.

He starts to explain his tardiness. "Well, my friends came by last night to see if I wanted to go drinking. I really did not want to go because I always seem to get into trouble when I am with them, but they are my friends. My wife has been hassling me about a job. I haven't worked since being laid off from the tire plant about a year and a half ago. So, to get a little peace and quiet, I thought I would get out of the house for a while. We stayed out drinking until 3:00 A.M. because none of us had to get up to go to work. By the time I got home, I was really out of it. I drank way too much. My wife and I started fighting again, and after I pushed her down, I crashed into the bed. I intended to be on time, but when the alarm went off, my wife started again. So here I am, and I'm late. So what are you going to do to me—put me in jail? Big deal! I don't really care."

57. As the supervising probation officer, how would you characterize John as indicated by the pattern in his criminal history?
   a. John is aggressive with violent tendencies.
   b. John is a petty thief.
   c. John is a repeat property offender.
   d. John has a tendency to commit victimless crimes.

58. During this initial visit, you realize that it will be almost impossible to communicate with this probationer. Therefore, you decide to
   a. advise him to leave and come back when he gets his attitude together.
   b. review the conditions of probation and stress the importance of obeying those conditions.
   c. write a note to the judge informing him that John should have his probation revoked.
   d. become hostile to let him know that you can be just as tough and hard.

59. You recognize that this offender will be difficult to supervise because there are so many problems and issues. You do a "risk and needs" assessment of his returning to crime. You discover that John has a high need level and is at a high risk for returning to crime. You
   a. do nothing and hope that that he violates probation quickly so you can get him off your caseload.
   b. conclude that he is hopeless and nothing can be done to help him.
   c. change his supervision level from maximum to medium so that you see him only once a month instead of biweekly.
   d. prioritize his needs and develop a plan that helps him address the most serious needs first.

60. Six months into supervision, John informs you that his uncle has hired him as a plumber's helper and plans to teach him the trade. John confides to you something that you had already figured out—that he cannot read. You advise him to
   a. find another job that will not require reading.
   b. enroll in the night literacy program at the local high school.
   c. tell his uncle that he is not interested in learning plumbing.
   d. fake it.

Directions: Read the following passage and then answer questions 61 through 65.

The issue of maintaining DNA files on criminals and parolees is a contentious one. Some say that requiring all criminals to submit material for a national DNA "databank" will help to prevent future crimes and to prosecute repeat criminals effectively. However, others object, saying that such a databank is a violation of the privacy of individual citizens. And the financial costs to taxpayers of maintaining such a database may be extremely high.

A federal law passed in 2000 requires certain parolees to provide a sample of their blood for a national DNA database, which would be maintained by the FBI. This law applies primarily to those convicted of sexual assault or other violent crimes.

In September 2003, Governor James McGreevey of New Jersey signed legislation that requires all newly convicted criminals to submit saliva for the DNA database, regardless of their crime. The law also applies to offenders on parole or probation. Officials at the time estimated that this new law would increase the statewide databank to more than 140,000 samples of DNA. The state budgeted $8 million to fund processing the DNA for the databank, which would require the work of 40 scientists.

However, in October of that same year, the Ninth Circuit Court of Appeals in San Francisco, California, ruled that requiring parolees to provide DNA samples is a violation of their right to privacy. The court sited the Fourth Amendment clause against illegal search and seizure. A dissenting judge in the case stated that parolees had diminished privacy rights, but the court's decision ruled against the DNA requirement.

The debate over DNA databanks will continue to be argued in the legislatures and the courts. State and federal governments will strive to find a balance between parolees' privacy as American citizens, the costs of the databank to taxpayers, and the potential benefits of DNA tracking for preventing and prosecuting future crimes.

61. Which of the following best expresses the main idea of the passage?
   a. California and New Jersey are two states that maintain DNA databanks on all criminals, a system that costs about $8 million.
   b. Requiring convicted criminals to submit DNA samples for databanks is a many-sided issue, which has not yet been resolved.
   c. Parolees give up their right to privacy when they commit a crime, and they must submit DNA samples to databanks, according to federal law.
   d. DNA databanks are far too expensive for the little benefit they generate, and are not a good expenditure of taxpayers' money.

62. Which of the following details from the passage does NOT directly support the main idea?
   a. New Jersey passed legislation requiring DNA samples from all convicts and parolees.
   b. A San Francisco court ruled that requiring DNA samples violates privacy rights.
   c. The New Jersey databank may eventually contain 140,000 samples of DNA.
   d. One judge stated that parolees have diminished privacy rights.

63. Which of the following sentences best summarizes the facts in the passage?

   a. In response to a federal law requiring some convicted criminals to submit DNA samples, New Jersey passed legislation requiring DNA testing of all convicts and parolees, while a San Francisco court ruled such a requirement unconstitutional.

   b. DNA profiling is still a hotly debated issue, with different courts coming down on different sides.

   c. San Francisco upheld and extended the federal government's DNA sample mandate, while a New Jersey court ruled such a requirement unconstitutional.

   d. The Ninth Circuit Court of Appeals in San Francisco overturned a federal mandate to collect DNA samples from convicted criminals.

64. Which of the following would make the best concluding sentence for this passage?

   a. Legislators in states such as Wyoming and Utah have expressed uneasiness with the federal government's DNA databank mandate.

   b. Also, the San Francisco court may yet reverse its decision.

   c. Only time will tell which way the debate over the DNA databanks will ultimately end.

   d. Obviously, the future of American taxpayers depends on a DNA database.

65. Which of the following best describes the author's point of view in this piece?

   a. She believes that DNA databanks are necessary to keep criminals from committing repeat offenses.

   b. She believes that DNA databanks are an unconstitutional invasion of privacy.

   c. She believes that the debate over DNA databanks is unimportant and will blow over.

   d. She believes that the debate over DNA databanks is a complex one that will continue to be argued.

Directions: Read the following passage and then answer questions 66 through 70.

In 2004, a former New York state senator named Guy Velella was sentenced to one year in prison after being convicted of bribery. Three months later, he was released. This strange turn of events caused a flood of inquiry into the organization that orchestrated his release: the Local Conditional Release Commission (LCRC).

Founded in the mid-1990s, the LCRC was intended to review prison sentences and to reduce the sentences of selected nonviolent criminals. This act of mercy would theoretically decrease prison overcrowding and save money for the state. Prisoners released by the commission would have to agree to strict conditions, such as entering drug treatment or wearing ankle bracelets for monitoring. They would also be required to serve a mandatory year on probation.

However, by 2004, the prison population of New York State had greatly diminished, and the commission was releasing fewer and fewer prisoners. Many working in law enforcement were unaware that it even existed. In fact, the state senate (including Senator Velella) had voted to abolish the commission and others like it, but the bill died in the state assembly.

When the commission voted to release Senator Velella, however, lawmakers and others took notice and began to ask questions. How did the commission choose whom to release? How was its $386,000 budget spent? Why had it released celebrities such as Mark Gastineau, a former New York Jets player, even though he had been convicted of the violent crime of domestic abuse? Most important, to whom was the commission accountable?

Some defended the commission's existence, saying it was a well-run organization to help remove people from the prison system who would be better served by being in the community. Others called for its abolishment, as a secretive organization plagued by favoritism and ultimately unnecessary.

Under the storm of angry scrutiny, the panel's chairman, its three other members, and its executive director all resigned. The mayor selected a new chairman. However, the records of the commission's decisions were not made public, and many questions remained unanswered.

66. Which of the following is best describes the main idea of this passage?
    a. Senator Guy Velella of New York was released from prison after three months, prompting inquiries.
    b. The Local Conditional Release Commission for releasing nonviolent prisoners in New York came under scrutiny in 2004 for its secrecy and possible corruption.
    c. The Local Conditional Release Commission did not release its records to the public, despite requests that it do so.
    d. A commission that had outlived its usefulness, the LCRC was condemned in 2004.

67. Which detail could be added to the passage to support the idea that there were many unanswered questions about the Local Conditional Release Commission?
    a. It is still unclear whether the commission met in person to deliberate, despite the staff's high salaries.
    b. One senator wrote a letter advocating Velella's release, even as he voted to abolish the commission.
    c. The mayor's office said there had been no policy to tighten the release criteria because the board was independent.
    d. Eighteen more inmates were offered early release in the past year but did not take it, because they would be required to serve a year's probation.

68. Which of the following best summarizes the objections to the Local Conditional Release Board as described in the passage?
    a. The board did not have the full approval of the state legislature or the mayor's office.
    b. The board requires prisoners who are released to serve a period of probation.
    c. The board is expensive, unnecessary to prevent overcrowding, and arbitrary in its decisions.
    d. The board took bribes and played favorites in releasing prisoners.

69. Which of the following would make the best concluding sentence for this passage?
    a. Some prisoners are grateful for the commission's intervention—for example, the single mother who was released to care for her children.
    b. A former assistant district attorney calls the Local Conditional Release Commission "a backdoor out of jail."
    c. Perhaps the inquiry resulting from Velella's release may prompt changes in how it is run, but it seems the commission will continue to exist, for the time being, whether or not it proves to be effective.
    d. Fifteen prisoners were released by the commission from 1999 to 2004, leading to the question of how effective the commission can be in preventing prison overcrowding.

70. Which of the following best describes the author's point of view?

   a. He believes the Local Conditional Release Commission should be completely abolished.

   b. He suspects there are problems with the Local Conditional Release Commission, but he presents both sides of the case.

   c. He insists that the Local Conditional Release Commission, as a public service, is being unjustly maligned.

   d. He thinks that Senator Velella is the real source of wrongdoing, not the Local Conditional Release Commission.

Directions: Read the following passage and then answer questions 71 through 75.

At one time in the United States, many states had laws prohibiting convicted criminals—such as parolees and probationers, even those who had been convicted of very minor crimes—from registering to vote. Even after they had served their jail sentences and paid the penalty for their crimes, these men and women were barred from voting in state and national elections. An entire segment of American society was thus disenfranchised, and the nation's ideals of equality under the law were compromised.

In the 2004 election, nearly four million ex-felons, parolees, and probationers were prevented from voting in the southern United States. The stringent and unjust laws, which prevented ex-convicts from voting, not only robbed these individuals of their rights, but also may have influenced the outcome of a very closely decided electoral race.

Fortunately, most states have since repealed or modified laws prohibiting voting for parolees and probationers. The 2004 election may have helped to bring this problem to light, and great steps have been made in reinstating the voting rights of Americans who have served their jail time.

However, problems still remain. Many election officials are unaware of the changes in voting laws and continue to prevent ex-felons and parolees from voting.

As one example, New York State law guarantees voting rights for people on probation. Two civil rights groups (Demos and the Brennen Center for Justice) conducted surveys of all of the state's county election boards to gauge their knowledge of state voting standards. They found that 40% of the officials they surveyed were ignorant of the state's voting rights law. Worse, more than one-third continued to prevent parolees from voting, believing they were upholding the law.

Clearly, merely passing legislation to prevent disenfranchisement is not enough. What is now needed is education and enforcement. State and federal election officials must take the initiative to inform and educate local officials about voting rights laws. And they must carry out punishment against those who deny voters their rights.

71. Which detail from the passage does NOT support the idea that problems still exist for parolees attempting to vote?

   a. Nearly four million ex-felons were prevented from voting in 2004.

   b. One-third of surveyed election officials in New York continued to prevent parolees from voting.

   c. In New York, 40% of the surveyed officials were ignorant of the state's voting rights law.

   d. Two different firms conducted research and found similar data.

72. Which of the following best expresses the main idea of the passage?

    a. Disenfranchisement of parolees probably affected the outcome of the 2004 election, which proves how significant it is.

    b. The southern United States is the worst place for ex-convicts and parolees to attempt to become functioning members of American society.

    c. Studies show that election officials are often unaware of the laws regarding parolees who attempt to vote.

    d. Disenfranchisement of parolees is an ongoing problem in America, as shown by the 2004 election, and must be fought with education as well as legislation.

73. Which of the following details could be added to the passage to support the idea that education about parolee voting rights is needed?

    a. The total percentage of eligible voters who are denied voting rights is not known.

    b. Courts have ruled in some cases that prison inmates do not have all of the rights and privileges of other citizens of the United States.

    c. Many local election officials are volunteers and do not have extensive knowledge of the legal system or voting statutes.

    d. The death penalty is applied more frequently in southern states, which suggests that animosity toward criminals is high.

74. Based on the details and tone of the passage, what inference can you make about this author's feelings about ex-convicts?

    a. She is mistrustful of them and thinks they should be closely monitored.

    b. She is protective of them and thinks they should be granted greater rights.

    c. She is fascinated by them and thinks they should be studied.

    d. She is angered by them and thinks they should be punished further.

75. Which of the following would make the best concluding sentence for this passage?

    a. Other studies confirm the results obtained by Demos and the Brennen Center for Justice.

    b. Without these steps, the United States will continue to fail to live up to its ideals, and the disenfranchisement of parolees will remain a shameful fact of American life.

    c. Disenfranchisement and other abuses of power by the government must be met with decisive action.

    d. Parolees have a hard enough time without being stopped from voting.

Directions: Read the following passage and then answer questions 76 through 80.

The city of New York has taken a new approach to the rehabilitation of juvenile offenders. They have given them their own school.

Community Prep High School, located on Twenty-Ninth Street in Manhattan, was founded by the city as a school for high school–aged parolees. Dubbed "Last Chance High" in a 2004 *New York Times* profile, the school is, in many cases, the only thing standing between teenagers and a return to jail.

School officials estimate that every year 8,000 juvenile offenders are released from prison in New York State. Most have been attending school in prison, and many attempt to reenroll in their high schools. But many high schools, feeling that these students are likely to cause problems, refuse to accept them.

A New York State study found that 81% of offenders age 17 and under return to jail within 36 months of their release. The head of Community Prep, Tim Lasante, points out that the evidence suggests that most of these repeat offenders were not in the school building at the time of their arrest. Perhaps merely being in school, he suggests, may be an antidote to further crimes.

The odds may be against these students. Another study estimates that only one in eight students who has been in custody ultimately completes his or her high school education. It is far easier to return to crime than to school, especially for those who feel the school has rejected them.

That's where Community Prep comes in. Devoted to small classes, individual attention, a highly structured school day, and lots of counseling, the school aims to give paroled students another shot at their education.

The work is not easy. Many students drop out or come to school rarely, and those who do come to class are often defiant and disruptive. But the school has undoubtedly made a difference in the lives of at least a few of these young men and women. Several have gained enough credits—and credibility—to return to conventional high schools, and some have been accepted into charter schools.

76. Which of the following best expresses the main idea of this passage?
  a. Many high schools refuse to take former juvenile offenders as students for fear that they will cause problems and return to prison.
  b. Community Prep is a high school for former juvenile offenders located in New York City.
  c. Because former juvenile offenders often have difficulty completing high school and staying out of prison, Community Prep High School was created to help them.
  d. Some studies suggest that being in school can reduce the chances that a juvenile offender will return to prison.

77. Which of the following details from the passage does NOT support the idea that Community Prep is needed to help high school–aged parolees?
  a. A study shows that 81% of offenders 17 and under will return to jail within 36 months of their release.
  b. Many students drop out or come to school rarely.
  c. Many high schools, feeling that these students are likely to cause problems, refuse to accept them.
  d. One in eight students who has been in custody ultimately completes his or her high school education.

78. Which detail could be added to the passage to support the idea that having a separate high school is helping juvenile parolees?
  a. The percentage of graduates of Community Prep is greater than the average percentage of juvenile parolees who graduate from high school.
  b. The New York State Board of Education is considering requiring high schools to accept juvenile parolees.
  c. The peer pressure of urban life is likely to prevent many juvenile parolees from making school a priority.
  d. Juvenile parolees make up a very small percentage of the high school–aged population in New York State.

79. Based on this passage, what is the author's point of view about juvenile parolees?
  a. He considers them a danger to other students.
  b. He considers them in need of help.
  c. He considers them beyond help.
  d. He considers them unjustly accused.

80. Which of the following would make the best concluding sentence for this passage?

a. Carlos Negron is one of Community Prep's success stories, because he was accepted into a charter high school.

b. But the fact remains that one in eight juvenile parolees will complete high school, with or without Community Prep.

c. Meanwhile, New York State's adult crime rate remains high.

d. Community Prep is changing the face of juvenile rehabilitation, one student at a time.

Directions: Read the following passage and then answer questions 81 through 85.

There are many reasons that a prisoner may be denied parole. In the case of one high-profile prisoner, Mark David Chapman, parole has been denied three times, and the reasons are as complex as the crime.

Chapman was convicted of murdering former Beatle and international music icon John Lennon in 1980. He was sentenced in 1981 to 20 years to life in prison, and has been serving his sentence in Attica. He applied for parole in 2000, 2002, and 2004, and each time he was denied.

One member of the parole board during the 2004 appeal stated simply that releasing Chapman would "significantly undermine respect for the law," because he had demonstrated "extreme malicious intent." Although he acknowledged Chapman's good behavior during his prison term, his reasoning was that, because Chapman's culpability and intentionality in a violent crime was so well documented, there could be no justification for reducing his sentence.

Another, stranger reason has to do with another kind of punishment. Chapman has stated on several occasions that he killed Lennon in order to get attention. He was a "nobody" and seemed to think that murdering the famous singer would propel him into the limelight. Some members of the parole board have noted that releasing him from prison would probably make him a public figure again. His release would, in effect, bring him the kind of attention he sought in his crime and, in a way, reward him. The board decided that the less attention paid to Chapman, the better, and made this a factor in its decision to deny him parole.

Finally, part of the decision to keep Chapman in jail may have been a degree of concern about his physical safety. Chapman is confined separately from other prisoners in Attica. There is the possibility that, if he were released, his life would be in danger by any of the millions of Lennon's fans who resent Chapman's role in his death. The parole board did not mention this as a motivation, but it is possible that releasing Chapman would amount to putting his life in danger.

81. Which sentence best describes the main idea of this passage?

a. Mark David Chapman is serving 20 years to life in Attica prison, and when he applied for parole in 2000, 2002, and 2004, he was refused parole each time by the board.

b. Mark David Chapman, convicted murderer of John Lennon, has been denied parole for reasons related to his intentionality, his desire for fame, and the risks to his safety.

c. Releasing Mark David Chapman would significantly undermine respect for the law, because he demonstrated extreme malicious intent.

d. Millions of music fans all over the world mourn the death of John Lennon, killed in 1980 outside his New York City apartment building by John David Chapman.

82. Which of the following is NOT one of the three main reasons the author speculates that Chapman has been denied parole?
- **a.** the malicious intent of his crime
- **b.** the prisoner's desire for fame
- **c.** the iconic status of the victim
- **d.** the possibility of physical danger to the prisoner

83. Which detail could be added to the passage to support the idea that Chapman has been denied parole for his own safety?
- **a.** John Lennon has fans in every country of the world.
- **b.** Certain websites devoted to Lennon express a desire to harm Chapman.
- **c.** The parole board has several members with records of humanitarian service.
- **d.** Chapman has demonstrated negative behavior in prison.

84. Which of the following sentences best summarizes the events in Chapman's case?
- **a.** Chapman was convicted of killing Lennon in 1980, was sentenced to prison in Attica in 1981, and was denied parole in 2000, 2002, and 2004.
- **b.** Chapman killed Lennon in order to get attention, and tried to convince the parole board to release him three different times.
- **c.** Chapman killed John Lennon in cold blood in 1980, was sentenced to prison in Attica in 1981, and was denied parole in 2000, 2002, and 2004 after serving 20 long years in prison.
- **d.** Chapman was convicted of killing Lennon in 1980 and has so far served 26 years in Attica.

85. Which of the following is the best concluding sentence for this passage?
- **a.** Notoriously strict, the Attica parole board has outdone themselves on this one, and history will judge them harshly.
- **b.** John Lennon's fans will forever mourn him, and it seems just that his killer will continue to rot in a prison cell.
- **c.** A further examination of Chapman's intentionality must take into account his mental health at the time of the murder of which he has been convicted.
- **d.** Thus, in the eyes of the parole board, Chapman's own intentional bid for fame through murder, and the possibility that this very notoriety may put him in danger, combined to keep him in prison, in this strangest of all parole cases.

Directions: Read the following passage and then answer questions 86 through 91.

At some points in our nation's history, lifetime jail sentences were few and far between. When such sentences were applied, they rarely meant a prisoner would die in jail. However, in recent years far more "lifers" are serving time in our nation's prisons, fewer life sentences have been commuted, and more and more prisoners are serving life.

Life sentences are typically handed out only for the most violent crimes. According to statistics released by state corrections departments between 1988 and 2001 and reported in the *New York Times*, 63% of life sentences are handed out for murder, 18% are for other violent crimes, and 16% for drug-related crimes.

However, lifers make up a surprisingly high percentage of the prison population. A *New York Times* survey revealed that about 132,000 prisoners, or about 1 in 10, are serving life sentences. Forty states made their statistics available for the survey, and 39 of those states had seen the number of lifers increase over the last ten years. In fact, more than two-thirds of the states had the number of lifers increase by 50% or more.

Not all of these lifers will necessarily stay in prison until they die. Many have a chance for parole. But there seems to be an increase in sentences of "life without parole." Sentences of life without parole increased from being 20% of life sentences in 1993 to being 28% in 2003.

Even if an inmate is eligible for parole, the Board of Pardons must first approve him or her, and then the governor of the state must approve the commutation of his or her sentence. In Pennsylvania between 1971 and 1979, 267 prisoners serving life sentences were recommended for commutation by Board of Pardons. Of these, 251 had their sentences commuted by Pennsylvania's governor. In contrast, between 1995 and 2001, only four lifers were recommended for parole by the board, and not a single one of them was approved by the governor.

This decrease in the number of lifers paroled may have many causes. One is increased opposition to the death penalty, which in some cases has led to decreases in death penalty sentences. The Supreme Court ruled in 2003 that the death penalty couldn't be applied to minors. In order to punish violent juvenile offenders, and unable to sentence them to death, juries often sentence them to life without parole instead.

86. Which of the following sentences best expresses the main idea of the passage?
   a. At some points in our nation's history, lifetime jail sentences were few and far between.
   b. An increasing percentage of the U.S. prison population serves life sentences without parole.
   c. An increasing percentage of the U.S. prison population serves life sentences, and paroles and pardons seem to be decreasing, perhaps partly in response to fewer death sentences.
   d. The change in the number of lifers paroled may have many causes.

87. Which of the following details from the passage supports the idea that the number of life sentences is increasing?
   a. Of life sentences, 63% are handed out for murder.
   b. About 132,000 prisoners, or about 1 in 10, are serving life sentences.
   c. More than two-thirds of states had the number of lifers increase by 50% or more.
   d. In Pennsylvania, between 1995 and 2001, only four lifers were recommended for parole by the board.

88. Which of the following sentences best summarizes the paragraph that begins "Even if an inmate is eligible for parole. . ."?
   a. In Pennsylvania, the number of prisoners recommended for parole and the number of pardons granted by the governor have both decreased significantly since the 1970s.
   b. In Pennsylvania, prisoners are subject to a complicated system whenever they attempt to apply for parole.
   c. In Pennsylvania, between 1971 and 1979, 267 prisoners serving life sentences were recommended for commutation by the Board of Pardons.
   d. Pennsylvania did not parole a single prisoner serving a life sentence between 1995 and 2001.

89. Which of the following details from the passage supports the idea that there is increased opposition to the death penalty?
   a. Life sentences are typically handed out for only the most violent crimes.
   b. Sentences of life without parole increased from being 20% of life sentences in 1993 to being 28% in 2003.
   c. Over the last ten years, 39 of those states had seen the number of lifers increase.
   d. The Supreme Court ruled in 2003 that the death penalty could not be applied to minors.

90. What can be inferred about the commonwealth of Pennsylvania from the details in this passage?
   a. More violent crimes occurred in Pennsylvania in the 1990s than in the 1970s.
   b. Opposition to releasing prisoners with life sentences has increased in Pennsylvania.
   c. The governor of Pennsylvania has problems with the parole board.
   d. The parole board of Pennsylvania is more personally involved with prisoners than they were in the 1970s.

91. Which of the following would make the best concluding sentence for this passage?
   a. Although there may be many causes, the fact that more prisoners than ever are spending their lives in jail with no possibility for release is well documented and will likely be an issue within the justice system for years to come.
   b. However, sentencing a juvenile to life in prison without parole is tantamount to sentencing them to death in prison, an unjustifiable act no matter what the minor's crime.
   c. Studying the incidence of life without parole sentences in states where the death penalty is frequently used may shed light on the causality of these changes.
   d. Why anyone would want to sentence another human being to death is beyond me, and life in prison is obviously a better solution.

92. Which of the following sentences is grammatically correct?
   a. Since being released from prison, Joanna has demonstrated excellent behavior.
   b. Since being releasing from prison, Joanna has demonstrated excellent behavior.
   c. Since being released from prison, Joanna has demonstrate excellent behavior.
   d. Since releasing from prison, Joanna demonstrating excellent behavior.

93. Which sentence do you feel is the most clearly written?
   a. Although graffiti and window breaking are not as serious crimes as robbery, they can lead to it.
   b. Although graffiti and window breaking are less serious crimes than robbery, these minor crimes can lead to bigger ones.
   c. Although graffiti and window breaking is less serious than robbery, it can lead to them.
   d. Graffiti and window breaking aren't too bad as robbery, these minor crimes can lead to bigger ones.

94. Which of the following sentences is punctuated correctly?
   a. Not all repeat criminals commit crimes similar to their original offense, some are jailed for breaking parole, while others may move on to more serious crimes.
   b. Not all repeat criminals commit crimes similar to their original offense; some are jailed for breaking parole; while others may move on to more serious crimes.
   c. Not all repeat criminals commit crimes similar to their original offense; some are jailed for breaking parole, while others may move on to more serious crimes.
   d. Not all repeat criminals commit crimes similar to their original offense; some are jailed for breaking parole. While others may move on to more serious crimes.

95. Which of the following sentences is grammatically correct?
   a. Officer Patterson checked in with his parolees regularly, and he took careful notes.
   b. Officer Patterson checking in with his parolees regularly, and he took careful notes.
   c. Officer Patterson checked in with his parolees regularly, and he taked careful notes.
   d. Officer Patterson check in with his parolees regularly, and he take careful notes.

96. Which sentence do you feel is the most clearly written?
   a. Although Sarah's client's criminal record made her nervous, her training had taught her to focus on it for the best results.
   b. Although her client's criminal record made Sarah nervous, she had learned to focus on her training for the best results.
   c. Although Sarah was made nervous by the criminal record of her client, her training had taught her to focus on it for the best results.
   d. Although the criminal record of Sarah's client made her nervous, her training had taught her to pay attention to it for the best results.

97. Which of the following sentences is punctuated correctly?
   a. Will you please return to my office, which is right around the corner?
   b. Will you please return to my office which is right around the corner?
   c. Will you please return to my office, which is right around the corner.
   d. Will you please return to my office which is right around the corner.

98. Which of the following sentences is grammatically correct?
   a. I should of remembered to speak to Officer Morales.
   b. I should of remembered to spoken to Officer Morales.
   c. I should have remember to speak to Officer Morales.
   d. I should have remembered to speak to Officer Morales.

99. Which sentence do you feel is the most clearly written?
   a. Why this law is like it is, is something I don't know.
   b. I don't know the reason this law works this way.
   c. The reasons for the implications of this law are something I don't claim to understand.
   d. What the law is doing or the reasons for it or why is something I don't know.

100. Which of the following sentences is punctuated correctly?
   a. Brooklyns' parole officers face unique challenges, but the officer's record of meeting these challenges is good.
   b. Brooklyns' parole officers face unique challenges, but the officers' record of meeting these challenges is good.
   c. Brooklyn's parole officers face unique challenges, but the officers' record of meeting these challenges is good.
   d. Brooklyn's parole officers face unique challenges, but the officer's record of meeting these challenges is good.

► Answers

1. a. The primary goal of the treatment agent is to understand and change the behavior of the offender. Although it may overlap with some of the other roles (being a service broker and an advocate), the primary goal is to help the offender learn behavior that is more law abiding and productive. Choice **b** is incorrect; it describes the primary goal of the broker. Choice **c** is incorrect; it describes the primary goal of the advocate. Choice **d** is incorrect; it describes the primary goal of the law enforcer.

2. b. Most probation and parole officers cite the lack of training and skills necessary to do treatment and therapy with clients. Choices **a**, **c**, and **d** are incorrect. There is no research to indicate that these are reasons that probation and parole officers fail to do more treatment with clients.

3. c. The probationer has been in compliance with conditions and followed all of the rules as ordered by the court. Dropping the curfew can be a reward for compliance and encouragement for him to continue his law-abiding and productive behavior. Choice **a** is incorrect because conditions can be and often are amended during the probationer's term to deal with changing circumstances. Choice **b** is incorrect. Technical violations or new arrests will likely result in an amended probation order or revocation. Choice **d** is incorrect. To make the curfew earlier punishes the probationer.

4. b. A new arrest, especially for a violent felony such as robbery, is likely to result in revocation of the probationer's probation privilege. Choices **a** and **c** are incorrect. Although these are technical violations or violations of administrative rules, they are not likely to result in revocation unless they're reoccurring violations of several rules over a period

of time. Choice **d** is incorrect because requesting to travel outside the jurisdiction is not a violation of rules. However, traveling out of the jurisdiction without permission is a violation of rules.

5. d. Neither the probation department nor its employees can be sued in this case because the probationer got the job without the assistance of the probation department. If the officer had made the job referral and secured the job but failed to warn the employer of his past criminal history, the department could be sued. Choice **a** is incorrect; the probation officer did not secure the employment or assist him in securing employment. Choice **b** is incorrect. Probation and parole officers can be sued. Choice **c** is also incorrect. The officer could not be held liable for failure to supervise.

6. a. Restitution is the payment to the victim of a crime for the reimbursement of expenses caused by the offense. This could include medical bills and damage or loss of property. Restitution is paid in addition to fines, court costs, or fees. Choice **b** is incorrect. Retribution is a "purpose of punishment." The offender pays his or her debt to society by being punished for the offense. Choice **c** is incorrect. The probation department charges probation fees for supervision. Choice **d** is incorrect. A court can levy a fine as a part of the statutory penalty for the offense.

7. a. As a means of punishment, retribution requires that the offender pay his or her debt to society for the harm caused by the offense. Choice **b** is incorrect. This means of punishment argues that locking up or incapacitating the offender protects society from the potential criminal activities. Choice **c** is incorrect. The goal of rehabilitation is to change the offender's behavior so that he or she becomes a law-abiding, productive citizen. Choice **d** is incorrect. The deterrence goal of punishment aims to make the punishment so painful and unpleasant that the offender will no longer get involved in criminal behavior and the general population will not commit crimes because of the fear of punishment.

8. d. The number of dependents an offender has is not a major variable in the assessment for his or her parole release. Choices **a**, **b**, and **c** are incorrect. Most important for the consideration of parole release are institutional conduct, time served, and prior criminal record.

9. b. The parolee has an interest to be protected; therefore, under the Constitution, he is entitled to certain protections. The Supreme Court ruled in the case of *Morrissey vs. Brewer* that parolees are entitled to certain due process protections, which include a hearing and representation by counsel. Choice **a** is incorrect. Even though parole is a privilege, the parolee stands to lose conditional freedom. Therefore, the parolee is entitled to protections and procedural safeguards. Choice **c** is incorrect. He was entitled to both a hearing and an attorney. Choice **d** is incorrect. Even though parole is administrative, there are rights at stake and the parolee's rights must be protected. In an appeal to the Supreme Court in the case of *Morrissey vs. Brewer*, the court found cause to intervene to insure that parolees were not deprived of due process rights.

10. b. Probationers are required to maintain contact with the probation department and keep supervising officers informed of address changes. When probationers fail to maintain contact for a specified period of time, usually defined by court policy or statute, they are classified as absconders in violation of probation conditions. Choice **a** is incorrect. Probation revocation is primarily based on technical violations and new arrests. However, absconding can also be a reason for revocation, and when located and arrested, absconders are usually revoked and the prison sentence imposed. Choices **c** and **d** are incorrect. This is not a term used to identify probationers who are in need of special treatment or who are being considered for early termination. A person is considered for early termination only if there is exemplary conduct.

11. c. The PSI indicates the offense was committed after several hours of drinking, and the offender has had issues with alcohol in the past. The judge concludes alcohol is a problem and orders the probationer to address the problem through mandatory attendance at Alcoholics Anonymous meetings. Choices **a**, **b**, and **d** are incorrect. Although these are conditions that the judge may impose, they would not be directly related to the drinking problems of these two young men.

12. c. *Street time* is the time that the probationer or parolee spends in the community under supervision. Choices **a**, **b**, and **d** are incorrect. None of these is an appropriate definition for *street time* as used in probation and parole.

13. d. Many probation and parole departments are being forced to do more with less. They are required to provide more services to larger caseloads, while resources to fund these services are being cut severely. Volunteers can assist in providing many of these services. Many volunteers are intelligent, educated individuals. Student interns make good volunteers. Choice **a** is incorrect. Many volunteers are people who are involved in professions or students pursuing degrees in higher education. Choice **b** is incorrect. Probation and parole officers have plenty of work to do. Officers often supervise large caseloads, perform tasks for the court, and write reports. Choice **c** is incorrect. Sometimes employees fear that volunteers are there to take their jobs, but this is definitely not the case and is not consistent with the goal of using volunteers to provide assistance and unbudgeted ancillary services.

14. b. Protection of a person's confidentiality is crucial, and especially important as you deal with those under court supervision. Choice **a** is incorrect. You could face being reprimanded, or even being dismissed for providing information regarding an offender supervised by your office. Violating a client's right to privacy to satisfy someone's curiosity is never acceptable. Choices **c** and **d** are incorrect. Of course, these actions are a bit drastic. You must at all times portray a professional image, especially in dealing with the public. Your image, as well as the image of the department, is important.

15. c. It is not unusual for a person to request permission to travel for legitimate reasons. The court will usually grant the request unless the probationer has had major problems in complying with conditions of supervision. Choice **a** is incorrect. There is no reason to deny the request unless there have been supervision problems. Choice **b** is incorrect. Probationers should never be encouraged to lie. Choice **d** is incorrect. There is no need to violate the probationer's privacy in this case. It is inappropriate for the officer to do so.

16. a. There is a risk of flight. Parolees have little to lose if they are facing a return to prison for completion of an old sentence or serving time for a new charge. Choice **b** is incorrect. Morally, this may be important to some, but legally, it has no effect on decisions made by criminal justice officials. Choice **c** is incorrect. Criminal justice officials should not use detention prior to trial for that purpose. Choice **d** is incorrect. The parole board is an administrative board but does not operate in complete autonomy.

17. d. This is potentially damaging information. Inmates are required to refrain from making contact with the victim. It is a serious matter if this inmate is contacting the victim with threats. The senior officer and the warden must be informed of this behavior. Choice **a** is incorrect. Doing nothing, especially in this case, is not an option. Contacting the victim is a serious matter even if threats are not made. If the inmate is released and harms the victim, and the parole officer knew it and did nothing about it, there could be cause for liability. Choice **b** is incorrect. You must follow procedure in handling these charges. Choice **c** is incorrect. It is not the responsibility of the counselor to assess and make decisions about allegations. It should be reported to senior level administrators, who will then determine how to proceed.

18. c. Probation is an alternative to incarceration; the imposition of the prison sentence is delayed. The probationer must abide by court-ordered conditions. Failure to do so may result in the revocation of conditional freedom and imposing the original sentence. Choice **a** is incorrect. Parole is granted after a person has served at least one-third of the prison sentence. He or she is eligible for release by the parole board into the community for supervision by parole authorities. Choice **b** is incorrect. Commutation is an act of executive clemency. It gives the inmate some benefit, such as the modification of the sentence. Choice **d** is incorrect. A pardon is an action by the governor to exempt a convicted person from the penalties of an offense or crime.

19. b. First-time offenders are likely to receive probation, especially when they have committed a less serious offense such as a property offense. The criminal justice system tends to be more lenient on property offenders. Choice **a** is incorrect. Violent offenders are less likely to be granted probation, and being a repeat violent offender reduces those chances even more. Choice **c** is incorrect. Chronic offenders who have prior incarcerations are less likely to receive probation. The risk of recidivism is high. Choice **d** is incorrect. An individual who is already on parole is likely to go to prison if there is another offense.

20. a. Probationers are usually low-income employees who can't afford to pay an additional fee for supervision. A fee program requires very specific guidelines to set the parameters of how much offenders will pay. This is usually based on the amount of income and expenses an offender has, and must have provisions for indigents. Probation officers should never collect fees, only monitor the payment of fees. The exchange of currency between the probation officer and the probationer gives an appearance of impropriety and can set the stage disputes or illegal activity. Choices **b**, **c**, and **d** all represent arguments in support of fee collection practices. All of these arguments have been used to support fee collection.

21. d. Most probation and parole officer jobs require a degree in the social or behavioral sciences. Most agencies seek persons with training in sociology, criminology/criminal justice, and psychology. Candidates should have an understanding of human behavior and the workings of society as well as an understanding of the workings of the criminal justice system and its agencies. Choices **a**, **b**, and **c** are incorrect. Probation and parole officers should not be judgmental, hostile, intimidating, easily intimidated, and immature. Because of the type of clients, the officer must be self-confident, mature, and always professional.

22. c. Given the number of responsibilities and limited time to do all of these jobs, a probation or parole officer must learn time management and organization techniques. In most agencies, officers are being called upon to do more with less. Failure to develop management techniques will result in officer stress and burnout. Choices **a** and **d** are incorrect. Although these are valuable qualities for probation officers to have, these are not the most important qualities for the scenario described. Choice **b** is incorrect. As a newly appointed probation officer, it is not a good idea to attempt to get a lighter caseload.

23. d. Because his case had been adjudicated in juvenile court, it could not be transferred to adult criminal court, where he would be tried again for the same crime. The U.S. Supreme Court in *Breed vs. Jones* ruled that juvenile adjudication for violation of a criminal statute is equivalent to a court trial; therefore, the double jeopardy clause applies. Choices **a**, **b**, and **c** are incorrect. Although these are concerns you would have if juveniles were transferred for trial in adult criminal court, it is not the major concern in this case. The major concern is the violation of the double jeopardy clause of the Fifth Amendment.

24. b. The case should be sent back to the court psychiatrist to report the strange behavior of the office visits, especially because there were concerns about competency from the beginning. Choice **a** is incorrect. There has been no violation of probation conditions to justify a request for probation revocation. Choice **c** is incorrect. This is a bad attitude for a professional to have, and there is nothing to be accomplished by taking this action. Choice **d** is incorrect. This is inappropriate professional conduct. There has been no crime committed or ethical violation, nor is there proof of judicial misconduct.

25. c. The temptation to engage in criminal behavior has not been identified as a cause of officer stress and burnout. Choices **a**, **b**, and **d** are incorrect. All of these factors have been identified as causes of officer stress and burnout.

26. **d.** As a broker, you have a responsibility to refer clients to those community resources that can assist them with their problems. Because she fears for her safety, it is appropriate to refer Annie to an agency that can help her and grant her safety. Choices **a** and **b** are incorrect. Doing nothing or ignoring clients who seek your help is never an option. Dismissing the claims of abuse as insignificant or figments of an alcoholic imagination is unprofessional. It is the responsibility of the supervising officer to assist as much as possible. Choice **c** is incorrect. There is no basis for referral to court for violation of probation conditions.

27. **a.** Probation departments are concerned about the image of probation as "too lenient." Many agencies have combined a service model with a control model, to create an approach in which there is still emphasis on assisting with problems and employment issues, but there is also concern with the enforcement of the rules and the control of the behavior. Random drug tests, unannounced visits, and closer contact with police departments are important in probation practice. Choices **b**, **c**, and **d** are incorrect. These all indicate a lessening of control by the probation department. These will result in less public support.

28. **c.** As an officer who has been on the job for a number of years, you should warn the new officer of the dangers involved in developing this kind of relationship with offenders. Most probation agencies have policies that prohibit fraternization with offenders. Probation officers are employed by the courts to supervise the offenders and enforce the rules of the court. Developing this kind of relationship is likely to diminish the probationer's respect for the officer, weaken his authority and ability to do the job effectively, and possibly lead to disciplinary action. Such activities should be stopped immediately. Choice **a** is incorrect. As a new and inexperienced officer, he should get this kind of advice from an older, more experienced officer. Choice **b** is incorrect. If talking to the officer does not work and the fraternizing with probationers after hours continues, it may be a good idea to discuss this issue with the probation supervisor. However, talking to the officer is the first action that should be taken. Choice **d** is incorrect. As an employee of a public agency, it does matter what an officer does after work hours. Carrying that badge identifies you as an employee of the court, charged with upholding and enforcing the rules of the court 24 hours a day, seven days a week.

29. **b.** You should report the information about the inmate's proposed employment. Institutional service will include it as a part of the inmate's parole plan, to be presented to the parole board for review. Choice **a** is incorrect. You have been asked to verify employment. You should report if he has been promised a job at the facility as well as provide some information about the place of employment. Choice **c** is incorrect. It is not only unprofessional but also criminal. Choice **d** is incorrect. You should not contact the parole board. That action is inappropriate.

30. **c.** The best course of action is to seek advice from your supervisor and the legal counsel for the department. There are public safety concerns, but there are also liability issues to be considered. Stringent federal and state laws exist regarding the disclosure of medical information. Agencies have policies and procedures regarding the dissemination of information regarding persons who are HIV positive. Choice **a** is incorrect because it violates the rules of confidentiality. Choice **b** is

also incorrect. The probationer has not violated the conditions of his probation. He may be at risk of infecting someone even in prison. Choice **d** is also incorrect. Doing nothing is not an option. This attitude is not professional or appropriate.

31. b. Choices **a**, **c**, and **d** are incorrect because you are dismissing Diane's efforts to do better in life. By assisting in developing a plan and allowing her to take the lead, you can determine if she is serious and willing to set and work toward goals.

32. c. A main responsibility of an officer is to direct clients to community resources to assist them with a problem. Choice **a** is incorrect because at this time Diane needs help, not punishment. She reported her behavior to you because she wants help. Agencies generally have policies regarding court notification and procedures to determine the course of action for substance abuse. Notifying the judge is appropriate, but recommending revocation may not be. Treatment protocol may include provisions for probationers who relapse, other than revocation. Choice **b** is incorrect. She has told you that she feels depressed. As the officer, you should not make her feel worse about her behavior. Choice **d** is incorrect because an officer should provide guidance and should never encourage a probationer to commit a crime to get arrested and hopefully revoked. This behavior is unethical.

33. d. This is the correct answer because counselors at the domestic violence program are familiar with such threats and understand the concerns about safety that a spouse may have. There is a history of domestic violence, and the counselors can advise her on her best plan of action. Choices **a** and **b** are incorrect because you are dismissing her fears for her safety. Because there is some history of past abuse, her fears should not be taken lightly.

Choice **c** is incorrect because calls to family members will do little to address her concerns. There is no reason to arrest the family members. The family can advise, but ultimately Diane's husband makes his decisions.

34. b. He demonstrates an irresponsible and immature attitude in every aspect of his life. His employment and his marital and military history are indicative of this type of behavior. At age 23, he is receiving public assistance without having any apparent disability that would prevent employment. Choices **a**, **c**, and **d** are incorrect. He had a close relationship with his father, and he has not been unfairly labeled. He could have finished school or taken the initiative to get a trade. He had an opportunity to make his life better and pick up a skill in the military. He failed to do any of those things.

35. d. As a juvenile, he had five arrests and convictions for property offenses. As an adult, he has felony convictions for burglary, auto theft, and receiving stolen property. He has one misdemeanor conviction for theft. Choice **a** is incorrect. He has only one misdemeanor conviction for simple assault. Choices **b** and **c** are also incorrect. There are no drug-related offenses or victimless crimes in his criminal history.

36. c. Johnny's father was a strong disciplinarian who maintained order in the house. After the father died, order broke down because the mother was not a strong disciplinarian. Family life seemed to deteriorate after the death of Johnny's father. Choice **a** is incorrect. The home was not dysfunctional from the beginning; the father maintained strong discipline. Choices **b** and **d** are also incorrect. There was no violence in the home or even involvement in criminal activity until after the father's death.

37. b. Encouraging him to pursue a trade but allow him to take the initiative in starting the process is the best response. The officer will be able to determine if he will follow through. As in the past, he may not pursue a trade, but the officer should encourage him to develop a plan and stick to the plan. Choice **a** is incorrect. It is unprofessional for an officer to laugh at a client who shares plans for bettering his life. Choices **c** and **d** are also incorrect. It is unlikely that the judge would revoke his probation on this technical violation. Threats are not helpful, especially when a probationer has begun to make some effort to learn a trade and secure stable employment. Also, an officer should never encourage any violation of probation conditions, even if it is a technical violation. Failure to maintain employment is a violation of probation conditions.

38. b. Choice **b** is correct. Currently she is not violent nor a risk to public safety; therefore, prison is not an appropriate sanction. The case study reflects characteristics of a person who has multiple needs that can be best dealt with in the community. Supportive interventions will assist in developing behavior that will lead to responsible actions and connectivity to the community. Choices **a**, **c**, and **d** are incorrect. Her history does not support prison incarceration. However, her behavior could indicate the need for an evaluation to determine the appropriateness for inpatient mental health or alcohol treatment.

39. a. Even though Carolyn's husband is on probation, he is still supportive of her doing the right thing. She is close to her siblings. Having a support system is an important factor in rehabilitation. Choice **b** is incorrect. Having children can influence a person's behavior. Studies have shown that married people with children do better under supervision because they have a stake in conformity. It gives them a reason to stay out of trouble. Not having children is not an advantage to influence

rehabilitation. Choice **c** is also incorrect. Being unemployed and having no skills is a disadvantage. Choice **d** is incorrect. There is no mention of her race.

40. a. The probation officer should always encourage the probationer, especially when he or she is attempting to do better with his or her life. The officer should never do the work but instead encourage, help, and direct the probationer to resources that can help. Choices **b**, **c**, and **d** are incorrect. These responses seem to demonstrate unwillingness by the officer to help or encourage the probationer. Being at home alone each day is probably one of the reasons that she drinks.

41. b. Carolyn needs counseling and should be referred to a counselor who can help her with depression. The judge can amend the probation order to require her to receive counseling. Continued depression can only lead to more physical and emotional problems. Choices **a** and **d** are incorrect. Doing nothing is never an option. Using probation revocation is a way to avoid taking action to help. Neither of these responses shows a willingness to help by the officer. Choice **c** is incorrect. Officers are not trained to do the type of counseling that Carolyn needs.

42. a. He admits that he is addicted. His drug addiction costs approximately $400 to $500 each day. He has no job and little employment history. He gets his drugs by committing crimes to get the money to buy them. His crimes are "drug related." An appropriate community-based intervention would be inpatient drug treatment. Choice **b** is incorrect. There is no evidence in the case history to indicate violent tendencies. His crimes have been property crimes to secure money to buy more drugs. In some cases, a history of repeated property crimes would warrant consideration of incarceration. Choice **c** is incorrect. The role of the officer is not to encourage violations as a solution to employment problems, but to help the offender to find ways to stay out of prison and be productive. Choice **d** is incorrect because, even though the marriage is unstable, Billy's wife may be willing to stay with him to help him to get better. There is no evidence of abuse.

43. c. There is no indication of violent behavior. All his offenses are related to getting money for drugs. Choices **a**, **b**, and **d** are incorrect. These are all major problems that can be the causes of criminal offenses.

44. d. Billy has no job or job skills. He admits drug addiction and does not believe that his drug addiction can or will get better. An appropriate response for this behavior is to recommend intensive drug treatment. Choices **a**, **b**, and **c** are incorrect. Given the negatives in his life plus his negative attitude, his chances of success are not excellent, good, or even fair. Because of the drug addiction, he is not able to understand the things that he will lose by going to prison.

45. a. His delinquent behavior does not seem to be deterred by punishment, and he has not responded to rehabilitative efforts to help him. He has been sentenced to probation and committed to a juvenile correctional facility. Choices **b**, **c**, and **d** are incorrect. He is not aggressive; his offenses are largely property offenses and public order crimes (i.e., liquor violations). There have been a number of attempts to help this young man through the care and concern of those in juvenile court. Finally, his delinquent behavior started prior to his incarceration.

46. b. There is evidence to show that, when juveniles are placed in adult prisons, they are more likely to be beaten, raped, and assaulted. Choices **a** and **d** are incorrect because they argue in favor of incarceration in an adult facility. Choice **c** is incorrect. Evidence does not support a difference in the maintenance costs for juveniles and adults in an adult prison.

47. c. His behavior has not been deterred by the punishment or the treatment efforts in juvenile court. Choices **a**, **b**, and **d** are incorrect. These responses seem to demonstrate an attempt to explain his behavior and keep him under the jurisdiction of juvenile court. Arguing that he does not understand the seriousness of his behavior or that his behavior is not serious enough to warrant severe punishment is an attempt to rationalize his behavior.

48. c. The probation officer should always encourage the probationer, especially when it involves the probationer attempting to do better with his or her life. The officer should never do the work, but encourage, help, and direct the probationer to resources that can help. Career counseling can help to see what he needs to do to improve his chances of getting suitable employment. Choices **a**, **b**, and **d** are incorrect. These responses seem to demonstrate an unwillingness by the officer to help or encourage the probationer. The officer should not do the probationer's work, but seek to encourage him in trying to do better.

49. b. Officers should not act too quickly with these kinds of reports, especially if they are coming from other probationers. It is important to talk with the probationer to let him know that to continue to dance at these bars is in violation of probation conditions. If the behavior continues, he could lose conditional freedom. Choice **a** is incorrect because it is unwise to file a violation report to revoke probation on hearsay. This is a technical violation that is unlikely to result in revocation. It is better to talk with the probationer to remind him of the agreement that was made between him and the court. Choices **c** and **d**

are incorrect. It is an unacceptable practice to involve other probationers in case management activities involving probationers. Given the resource workload of many police departments, it is unlikely that police would engage in undercover surveillance to catch someone dancing in a bar.

50. b. It is always a good idea to address all potential problems during the initial visit. They were important enough to be included in the presentence investigation report, thus they should be addressed at the first visit. The initial probation supervision plan must address needs and deficiencies, i.e., counseling for alcohol abuse and anger management. Choices **a** and **d** are incorrect. You should never wait to address or ignore completely a potential problem. If it was important enough to include in the PSI, the supervising officer should address it during the initial meeting. This is a major reason that officers receive a file folder containing the case information before the initial visit.

51. d. Her chances of success under parole supervision after release are poor. She has not secured employment, and she refuses to live with her mother, so living arrangements are unsettled. It is likely that she has a drug problem but refuses to admit it or seek treatment. There have been questions raised about her possible criminal activity while in prison. Finally, in prison, she has maintained contact with friends who are suspected drug dealers. All of these predict failure if she is released into the community on parole. Choice **a** is incorrect. She may have friends who are supportive of her but may encourage criminal activity. Associating with these "supportive" friends may not be conducive to Joyce staying out of trouble. Choice **b** is incorrect. She has made satisfactory adjustment in prison because she no longer fights other inmates

and she has kept a job in the prison laundry. However, the adjustments she has made during the 18 months of incarceration will not predict success given her initial problems. Choice **c** is incorrect. She has a drug problem but refuses to admit or seek treatment.

52. a. Her initial adjustment was poor, but she soon settled in to prison life. There are still concerns about her possible release on parole, but her adjustment in prison has been satisfactory. Choices **b**, **c**, and **d** are incorrect. There is no evidence to indicate that she has learned how to play the "con" game with prison personnel. Neither is there evidence from prison staff that she negatively influences or manipulates other inmates.

53. c. As her institutional parole officer, you are responsible for helping her prepare for life outside of the prison system. Acquiring a skill is an important step in that preparation. If she has shown a desire to gain a skill, she should be encouraged. Choices **a** and **c** are incorrect for the aforementioned reasons. She should be prepared for life outside prison. Generally, inmates return to prison within two years of being released, and a major factor is unemployment. Choice **d** is incorrect. She has not violated prison rules. If so, there is a procedure to be followed within the prison structure.

54. d. This is hearsay information. Inmates know she is eligible for parole and may attempt to sabotage her chances. The best action to take is to talk with Joyce. Choice **a** is incorrect. It would be inappropriate to report hearsay to the parole board without verifying it first. Choice **b** is incorrect. Using other inmates as prison snitches is not a good practice. Choice **c** is also incorrect. You should make Joyce aware that you know there is talk of criminal activity. She should also know that you are watching her actions. She should also be reminded of what is at stake for her.

55. a. Living with her mother will provide stable living arrangements until she is able to find and afford her own living quarters. Choices **b** and **c** are incorrect. Her living arrangements should be suitable for staying out of trouble and obeying the conditions of parole. "Living with suspected criminals or just anywhere" may give her shelter but present her with opportunities to commit crime. Choice **d** is also incorrect because she will not have the resources or the ability to find an apartment before she leaves prison.

56. b. Working for police in this capacity would require her to be in the company of people who are criminal, which would not be conducive to her staying out of trouble. It also violates her condition of parole to avoid associating with criminals. It also places her in harm's way if drug dealers identified her as an informant. Choices **a**, **c**, and **d** are incorrect. These are all conditions of parole.

57. a. John's violent behavior started at age 14 when he was arrested for cutting a fellow student with a razor. He has had three misdemeanor arrests for assaults and was convicted on one of those charges. He is on felony probation for serious assault. Choices **b**, **c**, and **d** are incorrect. He has had only one arrest and conviction for burglary and no arrests for victimless crimes. The majority of his crimes have been for violent offenses.

58. b. Because of John's attitude at this point, he will not be receptive to communication and any attempt to discuss his lateness will be met with hostility. Therefore, the best action to take is to review the court-ordered conditions. You must remind him of the importance of obeying the conditions, which include showing up for appointments on time. Choices **a** and **d** are incorrect. Despite

his attitude, you must remain professional. Often, the probationer will express an attitude of resistance that he could not display in the presence of the judge. As the officer, you must always be in control, but you must not become combatant or hostile. Choice **c** is incorrect. Although John has made a bad impression on the officer, and the officer realizes that this will be a tough probationer, John has not violated the conditions of probation. Revocation of probation must be based on violation of probation rules, usually a new arrest violation.

59. d. John has many needs and issues, including aggressive tendencies, persistent unemployment, lack of job skills, possible drinking problem, marital problems, immaturity, literacy issues, etc. It would be a good idea to prioritize these needs to address those that are most serious and important for complying with probation conditions (i.e., finding employment). Choices **a**, **b**, and **c** are incorrect. Doing nothing and hoping for a new crime is never an option. This case seems hopeless, and if things don't change, he will be back in court for probation violations. The officer does not have the option of changing the supervision level of a probationer. That action can only be taken through an amended probation order from the judge and for a good reason. If the person has made sufficient progress, you can request that the supervision level be changed from maximum to medium. If an offender commits a new crime but is restored to probation supervision, you may request that his or her supervision level be changed from medium to maximum.

60. b. Because he seems to be excited about this opportunity, advise him to enroll in the literacy program and help him to get the information and make the necessary contacts. Having a job and possibly learning a skill can make a difference in his life and his behavior. Choices **a**, **c**, and **d** are incorrect. These responses show little concern for an individual who is at least trying to change and improve his life. Six months earlier, you would have thought that he would be incarcerated by now. John will still have to take the initiative to go through with the class, while he receives some guidance and support from you as the officer.

61. b. The author of this passage brings up several sides of the issue of requiring DNA samples from criminals, and states in the introductory and concluding paragraphs that the issue is still in dispute. Choice **a** contains incorrect information and is, therefore, not the best statement of the main idea. The passage mentions California but states that the requirement for all convicted criminals to submit DNA samples was overturned. The number $8 million was mentioned only in connection to the New Jersey legislation. Additionally, this sentence does not mention the main idea of the passage, which is the debate over requiring DNA samples. Choices **c** and **d** are both opinions expressed by people mentioned in the passage, but they do not state the main idea of the passage itself. A judge stated that parolees do not have the same rights to privacy, as in choice **c**, but this is not the position of the author of the passage. The passage mentions the high cost of the DNA databanks as a possible problem but does not state the opinion that the costs are too high to make them effective.

62. c. This detail, although it relates to the DNA databank, is the only one that does not address the debate about DNA databanks. The size of the databank is not part of the debate about whether or not it is a good idea. Choice **a** is incorrect. This detail supports the main idea that DNA databanks are controver-

sial, by showing what one state has done to support them. Choice **b** is incorrect. This detail supports the main idea that DNA databanks are controversial by showing that the San Francisco court ruled against them. Choice **d** is incorrect. This detail also shows that the DNA databanks are controversial by referring to the dissent that existed even within a single court. This is not the correct answer, because it does support the main idea.

63. a. This sentence includes the facts about the issue at stake, the federal law, and the response of New Jersey and San Francisco. It does not make any judgments or draw conclusions from facts but correctly summarizes the most important ones. Choice **b** is incorrect. This sentence summarizes the main idea of the passage but does not include the facts within the passage that lead to the main idea. This is not a good summary of the facts themselves. Choice **c** is incorrect because it is an inaccurate description of the facts in the passage. San Francisco, not New Jersey, ruled the federal government's DNA sample mandate unconstitutional; New Jersey upheld it, and even expanded on it. This statement is false and, therefore, not a good summary. Choice **d** is incorrect. This is an accurate description of one fact in the passage, but it does not include the other major facts. It does not summarize the facts of the passage.

64. c. The focus of the passage has been on the debate over the legitimacy of DNA databanks, and this sentence best ends the passage by stating that the debate is not yet concluded. Choice **c** is the only sentence that effectively ends the passage by wrapping up its main ideas. Choice **a** adds another detail that somewhat supports the author's point of view, but it does not effectively end the passage. A new detail implies that there is more to say on the topic and does not create a sense of closure. Choice **b** is incorrect. This detail refers to an earlier paragraph, and it brings up a new detail that may need further comment. This is not the best concluding sentence, because it does not sum up the passage and effectively end it. Choice **d** is incorrect. This sentence does not fit the author's tone in the rest of the passage. The sentence expresses an opinion that the author has not expressed in the passage, and the use of the word *obviously* implies an opinionated tone the rest of the passage did not have. If the author has not already stated an opinion about the DNA databank debate in the passage, the concluding sentence is not the best place to do so.

65. d. The author states at the beginning of the passage that the debate over DNA databanks is complex and at the end of the passage states that the issue will continue to be worked out. She does seem to believe the issue is important, but does not take a side within the passage. Choice **a** is incorrect. Although the author states that this is the view of some within the courts, she does not state it as her own opinion, and the tone of the passage does not suggest that this represents her point of view. Choice **b** is incorrect. Again, although the author states that this is the view of some within the courts, she does not state it as her own opinion, and the tone of the passage does not suggest that this choice represents her point of view. Choice **c** is incorrect. Although the author mentions that only time will tell how the issue will be resolved, she does not imply that it is unimportant or that people will stop caring about the issue of DNA databanks. The tone of the passage implies that she believes this is an important issue.

66. b. This sentence describes the central issue of the passage and the events the passage details in a concise way. Choice **a** is incorrect. This

sentence describes the first major detail of the passage, but it does not describe the main idea of the passage. Choice **c** is incorrect. This sentence describes a detail near the end of the passage, but does not express the main idea of the passage. Choice **d** is incorrect. This sentence states an opinion about the commission described in the passage, but it does not summarize the main idea as it is written.

67. a. This detail addresses one issue that was unclear regarding the commission, and supports the larger idea that there were unanswered questions about the LCRC. Choice **b** is incorrect. This detail refers to the contradictory feelings that some had about the commission, but it does not demonstrate the unanswered questions about the commission itself. Choice **c** is incorrect. This detail shows a question that was answered about the commission, so it does not support the larger idea that there were unanswered questions. Choice **d** is incorrect. This is a detail about the commission's activities that is not unclear, so it does not support the idea that there were unanswered questions.

68. c. This sentence describes each of the major objections to the commission that are mentioned or alluded to in the passage, summarizing them concisely and accurately. Choice **a** is incorrect. This fact does not appear in the passage, so this sentence is not a good summary of the objections described in the passage. Choice **b** is incorrect. This sentence contains a fact that appears in the passage, but the probation required by the commission was not one of the major objections to its existence. This sentence is not a good summary of the objections described in the passage. Choice **d** is incorrect. This allegation may have been suspected about the commission, but it does not appear in the passage, and it does not include all of the objections to the commission that are described. This is not an effective summary.

69. c. This sentence refers back to the beginning of the passage, mentions the events that have occurred, and makes a cautious prediction for the future. It draws the passage to a close by summarizing and drawing conclusions about the passage in a definitive way. This is the best concluding sentence. Choice **a** is incorrect. This sentence brings up a whole new aspect of the commission. It seems to lead to a different line of inquiry and does not summarize the passage as it exists or brings it to a close, but instead ends it on a cliffhanger. This is not the best concluding sentence for this kind of passage. Choice **b** is incorrect. This sentence may have been effective earlier in the passage, but it does not summarize or draw conclusions about the passage or bring it to a satisfactory close. This is a detail sentence and not an effective concluding sentence. Choice **c** is incorrect. This detail adds new information to the passage, but it does not summarize the passage and draw broad conclusions to bring the passage to a close. This sentence may be placed earlier in the passage, but it is not an effective concluding sentence.

70. b. The tone of the passage and its emphasis on unanswered questions about the commission imply that the author suspects that some problems exist, but he does not advocate any particular opinion or action. The author presents the facts of the case on both sides without explicitly voicing his opinion, although his suspicion is clear. Choice **a** is incorrect. Nowhere in the passage does the author state or imply that the commission should be abolished, although he does imply that there are some problems with the way it is run. This sentence is too extreme to describe the author's point of view accurately.

Choice **c** is incorrect. Although the author mentions that some people do believe that the commission is a good public service, he does not express that opinion himself, and his emphasis on unanswered questions implies that he suspects that some of the suspicion of the commission may be just. Choice **d** is incorrect. Nothing in the passage states or implies that the author feels that Senator Velella is to blame for the actions or existence of the commission. The focus of the passage is on the commission, and it is inaccurate to state that the author's point of view is that Velella is the guilty party.

71. a. This detail describes the situation in 2004, not when the passage was written. It does not support the idea that problems still exist for parolees attempting to vote even now, long after the election. Choice **b** is incorrect. This detail does support the idea that problems still exist for parolees attempting to vote by showing that officials still prevent them from voting. Choice **c** is incorrect. This detail does support the idea that problems still exist for parolees attempting to vote by demonstrating that ignorance of their rights to vote still exists. Choice **d** is incorrect. This detail does support the idea that problems still exist for parolees attempting to vote by alluding to well-verified data that suggests problems exist.

72. d. This sentence from the final paragraph expresses the main idea and summarizes the significance of all the facts presented in the passage. All of the details in the passage support this statement. Choice **a** is incorrect. This sentence summarizes the first part of the passage but expresses only part of the main idea. The idea that parolee disenfranchisement is significant is part of the main idea, but this sentence does not include the latter half of the passage about ongoing problems and the potential solutions. Choice **b** is incorrect. Although the passage mentions the southern states, no conclusions about the region are mentioned. This sentence does not describe the main focus of the passage on the problem of parolee disenfranchisement and what can be done. Choice **c** is incorrect. This sentence describes a detail that supports the main idea, but it does not describe the main idea of the passage.

73. c. This detail shows that election officials may not have all the information they need about parolee voting rights, so they need more education about those rights. This is the only detail that supports the larger idea. Choice **a** is incorrect. The total percentage of those who are denied voting rights is not a relevant fact to ensure parolees know their rights. This detail does not support the need for education about parolee voting rights. Choice **b** is incorrect. This detail refers to prison inmates, not parolees. It does not support the need for education about parolee voting rights. Choice **d** is incorrect. This fact about the justice system in the southern states is followed by a dubious conclusion and is not related to education about parolee voting rights.

74. b. The author thinks that parolees should not be denied the right to vote, which shows that she thinks they should be granted greater rights than they have in some cases. Her attitude toward ex-convicts is a protective one, because she believes they are being abused and denied what is rightfully theirs. This choice best describes the author's feelings in the passage. Choice **a** is incorrect. The author does not make any statements about monitoring ex-convicts in the passage, nor does she suggest mistrust with her tone. Her mistrust is toward those who refuse to allow ex-convicts to vote, not toward the ex-convicts themselves. Choice **c** is incorrect. The author is clearly interested in ex-convicts, but her tone does not suggest an interest on the level

of fascination, and she does not mention studying ex-convicts. She seems more interested in how the voting system treats ex-convicts than in the ex-convicts themselves. Choice **d** is incorrect. Although the author's tone can sometimes sound angry, her anger does not seem to be directed at ex-convicts, but rather at the problems preventing them from voting. Her insistence that they be granted their right to vote does not suggest that she thinks they should be further punished, rather the opposite.

75. b. This sentence brings the passage back to the assertion made at the beginning and lays out the reasons and consequences for the actions advocated in the last paragraph, while striking a decisive closing note. This is the best sentence for the conclusion. Choice **a** is incorrect. This detail may make sense earlier in the passage, but it is not a good concluding sentence because it does not summarize or draw conclusions about the main ideas of the passage. Choice **c** is incorrect. This sentence strikes a decisive closing note, but it introduces an idea that is absent from the rest of the passage: that disenfranchisement of parolees is an abuse of power by the government. The tone of this sentence does not fit the rest of the passage and undermines the carefully worded argument. This is not the best concluding sentence. Choice **d** is incorrect. Although this sentence does strike a note of finality or closing, it is in an entirely different tone from the rest of the passage. The language is much more casual than the preceding sentences, and the considerations are not the lofty ideological ones that have defined most of the passage. This is not the best conclusion to summarize, wrap up, and encapsulate this passage.

76. c. This sentence summarizes the statistics about juvenile offenders and links them to Community Prep. Both the problems of juvenile offenders and the creation of Community Prep are part of the main idea of this passage, and this is the only sentence that effectively states both aspects of the main idea. Choice **a** is incorrect. This is a detail that appears in the passage, but it is not the main idea. This sentence does not mention Community Prep, which is the focus of the passage, and it does not include references to the many other statistics and problems regarding juvenile offenders. This sentence is not broad enough to be an effective statement of the main idea. Choice **b** is incorrect. This sentence mentions the existence of Community Prep, which is the focus of the passage, but it does not describe the reasons for its creation, which take up most of the passage. The statistics and descriptions of the problems facing juvenile offenders are part of the main idea, along with the existence of Community Prep. This sentence is not complete enough to be an effective statement of the main idea. Choice **d** is incorrect. This is a misstatement of a detail in the passage, because the idea that staying in school can prevent repeat offenses does not come directly from a study but from the head of Community Prep. This idea is an important part of the passage, but it is not broad enough to be the main idea of the passage.

77. b. This detail about the students at Community Prep suggests that going to a special high school may not be helping these students to stay in school. This is the only detail that does not support the idea that Community Prep is needed to help high school–aged parolees. Choice **a** is incorrect. This statistic shows that repeat offenses by juvenile parolees are a problem, which suggests that a measure such as Community Prep is needed. This detail does support the idea that Community Prep is needed to help high school–aged parolees.

Choice **c** is incorrect. This detail shows why many juvenile offenders cannot return to regular high schools and supports the idea that Community Prep is needed to help high school–aged parolees. Choice **d** is incorrect. This statistic, taken before the existence of Community Prep, shows how difficult it is for juvenile parolees to complete their education and supports the idea that Community Prep is needed to help high school–aged parolees.

78. a. This detail shows that more parolee students are graduating as a result of their involvement in Community Prep, and supports the idea that having a separate high school is helping them. Choice **b** is incorrect. This detail may affect the overall status of juvenile parolees in the school system, but it does not relate directly to Community Prep. Adding this detail would not support the idea that having a separate high school is helping high school parolees. Choice **c** is incorrect. This detail shows why it is difficult for many juvenile parolees to complete school, but it does not relate directly to Community Prep. Adding this detail would not support the idea that having a separate high school is actually helping juvenile parolees. Choice **d** is incorrect. This detail does not relate directly to Community Prep and actually suggests that juvenile parolees are not very important because they make up a very small percentage of the high school–aged population. This detail does not support the idea that having a separate high school is helping juvenile parolees because it is not related to the separate high school at all.

79. b. The author of this passage includes statistics and others' opinions about the challenges facing juvenile parolees, and his cautiously enthusiastic description of Community Prep suggests that he thinks these students are troubled and in need of help. He does not describe parolees in negative language, but focuses on the possibilities for their rehabilitation. It is logical to conclude that he considers them in need of help. Choice **a** is incorrect. Although the author does state that some high school administrators may not wish to have juvenile offenders in their schools because of the possibility that they may cause problems, he does not express such an opinion himself. His focus in the passage is on efforts to help juvenile offenders to finish school and stay out of jail, not on protecting other students from them. It does not seem logical to conclude that he considers juvenile offenders a danger to other students. Choice **c** is incorrect. Much of the passage focuses on the grim odds for juvenile offenders staying in school and out of prison, but the author's focus on Community Prep suggests that he does not think they are beyond help. The concluding paragraph suggests that there is some progress being made in helping juvenile parolees. It does not seem logical to conclude that the author believes they are beyond help. Choice **d** is incorrect. The author does not mention the guilt or innocence of any particular juvenile parolee, nor make generalizations about his or her guilt or innocence. He does not even suggest that traditional high schools are unjustly accusing juvenile parolees of causing trouble. It does not seem logical to conclude that the author thinks juvenile parolees are unjustly accused.

80. d. This sentence makes reference to the problems in juvenile rehabilitation described by the statistics in the first half of the passage and mentions the aims and achievements of Community Prep in a tone that successfully brings the passage to an end. This sentence does not introduce any new details but mentions the main idea or focus of the passage while drawing a conclusion about what may

lie in the future. Choice **a** is incorrect. This sentence brings in a new detail about a student at Community Prep. This student's story may make a good conclusion to the passage about Community Prep, but introducing the story in the last sentence does not help to bring the passage to a close. This statement does not make reference to the main ideas of the passage and is not the best concluding sentence. Choice **b** is incorrect. This sentence repeats a detail from the passage, but its tone is completely different from the rest of the passage. Although most of the passage is optimistic about Community Prep helping juvenile parolees to escape the statistics about repeat offenders and dropping out of school, this sentence adopts a more cynical tone about their chances. This is not a good concluding sentence because it does not fit the rest of the passage. Choice **c** is incorrect. This sentence introduces a new, unrelated detail into the passage. It does not relate to the content of the passage or bring the passage effectively to a close. Introducing a new detail is not the best way to write a concluding sentence, and the lack of summary or reference to the rest of the passage means that this is not the best concluding sentence.

81. b. This sentence includes each major point of the passage and no additional information. Choice **a** is incorrect. This sentence includes details about Chapman's prison sentence but does not mention why he was jailed or why he has been denied parole, which is the primary focus of the passage. This sentence does not adequately describe the main idea. Choice **c** is incorrect. This sentence describes the position of one of the members of Chapman's parole board, but it does not describe the main idea of the passage itself. Choice **d** is incorrect. This sentence is primarily about John Lennon, while the passage is primarily about Mark David Chapman and the denial of his parole. This sentence does not reflect the main idea of the passage.

82. c. Although John Lennon, the murder victim, does have iconic status, this is not one of the direct reasons the author speculates that Chapman may have been denied parole. Lennon's iconic status may be a reason that Chapman is in physical danger upon release, but it is not directly a reason for the parole board to deny his parole request. Choice **a** is incorrect. This is the reason stated by the parole board as the cause for denial of Chapman's parole request and the subject of the first paragraph of the passage. This is one of the reasons, as speculated by the author, that Chapman was denied parole. Choice **b** is incorrect. Chapman's desire for fame is the subject of paragraph 2 of the passage, and the parole board notes that releasing him would, in effect, make him famous. His desire for fame in committing the crime is one of the reasons the board decided to deny him parole. Choice **d** is incorrect. This is stated in the final paragraph as one of the main reasons Chapman's parole may have been denied. The precautions taken to protect Chapman indicate that he may be in physical danger, and the author speculates that this is one of the reasons he was denied parole.

83. b. This is the only detail that indicates possible physical harm to Chapman if he were released into society. This detail would support the idea that Chapman was denied parole because of concerns about his physical safety. Choice **a** is incorrect. The fact that John Lennon has fans in every country does not necessarily mean that the man convicted of killing him would be in danger upon release. This detail does not directly support the idea that Chapman was denied parole for his own safety. Choice **c** is incorrect. The

record of the parole board does not necessarily have any bearing on its reasons for releasing Chapman. A devotion to humanitarian ideals and service would not imply a concern for Chapman's safety unless there was some indication that he was in danger. This detail does not directly support the idea that Chapman was denied parole for his own safety. Choice **d** is incorrect. Chapman's negative behavior in prison may be another reason to deny him parole, but it has no relation to his physical safety upon release. This detail does not support the idea that he was denied parole to protect his safety.

84. a. This is the only sentence that includes all the important facts of Chapman's case and no unnecessary information. The summary includes main events and dates in order, but leaves out the reasons or extra details or descriptions that would be included in the passage but not in a summary. Choice **b** is incorrect. This sentence contains speculation about Chapman's motives and does not include the dates of events in the case. Because it includes extra details and does not contain all of the relevant facts, this is not the best summary of the events of the case. Choice **c** is incorrect. This sentence contains extra judgments about Chapman's motivations and the nature of his prison term. The redundancy of the sentence means that it is not the best summary of the events of the case. Choice **d** is incorrect. This sentence does not contain any information about Chapman's attempts at parole. Because it does not include all of the relevant facts, this choice is not the best summary of the events of the case.

85. d. This sentence summarizes and puts into context the three main ideas of the passage and brings the passage to a decisive close. This is the only sentence that does both of these things in a tone that fits the rest of the passage, and it is the best sentence to conclude the passage. Choice **a** is incorrect. This sentence brings the passage to a close, but it introduces a new detail about the parole board and uses a judgmental tone, which is not in keeping with the rest of the passage. This sentence does not fit the passage and would not make the best concluding sentence. Choice **b** is incorrect. This sentence is written in an emotional and opinionated tone that is not in keeping with the rest of the passage, and it does not effectively summarize or put into context the details of the passage. This is not the best concluding sentence. Choice **c** is incorrect. This sentence introduces a new detail that relates to a previous paragraph. This detail may make sense earlier in the passage, but it does not bring the passage effectively to a close, and it is not the best concluding sentence.

86. c. This is the only sentence that includes all of the major ideas from the passage and connects them into one cohesive main idea. Choice **a** is incorrect. This is the introductory sentence of the passage, but it does not have much to do with the main idea of the passage. The passage focuses on the current state of life sentences in the United States, not the historical record. Choice **b** is incorrect. This sentence does state one of the main ideas of the passage, but it fails to include several of the other aspects of the passage's discussion of life sentences. The sentence is not complete enough to express the main idea accurately. Choice **d** is incorrect. This sentence is found in the passage, but it does not address all of the main ideas of the passage. This sentence mentions only the reasons for the changes in life sentences, not what those changes are or what the reasons are, and is, therefore, not the best expression of the main idea of the passage.

87. c. This statistic is the only one demonstrating an increase in the number of life sentences. This detail supports the idea that the number of life sentences is increasing. Choice **a** is incorrect. This statistic shows the reason for many life sentences but does not indicate whether the number of these sentences is increasing. Choice **b** is incorrect. This statistic shows the percentage of life sentences in the total prison population but does not indicate whether life sentences are increasing. Choice **d** is incorrect. This statistic is part of a detail that shows that paroles are decreasing but does not indicate whether life sentences are increasing.

88. a. This sentence summarizes the meaning of the statistics mentioned in the paragraph and expresses the main idea: that parole requests and pardons have both decreased. This choice is the only sentence that summarizes the meaning of the paragraph. Choice **b** is incorrect. This sentence summarizes the first sentence of the paragraph but neglects to include a summary of all the statistics which follow and their meanings. Although it does contain some summary, this choice is not the best summary of the paragraph. Choice **c** is incorrect. This choice is a sentence from the paragraph, not a summary of the ideas of the paragraph. This sentence contains only one set of details and is not a summary of the entire paragraph. Choice **d** is incorrect. This sentence summarizes some of the information from the paragraph but does not summarize the meaning of the entire paragraph.

89. d. This is the only detail that applies directly to the death penalty, and because it shows that the death penalty was outlawed in certain cases, it supports the idea that opposition to the death penalty has increased. Choice **a** is incorrect. This detail applies only to life sentences and does not support the idea that opposition to the death penalty has increased. Choice **b** is incorrect. This detail shows an increase in life without parole but does not demonstrate anything about the death penalty. This detail does not support the idea that opposition to the death penalty has increased. Choice **c** is incorrect. This detail shows an increase in the number of life sentences but does not apply directly to the death penalty. This detail does not support the idea that opposition to the death penalty has increased.

90. b. Because the number of prisoners paroled has gone down, it is correct to infer that opposition to releasing prisoners has increased, at least among those who have the power to affect releases. This is the only logical inference from the details in the passage. Choice **a** is incorrect. There is no evidence to suggest that more violent crimes were committed in Pennsylvania. Even if fewer prisoners with life sentences are being released, this does not mean more prisoners are being sentenced to life, nor that more violent crimes are being committed. Choice **c** is incorrect. There is no implication that the decrease in the number of lifers released is related to problems between the governor and the parole board. Both the number of recommendations and the number of sentences commuted have gone down in the statistics quoted, a fact which suggests that the governor and the board are in agreement. Choice **d** is incorrect. Nothing in the passage suggests that the parole board of Pennsylvania has ever been personally involved with prisoners; in fact, the decrease in parole recommendations suggests the opposite. This is not a logical inference.

91. a. This sentence summarizes the main ideas of the passage that precede it, and brings the passage to a decisive close. This is the only choice that performs these two functions

without including extra details or opinions that are not in keeping with the tone of the passage. Choice **b** is incorrect. The word *unjustifiable* indicates a strong opinion, which is not in keeping with the factual tone of the rest of the passage. This sentence also fails to summarize the main points of the passage, which makes it not the best choice for a concluding sentence. Choice **c** is incorrect. This sentence is in keeping with the tone of the passage but introduces a speculation that calls for more information, and does not bring the passage to a close. It also fails to summarize the main points of the passage, and so it is not the best choice for a concluding sentence. Choice **d** is incorrect. This sentence is written in a first-person, emotional, and opinionated tone and does not fit the factual tone of the rest of the passage. It also fails to summarize the main points of the passage, and so it is not the best choice for a concluding sentence.

92. a. This sentence uses the past tense of each verb correctly. Choice **b** is incorrect. The verb phrase *being releasing* is an incorrect use of the past tense of the verb. Choice **c** is incorrect. The verb phrase *has demonstrate* is an incorrect use of the ongoing past tense of the verb. Choice **d** is incorrect. Using the gerund forms of the verbs *release* and *demonstrate* without helping verbs is an incorrect use of the past tense of these verbs in this sentence.

93. b. This sentence uses correct grammar and has a clear antecedent for every pronoun. The meaning of the sentence is clear. Choice **a** is incorrect. The words *they* and *it* are pronouns without clear antecedents, making the sentence unclear about which pronouns refer to *graffiti*, *window breaking*, or *robbery*. In addition, the phrase *are not as serious crimes as robbery* is grammatically incorrect without the word *is* before the word *robbery*. Choice **c**

is incorrect. The pronouns *it* and *them* are very unclear in this sentence, and the singular verb *is* refers incorrectly to the two nouns *graffiti* and *window breaking*. The meaning of the sentence is unclear. Choice **d** is incorrect. The phrase *aren't too bad as robbery* is grammatically incorrect; it should read *aren't as bad as robbery*. In addition, the comma makes this a run-on sentence, and the cause and effect of the sentence are unclear.

94. c. This sentence correctly uses a semicolon to connect two independent clauses, and a comma to connect two dependent clauses within the same sentence. Choice **a** is incorrect. This sentence incorrectly uses a comma to connect two independent clauses, making it a run-on sentence. Choice **b** is incorrect. This sentence correctly uses a semicolon to connect two independent clauses, but it incorrectly uses a semicolon to connect dependent clauses within the same sentence. Choice **d** is incorrect. This sentence incorrectly separates two dependent clauses with a period, so that the final clause is an incomplete sentence.

95. a. This sentence correctly uses the simple past tense of the verbs *check* and *take*. Choice **b** is incorrect. Using the gerund form of the verb *check* is incorrect when talking about an action that happened in the past. Choice **c** is incorrect. The correct past tense form of the verb *take* is *took*, not *taked*. Choice **d** is incorrect. The verbs *check* and *take* in this sentence are in the present tense plural form, which is incorrect because they are intended to describe actions taken by one person in the past.

96. b. This sentence makes clear who has the criminal record (Sarah's client) and what Sarah is focusing on (her training). This is the only sentence that is entirely clear on these two issues. Choice **a** is incorrect. The pronoun *it* in this sentence has no clear antecedent and

could refer to the training or the criminal record. Choice **c** is incorrect. The first half of this sentence is unnecessarily complex, and the pronoun *it* has no clear antecedent. Choice **d** is incorrect. This sentence rearranges the first half of the sentence effectively, but leaves the pronoun *it* with no clear antecedent.

97. a. This sentence separates two dependent clauses with a comma, and ends the interrogative sentence correctly with a question mark. Choice **b** is incorrect. This interrogative sentence ends correctly with a question mark but does not separate two dependent clauses with a comma. Choice **c** is incorrect. This sentence correctly separates two dependent clauses with a comma but does not end the interrogative sentence with a question mark. Choice **d** is incorrect. This sentence does not separate the two dependent clauses with a comma and also fails to end the interrogative sentence with a question mark.

98. d. *Have remembered* is the correct conjugation of the verbs *have* and *remember* to show an action that occurred (or, in this case, should have occurred) in the past. The word *of* is incorrect in this verb phrase, and the verb *remember* must be in the past tense. Choices **a** and **b** are incorrect. *Should of remembered* is an incorrect version of the verb phrase *should have remembered*. In addition, in choice **b**, the verb *speak* should be in its root form *to speak*, not conjugated as *to spoken*. Choice **c** is incorrect. This sentence correctly uses the word *have*, not *of*, but the verb *remember* is not conjugated correctly.

99. b. This sentence clearly states the writer's lack of knowledge about the reason for the law without repetition, unnecessary complexity, or incorrect grammar. Choice **a** is incorrect. This sentence's repetition of the word *is* is incorrect for written English and makes this a run-on sentence. It also introduces repetition, which makes the sentence less clear. Choice **c** is incorrect. This sentence is unnecessarily complex and obscures the meaning of the writer's statement. Choice **d** is incorrect. This sentence breaks down the statement too much and uses the singular verb *is* incorrectly to refer to all the parts. It is confusing to read and grammatically incorrect.

100. c. This sentence correctly uses the apostrophe before the *s* in *Brooklyn's*, because Brooklyn is a singular noun, a place where the parole officers work. The apostrophe is also correctly placed after the *s* in *officers'* to show a possessive form of the plural noun *officers*. Choice **a** is incorrect. The apostrophe is incorrectly placed after the *s* in *Brooklyns'*, even though Brooklyn is a singular noun. The apostrophe is also incorrectly placed before the *s* in *officer's*, because multiple officers need to be described with the possessive noun. Choice **b** is incorrect. The apostrophe is correctly placed after the *s* in the plural noun *officers'*, but incorrectly placed after the *s* in the singular noun *Brooklyns'*. Choice **d** is incorrect. The apostrophe is correctly placed before the *s* in the singular noun *Brooklyn's*, but incorrectly placed before the *s* in the plural noun *officer's*.

14 ▶ Practice Test 7

This is the seventh and final practice test in the book based on the most commonly tested areas on the probation officer and parole officer exams. The practice test consists of 100 multiple-choice questions in the following areas: job responsibilities, case studies, writing skills, and reading comprehension. The number of questions and the time limit of the actual probation officer or parole officer exam can vary from region to region. Allow yourself three hours to complete this practice test.

A version of this practice test is available through the LearningExpress online link, if you prefer to take it on the computer.

Practice Test 7

1.	ⓐ	ⓑ	ⓒ	ⓓ	36.	ⓐ	ⓑ	ⓒ	ⓓ	71.	ⓐ	ⓑ	ⓒ	ⓓ
2.	ⓐ	ⓑ	ⓒ	ⓓ	37.	ⓐ	ⓑ	ⓒ	ⓓ	72.	ⓐ	ⓑ	ⓒ	ⓓ
3.	ⓐ	ⓑ	ⓒ	ⓓ	38.	ⓐ	ⓑ	ⓒ	ⓓ	73.	ⓐ	ⓑ	ⓒ	ⓓ
4.	ⓐ	ⓑ	ⓒ	ⓓ	39.	ⓐ	ⓑ	ⓒ	ⓓ	74.	ⓐ	ⓑ	ⓒ	ⓓ
5.	ⓐ	ⓑ	ⓒ	ⓓ	40.	ⓐ	ⓑ	ⓒ	ⓓ	75.	ⓐ	ⓑ	ⓒ	ⓓ
6.	ⓐ	ⓑ	ⓒ	ⓓ	41.	ⓐ	ⓑ	ⓒ	ⓓ	76.	ⓐ	ⓑ	ⓒ	ⓓ
7.	ⓐ	ⓑ	ⓒ	ⓓ	42.	ⓐ	ⓑ	ⓒ	ⓓ	77.	ⓐ	ⓑ	ⓒ	ⓓ
8.	ⓐ	ⓑ	ⓒ	ⓓ	43.	ⓐ	ⓑ	ⓒ	ⓓ	78.	ⓐ	ⓑ	ⓒ	ⓓ
9.	ⓐ	ⓑ	ⓒ	ⓓ	44.	ⓐ	ⓑ	ⓒ	ⓓ	79.	ⓐ	ⓑ	ⓒ	ⓓ
10.	ⓐ	ⓑ	ⓒ	ⓓ	45.	ⓐ	ⓑ	ⓒ	ⓓ	80.	ⓐ	ⓑ	ⓒ	ⓓ
11.	ⓐ	ⓑ	ⓒ	ⓓ	46.	ⓐ	ⓑ	ⓒ	ⓓ	81.	ⓐ	ⓑ	ⓒ	ⓓ
12.	ⓐ	ⓑ	ⓒ	ⓓ	47.	ⓐ	ⓑ	ⓒ	ⓓ	82.	ⓐ	ⓑ	ⓒ	ⓓ
13.	ⓐ	ⓑ	ⓒ	ⓓ	48.	ⓐ	ⓑ	ⓒ	ⓓ	83.	ⓐ	ⓑ	ⓒ	ⓓ
14.	ⓐ	ⓑ	ⓒ	ⓓ	49.	ⓐ	ⓑ	ⓒ	ⓓ	84.	ⓐ	ⓑ	ⓒ	ⓓ
15.	ⓐ	ⓑ	ⓒ	ⓓ	50.	ⓐ	ⓑ	ⓒ	ⓓ	85.	ⓐ	ⓑ	ⓒ	ⓓ
16.	ⓐ	ⓑ	ⓒ	ⓓ	51.	ⓐ	ⓑ	ⓒ	ⓓ	86.	ⓐ	ⓑ	ⓒ	ⓓ
17.	ⓐ	ⓑ	ⓒ	ⓓ	52.	ⓐ	ⓑ	ⓒ	ⓓ	87.	ⓐ	ⓑ	ⓒ	ⓓ
18.	ⓐ	ⓑ	ⓒ	ⓓ	53.	ⓐ	ⓑ	ⓒ	ⓓ	88.	ⓐ	ⓑ	ⓒ	ⓓ
19.	ⓐ	ⓑ	ⓒ	ⓓ	54.	ⓐ	ⓑ	ⓒ	ⓓ	89.	ⓐ	ⓑ	ⓒ	ⓓ
20.	ⓐ	ⓑ	ⓒ	ⓓ	55.	ⓐ	ⓑ	ⓒ	ⓓ	80.	ⓐ	ⓑ	ⓒ	ⓓ
21.	ⓐ	ⓑ	ⓒ	ⓓ	56.	ⓐ	ⓑ	ⓒ	ⓓ	91.	ⓐ	ⓑ	ⓒ	ⓓ
22.	ⓐ	ⓑ	ⓒ	ⓓ	57.	ⓐ	ⓑ	ⓒ	ⓓ	92.	ⓐ	ⓑ	ⓒ	ⓓ
23.	ⓐ	ⓑ	ⓒ	ⓓ	58.	ⓐ	ⓑ	ⓒ	ⓓ	93.	ⓐ	ⓑ	ⓒ	ⓓ
24.	ⓐ	ⓑ	ⓒ	ⓓ	59.	ⓐ	ⓑ	ⓒ	ⓓ	94.	ⓐ	ⓑ	ⓒ	ⓓ
25.	ⓐ	ⓑ	ⓒ	ⓓ	60.	ⓐ	ⓑ	ⓒ	ⓓ	95.	ⓐ	ⓑ	ⓒ	ⓓ
26.	ⓐ	ⓑ	ⓒ	ⓓ	61.	ⓐ	ⓑ	ⓒ	ⓓ	96.	ⓐ	ⓑ	ⓒ	ⓓ
27.	ⓐ	ⓑ	ⓒ	ⓓ	62.	ⓐ	ⓑ	ⓒ	ⓓ	97.	ⓐ	ⓑ	ⓒ	ⓓ
28.	ⓐ	ⓑ	ⓒ	ⓓ	63.	ⓐ	ⓑ	ⓒ	ⓓ	98.	ⓐ	ⓑ	ⓒ	ⓓ
29.	ⓐ	ⓑ	ⓒ	ⓓ	64.	ⓐ	ⓑ	ⓒ	ⓓ	99.	ⓐ	ⓑ	ⓒ	ⓓ
30.	ⓐ	ⓑ	ⓒ	ⓓ	65.	ⓐ	ⓑ	ⓒ	ⓓ	100.	ⓐ	ⓑ	ⓒ	ⓓ
31.	ⓐ	ⓑ	ⓒ	ⓓ	66.	ⓐ	ⓑ	ⓒ	ⓓ					
32.	ⓐ	ⓑ	ⓒ	ⓓ	67.	ⓐ	ⓑ	ⓒ	ⓓ					
33.	ⓐ	ⓑ	ⓒ	ⓓ	68.	ⓐ	ⓑ	ⓒ	ⓓ					
34.	ⓐ	ⓑ	ⓒ	ⓓ	69.	ⓐ	ⓑ	ⓒ	ⓓ					
35.	ⓐ	ⓑ	ⓒ	ⓓ	70.	ⓐ	ⓑ	ⓒ	ⓓ					

▶ Practice Test 7

1. Which of the following probationers would most likely be successful under probation supervision?
   a. a drug-addicted probationer with a history of repeat property offenses
   b. a probationer with a family and steady employment
   c. an unemployed probationer who lives at home with his parents
   d. a probationer who has frequent problems with drug abuse

2. Robert is on probation for felony DUI. As a condition of probation, he is prohibited from having a driver's license or operating a motor vehicle. You discover that he has been driving to and from work each day. When you confront him with the issue, he informs you that he has been driving to and from work because his place of employment is ten miles from his home. As his probation officer, you should
   a. suggest that he find new employment within walking distance.
   b. suggest that he quit his job.
   c. advise him to use public transportation or have someone drive him to work.
   d. charge him with a new crime.

3. A probationer with a history of alcohol abuse informs you that she is drinking again and wants you to help her before the problem gets worse. You respond by saying that
   a. she should violate her conditions of probation so you can recommend revocation and jail time.
   b. she should try to resolve the problem herself.
   c. you will refer her to a community resource that can help her with her problem.

   d. you will prepare a violation report for the courts to have her probation revoked.

4. Which of the following is NOT likely to be a condition of parole?
   a. You will report to your parole officer as instructed.
   b. You will associate with known felons and ex-cons to assist you in your transition back into the community.
   c. You will maintain suitable employment.
   d. You will notify the parole officer of any change of address or employment.

5. The wife of a parolee calls to inform you that, since her husband's release from prison, he has been drinking and staying out late at night. Which of the following is the correct response?
   a. You request that the parolee to come to your office to talk about the accusations made by his wife.
   b. You issue a warrant for his arrest.
   c. You submit a parole revocation report to the parole board.
   d. You do nothing.

6. You have been asked to verify the employer and home address provided by an inmate in his pre-parole plan. While conducting the investigation, you discover that the inmate has not been truthful. His family members are opposed to him living at home, and the prospective employer indicated that he did not offer the offender employment. What should you do?
   a. You should write a report to the sentencing court recommending that additional time be added to the parolee's sentence.
   b. You should report the facts of your investigation to the institutional parole officer.
   c. You should inform the parole board of the discrepancies and recommend denial of parole.

d. You should ignore the discrepancies because the inmate has spent enough time in prison and deserves release.

7. The parole board is responsible for determining the eligibility of an inmate for and the conditions of release. The wife of a parolee calls to request that the court amend her husband's parole order to include mandatory church attendance. She states that not attending church is probably the reason for her husband's problems. Which of the following is the best response to her request?

a. You advise her that you will request the court to amend her husband's parole order to include the condition of mandatory church attendance.

b. You talk to the parolee and convince him that he must attend church as a condition of parole or he will face probation revocation.

c. You inform the woman that the judge cannot require a parolee to attend church as a condition of parole because it would be in violation of his First Amendment rights.

d. You do nothing, even though you told her that you would take care of the matter.

8. When a probationer makes the initial visit with the probation officer, which of the following is likely to be true?

a. The officer files a delinquency report to have probation revoked, because the probationer is 30 minutes late.

b. The officer explains the rules and conditions of probation.

c. The officer modifies the conditions that are considered unnecessary for this probationer.

d. The probationer informs the officer that there are conditions that he will not follow because they interfere with his lifestyle.

9. Another probation officer in your office has been acting in an unprofessional manner with a probationer. The officer despises the probationer and thinks the offender should have been sentenced to prison. Even after you have had several conversations with the probation officer about this issue, you observe the probation officer continually harassing the probationer for frivolous things and making jokes about him to other staff members. What would be the next step to take?

a. You agree that the officer should revoke probation and send the offender to prison.

b. You advise the probationer to tough it out and ignore the officer.

c. You inform the officer that you are going to bring this matter to the attention of your supervisor.

d. You tell the probationer that his officer's behavior is the way things are done around here.

10. In the last few years, there have been several attempts to abolish parole. Which of the following is a good reason NOT to abolish parole?

a. The absence of parole supervision leaves the parolee without assistance in establishing positive relationships to assist his or her transition back into the community.

b. Parole takes much of the burden off the court system.

c. Parole provides important post-custody supervision for the released inmate.

d. There have been no good reasons to keep parole.

11. The presentence investigation report of a probationer who has been assigned to your caseload indicates he has had three arrests for aggressive behavior and an incident of domestic violence. The conditions of probation do not address the apparent aggressive tendencies. What do you do?

a. You do nothing; your responsibility is to enforce the conditions of probation as ordered by the courts.

b. You plan to discuss this information with the probationer on his first visit and decide what to do from that point.

c. You refer the case back to the court and reprimand the judge for failure to address this behavior.

d. You use this information to show that the probationer poses a danger and request revocation of probation.

12. An inmate has been denied parole for the third time in six years. He tells his institutional parole officer that he is going to appeal the decision because he was denied access to an attorney at all three parole hearings. Which of the following is the best response to his statement?

a. You inform him that he was not entitled to an attorney because he had no present private interest to be protected because he was already incarcerated.

b. You encourage the appeal because inmates have a right to counsel at parole release hearings.

c. You approach parole board members about the unfair treatment of the inmate.

d. You assist the inmate in finding an attorney to represent him for the appeal.

13. A female inmate with previous charges of prostitution indicates in her parole release plan that she has secured a job at a restaurant called The Lion's Den. Verification of this employment reveals that the "restaurant" is really a topless bar that is under investigation for prostitution. What do you tell her?

a. You tell her that you know about her prospective employer, but you won't inform the parole board.

b. You tell her this job is not suitable employment, but you will work with her to find a more appropriate place to work.

c. You tell her that you know about her place of employment but will keep quiet for a little "hush money."

d. You do not talk to the inmate but go directly to the parole board with the information.

14. You discover that a volunteer whose assignment is to assist probationers with remedial reading has been harassing probationers about attending church and bible studies and has been using volunteer time to teach bible lessons. The probationers tell you they are tired of being constantly harassed and reminded that they are "going to hell." What is the appropriate response?

a. You schedule a meeting with the volunteer to determine if there is truth in the allegations and, if so, to discuss the consequences of her actions.

b. You do nothing.

c. You encourage the volunteer to continue but in a more discreet manner.

d. You report your findings to your supervisor.

15. What does mean when an offender's parole is revoked?

  a. The probationer is placed on shock probation.

  b. The court takes away the conditional freedom of a parolee.

  c. The parole board decides to send the parolee back to prison to complete his or her term.

  d. The court sentences the parolee to serve more time in prison.

16. Walt, an 18-year-old man on your caseload, lives with his sister in a neighborhood known for extensive criminal activity. He has been arrested several times, always in this neighborhood, with his best friend. Walt is also known as a major player in the drug business. He could live in a more stable neighborhood with his mother, who has tried repeatedly to get him to move, but he refuses. His mother, fearful that her son will die in this neighborhood, comes to you for help. What is your response?

  a. You tell her that there is nothing you can do because Walt is an adult.

  b. You request that the judge amend the probation order to require Walt to move out of this neighborhood.

  c. You write a probation violation report requesting that the probation be revoked.

  d. You wait until he gets arrested and then recommend revocation and prison time.

17. An employer, who recently hired one of your parolees for a laboring construction job, calls to report that the parolee stole the employer's tools and hasn't come to work since. He demands that action be taken. What is your response?

  a. You call the police to have the parolee arrested.

  b. You notify the judge that you will be filing a motion to request revocation of parole.

  c. You make contact with the parolee to see why he didn't report to work and what he knows about the missing tools.

  d. You tell the employer that it is his responsibility to find his own tools because the parole department is not in the lost-and-found business.

18. When the parole board considers the release of an inmate, which of the following are the most important factors it looks for in the parole plan?

  a. prospective employment, treatment plans, and suitable living arrangements

  b. age of parents, family history, and remorse by the inmate

  c. treatment plans, restitution payments, and suitable living arrangements

  d. prospective employment, hobbies, and age

19. Joyce, a single mother with three children, is on probation for forgery. She has been ordered to pay a fine, court costs, and probation supervision fees. She is presently 12 months behind on all of her fees. You know that she is living with her mother and working two jobs to make ends meet. What is the best action to take?

  a. You prepare a violation report requesting revocation of her probation for a technical violation—failure to pay fees.

  b. You recommend a 30-day jail term to scare her into paying the delinquent fees.

  c. You report the violation to your supervising officer so he will make a decision about the case.

  d. You request an amended probation order to waive fees until she can pay.

20. A student at the local university is working with you as a probation case aide. You discover that she is discussing information contained in a case file with one of her friends in the school cafeteria about another friend who is on probation. What should you do?

a. You should report her actions to your supervisor and the university internship coordinator to determine a course of action.

b. You should do nothing because she is a student and didn't know better.

c. You should have her arrested for violating rules of privacy and confidentiality.

d. You should start to look into her criminal history because she may acquainted with probationers.

21. Probation conditions may be categorized as either standard or special conditions. *Standard conditions* apply to all offenders placed on probation. *Special conditions* are those given to a particular probationer because of a specific need. Which of the following conditions would be a special condition?

a. You will obey all laws and commit no other crime.

b. You maintain suitable employment.

c. You will not leave the jurisdiction without permission.

d. You will attend anger management classes.

22. Which of the following statements is true of the presentence investigation report (PSI)?

a. The defendant and the defense attorney prepare the PSI prior to the beginning of the trial.

b. The PSI is used to determine guilt or innocence.

c. The PSI provides recommendations for sentencing and treatment plans after the offender has been convicted of a crime.

d. The PSI is prepared by the district attorney's office for use during the trial.

23. A probationer on your caseload has been unemployed for the past eight months. Each time you attempt to talk about the subject of unemployment, the probationer starts to talk about general unemployment problems and the "bad economy." Realizing that the conversation has drifted from the original purpose, how can you bring it back on point?

a. You encourage the probationer to identify issues that are within his control and to address these issues as he prepares a job search plan.

b. You prepare a probation violation report, citing failure to maintain employment.

c. You allow the probationer to continue to talk; it is healthy for him to express himself.

d. You request an amended probation order that waives the employment condition.

24. In many jurisdictions, probation and parole officers are considered to be law enforcement officers and are required to complete firearms training and carry weapons. Which of the following arguments would support the practice of officers carrying firearms?

a. Carrying a weapon makes the officer feel more powerful and authoritative.

b. There has been an increase in officer victimization during field visits in the community.

c. Showing a probationer or parolee a firearm helps to coerce the offender into compliance.

d. Carrying a weapon associates the role and authority of a probation or parole officer with those of police officers.

25. You find that an 18-year old on your caseload has repeatedly violated his court-ordered curfew. Despite several warnings, he continues to stay out past his 11:00 P.M. curfew. What should you do?

a. You should talk to the probationer about why he consistently stays out after 11:00 P.M. and determine a reasonable course of action.

b. You should take no action because an 11:00 P.M. curfew for an 18-year-old is unreasonable.

c. You should file a probation violation report recommending weekend jail time.

d. You should file a violation report requesting probation revocation and a prison sentence.

26. If you were making an argument that there are many advantages for probation and parole, which of the following statements would you NOT include in your argument?

a. Probation and parole supervision is less expensive than incarceration.

b. Releasing dangerous offenders into the community increases the risk of harm to the citizens.

c. A standard condition of probation and parole is to require offenders under supervision to be employed.

d. Both provide more meaningful opportunities than prison for the offender to become rehabilitated and productive, which then diminishes the propensity to commit crimes.

27. You receive notice that a probationer who has been ordered to receive drug treatment has been denied access to a nonprofit drug addiction program. The regulations of this program prohibit services to those convicted of a felony offense. As an advocate for the probationer, what do you do?

a. You leave it up to the probationer to find a program that will accept him.

b. You investigate to see if the nonprofit agency will negotiate and change its regulations so offenders can enter the program.

c. You inform the judge that the probationer cannot receive the services in the community and should be revoked and sent to prison to receive services.

d. You encourage the probationer to sue the agencies that denied him services.

28. Daniel was convicted of "indecency with a child." He was sentenced to probation and ordered to register as a sex offender. He was ordered to avoid employment that involved children. Six months into his term, you discover that he has not registered and has taken a job with an agency, *Children First*, which provides services to children of incarcerated parents. Which of the following is the correct response to this situation?

a. You file a request to have probation revoked because Daniel has violated probation conditions.

b. You advise Daniel that, if he quits his job and registers as a sex offender, you will not inform the court of his violations.

c. You allow Daniel to remain on probation and keep his job if he will independently seek mental health counseling.

d. You do nothing because he needs the job to stay compliant with probation conditions.

29. A probationer requests authorization to move to another state where he has family and the promise of a job. He believes that moving would be in his best interest. What should you do?

  a. You should tell him that he cannot move until he has served at least one-third of his probation term.

  b. You should terminate his probation in the convicting state and allow him to move.

  c. You should allow him to move if the receiving state agrees to supervise him.

  d. You should ignore his request.

30. Which of the following would NOT be compatible with the rehabilitation theory of punishment?

  a. placing an offender in a drug treatment program to deal with his or her drug addiction

  b. recommending to the judge that the offender be given counseling for the psychological problems associated with his or her offense

  c. referring an offender to a job-training program to assist in securing employment

  d. recommending that the offender be sent to prison to serve 100% of the sentence to pay his or her debt to society

Directions: Read the following case study and then answer questions 31 through 35.

Robert, an 18-year-old man, is on probation for burglary and possession of crack for resale. Although these are his first offenses as an adult, he has an extensive juvenile criminal history, which includes several property offenses, three possession charges, and two aggravated assaults. He served a 90-day shock probation term and has been under felony probation supervision for the last year.

In a year, he has made only three payments toward his probation costs, which include fine and court costs ($348); restitution ($1,000), and $20 monthly probation fees ($20 monthly). He has worked only two months in the last year. Because he dropped out of school in the ninth grade, obtaining a job is even more difficult. He is still classified as maximum supervision because his reporting has been infrequent.

Recently, there has been some concern about his activities. When you conduct a home visit, you find him intoxicated with other felony probationers. The police inform you that they are watching Robert because they got a tip that he was selling drugs and bragging about "better selling," owed to techniques he learned while in prison for 90 days. One morning at 2:00 A.M., you receive a call from police informing you that Robert was taken to the emergency room, suffering from a drug overdose, but that he disappeared before he could be treated. Robert denies that this incident happened.

Robert lives with his 17-year-old girlfriend and their two-year-old son. She recently confided in you that Robert is abusive and sometimes violent toward her and the child. She has also said that he steals her food stamps to buy drugs. She refuses to press charges and vows to deny everything if you tell anyone else.

Attempts to revoke Robert on technical violations have been met with resistance by the judge, who refuses to consider revocation unless a crime has been committed and charges filed. The PSI says that Robert enjoys building things and that he was a Golden Gloves boxing champion for his district when he was younger.

31. As you review Robert's case, his juvenile and adult criminal history indicates that

  a. Robert's only crime-related problem is repeated property offenses.

  b. Robert is a dangerous violent offender who should be locked up.

  c. as a juvenile, Robert was involved in criminal behavior but has aged out.

  d. Robert has been involved with many drug-related and property offenses over the years.

32. Robert's behavior and lifestyle are in violation of several conditions of his probation. Based on the information provided in the case study, which of the following is NOT one of those violations?

a. failure to maintain suitable employment

b. association with known felons

c. failure to receive counseling as ordered for aggressive and violent tendencies

d. failure to report as ordered

33. Robert was given shock probation of 90 days. What is shock probation?

a. The judge sends the probationer to a mental health facility for treatment, if he or she suspects mental disorders.

b. The judge orders a short prison stay prior to placing the offender on probation.

c. The judge defers prosecution and places the individual on probation; the offender accepts moral responsibility for the offense.

d. The probationer agrees to spend time in a work-release center prior to being placed on probation.

34. What are Robert's chances of success under probation supervision?

a. Excellent; he has carpentry skills that will enable him to become productively employed.

b. Good; he has a family who helps him maintain stability and gives him a stake in traditional values.

c. Fair; although he needs motivation, he is on the road to becoming a productive, law-abiding citizen.

d. Poor; he has no job, no desire to obtain one, is suspected of using and selling drugs, gets drunk with other felons, and steals from his girlfriend to buy drugs.

35. If the police arrest Robert for possession of drugs for resale, what action should you, as his supervising officer, take?

a. You should use the arrest as an opportunity to get Robert into a drug counseling/treatment program.

b. You should request revocation of Robert's probation and recommend time in prison.

c. You should recommend that Robert be restored to probation supervision with orders to pay fees, maintain employment, and support his dependents.

d. You should refuse to file a probation violation report because the judge refuses to revoke Robert's probation and send him to prison.

Directions: Read the following case study and then answer questions 36 through 39.

For the past two years, you have been the institutional parole officer for Debra, a 35-year-old woman who is serving a 20-year sentence for two counts of attempted murder and two counts of aggravated assault. Debra shot her boyfriend during an argument after she accused him of having an affair. She also shot another man who attempted to break up the fight. When police arrived, she told them that she had committed the crime. Later, she expressed her remorse to the victims' families. She has two juvenile arrests for prostitution, and as an adult, Debra has ten arrests and six convictions. Four of the convictions were for assault and battery. She had two convictions for receiving stolen property and forgery. She has also been arrested several times for prostitution and disorderly conduct. She has served seven years of her 20-year sentence. This is her first prison incarceration. She will be eligible for parole next year.

Debra is an only child who grew up very poor. Her father worked at the shipyard in North Carolina and made decent money. Because of his excessive gambling, he did little to take care of his family. Debra's mother died when she was four, and her father remarried and sent Debra to live with her grandmother. By the time Debra was 14, her grandmother had put her out of the house for incorrigible behavior. Debra was homeless, living on the streets, and prostituting to survive at age 14.

At age 17, Debra married a cocaine addict and soon became addicted herself. The marriage deteriorated, and he left her for another woman, who later killed him. Debra then met Harry, and they married. They lived together for two years and, in the beginning, had a good relationship. Debra says Harry started drinking, gambling, and having affairs with other women. She eventually shot him as well.

Debra dropped out of school in the eighth grade. She was a poor student who missed a lot of school. She says she hated school and saw no value in it when you could make money on the streets. Since being incarcerated, she has completed the requirements for a GED and received training and a license in cosmetology. She has had mostly unskilled jobs. Her longest period of employment was when she worked for five years as a housekeeper for a family, before she was incarcerated.

She began drinking heavily at age 13 and began using drugs at age 15. By age 19, she was addicted to crack cocaine. While incarcerated, she has received counseling for her drug use. She says that she has been drug-free since she entered prison.

36. Although Debra has been ordered to have no contact with the victims of her crimes, she confides to you that an ex-boyfriend has been calling and writing her for the past year. She also tells you that he has asked her to come and live with him once she is released from prison. She asks you for your advice. How do you respond?
   a. You report to the prison authorities that she has been contacting the victim of her crime and recommend that she be punished.
   b. You suggest that she should find other living arrangements because this scenario would not be acceptable to the parole board.
   c. You recommend to the parole board that her parole should be denied because she has violated prison rules by contacting the victim.
   d. You say nothing and keep quiet about her contact with her ex-boyfriend and the proposed living arrangements.

37. During a conversation with Debra about her preparation for parole and possible release, she confides that she is afraid of being released. She says she is afraid that she will drift back into her old lifestyle. What recommendation would you make to Debra?
   a. You recommend that Debra commit another crime to lengthen her sentence.
   b. You recommend that Debra approach the parole board and ask if she could max out or serve all of her sentence.
   c. You recommend that Debra request to go to a work-release center or a halfway house before being released.
   d. You recommend that Debra not bother you with this because there are other inmates with more serious concerns.

38. As you read Debra's case file, you notice that she has had drug treatment, as well as academic classes and vocational training, while incarcerated. However, you are concerned that she has never had counseling to focus on her violent tendencies. You recommend that she should receive additional counseling for the next year. How do you justify your recommendation?

   a. You point out that Debra grew up as the victim of her father and grandmother's abuse.

   b. You point out that Debra was abused by her husband and ex-boyfriend.

   c. You point out that additional counseling will likely impress the parole board.

   d. You point out Debra's criminal history, including the offenses for which she is serving time, which shows a pattern of violent behavior.

39. How would you evaluate Debra's chances of success if she were released on parole?

   a. Poor; Debra will not succeed because she has no GED and no marketable skills.

   b. Poor; Debra will fail because she has not accepted responsibility or remorse for her behavior.

   c. Good; Debra will succeed because she has been productive in prison, getting her GED and a cosmetology license.

   d. Poor; Debra does better in prison than in the community, so she should stay in prison.

Directions: Read the following case study and then answer questions 40 through 43.

Sheila is a 19-year-old woman who was convicted and given ten years probation for five counts of possession of a controlled substance. She and her boyfriend sold cocaine, speed, and heroin to an undercover police officer. She denies that she sold anything but says that her boyfriend may have had drugs. He is now serving a ten-year prison term for his conviction. She has no juvenile or adult criminal record.

Sheila grew up with her mother and two younger sisters but never knew her father. Her mother married when Sheila was six years old. She got along well with her stepfather until he became overly protective and harsh with Sheila and her two sisters.

When she turned age 17, Sheila moved in with her boyfriend and lived with him for two years before he was arrested. She was pregnant when she was arrested but had a miscarriage soon after. She was an average student but dropped out of high school in the tenth grade. She plans to get her GED soon. Sheila has no employment history and no desire or plans to work. She wants to be a homemaker with a large family. Presently, she has no visible means of income.

She has used many different kinds of drugs and is now addicted to speed. One of the conditions of her probation is that she spend 60 days in a clinic for drug treatment. She denies having a drug problem and believes that going to the clinic for drug treatment is a waste of time.

In addition to receiving drug treatment, Sheila has been ordered to get her GED, find suitable employment, and move out of the neighborhood where she lived with her boyfriend. Crime rates there are high, and it is known as an area where a person can get any kind of drug that he or she wants. However, Sheila has refused to move and still lives in the same neighborhood.

40. During her initial visit into your office, she again denies being involved in any sale or use of drugs. She further denies any addictions, even though she admits to experimenting with some different drugs. What is likely to be the major obstacle to Sheila's rehabilitation?

   a. She is too young to understand the seriousness of her crime.

   b. She refuses to take responsibility for her actions.

   c. She grew up in a dysfunctional home.

   d. She has a past criminal history.

41. Sheila does not have high school diploma, GED, job skills, or employment history, and lacks the desire to find and maintain employment. Her goal is to be a homemaker with a large family. How can you motivate her to get her GED, find employment, and change her present living arrangements?

a. You can remind her that she is in violation of probation conditions but then encourage her to develop a plan to get her GED as well as a job.

b. You can recognize that you cannot motivate her and request that her probation be revoked.

c. You can do nothing and just wait for her to mess up and then request revocation.

d. You can notify her landlord that she is on probation and request that he evict her from her apartment.

42. Sheila continues to live in her apartment. She pays her bills and periodically purchases new furnishings, despite no visible source of income. You become even more concerned when another probationer tells his officer that Sheila sells drugs and engages in prostitution. You

a. ignore the rumors and conclude that her mother and stepfather are helping her financially.

b. hope that she gets arrested so that she can be revoked and removed from your caseload.

c. submit a violation report to the judge requesting a 30-day shock probation period, based on her refusal to abide by the conditions of probation.

d. ask the police to spy on Sheila and arrest her at the first sign of criminal behavior.

43. A week before she goes to court on the probation violations, Sheila informs you that she has been offered a job at a local restaurant; meanwhile, she says she wants to get her GED and asks you for help. You respond by

a. referring her to the adult literacy program, giving her all of the information, and waiting for her to follow up on the information.

b. dismissing her actions as an attempt to stay out of prison.

c. telling her that she should wait until she gets to prison to get her GED.

d. leaving it up to her to get the information and follow through.

Directions: Read the following case study and then answer questions 44 through 46.

Michael is a 19-year-old man serving a 15-year sentence for burglary, receiving stolen property, and theft. Michael was hooked on cocaine and heroin. He could not afford his addiction nor stop using drugs so he resorted to stealing to keep up with his habit. He is still addicted to drugs but says that he has been drug-free for the last two months. Michael has had six arrests and three convictions as a juvenile. He was on probation for six months but has had no incarcerations. His adult criminal history has consisted largely of property offenses to get money for drugs.

Michael is the oldest of five children, whose father was gone much of the time because he was in the military. The family spent two years overseas. His father was seriously addicted to drugs when he returned from Vietnam. Michael has no contact with his father but has a close relationship with his mother. He has never been married, mainly because of his drug addiction.

He dropped out of school in the eighth grade. He was a poor student and was disruptive and suspended often. He got his GED but has never held a job. Michael enlisted in the navy; however, he was issued a dishonorable discharge after six months of service because of drug use.

44. Reading Michael's case file information, it is apparent that his criminal behavior is the result of
   a. a home from which the father was absent much of the time.
   b. his addiction to drugs.
   c. rebellion because he was released from the navy.
   d. his rebellion against his father for being addicted to drugs.

45. What would be your priority as Michael's institutional counselor in developing his treatment plan?
   a. intense drug therapy
   b. employment counseling
   c. rebuilding the relationship with his family
   d. finding the right prison job

46. After one-and-a-half years in prison, Michael presents you with a program plan he has been thinking about. He would like to get into a vocational training program in prison and participate in a drug support group called Boys Against Drugs (BAD). He also would like to reestablish a relationship with his family, especially his father. You respond by
   a. informing him that you think that he is trying to con the warden and the parole board with his change in behavior.
   b. encouraging him to continue these positive efforts and assure him that you will do whatever you can to assist him.
   c. telling him that you don't believe that he will follow through on his plans.
   d. telling the other counselors and correctional officers to watch him because he must be up to something.

Directions: Read the following case study and then answer questions 47 through 49.

Daniel is a 25-year-old man convicted of robbery and theft. He was given a five-year probation term. He and a friend stole the nightly deposit from the manager of Golden Fried Chicken as she was making a deposit at the bank. He confessed and apologized to the victim. He later stated that he regretted leaving his home that night. His friend admitted that it was not Daniel's idea to rob the young lady. He has no juvenile or adult criminal history, and this is his first offense.

Daniel has three sisters and grew up in a lower middle class neighborhood in a stable family. The family is close and was surprised by Daniel's criminal behavior. He is not married but has a girlfriend he hopes to marry. Daniel dropped out of school in the ninth grade. He was a poor student who was absent from school much of the time. Since he has been on probation, he has worked at a gas station. His employer describes him as a dependable employee who is good at organizing and taking care of equipment and tools. His employer has offered him the position of tool supervisor. Daniel has a heart problem and, therefore, cannot do heavy laboring work.

His family has planned to move to Indiana because his father's job has transferred him to another office. Daniel is totally dependent upon his family for financial and emotional support. He does not want to leave his job or his girlfriend, but he doesn't know if he can make it without his family.

47. Daniel received a five-year probation term for robbery and theft. There are a number of reasons the court decided to grant probation. Which of the following is probably NOT a consideration in granting him probation?
   a. He is a first-time offender.
   b. He accepted responsibility, expressed remorse, and apologized to the victim.
   c. He has a stable family and strong family support.
   d. He was under the influence of drugs at the time of the offense.

48. Since Daniel is serving a felony probation term, his parents want to know if it is possible for Daniel to leave the jurisdiction and move to another state. In reply to their concerns, you tell them that
   a. no, he cannot leave because of a felony conviction in his home state.
   b. yes, he can move but only after he has served a third of his sentence.
   c. yes, he can move to another state if the receiving state agrees to supervise him.
   d. he may move to another state if he serves prison time in the receiving state before being placed on probation.

49. Is there any advantage for Daniel if he chooses to stay where he is instead of traveling with his family?
   a. It allows him to keep his job, have more stability, and become emotionally and financially independent.
   b. It allows the probation department to keep an eye on him because there is a high risk of recidivism.
   c. It makes it easier to revoke him if he violates conditions of probation.
   d. There are no advantages; Daniel cannot make it without his family.

Directions: Read the following case study and then answer questions 50 through 54.

Kenny is a 35-year-old man with both a juvenile and adult criminal record. As a juvenile, he was on probation twice and spent time in a juvenile institution. As an adult, he was incarcerated twice for burglary, receiving stolen property, and possession of cocaine. He admits that his crimes as a juvenile and as an adult were related to his drug habit. He was addicted to cocaine, heroin, and Lortabs, and would do whatever it took to get the drugs he wanted. He confesses that he once stole his mother's money allotted for monthly bills to buy drugs.

During his last incarceration, he decided to apply for participation in a therapeutic community, a move that he admits saved his life. The program offered intense individual and group drug therapy, which helped him to confront his drug use and some of the reasons for that drug use. For the past six years, he has been clean. He is now married, employed, and serving as a counselor for a young men's organization in his community. He is also pursuing a degree in social work at the local university. He hopes to get a master's in social work and work as a juvenile social worker.

A year and a half ago, he was hired by the probation and parole department as a paraprofessional, who serves as an aide to probation and parole officers. Reactions to his hiring have been mixed. Some of the office personnel see it as a way to have someone who comes from the same environment as the offenders and can relate to them in the office. Others who oppose this practice argue that it is likely that Kenny will identify too much with the offenders, which will ultimately cause problems.

50. What is a paraprofessional?
   a. a person who does not have the same status as a full-time probation or parole officer but assists in the supervision process as a paid probation/parole aide
   b. a person who once held the position of probation/parole officer but was demoted
   c. a person hired by the probation/parole department to spy on the activities of probation and parole clients
   d. a person hired by management to replace probation and parole officers who have become ineffective

51. How can Kenny be an asset to the probation and parole officers with whom he works?

   a. He really can do nothing to assist in supervision because he has no training and qualifications.

   b. He can help officers who may be from a different background to understand and help offenders become more comfortable, open, and honest.

   c. He can increase the costs of supervision, which sends a message to the administration that more money is needed.

   d. He can help officers by providing information about the illegal activities of clients.

52. As the department supervisor who hired Kenny, you have discovered that some staff members have refused to work with him or train him in techniques of supervision. How should you approach the situation?

   a. You should call a staff meeting to name openly the staff members in question and point out that Kenny may one day have their jobs.

   b. You should meet with the staff members to discuss their concerns and reassure them that Kenny can't and will not take their jobs.

   c. You should recommend the dismissal of these staff members.

   d. You should fire Kenny to maintain the morale of the department.

53. Kenny has been asked to work with a probationer who was his childhood friend. He had also served time with this young man in state prison when they both were 18 years old. He further admitted that he feels reluctant to work with this former friend. How do you respond?

   a. You suggest that Kenny work with the client and try to get information on any illegal behavior.

   b. You report Kenny's insubordination to the supervisor.

   c. You understand Kenny's dilemma and decide to assign him another probationer.

   d. You tell Kenny that he has to work with him or be fired.

54. A probationer brags to Kenny that he has been involved in some recent unsolved burglaries of local businesses. These businesses have lost quite a bit of money in these burglaries, and the business community has been demanding that these crimes be solved. What should you do with the information Kenny gave you?

   a. You should keep your mouth closed because you have too much going on with your caseload without putting additional stress on yourself.

   b. You should provide the information to local law enforcement authorities so they can begin an investigation.

   c. You should tell Kenny to demand "hush money."

   d. You should contact the businesses to determine if they have reward money and then make a decision about what to do with the information.

Directions: Read the following case study and then answer questions 55 through 60.

John was a smart and successful attorney and an ambitious person. He owns stock in a farm equipment company, a thriving automobile company, and a large motel. Prior to his conviction, he was a prominent member of his community and was considered a model citizen. He had close associations with public officials and was always a friend of law enforcement. He had an annual party for public officials and law enforcement officers. He was convicted of receiving stolen property and disposing this property through a convicted felon, and he was sentenced to probation. While on probation, John had a problem with reporting and allowing the officer to visit him in the field. He did not see himself as a criminal and felt that contact with a probation officer was beneath him.

After being on probation for a year, he was arrested for receiving stolen property. The probation officer recommended continued probation with amended conditions. The judge did not concur with the probation officer's recommendation and revoked John's probation. The judge sentenced him to five years in prison. The judge stated that, by revoking John's probation, he wanted to send a clear message to the public: "If you do the crime over and over again with no regard for the law or legal system, you will pay, regardless of who you are and who you know." John, his family, and friends in the legal community were clearly shocked by the judge's decision.

John served one-and-a-half years of his five-year term and became eligible for parole. When John arrived at the correctional classification center, he was hostile and angry because he was being treated as a common criminal. He argued that he was not a threat but rather a supporter of the community. He maintained that he was not a criminal but a shrewd businessman and that his business practices were no different than those of other people that he knew.

John was finally sent to a correctional center, where he was given a job in the prison library. He has updated the library holdings and has procured two extra computers for inmates to enable them to take their high school equivalency tests. There have been no documented disciplinary problems.

When he first arrived at the prison, John refused to have anything to do with the other inmates, constantly reminding them that they were criminals and he was not. Later, he made friends with some of the inmates. Six months ago, the police discovered that John had been continuing his property business within the prison. This time, it was noted that John now had a flourishing drug trade in and outside the prison, employing prison guards and inmates that he had befriended. This drug and property business resulted in five inmates receiving additional prison time and in three guards being fired. Even though the investigators knew that John is the leader, they needed more proof. Even though there were hints, no one would state that John was the leader. One inmate, who told investigators that he was willing to identify the main leader, suddenly "committed suicide."

Now, John is being considered for parole, and, in your mind, the issue of his drug business is still unresolved. The parole release hearing is soon, and John is demanding that the state provide an attorney to represent him.

55. How would you characterize John?
  a. John is an upstanding citizen who made a mistake and received a harsh prison sentence.
  b. John is a repeat offender who uses his money and associations to manipulate people and the criminal justice process
  c. John is a shrewd businessman who sometimes bends the rule of law to make a profit.
  d. John is an innocent man who is the victim of jealous competitors and vindictive judges and police officers.

56. As you review John's case, what do you see as the major impediment to his rehabilitation?
a. the police who will continue to harass him and accuse him of illegal activities
b. the stigma attached to the criminal label
c. John's refusal to accept responsibility or show remorse for his behavior
d. John's lack of family and community support

57. John has demanded to have an attorney present to represent him at the parole release hearing because it is his due process right. How do you respond?
a. Because he knows people in high places, you make sure that he has counsel.
b. You remind him that inmates are not entitled to counsel at release hearings but can have an advocate.
c. You report directly to the parole board that John is being difficult and should remain in prison.
d. You give him names of attorneys who could file a lawsuit against the prison for violation of his due process rights.

58. John's wife recently informed you that neighbors in the gated community where they have lived for the past 15 years were concerned about John moving back into the community and about the danger that he may pose to residents. You should respond to her concerns by informing her that
a. John is dangerous and could be a threat to the community.
b. John's crimes have been property offenses, and he has shown no indications of being a threat to the community.
c. he is a threat to the community and to their children.
d. the pattern of violence in his criminal history suggests he's a threat.

59. The parole board voted to deny John's parole and given him a new hearing date. Which of the following statements is likely the reason for the board's denial?
a. There is a pattern of violent offenses in John's background.
b. The judge ruled that he should be denied parole.
c. There were concerns about some alleged criminal conduct in prison that needed further investigation.
d. There was a concern about John being a flight risk and leaving the jurisdiction.

60. If John were released on parole, what would be his chances for success?
a. His prospects are excellent, because he has business, family, and friends to support him.
b. His prospects are not good, because he has never viewed his behavior as criminal, and there are allegations that his criminal behavior has not stopped in prison.
c. His prospects are good, because he has the connections to keep him out of the court system.
d. His prospects are very good, because he has been innocent from the beginning.

Directions: Read the following passage and then answer questions 61 through 65.

Many think the function of the parole officer is primarily enforcement. Officers are considered tough, unforgiving, and hard on former criminals, especially juveniles, in order to attempt to keep them out of further trouble.

In New Jersey, however, a program called the Village Initiative aims to take a different approach to parolees and those who supervise them. Under this program, a traditional parole officer is accompanied by a doctor, and sometimes by other health and social services professionals, while visiting the homes of juvenile offenders. The doctor will check up on the health of the parolee and his family and, when necessary, ask questions about their well-being and activity.

Former criminals, many of whom struggle with poverty and gang violence as well as drugs and other dangers, are at great risk of becoming recidivist or repeat offenders. Along with being a means of philanthropy, the Village Initiative aims to reduce recidivism by offering a human side to the parole process. Seeing state officials and officers as resources or as friends can give the parolee the courage to ask questions and to develop self-esteem. The program assists offenders to feel less alone in their struggle to stay out of trouble and demonstrates that the state is trying to help offenders rather than try to catch them doing something wrong.

So far, it seems the theory may be working. County statistics show that recidivism of juveniles who have been part of the Village Initiative has decreased from 37% to 5% over the last five years. Most agree that further evaluation is necessary to determine the effects of the program on recidivism, but initial results are promising.

The name of the initiative comes from the proverb "It takes a village to raise a child."

61. Which sentence best expresses the main idea of this article?
   a. Parole officers are not always the tough enforcers that they seem to be, despite the perceptions by many juvenile offenders.
   b. Recidivism in the county that utilizes the Village Initiative has decreased from 37% to 5%.
   c. The Village Initiative aims to decrease recidivism by having doctors visit parolees.
   d. Juvenile parolees often think that the system is against them, which may prevent them from asking for help when they need it.

62. Which of the following details supports the idea that a visit by a doctor can change juvenile offenders' perceptions?
   a. It can give the impression that the state is trying to help them, rather than trying to catch them doing something wrong.
   b. The name of the initiative comes from the proverb "It takes a village to raise a child."
   c. These former criminals, many of whom struggle with poverty and gang violence as well as drugs and other dangers, are at great risk for recidivism.
   d. Most agree that it will take more time for studies of the project's effects to be determined.

63. Which of the following details could be added to the article to support the idea that recidivism is a problem among juvenile offenders?
   a. Experts say that many at-risk youth at the Village Initiative do not have access to health services.
   b. Some studies show that attending high school is the best way for juvenile offenders to keep out of trouble.
   c. Statistics indicate that a high percentage of young parolees in the Village Initiative will be arrested again.
   d. One research firm's findings suggest that the Village Initiative has an unusually high rate of juvenile crime.

64. What can be inferred about juvenile offenders from the decreased recidivism statistics in the article?
   a. Juvenile offenders are resentful of the presence of the government in their lives.
   b. Juvenile offenders respond well to positive interactions with officials.
   c. Juvenile offenders are unique to the Village Initiative.
   d. Juvenile offenders are the same everywhere.

65. Which of the following sentences would make the best concluding sentence for this article?

a. In the Village Initiative, proverbs don't count for much in a world in which every influence only steers young people back into a life of crime.

b. The Village Initiative is financed through the office of the attorney general, which provides grants for such programs.

c. In the Village Initiative, the juvenile justice system seems to be proving the proverb right by taking an extra interest in the lives of its youngest offenders.

d. In the Village Initiative, Officer James Pruden is one of the doctors who visits the homes of juvenile offenders and provides free health care and advice.

Directions: Read the following passage and then answer questions 66 through 70.

Why would a convicted criminal ask for a death sentence instead of a sentence of life in prison without parole? Given the precedent of a case in Alabama, he may have a good reason for doing so.

In 1988, a jury in Alabama convicted Walter McMillian of capital murder. The jury recommended a sentence of life in prison without parole. However, Judge Robert E. Lee Key, Jr. overrode the jury's verdict and decided to sentence McMillian to death.

There were many who were not about to see McMillian executed without a fight. His case became a cause for anti–death penalty activists. Several activist lawyers took up his case. The prosecutors ultimately admitted they had used perjured testimony in the trial, and the guilty verdict was overturned. Five years after his original sentence, McMillian was released from prison.

In a newspaper interview, one of McMillian's lawyers expressed the significance of the case. "Had there not been that decision to override," he said of the original judge's decision, "[McMillian] would be in prison today."

Now many defendants in Alabama are hoping to replicate McMillian's success. By seeking a death penalty, they are hoping to attract the attention of activists and lawyers who oppose the death penalty. Many believe the death penalty is wrong, and they are willing to invest time and money in helping those on death row.

There are far more activists opposed to the death penalty than there are opponents of life imprisonment. Very little effort nationwide is devoted to fighting the convictions of those who have been sentenced to life. But to many prisoners, dying in prison at the end of a life sentence is just as bad, if not worse, than dying by execution.

Seeking the death penalty is a risky move for convicted criminals. They may not attract the helpful attention they hope for. Even if they do, the efforts of those who would like to help them may not be effective, and their sentence may be ultimately carried out. However, to many, the risk is worth the chance of overturning their sentence entirely.

66. Which sentence best expresses the main idea of this article?

a. Walter McMillian was a convicted murderer who was released because of the misguided efforts of anti–death penalty activists.

b. There are far more opponents of the death penalty than there are opponents of life imprisonment.

c. In 1988, Walter McMillian was convicted of capital murder and sentenced to life in prison without parole, but the judge overrode the sentence and gave him the death penalty.

d. Many convicts in Alabama seek death sentences in hopes of gaining help from anti–death penalty activists, as in the case of Walter McMillian.

67. Which detail from the article directly supports the idea that death penalty cases receive more attention?

a. The prosecutors ultimately admitted they had used perjured testimony in the trial, and the guilty verdict was overturned.

b. There are far more opponents of the death penalty than there are opponents of life imprisonment.

c. Very little effort nationwide is devoted to fighting the convictions of those who have been sentenced to life.

d. However, to many, the risk is worth the chance of overturning their sentence entirely.

68. Which sentence best summarizes the events in McMillian's case?

a. Walter McMillian was a convicted murderer who was released because of the misguided efforts of anti–death penalty activists.

b. Walter McMillian was convicted of murder and sentenced to life in prison without parole, but when the judge overrode the sentence and gave him the death penalty, anti–death penalty activists took his case and ultimately uncovered evidence that overturned the verdict entirely.

c. In 1988, Walter McMillian was convicted of capital murder and sentenced by a jury to life in prison without parole; however, the decision was overturned by the judge, who sentenced McMillian to the death penalty instead, setting a precedent that would prove important to many prisoners in similar situations to McMillian's.

d. Walter McMillian was sentenced to life in prison, but then the sentence was changed to death, and he was eventually released.

69. What can be inferred from the fact that many death row sentences are overturned as a result of anti–death penalty activists' interest?

a. Other sentences that receive less attention may also deserve to be overturned.

b. Death row criminals are usually innocent.

c. Anti–death penalty activists are helping guilty people go free.

d. Juries tend to make more mistakes in death row cases than in other cases.

70. Which of the following is the best concluding sentence for this article?

a. Bryan Stevenson, one of McMillian's lawyers, is the director of the Equal Justice Initiative of Alabama.

b. McMillian's case serves as a poignant reminder of how easily someone can be wrongly accused and convicted, and how important it is for activists to take a stand to defend those facing death.

c. Although convicted violent criminals seek loopholes to avoid facing punishment, the legal system must take steps to avoid letting the efforts of activists help guilty people escape from their just punishment.

d. The philanthropic efforts of anti–death penalty activists such as those who helped McMillian may have created a new group of prisoners willing to risk death in order to avoid a life behind bars.

Directions: Read the following passage and then answer questions 71 through 75.

Child welfare agents, parole officers, and prison wardens are often forced to deal with many of the same challenges. Each position is considered by some to be less glamorous than that of a police detective, attorney, or other more high-profile law enforcement agent, and is often noticed only when something goes wrong. Attention focuses on parole officers when a parolee commits another crime. Criticism is leveled at child welfare agents when a child slips through the system's cracks. Wardens are scrutinized when poor conditions in prisons are reported. Little notice is given to the hard work and successes that make up most of these officers' days.

In Cook County, Illinois, a woman who has faced the challenges of all of these jobs has been chosen to bring all of her experience and skill to bear in a new line of work. Brenda Welch was appointed by a U.S. district judge to be the compliance administrator for the county juvenile temporary detention center. The center is in dire need of change, and Welch is clearly the right person for the job.

Welch got her start as a parole officer in the Illinois Department of Corrections. Later, she worked in a prison environment, as an assistant warden at the Joliet Correctional Center. Her most recent job was at the DuPage County Children's Center, which oversees cases involving child abuse as an extension of the county's state's attorney's office.

As a parole officer, prison warden, and child welfare agent, Welch has been in some of the most challenging positions in law enforcement, and she has developed a reputation for getting things done.

The Cook County Juvenile Detention Center has been under scrutiny from civil rights groups such as the ACLU, who have lodged complaints of abuse of its underage inhabitants by staff. Welch's arrival at the center is intended to bring about much-needed change. The ACLU has expressed confidence in Welch's ability to make the center a better place for rehabilitating young people.

71. Which sentence best expresses the main idea of this article?
   a. Brenda Welch is an exception to the rule that parole officers are noticed only when something goes wrong.
   b. The Cook County Juvenile Detention Center is in great need of a leader with experience in a number of fields.
   c. Brenda Welch's experience as a parole officer, prison guard, and child welfare agent make her an ideal candidate for head of the juvenile detention center.
   d. Child welfare agents, parole officers, and prison wardens are often forced to deal with many of the same challenges.

72. Which detail from the article does NOT support the idea that parole officers, prison workers, and child welfare workers have something in common?
   a. Each position is considered by some to be less glamorous than that of a police detective, attorney, or other more high-profile law enforcement agent.
   b. Little notice is given to the hard work and successes that make up most of these officers' days.
   c. Her most recent job was at the DuPage County Children's Center, which oversees cases involving child abuse as an extension of the county's state's attorney's office.
   d. As a parole officer, prison warden, and child welfare agent, Welch has been in some of the most challenging positions in law enforcement.

73. Which sentence best summarizes Welch's career?

a. Brenda Welch worked in various capacities in Illinois before being tapped for the job as head of the juvenile detention center in Cook County.

b. Brenda Welch worked as a parole officer, then as an assistant warden, then at a children's center that oversaw cases involving child abuse, before accepting a job as head of the juvenile detention center.

c. Welch got her start as a parole officer in the Illinois Department of Corrections; later, she worked in a prison environment as an assistant warden at the Joliet Correctional Center; and her most recent job was at the DuPage County Children's Center, overseeing cases involving child abuse as an extension of the county's state's attorney's office.

d. Brenda Welch is a woman who works in law enforcement.

74. What can be inferred from the details in the article about Welch's experience in her previous jobs?

a. Welch probably hated her three previous jobs, which is why she is taking the detention center job.

b. Welch probably learned things at her previous jobs that will help her in her new job at the detention center.

c. Welch was probably a very tough prison warden, who made many enemies among the inmates.

d. Welch probably did a better job as a parole officer than as a child welfare worker.

75. Which of the following sentences best describes the author's point of the view?

a. The author is leery of law enforcement professionals such as Brenda Welch and thinks all inmates and prisoners should be afraid of them.

b. The author is in favor of tough standards for law enforcement and hopes that Brenda Welch will crack down in the juvenile detention center.

c. The author thinks that being a detective is more glamorous than being a parole officer.

d. The author admires people like Brenda Welch who can deal with the challenges of jobs in law enforcement.

Directions: Read the following passage and then answer questions 76 through 80.

The technology of Global Positioning Systems, or GPS, is now being used as a tool for parole officers and law enforcement officials to keep track of certain parolees.

In 2004, Massachusetts became one of the first states to authorize GPS tracking of certain paroled sex offenders in the state. The law was applied only to those offenders deemed most likely to commit similar crimes again.

These parolees, in addition to having regular meetings with their parole officers, were fitted for an ankle bracelet and a GPS unit to be worn around the waist. Authorities would be alerted electronically if the bracelet was cut or the GPS unit was removed a certain distance from the bracelet, ensuring that the parolee would keep the units on or be pursued.

Together, these two parts of the GPS system show the parole officer exactly where the parolee is at any time. This is an easy and reliable way to track the offenders as they go to and from their jobs and appointments. Most important, the GPS system alerts parole officers if the parolee ever enters an "exclusion zone." For sex offenders, these exclusion zones include schools, playgrounds, and the homes of former victims.

Massachusetts has some reason to hope the GPS project will be successful. The Middlesex County sheriff's office in Massachusetts has successfully used GPS tracking to monitor inmates on a work-release program. The GPS bracelets ensured that the inmates were appearing at their assigned jobs. Senator Steven C. Panagiotakos, who sponsored the budget provision for the program, has cited evidence that such tracking programs have been successful in preventing repeated offenses in other states.

Parolees are still required to check in with their parole officers in person, so the new technology will not replace parole officers.

76. Which sentence best expresses the main idea of this article?
a. Massachusetts has begun to use GPS technology to keep track of paroled sex offenders.
b. GPS technology will never replace visits to a real parole officer.
c. GPS technology has been effective in preventing repeat offenses in some states.
d. The GPS system for tracking parolees involves two pieces that cannot be separated.

77. Which detail from the article does NOT support the idea that GPS systems will make it easier to keep track of former criminals?
a. Together, these two parts of the GPS system could show the parole officer exactly where the parolee is at any time.
b. The GPS system alerts parole officers if the parolee ever enters an "exclusion zone."
c. The GPS bracelets ensured that they were appearing at their assigned jobs.
d. Senator Steven C. Panagiotakos sponsored the budget provision for the program.

78. Which detail could be added to the article to support the idea that GPS systems will make the state safer?
a. Not all states can afford this high-tech monitoring system.
b. Many activists view the GPS monitors as an invasion of privacy.
c. Officers are equipped to respond quickly if a GPS monitor shows that a parolee has entered an exclusion zone.
d. Massachusetts already has one of the lowest crime rates in the nation.

79. Which choice best describes the author's point of view?
a. The author worries that GPS tracking will lead to abuse of power by parole officers.
b. The author believes that GPS tracking has the potential to help parole officers.
c. The author believes that GPS tracking will one day replace parole officers.
d. The author believes that GPS tracking will be of no use to parole officers.

80. Which of the following sentences would make the best concluding sentence for this article?
a. This effort is part of a worldwide increase in the use of Global Positioning Systems, which have the potential to be the next major technological trend of the 21st century.
b. Senator Panagiotakos has a proven record of being tough on crime, so residents can rest assured that he has their best interests at heart.
c. The commonwealth of Massachusetts hopes that GPS systems will make parole officers' jobs easier and make the state safer for everyone.
d. The ankle and waist attachments are made to be comfortable and wearable for parolees so that wearing them is not a punishment in itself.

Directions: Read the following passage and then answer questions 81 through 85.

Identity theft is one of the largest and fastest-growing categories of financial crime in the United States. At the same time, it is one of the most difficult to prevent and to prosecute. Federal law enforcement officials, credit card companies, and individual consumers are all struggling to combat this virulent new strain of criminal activity.

Identity theft comes in many forms. Among the most common is the use of an existing credit card number or bank account by someone not authorized to do so. According to surveys by the independent research firm Javelin Strategy and Research and the Better Business Bureau, about nine million people, or 4% of the American population, are victimized by this kind of identity theft each year.

New account fraud, in which a victim's social security number or other personal data is used to open new accounts or lines of credit, is more difficult for a victim to repair. The Javelin study found that about three million Americans each year fall prey to this kind of identity theft.

Much of this fraudulent information and spending occurs through the Internet. A survey conducted by Cybersource of more than 400 online retailers estimated that more than $3 billion was lost to online fraud in 2005, compared to $1.5 billion in 2000.

Fortunately, federal law enforcement officials are becoming more skilled at finding and prosecuting large-scale identity theft operations. In March 2006, seven people around the country were arrested in connection with a complex web of illegal identity information trading through websites. Much of the stolen credit and identity information passes through these sites, and officers were able to infiltrate the sites anonymously and track down the perpetrators.

In addition, credit card holders are becoming better educated about the dangers of identity theft and what they can do to prevent their own information from being stolen. Using caution when giving out credit card information, ensuring that websites are secure, and requiring that retailers ask for verification of credit card holders' identities are some of the ways individuals can help to reduce their risk.

81. Which sentence best expresses the main idea of this article?
- **a.** Identity theft is widespread and fast growing, but law enforcement and individuals are learning to combat it.
- **b.** The Internet is the site of most identity theft, and the numbers are increasing each year.
- **c.** Existing account fraud is more common than new account fraud, although the latter is harder to repair for the victim.
- **d.** Law enforcement officials, credit card companies, Internet companies, and consumers all have something to lose in identity theft.

82. Which detail from the article supports the idea that identity theft is a fast-growing category of crime?
- **a.** About nine million people each year are victimized by this kind of theft.
- **b.** About three million Americans each year fall prey to this kind of identity theft.
- **c.** More than $3 billion was lost to online fraud in 2005, compared to $1.5 billion in 2000.
- **d.** Seven people were arrested around the country in connection with a complex web of illegal identity information trading through websites.

83. Which of the following sentences best summarizes the results of the Javelin study as cited in this article?
   a. About 12 million people each year have their identities stolen.
   b. About nine million people each year suffer from existing account identity theft, and three million are victimized by new account fraud.
   c. More difficult for a victim to repair is new account fraud, in which a victim's social security number or other personal data is used to open new accounts or lines of credit; about three million Americans each year fall prey to this kind of identity theft.
   d. More than $3 billion was lost to online fraud in 2005, compared to $1.5 billion in 2000.

84. Which of the following details could be added to the article to support the idea that federal agents are learning how to combat identity theft?
   a. Federal agents deal with many forms of international and organized crime and have more authority than state or local officials when it comes to online theft.
   b. Some have speculated that many of the most effective large-scale identity thieves probably come from the ranks of former federal law enforcement officials.
   c. Credit card companies increasingly issue warnings to their customers about the dangers of identity theft and the steps they can take to help prevent it.
   d. New FBI agents are required to possess high levels of technological savvy, so they are able to keep up with the rapid pace of developments in identity theft.

85. Which of the following sentences would make the best concluding sentence for this article?
   a. Many consumers are still convinced that identity theft can never happen to them.
   b. With diligence, both individuals and law enforcement can help to change the trend and lower the incidence of identity theft.
   c. Identity theft actually makes up a small percentage of financial crimes worldwide, both in the number of incidents and in dollar amounts.
   d. I know I'll never be giving my credit card number to a stranger online!

Directions: Read the following passage and then answer questions 86 through 91.

The United States is one of the only countries in the world that sentences prisoners to life in prison without parole. No matter how brutal the crime, most other nations rarely exercise such punishment, although they may mete out harsher penalties in different ways.

Although some justice systems may sentence a prisoner to life in prison, parole is almost always an option. Western European countries consider a served sentence of 10 to 12 years to be extremely harsh. Even Mehmet Ali Agca, who attempted to kill Pope John Paul II, was released by Italian authorities after 19 years in prison.

Mexico, the United States' nearest neighbor, has become a haven for fugitives facing a life sentence in the United States. The country will not extradite any defendant facing a life sentence.

In some parts of the Islamic world, punishments for capital crimes can be extremely harsh. Islamic law often calls for corporal punishment or mutilation. However, even in these justice systems, prisoners are not sentenced to a life in prison without possibility of release.

The reasons for this difference may be rooted in the religious origins of American culture. The Puritan and Calvinist traditions of the early English settlers may have laid the foundation for the present day's preference for harsh justice for those known to have committed crimes.

In the words of Michael H. Tonry, a University of Minnesota professor of law and public policy, this tradition implies that "You deserve what you get, both good and bad." Tonry, who is also an expert on comparative punishment, mentions that this tradition may also be the reason that the United States does not employ the systems of welfare that are popular in many European nations.

An American sense of the importance of self-reliance and, by implication, taking ultimate responsibility for one's crimes, may be the most significant reason for the American dependence on immutable life sentences.

86. Which sentence best expresses the main idea of this article?
- **a.** The legal code of the Islamic world is one of the harshest, often sentencing prisoners to corporal punishment or mutilation.
- **b.** The religious tradition of the Puritans still affects American life today.
- **c.** The United States is one of the few nations in the world that enforces life sentences, perhaps because of its religious traditions.
- **d.** Comparative punishment is a fascinating field that reveals cultural, religious, and economic factors at play in the traditions of various legal systems.

87. Which detail from the article does NOT support the idea that most other countries do not enforce sentences of life without parole?
- **a.** Although some justice systems may sentence a prisoner to life in prison, parole is almost always an option.
- **b.** Mehmet Ali Agca, in an attempt to kill Pope John Paul II, was released by Italian authorities after 19 years in prison.
- **c.** Mexico will not extradite any defendant facing a life sentence.
- **d.** In some parts of the Islamic world, punishments for capital crimes can be extremely harsh.

88. Which detail supports the idea that life sentences without parole are part of an American tradition?
- **a.** Western European countries consider a served sentence of 10 to 12 years to be extremely harsh.
- **b.** Mexico, the United States' nearest neighbor, can become a haven for fugitives facing a life sentence in the United States.
- **c.** Michael H. Tonry is a University of Minnesota professor of law and public policy.
- **d.** An American sense of the importance of self-reliance and, by implication, taking ultimate responsibility for one's crimes.

89. Which sentence best summarizes Professor Tonry's opinions on the legacy of the Puritan tradition?
- **a.** The Puritan and Calvinist traditions of the early English settlers may have laid the foundation for the present day's preference for harsh justice for those known to have committed crimes; this tradition implies that "You deserve what you get, both good and bad," and may also be the reason that the United States does not employ the systems of welfare that are popular in many European nations.
- **b.** Puritans believed that everyone deserved what they got, and so do present-day Americans.
- **c.** The Puritan tradition of self-reliance and responsibility may help explain both life sentences without parole and the resistance to a welfare state.
- **d.** Puritans fled the morally relaxed climate of Europe to establish a community of high standards in the New World, and their legacy lives on in the current climate of life sentences without parole and resistance to welfare in favor of self-reliance.

90. Which of the following best describes the author's point of view?

   a. The author is cautiously opposing life sentences without parole and thinks the United States should learn from its European counterparts.

   b. The author is curiously inquiring about the reasons for the uniqueness of the American justice system.

   c. The author is bravely exposing the Puritan tradition and thinks the United States justice system should be reformed.

   d. The author is totally advocating the American tradition and believes that life sentences without parole are justified and effective.

91. Which of the following sentences would make the best concluding sentence for this article?

   a. The American system is obviously superior to many in the world, because it chooses life imprisonment over the death sentence.

   b. Prison conditions can vary throughout the world, so a life sentence may not mean the same thing in the United States that it does in a Third World country.

   c. The states with the highest percentages of life sentences also tend to have the highest percentages of death sentences.

   d. The uniqueness of the life sentence in the American justice system may indicate something about American culture and history that is worth examining in the context of the larger world.

92. Which of the following sentences is grammatically correct?

   a. When someone's spent time in jail, it ain't easy for them to start over.

   b. When someone has spent time in jail, it isn't easy for them to start over.

   c. When someone's been in jail, it ain't easy for them to start over.

   d. When someone has spent time in jail, it isn't easy to start over.

93. Which sentence do you feel is the most clearly written?

   a. A program called Books Through Bars exists, which its function is to give books to inmates in jail.

   b. A program called Books Through Bars gives books to inmates in jail.

   c. Giving books to inmates in jail is what a program called Books Through Bars does.

   d. It's giving books to inmates in jail that does a program called Books Through Bars.

94. Which of the following sentences is punctuated correctly?

   a. When Officer Jackson sees parolees, he spends time discussing each one's problems.

   b. When Officer Jackson sees parolees', he spends time discussing each one's problems.

   c. When Officer Jackson sees parolees, he spends time discussing each ones problems.

   d. When Officer Jackson sees parolees', he spends time discussing each ones problems'.

95. Which of the following sentences is grammatically correct?
  a. On the night of May 22, the couple had a fight.
  b. On the night of May 22, the couple has them a fight.
  c. In the night of May 22, the couple had a fight.
  d. In the night of May 22, the couple having a fight.

96. Which sentence do you feel is the most clearly written?
  a. A record of effort and achievement from their parolees is all what parole officers want to see.
  b. All parole officers want to see from their parolees, a record of effort and achievement.
  c. Every parole officer wants to see a record of effort and achievement from his or her parolees.
  d. From their parolees, all parole officers want a record of effort and achievement.

97. Which of the following sentences is punctuated correctly?
  a. After the collision the driver, Harold Lloyd drove quickly away.
  b. After the collision, the driver, Harold Lloyd, drove, quickly, away.
  c. After the collision, the driver Harold Lloyd, drove quickly away.
  d. After the collision, the driver, Harold Lloyd, drove quickly away.

98. Which of the following sentences is grammatically correct?
  a. If Officer Sharon hadn't of been there for me, none a this could have happened.
  b. If Officer Sharon hadn't been there for me, none of this could have happened.
  c. If Officer Sharon hadn't of been there for me, none of this could have happened.
  d. If Officer Sharon hadn't been there for me, none a this could have happened.

99. Which sentence do you feel is the most clearly written?
  a. It's better than the attic, the cellar, for keeping contraband.
  b. Keeping contraband it's better the cellar than the attic.
  c. It's better for keeping contraband, the cellar than the attic.
  d. The cellar is better than the attic for keeping contraband.

100. Which of the following sentences is punctuated correctly?
  a. It's difficult to understand the law, because its wording is often complicated.
  b. Its difficult to understand the law, because its wording is often complicated.
  c. It's difficult to understand the law, because it's wording is often complicated.
  d. Its difficult to understand the law, because it's wording is often complicated.

▶ Answers

1. b. A probationer who has a family and is employed risks losing those things if he or she violates the conditions of probation. Choice **a** is incorrect because the probationer is addicted to drugs and has a previous record of offending, both of which reduce his or her chance of success. Choice **c** is incorrect because unemployment can result in unconstructive time, which often leads to criminal behavior. In most jurisdictions, maintaining employment is a condition of probation; therefore, being unemployed can be considered a violation of probation. Choice **d** is incorrect because ongoing problems with drug abuse can lead to criminal behavior as well as violations of other conditions (i.e., unemployment and associating with other felons).

2. c. This choice allows Robert to maintain employment while remaining in compliance with probation conditions. Many times, probationers use the excuse that they do not have a vehicle as a reason for noncompliance. Often, unless restricted by law, the probation officer can petition the court to modify the condition to allow the probationer to drive to work. Choice **a** is incorrect because it is not considerate of Robert's efforts to maintain steady employment, which can be difficult for a convicted felon. Choice **b** is incorrect because he is *required* to maintain employment as a condition of probation. Choice **d** is incorrect because this choice represents a technical violation of a probation condition, not a new offense.

3. c. One of the roles of a probation officer is to be a "broker of services," connecting probationers to community resources that address the problems that may interfere with their efforts to become law-abiding citizens. Choice **a** is incorrect because you should not encourage

violation; jail time is not the answer for a drinking problem. Choice **b** is appropriate, and choice **d** is incorrect because she has not violated probation conditions.

4. b. A standard condition of parole is not to associate with felons. Association with offenders will, in many situations, lead to criminal behavior. Choices **a**, **c**, and **d** are incorrect because they are all requirements for offenders under parole or supervision.

5. a. It is critical for the parole officer to investigate and verify information before deciding upon an appropriate action or imposing a sanction. In this situation, the officer must proceed with caution, because the parolee's wife provided the information. Choices **b** and **c** are incorrect because sometimes spouses will get angry and try to get an offender into trouble, and then later recant and admit that they made up the accusations. Choice **d** is not acceptable. It is the responsibility of the parole officer to initiate an inquiry to determine the legitimacy of the wife's statements. Ignoring the allegations or acting prior to an investigation is unadvisable.

6. b. At this point, the responsibility is simply to verify the information and report the findings. Choice **a** is incorrect because parole is an administrative matter and, because no new crime has been committed, the court should not be involved. Choice **c** is incorrect. The investigating officer's responsibility is to verify the information and report it to the institutional parole officer, not to the paroling authority. Prison personnel and the parole board will decide how to use the information in assessing readiness for release. Choice **d** is incorrect. Ignoring the discrepancies is not an option. It is mandatory that the investigating officer report the results of an investigation.

7. c. An alternative suggestion would be to advise the wife to address the issue with her husband to see if they can resolve the matter themselves. If not, maybe he would agree to listen to somebody who can provide guidance from the faith-based community. Choices **a** and **b** are incorrect because the U.S. Supreme Court has ruled that you cannot make a person attend church or accept particular religious beliefs, because it is in violation of the First Amendment of the Constitution. Choice **d** is incorrect. Such behavior could lead to future difficulties between you and the probationer's spouse, and could strain your relationship with the probationer and, ultimately, your employer.

8. b. The most important function of the initial meeting is to ensure that the probationer has a basic understanding of his or her responsibility regarding the court order and conditions of probation. This time is also used to get input from the probationer in the development of the probation plan, including the necessary requirements for supervision and services. The offender and the probation officer can take this time to establish a rapport and to set the stage for ongoing communications. Choice **a** is incorrect. There may be a legitimate reason for his tardiness on the first visit, for instance, having difficulty finding the office. Being late for office visits is not a reason to recommend probation revocation. However, if the probationer continuously misses his reporting date, the officer would be justified in taking action. Choice **c** is incorrect because the probation officer does not have the authority to amend conditions of probation. This responsibility lies with the court, and only the judge can change or amend conditions of probation, usually based on a recommendation from the probation officer. Choice **d** is incorrect. The offender must understand that probation is a privilege and that the conditions of probation must be followed in order to keep that privilege. Ignoring probation conditions could result in additional sanctions, revocation, or incarceration.

9. c. If you are aware of this situation and are unable to resolve it, you should bring it to the attention of your supervisor so that he or she can take appropriate action. Any officer supervising a probationer must remain nonjudgmental and professional; personal feelings should never interfere. Working in the criminal justice system, you will often encounter people who have said or done things that are offensive to you as an officer or the community at large. But, nonetheless, you must maintain your professionalism. Choice **a** is incorrect. A probation revocation request must be based on the violation of court-ordered conditions—either chronic or persistent technical violations—or new arrests. Choice **b** and **d** are incorrect. Both of these responses ignore the real problem and allow the probation officer to continue with his inappropriate behavior. Knowing about a problem and not reporting it may make you just as culpable as the individual creating the problem.

10. a. and c. Parole benefits society because it provides released inmates with the guidance needed to assist them with their transitions into the community. Choice **b** is incorrect because parole is not a judicial function. Choice **d** is incorrect. Choices **a** and **c** are reasons to advocate for parole.

11. b. The initial visit helps to address any potential problems or questions raised in the presentence investigation report. After this visit, the officer can determine the appropriate action to take, if any. If the situation warrants, the officer may choose to note this information for future reference. On the other hand, the officer may want to confer with a supervisor to determine whether this matter should be brought back to the attention of the court. An addition or modification of the probation order may be appropriate. Choice **a** is incorrect because, if there is a problem with aggressive behavior, you want to address it immediately. Choice **c** is incorrect. Demeaning the bench is inappropriate, and a reprimand or disciplinary action toward you may result. Courts have a great interest in doing right and usually can be approached in an appropriate manner. Choice **d** is incorrect because there has been no technical or new arrest violation of the conditions.

12. a. Parole is a privilege, an act of mercy. The decision to grant parole is based largely on the paroling authority's assessment of the inmate's progress toward rehabilitation. Because the inmate is already incarcerated, he has no "present private interest" to be protected (*Menechino v. Oswald*, 1970). An advocate may be present, but the inmate is not legally entitled to an attorney. Choices **b** and **d** are incorrect for this reason. The inmate is not legally entitled to an attorney. Choice **c** is incorrect because it is inappropriate for a parole officer to criticize the parole board about a decision.

13. b. Because the inmate is in prison, she may not be aware of the nature of this business. As the officer assisting the inmate in her transition back into society, you should explain why this work environment is not acceptable and help her find suitable employment. Choices **a** and **d** are incorrect because these actions set the stage for potential violations. If the officer approves this employment, he or she must notify the parole board. At the same time, the inmate should be made aware that her employment may cause her violations if she's not careful about her behavior. Choice **c** is incorrect because this action is not only unethical, it is criminal.

14. a. and d. Volunteers are carefully screened and attend orientation and training before having contact with probationers. However, it is not uncommon for situations like this to occur. The first step is to discuss this issue with your supervisor to determine a course of action, which could include additional training, counseling, a reprimand, or severing the volunteer's relationship with the program. When a decision is made, the volunteer should be informed of the consequences of this behavior and the subsequent course of action. Volunteers are valuable assets and can provide much needed services to probationers. However, constant oversight and continuous training is necessary. Choice **b** is incorrect. Doing nothing is never an option when there is a problem. Choice **c** is incorrect. Legitimate organizations provide bible study for offenders on probation, and probation agencies usually collaborate with community faith-based organizations for this service.

15. c. Parole is an administrative matter that is handled largely by the parole board, not the courts. The parole board has this authority. Choice **a** is incorrect. Shock probation occurs when the judge orders a short prison stay as a condition of probation. Choices **b** and **d** are incorrect. The courts do not revoke parole; parole is handled largely by a parole board.

16. b. Probation officers can request amendments to probation conditions if they aid in rehabilitation and law-abiding behavior. Choice **a** is incorrect. As Walt's probation officer, you should take action in his best interest. Choice **c** is incorrect. If his "several" arrests occurred prior to Walt being placed on probation, you cannot file a request to have probation revoked. Choice **d** is incorrect. This action indicates that the officer is waiting for an opportunity to get Walt off his caseload. The role of the officer should be to help the offender abide by the conditions of probation and avoid future contact with the criminal justice system.

17. c. It is not unusual for employers to accuse a parolee first if something comes up missing or wrong. The parole officer should not act too quickly in this situation but try to make contact with the parolee to determine what happened. If contact cannot be made, the probation officer should file a request for a warrant to arrest and detain this offender as an absconder. Often, the employer will find the missing tools or discover that another employee committed the crime. Choices **a** and **b** are both incorrect. Both actions are hasty and could be wrong. Choice **d** is incorrect. You should never take this approach with employers, especially those who are willing to hire offenders. This attitude instills a negative image for public service agencies.

18. a. Parole board members determine readiness for parole based upon numerous criteria; they often look at what kind of employment the parolee will have and where the parolee will live, and then they can determine if the location is accessible to needed treatment services and conducive to reintegration. Choices **b**, **c**, and **d** are incorrect. The ages of the inmate's parents, family history, hobbies, and the inmate's age are not considered to be important factors. Although remorse from the inmate is important, the board will get that information by either asking the inmate and/or looking at the presentence investigation report and prison records. An inmate given a prison sentence is usually not given an order to make restitution payments.

19. d. It is obvious that she cannot pay. Judges are reasonable and will usually amend the order

or waive the fees if the probation officer determines that the probationer does not have the ability to pay and is not just ignoring the court orders. Choices **a** and **b** are incorrect. Revoking probation and sending her to prison will create even more problems. The impact of her spending time in prison would devastate her family. Choice **c** is incorrect. To hand off the problem to your supervisor is not the thing to do. Working in probation requires common sense and logic, coupled with the ability to work within the parameters of agency policies and procedures. Keeping this in mind, probation officers must have the ability to be responsible and make decisions on their own.

20. a. You, your supervisor, and the university internship coordinator must decide if there are justifiable reasons to allow this intern to continue. If not, the student should be terminated from the internship. The justification for termination must be documented and retained in the appropriate records. Violation of policies regarding confidentiality is a serious issue. Choice **b** is incorrect. By the time a student has reached the point of doing an internship in a criminal justice program, he or she knows the importance of client confidentiality. As a part of many internship programs, participating students are required to sign statements of confidentiality. Lack of knowledge is not an excuse. Choice **c** is incorrect because this situation is not a criminal matter. Choice **d** is incorrect because this action would not be ethical. As a requirement for interning, students must have their criminal histories checked.

21. d. In this case, the offender has a history of aggressive behavior or inability to control anger. Choices **a**, **b**, and **c** are all incorrect. Theses are standard conditions that all probationers are required to follow.

22. c. The PSI is prepared by the probation department to assist the judge in determining the appropriate sentence and to provide guidance in probation supervision. Choices **a**, **b**, and **d** are incorrect. The PSI is not prepared by the defense attorney or the district attorney and is not used to determine guilt or innocence. The judge orders the PSI after a determination of guilt and before sentencing.

23. a. It is important for the probationer to deal with unemployment issues. Probationers should never be encouraged to talk in generalities but rather in specifics about their own unemployment: "Why can't *I* find a job?" Then, the probationer should develop a plan to address the question of his unemployment. Choice **b** is incorrect. It is unlikely that the judge would revoke probation for this technical violation alone. Prison is not a solution to the problem. Choice **c** is incorrect. The probationer should be encouraged to talk specifically about his situation and then develop a plan of action. Choice **d** is incorrect because there is not a legitimate reason for the probationer to be unemployed.

24. b. In recent years, the victimization of probation and parole officers has increased, and as a result, officers are more concerned about their safety when they make field contacts. It has been noted that police and warrant enforcement officers are often unwilling to go into high-crime areas to enforce warrants, leaving the officer responsible for serving these warrants. Therefore, officers are demanding more protection and more defensive training. Choices **a** and **d** are incorrect. Portraying an image of power and authority may be detrimental to the relationship between the probation officer and the probationer by giving the perception that the probation officer is more of a law enforcer than a supportive guide. Choice **c** is incorrect. Using a firearm to scare a probationer or parolee into compliance is not only unprofessional but also unethical and, in some cases, criminal. This is absolutely an unacceptable practice.

25. a. Determining the probationer's reasons for being out later than 11:00 P.M. will sometimes generate options for resolving the situation. For example, if the probationer is satisfying all other conditions of probation, he may see an amendment to the curfew as an incentive to continue abiding with the conditions of the court. On the other hand, you may want to reason with the probationer and explain the potential consequences of late hours, holding fast to the time frame of the curfew. Choice **b** is incorrect. As an officer, you are responsible for enforcing the court-ordered conditions of probation whether or not you agree with them. However, in most instances, the probation officer has some discretion to petition the court to make amendments to probation conditions. Choices **c** and **d** are incorrect. The sanction does not fit the crime. Although this probationer needs to be made aware of the seriousness of probation, recommending shock incarceration or probation revocation is drastic. The judge would be unlikely to follow either of these recommendations on a single minor technical violation. If the situation remains unresolved or other violations occur as a result of staying out past the curfew, weekend jail time may be an option.

26. b. A major concern of those who oppose probation and parole is that many of these offenders are dangerous and pose a threat to citizens, because probation and parole are not viewed as "real punishment." As a result, the perception is that society is not protected from the potential criminal acts of these offenders. Choice **a** is incorrect. One of the attractive features of probation and parole is the reduced cost. Incarceration can cost from $10,000 to $35,000 per year per inmate, whereas probation and parole supervision may cost from $600 to $1,500 per year, per offender. Choice **c** is incorrect. Probationers and parolees are required to be employed as a condition of supervision because (a) it limits excessive idle time; (b) it allows the offender to take care of his or her family; and (c) it gives the offender a "stake in conformity." Some studies have found that unemployment is one of the most significant factors related to criminal offending and failure under supervision. Choice **d** is incorrect. Prisons are often viewed as breeding grounds for criminal behavior. Criminals can often learn additional criminal techniques in prison. Parole should come at a time when the inmate can benefit from conditional release and avoid further association with the prison subculture. On the other hand, probation gives the offender the opportunity to avoid the negative impact of exposure to the prison subculture and, instead, to capitalize on the positive influences available in the community.

27. b. The officer-as-advocate realizes that some agencies will deny services to probationers, because they see them as undeserving or threatening. Furthermore, the advocate fights for the rights of the offender in need of help. As the advocate, you attempt to remove barriers that prevent the client from receiving the needed help. Choice **a** is incorrect. Connecting offenders to community resources is a probation task. Often, offenders lack the knowledge about available resources and interpersonal skills to deal with these agencies, which can lead to frustration and more antisocial behavior on the part of the offender. Choice **c** is incorrect. There are no legitimate grounds for revocation. Revocation should be based on excessive technical violations or new arrest

violations. Choice **d** is incorrect. Litigation should never be encouraged. Usually, offenders do not have the finances to hire an attorney to pursue a legal recourse.

28. a. Daniel is in serious violation of probation conditions. He has failed to comply with two very important conditions of his conditional release, and there is little reason to believe that he will abide by the other rules of probation. Choice **b** is incorrect. The judge should be informed of these serious violations immediately. Failure to do so jeopardizes your job and your credibility with the judge. Although you want to assist the probationer, you have a responsibility to enforce the court-ordered conditions and ensure the safety of citizens—in this case, children. Choices **c** and **d** are incorrect. He should not be allowed to continue his employment. There is also the issue of "liability": The probation agency can be sued for failure to warn a third party of an offender's risk for recidivism and failure in "the duty to protect."

29. c. Because of the Interstate Compact, a probationer may be allowed to move for employment or family purposes if the receiving state agrees to supervise the probationer while he or she lives in that state. The probationer must report to the supervising state's probation department. If there is a new offense or if there are other violations, the probationer is sent back to the convicting state. Choice **a** is incorrect. There is no stipulation on the amount of time on probation the probationer must complete before requesting a move to another state. Choice **b** is incorrect. As a probation officer, you do not have the authority to terminate a probationer's probation term. Choice **d** is incorrect. Ignoring a request is never a solution.

30. d. This is more compatible with the "get tough" approach on crime, which stresses retribution, mandatory sentencing, and incapacitation as punishments. Choices **a**, **b**, and **c** are incorrect because they are all strategies used by the rehabilitation model.

31. d. Robert's juvenile criminal history is characterized by arrests for several property offenses and three possession charges. His adult history follows a similar pattern of drug-related and property offenses. Choice **a** is incorrect. Robert has established a history of both property and drug-related offenses. Choice **b** is incorrect. Robert would not be correctly classified as a dangerous violent offender. Although he was arrested as a juvenile for aggravated assaults and has been accused by his girlfriend of being violent and abusive to her and their child, there is nothing to indicate that he is violent and dangerous. However, the probation officer should recommend counseling to address the aggressive and violent behavior that Robert has exhibited. Choice **c** is incorrect. Robert has not aged out of criminal behavior. He is 18 years old and has already been convicted of two major felonies. In most states, a person is not considered an adult until age 18. It seems that he is establishing a history of adult criminal offenses.

32. c. There is no information in the case to indicate that Robert has been ordered to receive counseling for aggressive and violent tendencies. If the information given by his girlfriend is correct, then his probation conditions should be amended to include counseling. Choices **a**, **b**, and **d** are all incorrect. Robert is in violation of all of these conditions. He worked only two months of the entire year; he reports infrequently and gets drunk with known felony probationers. Additional sanctions should be considered if he does not curtail this activity.

33. b. The judge sends the offender to prison for a short stay (30, 60, 90, or 120 days). After the

short stay, the judge orders the offender back to on probation. Most studies regarding shock probation indicate that it yields little success. Many offenders respond as Robert did—they learn better techniques of criminal behavior. Choice **a** is incorrect. The practice has nothing to do with mental health treatment or testing. Choice **c** is incorrect. This refers to the practice of deferred prosecution probation that is used in some jurisdictions. Choice **d** is incorrect. Work release is usually imposed as a condition of probation or as a reintegration opportunity for offenders returning to the community from prison, to provide a structured, minimum-custody, community-based residential sanction that allows the offender to work while under intensive supervision.

34. d. Robert has no job and did not graduate from high school. He appears to have no concern for abiding by the rules of probation, is under suspicion of selling drugs, and openly brags about "better" skills acquired in prison. Although he has carpentry skills and boxing experience, which he could use to become productive, he seems to have little or no interest in doing what is right. He is addicted to drugs and allegedly steals his girlfriend's food stamps to buy drugs. He seems to be immature and irresponsible as well. The probability of Robert committing additional crimes is high. Choice **a** is incorrect. Although he has carpentry skills, he seems to have little or no interest in pursuing that interest. Choice **b** is incorrect. There is no proof that he is close to his child or has made attempts to take care of his family. Choice **c** is incorrect. It seems that he is on the way to becoming a career criminal rather than a law-abiding citizen.

35. b. Robert should be revoked and sent to prison because he has failed to abide by the rules of probation. He has failed to pay assessed fees, failed to maintain suitable employment, failed to support his dependents, associates with known felons, gets drunk, and uses drugs. He is irresponsible and has a bad attitude toward his behavior and the probation conditions. He fails to understand the benefits or the requirements of probation. He has not been amenable to efforts to help him. Because of his attitude, it appears that he has no rehabilitation potential. Choice **a** is incorrect. Robert is not a good candidate for referral to drug treatment. He is the kind of offender who would use drug counseling/treatment to avert a prison sentence. It is not likely that he would take it seriously, but rather use it to "beat the system." Choice **c** is incorrect. Robert should not be restored to probation supervision. He has not followed the conditions of his parole, and it is unlikely that he would follow them if probation supervision were restored. Choice **d** is incorrect. If there is a new arrest or new crime, the probation officer has an obligation to file a report.

36. b. Because the relationship ended in such a violent manner, living together once she is released would not be acceptable to the parole board. She should find other living arrangements. Choices **a** and **c** are incorrect. She has not initiated any contact with him. Her ex-boyfriend has initiated all contact. Prison officials can decide if it is inappropriate to receive calls and letters and act accordingly. Choice **d** is incorrect. It is unethical for the officer to conceal information that may have influence parole release decisions.

37. c. Work release allows the inmate to work in the community during the day but return to the facility at night. It helps to prepare the inmate for reintegration into the community. It will also help Debra find employment prior to her release and help her deal with her apprehension about returning to the outside world. Choices **a** and **b** are incorrect. Inmates should never be encouraged to commit new crimes. Fear of returning to a society that has changed in seven years is understandable, but the solution is not avoiding it by committing a new crime or by asking to remain in prison. Parole is designed to come at a time when inmates can benefit from it. Parole allows inmates to avoid continued socialization into the prison culture. Choice **d** is incorrect. The institutional parole officer also serves as a counselor to the inmates. This inmate has a legitimate concern about being released. The officer has the wrong attitude by seeming to dismiss Debra's concerns.

38. d. Prior to the attempted homicides and aggravated assaults, Debra had four prior convictions for assault and battery, indicating some tendency for aggressive behavior. Past behavior is a strong predictor of future behavior. If there is an aggression problem, it should be dealt with before she is released from prison. Choices **a** and **b** are incorrect. There is no evidence in the case files to indicate that her family or the men in her life abused her. Choice **c** is incorrect. The purpose of rehabilitative efforts is to benefit the offender, not to impress the parole board.

39. c. Although she has a substantial record, she now has her GED and a marketable skill. Past arrests for prostitution indicate a lack of money. Choice **a** is incorrect because she earned a GED and a cosmetology license. Choice **b** is incorrect because she has expressed remorse and accepts responsibility. Choice **d** is incorrect. Keeping someone in prison because they seem to do better there is wrong.

40. b. Sheila refuses to take responsibility for her actions. She denies being involved in the sale of drugs or being addicted to drugs. Failure to take responsibility for her actions indicates irresponsibility in other areas of her life. Choice **a** is incorrect. At age 19, she should understand the seriousness of her criminal behavior. Choice **c** is incorrect. There is no indication that she grew up in a dysfunctional home. Choice **d** is incorrect. She had no past juvenile or adult criminal history.

41. a. Sheila must be reminded that she is in violation of probation and that, if she does not begin complying immediately, she is at risk of being revoked. At the same time, the officer must encourage her and help her to develop a plan for getting a GED and looking for a job. She has never had employment and probably does not know how to get a GED. Choices **b** and **c** are incorrect. Although this probationer presents a challenge for supervision, the officer should not be so quick to give up. Both of these alternatives indicate a defeatist attitude or a "it's not going to work so why try" attitude. That attitude not only is bad for the client, but also leads quickly to officer burnout. Choice **d** is incorrect. The officer is violating the rules of confidentiality by informing the landlord that Sheila is on probation. Also, asking the landlord to evict the offender is not an acceptable way to handle this situation.

42. c. It is obvious that Sheila does not understand the seriousness of her conviction and the importance of abiding by the conditions of probation. She has refused to comply with the most important rules of probation. Probation is a privilege that allows her to keep her conditional freedom. Hopefully, shock probation can "shock" her into the reality of her present legal status. If this tactic does not work, revocation is the next alternative. Choice **a** and **b** are incorrect. Both require no action by the officer. An officer should never

ignore possible indicators of illegal behavior. Even without the rumor, there are some inconsistencies. She has no income, yet she lives in an apartment, pays her bills, and has even purchased new furnishings since her boyfriend has been incarcerated. An officer should not be waiting and hoping for a client to get arrested. Choice **d** is incorrect. Given the workload of most police departments, spying for the probation department is not a major priority.

43. a. You should help her get started by giving her information about the literacy program, while letting her follow through on the information. Choices **b**, **c**, and **d** are incorrect. All of these responses show little willingness by the probation officer to help the client.

44. b. Michael is seriously addicted to drugs. His criminal behavior is the result of getting money to support his drug habit. He has never worked, so his only alternative is to commit crimes to obtain the money. Choice **a** is incorrect. This may have been a contributing factor to his drug use but is not the main cause of the criminal behavior. Choice **c** is incorrect. He was already addicted to drugs when he entered the navy. He was discharged because of his drug use. Choice **d** is incorrect. His father's addiction may have been a contributing factor to the drug addiction, but it's not the main reason for Michael's criminal behavior.

45. a. Because his addiction to drugs affects every other aspect of his life, dealing intensely with the drug problem should be priority. Choices **b** and **d** are incorrect. Employment and employment counseling are important issues. Michael's drug addiction is top priority, and until it is addressed, employment issues are insignificant. Choice **c** is incorrect. Although addressing family relationships is part of drug treatment, this is not the major issue. Family relationships may be an underlying cause of

Michael's addiction, but you cannot determine this until you start to address the addiction.

46. b. As his institutional parole officer, you encourage him and provide whatever assistance you can. If he takes the initiative to make some changes in his life to prepare for freedom on the outside, it is always a good idea to encourage that behavior. Choices **a**, **c**, and **d** are negative and do little to support or provide encouragement to an inmate who has made progress toward rehabilitation.

47. d. There is no indication that Daniel was under the influence of drugs at the time of the offense. Choices **a**, **b**, and **c** are incorrect. It is likely that all of these facts were considered favorable and resulted in Daniel being granted probation. Whether the offender is a first-time offender, is remorseful, and has family support are factors that are usually considered.

48. c. Under the terms of the Interstate Compact, a probationer may request permission to move to another state. The request will usually be granted if the receiving state agrees to supervision requirements; however, the original jurisdiction is still ultimately responsible for the probationer. Choice **a** is incorrect. Felons are not excluded; individuals convicted of felonies may request permission to move. Choice **b** is incorrect. There is not a stipulation on the amount of time that a person must serve before applying for this benefit. Choice **d** is incorrect. The receiving state cannot modify the conditions of probation to include additional requirements. Any modification of the probation conditions must be done by the state of origin.

49. a. Daniel has a job that he likes and needs to gain some financial and emotional independence from his parents. Choice **b** is incorrect. There is no indication that there is a major risk of recidivism. Choice **c** is incorrect. It may be easier for the probation department

to revoke him if there is a reason to return him to his home state. Choice **d** is incorrect. There are some advantages for Daniel.

50. a. Many jurisdictions use paraprofessionals to assist probation and parole officers as case aides. These aides are usually from the same environment, race, social class, and cultural background as many of the offenders. Frequently, these paraprofessionals are ex-offenders who are hired as probation and parole case aides. It provides them an opportunity for employment, even though they are paid at a lower salary. Choice **b** is incorrect; a paraprofessional is not a demoted officer. Choices **c** and **d** are incorrect. This person has not been hired to spy on the activities of clients or to replace officers whom the administration has come to view as ineffective. These individuals do not have the qualifications to replace probations and parole officers.

51. b. The paraprofessional usually shares the same or a similar background as the offenders. His or her presence can make the offender feel more comfortable to be open and honest. Ultimately, everyone can benefit from the presence of a paraprofessional. Choice **a** is incorrect. Even though paraprofessionals do not have the same qualifications as probation and parole officers, they can provide valuable assistance at lower costs. Choice **c** is incorrect. Paraprofessionals are hired and paid lower salaries; they provide assistance at lower cost. Choice **d** is incorrect. The paraprofessional is not to be used as a spy on clients because that practice would cause many problems.

52. b. Staff resistance to volunteers or paraprofessionals is not new. Staff members may feel that volunteers or paraprofessionals may intend to take their jobs. This is only true in rare instances. Choices **a** and **c** are incorrect. To call a meeting and publicly identify and chastise these staff members is wrong. They may have some concerns as well as insecurities, which should be addressed privately and individually. To dismiss these staff members is also wrong. To take either of these actions will result in more problems for you and the entire staff. Choice **d** is incorrect. Firing Kenny will not solve the problem. If the presence of a nonprofessional can cause morale problems, then there were probably morale problems before.

53. c. This situation puts Kenny in a difficult position. The most appropriate thing to do is to assign him a different probationer. Choice **a** is incorrect. You would not put anybody in that position, especially an ex-offender. Choices **b** and **d** are incorrect. You should not fire Kenny nor view his reluctance as insubordination. He is only expressing his discomfort about the situation.

54. b. You have a responsibility to report illegal conduct to law enforcement, especially when there is repeated behavior (serial crimes). Choice **a** is incorrect. You have a responsibility to share the information with legal authorities and allow them to pursue it. Choices **c** and **d** are incorrect. This behavior, called blackmail, is unprofessional and criminal.

55. b. John has committed at least two felonies that resulted in convictions. He manipulates people to get his way. Choices **a**, **c**, and **d** are incorrect. These are justifications for behavior that is unacceptable.

56. c. He does not acknowledge that his behavior is criminal. Choices **a**, **b**, and **d** are incorrect. John clearly has friends in the community, and the case study notes his good relations with the law enforcement community. Furthermore, the statement that John's acquaintances were "shocked" at his sentence suggests that the community does not feel he's a criminal and will not stigmatize him with such a label.

57. b. Not having an attorney present is not a violation of due process rights (so choice **d** is incorrect). John is not entitled to an attorney. He is seeking a privilege, not a right that he is entitled to, so his rights are not in danger. Choice **a** is incorrect. As a parole officer, you cannot ensure that he has counsel. Officers should never let inmates intimidate them. Choice **c** is incorrect. You do not report directly to the parole board. If the parole board needs to know something, you should include it in the case file.

58. b. John's criminal history shows no pattern of violent offending. There is no threat of harm to the community. Choices **a**, **c**, and **d** are incorrect. His crimes are property offenses.

59. c. He was being investigated for alleged criminal conduct while in prison. Choice **a** is incorrect. There is no indication that he has committed anything other than property offenses. Choice **b** is incorrect. The judge does not make parole decisions, because parole is not a judicial function. Choice **d** is incorrect. John has family, friends, and support. He is not likely to disappear.

60. b. He has never acknowledged that he has committed crimes, and he is under investigation for continued criminal behavior while in prison. Choices **a**, **c**, and **d** are incorrect. John was found guilty of his charges; therefore, family, friends, and business were not enough to keep him from criminal behavior.

61. c. This sentence describes the goal and function of the Village Initiative, which is the focus of the article. Choice **c** is the only sentence that accurately describes the article's main idea. Choice **a** is incorrect. This idea appears in the article, but it is not the main idea. The idea that a parole officer is not always an enforcer is one of the ideas behind the Village Initiative. However, the main idea of the article has to do with the Village Initiative, not the reputations of parole officers. Choice **b** is incorrect. This is a detail from the article but is not the main idea. This detail does not mention the Village Initiative, which is the main focus of the article and what may be behind the decrease in recidivism. Choice **d** is incorrect. This is an opinion from the article, but it is not the main idea. The overall effort of the Village Initiative, not only their effort to battle the misperceptions about juvenile offenders, is the main idea.

62. a. This detail describes both how juvenile parolees tend to view the government and how they may view government intervention after visits from doctors. This detail supports the idea from the article that the Village Initiative tries to change juvenile offenders' perspectives. Choice **b** is incorrect. This detail describes where the name of the initiative came from but does not support or address the idea that juvenile offenders' perceptions are changed by doctors' visits. Choice **c** is incorrect. This detail describes the problems juvenile offenders face, but does not directly address and support their perceptions or how those perceptions may be changed by doctors' visits. Choice **d** is incorrect. This detail complicates the idea that the Village Initiative is having a positive effect, by stating that more time is needed to assess the results. This detail does not directly support or address the idea that doctors' visits can change juvenile offenders' perceptions.

63. c. This detail suggests that many juvenile parolees will commit crimes again, and it is the only detail in support of the idea that recidivism, or repeat crimes, is a problem among juvenile offenders in the Village Initiative. Choice **a** is incorrect. This detail addresses young potential juvenile offenders but relates to health care, not repeat crimes. Choice **b** is incorrect. This detail may suggest

a solution for juvenile offenders to avoid a criminal life, but it does not show or suggest that recidivism is a problem. Choice **d** is incorrect. This detail suggests that youth crime in general is a problem in the Village Initiative, but it does not directly address repeat crimes by juvenile offenders. It does not directly support the idea that recidivism is a problem.

64. b. The decrease in repeat offenses by juvenile offenders in the program suggests that visits by doctors have had a positive effect and that juvenile offenders are responding to the positive interactions they have had with doctors. Choice **a** is incorrect. The decrease in repeat offenses by juvenile offenders does not indicate resentment, so this inference does not make sense. Choice **c** is incorrect. The decrease in repeat offenses by juvenile offenders does not mean that the Village Initiative is the only place that helps juvenile offenders, so this inference does not make sense. Choice **d** is incorrect. The statistics do not support this statement that juvenile offenders are the same everywhere; this inference does not make sense.

65. c. This sentence refers to the sentence immediately preceding it, recaps the main idea and focus of the article, and brings the article to a decisive close. This is the best concluding sentence because it maintains the tone of the article and summarizes the main ideas without introducing new ideas or details. Choice **a** is incorrect. Although it could bring the article to a decisive close, this sentence is not in keeping with the tone of the article, nor does it allude to the main idea and details of the article. A sentence focusing on the difficulties of young parolees' lives rather than the effects of the Village Initiative does not make sense as the concluding sentence for an article specifically about the Village Initiative. Choice **b** is incorrect. This sentence introduces a new detail to the article and should not be placed at the end. Although this detail may make sense earlier in the article, it does not summarize or finalize the article and so it does not make a good concluding sentence. Choice **d** is incorrect. This sentence introduces a new detail to the article and should not be placed at the end. Although this detail may make sense earlier in the article, it does not summarize or finalize the article and does not make a good concluding sentence.

66. d. This sentence expresses the goal of convicted criminals (to get help with their case from activists) and their actions to achieve it (by seeking the death penalty), as well as their reason for hoping this will work (the case of Walter McMillian). This is the only sentence that expresses the entire big picture that the article describes without including minor details. Choice **a** is incorrect. This sentence describes only the case of Walter McMillian, not the larger idea of convicts who seek the death penalty. This sentence also expresses an opinion (that activists are misguided), which is not expressed in the article. This is not the best expression of the main idea of this article. Choice **b** is incorrect. Although this sentence appears in the article, it is a detail and not the main idea. Choice **c** is incorrect. Although this sentence is a good summary of the case of Walter McMillian, it does not include the main focus of the article, which is that many convicts seek the death penalty hoping to achieve the same results as McMillian. This sentence is not broad enough to express the main idea of the passage.

67. b. This detail states that there are more activists devoted to opposing the death penalty, which suggests that death penalty cases will get attention from more people, directly supporting the idea that death penalty cases receive more attention. Choice **a** is incorrect.

This detail describes the results of the McMillian case and the reason it was overturned, but it does not directly mention the attention given to death penalty cases or even the attention paid to this particular case. Choice **c** is incorrect. This detail states that little attention is given to cases involving life sentences, but it does not necessarily imply that more attention is given to death penalty cases. Although this detail relates to the article, it does not directly support the idea that death penalty cases receive more attention. Choice **d** is incorrect. This detail describes the state of mind of convicted criminals who seek the death penalty, but does not directly mention or support the idea that death penalty cases receive more attention.

68. b. This sentence includes all of the relevant facts from McMillian's case (and only his case) and no unnecessary details or opinions. This is the best summary of the case. Choice **a** is incorrect. This sentence mentions some of the facts from McMillian's case, but it expresses an opinion, which is not an element of a summary. This summary is incomplete, and the opinion keeps it from being strictly a summary, so this is not the best choice. Choice **c** is incorrect. This sentence includes most of the elements of McMillian's case but fails to note how and why his verdict was overturned, instead including information about the implications of the case for others. This speculation about the case's impact is not part of a summary of the case itself, so this is not the best choice. Choice **d** is incorrect. This sentence includes some of the facts of the case, but none of the reasons that these events occurred. Without cause and effect, this is an ineffective and confusing summary, and it is not the best choice.

69. a. Because increased attention finds reasons that death penalty cases should be overturned, a logical inference may be that this attention may uncover the same kinds of reason in other cases. This is not necessarily related to the guilt or innocence of death row convicts or other convicts, but to the elements of the legal system that allow a verdict to be overturned and used by activists. This is the only one of these choices that can logically be inferred from the fact that many death row sentences are overturned. Choice **b** is incorrect. The fact that cases are overturned does not necessarily mean that the former convict is innocent. "Many death row sentences" is not the same as most or all death row criminals. This is not a logical inference. Choice **c** is incorrect. The fact that cases are overturned may mean that innocent people are being released from death row. It is not logical to infer that activists are helping guilty people. Choice **d** is incorrect. Because death penalty cases receive more attention, mistakes are often brought to light, but this does not mean that there are more mistakes in death penalty cases than in cases that do not receive the same kind of attention, whereby mistakes may not be noticed. This is not a logical inference.

70. d. This sentence mentions the important facts of the article (McMillian's case and the efforts of activists and convicts) and draws a conclusion about them in a way to draw the article to a close. The sentence does not include new details nor opinions that are not found in or supported by the article, but only summarizes and concludes the article. Choice **a** is incorrect. This sentence is a new detail, which could have been included earlier in the article but which does not make a good concluding sentence. This sentence does not summarize the article or bring it to an effective close. Choice **b** is incorrect. This sentence mentions the important facts of the article, but serves mostly to express a strong anti–death penalty

opinion, which is absent from the rest of the article. The tone of this sentence does not fit with the rest of the article, so this is not the best concluding sentence. Choice **c** is incorrect. This sentence mentions some of the important facts of the article, but expresses a strong anti-activism stance, which is absent from the rest of the article. The tone of the sentence does not fit with the rest of the article, so this is not the best concluding sentence.

71. c. This sentence describes Brenda Welch's experience in three major related fields and her new job. Her experience and the benefits of that experience are the main idea of the article. Choice **a** is incorrect. This sentence does not include the fact that Welch will be taking a new job based on her previous experience and mentions only one of the three major jobs that gave her that experience. This sentence makes a statement that is true in the context of the article but is too incomplete to be a good expression of the main idea. Choice **b** is incorrect. This is a detail from the article, not the main idea. This sentence does not mention Brenda Welch or her experience, which are the main focus of the article. Choice **d** is incorrect. This is the first sentence of the article and states one of the ideas of the article, but it does not mention Brenda Welch, the main focus of the article. This is not the best expression of the main idea of the article.

72. c. This detail mentions that Welch worked as a child welfare worker, but does not directly suggest that this job had something in common with the jobs of parole officers or prison workers. This is the only detail that does not directly support the idea that these three jobs have something in common. Choice **a** is incorrect. This sentence compares the positions of parole officers, prison workers, and child welfare workers by stating that each is considered less glamorous than some other jobs. This detail does support the idea that these three jobs have something in common, so it is not the best choice. Choice **b** is incorrect. This sentence compares the positions of parole officers, child welfare workers, and prison workers by stating that each job is mostly hard work and successes. This detail does support the idea that these three jobs have something in common, so it is not the best choice. Choice **d** is incorrect. This detail mentions that Welch has held the jobs of parole officer, prison worker, and child welfare agent and that each was challenging. This suggests that these three jobs have something in common, supporting this main idea, so this is not the best choice.

73. b. This sentence mentions each aspect of Welch's career without any additional information. This is the best summary of her career. Choice **a** is incorrect. This sentence does not include the various stages of Welch's career before the detention center or even mention that she worked in law enforcement. This sentence is too vague and incomplete to make an effective summary. Choice **c** is incorrect. This sentence includes too much detail about Welch's three previous jobs to be an effective summary. It also fails to mention her new job at the detention center. This sentence is both too long and too incomplete to make a good summary. Choice **d** is incorrect. This sentence does not include enough information about Welch's career to make a good summary. It is a statement of her identity, not a chronological summary. This is not the best summary of her career.

74. b. The article shows that the three jobs Welch held have much in common and that the ACLU has confidence that she will do a good job at the detention center. From this, it can

be inferred that she probably learned skills at these previous jobs that will help her in her new job at the detention center. Choice **a** is incorrect. It seems unlikely that Welch hated her previous jobs, because they were all in law enforcement, and she is taking another job in law enforcement. However, we cannot infer whether she liked or disliked her jobs from the details given in the article. This is not a logical inference. Choice **c** is incorrect. Because Welch is taking a job in which she will need to help prevent abuses of prisoners, it seems unlikely that she has a reputation for making enemies among inmates. However, the article does not give enough information one way or another about Welch's reputation among prisoners to make this judgment. This is not a logical inference. Choice **d** is incorrect. There is no indication in the article that Welch was better at one of her jobs than at any other job. This is not a logical inference.

75. d. The author spends time talking about the challenges of various law enforcement jobs and holds up Brenda Welch as an example of someone who does all of these jobs well. Her tone and the details she includes suggest that she admires law enforcement professionals who live up to the challenges of their jobs. Choice **a** is incorrect. Nothing in the author's tone suggests that she is fearful of law enforcement professionals or that she thinks prisoners should be afraid of them. Her tone is primarily positive and does not suggest a cautious or frightened point of view. Choice **b** is incorrect. The author does not seem to advocate any specific course of action for law enforcement professionals and focuses on the challenges of doing any law enforcement job effectively and fairly, not on the need to crack down. This is not an accurate description of the author's point of view. Choice **c** is incorrect. Although the author mentions that some people consider positions such as detective to be more glamorous than positions such as parole officer, she does not express this opinion herself. Her tone suggests that that opinion is inaccurate and part of the challenge of being a parole officer. This sentence is not an accurate description of her point of view.

76. a. This article is primarily about the new use of GPS technology to track parolees in Massachusetts. Choice **b** is incorrect. The article mentions that GPS systems will not replace parole officer visits, but it does not assert that this will *never* happen. This speculation is not the main idea or focus of the article. Choice **c** is incorrect. This detail is cited by the senator who advocated GPS tracking in Massachusetts, but the focus of the article is on the enactment of the system in Massachusetts, not its success or failure in other states. Choice **d** is incorrect. This is a detail about how the GPS system works, but it is not the main idea of the article.

77. d. This is a detail about the GPS program, but it relates to its origin and funding and does not directly support the idea that GPS systems will make it easier to track former criminals. This is the only detail that does not support this idea. Choice **a** is incorrect. This detail supports the idea that the GPS system will make it easier to track former criminals by stating that the system will show officers where the parolee is at any time. Choice **b** is incorrect. By showing that the GPS system can alert authorities when a parolee enters an off-limits area, this detail supports the main idea that the GPS system will make it easier for officers to track former criminals. Choice **c** is incorrect. By citing results from an earlier use of the GPS system that showed that parolees' movements could be effectively monitored with the system, this detail supports the idea that the GPS system will make it easier for officers to track former criminals.

78. c. This detail shows that the GPS system will be effective in preventing crime because officers can respond quickly to electronic alerts and apprehend criminals. This supports the idea that the systems will make the state safer. Choice **a** is incorrect. This detail does not relate to the idea that GPS systems will make the commonwealth of Massachusetts safer, because it mentions only the ability of other states to enact this system. Choice **b** is incorrect. This detail shows opposition to the GPS system and does not support the idea that the GPS system will make the state safer. Choice **d** is incorrect. This detail shows that Massachusetts already has low crime, which does not support the idea that the GPS system will help to prevent crime and make the citizens safer.

79. b. The tone of the article and the details the author chooses to include suggest that he believes that GPS tracking will help parole officers and make their jobs easier. Choice **a** is incorrect. The author does not mention the possibility that GPS tracking may lead to an abuse of power and, instead, seems optimistic about the project. This is not the best description of the author's point of view. Choice **c** is incorrect. The author clearly states that the GPS system will not replace parole officers and does not suggest in content or tone that he believes this will happen someday. This choice does not make sense as a description of the author's point of view. Choice **d** is incorrect. The author's tone and the details he includes suggest that he believes the GPS system will be of use to parole officers. This sentence does not make sense as a description of the author's point of view.

80. c. This is the only sentence that summarizes the main ideas of the article and draws conclusions about them, while bringing the article effectively to a close. Choice **a** is incorrect. Although this is a summarizing statement that may bring the article effectively to a close, it brings up a new issue (the global use of GPS systems) and does not mention the focus of the article (the specific use of GPS systems for Massachusetts parolees). This sentence does not maintain the focus of the article or summarize its main ideas, so it is not the best concluding sentence. Choice **b** is incorrect. Although Senator Panagiotakos is mentioned, he is not the main focus of the article. The tone of this sentence is more opinionated than the rest of the article, and it does not maintain the focus of the article on GPS tracking of parolees. This is not an effective concluding sentence. Choice **d** is incorrect. This is a detail about how the GPS tracking system will work in practicality, not a sentence that summarizes and concludes the article. This detail may make sense in the article, but it is not the best concluding sentence.

81. a. This is the only sentence that captures the main ideas of the article without including additional details. Choice **b** is incorrect. Although the article mentions that the Internet is a major location of identity theft, it does not say "most," and this point is not the main focus of the article. This sentence is not accurate or broad enough to be an effective statement of the main idea. Choice **c** is incorrect. This detail can be found from the article, but it is not the main idea. Choice **d** is incorrect. Although this statement may be true, it is not stated or implied in the article, and this sentence does not describe the article's focus.

82. c. By showing that the amount of fraud in 2005 was greater than in 2000, this detail shows that identity theft is growing fast. This is the only detail that compares numbers over time, rather than just its size at one point, to show the growth of identity theft. Choice **a** is

incorrect. Although this number shows that identity theft is a large problem, it does not show that it is growing fast, because only one statistic is stated and the detail does not show growth over time. Choice **b** is incorrect. Although this number shows that identity theft is a large problem, it does not show that it is growing fast, because only one statistic is stated and the detail does not show growth over time. Choice **d** is incorrect. This detail relates to preventing identity theft and does not show that identity theft is growing fast. This detail does not support the main idea.

83. b. This sentence is an accurate summary of the two major findings of the Javelin study and does not include any extra information. Choice **a** is incorrect. This is an inaccurate summary of the Javelin study, because it adds two unlike numbers together. Also, someone victimized by one kind of theft may have been a victim of the other as well and, therefore, should not be counted twice, so the total may not be 12 million people. In addition, this summary does not show what identity theft means in this study. This sentence is not accurate or complete enough to make an effective summary. Choice **c** is incorrect. This sentence is not a summary, because it includes only the details about new account fraud from the Javelin study. Choice **d** is incorrect. This summary refers to the Cybersource study, not the Javelin study.

84. d. This detail shows that the FBI includes increasing numbers of tech-savvy agents, so as an organization, it is learning how to combat identity theft. This is the only detail that relates directly to the increased learning and ability of federal agents with regard to identity theft. Choice **a** is incorrect. This detail relates to the authority of federal agents to deal with Internet crimes, but it does not support the idea that they are learning how to more effectively combat identity theft. This detail seems related, but it does not directly support the main idea. Choice **b** is incorrect. Although this speculation would suggest that there are some federal agents who are experts at identity theft, this detail does not support the idea that the federal agencies themselves are getting better at combating identity theft. By suggesting that the most talented federal agents join the ranks of identity criminals, this detail implies that federal agents are getting worse, not better, at combating identity theft. Choice **c** is incorrect. This detail relates to credit card companies and consumers, not to federal agents.

85. b. This is the only sentence that mentions the main points of the article, draws conclusions, and brings the article to an effective close without including new details or breaking the article's tone. This is the best concluding sentence. Choice **a** is incorrect. This is a detail that may make sense earlier in the article, but it is a new detail and does not make a good concluding sentence. Choice **c** is incorrect. This sentence is a new detail and does not summarize the article or draw conclusions. It also strikes a tone that goes against the main idea of the article, that identity theft is a real threat. This is not a good concluding sentence. Choice **d** is incorrect. Although this sentence is related to the paragraph about consumers exercising more caution to prevent identity theft, the first-person tone is not in keeping with the rest of the article. Because it also does not summarize the main ideas of the article, this is not the best concluding sentence.

86. c. This is the only sentence that describes the overarching ideas of the article and does not focus on details. Choice **a** is incorrect. The information about Islamic punishment is a detail in the article meant to contrast with the American system, not the main idea of the article. Choice **b** is incorrect. Although the effect of the religious traditions of the Puritans is one of the major ideas of the article, this sentence does not mention the existence of life sentences in the United States, which is the context for the discussion of the Puritans and the main idea of the article. Choice **d** is incorrect. The article only briefly mentions the study of comparative punishment, so it is not the main focus or idea of the article.

87. d. This is the only detail that does not directly show that other countries do not enforce life sentences. This detail focuses on the punishments that Islamic countries do enforce, and does not directly support the main idea that other countries do not enforce life sentences. Choice **a** is incorrect. This detail shows that, although some countries may have life sentences, they are almost never enforced. This detail directly supports the main idea, so it is not the correct answer. Choice **b** is incorrect. This detail shows an example of someone who did not receive a life sentence. This supports the main idea that other countries do not enforce sentences of life without parole, so it is not the correct answer. Choice **c** is incorrect. This detail shows Mexico's opposition to life sentences and directly supports the idea that other countries do not enforce life sentences, so it is not the correct answer.

88. d. This is the only detail that mentions an American tradition, supporting the idea that life sentences without parole may be part of an American tradition of self-reliance and responsibility. Choice **a** is incorrect. Although this sentence contrasts American ideas with Western European ones, it does not mention or support the idea of an American tradition, which includes life sentences. Choice **b** is incorrect. Although this sentence mentions the United States twice, it does not include any detail relating to American traditions and does not support the main idea. Choice **c** is incorrect. Although Tonry explains the idea of the American tradition in the article, the fact that he is a professor does not directly support the idea that life sentences are part of an American tradition.

89. c. This is the only sentence that includes all of the major points of Professor Tonry's opinion without including unnecessary or irrelevant details. Choice **a** is incorrect. This sentence is not a summary, because it includes all the details from the paragraph and does not stick to the main points of Professor Tonry's opinion. It includes too much information to be an effective summary. Choice **b** is incorrect because it is a vague and incomplete summary of Professor Tonry's opinion and does not include his connection to life sentences and the welfare state. This sentence does not include enough information to make an effective summary. Choice **d** is incorrect. This sentence includes information, which does not appear in the article's description of Professor Tonry's opinion. Although it does contain the main ideas of Professor Tonry's opinion in some form, this sentence includes too much extra information to be an effective summary.

90. b. The author's tone is factual and inquisitive, and does not take any of the strong *pro* or *anti* stances implied in the other choices. The tone of the article implies curious inquiry and comparison on the part of the author, not advocacy of any change or reform. Choice **a** is incorrect. The author does not imply that the Western European system is better or worse than the U.S. system but carefully notes their differences. Although the article may imply that it is a good idea to learn about other justice systems, there is no evidence that the author opposes life sentences. Choice **c** is incorrect. The author does

not imply that the Puritan tradition is a negative one or that the U.S. justice system should be reformed. The article is not written as an exposé nor does it advocate change, but rather it has an inquisitive tone. Choice **d** is incorrect. The author is careful not to state an opinion for or against life sentences or to state that one justice system is better or worse than another. There is nothing in the article to imply that this sentence describes his point of view.

91. d. This sentence mentions the main ideas of the article and draws a conclusion that is in keeping with the tone of the rest of the article, without including any new or unnecessary details. Choice **a** is incorrect. This sentence is not in keeping with the tone of the rest of the article. It expresses an opinion that is not expressed or supported anywhere else in the article. This sentence does not make sense as a conclusion to this article. Choice **b** is incorrect. This is a detail that may make sense in the article, but it introduces a new idea and does not summarize the ideas of the article, so it is not the best concluding sentence. Choice **c** is incorrect. This sentence introduces a new detail and does not summarize the article or draw conclusions. This is not a good concluding sentence.

92. d. This sentence is grammatically correct.

93. b. This sentence has the clearest meaning.

94. a. This sentence correctly places an apostrophe in the word *one's*, which is a possessive pronoun referring to *problems*. No other apostrophes are necessary. Choice **b** is incorrect. This sentence correctly places an apostrophe in the possessive pronoun *one's*, but incorrectly places an apostrophe after the word *parolees*, which is not a possessive noun and does not need an apostrophe. Choice **c** is incorrect. This sentence does not include an apostrophe in the word *ones*, which is a possessive pronoun referring to *problems*. Choice **d** is incorrect. This sentence incorrectly places apostrophes both in the word *parolees* and the word *problems*. Neither of these is a possessive noun, so neither should not receive an apostrophe.

95. a. This sentence correctly uses the phrase *on the night of* to identify the time and correctly conjugates the verb *have* in the past tense *had*. Choice **b** is incorrect. The verb *have* is incorrectly conjugated as *has them*. Because it is a simple past tense verb, the word should be *had*. Choice **c** is incorrect. This sentence incorrectly uses the phrase *in the night of* to identify the time the fight took place. The word *on* should be used instead of *in*. Choice **d** is incorrect. This sentence incorrectly uses the phrase *in the night of* instead of the correct *on the night of*. Additionally, the verb *have* is incorrectly conjugated as *having*. The past tense verb should be *had*.

96. c. This is the only sentence that uses the word *every* to clarify the inclusion of all parole officers, rather than the word *all* that could mean *the only thing* in the context of this sentence about what officers want from their parolees. The structure of the sentence is simple and straightforward, and the meaning is unmistakable. Also, this sentence uses the correct pronouns *his or her* to modify *Every parole officer*. Choice **a** is incorrect. The phrase *all what parole officers want* is grammatically incorrect, and it is unclear in the sentence whether *all* applies to *every parole officer* or to *the only thing that parole officers want*. Choice **b** is incorrect. This sentence is grammatically incorrect because it lacks a verb for the subject *parole officers*. In this sentence, it is also unclear from the placement of the word *all* whether the word implies *every parole officer wants* or *the only thing parole officers want*. Choice **d** is incorrect. This sentence puts the subject *parole officers* confusingly in the mid-

dle of the sentence. The structure of the sentence also makes it unclear whether the parole officers receive a record of good behavior from the parolees, or want the parolees to have a record of good behavior. This is not the clearest sentence.

97. d. This sentence correctly places a comma after the initial phrase, separating this dependent clause from the rest of the sentence. It also correctly places two commas around the proper name describing the previous noun *the driver*. Choice **a** is incorrect. This sentence correctly places commas around the proper name describing the previous noun *the driver* but fails to place a comma after the initial dependent clause *after the collision*. Choice **b** is incorrect. This sentence incorrectly places commas after the word *drove* and *quickly*, which are not separate phrases and do not require commas. Choice **c** is incorrect. This sentence correctly places a comma after the initial dependent clause. However, there is no comma separating the subject *the driver* from the descriptive name *Harold Lloyd*, and the comma after *Harold Lloyd* only makes the sentence more confusing. This sentence is incorrectly punctuated.

98. b. This sentence correctly omits the unnecessary word *of* from the phrase *hadn't been there*. It also correctly uses the prepositional word *of* in the phrase *none of this*. Choice **a** is incorrect. This sentence incorrectly includes the unnecessary word *of* in the phrase *hadn't of been there*. It also incorrectly uses the phrases *none a this* instead of the correct phrase *none of this*. Choice **c** is incorrect. This sentence incorrectly includes the unnecessary word *of* in the phrase *hadn't of been there*. Choice **d** is incorrect. This sentence replaces the prepositional word *of* in the phrase *none of this* with the incorrect abbreviation *a*.

99. d. This sentence clearly states the two places and makes clear which is better than the other in a straightforward way. Choice **a** is incorrect. The structure of the sentence makes it unclear whether the cellar or the attic is actually the better one for keeping contraband. Choice **b** is incorrect. This sentence has an awkward grammatical structure, and the choice to place the verb *keeping* at the beginning of the sentence makes its meaning unclear. Choice **c** is incorrect. This sentence has an unclear grammatical structure and leaves the reader unsure about whether the cellar or the attic is better.

100. a. This sentence correctly uses an apostrophe in the word *it's* when it is being used as an abbreviation for *it is*, and correctly does not use an apostrophe when the word *its* is being used as a possessive for the noun *wording*. Choice **b** is incorrect. This sentence correctly does not use an apostrophe when the word *its* is being used as a possessive for the noun *wording*. However, it fails to use an apostrophe in the word *it's* when it is being used as an abbreviation for *it is*. Choice **c** is incorrect. This sentence correctly uses an apostrophe in the word *it's* when it is being used as an abbreviation for *it is*. However, it incorrectly uses an apostrophe when the word *its* is being used as a possessive for the noun *wording*. The word *its* does not take a pronoun when it is being used as a possessive. Choice **d** is incorrect. This sentence incorrectly does not use an apostrophe in the word *it's* when it is being used as an abbreviation for *it is* and incorrectly uses an apostrophe when the word *its* is being used as a possessive for the noun *wording*. The word *its* should contain an apostrophe only when it is being used as an abbreviation, not when it is being used as a possessive pronoun.

15▶ The Interview

An interview is a meeting between an agency's hiring decision maker(s) and a candidate for employment. Typically, this exchange either occurs in a face-to-face session individually or, more often, is conducted by a panel of interviewers. The interview provides the agency an opportunity to review a candidate personally for potential selection for employment. The interview allows the candidate an opportunity to highlight his or her education, experience, and character traits verbally to the potential employer.

▶ What They Are Looking For

Basic Understanding of Criminal Justice Issues

Although employers may select candidates for interview who do not have a criminal justice/criminology degree, a desirable candidate is one who is aware of the issues specific to a criminal justice agency such as probation or parole. Candidates should be able to demonstrate knowledge in the areas typically associated with the supervision of criminal offenders in a community setting. Some examples would include recidivism, victimization, security threat groups (gangs), drug trafficking and use, and risk management. In addition to these areas, it is helpful for a candidate to possess information regarding modern trends in criminal activity, sentencing guidelines, and community corrections practices.

Job-Specific Knowledge and Skills

A candidate who possesses knowledge, skills, and training in an area specific to the various tasks and duties associated with probation and parole work is generally favored in the selection process. Candidates who hold applicable certifications such as firearms, CPR, substance abuse treatment, drug/alcohol testing, and self-defense or martial arts should highlight those skills in the interview process.

Additionally, candidates who have prior work experience in corrections, and specifically community corrections, are generally preferred. These individuals, although maybe not trained in the specific style a department prefers, have applicable experience in the performance of the various tasks and duties associated with the specific position. A candidate's experience does not necessarily have to be a previous employment experience. A candidate who has completed a full-time agency placement experience such as an internship, or a part-time agency placement such as a practicum, or who has volunteered with a comparable agency, can possess quite a bit of knowledge and understanding of the nature of the work he or she will be asked to perform.

Self-Confidence

Probation and parole officers are consistently called upon to make immediate, crucial, and life-changing decisions. As such, the people serving in these positions need to demonstrate a high level of confidence in their interactions with other people. A candidate who presents him- or herself as shy, timid, or reserved will create doubt in the interviewers' minds about his or her ability to make the tough decisions that is necessary for the job. Conversely, a candidate who appears overly confident may give the impression of arrogance or an impression that he or she is unteachable. Interviewers

will also view this expression of overconfidence negatively.

Demonstration of Ethical Behavior

With the discretion afforded probation and parole officers, agency administrators are undoubtedly looking for candidates whom they can rely upon to look out for the organization's best interests. Probation and parole officers are often placed in positions of trust within the criminal justice system and, as such, are privy to confidential and sensitive information. An organization's decision makers want to select employees whom they can trust with sensitive information and who will not create problems in the workplace.

Time Management Skills

With the high volume of offenders supervised by the various forms of community corrections, use of allotted time is crucial to the success of the probation and parole officer. The interviewer is likely to include an opportunity for the candidate to provide descriptions and examples of prior experience to determine how efficiently and effectively a candidate can use his or her time. A candidate who can demonstrate the ability to manage multiple tasks simultaneously will impress an interviewer. Furthermore, a candidate who can express good judgment in the prioritization of tasks will also have an advantage.

▶ How to Prepare for the Interview

Do the Homework

A candidate pursuing employment in a professional career field such as probation and parole should definitely possess a significant amount of knowledge about the organization he or she is interviewing with. A candidate should know as much about the organization and its administrators as possible. Knowing the history of the organization can help a candidate answer questions about politics and structure, and knowing about the administration of an organization will help a candidate form responses that are tailored to the agency's goals and priorities. Generally, a candidate who is well prepared with prior knowledge of the organization is viewed favorably by interviewers as someone who is obviously interested in working for them. This effort can also lead the interviewers to believe that the candidate desires to and, more likely, will remain with the organization for a significant period, which is favorable to an employee who leaves after only a short stay.

One of the first steps in "doing the homework" occurs when a candidate is invited to interview with an agency. At that point, the candidate should ask with whom he or she will be interviewing. The response will give the candidate some insight into not only who the actual interviewer is going to be, but also how many potential interviewers may be involved. This information can be valuable in helping prepare for the interview itself.

More and more criminal justice agencies are utilizing the Internet to share information with the public through their websites. A candidate can use his or her preferred search engine (i.e., Google, Yahoo!, etc.) to locate information on the agency. Often, the agencies' websites will include posted announcements regarding the recent actions or business of the agency. In addition, a website is likely to include the names of the agency's top administrators and will possibly provide a brief biography for each. A candidate for employment can gain quite a bit of knowledge using the Internet to locate information. A further search by a candidate on the specific person or people who will conduct the interview can yield helpful information as well.

Create a List of Questions You Might Anticipate Being Asked

In addition to the most common questions listed at the end of this chapter, candidates should prepare themselves to address questions specific to their education and employment history as outlined and demonstrated through the application and resume. If a can-

didate has a gap in his or her employment, an employer is going to want an explanation for that time. If a candidate's resume indicates a significant number of changes in employment or even in career fields, an interviewer is likely to address that as well.

To be successful, a candidate should think of him- or herself as the interviewer and conduct a review of the resume and application. It may be additionally helpful for a candidate to seek out a friend or family member to review the application materials and to formulate potential questions from them. The more aware a candidate is of potential questions raised from his or her submitted materials, the more likely he or she can avoid surprise questions.

Create a List of Questions You Would Like to Ask

A candidate should arrive at the interview prepared to engage in conversation. Candidates should remind themselves that this meeting is an interview, not an interrogation. To engage thoughtfully in conversation, a candidate should have some questions prepared in writing. This action will also help guide him or her through the conversation. Typically, at the end of the meeting, interviewers will, at the very least, give the candidate an opportunity to ask any questions he or she may have. Sometimes this is just a polite gesture, although, at other times, the interviewer may use this portion of the interview to gain further insight into what a candidate may value or what he or she believes about the agency. Candidates should not make the mistake of appearing as if they know everything there is to know about that agency, even if they think that they do.

Often, the interview itself will guide the questions a candidate may have regarding the agency or the job specifically. However, preparing his or her answers to a standard list of questions assists a candidate with nerves or anxiety he or she may feel throughout the interview. These questions not only solicit information for the interviewer's use, but also provide an opportunity for the candidate to project a desire to become a part of that agency.

Role-Play to Practice the Interview

Entry-level positions in the field of probation and parole often attract young professionals who have just obtained their college degrees. As such, these individuals may lack experience in interviews tailored to a professional career field. Interviews for part-time or temporary employment are just not the same as those interviews looking to establish a relationship with a career-minded individual. The candidate has more to lose or to gain during an interview for a position he or she wants to acquire in order to establish or advance his or her career. Additionally, the person(s) conducting the interview have more at stake as well.

Practicing the interview beforehand is the best way for a candidate to reduce some of the stress and anxiety produced during a first or early attempt at a professional interview. The practice also gives the candidate the opportunity to polish his or her responses and be reminded of the messages he or she is giving with their nonverbal cues and body posture. More and more colleges and universities are offering career services to their graduates. These services include the creation or improvement of a resume, job searching, and interview preparation. It is not uncommon for the interview preparation service to include mock interviewing as well as videotaping the interview. A videotape of the interview can assist a candidate in critiquing he or her responses and realizing how nonverbal cues can affect the impression an interviewer gets of the candidate.

▶ What to Do during the Interview

Dress for Success

As professionals, probation and parole officers are expected to dress professionally. Most organizations in the field will have specific dress codes for the employees to follow. However, a candidate can assume that at the very least he or she should approach the interview with as much formality in his or her style of dress as possible. Business professional attire is completely appropriate for the interview. A candidate's physical appearance is going to make the first impression on the interviewer(s). Therefore, a candidate's clothes should be color coordinated and neatly pressed, as well as properly fitted.

Arrive Early

One of the most consistent issues administrators face with employees is tardiness and attendance problems. A candidate who arrives late for the interview will be sending a message that he or she does not manage time well. Even if the interview is the first appointment of the day, a candidate should plan to arrive in the office early. A safe time frame is about 15 minutes prior to the scheduled appointment. Candidates should anticipate delays in traffic or difficulty in finding parking, especially in metropolitan areas.

An organization may require a candidate to complete an application or sample writing exercise on-site before the interview. Arriving early for the appointment allows a candidate to complete this expectation in a timely fashion without feeling rushed. Keep in mind that often the organization's receptionist is the first line of review.

Think before Speaking and Give Clear Answers

During the interview, a candidate should give responses in a timely manner—and *never* interrupt—to avoid appearing that he or she is attempting to out-think the interviewer. Candidates should carefully consider what the interviewer is asking and how they could best respond before answering a question. A candidate should be prepared to answer follow-up questions based on his or her answer to an interviewer's question. As such, candidates should consider the possible questions, born out of their own responses, that they may have to face.

A candidate should consider not only *what* he or she is going to say, but also *how* he or she is going to say it. Candidates should answer questions without providing too information that the question does not call for. Interviewers are likely looking for someone who expresses confidence and truth in his or her answers, but who can also stay on point in his or her response. These skills carry over into the field of community corrections work, especially in the area of court testimony.

Use Examples to Support Responses and Statements

Candidates who can demonstrate personal knowledge of the areas being questioned are more likely to have a successful interview. One way a candidate can demonstrate this knowledge is to provide examples as part of his or her response to a question. This technique gives the candidate the opportunity to refer to his or her previous experience with or understanding of the topic being discussed. A candidate who formulates a response that includes an applicable example will undoubtedly impress the interviewer.

Don't Forget the Goal

A mistake that a candidate can make is to leave the interview without taking the opportunity to share his or her skills and abilities with the interviewer(s). Some administrators are simply better at the task of interviewing than are others. With that in mind, a candidate should be prepared to offer the interviewer(s) an opportunity to get to know his or her attributes better. If an interviewer has not asked about a candidate's particular strength or area of expertise, the candidate should take the opportunity to drive the conversation toward that area. In this regard, the interview can be thought of, on the candidate's part, as a sales pitch. The candidate's task is to prove that he or she is the right person for the position. Relying too heavily on the interviewer's own skill in this area could prove to be costly for the candidate.

▶ What to Do after the Interview

Write a Thank-You Note

A note of thanks should be written within 48 hours of the interview to everyone who actively participated in the interview. Standard contents of this note include:

- A genuine expression of thanks for the opportunity to meet and discuss qualifications
- A description of the position's expectations to be placed upon the successful candidate
- A comparable outline of the candidate's qualifications related to the expectations
- Additional information that was not shared during the interview that is relevant to the position
- A closing paragraph that reiterates the candidate's desire to obtain the position, including a statement indicating a follow-up phone call

It is more important to send a well-written, thoughtful expression of gratitude and interest in the position than it is to mail out a form letter as rote. If the note reflects the candidate's enthusiasm for the position, it may give him or her additional leverage for the position. Likewise, a candidate who does not follow the protocol of writing the note may be looked upon by the interviewer as rude and/or ignorant.

Make a Phone Call

Approximately one week after mailing the post-interview note, a candidate should call the interviewer by telephone. If the candidate is routed through an agency's receptionist, he or she should indicate that the interviewer is expecting the call, because the post-interview note indicated that the candidate would be making this follow-up call. The phone call should consist of the following:

- Request for assurance that the note arrived
- Discussion of areas that seemed to elicit a positive response from the interviewer during the interview

- Discussion of additional information shared with the interviewer in the note but not during the interview
- Clarification of any aspect of the position or agency that remains unclear for the candidate
- Mention of any recent news or occurrence that could have an impact on the agency or the field
- Discussion or review of the timeline for reaching a decision about the position

While other candidates wait for the interviewer to phone them with a job offer or a request for a follow-up interview, a candidate who has followed up with a phone call has assuredly positioned him- or herself in the memory of the decision maker. A follow-up phone call can demonstrate to an organization that the candidate possesses the ability to show initiative and is genuinely interested in the position. Also, the candidate can possibly gain some insight into the process and learn what steps he or she can expect to follow. Or, if the candidate learns that he or she has not be selected for the position, he or she can take the opportunity to elicit feedback on the areas that need improvement.

Commonly Asked Interview Questions

- What are your long-range and short-range goals and objectives?
- Do you see yourself in this position in five years? Why?
- What are your long-range career objectives?
- What are the rewards you anticipate receiving from your career?
- Why did you choose probation or parole as a career?
- Do you prefer working alone or in a group setting?
- Have you ever had difficulty with a supervisor? How did you resolve the conflict?
- What do you consider to be your greatest strengths and weaknesses?
- What criticisms have you received regarding your work performance?
- How would you describe yourself?
- Why should our organization hire you?
- Why do you feel qualified for this position?
- How would you define success?
- In what ways do you think you can make a contribution to this field?
- What relevant experience do you have to make you successful in this field?
- Do you consider yourself a leader or a team player?
- How you would describe the ideal supervisor?
- Describe the workload in your current (or most recent) job.
- Which is more important, creativity or efficiency? Why?
- Describe the most rewarding experience of your career thus far.
- If you were hiring someone for this position, what qualities would you look for?
- How do you work under pressure? Can you give examples?
- Can you give us an example of how you deal with conflict?
- What is one of the hardest professional decisions you've ever had to make?
- How well do you adapt to new situations? Can you give examples?
- Why did you decide to seek a position in this company?
- What are your expectations regarding promotions and salary increases?
- Are you willing to relocate as a requirement of the job?
- What have you accomplished that shows your initiative and willingness to work?
- Can you explain the gap in your employment history?

16 ▶ The Physical, Medical, and Psychological Exams

▶ Physical Fitness Testing

Field work in probation and parole requires an officer to be physically fit and possess a reasonable amount of strength and agility. Officers consistently stand for long periods of time and walk during the completion of their assigned duties. Additionally, responding to emergencies often requires these officers to run, climb stairs, and navigate obstacles such as furniture, equipment, and fences. Officers must be able to confront an offender and/or other threatening person physically, as well as to arrest or physically restrain someone. Because of the potential for an officer to be called upon to perform these duties, some jurisdictions require candidates to undergo a physical test to measure strength, agility, and stamina.

The scope of the physical test is established by policy so as to avoid discriminatory requirements, but will require a clear standard of performance. Candidates can expect the requirements to be consistent with the completion of various duties associated with the physical nature of the probation or parole officer job. These tests will include a series of tasks and exercises a candidate must perform. Some of these tests will be measuring specific job-related tasks, while others will be measuring overall physical fitness.

A candidate should be prepared in advance for the physical conditioning portion of the test. These testing procedures measure a candidate's aerobic capacity, physical strength, flexibility, and overall endurance. These tests typically are given to groups of candidates and are likely to be held in a gymnasium or an outside recreation or sports facility.

Advanced Preparation

Candidates who have an established training regimen typically perform better under physical fitness testing. The longer a candidate has been training, the more likely he or she will meet or exceed the minimum standards acceptable for probation and parole officers. A minimum six-month training program is recommended for candidates considering taking the physical fitness portion of the probation and parole officer examinations. This duration of time allows an individual to incorporate not only specific exercises into his or her routine, but also a level of wellness leading to overall fitness.

Candidates may consider involvement with a competitive or recreational sports league or with some other regular participation in sports-related activities and exercise. Involvement with sports is a good way to begin to improve one's physical health and fitness. This type of exercise is generally fun for the participant and often leads to other forms of exercise.

In addition to sports-related exercise, a candidate should begin to consider flexibility training and aerobic exercise. Flexibility training will assist with physical fitness in a variety of ways—most important, by helping to avoid injury, General flexibility during the performance of specific exercises allows for maximum results on physical activities and exercise.

Anticipated Physical Fitness Exercises

Running

In a physical fitness test, candidates will undoubtedly be asked to complete some form of running exercise. The most common types of running exercises used in testing include distance running (usually one to two miles); timed running (usually 15 to 30 minutes); or sprint running, such as a 40-yard dash or shuttle running.

Obstacles

Candidates should anticipate some form of obstacle course. Depending upon the location of the testing, an obstacle course can be very elaborate or can be as simple as chalk lines or rubberized cones. If the test is to be given at a corrections or law-enforcement academy, a more elaborate obstacle course should be expected. If a test is to be given at an office location or gymnasium, it is likely the obstacle course will be makeshift or mobile.

Weight Lifting

This form of physical fitness testing is less likely, simply because of its specific equipment requirement. However, when this form of testing is used, it usually incorporates three to five specific weight lifting exercises. These exercises are designed to measure a candidate's physical strength in separate muscle groups.

Anticipated Job-Specific Tasks

Physical Restraint

Candidates can be called upon to perform an exercise involving the restraint of another individual typically by using techniques demonstrated at the time of the test. This form of testing allows for the evaluation of a candidate's ability to confront another person physically with the correct combination of technique and force necessary for the situation. This form of testing often will require a candidate to be confronted by someone in various ways, so that the candidate has to make a quick decision on technique and force to use.

Handcuffing

Probation and parole officers can find themselves in a position to take an offender into custody. Therefore, proper handcuffing techniques are essential to the task. Candidates can be tested on their ability to use the techniques demonstrated at the time of testing, giving examiners an opportunity to see how a candidate will perform in the field under simulated conditions.

Carrying Items

A probation or parole officer consistently carries equipment; therefore, a candidate's ability to lift and carry a significant amount of weight is measured. To test this ability, examiners will typically use a utility bag or box weighted accordingly. Candidates are asked to stand and lift and then to carry these items over a specified distance or to stack them to a certain height.

What to Wear

Because candidates will be called upon to perform various physical tasks and exercises, a candidate should wear clothing that suits the occasion. Athletic attire that is comfortable and allows for maximum flexibility is recommended. Candidates should also plan to wear tennis shoes, sneakers, or another type of athletic footwear. A candidate should plan for inclement weather, because examiners may choose to continue with testing despite less than favorable weather conditions.

▶ Psychological Testing

Because of the great deal of responsibility that probation and parole officers have, they consistently operate under high-stress conditions. Depending upon the specific jurisdiction or organization, candidates for employment in these fields may be required to undergo psychological testing. This testing is one way that agencies can provide a standardized form of evaluation to augment the typically subjective interview process. This form of testing can also provide feedback for administrators looking for specific character traits as a fit for a specific position or population to be served. Overall, the purpose in psychological testing is to ensure a candidate can handle the psychological and emotional demands of the job.

What to Expect

Written Portion

Most forms of standardized psychological testing will include some form of a written test. This test will ask for a candidate to respond to various prompts and usually utilizes a multiple-choice format. These tests can vary in length, from a dozen questions to several hundred questions. Often, these questions are designed to ask a candidate the same question, but in various forms to determine consistency of response. A commonly used form of this testing is the Minnesota Multiphasic Personality Inventory (MMPI) test. This test uses approximately 550 true/false questions and takes about an hour and a half to complete. From this test, an examiner can produce a general profile of a candidate that can detect possible problems or concerns with a candidate's attitudes, beliefs, and behavior.

Psychological Interview

This form of testing is generally conducted by a psychologist or psychiatrist contracted by the agency specifically to perform evaluations of candidates for employment. These examinations can be very costly for agencies; therefore, it is not uncommon for this form of testing to occur at the end of the selection process and only with candidates being seriously considered for employment. Typically, the person conducting the psychological interview will have the results of the written portion of the psychological examination, and will follow up on areas that raise attention or concern.

How to Prepare

A candidate cannot study for a psychological test. However, reducing the stress and anxiety typically associated with undergoing psychological testing for the first time is a great strategy. Candidates should not attempt to outsmart the examiner by second-guessing what the interviewer is asking. Candidates should provide honest answers to the questions being asked of them; otherwise, the examiner would note discrepancies in the responses. Staying on point with responses is also a smart strategy. A candidate should not venture into assumptions or away from the question being asked. Remaining calm and relaxed is key to successfully completing psychological testing. Otherwise, a candidate may have trouble focusing on what is being asked. Overall, candidates should remember that they are who they are. Regardless of how much he or she tries to impress an examiner, ultimately an examiner is going to have a pretty clear understanding of the candidate's belief systems and other personality characteristics.

▶ Medical Testing

Since the passing of the Americans with Disabilities Act, organizations will typically postpone any form of medical testing until a conditional offer of employment has been made. Otherwise, a medical examination may uncover a candidate's disability and thereby contaminate the hiring process. It can be anticipated that certain positions within the field of probation and parole will require an individual to receive medical clearance. These positions may include offender transportation, tactical and field units, along with warrant officers.

Applicants should anticipate a conditional offer of employment prior to this form of testing, and sometimes prior to any of the testing discussed within this chapter. An organization must make every effort to explore reasonable accommodations to address disabilities to assist a candidate in performing the essential duties of the position. If reasonable accommodations cannot be determined, a candidate can be denied employment on the basis that his or her disability conflicts with the essential functions of the position.

Typically, candidates who are asked to complete a medical examination will undergo a routine or standard physical exam. The physician will likely measure blood pressure and the candidate's height-to-weight ratio, and observe the standard heart and lung functions, as well as visually inspect the eyes, ears, nose, and throat. It is also possible for a candidate to be asked to provide a blood and/or urine sample to accompany these other tests and to determine conditions not visible to the routine observation.

Drug Testing

It is very common for probation and parole officer candidates to be required to submit to one of various forms of testing to determine the presence and use of illicit chemical substances. Common testing procedures would involve breath (for alcohol), urine, or blood samples. In addition, an agency may utilize a testing procedure that calls for a sample hair follicle. Standard policy usually dictates that probation and parole officers remain drug-free while employed in that capacity. As probation and parole officers commonly provide community supervision for persons identified as drug users, these officers must model behavior consistent with the goals of the community supervision. These goals certainly include refraining from and/or treatment for substance use.

Common drug concerns for candidates would be marijuana, cocaine, methamphetamine, and heroin. However, other forms of substance use are often included, such as narcotic analgesics (opium based), benzodiazepines, barbiturates, and other stimulants. A person's prescription use of these substances cannot be used to eliminate a candidate from employment, as long as verification from the prescribing physician is obtained.

ADDITIONAL ONLINE PRACTICE

Whether you need help building basic skills or preparing for an exam, visit the LearningExpress Practice Center! Using the code below, you'll be able to access additional online practice. This online practice will also provide you with:

Immediate scoring

Detailed answer explanations

Personalized recommendations for further practice and study

Log in to the LearningExpress Practice Center by using this URL: **www.learnatest.com/practice**

This is your Access Code: **5829**

Follow the steps online to redeem your access code. After you've used your access code to register with the site, you will be prompted to create a username and password. For easy reference, record them here:

Username: _____   **Password:** _____

With your username and password, you can log in and access your additional practice materials. If you have any questions or problems, please contact LearningExpress customer service at 1-800-295-9556 ext. 2, or e-mail us at **customerservice@learningexpressllc.com**.

NOTES

NOTES

NOTES

NOTES

NOTES

NOTES

NOTES

Special FREE Offer from LearningExpress

LearningExpress guarantees that you will be better prepared for, and score higher on, the probation or parole officer exam

Go to the LearningExpress Practice Center at www.LearningExpressFreeOffer.com, an interactive online resource exclusively for LearningExpress customers.

Now that you've purchased LearningExpress's *Probation Officer/Parole Officer Exam*, you have **FREE** access to:

- **Two full-length probation/parole officer practice tests** that mirror official probation and parole officer exams
- **Multiple-choice questions covering** job responsibilities, case studies, reading comprehension, and writing skills
- **Immediate scoring** and **detailed answer explanations**
- Benchmark your skills and focus your study with our **customized diagnostic reports**

Follow the simple instructions on the scratch card in your copy of *Probation Officer/Parole Officer Exam*. Use your individualized access code found on the scratch card and go to www.Learning ExpressFreeOffer.com to sign in. Start practicing online for the probation or parole officer exam right away!

Once you've logged on, use t̶ _____ ̶ ̶ ̶ ̶ ̶ ̶ newly created password for easy reference:

Access Code: _____